Enchiridio

A Manual o

*Consisting of
a brief description of the origins and history of the Rosary
prayers, devotions, and variations of the same
with writings from saints and popes
compiled from approved sources*

by
Paul A. Böer, Sr.

VERITATIS SPLENDOR PUBLICATIONS
et cognoscetis veritatem et veritas liberabit vos (Jn 8:32)
MMXIII

ALL RIGHTS RESERVED.

This typography of this publication is the property of Veritatis Splendor Publications and may not be reproduced, stored in a retrieval system, or transmitted in any form or by any means, in whole or in part, without written permission from the Publisher, except as permitted by United States and International copyright law.

Copyright © 2013. Veritatis Splendor Publications.

AD MAJOREM DEI GLORIAM

Preface

The Rosary has always been a significant force in my life.

I have very clear and dear memories of kneeling with my sister, mother and father around my parents' bed saying the Rosary. This was a nightly ritual for us. So much so that it was only very rarely interrupted. Indeed if we had guests on any particular evening, we still retired to my parents' room to pray the rosary. Our guests, Catholic or not, were always invited to join us, but any lack of participation on their part did not prevent us from praying. After our prayers, we would rejoin our guests.

The Rosary became the spiritual warp and woof of my family's life. On any car trip, my father would pull out his beads and lead us in prayer. My family prayed the Rosary in hotel rooms, the homes of relatives and friends, in tents on camping trips, and in countless other places. The Rosary was quite literally THE prayer of our family.

As I grew into young adulthood, I prayed the Rosary only infrequently. Even though I wandered far from the faith during these years, I always had a Rosary in my desk drawer. Because of my neglect, I soon forgot the rubrics of praying it, but I still reached for it in times of crisis – during my father's open heart surgery and again when he received the initial diagnosis of cancer. I prayed it with my father and sister the night of my mother's death, and again, I prayed it on the death of my father.

Through the grace of God and the prayers of my family, I long ago returned to the faith of my parents. And as I have aged, the Rosary has become increasingly dear to me, and with it, My Beautiful Blessed Mother Mary.

Now I am trying to bring this love to my own family – marveling at the discipline of my parents in their own faithfulness to prayer.

Relying on the grace of God through the intercession of His Most Blessed Mother, I look forward to the day when my adult children will themselves rediscover their faith and again pick up the beads of prayer. And I am watching with joy how Our Blessed Mother is leading my younger children into the Heart of Christ.

It is for such as these and for other families who are struggling to keep the faith in this very dark world that I put together this manual on the Most Holy Rosary.

St. Pio of Pietrelcina stated "The Rosary is THE WEAPON." Outside of Holy Mass, perhaps we have no greater weapon against the enemy and the powers of darkness. Our Blessed Mother, herself, promises that those who devoutly pray the Rosary shall find in it powerful armor against hell, a means of destroying vice, decreasing sin, and defeating heresy.

My prayer is that Our Precious Lord through the intercession of His Most Blessed Mother will use this manual to touch the hearts of its readers and bring them closer to His Sacred Heart as well as the Immaculate Heart of His Mother. And that in some small way it may be used to promote Our Lady's Rosary among the faithful.

All praise, honor, and glory to the Sacred Eucharistic Heart of Jesus, through the Immaculate and Sorrowful Heart of Mary, in union with Joseph, her most chaste spouse. Amen.

Paul A. Böer, Sr.
Feast of the Holy Rosary, 2013

CONTENTS

Preface 5
The Excellence of the Rosary 13
    I. The Name of this Devotion 14
    II. The Origin of the Rosary 19
    III. The Power of the Rosary 25
    IV. The Excellence of the Various Parts of the Rosary 32
        (a) The Sign of the Cross 32
    V. The Excellence of the Various Parts of the Rosary 38
        (b) The Apostles' Creed 38
    VI. The Excellence of the Various Parts of the Rosary 44
        (c) The Glory be to the Father 44
    VII. The Excellence of the Various Parts of the Rosary 49
        (d) The "Our Father" 49
    VIII. The Excellence of the Various Parts of the Rosary 55
        (e) The Hail Mary 55
    IX. The Prayer to increase the Three Divine Virtues 60
    X. The Excellence of the Rosary in regard to Its Form 66
    XI. The Excellence of the Rosary on account of The Mysteries
    Commemorated 70
The Prayers Used in the Rosary 75
    The Sign of the Cross 75
    The Apostles' Creed 75
    The Our Father (The Lord's Prayer also known as Pater) 75
    Hail Mary (Angelic Salutation, also known as Ave) 76
    Glory Be (Gloria or Doxology) 76
    Fatima Prayer 76
    Hail, Holy Queen (Salve Regina) 76
    Collect of the Feast of the Most Holy Rosary of the Blessed Virgin ... 76
    Remember, O Most Gracious Virgin Mary (Memorare) 77
    Prayer to Saint Michael 77
    Prayer to St. Joseph 77
    Litany of the Blessed Virgin Mary 78
    The Mysteries of the Rosary 82
Our Lady's 15 Promises 85
How to Pray the Rosary 92
Other Methods of Praying the Rosary 113
    A Method of Saying the Rosary, the First in the *Golden Manual* 113

A Method of Saying the Rosary, the Second in the *Golden Manual*......123
A Method of Saying the Rosary, the Third in the *Golden Manual*.........132
Methods for Saying the Rosary from St. Louis de Montfort................142
    First Method 142
    Second, Shorter Method of Celebrating the life, death and heavenly glory of Jesus and Mary in the Holy Rosary and a method of restraining our imagination and lessening distractions. 148
    Third Method of Fr. de Montfort for saying fruitfully the holy Rosary, for the use of the Daughters of Wisdom. 149
    Fourth Method Summary of the life, death and passion and heavenly glory of Jesus and Mary in the holy Rosary. 158
    Fifth Method 150 Motives Impelling us to say the Rosary 171
A Scriptural Rosary with Meditations by Blessed Dom Columba Marmion, O.S.B. 184
Meditations from The Mystical City of God A thought for each Hail Mary, taken from the "Mystical City of God," by Sister Mary of Jesus of Agreda..196
54 Day Rosary Novena 211
    The Joyful Mysteries 211
        Prayer before the recitation...211
            In petition 211
            In thanksgiving..211
        The Annunciation 212
        The Visitation 212
        The Nativity 213
        The Presentation 213
        The Finding Of The Child Jesus In The Temple...................213
        Spiritual Communion:..214
            In petition 214
            In thanksgiving..214
        Prayer...215
    The Sorrowful Mysteries 215
        Prayer before the recitation...215
            In petition 215
            In thanksgiving..216
        The Agony..216
        The Scourging..217
        The Crowning With Thorns..217
        The Carrying Of The Cross 217

The Crucifixion	218
Spiritual Communion	218
In petition	219
In thanksgiving	219
Prayer	219
The Glorious Mysteries	219
Prayer before the recitation	219
In petition	220
In thanksgiving	220
The Resurrection	221
The Ascension	221
The Descent of the Holy Ghost	221
The Assumption Of Our Blessed Mother Into Heaven	222
The Coronation Of Our Blessed Mother In Heaven As Its Queen	222
Spiritual Communion	223
In petition	223
In thanksgiving	223
Prayer	224
Other Chaplet Prayers	225
Chaplet of the Twelve Privileges of Our Lady	225
Rosary of the Seven Dolours	228
Chaplet of the Immaculate Conception	231
Chaplet of the Immaculate Heart of Mary	232
The Franciscan Crown or Seraphic Rosary	235
The Rule of the Mother of God of St Seraphim of Sarov	239
Meditation for the Feast of The Holy Rosary, 5 October 1879 Blessed John Henry Cardinal Newman	249
The Secret of the Rosary by St. Louis de Montfort	253
A White Rose	253
A Red Rose	254
A Mystical Rose Tree	256
A Rosebud	257
FIRST DECADE The surpassing merit of the Rosary as seen in its origin and name.	259
First Rose	259
Second Rose	259
Third Rose	261
Fourth Rose	265

- Fifth Rose 267
- Sixth Rose 269
- Seventh Rose 270
- Eighth Rose 272
- Ninth Rose 275
- Tenth Rose 276

SECOND DECADE The surpassing merit of the Rosary as seen in the prayers which compose it. 278
- Eleventh Rose [The Creed] 278
- Twelfth Rose [The Our Father] 280
- Thirteenth Rose 286
- Fourteenth Rose 288
- Fifteenth Rose 290
- Sixteenth Rose 291
- Seventeenth Rose 294
- Eighteenth Rose 296
- Nineteenth Rose 297
- Twentieth Rose: Brief explanation of the Hail Mary 299

THIRD DECADE The surpassing merit of the holy Rosary as a meditation on the life and passion of our Lord Jesus Christ 302
- Twenty-first Rose: The Fifteen Mysteries of the Rosary 302
- Twenty-second Rose: The Meditation of the Mysteries makes us resemble Jesus 305
- Twenty-third Rose: The Rosary is a Memorial of the Life and Death of Jesus 306
- Twenty-fourth Rose: Meditation on the Mysteries of the Rosary is a great means of perfection 308
- Twenty-fifth Rose: The Riches of Holiness contained in the Prayers and Meditations of the Rosary 310
- Twenty-sixth Rose 313
- Twenty-seventh Rose 315
- Twenty-eighth Rose 319
- Twenty-ninth Rose 321
- Thirtieth Rose 323

FOURTH DECADE The surpassing merit of the holy Rosary as seen in the wonders God has worked through it. 326
- Thirty-first Rose 326
- Thirty-second Rose 328
- Thirty-third Rose 329

Thirty-fourth Rose 333
Thirty-fifth Rose 334
Thirty-sixth Rose 335
Thirty-seventh Rose 336
Thirty-eighth Rose 337
Thirty-ninth Rose 338
Fortieth Rose 339
FIFTH DECADE How to say the Rosary worthily 341
Forty-first Rose 341
Forty-second Rose 343
Forty-third Rose 345
Forty-fourth Rose 347
Forty-fifth Rose 351
Forty-sixth Rose 352
Forty-seventh Rose 356
Forty-eighth Rose 361
Forty-ninth Rose 366
METHODS FOR SAYING THE ROSARY 368
First Method 368
Second, Shorter Method of Celebrating the life, death and heavenly glory of Jesus and Mary in the Holy Rosary and a method of restraining our imagination and lessening distractions. 374
Third Method of Fr. de Montfort for saying fruitfully the holy Rosary, for the use of the Daughters of Wisdom. 375
Fourth Method Summary of the life, death and passion and heavenly glory of Jesus and Mary in the holy Rosary. 384
Fifth Method 150 Motives Impelling us to say the Rosary 397
Appendix 409
The Principal Rules Of The Confraternity of the Holy Rosary 409
On the Power and Dignity of the Rosary 410
On the Dignity of the Hail Mary 411
Selected Papal Documents on the Rosary 415
Supremi Apostolatus Officio On Devotion Of The Rosary 415
Superiore Anno On The Recitation Of The Rosary 423
Quod Auctoritate Proclaiming An Extraordinary Jubilee 428
Vi E Ben Noto On The Rosary And Public Life 436
Quamquam Pluries On Devotion To St. Joseph 440
Octobri Mense On The Rosary 447
Magnae Dei Matris On The Rosary 461

Laetittiae Sanctae Commending Devotion To The Rosary 476
Iucunda Semper Expectatione On The Rosary 487
Adiutricem Populi On the Rosary 497
Fidentem Piumque Animum On the Rosary 510
Augustissimae Virginis Mariae On The Confraternity Of The Holy Rosary 518
Fausto Appetente Die On St. Dominic 527
Ingravescentibus Malis On The Rosary 534
Ingruentium Malorum On Reciting The Rosary 543
Grata Recordatio On The Rosary 550
Christi Matri On Praying the Rosary During the Month of October . 556
Marialis Cultus Apostolic Exhortation For The Right Ordering And Development Of Devotion To The Blessed Virgin Mary 562
Redemptoris Mater On The Blessed Virgin Mary In The Life Of The Pilgrim Church 619
Rosarium Virginis Mariae On the Most Holy Rosary 706

The Excellence of the Rosary

Conferences for Devotions in honor of The Blessed Virgin

BY
REV. M. J. FRINGS

NEW YORK
JOSEPH F. WAGNER

Nihil Obstat
REMIGIUS LAFORT, D.D.
Censor

Imprimatur
JOHN CARDINAL FARLEY
Archbishop of New York

NEW YORK, September 19, 1912

Copyright, 1912, by JOSEPH F. WAGNER, NEW YORK

Enchiridion Sanctissimi Rosarii

I. The Name of this Devotion

"I was exalted as a rose plant in Jericho."—Eccles. xxiv, 18.

My dear brethren, when Pope Pius IX, on May 23, 1877, gave audience to a number of pious pilgrims he said to them: "Have courage, my dear children! I exhort you to fight against the persecution of the Church and against anarchy, not with the sword, but with the rosary, with prayer and good example." This Pope, who with great wisdom and strong hand has guided for thirty-two years the bark of Peter, which in many violent storms had been rocked to and fro, he who well knew the great dangers of our times, regarded the rosary as a conquering weapon.

What great confidence his successor, Pope Leo XIII, placed in the veneration and invocation of the Blessed Virgin Mary, by means of the rosary! He exhorted all Christianity to pray the rosary daily during the month of October, in order to obtain assistance in these distressing times. In his brief on this occasion Leo XIII says: "It has been a favorite and prevalent custom of Catholics, in times of need and danger, to take refuge in Mary, and to seek consolation from her motherly concern."

Thus the firm reliance and confidence rightly placed by the Catholic Church in the mother of God is stanchly avowed.

As a matter of fact, Mary, the immaculate Virgin, free from original sin, the chosen mother of God, is endowed with such power by her Son, as no other creature, man or angel, has ever received or can receive.

The efficacy of this great devotion to the great Queen of Heaven had been demonstrated especially when false teachings, depravity, or other great enemies threatened disaster to Christians.

History, early and recent, relates how public and private devotion to the mother of God was held in times of calamity and distress, and how these prayers were heard, and help was granted. Thus originated the exalted titles which Catholics give to the Blessed Virgin, such as Help of Christians, Refuge of Sinners, etc.

To these titles was added another, when under date of December 10, 1883, Leo XIII directed that the title "Queen of the Rosary" be added to the Litany of the Blessed Virgin. In his brief the Holy Father expresses the desire that all the faithful practise daily the devotion of the rosary. If, therefore, the rosary is considered of such great power and efficacy by the head of the Church, the representative of Christ, it is befitting that we heed his words and pray often and devoutly by means of the rosary.

If this prayer were better understood it would be prayed with more devotion, and greater benefit would come from it. In order, then, to spread a better knowledge, and to urge the devout recital of the rosary, let us contemplate this devotion in a course of instructive addresses. The name rosary may be the subject of to-day's discourse.

The devotion of the rosary consists in the recital of a fixed number of Our Fathers and Hail Marys, combined with the meditation on certain mysteries from the lives of Jesus and Mary. The name rosary is significant. It is a symbol of Mary, also of the devotion to her. We will endeavor to make this clear.

The realm of nature is the symbol of the realm of grace, as the realm of grace is a symbol of the realm of glory. It was God's intention to let His earthly creation be a reflection of the divine perfections, of the supernatural, of divinity, so that man might perceive the supernatural through created things, and thus more readily understand it. "For the invisible things of him, from the creation of the world, are clearly seen, being understood by the things that are made" (Rom. i, 20).

Our first parents obtained a clear conception of the supernatural through the natural things of this life. Nature was to them an open book, in which they could read the divine perfections. Through sin the understanding of man was dimmed and he failed in the interpretation of nature. Instead of being led to God through it, he allowed himself to become estranged, and from a master became the slave of nature.

Then Christ came and redeemed the world from the slavery of sin and again granted to man the clear conception of the true God, as also the right understanding of nature. This is verified in the saints and we have a beautiful example in St. Francis of Assisi. About his interpretation and meditation of nature St. Bonaventure says: "He considered all things created as original from God, and saw in each creature the Creator and Preserver."

Everything in nature was to him a symbol of spiritual life. He took delight especially in flowers, because they reminded him of the flower from the root of Jesse, which refreshens and gladdens the whole world.

See, my dear brethren, this is the correct, the Christian way of contemplating nature. The spiritual world is reflected in the visible.

And Jesus being the King and Mary the Queen in the realm of grace and glory, nature contains symbols that refer to Jesus and Mary. All things of this creation: from the flowers of the valley to the brilliant stars that illumine the night, all things in nature are symbols of the glorious mother of God. Among many such symbols used in Holy Scripture we find Mary called the mystical rose. The Church therefore regards the rose as a symbol of Mary. Let us see in what the likeness consists.

If on a summer's day we enter a garden, where various flowers through their form, color and sweet odor delight and refresh us, our eye is chiefly attracted by the rose. We are especially well pleased with it. The rose is the queen of flowers in form, color and fragrant odor, because of its beauty.

Let us turn now our gaze to the spiritual garden, the Church of Christ. The various flowers there are the faithful, adorned with piety and virtue, and spreading the fragrance of saintliness with which God is pleased. In the Canticle of Canticles the Lamb of God is pictured as feeding among the lilies. A beautiful thought! It tells us how the Lamb of God, our divine Saviour, is fond of the flowers of God, the God-loving souls, as is the lamb of the lilies.

And in this garden of God, the Holy Church, Mary is the rose, the pride of the garden, the queen of the flowers. The rose is therefore the most beautiful symbol of Mary, of all saints the queen, exalted above all saints in sublimity, beauty, gentleness and sweetness. Therefore, because Mary is among the saints what the rose is among flowers, she is called "the mystical rose." And the name rosary is to remind us of this.

The rose, furthermore, signifies the virtuous life of Mary the virgin. The rosebud is a beautiful symbol of virginity. It is hidden as under a veil. Lovely is the Christian virgin, hidden in the garb of innocence like a rosebud. Mary is the Virgin of Virgins, and can above all be compared to the fair and undefiled rosebud.

The open, blooming rose is an emblem of pure motherhood. Like the opened radiant rose the Christian mother is in the full vigor of life; her heart open with true love for her husband and children; and she unfolds her soul to heaven, so that through prayer she may receive the needed assistance for herself and hers. Through her good example in Christian virtues she spreads around her the fragrance of a God-pleasing life, and encourages those who associate with her to imitate her virtues.

Mary is the immaculate virgin and mother, mother of God, and of all mankind. She is the most noble and perfect of all mothers. Like a magnificent rose she shines in the splendor of her virtues, and is the perfect example for all mothers. Because her heart is fired with love for God and man, she is, as St. Jordanus says, likened to the flaming red rose.

There is no rose but has its thorns. The thorns are a figure of suffering, of sorrow, of the temptations in life, under which only a truly virtuous life can thrive.

St. Brigid relates in her revelations how she at one time was downcast because the enemies of Christ were so powerful, and how she was consoled by the mother of God herself, who told her to remember the rose among the thorns. "The rose," so said Mary, "gives a fragrant odor; it is beautiful to the sight, and tender to the touch, and yet it grows among thorns, inimical to beauty and tenderness. So may also those who are mild, patient, beautiful in virtue, be put to a test among adversaries. And as the thorn, on the other hand, guards, so do wicked surroundings protect the just against sin by demonstrating to them the destructiveness of sin."

The life of Mary was interwoven with many sorrows and she is justly called "a rose among thorns." St. Brigid says: "The Virgin may suitably be called a blooming rose. Just as the gentle rose is placed among thorns, so this gentle Virgin was surrounded by sorrow."

The rose obtains its life through the stem, to which it is closely united. A rose broken from the stem will soon wither. So Mary received all her graces from Jesus, with whom she was united through the liveliest faith and ardent love.

Mary is in truth a spiritual, a mystic rose. The rose therefore is a fitting symbol of the virtuous life of the mother of God. As mystical rose she deserves our admiration and veneration, and she must be our example and model in all Christian virtues, the model of a true spiritual life.

The name rosary, therefore, is well suited to this devotion. For it is a wreath of spiritual roses, as it were, which we place at the feet of Mary, in order to show our love and veneration.

The rose has, moreover, been at all times regarded as a symbol of love. It was already the custom of the early Christians to adorn on feast days the pictures and statues of the saints with wreaths of roses, especially on feast days of the Blessed Virgin.

St. Dominic, inspired and instructed by Mary, formed from the beautiful and efficacious prayers, the Our Father and the Hail Mary, together with the principal mysteries from the lives of Jesus and Mary, a beautiful wreath, and called it the "Rosary."

The threefold mysteries represented in the devotion again give it a resemblance to the rose. The green of the rose is the color of hope and confidence. It is represented in the glorious rosary. The thorns are represented in the sorrowful rosary. The beautiful red petals of the rose, finally, are represented in the joyful rosary, in the glories of Jesus and Mary.

Thus is shown therefore the deep and significant meaning of the name rosary. And as the rosary reminds us of all the virtues, the spiritual beauty and sublimity of Mary, and as it is a worthy manifestation of our love and veneration for the mother of God it is meet that we hold the rosary in high esteem. And Mary finds delight in this devotion, for it reminds her of all the good God did for her, and for which all nations pronounce her blessed.

Oh, let us then resolve to wind this wreath frequently, to lay it often at the feet of the noble, the gracious queen of the Rosary!

II. The Origin of the Rosary

"The Highest himself hath founded her."—Ps. lxxxvi.

My dear brethren, in our consideration on the rosary let us to-day reflect upon its origin.

Its origin and age bestow on this devotion a great dignity. From the earliest times of Christianity it has been the custom of the Christians to observe in their prayers method and perseverance. Thus it was the custom of the hermits of the Orient, as far back as the fourth century, to devise a sequence of certain prayers, which they counted on pebbles. We also know that long ago in England a so-called Paternoster-cord was used for this purpose. St. Gregory, at the end of the fourth century, spoke of such a method of devotion in veneration of the Blessed Virgin Mary. This pious bishop thought a wreath of spiritual roses would be more pleasing to the blessed Virgin than the natural roses with which the faithful adorned her altar. He selected, therefore, a number of prayers, in praise of the blessed Virgin, and united them into a wreath. And this was the origin of the rosary, woven by pious hands for the veneration of Mary, the mystical rose.

In the fifth century, St. Brigid urgently commended the devotion of the rosary, and she chose as its prayers the Our Father, the Hail Mary, and the Creed, and united them into a wreath of prayers. In order to count their recital she strung little beads of stone or wood and made a wreath of them.

This custom subsequently spread through all Christian lands, and through the centuries, to our own days. That this devotion was always in great favor and esteem among pious Christians may be concluded from the fact that in the grave of St. Norbert, who died in 1134, a rosary similar to ours was found.

We have proof, then, that the devotion of the rosary, such as we have it, was practised already in the early days of Christianity. And it was practised not only by monks and nuns, but found adherents among all the faithful.

The particular manner in which we now pray the rosary was brought into vogue by St. Dominic. This is attested by the tradition of six centuries. Twelve Popes bear witness to this fact. We will now speak of the introduction by St. Dominic, and will also refer to the great efficacy of this devotion since its inception. May our reflections contribute to the greater honor of God, and of the glorious Queen of the rosary.

I. The devotion of the rosary in its present form dates its origin from the thirteenth century, and St. Dominic was selected by God as the instrument of its introduction. Spain was the home of this great saint. In one of the valleys of Castile there is situated an humble little village named Calarunga, where his parents possessed a small estate. He was born there in the year 1170. While being baptized his sponsor saw, as if in a vision, a brilliant star over the forehead of the future saint, shedding its brilliant light through the church. As Dominic advanced in years he increased in wisdom, virtue and piety. In due time he devoted himself to theology, believing that in this pursuit alone he could find the wisdom of God. Not in the pleasures of this world, but in the knowledge of God, he sought his pastime. His favorite place was the church and the solitude of the sanctuary. Two incidents from his schooldays throw a light upon his character. At the time of a famine Dominic gave all that he possessed to the poor, even all but the necessary clothes, and when he had nothing more to give, he sold even his beloved books and gave the proceeds to the poor. When berated by people for his excessive generosity, he said: "How could I dare indulge in these lifeless books, when human lives are in danger of starvation?" At another time St. Dominic met a woman who was weeping bitterly because she had no money with which she could release her brother, who had been imprisoned by the Saracens. Dominic offered to sell himself into bondage to release this brother; but since God had destined him to release sinful mankind from the bondage of sin, of error and unbelief, He did not permit Dominic to do as he offered.

At the age of twenty-five he was appointed upon the chapter of the cathedral at Osma. Here he was conspicuous among his brethren on account of his humility, holiness, and zeal for prayer. He spent nine years in Osma, during which time divine Providence prepared him for his important and great vocation. This vocation became plain to him when, in the year 1204, he went to France and saw the terrible devastation which the prevailing heresies had wrought against the Church of Christ. The sight of this disaster nearly broke his heart. The poison of heresy had spread among the faithful with great rapidity, and principally in southern France. From the city of Albi the heretics had assumed the name Albigenses. These Albigenses discarded the doctrines of Christianity and constructed new doctrines that played havoc with morality and social order. They were violent enemies of Church and State, and preached disobedience and rebellion against spiritual and temporal authority. An enemy of the Church is invariably also an enemy of the State; history and experience prove this.

In southern France the Albigenses secured the support of Prince Raimond, of Toulouse, a wealthy and mighty, but, at the same time, a most godless and immoral prince of that time. He had several wives; associated with heretics, and even gave his children to be educated by them. This prince undertook the leadership of the heretical Albigenses, and with them, and other rabble by which France at that time was overrun, scoured the country, robbing and plundering wherever they went. This lawless band, under the direction of this godless prince, robbed churches of their treasures, murdered priests, even tore open the tabernacles and desecrated the most holy Sacrament. A messenger of Pope Innocent III was murdered by one of these knaves, who then found the protection of this depraved prince. Under these conditions the Pope finally saw the necessity of preaching a crusade against these heretics, who surpassed even the Saracens in the outrages committed. A terrible war then ensued, in which these enemies of Church and State were subdued, but not converted. For this there was necessary an extraordinary spiritual effort, and divine Providence had already prepared the instrument. St. Dominic was the tool in the hand of God to introduce and apply an efficacious remedy, and this remedy was the rosary.

Dominic had for many years taught the doctrines of the Catholic Church to the heretics, and had converted a number of them, but not enough to satisfy his holy zeal. He often turned with humility to God and besought Him with tears, and deeds of penance, that He might let him know how to accomplish better results. Since childhood he had been a faithful servant of Mary, and had often said that the devotion to her was a powerful means of converting heretics and sinners.

Finally his prayers were heard in a miraculous way. One day, while on his way from Toulouse, Dominic threw himself down on his knees and resolved not to cease praying until his prayers were heard. Then, so the legend tells us, the glorious Queen of heaven appeared to him, spoke words of encouragement, and taught him how to pray the rosary, assuring him that this would be the right weapon to conquer error and sin. With joy Dominic arose and returned to Toulouse, and began to spread the use of the rosary, as Mary had taught him and in the way we now recite it. He preached this devotion, explained it, and taught the people how to pray it. It proved indeed a most efficacious means for the conversion of apostates, heretics, and sinners. Since the lack of knowledge in matters of faith had been the real cause why heresy so quickly spread, the principal truths of faith and morals were now communicated to the people through the rosary, and the principles of a Christian life were taught them in this most sublime prayer of the Church. This was bound to bring results, and we will give now some thought to these results.

II. According to the historians of those ages the effects of the rosary sermons of St. Dominic were truly wonderful. In all cities where he preached, the people gathered in great numbers to hear his heaven-inspired words and to pray the rosary with St. Dominic. Sinners were converted, the faithful were strengthened and fortified, and many thousands of those who had been led into heresy opened their hearts again to the true faith and returned to the holy Church. The inspired words of St. Dominic met with such splendid results that, even if the tradition did not tell us so, the miraculous effects of this devotion would prove its heavenly inspiration, and Pius IX, Leo XIII, as many Popes before them, have publicly avowed their belief that St. Dominic received the rosary from our blessed Mother.

The promise which Dominic received was fulfilled. Where all other means had failed, the humble prayer of the rosary accomplished the victory over heresy. Thus divine wisdom and infinite power make use of humble things to effect great achievements. Of this the great work of the redemption gives us an example. God made the Cross the instrument of the redemption. The despised Cross, once a shame and disgrace, was raised on the height of Calvary and became the instrument of the redemption for all the world, the fountain of grace, a blessing for time and eternity, the symbol of victory and glory.

St. Paul, in his first letter to the Corinthians, writes: "And I, brethren, when I came to you, came not in loftiness of speech or of wisdom, declaring unto you the testimony of Christ. For I judge not myself to know anything among you, but Jesus Christ, and him crucified. And my speech and my preaching was not in the persuasive words of human wisdom, but in the showing of the spirit and power. That your faith might not stand on the wisdom of men, but on the power of God. But we preach Christ crucified, unto the Jews indeed a stumbling block, and unto the Gentiles foolishness: But unto them that are called, both Jews and Greeks, Christ the power of God, and the wisdom of God; for the foolishness of God is wiser than men; but the foolish things of the world hath God chosen, that he may confound the strong. That no flesh should glory in his sight" (I Cor. i and ii). And so did God choose the rosary, this humble prayer, to work such great things, that human effort had not been able to accomplish. What an incentive to put all our trust in God, rather than in our own strength!

The devotion of the rosary soon spread from southern France to all other Catholic lands, and all peoples welcomed it with joy and prayed it with great zeal. Rosary societies were formed and approved of by the Popes, and were richly endowed with many indulgences. Ever since there has been no other prayer practised so diligently as the rosary. And often there have been recorded miraculous effects of this devotion, no less miraculous than the conversion of the heretics in the south of France.

The devotion as now practised is therefore in use over seven hundred years. The wonderful origin, its great age and the remarkable miracles that were wrought by its use at all times, bestow a great dignity on this devotion.

When we consider the conditions that prevailed at the time of the origin of the rosary, and for the betterment of which divine Providence provided this devotion, we can not fail to realize a similarity of conditions in our own times. Materialism and unbelief, connected with widespread immorality, are now prevalent as they were then. They are causing great injury to Church, State, and homes, and will become more destructive if not checked by the right weapon. Pope Pius IX, as also Pope Leo XIII, have declared the rosary to be that weapon, and have exhorted Christianity to resort to the zealous use of it. If all Christians would follow the advice of these supreme Pontiffs, we should soon see the Catholic faith and good morals come into their own again, and ample blessing would, through this devotion, be bestowed upon private and public life. All the insistent endeavors of world-wise scholars and reformers will be of no avail if God's blessing does not rest upon their work. Only then, when the true faith and a life of faith are made the standard of public and private merit and ethics, will the temporal, no less than the eternal, welfare of nations and of individuals be assured.

Let us, through the rosary, call to Mary for her powerful intercession in the battle of the Church against the enemies of faith and morals, and with her intercession we shall be sure of victory. Amen.

III. The Power of the Rosary

"Lo, here is the sword of Goliath. . . . There is none like that, give it to me."—I Kings xxi, 9.

SYNOPSIS.—*David, with God's assistance, his only weapon a pebble, slew the giant. God gives us, as our weapon, the rosary. This has proven efficacious in the battles of the Church against heretics and heathen armies. Examples: Albigenses; Turks at Lepanto and Belgrade; many epidemics abated or averted by the power of the rosary. This devotion is just as powerful for the individual and for the family.*

God has shown us that He wishes many to co-operate with the Church and with the Christian in their fight for faith and salvation. Let all use this weapon.

My dear brethren, in the first book of Kings we read how the Philistines went forth to battle against the Israelites. The Philistines arrayed their forces on a mountain, and the Israelites occupied a mountain on the opposite side, so that the valley was between them. Then there went out from the hordes of the Philistines a man named Goliath, a giant of enormous strength, who challenged the Israelites to let one of their men fight him hand to hand, the result of this contest to decide the victory or defeat of either army. A youth named David, inspired and urged by the spirit of God, went forth with a few smooth stones and a sling to meet this Philistine, and as Goliath rushed toward him David cast the stones with the sling and struck the Philistine in the forehead, and he fell upon his face to the earth. David then ran and stood over the Philistine and took his sword and slew him. Israel thus gained the victory over the Philistines. But when for this victory exceeding praise was given to David, King Saul became angry and sought the life of the youthful hero. In his flight David came to Nobe. Not having any weapon, he said to the high priest Achimelech: "Hast thou here at hand a spear or a sword?" The high priest answered: "Lo, here is the sword of Goliath, whom thou slewest in the valley of Terebinth, if thou wilt take this, for there is no other but this." And David said, "There is none like that, give it me."

These last words, which I have made the text for my address to-day, we may fitly apply to the holy rosary. For the rosary has ever since its origin proven itself a conquering weapon for the Church, as also well as for the individual Christian, against the most powerful enemies of God and of His Church. Let us consider the fact for the greater glory of God and of the Queen of the rosary.

A Manual of the Most Holy Rosary

Since the introduction of the rosary by St. Dominic, for more than six hundred years therefore, the great victories of Christianity against the many and ferocious enemies of the Church are ascribed to the devotion of the rosary. The Church has at all times had enemies, who with all their power and in all their evil ways have opposed and persecuted her. Nor is this surprising. Ever since Satan succeeded in beguiling our first parents into sin, he has continued to sow dissention among mankind. Beginning with Cain and Abel, there have been children of God who obeyed God's commandments, and, on the other hand, children of Satan, as holy Scripture calls them, who seek their salvation in the pleasures of this life. Since the time of Cain and Abel, mankind has been split into two divisions, one seeking the kingdom of God, the other the kingdom of the world, the kingdom of Satan.

When our Saviour conquered Satan He left him power over those who make themselves slaves to the sensual pleasures, and thus there exists an evil force against the Church, and it will exist to the end of time. This is a fact that we must keep in view in order to fully understand and judge the conditions. The realm of darkness, Satan's realm, stands opposed to the realm of Christ. Satan and his adherents carry on the warfare against the Church of Christ, as they assaulted Christ Himself. "As they have persecuted me, they will also persecute you," so did Christ prophecy.

The Church of Christ demands the subjection of the flesh; she preaches against luxury, pride and selfishness. She preaches chastity and submission to the commandments of God; she preaches penance alike to those of high and low station in life. This angers all those who would indulge in the evil things of this world. They cry: "Let us break her bonds asunder; and let us cast away her yoke from us." But as Christ foretold the persecution of His Church, so He also foretold that the gates of hell would not prevail against her. The Church of God will in due time conquer all her enemies, some will be converted, while others who are obstinate will perish in the battle. In all these battles and victories of the Church, Mary, blessed mother of her divine Founder, co-operates with the Church through her intercession. Mary was already spoken of in paradise as the one who would come to tread upon the head of the serpent, the spirit of darkness. This she has done by becoming the mother of God, by bringing forth the Redeemer. And as Jesus through Mary's co-operation came into this world, so He desires her co-operation in ruling the world. The history of the contests and Victories of the Church verify this throughout the centuries.

The evil spirit has a twofold weapon with which he assails and combats God's Church; namely, the godless rulers of the world and heresy. Through the godless authorities of the world Satan has endeavored since the beginning to crush the Church; through heresy he attempts to destroy the Church by internal dissension. Both weapons are used together, for heresy and calumny can not prevail without substantial support, and heretics seek worldly power and assistance. On every page of Church history we find recorded the clashes planned by these evil forces, from which the Church always came out not conquered, but a conqueror.

The history of the veneration of Mary tells us that the Blessed Virgin Mary helped to win these victories. During the early times, when fierce battles against the Church were raging, bishops and priests knew of no more efficacious means to avert these dangers than to exhort the faithful to pray to the Blessed Virgin. Thus we read in history that the holy bishops and martyrs Ignatius and Irenaeus did this in the second century, and in the third century it was Pope Calixtus who advised the faithful to take refuge with the Blessed Virgin in time of persecution of the Church. And so on through all Christian times.

Since the introduction of the rosary by St. Dominic all great victories have been credited to the devotion of the rosary. The first great conquest of the Church effected by the rosary was the victory over the Albigenses, who had spread heresy in southern France and had caused great havoc in Church and State.

St. Bernard complained in those times: "The churches are empty, the people without priests, the Sacraments without reverence.

People on their deathbed refuse the assistance of the Church, ridicule penance."

How the weapon with which this heresy was conquered was the rosary we have related in a previous sermon. This was the first glorious victory through the devotion of the rosary. It was the sword with which the Church slew the proud Goliath of heresy.

Another wonderful victory through this miraculous weapon of Christianity was the defeat of the Turkish navy at Lepanto, on October 7, 1571. The so-called reformation, of which Martin Luther was the originator, had spread over the whole of Europe, bringing in its trail destruction, dissension and war. The Turks, who had long thirsted for vengeance upon the Christians, found situations favorable for their plans. They gathered all their forces to assail the Christian lands. The princes of Europe were either indifferent, or were besieged with difficulties in their own lands, and Luther even said he preferred the Turks to the papacy. Pope Pius V alone realized the great danger that threatened Christianity and he called upon the Christian people to defend country and Church against the common enemy.

The Christian forces which could be assembled were very small compared with those of the Turks. Nevertheless Pius V knew of another power which he realized would be a mighty ally. With all his energy he exhorted his people to implore the Blessed Virgin and glorious Queen of heaven, through the rosary, to come to the assistance of the Christian army. It was, as Leo XIII said in his Commendation of the rosary, an ennobling sight, which drew the eyes of the whole world; on one side, not far from the Corinthian Sea, the Christians prepared to sacrifice life for religion and country; while gathered on the other side, imploring through the rosary Mary's assistance for the fighting Christians, were many Christians unable to take up arms.

The small army of Christians attacking the great force of the Turkish fleet was an undertaking similar to the assault of David upon the giant Goliath. On October 7, 1571, the deciding battle was fought, in the Bay of Lepanto. The battle raged from six o'clock in the morning until six o'clock at night. It was one of the most terrific battles ever fought. And, lo! in the evening, toward six o'clock, the battle ended in the victory of the Christians over their powerful enemy. This wonderful victory of the Christians was undoubtedly due to the assistance of the Blessed Virgin. Pope Pius V so declared, and in memory of this wonderful achievement he added to the litany of the Blessed Virgin the supplication: "Help of Christians, pray for us!" He also ordained that the anniversary of this victory be celebrated as the feast of "Our Lady of Victory," which Gregory XIII subsequently styled the "Feast of the Rosary."

In the annals of the Church there is another great victory over the Turks recorded which once more demonstrated the power of the rosary. It was the great victory in the campaign against the Turks at the beginning of the eighteenth century.

After the Turks had been defeated at sea, they endeavored to conquer on land. They forced their way to Hungary, and had taken possession of eight provinces, when Emperor Charles VII sent an army against them under the command of Prince Eugene. This army was composed of only seventy thousand men. With this meager force Prince Eugene defeated two hundred thousand Turks and laid siege to Belgrade, their stronghold.

Prince Eugene, before engaging the enemy, implored the help of the Blessed Virgin, through the rosary, and then with confidence in God's assistance went to battle and to glorious victory. Thirty thousand Turks were slain on the battlefield; the others fled. The rosary again had won the victory, and on the feast day of the Blessed Virgin.

In the same manner as the rosary was a successful weapon against heretics and other enemies of the Church, it has demonstrated its wonderful efficiency in individual cases of stress, and of such I will mention a few instances. In the year 1578 a fearful epidemic devastated the city of Pavia. The terrified people made a public vow to build a chapel to our Blessed Lady of the Rosary if the epidemic would cease. And the very day the vow was made the epidemic did abate. A similar case happened in Cologne, where people were saved from an epidemic after such a vow had been made. That cases like these are innumerable' is manifested by the many chapels built as a result of such vows, and by the votive tablets in pilgrimage churches dedicated to Mary. Sight is restored to the blind, hearing to the deaf, speech to the dumb, the use of their limbs to the crippled, diseases of all kind are cured, by invoking the intercession of the Blessed Virgin by means of the devotion of the rosary.

The conversion of a hardened sinner is, after all, a greater miracle than all cures of disease. And such conversions to this day are as numerous as they were at the time the rosary was introduced. Entire nations, provinces and cities have been converted to God through his devotion. Blessed John, a companion of St. Dominic, wrote a book about the miraculous power of the rosary. The blessed Alanus de la Roche tells of a bishop, in whose diocese morality was decadent, who finally took up the devotion to the rosary, explained it to his people, prayed it with them, and had it introduced in all parishes. Soon the people abandoned their evil ways.

St. Clement Hofbauer assures us: "When I am called to a sick man of whom I know that he is averse to making his peace with God, on the way I pray my rosary, and when I reach him I am sure to find him desirous to receive the Sacraments."

The holy doctor Alphonsus of Liguori relates from his experience: "The walls of Jericho did not collapse more quickly at the trumpet call of Josue than false teachings disappear after the earnest praying of the rosary. The swimming pool of Jerusalem was not as healing for the bodily sick as the rosary is as remedy for the spiritually diseased."

These few examples, to which I could add hundreds of other similar instances, prove the miraculous efficacy of the rosary. Oh, that all Christians would grasp this weapon to attack and conquer all enemies of Church and soul!

Great dangers threaten the spiritual weal of the individual, family and community. Let us, then, arise and grasp the mighty sword which is like to none, the holy rosary, and let us attack with it the Goliath of our times, corruption and godlessness. As David courageously met the enemy of Israel with the humble sling in his hand and conquered because God was with him, so let us face the enemies of Christendom and of our salvation, with the humble wreath of the rosary in our hands, and the intercession of the Blessed Virgin will secure for us God's grace and assistance, and with God to fight our battles, who will do us harm? Amen!

IV. The Excellence of the Various Parts of the Rosary

(a) The Sign of the Cross

"The foundations thereof are in the holy mountains."—Ps. lxxxvi, I.

Dear brethren, we have seen in our previous discourses upon the rosary how for more than six centuries the rosary has proved itself a great, indeed a marvelous, power and help in times of stress. This, of course, was apparent from its very origin. It was a special instrument of divine Providence in troublous times of Church and Society. The various parts of the rosary are admirably adapted to exercise such great power and efficacy. The Our Father, the Hail Mary, the Creed, the Glory be to the Father, and the Sign of the Cross, which are said in reciting the rosary, are the most beautiful, I the holiest and most excellent of prayers, and for this reason also the most potent and efficacious. The mysteries of our holy faith, which are at the same time meditated upon, embrace the entire work of our redemption, in its work (joyful mysteries), its accomplishment (sorrowful mysteries), and in its fruits (glorious mysteries). Meditation combined with prayer as it is contained in the rosary renders it a perfect prayer. The rosary furthermore is the best means of honoring Mary, and therefore it is the best means for obtaining Mary's powerful intercession.

That we may understand and perceive the whole beauty and excellence of the rosary let us closely view its component parts, and we will begin to-day by considering the opening of the rosary, namely the sign of the Cross. This has a most sublime meaning, and has of itself great power and efficacy. It is a sign of honor, of blessing and of power. In this threefold aspect let us consider it to-day.

I. The sign of the Cross is, first of all, a mark of honor. It reminds us of the holy Trinity and of our relation to the triune God. The Father has created us, the Son redeemed us, and the Holy Ghost has sanctified us. God the Father created us after His own image, and therefore we bear a resemblance to God in our souls. Our soul is a spirit, as God is a spirit. It has understanding and free will; it can be holy; it can become perfect, since our heavenly Father is perfect. Our soul is immortal, as God is immortal, and it is destined to partake in heaven of divine glory and happiness. Is there not in this resemblance and likeness to God an unspeakably high dignity and glory for man? We are reminded of this by the sign of the Cross. The Son of God redeemed us through the Cross. After sin had reduced the human race to a state of ignominious bondage the Son of God, moved by infinite love, became incarnate for us, in order to make satisfaction for our sins and to remove from us their awful consequences. From slaves of sin and of the devil, He has made us just and children of God. Having been redeemed, we now call God our Father; and Jesus, the Son of the eternal Father, calls us His brethren. Of all this we are reminded by the Cross, for we were redeemed through the Cross, and became children of God and heirs of heaven. Thus the Cross is the glorious sign of our redemption. The Holy Ghost sanctifies us by dwelling in us and making of us His temples. What an honor for us! The sign of the Cross reminds us of this honor.

In truth is therefore this sign a mark of the highest honor, and the Christian's greatest glory. In this sense the Apostle wrote to the

Galatians: "But God forbid that I should glory, but in the Cross of our Lord Jesus Christ" (Gal. vi, 14). This means, according to Saint Chrysostom: "I glory only in the Cross of our Lord Jesus Christ, namely, in the faith, in grateful remembrance and contemplation of the benefactions of the Cross, through which we were redeemed and have received the grace to lead a devout life and to strive for eternal happiness. In the Cross we recognize thoroughly the enormity of our guilt and the boundless love of God."

With what love and devotion should we, then, make the sign of the Cross! As often as we sign ourselves with the Cross we profess our belief in the holy Trinity, and in the merciful and blessed work of the redemption, and express our gratitude to the holy Trinity, Father, Son and Holy Ghost. It is hard to believe that there are Christians who are ashamed to make the sign of the Cross; and yet: there are many such nowadays. Some act so from motives of cowardly human respect; others because their faith is dead. But to be ashamed of the Cross means a denial of our faith. At all times the sign of the Cross has served as a public and solemn profession of the Christian faith. Thus did in the days of persecution the faithful profess their belief in Christ, and seal their profession with their blood, as the acts of the martyrs record. When the holy Bishop Polycarp was brought before the heathen judge, who said to him, "Deny Christ and you will be free!" Polycarp's reply was worthy of a true Christian. "It is now over sixty years that I have served Him, and He never did me any harm. How, then, can I deny my beloved Master, King and Saviour?" So speaks the true Christian when an attempt is made to make him deny his God and Redeemer. The sign of the Cross also serves as a mark of distinction from those sects, which centuries ago separated themselves from the mother Church and abandoned the beautiful custom of making the sign of the Cross. It is a great crime, then, to be ashamed of a sign which serves for our honor and distinction. And Jesus Christ says, "For whosoever shall be ashamed of me, and of my words, of him shall the Son of Man be ashamed, when he shall come in his majesty, and of his father's, and of the holy angels" (Luke ix, 26). "But whosoever shall deny me before men, I will also deny him before my Father, who is in heaven" (Matt, x, 33). Thus does Jesus Christ express Himself concerning those who are ashamed of the glorious sign of the true Christian, and those who reject this sign with contempt.

II. The Cross is, furthermore, a sign of blessing. It reminds us, in the first place, as we have considered, of the source of all blessing, of all gifts and graces for body and soul. This source is the blessed Trinity. As often as we make the sign of the Cross we invoke the blessings of God upon us, for we owe all blessings to the infinite merits of our divine Saviour, who died upon the Cross for us. The ignominious instrument of torture and death, the Cross, has now become the instrument of life and the source of salvation. Hence the Church never dispenses blessing except in the sign of the Cross. St. Chrysostom says therefore: Every blessing in which we participate is accomplished through the sign of the Cross. When regeneration (Baptism) takes place, the sign of the Cross is employed. Whether we partake of that holy mysterious food or receive any other of the Sacraments, it is always under the sign of our victory, the sign of the Cross. We should, therefore, earnestly endeavor to have this sign in our homes, and often sign our foreheads with it; for it is the commemoration of our salvation and of our redemption. In making the sign of the Cross devoutly we say to God: Heavenly Father, behold not our sins which render us unworthy of thy grace, but the Cross of thy beloved Son, with which we sign our foreheads, which we profess with our lips and carry devoutly in our hearts. For the sake of Jesus' bitter death upon the Cross be merciful to us and grant us the assistance of thy grace in all our words and actions! This is the prayer which is contained in the sign of the Cross. That such prayer will not remain unheard is attested by numerous manifestations of grace which have been obtained through this sign, and the countless miracles which at all times have been performed through the same.

III. Finally, the Cross is a sign of power. Because Jesus upon the Cross conquered the arch enemy, redeemed mankind and merited for us all blessings and graces, there lies in the sign of the Cross a miraculous strength and efficacy. Jesus himself has said: "Everything that you ask the Father in my name, he will give you." The sign of the Cross calls for help and grace through the Blood of Christ shed upon the Cross. Would God deny such prayer? The sign of the Cross is a particularly powerful weapon against the malicious and cunning assaults of the devil. Of this St. Chrysostom says: "When in the fulness of faith you make the sign of the Cross upon your forehead no impure spirit will be able to tarry near you; for he beholds the sword that has given him the death blow." "Write the sign of the Cross upon thy brow," says St. Cyril, "so that the devils when they see the sign of the king may tremble and take flight." St Augustine tells us that our mere remembrance of the Cross puts the devil to flight, strengthens us against his assaults, and preserves us from his snares. The sign of the Cross provides us with a powerful weapon, wherewith we may conquer the unseen foe in every attack.

We know, too, from the testimony of Holy Writ, that the evil spirit can injure mankind not only in body and soul but also in earthly possessions. Thus the devil, by God's permission, slew Job's children, deprived him of his possessions and afflicted him with painful and loathsome maladies. Now, though Christ by His death has broken Satan's power, yet He has not completely removed it. For this reason the Church makes the sign of the Cross over people, blesses food and drink, dwellings, water, soil, in brief everything that Christians come in contact with. This she does in order to withdraw all these things from the injurious influence of the evil spirit, to unite them with the divine blessing and thus make them salutary. The grace before meals of Christians has the same purpose. It is indeed a sad token of ignorance, of indifference, or lack of faith, when in Christian homes grace before meals is disregarded, as not infrequently happens in our days. We know from the testimony of history that the sign of the Cross was also employed successfully against bodily evils. When St. Benedict was handed a glass of poisoned wine, the saint made the sign of the Cross over it, and behold the glass broke in his hand, and he was saved from death. St. Gregory of Nissa testifies that his sister during an illness desired her mother to make the sign of the Cross over her; and when it was done the illness left her. Through the sign of the Cross Bishop Fortunatus restored the sight to a blind man; St. Lawrence cured several others similarly affected. St. Roch cured the plague stricken, and the legend says that St. Corbinian brought the dead back to life by this same sign. The lives of the saints are replete with examples that testify to the miraculous power of the sign of the Cross.

Because the Cross is then a sign of honor, of blessing and power, because it is an effective remedy against evils of body and soul, the Church has always exhorted the faithful by word and example to make zealous use of the same at all times. Since the time of the Apostles the sign of the Cross has been made by the faithful in all their undertakings. Through this sign they dedicated their work to God and invoke the divine blessing upon it.

The Fathers teach that this custom originated with the Apostles; it is related even by a pious legend that Christ Himself at His ascension into heaven blessed the Apostles with this sign. How universal this custom was among Christians of the early centuries may be learned from the words of St. Chrysostom: "We find everywhere the sign of the Cross, it is used by princes and subjects, by women and men, by the slaves and the free. They all sign themselves with it by making it over their foreheads."

Let us then imitate the pious Christians of those days when faith was more lively and robust, and let us never be ashamed of this sign of honor! What would you think of a soldier ashamed of his colors? Let us not be ashamed of this sign, lest Jesus be ashamed of us, when He comes in power and majesty, with the Cross shining before Him like the sun. Let us not deprive ourselves of the manifold blessings of this sign, either through fear of our fellowmen or indifference. Let us make abundant use of this sign of power, so that we may participate in the blessing and protection that comes from the Cross, most especially when assailed by the enemies of our salvation. This sign of the Cross should be placed upon the forehead, lips and breast, before our prayers, for by this our thoughts, our words, and the emotions of our heart are consecrated and become more pleasing to God. This is the purpose of beginning the prayer of the rosary with the sign of the Cross. But, remember, it is not enough to make the sign merely with the fingers, our spirit must take part in making it, and it should be made with reverence, devotion, with a lively faith and firm confidence in the merits of Jesus Christ. Christians who make this sign thoughtlessly and without devotion deprive themselves of the great blessings of this holy sign. We, however, who have just contemplated this glorious token of salvation will use it with the greatest zeal and piety, and profess with it our faith in the blessed Trinity and in our holy mother Church. Amen.

V. The Excellence of the Various Parts of the Rosary

(b) The Apostles' Creed.

"For with the heart, we believe unto justice: but, with the mouth, confession is made unto salvation" (Rom. x, 10).

Dear Brethren: At the beginning of the Rosary, the Apostles' Creed is recited. Everything that we must believe, in order to attain to eternal life, is contained in this Creed. It puts in explicit words all that of which the sign of the Cross is the symbol. Tradition tells us that this profession of faith originated with the Apostles, and for this reason it is called the Apostles' Creed. To be sure not all the dogmas of the Catholic Church are declared in the twelve articles of the Creed, but any dogmas not expressly mentioned are included in the ninth article, which says: "I believe in the Holy Catholic Church." In these words the Catholic declares that he believes everything which the holy infallible Catholic Church teaches and requires of us to believe.

The Creed is, therefore, by its origin, as well as its contents, a truly holy and excellent prayer. It we duly appreciate this beautiful prayer we shall say it with more devotion, to the greater glory of God, and our own good.

I. "I believe in God." With these words I express my firm conviction that there is a God, and that everything that God has revealed is infallible truth, because God is truth itself and can neither deceive nor be deceived. With these words I submit my mind, my reason and my will to the infallible authority of God.

"I believe in God the Father." This means that I believe that in God there are three Persons, of whom the first Person is called the Father because He is the origin of all existence; because from all eternity He begot the Son, who is equal to Him in essence but different in Person. Further, He is our Father because He created us His children.

"I believe in God, the Father Almighty." It is befitting that at the beginning of the Creed the omnipotence of God should be emphasized. Our faith contains many mysteries, which no created understanding can comprehend. Because I firmly believe in the omnipotence of God I profess that to God nothing is impossible.

In His omnipotence, God, the Father, created the world, calling it into existence from nothing. Hence we say: "I believe in God, the Father Almighty, the Creator of heaven and earth." But God not only created the world, He also preserves and rules it through His omnipotence. As by virtue of His will He created the world, so does God cause it to continue in existence. A building erected by a master hand remains standing even though the master absent himself; yet the world, according to St. Augustine, could not continue to exist for one moment did not God preserve it. This world which God called forth from nothing would, the very moment that God should withdraw His almighty hand, fall back into nothing. "And how could anything endure if thou wouldst not?" Thus we read of God in the Book of Wisdom (ii, 26). Since we are then so utterly dependent upon God that at any moment He could cut the thread of our lives, how greatly should we fear to offend Him?

God not only preserves, but also rules the world; He is solicitous for all things; He orders and governs all things with wisdom and mercy to the end for which He created them. "The eyes of all hope in thee, O Lord: and thou givest them meat in due season. Thou openest thy hand, and fillest with blessing every living creature" (Ps. cxliv, 15-16). Of what little value is a flower which so soon withers? And yet the divine solicitude extends to this humble flower. Indeed, is not the flower of the field clothed more beautifully by the hand of God, than was Solomon in all his glory? What is there about a man of less account than a single hair of his head? And yet each of these hairs is counted, and not one falls from the head without the knowledge and will of God. We see how the care and providence of God extends to all things, even the most insignificant.

God, furthermore, orders and governs all things according to their appointed end. He created the world and all that is in it for His glorification and for the welfare of mankind, and provides in all things that this end may be attained. Nothing can withdraw itself from the rule of God. There is no blind chance, no blind fortune. The prophet Jeremias asks: "Who is he that hath commanded a thing to be done, when the Lord commandeth it not?" (Lam. iii, 37). "Thy providence, O Father, ruleth all things," so we read in the Book of Wisdom. And so God orders and disposes everything in our lives, that we may attain the eternal goal. We have but to commit ourselves to divine Providence and place our trust in God. For this reason we should exclaim with David: "The Lord ruleth me: and I shall want nothing. For though I should walk in the midst of the shadow of death, I will fear no evils, for thou art with me" (Ps. xxii).

In the first article we profess our faith, therefore, in the omnipotence of God, divine Providence, and all the divine attributes. God has created us and preserves us. But He has done still greater things for us. Is this possible? Yes, for God so loved the world that He sacrificed His only begotten Son for it. And this brings us to the second article, which comprises the truths we must believe of God the Son.

II. When the sin of our first parents had deprived us of the friendship of God as well as of our heirship to Heaven, there came to our rescue the second Person of the Godhead, the only begotten of the Father. The succeeding articles tell us of the love and sacrifice of the Son of God for our race.

The second article is: "And in Jesus Christ, His only Son, our Lord." What does this mean? It means I believe that He is the Son of God, God of God, true God of true God. It means I believe that He became incarnate for the sake of our salvation. It means I believe in the doctrines that He proclaimed, in the miracles that He performed. It means I believe in His presence in the holy Eucharist; in the effects of the holy Sacraments which He instituted. It means I believe in His holy Church, to which He transmitted His authority. To believe in Jesus Christ means, furthermore, to believe in His Passion and death, by which He redeemed the world; in His glorious resurrection and ascension. He is the Divine Master, and as such the supreme Lawgiver whom all creatures must obey. He is also the Judge of the universe, and as such will come again one day to preside at the general judgment, when He will judge all men according to their belief, according to the manner in which each one has observed or transgressed His commandments, used or neglected the means of salvation. Then will be the end of time; and mankind will go to its reward or to its punishment once and for all. All this is proclaimed in the articles of faith that treat of Jesus Christ. To believe in Jesus Christ means to believe everything that the Gospel teaches and everything which the holy, infallible Church requires us to believe.

The third chief part of the Creed declares what we must believe of the Holy Ghost, the third Person of the Godhead.

III. The Holy Ghost, the third Person of the Godhead, proceeds equally from the Father and the Son, from all eternity, and is of equal essence with the Father and the Son from eternity.

The Holy Ghost, sent by the Father and the Son, came down upon earth and took charge of the Church founded by Christ, in order to apply through it the fruits of redemption to mankind.

Only in the true Church of Christ can be found the fruits of the redemption; only in her is the true priesthood of the Lord. The fruits of the redemption here on earth are truth and grace, and in the hereafter eternal salvation. The divine truth, as proclaimed by Christ, is alone contained in the holy Catholic Church; and through the co-operation of the Holy Ghost it is preserved uncorrupted in this Church. The Church is the pillar and the beacon of the truth. She can not deviate unto the end of the world one tittle from the doctrine received from Christ, because the Holy Ghost guides the teaching Church in all truth, and sees to it that every truth is understood rightly by her and properly interpreted and explained. Hence, to submit ourselves to the Church's definition of the faith means to submit ourselves to the Holy Ghost. The Holy Ghost operates in the Church, through the priesthood, and thus applies to the faithful the fruits of the redemption, so as to sanctify them and prepare them for eternal happiness. Thus it is the Holy Ghost who sanctifies us, who makes us holy, as our Father in heaven is holy; who leads us to perfection, as our Father in heaven is perfect.

"I believe in the Holy Catholic Church," is the next article of our Creed. The Holy Ghost lives and operates in the Church. This Church is a "Communion of Saints," a communion of faithful, part of whom have already entered eternal life of bliss, and is called the Church Triumphant; another part is being cleansed from the remnants of sin in the place of purification, and is called the Suffering Church; a third part is still struggling on the battlefield of the world for the crown of eternal life, and is called the Church Militant. All are true members of this great community of saints and children of God, allied through the bond of love. This doctrine is very consoling to us. It opens to us, as it were, even during our earthly life, the portals of eternity. We may enter these in spirit, and seek and find help and consolation amongst our glorified brethren, and also carry help and consolation to our suffering brethren. One thing alone bars us from this glorious communion and shuts heaven against us, and that is sin. But in the Church there is provided for repentant sinners the Absolution from Sins, the remission of sin and its penalty. When we finally die in the grace of God our soul shall enjoy eternal life, and our glorified body shall be joined to it on the great day of resurrection.

This, then, is what we are taught to believe in the Apostles' Creed. When we say this Creed with devotion and perfect faith, we honor and glorify first of all the Blessed Trinity. But we refresh also the teaching of the Gospel in our minds, and thus strengthen our faith. It is an excellent means of awakening exalted sentiments of faith within us, and of inspiring us to a courageous profession of our holy religion.

The Creed is possessed of great power against the temptations of the evil one. The Apostle exhorts us "to resist the devil strong in faith" (I Pet. v, 8), and Holy Scripture calls the faith a shield against which the darts of Satan are broken. Thus is the Creed, according to its origin, and its contents, and efficacy, a holy and excellent prayer. In conclusion, let me quote an exhortation from St. Augustine: "Forget not," he says, "to recite the profession of your faith when you rise in the morning, nor when retiring at night; repeat it frequently, for its repetition is salutary for you, that no forgetfulness may arise. Your creed should be your mirror. Examine yourself therein as to whether you firmly believe everything you profess to believe, and rejoice daily in the possession of faith." Well, then, let us bear in mind this beautiful advice. Let us say the Creed daily, in order to strengthen ourselves in the faith but especially let us say it with great devotion as part of the holy Rosary. If here below we are true to the faith we shall one day behold in reality what we now see only with the eyes of faith, and in this vision enjoy eternal glory and bliss without end. Amen.

VI. The Excellence of the Various Parts of the Rosary

(c) The Glory be to the Father

"Thou art worthy, O Lord our God, to receive glory, and honor, and power: because thou hast created all things."—Apoc. iv, II.

Dear Brethren, we know that the "Glory be to the Father" occurs very frequently in the prayers of the Church and in our private devotions. In the Rosary it is repeated with every decade. This prayer of praise is of great significance for the Christian life. In order to understand its meaning better we must join in spirit the choirs of the blessed before the throne of God. Isaias, the great prophet of the Old Testament, to whom was vouchsafed a profound insight into the mysteries of God, had a vision of heaven, and he says, "I saw the Lord sitting upon a throne high and elevated, and his train filled the temple; upon it stood the seraphims: . . . and they cried one to another, and said: Holy, holy, holy, the Lord God of hosts; all the earth is full of his glory" (Is. vi, I). So also did John, the beloved disciple of Jesus, have the grace to see heaven, and he saw the angels of heaven, and with them the whole army of the saints and all the nations, tribes and peoples, standing before the throne in sight of the Lamb, and with a loud voice they praised God, who sat upon the throne, and the Lamb, who is the Lamb of God (Apoc. vii, 11).

Thus God has made known to us, through both these prophets, in what the unceasing occupation of the blessed in heaven consists. They behold the magnificent beauty of God and praise Him on account of His majesty, power and love, and this occupation of the dwellers in heaven should also be the task of the dwellers upon earth. It is indeed the duty of mankind, and an indispensable obligation. King David acknowledged this when he said: "I will bless the Lord at all times, his praise shall be always in my mouth" (Ps. xxxiii).

Therefore, our whole life and endeavor should be one uninterrupted "Glory be to the Father, and to the Son, and to the Holy Ghost."

We will make this obligation the subject of our consideration.

I. The happy inhabitants of heaven as they behold God in His indescribable splendor extol Him with hymns of praise. To know God and to serve Him, to glorify Him, this is the supreme end of man, not only when he is admitted to heaven, but even here on earth. God himself tells us this through the Prophet Isaias. "In order," thus He speaks, "that man should glorify me, therefore have I created him and brought him forth from nothing."

We mortals as yet can not behold God as the blessed do in heaven; but we do behold Him in His works, and know Him from His revelation given us through the prophets, and through Jesus Christ, our Lord.

The works through which God has revealed Himself to us are creation, redemption and sanctification. Creation is a vast book which speaks to us unceasingly of God, and it is intelligible to all. If we contemplate the magnificence of the starlit sky we must exclaim with David: "The heavens show forth the glory of God, and the firmament declareth the work of his hands" (Ps. xvlii). Yet not only the heavens, but also the earth shows us, at every step, the omnipotence of God, His wisdom and love. Mountain and valley, forest and field, river and ocean, they all remind us of God, their creator. Every flower of field and meadow is a great masterpiece, which no mortal man could create.

The animal world presents still greater marvels for our consideration. The waters teeming with millions of animals of all kinds, from the smallest jellyfish to the ship-destroying monsters, the beasts of the forest, the birds of the air, they all are called into existence by God, and God has not merely called all these creatures into existence, but His providence preserves them, and not even a sparrow falls from the roof without His knowledge.

But we have not yet considered the masterpiece of creation: man, the creature with an immortal soul, created according to God's own image and likeness. In man body and soul are joined together in a wonderful unity, so that man presents in himself a combination of the spiritual and material.

Man is the masterpiece of creation, and all creation is for his service. "Thou hast made him a little less than the angels, thou hast crowned him with glory and honor; thou hast set him over the work of thy hands" (Ps. viii, 6).

In very truth we may say, therefore, the universe speaks to our mind and heart in powerful and impressive language. This language is its beauty, its appropriateness, its greatness.

But yet more plainly than creation does the redemption proclaim the glory of God. It is "not the immensity of the heavenly bodies," says St. Gregory, "not the brilliancy of the stars, not the adornment of the universe, not the preservation of the world, that point so much to the glory of the divine power and omnipotence, as does that divine condescension to the feebleness of nature."

Jesus Christ, the Son of God, descended from heaven and brought into the world a truer and fuller knowledge of God. The ancient people knew there was a God, but they knew Him not. The knowledge of the true God was drowned in paganism. Even among the Jews small had become the number of those who still possessed an undefiled knowledge of God. In the Old Testament there was only an intimation of the blessed Trinity, not a clear knowledge. Then Jesus Christ brought to us the knowledge of the Triune God. In Him the divine attributes of love, sanctity, justice, wisdom, omnipotence and mercy were presented to our minds so that we can comprehend them. He made known to us the merciful decrees which God had ordained for our temporal and eternal welfare. Through His bitter passion and death He reconciled us to the Father, and acquired for us the heirship of heaven. He founded the Church, the kingdom of God upon earth, and He rules it through the Holy Ghost, who proceeds from Him and the Father.

Through this Church are applied the glorious fruits of the redemption. Through this Church God would sanctify all mankind and lead them to eternal salvation. The Church and the communion of the saints reveal to us God's glory and love far more than all the wonders of the world. A single saint is a greater miracle of the divine grace than the whole universe. The redemption made of earth a preparatory school for heaven, and it behooves us, as St. Augustine says, in this life to give praise to God, because in heaven our work will be an eternal proclamation of the divine praises. Our whole earthly life, as a befitting preparation for heaven, should be an imitation of the life of the blessed in heaven. It ought to be a perpetual praise of God, until after a happy death we are admitted to the ranks of the celestial choirs.

II. Jesus Christ, the Incarnate Son of God, who has brought to us the true knowledge of God, taught us also the true worship of God. After He had accomplished the work of the redemption and had founded the Church, He returned to heaven. Before this, however, He provided that He should also remain here upon earth. He instituted the most Holy Eucharist, the holy Sacrifice of the Mass, and thus remains in His Church until the end of time. Jesus, the Head of the Church, offers Himself to the Father unceasingly in the holy Sacrifice of the Mass. Thus the glorification of God takes place here upon earth as unceasingly as it does in heaven. The praise of God takes place here on earth, furthermore, through the' ecclesiastical hourly prayer, in which all the priests and religious of the Church unite throughout the world. The Church dedicates the Sunday exclusively to the praise and service of God. This day is to remind us of the creation accomplished by the Father, of the redemption accomplished by the Son, and of the sanctification accomplished by the Holy Ghost. On this day especially are the members of the Church invited to contemplate these great works of God, and praise and thank Him for the same.

The entire year has been divided by the Church into three great festival cycles, Christmas, Easter, and Pentecost, and thus is consecrated to the Triune God.

We are exhorted to receive the holy Sacraments, and thus participate in the fruits of the redemption, sanctifying ourselves by a Christian life. A truly Christian life is the best and highest worship of God here below, as it makes us worthy to be associated with the heavenly choirs, there to continue eternally our praises in the blissful vision of God.

We see then how the Church admonishes us to make our whole lives and all our works an unending "Glory be to God." In order that this may be accomplished we must above all things be faithful children and living members of the Church, brethren of Jesus Christ.

We must diligently and devoutly obey the Commandments, and receive the Sacraments. The light of faith should lead us and hope should draw us heavenward, the love of God and of our neighbors must fill our hearts. He who possesses these virtues is indeed in possession of all other virtues. Love is the bond of perfection, for who so loves God and his neighbor has fulfilled the law. We should make a good intention the first thing in the morning, and renew it frequently throughout the day. This certainly is not difficult. St. Paul exhorts us urgently to make this good intention in the words: "Therefore, whether you eat or drink, or whatsoever else you do; do all things for the glory of God" (I Cor. x, 31)

To make this good intention, the "Glory be to the Father" is especially appropriate. If we utter the same frequently and devoutly we shall makes our lives a continual praising and glorifying of God, a perpetual prayer. Glory be to the Father, who has created us; to the Son, who has redeemed us; and to the Holy Ghost, who sanctifies us. Glory be to the Holy Trinity through all our thoughts, words and works, as glory was to God in the beginning, when He created heaven and earth, as now, and so too through all eternity in heaven. Yes, we will glorify God here below with the militant Church, so that we may be worthy to behold Him one day with the triumphant Church, and to praise Him in blissful rapture for all eternity! Amen.

VII. The Excellence of the Various Parts of the Rosary

(d) The "Our Father"

"Lord, teach us to pray."—Luke xi, I.

Dear Brethren: The holiest, the most beautiful and most perfect, and for this reason the most efficient prayer is the "Our Father."

This prayer comes from Our Lord himself, who gave it to His disciples when they urged that He should teach them how to pray. The "Our Father," therefore, had its origin with God himself, and, therefore, is the holiest of prayers. It is a petition to His heavenly Father, composed by the God-man and bequeathed to us, His brethren. In this petition is contained everything we may ask for. Tertullian says in his writings that the "Our Father" contains not merely the things for which man ought to ask God, but also everything the Lord has taught and ordained, so that the whole Christian doctrine is briefly contained therein. The separate petitions are arranged according to their importance, and follow one another in a most appropriate way. Therefore, the "Our Father" is according to its origin, as also according to its contents and its form, the perfect prayer.

The divine Saviour promised that everything we ask of our Father in heaven He will give us. When we recite the "Our Father" we not merely pray in the name of Jesus, but in His own words. Hence the Lord's Prayer is to God the most pleasing prayer, and for that reason the most efficient and powerful of prayers. It is evident from the history of the Church that the Lord's Prayer has, at all times been held by the faithful in the highest esteem. It was used, as the fathers tell us, not only in public, but also in private devotions.

This holy, excellent and most efficacious prayer forms a part of the Rosary, and we will give it our consideration, in order the better to understand it, to appreciate it more fully, and to say it more devoutly.

Enchiridion Sanctissimi Rosarii

I. The "Our Father" consists of a preface and seven petitions. The preface is intended to lift up our thoughts to God. Holy Scripture admonishes us to such preparation, "Before prayer, prepare thy soul: and be not as a man that tempteth God" (Eccles. xviii, 23). When beginning to pray we should present to our mind God as He is enthroned in heaven. We should approach God in humility and reverence with childlike confidence and love. Thus prepared for prayer we will be pleasing to God. To give our mind this disposition is the purpose of the preface: "Our Father, who art in heaven." Hence this preface should be said with devotion and piety.

The seven petitions of the "Our Father" contain everything a Christian ought and may ask for. But what may and should a Christian ask for? For all things necessary and serviceable for the proper fulfilment of his life work. This prayer contains petitions for everything necessary for the attainment of the last end for which we were created, and that is, in the first place, the glorification of God, and, in the second place, our eternal salvation. In the first four petitions Christ teaches us and commands us to beseech for the things that pertain to this last end, and in the last three petitions for protection against the things which hinder the attainment of this end.

1. The glory of God is the first and chief purpose of all creation, as also of redemption and sanctification. It should be the occupation of all mankind, as it is the occupation of the blessed in heaven. We glorify God when we recognize Him as the highest good; when we love Him above all things, with a childlike love, serve Him faithfully, worship Him in all our thoughts, words and actions. As we are unable to do this by our own strength we must seek the assistance of grace, which we do in the words of the first petition: "Hallowed be Thy name." By the words "Thy name" must be understood here, God himself, as He has revealed Himself to us and this petition is equivalent to saying: "Thou, O God, shalt be glorified by us and by all mankind." We ask in the first petition that God may not be blasphemed, but rightly known, truly loved and

duly revered. We implore God in this petition to enlighten the heathen that yet stand in the shadow of death, and all unbelievers and heretics, that they may learn to know and adore Him; and to grant sincere conversion to all sinners. We also ask, for ourselves and our fellow Christians, the grace to grow in the knowledge of God, in His love and service and in Christian perfection, so that thereby God may ever be glorified more and more. A truly Christian life is our highest glorification of God, hence to obtain this grace we must diligently pray.

This petition is placed first, because it is the most necessary to the glorification of God and to our salvation. It is also the foundation of the other petitions.

2. In the second petition "Thy kingdom come," a threefold kingdom of God is meant, for the coming of which we pray. It is the kingdom of God about us, in us and above us. The kingdom of God about us is the Church of Christ. Christ founded it as His divine kingdom on earth, to glorify God and lead mankind to Salvation. We ask that God may grant to all men grace to recognize our holy Church as *the* divine institution, to submit themselves to her authority, and to become members of this Church find order to properly worship the true God, to glorify Him, and thus work their salvation.

The kingdom of God is within us, when we allow ourselves to be ruled and guided not by the spirit of the world, but by the spirit of God. "Those who are moved by the spirit of God are God's children." In his soul is the kingdom of God established whose faith agrees with the teaching of the Church, who hopes, loves and lives in the true faith.

The kingdom of God above us is the kingdom of heaven. The Church on earth is the kingdom of truth, of grace, of virtue; it will become in heaven the kingdom of glory.

Through this triple kingdom God is glorified on earth and in heaven, and this is the first and chief aim of every created thing.

Through this threefold kingdom we gain salvation, happiness and eternal life. That this threefold dominion of God may come to us and to all mankind we ask the Father in heaven in the second petition.

In order that what we ask for in the second petition may be attained we must comply with the third petition: "Thy will be done on earth, as it is in heaven." Almighty God is the supreme ruler of heaven and earth. All creatures in heaven and earth must submit themselves unconditionally to His holy will. God makes His will known to us through His commandments, and through His holy Church. We must be ready and willing at all times to do the will of God, and to submit to it in all things. We must obey His commandments, we must gladly and humbly submit ourselves to His dispensations, no matter what they may be. That God's will may at all times be done by us, and in us, and in all things, this should be our ardent desire, not with a servile fear but with filial love, as Jesus has taught us by His word and example. But this far surpasses our own strength and for this reason Jesus teaches and enjoins us to beg the Father that He may grant to us and to all mankind the grace to do at all times His holy will. By this faithful submission of our wills to the will of God we glorify God in the most perfect way.

3. In our earthly pilgrimage to heaven we require divine assistance in order to live our corporal and spiritual life according to the divine Will. For this reason Christ instructs us to pray in the fourth petition: "Give us this day our daily bread." That means: Give us, O God, what we stand in need of for body and soul that we may live according to Thy holy will.

We depend upon God in all things. He is our Creator and also our Preserver. We could not live a single moment without his aid. As we are composed of body and soul our wants are twofold, we have requirements for the body and others for the soul. We stand in need of food, shelter and clothing for body. All, rich and poor alike, must petition God for these, for each one stands in God's hand. God can cast the rich man down like Job, and free the poor man from all want. The word bread includes all necessities of life. "Give me neither beggary nor riches: give me only the necessaries of life" (Prov. xxx, 8).

That we are told to pray for our daily bread should remind us that we must not be too solicitous for the morrow. He who gives unto us to-day will also provide for us to-morrow if we humbly ask Him. We say: *Our* bread, because it is our duty to earn it in an honorable manner by industry and labor. "He who toils not, shall not eat." We say also *our* bread, and not *my* bread, because we wish the poor who can not help themselves to have it as well as we ourselves, and we must share it with them as much as our means allow.

As our body requires nourishment, so does our soul. The food of the soul is the word of God, and the Bread of Life that came down from heaven. We must partake of this Bread of the soul by hearing the word of God, by reading and meditation, and by receiving the Sacraments.

Thus has Jesus in the four first petitions taught and commanded us to ask for everything that is necessary for the attainment of our last end. In the three remaining petitions He instructs us to pray for protection against all things which are obstacles to the attainment of that end.

II. In these three petitions we ask that everything may be averted that would hinder us from attaining our true goal, our salvation and the glorification of God.

1. This obstacle, however, is sin and its evil consequences and these three petitions have reference to sin and its evil consequences. We, like all men, are sinners, and in our sins we can not worship God properly, nor can we attain our salvation if God does not show mercy to us. For this reason we humbly implore God in the fifth petition: "Forgive us our trespasses." In these words we implore God to grant unto us and to our fellow men a sincerely contrite heart and to graciously forgive us our sins and the punishment due for them. As a condition of forgiveness, however, God exacts from

us that we forgive those who have offended us, as fully as we desire that God forgive us. Therefore, we add: "As we forgive those who trespass against us."

2. In the sixth petition we implore God that He would graciously preserve us from falling into sin. "Lead us not into temptation." With these words we urge God that He should keep from us temptation to sin, or, if through temptation He desires to try us, that He grant us abundant graces to conquer it. Temptations do not come from God, but from our own nature, from Satan and from the world. God permits them in His wisdom to try our love for Him, to preserve us in humility, and to strengthen us, to animate our zeal for virtue and to increase our merits. God will assist us in temptation if we are exposed to it without any fault of ours.

Those, however, who court the danger will perish in it. They can not expect divine assistance who wilfully seek temptation and sin.

3. The seventh and last petition is "But deliver us from evil." After asking God not to lead us into temptation we urge Him to preserve us from evil of soul and body. We confidently trust God to guide us according to His wisdom and mercy, and to deliver us from everything which is an obstacle to our salvation, even if in our own shortsightedness we may think it good and desirable.

We conclude the "Lord's Prayer" with the little word "Amen," which is equivalent to "So be it." With this single word we confirm all our petitions. It means: "O God grant us these things for which we have just prayed."

Truly this prayer, taught us by Our Lord, is of high dignity and importance. It is not alone a prayer, but a sermon as well. It is a prayer which comprises in itself all other prayers. It is a prayer of praise, of thanksgiving and supplication. It is, therefore, appropriate for all occasions. Are you discouraged and faint-hearted, go and say the "Our Father." The thought that you have an all-merciful Father in heaven will lift you up, inspire you with confidence and comfort you. Do self-love and pride strive for the mastery within you, go and say, "Hallowed be Thy name." Is anger and malice in your heart, say, "Forgive us our trespasses at we forgive those who trespass against us." If impatience is your fault say, "Thy will be done on earth, as it is in heaven." When beset by temptation invoke God: "Lead us not into temptation," and in trial and adversity beseech God: "Deliver us from evil."

O that this holy and sublime prayer would be properly understood and appreciated. What blessings it would produce everywhere. May then our contemplation contribute with the blessing of God toward our own love of this wonderful prayer and greater devotion in its recital.

VIII. The Excellence of the Various Parts of the Rosary

(e) The Hail Mary.

"And the angel said to her: Hail, full of grace, the Lord is with thee, blessed art thou among women."—Luke i, 28.

Dear Brethren: To-day there is offered for our consideration one of the sweetest of prayers of our holy Religion. It is the "Hail Mary," or Angelical Salutation, which we say so often, particularly in the Rosary. Considered in its origin, its contents, and in its efficacy it is beautiful and sublime, and, with the exception of the Lord's Prayer, the most excellent. Its origin is to be had in the words which the Archangel Gabriel addressed to blessed Mary, ever virgin. To these have been added the words of St. Elizabeth on the occasion of Mary's visit, and the holy Church has completed the prayer with a consoling supplication. Its very origin, therefore, makes this prayer a holy and venerable one.

The words of salutation are brief, but they contain everything that one could ever say in praise of the Virgin Mother of God.

The petition includes briefly everything for which we may ask Mary.

Enchiridion Sanctissimi Rosarii

Let us then give our attention to this beautiful prayer in the name of Jesus and Mary, His blessed mother.

I. I said, that in the first part of the "Hail Mary" all the privileges and glories which made the blessed Virgin so worthy of praise are contained. A closer examination will show us how true this is. Let us transport ourselves in spirit to Nazareth, to the quiet little room where Mary is praying in deepest devotion. Suddenly there enters this room one of the most exalted spirits that stand at the throne of the Creator. What does this messenger from heaven desire of this humble virgin, unknown to the world? He desires no less than her participation in our redemption. The only begotten Son of God, in His infinite love for mankind, has offered to take upon Himself human nature, to atone for our sins and to redeem us. The time appointed by God's providence, when this great work was to be consummated, had now come. Mary, in the divine counsels, is destined to be the mother of the Saviour. The celestial messenger appears to bring this message to her, and to obtain her consent. God desired that Mary should voluntarily cooperate in the redemption.

Mary cooperated in our redemption by proving herself worthy to be called to the divine motherhood, as far as this is possible for a human being. This she did by cooperating faithfully with the abundance of grace granted her by God, and thus proving herself worthy to become the mother of the Saviour. Through her virginity she rendered herself worthy according to the body, and through her most profound piety and humility according to the spirit. Both virtues stand forth most brilliantly in the annunciation of the angel. But she wished rather to forego the exalted dignity of divine motherhood, than relinquish the virginity which she had dedicated to God. And when the highest dignity which can be bestowed upon a creature was announced to her, she called herself the handmaid of the Lord. Mary, when convinced of the will of God, humbly consented, saying, "Behold the handmaid of the Lord, be it done unto me according to thy word."

Through this consent Mary conferred upon the world an unspeakable great blessing, for which we should be eternally grateful to her. By this consent she became the second Eve, me spiritual first parent of the redeemed race.

The angel, recognizing in Mary his future queen, now reverently set forth in brief words all the prerogatives which God had granted her, and was about to bestow upon her. These prerogatives are: (1) the fulness of grace which God had already granted unto her; (2) the dignity of mother of God which He now granted her, and, finally (3), the veneration and glorification which on account of this fulness of grace and this dignity she would partake of in heaven and earth.

The first privilege, fulness of grace, which she had received from God, the angel expressed with the words "full of grace." These words mean: thou art filled with all the divine graces in a measure possible to no other creature; thou hast received to the full all graces. As God will exalt thee to a dignity beyond that of the most exalted spirits of heaven, so He has granted you more and greater graces than even to the Seraphim and Cherubim. Now since thou hast cooperated in a perfect manner with all these graces, thou hast become the most virtuous, the holiest, the most perfect of all creatures. Therefore, art thou worthy to become the mother of the Most High.

Mary's second privilege which the angel mentioned was her elevation to the dignity of mother of God. "The Lord is with thee," that is, God has bestowed upon thee every grace, and, finding thee worthy, thou art to be the mother of His Son, to cooperate in the redemption and the salvation of the world.

In the words "The Lord is with thee" is expressed the intimate relationship of Mary to God, accomplished by the Incarnation. Not merely through the fulness of His grace and love is God with her, but even according to the flesh God is intimately united to her.

Mary's third privilege announced by the angel is the exalted veneration which she merits for her dignity and sanctity. The angel expresses this in the words "Blessed art thou among women." The angel had reference to the promise given by God in Paradise, that there would come a woman who should crush the serpent's head. He had in mind also the renowned women of the old law who had rescued the people of God from peril and oppression, and who were for this reason blessed by the people, such as Judith and Esther. These heroic women were glorious prototypes, pointing to Mary who was to crush the serpent's head, to destroy the designs of Lucifer, and to save the human race from destruction. Yes, truly, Mary is blessed by God among all women, and is herself an infinite blessing for the entire world. The Lord hath done great things in her. She realized this herself, in those prophetic words, "Behold from henceforth all generations shall call me blessed, for he that is mighty hath done great things to me, and holy is his name." And so it has been, and ever will be, as long as the sun illumines the earth. For more than nineteen centuries the people and nations have joyfully repeated the angel's words, "Blessed art thou among women." By precept of the Church we add the words "and blessed is the fruit of thy womb, Jesus," in order to join to our praise of Mary that of Jesus, from whom and on whose account she received all her privileges, and for whose sake she receives all this praise.

II. After the prayer of praise in the "Hail Mary" there follows the prayer of supplication which the Church has added. This supplication is "Holy Mary, mother of God, pray for us sinners, now, and at the hour of our death. Amen." A short petition, but a significant one by which we invoke Mary's intercession in all our needs. The words holy Mary, mother of God, form the opening of this petition. They repeat the truth contained in the prayer of praise, and are at the same time calculated to arouse our confidence in Mary. The name "Mary" alone should awaken our confidence in the blessed Virgin, because the name Mary means sovereign. Mary, is indeed a sovereign, a ruler. As mother of the King of heaven and earth, she is the Queen of heaven and earth, and our lady, our queen as well. Mary means also star of the sea. As star of the sea

Mary is to mankind what a kindly star is to the sailor who finds himself on the stormy waters. This world resembles an ocean, where storms and perils abound to the menace of body and soul. The winds and storms of temptations rise, the dangerous rocks of oppression threaten, the stormy waves of passion, of pride, of ambition, of avarice, of anger, envy, revenge, avidity beat upon us. All these dangers trouble the heart and fill it with sorrow and fear. And as the star leads the sailor to a safe haven, so Mary is to us the kindly star that inspires us with consolation and confidence and brings us rescue.

Holy Mary, mother of God! As mother of God Mary possesses the power of mediation with her divine Son. The angels and saints all together can not have the influence that Mary exercises. The holy fathers and teachers refer to this power, when they say Mary is omnipotent through her intercession, as God is omnipotent in Himself. Thus the opening of the supplication inspires veneration and confidence in Mary. With this veneration and confidence then we ask, "Pray for us sinners." Thou, the holy one, the powerful and good, pray for us miserable sinners, not worthy to approach God and be heard. Pray for us in all our temporal and spiritual necessities, in every danger of body and soul. Pray above all, to obtain for us the grace of a perfect conversion and repentance, and the grace of perseverance until the end of life. Pray for us, holy Mary, mother of God, now, while it is yet time for us to merit salvation, but pray for us especially when that solemn and sad hour of death has arrived. In that dark hour will be decided our eternal destiny; at that dread hour forsake us not, Pray for us now, and at the hour of our death.

We have seen what an excellent prayer the Hail Mary is. It follows that it is also an efficacious prayer. When the Hail Mary was uttered for the first time by the Archangel it ushered in the most stupendous of all miracles. And whenever we devoutly repeat this salutation with faith and confidence, it will be for us also a means of grace and blessing. Whenever you salute Mary, says St. Bernard, she returns the greeting, she gives you in return consolation and blessing.

Let us then recite this beautiful and excellent prayer most diligently and piously, and let us give special preference to the devotion of the Rosary which is a garland woven to blessed Mary from this prayer of praise. The quarter of an hour spent in reciting the beads will bring us blessings in life and a happy death. How we shall rejoice when we behold Mary face to face and greet her with the words: Hail Mary, full of grace, the Lord is with thee, blessed art thou among women, and blessed is the fruit of thy womb, Jesus, to whom be praise for all eternity. Amen.

IX. The Prayer to increase the Three Divine Virtues

"And now there remain faith, hope, and charity, these three: but the greatest of these is charity."—I. Cor. xiii, 13.

Dear brethren, in beginning the Rosary one Our Father and three Hail Marys are said in supplication for the three divine virtues. These virtues are called divine because they have God for their Author or their object. In Baptism these virtues are infused into the soul together with sanctifying grace. Through sanctifying grace, received in Baptism, we are made children of God. From that moment there is imposed upon us the duty, as soon as we shall be able to use our reason, of thinking, speaking and acting as behooves the true children of God. This duty we perform if we imitate the example of Jesus Christ, and if we endeavor to be perfect as our heavenly Father is perfect. But as this cannot be done by human power, the Holy Ghost has willed to enable us to do so, by imparting to us, in Baptism, the three divine virtues. By the infused grace of faith God gives us a supernatural light, in addition to the natural light of our reason, with the aid of which we may comprehend His revelations. God bestows upon us thus, through the virtue of faith, a share in His own wisdom. The supernatural grace of hope turns our thought heavenward, gives us an incentive to co-operate with grace.

The supernatural virtue of charity renders us capable of loving God in a worthy and meritorious manner and of loving that which God loves.

As the child arrives at the age of discretion, and obtains the right use of reason, he is obliged to practise these virtues, and thus I strengthen his soul and grow in grace.

We are obliged to awaken frequently faith, hope, and charity towards God and our neighbor, in a practical manner. By the possession, practise and application of these three divine virtues we attain to Christian perfection. The more we learn to know these virtues, the more zealous we shall be in practising them, the more earnestly we shall strive for their increase, the more incessantly shall we pray for them.

Let us, therefore, take these three divine virtues for the subject of our consideration.

I. Faith is the first of the three divine virtues; it is the foundation of the other virtues. Without faith in God, in His revelations and promises, there can be no Christian hope, no Christian charity. For this reason faith is the foundation of virtuous living: Christian faith is a virtue infused by God into our souls by which we are enabled to believe firmly all that which God has revealed and which the infallible Catholic Church proposes for our belief.

An act of faith requires the use of the understanding and the use of the will. The mysteries surpass our natural understanding; they are, furthermore, to be believed in a supernatural manner, and we require, therefore, the supernatural light of faith, added to the natural light of our understanding, and we require also that our natural willpower be strengthened by the supernatural power of grace. This light and this power we receive in Baptism. The supernatural light of faith qualifies us to understand that the truths revealed by God are divine.

In order to believe it does not suffice to know the divine truths as the Church teaches them, we must also, of our own free will, assent to them, and acknowledge as divine truths even those mysteries which surpass our human understanding. To that extent faith is a matter of the will. God, through the light and the power of the grace of faith, comes to the assistance of our reason and will, in order that we may confidently submit both to divine revelation, that is, to God. In order that the infused virtue of faith may be meritorious for us, we must co-operate with grace by readily submitting our understanding and our will to divine revelation. Then this virtue of faith will not only be an infused one but, also, will be an acquired one and thus become a meritorious virtue. This actual and acquired virtue is for every adult the first condition of salvation. Still the acceptance of the divine doctrine is alone not sufficient for salvation. We must live in accordance with our faith; we must do good and shun evil. Such is the teaching of faith. "He truly believes who practises what believes," says St. Gregory, and St. James tells us that "Faith without works is a dead faith and avails nothing to salvation." A living faith is the first condition and the beginning of salvation. Eternal happiness consists, as we are aware, in the vision of God. The living faith is a beginning of this vision. We know God through the Christian faith, but only as in a mirror. "Now I know in part: but then I shall know even as I am known" (I. Cor. xiii, 12).

II. The second of the divine virtues is hope. Christian hope is a virtue infused into our souls by which we confidently expect of God everything which He has promised us through the merits of Christ. God has promised us eternal happiness, also all things which we stand in need of, and that are profitable for us in our endeavor to attain eternal happiness. Jesus has merited these for us, and God has promised them to us for the sake of the merits of Jesus Christ. And because God has promised them to us we must confidently expect and hope for them, because God is omnipotent, merciful and faithful to His promises.

A Manual of the Most Holy Rosary

This Christian confidence in God is bestowed by the virtue of hope, infused into our souls at Baptism. We must frequently exercise it in order to make it conducive to salvation.

The virtue of hope is based upon the virtue of faith. Faith informs us of the promises of God, and that He is all-powerful and faithful in fulfilling His promises. Without faith Christian hope would not be possible. This the Apostle Paul teaches in his Epistle to the Corinthians, in plain words: "Faith," he writes, "is the substance of things hoped for" (Heb. xi, i). Hope is really, therefore, an active faith in the mercy and generosity of God. Christian hope is just as necessary for salvation as faith. "For we are saved by hope." Thus the Apostle writes in the Epistle to the Romans (Rom. viii, 24). Hence, when we lose hope we forfeit our salvation.

Christian hope is in part desire, in part confidence. It is a lively desire for eternal happiness, for the possession of God and for the means which aid us in gaining salvation. It contains in itself a heartfelt desire for forgiveness of sins, and for liberation from the punishment due to sins. It includes an ardent longing for a virtuous Christian life. It is that hunger and thirst for justice of which Christ speaks in the eight Beatitudes. As God is the supreme good, combining every other good, so our desire for the blessed possession of God must be the sincerest, indeed, the sole, desire of our hearts. All other things we may desire only on God's account, and only in so far as they are the means to help us to the possession of God. Whoever experiences this desire will zealously pray for all things; he will be a man of prayer.

Christian hope is not only desire, but also confidence. God has promised us forgiveness of our sins and the grace to do the good that is required of us. He has promised us after a Christian life the eternal happiness of heaven. He is ready to fulfil His promises. The fulfillment of the divine promise depends, however, upon our own co-operation, upon our sincere good-will, upon our co-operation with grace. Our confidence must, therefore, never become presumption. The Apostle admonishes us to work out our salvation in fear and trembling. St. Francis de Sales calls confidence in God and distrust in ourselves the two balancing poles by the help of which we are enabled to keep our equilibrium. To distrust ourselves, and to have the fullest trust in God, this is the essence of Christian hope.

Christian hope is an essential condition for eternal happiness. By hope we anticipate life eternal. It is to us a pledge and a foretaste, and when we shall pass into eternity with this living hope, our hope will be transformed into possession of that which we have hoped for the possession of God, the supreme good.

III. Charity, the third of the divine virtues, is the virtue infused by God into our souls which enables us to love God above all things, and for His sake to love our neighbor as ourselves. That such divine charity surpasses human power is quite evident. It is inseparably united to sanctifying grace. He who possesses sanctifying grace possesses also the virtue of divine charity. He who loses sanctifying grace through mortal sin, loses also divine charity. The virtue of charity is a participation in the divine charity with which God loves us. It is a divine commandment that we must love God with our whole heart, with our whole soul, with our whole strength, and that we must love our neighbor as ourselves, for God's sake. To give oneself wholly to God, to prefer Him to all things, rather lose all things than offend Him, to seek to accomplish His holy will in all things, to observe His commandments, to offer up to God every thought, word, and deed, to work and suffer for God, to live and die for God, this is the true love of God.

"He that hath my commandments, and keepeth them; he it is that loveth me." Thus speaks the Son of God (John xiv, 21). To love God in this manner is made possible for us by the divine virtue of charity, received in Baptism. We may, however, co-operate with it and so fulfil God's commandments. Only in this manner does the infused virtue become an acquired and meritorious virtue. The Christian virtue of charity is the greatest of all virtues. It presupposes faith and hope because we must believe and hope in God before we can love Him: charity gives life to faith and hope.

Without charity, faith and hope are dead and avail not for salvation. Who so loves not remains in death. Charity is not merely the greatest of all virtues, but it contains all Christian virtues; it is the essence of the Christian life. Through Christian faith we participate in the divine knowledge, through hope in the divine power, and through charity we participate in the divine justice and sanctity. Christian charity renders us holy, as the heavenly Father is holy, and perfect as the Father in heaven is perfect. It is charity which here on earth unites us with God. "He who abides in charity abides in God and God in him." It is a virtue which continues for all eternity, when faith has become the vision, and hope the possession, of God.

The love of God is inseparably united to the love of our neighbor; for, as St. Augustine says, there are two commandments but only one charity, because there is no other charity with which we love our neighbor than that with which we love God. Who so says that he loves God, but does not love his neighbor, in him there is no divine charity.

We have seen, therefore, how the three divine virtues are the foundation of the Christian life, and that their practise constitutes Christian life. The true worship of God consists in practising these virtues which, at the same time, are the sole way to eternal bliss. Progress in the Christian life keeps pace with the activity of these virtues. This increase of virtue is, likewise, a gracious gift of God. We are ever obliged to co-operate with grace. We must strive for the increase of our faith, hope, and charity, by frequently practicing these virtues, by the worthy reception of the holy Sacraments, by attentively contemplating the divine truths and, especially, by humble and heartfelt prayer.

How feeble, indeed, is our faith, how wavering our hope, how insufficient our love of God and our neighbor. They need the strengthening grace of God.

To pray rightly, and to be worthy of being heard, we must awaken these fundamental virtues. Therefore, at the beginning of the

Rosary we say devoutly one Our Father and three Hail Marys to ask God for an increase of these virtues. Because faith, hope, and charity should be both the basis and the fruit of the Rosary. Amen.

X. The Excellence of the Rosary in regard to Its Form

"She reacheth therefore from end to end mightily, and ordereth all things sweetly."—Wisdom viii, 1.

The disposition of the heart is in prayer of more consequence than the manner of expression. Yet an appropriate form of prayer is helpful in avoiding distraction and in inducing devotion. Our Divine Saviour taught His disciples to make use of a special form of prayer, the "Our Father."

The form of the Rosary helps appreciably in rendering the Rosary the great prayer it is. The Rosary has been aptly called the "lay breviary." For many centuries the faithful joined in the reciting of the breviary. As late as in the eleventh century St. Peter Damian urgently exhorted the faithful to participate in the ecclesiastical "hours" of prayer. And when gradually participation in the ecclesiastical prayer ceased, Divine Providence supplied the Rosary to take for the laity the place of the breviary. It may thus properly be called the "lay breviary." In fact it reminds of the breviary of priests, for it contains verbal prayer and meditation, and the hundred and fifty "Hail Marys" of the Rosary correspond to the hundred and fifty psalms of the breviary.

Let us now consider how appropriate the form of the Rosary is, and how it renders the Rosary a perfect prayer.

The form makes the Rosary both an excellent devotion and a perfect prayer. Prayer is the first duty of all men. It is an article of faith that no man can work out his salvation without prayer. The real essence of prayer consists in the union of vocal prayer with meditation, or interior prayer. The true prayer is a conversation, or intercourse, of man with God. The combination of meditating with vocal prayer is an excellent means of participating in Divine grace.

Meditation makes us realize our needs, the faults which we should lay aside, and the virtues which we must acquire. Sin makes man blind, meditation opens his eyes. Vocal prayer alone is not of itself a protection from sin, daily experience teaches this. There are many who say vocal prayers and yet fall into grievous sin and remain in that state. The reason is because they omit the contemplative prayer. Those who combine vocal prayer with meditation do not easily incur God's disfavor, or if they do they at once resolve to amend and they lose no time in returning to God. A combination of meditation and vocal prayer is therefore calculated to preserve us from sin, and to rescue us from that state, if unfortunately we find ourselves in it. It is also the most effective means for us to reach Christian perfection and eternal salvation.

We should therefore combine with vocal prayers proper meditation if we desire our prayers to be more perfect. When we say the "Our Father," or the "Hail Mary," we should not merely utter the words with our lips, but should contemplate the purport of the words, lifting the mind to God, to whom we are praying, otherwise our prayer will be merely a prayer of the lips. Remember the words of our Divine Saviour: "These people glorify Me with their lips, but their hearts are far from Me."

In saying the Rosary we combine vocal prayer with meditation upon the Sacred Mysteries. Where there is time for it a longer meditation is very beneficial and of great spiritual advantage. But if time is lacking, or when the Rosary is said in common with others, one should at least at every decade briefly put the mystery before the mind. Pondering upon the mysteries whilst saying the prayers is ordinarily requisite to gain the indulgences attached to the Rosary.

The Rosary in its union of vocal prayer and meditation is a perfect prayer. The parts of the Rosary so appropriately succeed one another as to form a beautiful chain of prayers. We begin the prayers of the Rosary with the sign of the Cross, with which the Church commences all her prayers. This sign reminds us of the Most Holy Trinity in whose Name we were baptized, and to whom we belong absolutely, through creation, redemption, and sanctification. By making the sign of the Cross we place ourselves vividly in the presence of God, to whom we are praying, and awaken within us acts of faith, reverence, love, and confidence. Through the sign of the Cross there are dedicated to God in prayer the thoughts of the mind, the words of our lips, and the sentiments and feelings of the heart. Most assuredly the devout signing ourselves with the Cross is an excellent introduction and preparation for prayer.

Then follows most appropriately the Apostle's Creed. It declares more fully that which the sign of the Cross indicates. The twelve articles of the Creed contain that which we must firmly believe if we would be saved.

The Creed most properly opens the Rosary because it is the basis of our faith. The Joyful Rosary expounds the article of faith: "Conceived by the Holy Ghost, born of the Virgin Mary." The Sorrowful Rosary is a commemoration of the article: "Suffered under Pontius Pilate, was crucified, died and was buried." The glorious is founded upon the article: "Rose again from the dead, ascended into Heaven and sitteth at the right hand of God." Thus the entire Rosary is in truth a prayer of faith, and draws from the faith its force and efficacy.

After the Creed follows "Glory be to the Father," which is repeated at every decade of the Rosary as it is also said in the ecclesiastical "hours" after every Psalm. To give glory to God is our chief duty, it must be our intention in all our words and works. To give glory to God must also be our principal intention in saying the Rosary. As we repeat this doxology at the end of each decade, we should again raise up our mind and heart to God with fresh sentiments of faith, love, and confidence. This preserves us from distraction and gives new zeal to our prayers.

After the first "Glory be to God" we say one Our Father and three Hail Marys for the increase of the three divine virtues. The three divine virtues are the foundation of the right disposition which we must have, in order truly and worthily to honor God. St. Augustine says: "God is to be glorified through faith, hope, and charity. They are the corner-stone of the Christian life." And the Apostle says: "The just man liveth by faith" (Heb. x, 38), meaning that man lays the foundation for his justification through faith, receives the life of justification from faith, perseveres in this just life through faith, perfects this life through the light and the power of faith whence hope and charity proceed.

To promote this kind of life is the aim of the devotion of the Rosary. The more pious and virtuous we become, the more we glorify God and assure our temporal and eternal happiness.

These prayers are the introduction and preparation to the prayer of the Rosary, which combines meditation of the Mysteries with the recital of the Our Fathers and Hail Marys. The Rosary is a prayer indeed for the glory of God and for honoring and invoking Mary the Mother of God. The Mysteries of the Rosary contain that which God has done in order to glorify Himself and to redeem, sanctify, and save mankind. At the same time these mysteries from the lives of Jesus and Mary are fraught with touching examples for our own lives. In the devout contemplation of these mysteries, and in the application of the same to our own religious moral life, lie the gist of the prayers of the Rosary and the chief fruits which we should draw from this saving devotion.

Certain critics of the Rosary cannot understand why the Hail Mary is so frequently repeated. But in the repetition lies the strength of the prayer, for holy perseverance is expressed by this repetition. The psalmist in the one hundredth and thirty-fifth Psalm repeats twenty-six times the words: "For his mercy endureth forever." And the heavenly hosts proclaim their "Thrice Holy" for ever and ever.

We are perfectly right, therefore, in declaring that the Rosary is a thoroughly practical prayer, corresponding exactly to the necessities and peculiarities of our minds and hearts.

We might challenge the world to name a more beautiful, a more excellent prayer. The Church therefore numbers the Rosary amongst her most efficacious prayers, and she has endowed it richly with indulgences to induce the faithful to say it frequently.

XI. The Excellence of the Rosary on account of The Mysteries Commemorated

> "Unless thy law had been my meditation, I had then perhaps perished in my abjection."—Ps. cxviii, 92.

Dear Brethren: In our former considerations of the Rosary we have discussed the prayers of which the Rosary is composed. The second chief part of the Rosary is the fifteen Mysteries. They are called Mysteries because the truths which they contain are hidden and cannot be comprehended except by Divine revelation. These Mysteries and their significance will be the subject of our discourse to-day. It is the spirit and intention of the Church that these Mysteries be properly meditated upon while saying the Rosary. This we do by reflecting upon them, by applying to ourselves the lesson drawn! from them, and by resolving to amend our life or to perfect it according to this lesson.

I. The consideration of the Divine truths of salvation is absolutely necessary for all mankind, for no one can be saved who is not mindful of his salvation. We cannot attain happiness without serving and loving God. Yet he knows not God who does not give any thought to things divine. In order to learn to know God and to make progress in this knowledge we must contemplate the Divine attributes and perfections, and the works which proclaim them. The whole universe is preaching to us God's omnipotence, wisdom, and love. The heavens tell of God's glory, and the firmament proclaims the works of His hands. The tiny flowers in field and meadow, the birds in the tree, the stars in the sky, they all remind us of God and of His Omnipotence and Goodness. We ought not regard these things thoughtlessly, they give us food for salutary thought and meditation. They exhort us to show love and gratitude towards God, the merciful Father who has created all these things for us.

God so loved the world as to sacrifice for it His only begotten Son. The Son so loved Mankind that He became Man, suffered for us and died upon the Cross, in order to ransom us from sin and ruin. We learn to know not only the malice, horror, and guilt of sin, but also the infinite mercy and love of God by pondering on the works of God.

In the work of sanctification, specially ascribed to the Holy Ghost, we perceive fresh wonders of God's love. The Holy Ghost cleanses us from our sins and transforms us into children of God. He consoles us with heavenly consolation, and leads us with His hand, conducting us to Christian perfection and to life eternal. By considering these divine works, often and earnestly, we learn to know God, and become desirous of loving Him and serving Him faithfully. To make progress in the knowledge of these divine things is the sacred duty of a Christian. But in order to be saved it is not sufficient to know God; we must also know ourselves. For this reason St. Augustine besought God: "Let me know myself, and let me know Thee." We must learn to know our faults in order to correct them, and our evil inclinations so as to fight against them. We must ascertain what virtues we are lacking in so that we may strive to acquire them. We must understand the gravity of our sins to repent of them sincerely. Finally, we must understand our inability to acquire merit, so that we may seek from God grace, strength, and help.

It is necessary also that we understand clearly the duties which we have to perform.

If we were profoundly impressed by the excellence of the Divine Laws, of the magnificent rewards that will be the share of those who observe the Commandments, and of the terrible chastisement awaiting the transgressor, who would ever presume to transgress these Divine Commandments? And what is calculated to impress us with these truths if not serious reflection upon them?

The royal Prophet exclaims: "Blessed are they that search his testimonies; that seek him with their whole heart" (Ps. cxviii, 2).

Meditation has drawn numberless sinners from the depths of sin and protected untold numbers against sin. It is also, as St. Ignatius remarks, the shortest way to Christian perfection. Hence St. Teresa implores those who have not yet begun this meditative prayer, to do so in the name of God, and through the love of Christ, and no longer deprive themselves of this most precious and necessary good.

Objection may be made by some that they cannot meditate, that they have not the ability to do so. The reply is that for meditation no skill or science is required. When you reflect upon an article of faith, upon a commandment of God, upon sin or virtue, upon God, your duties, and then awaken acts of faith, hope and charity, contrition, and thanksgiving, followed by resolutions of amendment, petitions to God for His grace and assistance to keep these resolutions, you have made a very good meditation. This much any one can do.

Another objection may be advanced, that one has no time for it. A man living in the world has many business cares, but then the salvation of the soul is the chief business of man. Our Divine Saviour has said that one thing only is necessary, and this one thing is solicitude for the soul's welfare. David had the cares of governing a great kingdom, and yet he said: "O how have I loved thy law, O Lord, it is my meditation all the day." (Ps. cxviii, 97.) No, my brethren, time and ability are not lacking. If anything is lacking, it is the good will. Therefore let us all make the firm resolution to give in the future due consideration to Christian meditation so as to place our soul's welfare in safety.

II. The Mysteries of the Rosary offer us an easy method and material for our meditation. They give us a brief sketch of the life, passion, and death of Jesus Christ and the sorrows and joys of our Mother Mary. The fifteen Mysteries are divided into three parts: the Joyful, the Sorrowful, and the Glorious Mysteries.

The joyful Mysteries of the Rosary contain events from the youthful life of Jesus. These are the Annunciation, the Visitation of

Mary, the Nativity of Christ, the Presentation of Christ in the Temple, and the Finding of the Child Jesus in the Temple. These five Mysteries comprise the foundation of the work of the redemption. With all of them is intimately connected Mary, the Blessed Mother of the Redeemer.

These five Mysteries set before us the example of Jesus and Mary. To make of us children of God, the Son of God became incarnate, and He is for us the model of a child of God. Mary, His holy Mother, is in all things His faithful likeness and thus the model for us in the imitation of Christ.

The sorrowful Mysteries of the Rosary remind us of the work of redemption, through the passion and death of Jesus Christ. He begins His passion in the garden of Olives in an agony of sorrow. By the scourging He did penance for our sins of the flesh, and by the crowning with thorns, for our sins of the mind. Then He bore His Cross to the place of execution, and with it the sins of the world, in order to efface our debt upon this Cross. These Mysteries teach us how to partake of the merits of the redemption. The consideration of our sins, of their malice and guilt, and a sincere contrition for them is the first step. The second is the discipline of our flesh and its evil desires by temperance, chastity, and mortification. The third step is the discipline of the spirit by humble obedience towards God and His holy law. The fourth is the patient bearing of our cross, and the last is that we die completely to sin, and live only for Christ.

The glorious Mysteries of the Rosary tell us of the glorious fruits of the redemption. These are a new life of grace, resurrection from the dead, and admittance into heaven. They speak to us also of the mission of the Holy Ghost, whose work is to sanctify us. In Mary's assumption into Heaven we behold the most sublime work of the Holy Spirit, *viz.*, her holy life here upon earth and her coronation in Heaven, the reward of this holy life for all eternity. All these things are calculated to induce in us a devout Christian life. We behold what God has prepared for those who love Him, who live for Him, who work and suffer and die in His grace and love.

Thus the fifteen Mysteries give us a short summary of the lives of Jesus and Mary. The events selected are best calculated to awaken our faith, to strengthen our hope, to inflame our hearts with love for Jesus and Mary, and to animate us to imitate the lives of Jesus and Mary.

These Mysteries thus offer most excellent material for our meditations. They are so simple that every believing Christian may understand them, yet so profound and full of meaning that those most learned and advanced in the spiritual life may find therein ample food for edification. The public life of Jesus and Mary pass, as it were, before our eyes.

How fortunate did the Apostles esteem themselves to have known Jesus by sight, to have listened to the teachings from His own lips, to have gazed and meditated upon His holy life! We may draw the same profit from the diligent and devout meditation of the Mysteries of the Rosary.

If we daily say the Rosary, and picture the mysteries to ourselves, what advantage may we not draw from them for our life! It will be for us a daily intercourse and association with Jesus and Mary that will enlighten our minds, elevate and ennoble our hearts, and powerfully invite our will to a true life of virtue. The Rosary is, therefore, an admirable means to lead a truly Christian life, and an admirable means, consequently to attain eternal salvation. Let us all be zealous to avail ourselves of it and the Rosary will become a bond uniting us intimately with Jesus and Mary, and conducting us to the participation of their glory and happiness for all eternity. Amen.

The Prayers Used in the Rosary

The Sign of the Cross

In the name of the Father *(touch forehead)*, and of the Son *(touch heart)*, and of the Holy Spirit *(touch left then right shoulders)*. Amen

The Apostles' Creed

V. I believe in God, the Father almighty, Creator of Heaven and earth, and in in Jesus Christ, His only Son, our Lord. He was conceived by the Holy Spirit, and born of the Virgin Mary. He suffered under Pontius Pilate, was crucified, died and was buried. He descended into Hell. On the third day He rose again. He ascended into Heaven, and is seated at the right hand of God the Father Almighty. He will come again to judge the living and the dead.

R. I believe in the Holy Ghost, the Holy Catholic Church, the communion of saints, the forgiveness of sins, the resurrection of the body, and life everlasting. Amen.

The Our Father (The Lord's Prayer also known as Pater)

V. Our Father, Who art in heaven, Hallowed be Thy Name. Thy Kingdom come, Thy Will be done, On earth as it is in Heaven.

R. Give us this day, our daily bread, And forgive us our trespasses, as we forgive those who trespass against us. And lead us not into temptation, but deliver us from evil. Amen.

Hail Mary (Angelic Salutation, also known as Ave)

V. Hail Mary, Full of Grace, The Lord is with thee. Blessed art thou amongst women, and blessed is the fruit of thy womb, Jesus.

R. Holy Mary, Mother of God, pray for us sinners now, and at the hour of death. Amen.

Glory Be (Gloria or Doxology)

V. Glory be to the Father, and to the Son, and to the Holy Ghost.

R. As it was in the beginning, is now, and ever shall be, world without end. Amen.

Fatima Prayer

O My Jesus, * forgive us our sins, save us from the fires of Hell and lead all souls to Heaven, especially those in most need of Thy mercy. Amen.

Hail, Holy Queen (Salve Regina)

Hail holy Queen, mother of mercy, our life, our sweetness, and our hope. To thee do we cry, poor banished children of Eve. To thee do we send up our sighs, mourning and weeping in this valley of tears. Turn then, most gracious Advocate, thine eyes of mercy toward us. And after this our exile show unto us the blessed Fruit of thy womb, Jesus. O clement, O loving, O sweet Virgin Mary. Amen.

Collect of the Feast of the Most Holy Rosary of the Blessed Virgin

V. Pray for us, O Holy Mother of God.
R. That we may be made worthy of the promises of Christ.

Let us pray. O God, Whose only-begotten Son, by His life, death, and resurrection hath purchased for us the rewards of eternal life: grant, we beseech Thee, that, meditating on the mysteries of the most holy Rosary of the Blessed Virgin Mary, we may imitate what they contain and obtain what they promise. Through the same Jesus Christ, Thy Son, Who liveth and reigneth with Thee in the unity of the Holy Ghost, God, world without end.

Remember, O Most Gracious Virgin Mary (Memorare)

Remember, O most gracious Virgin Mary, that never was it known that anyone who fled to thy protection, implored thy help, or sought thy intercession was left unaided. Inspired with this confidence, I fly to thee, O Virgin of virgins, my Mother; to thee do I come; before thee I stand, sinful and sorrowful. O Mother of the Word Incarnate, despise not my petitions, but in thy mercy hear and answer me. Amen.

Prayer to Saint Michael

St. Michael the Archangel, defend us in battle; be our safeguard against the wickedness and snares of the Devil. May God rebuke him, we humbly pray, and do Thou, O Prince of the Heavenly Host, by the power of God, cast into Hell, Satan and all the other evil spirits, who wander throughout the world, seeking the ruin of souls. Amen.

Prayer to St. Joseph

To thee, O Blessed Joseph, we have recourse in our tribulations, and while imploring the aid of thy most holy Spouse, we confidently invoke thy patronage also. By that love which united thee to the Immaculate Virgin, Mother of God, and by the fatherly affection with which thou didst embrace the Infant Jesus, we humbly beseech thee graciously to regard the inheritance which Jesus Christ purchased with His Blood and to help us in our necessities, by thy powerful intercession.

Protect, O most provident Guardian of the Holy Family, the chosen children of Jesus Christ; ward off from us, O most loving Father, all taint of error and corruption; graciously assist us from Heaven, O most power protector, in our struggle with the powers of darkness; and as thou didst once rescue the Child Jesus from imminent peril to His life, so now defend the Holy Church of God from the snares of her enemies and from all adversity.

Shield each one of us with thy unceasing patronage that, imitating thy example and sported by thy aid, we may be enabled to live a good life, die a holy death, and secure everlasting happiness in Heaven. Amen.

Litany of the Blessed Virgin Mary

Italics are said by congregation if said in a group.

Lord, have mercy on us. *Christ have mercy on us.*
Lord, have mercy on us. *Christ, hear us. Christ graciously hear us.*
God, the Father of heaven, *have mercy on us.*
God the Son, Redeemer of the world, *have mercy on us.*
God the Holy Ghost, *have mercy on us.*
Holy Trinity, one God, *have mercy on us.*

Holy Mary, *pray for us.*
Holy Mother of God, *etc.*
Holy Virgin of virgins,
Mother of Christ,
Mother of the Church
Mother of divine grace,

Mother most pure,
Mother most chaste,
Mother inviolate,
Mother undefiled,
Mother most amiable,
Mother most admirable,
Mother of good counsel,
Mother of our Creator,
Mother of our Savior,
Virgin most prudent,
Virgin most venerable,
Virgin most renowned,
Virgin most powerful,
Virgin most merciful,
Virgin most faithful,
Mirror of justice,
Seat of wisdom,
Cause of our joy,
Spiritual vessel,
Vessel of honor,
Singular vessel of devotion,
Mystical rose,
Tower of David,
Tower of ivory,
House of gold,
Ark of the covenant,
Gate of heaven,
Morning star,
Health of the sick,
Refuge of sinners,
Comforter of the afflicted,
Help of Christians,
Queen of Angels,
Queen of Patriarchs,
Queen of Prophets,
Queen of Apostles,
Queen of Martyrs,

Queen of Confessors,
Queen of Virgins,
Queen of all Saints,
Queen conceived without original sin,
Queen assumed into heaven,
Queen of the most holy Rosary.
Queen of the family,
Queen of Peace,

Lamb of God, who takest away the sins of the world, *spare us, O Lord.*
Lamb of God, who takest away the sins of the world, *graciously hear us O Lord.*
Lamb of God, who takest away the sins of the world, *have mercy on us.*

Pray for us, O holy Mother of God,
That we may be made worthy of the promises of Christ.

Let us pray. Grant, we beseech Thee, O Lord God, unto us Thy servants, that we may rejoice in continual health of mind and body; and, by the glorious intercession of Blessed Mary ever Virgin, may be delivered from present sadness, and enter into the joy of Thine eternal gladness. Through Christ our Lord. *Amen.*

During Advent

Let us pray.
O God,
You willed that, at the message of an angel,
Your word should take flesh
in the womb of the Blessed Virgin Mary;
grant to your suppliant people,
that we, who believe her to be truly the Mother of God,
may be helped by her intercession with You.

Through the same Christ our Lord.
R. *Amen.*

From Christmas to the Purification

Let us pray.
O God,
by the fruitful virginity of Blessed Mary,
You bestowed upon the human race
the rewards of eternal salvation;
grant, we beg You,
that we may feel the power of her intercession,
through whom we have been made worthy
to receive the Author of life,
our Lord Jesus Christ your Son,
who lives and reigns with You forever and ever.
R. *Amen.*

During Paschaltime

Let us pray.
O God, who by the Resurrection of Your Son,
our Lord Jesus Christ,
granted joy to the whole world,
grant, we beg You,
that through the intercession of the Virgin Mary, his Mother,
we may attain the joys of eternal life.
Through the same Christ our Lord.
R. *Amen.*

Enchiridion Sanctissimi Rosarii

The Mysteries of the Rosary

Joyful Mystery of the Rosary

(Monday & Saturday)

- The Annunciation of the Lord to Mary
- The Visitation of Mary to Elizabeth
- The Nativity of our Lord Jesus Christ
- The Presentation of our Lord
- Finding Jesus in the Temple at age 12

Sorrowful Mystery of the Rosary

(Tuesday & Friday)

- The Agony of Jesus in the Garden
- The Scourging at the Pillar
- Jesus is Crowned with Thorns
- Jesus Carried the Cross
- The Crucifixion of our Lord

Glorious Mystery of the Rosary

(Wednesday & Sunday)

- The Resurrection of Jesus Christ
- The Ascension of Jesus to Heaven
- The Descent of the Holy Ghost

The Assumption of Mary into Heaven

Mary is Crowned as Queen of Heaven and Earth

Luminous Mystery of the Rosary

(Thursday)

The Baptism in the Jordan

The Wedding at Cana

The Proclamation of the Kingdom

The Transfiguration

The Institution of the Eucharist

Enchiridion Sanctissimi Rosarii

A Manual of the Most Holy Rosary

Our Lady's 15 Promises

Our Lady revealed to Blessed Alan de la Roche 15 benefits for those who devoutly pray the Rosary.

1. Whosoever shall faithfully serve me by the recitation of the Rosary shall receive signal graces.
   Signal Graces are those special and unique Graces to help sanctify us in our state in life. See the remaining promises for an explanation for which these will consist. St. Louis de Montfort states emphatically that the best and fastest way to union with Our Lord is via Our Lady [True Devotion to Mary, chapter four].

2. I promise my special protection and the greatest graces to all those who shall recite the Rosary.
   Our Lady is our Advocate and the channel of all God's Grace to us. Our Lady is simply highlighting that She will watch especially over us who pray the Rosary. (see <u>Lumen Gentium chapter VIII - Our Lady #62</u>) [a great more detail is available on this topic in True Devotion to Mary, chapter four, by St. Louis de Montfort]

3. The Rosary shall be a powerful armor against hell, it will destroy vice, decrease sin and defeat heresies.
   This promise, along with the next, is simply the reminder on how fervent prayer will help us all grow in holiness by avoiding sin, especially a prayer with the excellence of the Rosary. An increase in holiness necessarily requires a reduction in sin, <u>vice</u>, and doctrinal errors (heresies). If only the Modernists could be convinced to pray the Rosary! (see <u>Lumen Gentium chapter V - The Call to Holiness #42</u>) St. Louis de Montfort states "Since Mary alone crushed all heresies, as we are told by the Church under the guidance of the Holy Spirit (Office of the Blessed Virgin Mary)..." [True Devotion to Mary #167]

4. It will cause good works to flourish; it will obtain for souls the abundant mercy of God; it will withdraw the hearts of men from the love of the world and its vanities, and will lift them to

the desire for Eternal Things. Oh, that souls would sanctify themselves by this means.
This promise, along with the previous, is the positive part, that being to live in <u>virtue</u>. Becoming holy is not only avoiding sin, but also growing in virtue. (see <u>Lumen Gentium chapter V - The Call to Holiness #42</u>)

5. The soul which recommends itself to me by the recitation of the Rosary shall not perish.
Since Our Lady is our Mother and Advocate, She always assists those who call on Her implicitly by praying the Rosary. The Church reminds us of this in the <u>Memorare</u> prayer, "... never was it known that anyone who fled to your protection, implored your help or sought your intercession, was left unaided ..."

6. Whosoever shall recite the Rosary devoutly, applying himself to the consideration of its Sacred Mysteries shall never be conquered by misfortune. God will not chastise him in His justice, he shall not perish by an unprovided death; if he be just he shall remain in the grace of God, and become worthy of Eternal Life.
This promise highlights the magnitude of Graces that the Rosary brings to whomever prays it. One will draw down God's Mercy rather than His Justice and will have a final chance to repent (see promise #7). One will not be conquered by misfortune means that Our Lady will obtain for the person sufficient Graces to handle said misfortune (i.e. carry the Crosses allowed by God) without falling into despair. As Sacred Scripture tells us, "For my yoke is sweet and my burden light." (<u>Matthew 11:30</u>)

7. Whoever shall have a true devotion for the Rosary shall not die without the Sacraments of the Church.
This promise highlights the benefits of obtaining the most possible Graces at the hour of death via the Sacraments of Confession, Eucharist, and Extreme Unction (Anointing of the Sick). Being properly disposed while receiving these Sacraments near death ensures one's salvation (although perhaps with a detour through Purgatory) since a final repentance is

possible.

8. Those who are faithful to recite the Rosary shall have during their life and at their death the Light of God and the plenitude of His Graces; at the moment of death they shall participate in the Merits of the Saints in Paradise.
   Our Lady highlights the great quantity of Graces obtain through praying the Rosary, which assist us during life and at the moment of death. The merits of the Saints are the gift of God's rewards to those persons who responded to His Grace that they obtained during life, and so Our Lady indicates that She will provide a share of that to us at death. With this promise and #7 above, Our Lady is providing the means for the person to have a very holy death.

9. I shall deliver from purgatory those who have been devoted to the Rosary.
   Should one require Purgatorial cleansing after death, Our Lady will make a special effort to obtain our release from Purgatory through Her intercession as Advocate.

10. The faithful children of the Rosary shall merit a high degree of Glory in Heaven.
    This promise is a logical consequence of promises #3 and #4 since anyone who truly lives a holier life on earth will obtain a higher place in Heaven. The closer one is to God while living on earth, the close that person is to Him also in Heaven. The Catechism of the Catholic Church states "Spiritual progress tends toward ever more union with Christ." (Catechism of the Catholic Church paragraph 2014)

11. You shall obtain all you ask of me by recitation of the Rosary.
    This promise emphasizes Our Lady's role as our Advocate and Mediatrix of all Graces. Of course, all requests are subject to God's Most Perfect Will. God will always grant our request if it is beneficial for our soul, and Our Lady will only intercede for us when our request is good for our salvation. (see <u>Lumen Gentium chapter VIII - Our Lady #62</u>)

12. All those who propagate the Holy Rosary shall be aided by me in their necessities.
    If one promotes the praying of the Rosary, Our Lady emphasizes Her Maternal care for us by obtaining many Graces (i.e. spiritual necessities) and also material necessities (neither excess nor luxury), all subject to the Will of God of course.

13. I have obtained from my Divine Son that all the advocates of the Rosary shall have for intercessors the entire Celestial Court during their life and at the hour of death.
    Since Our Lady is our Advocate, She brings us additional assistance during our life and at our death from all the saints in Heaven (the Communion of Saints). See paragraphs 954 through 959 in the Catechism of the Catholic Church.

14. All who recite the Rosary are my Sons, and brothers of my Only Son Jesus Christ.
    Since the Rosary is a most excellent prayer focused on Jesus and His Life and activities in salvation history, it brings us closer to Our Lord and Our Lady. Doctrinally, Our Lady is our Mother and Jesus is our Eldest Brother, besides being our God. (see <u>Lumen Gentium chapter VIII - Our Lady #62</u>)

15. Devotion to my Rosary is a great sign of predestination.
    Predestination in this context means that, by the sign which is present to a person from the action of devoutly praying the Rosary, God has pre-ordained your salvation. Absolute certainty of salvation can only be truly known if God reveals it to a person because, although we are given sufficient Grace during life, our salvation depends upon our response to said Grace. (See Summa Theologica, Question 23 for a detailed theological explanation). Said another way, if God has guaranteed a person's salvation but has not revealed it to Him, God would want that person to pray the Rosary because of all the benefits and Graces obtained. Therefore the person gets a hint by devotion to the Rosary. This is not to say that praying the Rosary guarantees salvation - by no means. In looking at promises #3 and #4 above, praying the Rosary helps one to

live a holy life, which is itself a great sign that a soul is on the road to salvation. (See also paragraphs 381, 488, 600, 2782 in the Catechism of the Catholic Church.) In fact, St. Louis de Montfort says even more strongly that "an infallible and unmistakable sign by which we can distinguish a heretic, a man of false doctrine, an enemy of God, from one of God's true friends is that the hardened sinner and heretic show nothing but contempt and indifference to Our Lady..." [True Devotion to Mary, #30]

Reminder: these promises mean that, by faithfully and devoutly praying the Rosary, Our Lady will obtain for us the necessary Graces to obtain said promises. It is still up to each individual soul to <u>respond</u> to those Graces in order to obtain salvation.

Enchiridion Sanctissimi Rosarii

A Manual of the Most Holy Rosary

How to Pray the Rosary

1. SAY THESE PRAYERS...

IN THE NAME of the Father, and of the Son, and of the Holy Spirit. Amen. *(As you say this, with your right hand touch your forehead when you say Father, touch your breastbone when you say Son, and touch your left shoulder when you say Holy, and touch your right shoulder when you say Spirit.)*

I BELIEVE IN GOD, the Father almighty, Creator of Heaven and earth. And in Jesus Christ, His only Son, our Lord, Who was conceived by the Holy Spirit, born of the Virgin Mary, suffered under Pontius Pilate; was crucified, died, and was buried. He descended into Hell. The third day He rose again from the dead. He ascended into Heaven, and sits at the right hand of God, the Father almighty. He shall come again to judge the living and the dead. I believe in the Holy Spirit, the holy Catholic Church, the communion of saints, the forgiveness of sins, the resurrection of the body, and life everlasting. Amen.

OUR FATHER, Who art in Heaven, hallowed be Thy Name. Thy kingdom come, Thy will be done on earth as it is in Heaven. Give us this day our daily bread, and forgive us our trespasses, as we forgive those who trespass against us. And lead us not into temptation, but deliver us from evil. Amen.

HAIL, MARY, full of grace, the Lord is with thee. Blessed art thou among women, and blessed is the fruit of thy womb, Jesus. Holy Mary, Mother of God, pray for us sinners, now and at the hour of our death. Amen.

GLORY BE to the Father, and to the Son, and to the Holy Spirit. As it was in the beginning is now, and ever shall be, world without end. Amen.

O MY JESUS, forgive us our sins, save us from the fires of Hell; lead all souls to Heaven, especially those in most need of Thy mercy. Amen.

HAIL, HOLY QUEEN, mother of mercy; our life, our sweetness, and our hope. To thee do we cry, poor banished children of Eve. To thee do we send up our sighs, mourning and weeping in this vale of tears. Turn, then, most gracious advocate, thine eyes of mercy toward us. And after this, our exile, show unto us the blessed fruit of thy womb, Jesus. O clement, O loving, O sweet Virgin Mary. Pray for us, O holy Mother of God, that we may be made worthy of the promises of Christ. Amen.

O GOD, WHOSE only-begotten Son by His life, death and resurrection, has purchased for us the rewards of eternal life; grant, we beseech Thee, that by meditating upon these mysteries of the Most Holy Rosary of the Blessed Virgin Mary, we may imitate what they contain and obtain what they promise, through the same Christ our Lord. Amen.

ANNOUNCE each mystery by saying something like, "The third Joyful Mystery is the Birth of Our Lord." This is required only when saying the Rosary in a group.

2. IN THIS ORDER...

INTRODUCTION
1. IN THE NAME
2. I BELIEVE IN GOD
3. OUR FATHER
4. HAIL, MARY
5. HAIL, MARY
6. HAIL, MARY
7. GLORY BE
8. O MY JESUS

THE FIRST DECADE
9. ANNOUNCE
10. OUR FATHER
11. HAIL, MARY
12. HAIL, MARY
13. HAIL, MARY
14. HAIL, MARY
15. HAIL, MARY
16. HAIL, MARY
17. HAIL, MARY
18. HAIL, MARY
19. HAIL, MARY
20. HAIL, MARY
21. GLORY BE
22. O MY JESUS

THE SECOND DECADE
23. ANNOUNCE
24. OUR FATHER
25. HAIL, MARY
26. HAIL, MARY
27. HAIL, MARY
28. HAIL, MARY
29. HAIL, MARY
30. HAIL, MARY
31. HAIL, MARY
32. HAIL, MARY
33. HAIL, MARY
34. HAIL, MARY
35. GLORY BE
36. O MY JESUS

THE THIRD DECADE
37. ANNOUNCE
38. OUR FATHER
39. HAIL, MARY
40. HAIL, MARY
41. HAIL, MARY
42. HAIL, MARY
43. HAIL, MARY
44. HAIL, MARY
45. HAIL, MARY
46. HAIL, MARY
47. HAIL, MARY
48. HAIL, MARY
49. GLORY BE
50. O MY JESUS

THE FOURTH DECADE
51. ANNOUNCE
52. OUR FATHER
53. HAIL, MARY
54. HAIL, MARY
55. HAIL, MARY
56. HAIL, MARY
57. HAIL, MARY
58. HAIL, MARY
59. HAIL, MARY
60. HAIL, MARY
61. HAIL, MARY
62. HAIL, MARY
63. GLORY BE
64. O MY JESUS

THE FIFTH DECADE
65. ANNOUNCE
66. OUR FATHER
67. HAIL, MARY
68. HAIL, MARY
69. HAIL, MARY
70. HAIL, MARY
71. HAIL, MARY
72. HAIL, MARY
73. HAIL, MARY
74. HAIL, MARY
75. HAIL, MARY
76. HAIL, MARY
77. GLORY BE
78. O MY JESUS

CONCLUSION
79. HAIL, HOLY QUEEN
80. O GOD, WHOSE
81. IN THE NAME

3. WHILE TOUCHING THESE BEADS TO KEEP TRACK OF YOUR PROGRESS...

4. AND SILENTLY MEDITATING ON THESE "MYSTERIES", OR EVENTS FROM THE LIVES OF JESUS AND MARY...

On Monday and Saturday, meditate on the *"Joyful Mysteries"*
First Decade (Steps 9-22): The Annunciation of Gabriel to Mary (Luke 1:26-38)
Second Decade (Steps 23-36): The Visitation of Mary to Elizabeth (Luke 1:39-56)
Third Decade (Steps 37-50): The Birth of Our Lord (Luke 2:1-21)
Fourth Decade (Steps 51-64): The Presentation of Our Lord (Luke 2:22-38)
Fifth Decade (Steps 65-78): The Finding of Our Lord in the Temple (Luke 2:41-52)

On Thursday, meditate on the *"Luminous Mysteries"*
First Decade: The Baptism of Our Lord in the River Jordan (Matthew 3:13-16)
Second Decade: The Wedding at Cana, when Christ manifested Himself (Jn 2:1-11)
Third Decade: The Proclamation of the Kingdom of God (Mark 1:14-15)
Fourth Decade: The Transfiguration of Our Lord (Matthew 17:1-8)
Fifth Decade: The Last Supper, when Our Lord gave us the Holy Eucharist (Mt 26)

On Tuesday and Friday, meditate on the *"Sorrowful Mysteries"*
First Decade: The Agony of Our Lord in the Garden (Matthew 26:36-56)
Second Decade: Our Lord is Scourged at the Pillar (Matthew 27:26)
Third Decade: Our Lord is Crowned with Thorns (Matthew 27:27-31)
Fourth Decade: Our Lord Carries the Cross to Calvary (Matthew 27:32)
Fifth Decade: The Crucifixion of Our Lord (Matthew 27:33-56)

On Wednesday and Sunday, meditate on the *"Glorious Mysteries"*
First Decade: The Glorious Resurrection of Our Lord (John 20:1-29)
Second Decade: The Ascension of Our Lord (Luke 24:36-53)
Third Decade: The Descent of the Holy Spirit at Pentecost (Acts 2:1-41)
Fourth Decade: The Assumption of Mary into Heaven
Fifth Decade: The Coronation of Mary as Queen of Heaven and Earth

You are encouraged to copy and distribute this sheet.

www.HowToPrayTheRosary.net

How to Pray the Rosary

At the Crucifix

The following prayers are written as if they were Versicles (V) and Responses (R) in order to show clearly how the rosary is said with others. The first person says the versicle and the second person says the response. If more than two people are saying the rosary, then one person says the versicle, and the others together say the response.

V. I believe in God the Father Almighty, Maker of heaven and earth: And in Jesus Christ, His only Son, our Lord: Who was conceived by the Holy Ghost, Born of the Virgin Mary: Suffered under Pontius Pilate, Was crucified, dead, and buried: He descended into hell; The third day he rose again from the dead: He ascended into heaven, and sitteth on the right hand of God the Father Almighty: From thence he shall come to judge the quick and the dead.

R. I believe in the Holy Ghost: The holy Catholic Church: The Communion of Saints: The Forgiveness of sins: The Resurrection of the body: And the Life everlasting. Amen.

Move your fingers to the first Pater bead, which is the first bead next to the crucifix.

The First Pater Bead

V. Our Father, who art in heaven, Hallowed be thy Name. Thy Kingdom come. Thy will be done, On earth as it is in heaven. R. Give us this day our daily bread. And forgive us our trespasses, as we forgive them that trespass against us. And lead us not into temptation, But deliver us from evil. Amen.

Continue to the next bead, which is the first of three Ave beads.

The Three Ave Beads

Ask for Final Perseverance; or for a Good Death; or for Purity; or for Faith, Hope, and Charity.

V. Hail Mary, Full of Grace, The Lord is with thee. Blessed art thou amongst women, and blessed is the fruit of thy womb, Jesus.

R. Holy Mary, Mother of God, pray for us sinners now, and at the hour of death. Amen.

Move to the next Ave bead. Continue in this way to move to the next bead after concluding each prayer with the Amen.

Hail Mary…

Hail Mary…

On the Gloria Bead

V. Glory be to the Father, and to the Son, and to the Holy Ghost.
R. As it was in the beginning, is now, and ever shall be, world without end. Amen.

The Joyful Mysteries: The Childhood of Christ

The complete Rosary contains 15 decades of Aves–150 Hail Marys corresponding to 150 Psalms. (If you count the 3 Aves in the introduction, there are 153 total, an interesting number that corresponds to the miraculous catch of 153 fish recounted in the gospel of John.)

It is common to refer to only a third part of the complete Rosary as "one Rosary" because there is a long-standing custom of saying this much every day, cycling through the full Rosary every three days. Even when Our Lady appeared at Fatima, she requested that people say "a third part of the rosary" every day.

The First Decade

Fix your mind on the first mystery of the Rosary–The Annunciation of the Angel St. Gabriel to the Blessed Virgin–and ask for the grace of Humility.

On the Pater Bead

V. Our Father, who art in heaven, Hallowed be thy Name. Thy Kingdom come. Thy will be done, On earth as it is in heaven. R. Give us this day our daily bread. And forgive us our trespasses, as we forgive them that trespass against us. And lead us not into temptation, But deliver us from evil. Amen.

On Each of the 10 Ave Beads

V. Hail Mary, Full of Grace, The Lord is with thee. Blessed art thou amongst women, and blessed is the fruit of thy womb, Jesus. R. Holy Mary, Mother of God, pray for us sinners now, and at the hour of death. Amen.

After the Last Hail Mary

V. Glory be to the Father, and to the Son, and to the Holy Ghost. R. As it was in the beginning, is now, and ever shall be, world without end. Amen.

Aspiration after the Gloria

Say the Fatima Prayer written here, or some other aspiration. If several people are saying the rosary together, the leader says the first words up to the asterisk (*), and then the others join in.

O My Jesus, * forgive us our sins, save us from the fires of Hell and lead all souls to Heaven, especially those in most need of Thy mercy. Amen.

The Second Decade

Fix your mind on the second mystery of the Rosary—The Visitation of the Blessed Virgin to St. Elizabeth—and ask for the grace of Brotherly Love.

On the Pater Bead

V. Our Father, who art in heaven, Hallowed be thy Name. Thy Kingdom come. Thy will be done, On earth as it is in heaven. R.

Give us this day our daily bread. And forgive us our trespasses, as we forgive them that trespass against us. And lead us not into temptation, But deliver us from evil. Amen.

On Each of the 10 Ave Beads

V. Hail Mary, Full of Grace, The Lord is with thee. Blessed art thou amongst women, and blessed is the fruit of thy womb, Jesus. R. Holy Mary, Mother of God, pray for us sinners now, and at the hour of death. Amen.

After the Last Hail Mary

V. Glory be to the Father, and to the Son, and to the Holy Ghost. R. As it was in the beginning, is now, and ever shall be, world without end. Amen.

Aspiration after the Gloria

Say the Fatima Prayer, or some other aspiration.

O My Jesus, * forgive us our sins, save us from the fires of Hell and lead all souls to Heaven, especially those in most need of Thy mercy. Amen.

The Third Decade

Fix your mind on the third mystery of the Rosary—The Nativity of Our Lord Jesus Christ—and ask for the grace of the Love of Poverty.

On the Pater Bead

V. Our Father, who art in heaven, Hallowed be thy Name. Thy Kingdom come. Thy will be done, On earth as it is in heaven. R. Give us this day our daily bread. And forgive us our trespasses, as we forgive them that trespass against us. And lead us not into temptation, But deliver us from evil. Amen.

On Each of the 10 Ave Beads

V. Hail Mary, Full of Grace, The Lord is with thee. Blessed art thou amongst women, and blessed is the fruit of thy womb, Jesus. R. Holy Mary, Mother of God, pray for us sinners now, and at the hour of death. Amen.

After the Last Hail Mary

V. Glory be to the Father, and to the Son, and to the Holy Ghost. R. As it was in the beginning, is now, and ever shall be, world without end. Amen.

Aspiration after the Gloria

Say the Fatima Prayer, or some other aspiration.

O My Jesus, * forgive us our sins, save us from the fires of Hell and lead all souls to Heaven, especially those in most need of Thy mercy. Amen.

The Fourth Decade

Fix your mind on the fourth mystery of the Rosary–The Presentation of Our Lord in the Temple–and ask for the grace of the Spirit of Sacrifice.

On the Pater Bead

V. Our Father, who art in heaven, Hallowed be thy Name. Thy Kingdom come. Thy will be done, On earth as it is in heaven. R. Give us this day our daily bread. And forgive us our trespasses, as we forgive them that trespass against us. And lead us not into temptation, But deliver us from evil. Amen.

On Each of the 10 Ave Beads

V. Hail Mary, Full of Grace, The Lord is with thee. Blessed art thou amongst women, and blessed is the fruit of thy womb, Jesus. R. Holy Mary, Mother of God, pray for us sinners now, and at the hour of death. Amen.

After the Last Hail Mary

V. Glory be to the Father, and to the Son, and to the Holy Ghost.
R. As it was in the beginning, is now, and ever shall be, world without end. Amen.

Aspiration after the Gloria

Say the Fatima Prayer, or some other aspiration.

O My Jesus, * forgive us our sins, save us from the fires of Hell and lead all souls to Heaven, especially those in most need of Thy mercy. Amen.

The Fifth Decade

Fix your mind on the fifth mystery of the Rosary—The Finding of Our Lord in the Temple—and ask for the grace of Wisdom.

On the Pater Bead

V. Our Father, who art in heaven, Hallowed be thy Name. Thy Kingdom come. Thy will be done, On earth as it is in heaven. R. Give us this day our daily bread. And forgive us our trespasses, as we forgive them that trespass against us. And lead us not into temptation, But deliver us from evil. Amen.

On Each of the 10 Ave Beads

V. Hail Mary, Full of Grace, The Lord is with thee. Blessed art thou amongst women, and blessed is the fruit of thy womb, Jesus. R. Holy Mary, Mother of God, pray for us sinners now, and at the hour of death. Amen.

After the Last Hail Mary

V. Glory be to the Father, and to the Son, and to the Holy Ghost. R. As it was in the beginning, is now, and ever shall be, world without end. Amen.

Aspiration after the Gloria

Say the Fatima Prayer, or some other aspiration.

O My Jesus, * forgive us our sins, save us from the fires of Hell and lead all souls to Heaven, especially those in most need of Thy mercy. Amen.

Either continue on to the next five decades, or finish here with the Concluding Prayers. If you want to say more than a third part of the rosary in a day, it is advisable to say five decades at a time at different times of the day.

Traditionally the Rosary consists of three sets of mysteries, the Joyful, Sorrowful, and Glorious. However in October 2002, Pope John Paul II proposed five additional mysteries to the Rosary in his Apostolic Letter Rosarium Virginis Mariae. The Luminous Mysteries or Mysteries of Light provide opportunity for us to meditate on the public ministry of Jesus, those years between His childhood and His Passion. The pope made is clear that these were optional for the faithful. But since their proposal, they have become regularly used by the faithful.

The Luminous Mysteries: The Public Life of Christ

The Sixth Decade

Fix your mind on the sixth mystery of the Rosary–The Baptism of our Lord– and ask for the grace of to be true to your own baptism.

On the Pater Bead

V. Our Father, who art in heaven, Hallowed be thy Name. Thy Kingdom come. Thy will be done, On earth as it is in heaven. R. Give us this day our daily bread. And forgive us our trespasses, as we forgive them that trespass against us. And lead us not into temptation, But deliver us from evil. Amen.

On Each of the 10 Ave Beads

V. Hail Mary, Full of Grace, The Lord is with thee. Blessed art thou amongst women, and blessed is the fruit of thy womb, Jesus. R.

Holy Mary, Mother of God, pray for us sinners now, and at the hour of death. Amen.

After the Last Hail Mary

V. Glory be to the Father, and to the Son, and to the Holy Ghost. R. As it was in the beginning, is now, and ever shall be, world without end. Amen.

Aspiration after the Gloria

Say the Fatima Prayer written here, or some other aspiration.

O My Jesus, * forgive us our sins, save us from the fires of Hell and lead all souls to Heaven, especially those in most need of Thy mercy. Amen.

The Seventh Decade

Fix your mind on the seventh mystery of the Rosary–The Wedding at Cana– and ask for the grace of going to Jesus through Mary, His mother.

On the Pater Bead

V. Our Father, who art in heaven, Hallowed be thy Name. Thy Kingdom come. Thy will be done, On earth as it is in heaven. R. Give us this day our daily bread. And forgive us our trespasses, as we forgive them that trespass against us. And lead us not into temptation, But deliver us from evil. Amen.

On Each of the 10 Ave Beads

V. Hail Mary, Full of Grace, The Lord is with thee. Blessed art thou amongst women, and blessed is the fruit of thy womb, Jesus. R. Holy Mary, Mother of God, pray for us sinners now, and at the hour of death. Amen.

After the Last Hail Mary

V. Glory be to the Father, and to the Son, and to the Holy Ghost.
R. As it was in the beginning, is now, and ever shall be, world without end. Amen.

Aspiration after the Gloria

Say the Fatima Prayer, or some other aspiration.

O My Jesus, * forgive us our sins, save us from the fires of Hell and lead all souls to Heaven, especially those in most need of Thy mercy. Amen.

The Eighth Decade

Fix your mind on the eighth mystery of the Rosary–The Proclamation of the Kingdom of God–and ask for the grace of true repentance and trust in God.

On the Pater Bead

V. Our Father, who art in heaven, Hallowed be thy Name. Thy Kingdom come. Thy will be done, On earth as it is in heaven. R. Give us this day our daily bread. And forgive us our trespasses, as we forgive them that trespass against us. And lead us not into temptation, But deliver us from evil. Amen.

On Each of the 10 Ave Beads

V. Hail Mary, Full of Grace, The Lord is with thee. Blessed art thou amongst women, and blessed is the fruit of thy womb, Jesus. R. Holy Mary, Mother of God, pray for us sinners now, and at the hour of death. Amen.

After the Last Hail Mary

V. Glory be to the Father, and to the Son, and to the Holy Ghost.
R. As it was in the beginning, is now, and ever shall be, world without end. Amen.

Aspiration after the Gloria

Say the Fatima Prayer, or some other aspiration.

O My Jesus, * forgive us our sins, save us from the fires of Hell and lead all souls to Heaven, especially those in most need of Thy mercy. Amen.

The Ninth Decade

Fix your mind on the eighth mystery of the Rosary–The Transfiguration of Christ–and ask for the grace to truly desire holiness.

On the Pater Bead

V. Our Father, who art in heaven, Hallowed be thy Name. Thy Kingdom come. Thy will be done, On earth as it is in heaven. R. Give us this day our daily bread. And forgive us our trespasses, as we forgive them that trespass against us. And lead us not into temptation, But deliver us from evil. Amen.

On Each of the 10 Ave Beads

V. Hail Mary, Full of Grace, The Lord is with thee. Blessed art thou amongst women, and blessed is the fruit of thy womb, Jesus. R. Holy Mary, Mother of God, pray for us sinners now, and at the hour of death. Amen.

After the Last Hail Mary

V. Glory be to the Father, and to the Son, and to the Holy Ghost. R. As it was in the beginning, is now, and ever shall be, world without end. Amen.

Aspiration after the Gloria

Say the Fatima Prayer, or some other aspiration.

O My Jesus, * forgive us our sins, save us from the fires of Hell and lead all souls to Heaven, especially those in most need of Thy mercy. Amen.

The Tenth Decade

Fix your mind on the tenth mystery of the Rosary—The Institution of the Eucharist—and ask for the grace of a Love and Adoration of the Christ in the Blessed Sacrament.

On the Pater Bead

V. Our Father, who art in heaven, Hallowed be thy Name. Thy Kingdom come. Thy will be done, On earth as it is in heaven. R. Give us this day our daily bread. And forgive us our trespasses, as we forgive them that trespass against us. And lead us not into temptation, But deliver us from evil. Amen.

On Each of the 10 Ave Beads

V. Hail Mary, Full of Grace, The Lord is with thee. Blessed art thou amongst women, and blessed is the fruit of thy womb, Jesus. R. Holy Mary, Mother of God, pray for us sinners now, and at the hour of death. Amen.

After the Last Hail Mary

V. Glory be to the Father, and to the Son, and to the Holy Ghost. R. As it was in the beginning, is now, and ever shall be, world without end. Amen.

Aspiration after the Gloria

Say the Fatima Prayer, or some other aspiration.

O My Jesus, * forgive us our sins, save us from the fires of Hell and lead all souls to Heaven, especially those in most need of Thy mercy. Amen.

Either continue on to the next five decades, or finish here with the Concluding Prayers. If you want to say more than a third part of the rosary in a day, it is advisable to say five decades at a time at different times of the day.

The Sorrowful Mysteries: The Passion of Christ

The Eleventh Decade

Fix your mind on the sixth mystery of the Rosary–The Agony of Our Lord in the Garden–and ask for the grace of True Contrition for Your Sins.

On the Pater Bead

V. Our Father, who art in heaven, Hallowed be thy Name. Thy Kingdom come. Thy will be done, On earth as it is in heaven. R. Give us this day our daily bread. And forgive us our trespasses, as we forgive them that trespass against us. And lead us not into temptation, But deliver us from evil. Amen.

On Each of the 10 Ave Beads

V. Hail Mary, Full of Grace, The Lord is with thee. Blessed art thou amongst women, and blessed is the fruit of thy womb, Jesus. R. Holy Mary, Mother of God, pray for us sinners now, and at the hour of death. Amen.

After the Last Hail Mary

V. Glory be to the Father, and to the Son, and to the Holy Ghost. R. As it was in the beginning, is now, and ever shall be, world without end. Amen.

Aspiration after the Gloria

Say the Fatima Prayer written here, or some other aspiration.

O My Jesus, * forgive us our sins, save us from the fires of Hell and lead all souls to Heaven, especially those in most need of Thy mercy. Amen.

The Twelfth Decade

Fix your mind on the seventh mystery of the Rosary–The Scourging of Our Lord at the Pillar–and ask for the grace of the Spirit of Mortification.

On the Pater Bead

V. Our Father, who art in heaven, Hallowed be thy Name. Thy Kingdom come. Thy will be done, On earth as it is in heaven. R. Give us this day our daily bread. And forgive us our trespasses, as we forgive them that trespass against us. And lead us not into temptation, But deliver us from evil. Amen.

On Each of the 10 Ave Beads

V. Hail Mary, Full of Grace, The Lord is with thee. Blessed art thou amongst women, and blessed is the fruit of thy womb, Jesus. R. Holy Mary, Mother of God, pray for us sinners now, and at the hour of death. Amen.

After the Last Hail Mary

V. Glory be to the Father, and to the Son, and to the Holy Ghost. R. As it was in the beginning, is now, and ever shall be, world without end. Amen.

Aspiration after the Gloria

Say the Fatima Prayer, or some other aspiration.

O My Jesus, * forgive us our sins, save us from the fires of Hell and lead all souls to Heaven, especially those in most need of Thy mercy. Amen.

The Thirteenth Decade

Fix your mind on the eighth mystery of the Rosary–The Crowning with Thorns–and ask for the grace of Contempt for the World.

On the Pater Bead

V. Our Father, who art in heaven, Hallowed be thy Name. Thy Kingdom come. Thy will be done, On earth as it is in heaven. R. Give us this day our daily bread. And forgive us our trespasses, as we forgive them that trespass against us. And lead us not into temptation, But deliver us from evil. Amen.

On Each of the 10 Ave Beads

V. Hail Mary, Full of Grace, The Lord is with thee. Blessed art thou amongst women, and blessed is the fruit of thy womb, Jesus. R. Holy Mary, Mother of God, pray for us sinners now, and at the hour of death. Amen.

After the Last Hail Mary

V. Glory be to the Father, and to the Son, and to the Holy Ghost. R. As it was in the beginning, is now, and ever shall be, world without end. Amen.

Aspiration after the Gloria

Say the Fatima Prayer, or some other aspiration.

O My Jesus, * forgive us our sins, save us from the fires of Hell and lead all souls to Heaven, especially those in most need of Thy mercy. Amen.

The Fourteenth Decade

Fix your mind on the eighth mystery of the Rosary—The Carrying of the Cross— and ask for the grace to Carry Your Cross.

On the Pater Bead

V. Our Father, who art in heaven, Hallowed be thy Name. Thy Kingdom come. Thy will be done, On earth as it is in heaven. R. Give us this day our daily bread. And forgive us our trespasses, as we forgive them that trespass against us. And lead us not into temptation, But deliver us from evil. Amen.

On Each of the 10 Ave Beads

V. Hail Mary, Full of Grace, The Lord is with thee. Blessed art thou amongst women, and blessed is the fruit of thy womb, Jesus. R. Holy Mary, Mother of God, pray for us sinners now, and at the hour of death. Amen.

After the Last Hail Mary

V. Glory be to the Father, and to the Son, and to the Holy Ghost. R. As it was in the beginning, is now, and ever shall be, world without end. Amen.

Aspiration after the Gloria

Say the Fatima Prayer, or some other aspiration.

O My Jesus, * forgive us our sins, save us from the fires of Hell and lead all souls to Heaven, especially those in most need of Thy mercy. Amen.

The Fifteenth Decade

Fix your mind on the tenth mystery of the Rosary–The Death of Our Savior on the Cross–and ask for the grace of Final Perseverance.

On the Pater Bead

V. Our Father, who art in heaven, Hallowed be thy Name. Thy Kingdom come. Thy will be done, On earth as it is in heaven. R. Give us this day our daily bread. And forgive us our trespasses, as we forgive them that trespass against us. And lead us not into temptation, But deliver us from evil. Amen.

On Each of the 10 Ave Beads

V. Hail Mary, Full of Grace, The Lord is with thee. Blessed art thou amongst women, and blessed is the fruit of thy womb, Jesus. R. Holy Mary, Mother of God, pray for us sinners now, and at the hour of death. Amen.

After the Last Hail Mary

V. Glory be to the Father, and to the Son, and to the Holy Ghost. R. As it was in the beginning, is now, and ever shall be, world without end. Amen.

Aspiration after the Gloria

Say the Fatima Prayer, or some other aspiration.

O My Jesus, * forgive us our sins, save us from the fires of Hell and lead all souls to Heaven, especially those in most need of Thy mercy. Amen.

Either continue on to the next five decades, or finish here with the Concluding Prayers. If you want to say more than a third part of the rosary in a day, it is advisable to say five decades at a time at different times of the day.

The Glorious Mysteries: The Resurrection of Christ

The Sixteenth Decade

Fix your mind on the eleventh mystery of the Rosary–The Resurrection of Our Lord–and ask for the grace of Faith.

On the Pater Bead

V. Our Father, who art in heaven, Hallowed be thy Name. Thy Kingdom come. Thy will be done, On earth as it is in heaven. R. Give us this day our daily bread. And forgive us our trespasses, as we forgive them that trespass against us. And lead us not into temptation, But deliver us from evil. Amen.

On Each of the 10 Ave Beads

V. Hail Mary, Full of Grace, The Lord is with thee. Blessed art thou amongst women, and blessed is the fruit of thy womb, Jesus. R. Holy Mary, Mother of God, pray for us sinners now, and at the hour of death. Amen.

After the Last Hail Mary

V. Glory be to the Father, and to the Son, and to the Holy Ghost. R. As it was in the beginning, is now, and ever shall be, world without end. Amen.

Aspiration after the Gloria

Say the Fatima Prayer written here, or some other aspiration.

O My Jesus, * forgive us our sins, save us from the fires of Hell and lead all souls to Heaven, especially those in most need of Thy mercy. Amen.

The Seventeenth Decade

Fix your mind on the twelfth mystery of the Rosary–The Ascension of Our Lord into Heaven–and ask for the grace of Hope.

On the Pater Bead

V. Our Father, who art in heaven, Hallowed be thy Name. Thy Kingdom come. Thy will be done, On earth as it is in heaven. R. Give us this day our daily bread. And forgive us our trespasses, as we forgive them that trespass against us. And lead us not into temptation, But deliver us from evil. Amen.

On Each of the 10 Ave Beads

V. Hail Mary, Full of Grace, The Lord is with thee. Blessed art thou amongst women, and blessed is the fruit of thy womb, Jesus. R. Holy Mary, Mother of God, pray for us sinners now, and at the hour of death. Amen.

After the Last Hail Mary

V. Glory be to the Father, and to the Son, and to the Holy Ghost. R. As it was in the beginning, is now, and ever shall be, world without end. Amen.

Aspiration after the Gloria

Say the Fatima Prayer, or some other aspiration.

O My Jesus, * forgive us our sins, save us from the fires of Hell and lead all souls to Heaven, especially those in most need of Thy mercy. Amen.

The Eighteenth Decade

Fix your mind on the thirteenth mystery of the Rosary—The Coming of the Holy Ghost at Pentecost—and ask for the grace of Zeal.

On the Pater Bead

V. Our Father, who art in heaven, Hallowed be thy Name. Thy Kingdom come. Thy will be done, On earth as it is in heaven. R. Give us this day our daily bread. And forgive us our trespasses, as we forgive them that trespass against us. And lead us not into temptation, But deliver us from evil. Amen.

On Each of the 10 Ave Beads

V. Hail Mary, Full of Grace, The Lord is with thee. Blessed art thou amongst women, and blessed is the fruit of thy womb, Jesus. R. Holy Mary, Mother of God, pray for us sinners now, and at the hour of death. Amen.

After the Last Hail Mary

V. Glory be to the Father, and to the Son, and to the Holy Ghost. R. As it was in the beginning, is now, and ever shall be, world without end. Amen.

Aspiration after the Gloria

Say the Fatima Prayer, or some other aspiration.

O My Jesus, * forgive us our sins, save us from the fires of Hell and lead all souls to Heaven, especially those in most need of Thy mercy. Amen.

The Nineteenth Decade

Fix your mind on the fourteenth mystery of the Rosary—The Assumption of the Blessed Virgin, Body and Soul, into Heaven—and ask for the grace of a Tender Devotion to Mary.

On the Pater Bead

V. Our Father, who art in heaven, Hallowed be thy Name. Thy Kingdom come. Thy will be done, On earth as it is in heaven. R. Give us this day our daily bread. And forgive us our trespasses, as we forgive them that trespass against us. And lead us not into temptation, But deliver us from evil. Amen.

On Each of the 10 Ave Beads

V. Hail Mary, Full of Grace, The Lord is with thee. Blessed art thou amongst women, and blessed is the fruit of thy womb, Jesus. R. Holy Mary, Mother of God, pray for us sinners now, and at the hour of death. Amen.

After the Last Hail Mary

V. Glory be to the Father, and to the Son, and to the Holy Ghost. R. As it was in the beginning, is now, and ever shall be, world without end. Amen.

Aspiration after the Gloria

Say the Fatima Prayer, or some other aspiration.

O My Jesus, * forgive us our sins, save us from the fires of Hell and lead all souls to Heaven, especially those in most need of Thy mercy. Amen.

The Twentieth Decade

Fix your mind on the fifteenth mystery of the Rosary—The Coronation of the Blessed Virgin in Heaven by Our Lord—and ask for Perseverance in Grace.

On the Pater Bead

V. Our Father, who art in heaven, Hallowed be thy Name. Thy Kingdom come. Thy will be done, On earth as it is in heaven. R. Give us this day our daily bread. And forgive us our trespasses, as we forgive them that trespass against us. And lead us not into temptation, But deliver us from evil. Amen.

On Each of the 10 Ave Beads

V. Hail Mary, Full of Grace, The Lord is with thee. Blessed art thou amongst women, and blessed is the fruit of thy womb, Jesus. R. Holy Mary, Mother of God, pray for us sinners now, and at the hour of death. Amen.

After the Last Hail Mary

V. Glory be to the Father, and to the Son, and to the Holy Ghost. R. As it was in the beginning, is now, and ever shall be, world without end. Amen.

Aspiration after the Gloria

Say the Fatima Prayer, or some other aspiration.

O My Jesus, * forgive us our sins, save us from the fires of Hell and lead all souls to Heaven, especially those in most need of Thy mercy. Amen.

Conclusion of the Rosary

The Hail Holy Queen

Hail holy Queen, mother of mercy, our life, our sweetness, and our hope. To thee do we cry, poor banished children of Eve. To thee do we send up our sighs, mourning and weeping in this valley of tears. Turn then, most gracious Advocate, thine eyes of mercy toward us. And after this our exile show unto us the blessed Fruit of thy womb, Jesus. O clement, O loving, O sweet Virgin Mary. Amen.

Collect of the Feast of the Most Holy Rosary of the Blessed Virgin

V. Pray for us, O Holy Mother of God.
R. That we may be made worthy of the promises of Christ.

Let us pray. O God, Whose only-begotten Son, by His life, death, and resurrection hath purchased for us the rewards of eternal life: grant, we beseech Thee, that, meditating on the mysteries of the most holy Rosary of the Blessed Virgin Mary, we may imitate what they contain and obtain what they promise. Through the same Jesus Christ, Thy Son, Who liveth and reigneth with Thee in the unity of the Holy Ghost, God, world without end.

Obtain the Indulgences

If you are not aware of any unconfessed mortal sin on your soul, and you pray a third of the rosary continuously in a church, in a family, or in a religious community, you may gain a plenary indulgence if you say some prayers for the usual intentions of the Holy Father. You may apply the indulgence to the suffering souls in purgatory if you wish.

You do not need to call the Vatican to find out the Pope's prayer intentions; the usual intentions of the Holy Father have always been defined as the following: 1) The increase of the Catholic Faith; 2) the triumph of Holy Church; 3) the conversion of sinners; 4) peace and concord among Christian princes and rulers; and 5) the uprooting of heresy. No specific prayers are assigned, but it is customary to simply say an Our Father, *a* Hail Mary, *and a* Glory Be to the Father *for these intentions.*

Other Methods of Praying the Rosary

A Method of Saying the Rosary, the First in the *Golden Manual*

The Golden Manual was a book of prayers and devotions first published in the mid-nineteenth century. As such, it was written before the proposed Luminous Mysteries of Pope John Paul II.

With a meditation and prayer on each mystery, which is that commonly used in England.

✝ In the name of the Father, and of the Son, and of the Holy Ghost. Amen.

V. Hail, Mary, full of grace, the Lord is with thee.
R. Blessed art thou amongst women, and blessed is the fruit of thy womb, Jesus.

V. Thou, O Lord, wilt open my lips.
R. And my tongue shall announce thy praise.

V. Incline unto my aid, O God.
R. O Lord, make haste to help me.

V. Glory be to the Father, and to the Son, and to the Holy Ghost.
R. As it was in the beginning, is now, and ever shall be, world without end. Amen. Alleluia.

Except from Septuagesima to Easter; then for Alleluia say, Praise be to thee, O Lord, King of eternal glory.

The Five Joyful Mysteries

I. The Annunciation.

Let us contemplate, in this mystery, how the angel Gabriel saluted our Blessed Lady with the title "Full of grace," and declared unto her the Incarnation of our Lord and Saviour Jesus Christ.

Our Father. Ten Hail Marys. Glory be to the Father, &c.

Let us pray. O Holy Mary, Queen of Virgins; through the most high mystery of the Incarnation of thy beloved Son, our Lord Jesus Christ, wherein our salvation was begun, obtain for us, through thy most holy intercession, light to understand the greatness of the benefit he hath bestowed upon us, in vouchsafing to become our Brother, and giving thee, his own beloved Mother, to be our Mother also. Amen.

II. The Visitation.

Let us contemplate, in this mystery, how the Blessed Virgin Mary, understanding from the angel that her cousin St. Elisabeth had conceived, went with haste into the mountains of Judea to visit her, bearing her Divine Son within her womb, and remained with her three months.

Our Father. Ten Hail Marys. Glory be to the Father, &c.

Let us pray. O Holy Virgin, most spotless mirror of humility; by that exceeding charity which moved thee to visit thy holy cousin St. Elisabeth, obtain for us, through thine intercession, that our hearts being visited by thy Divine Son, and freed from all sin, we may praise and give thanks to him forever. Amen.

III. The Birth of our Saviour Christ in Bethlehem.

Let us contemplate, in this mystery, how the Blessed Virgin Mary, when the time of her delivery was come, brought forth our Redeemer, Jesus Christ, at midnight, and laid him in a manger, because there was no room for him in the inns at Bethlehem.

Our Father. Ten Hail Marys. Glory be to the Father, &c.

Let us pray. O most pure Mother of God; through thy virginal and most joyful delivery, whereby thou gavest to the world thy only Son, our Saviour, we beseech thee obtain for us, through thine intercession, the grace to lead such pure and holy lives in this world, that we may become worthy to sing, without ceasing, the mercies of thy Son, and his benefits to us by thee. Amen.

IV. The Presentation of our Blessed Lord in the Temple.

Let us contemplate, in this mystery, how the Blessed Virgin Mary, on the day of her purification, presented the child Jesus in the Temple, where holy Simeon, giving thanks to God, with great devotion received him into his arms.

Our Father. Ten Hail Marys. Glory be to the Father, &c.

Let us pray. O Holy Virgin, most admirable mistress and pattern of obedience, who didst present the Lord of the Temple in the Temple of God; obtain for us of thy blessed Son, that, with holy Simeon and devout Anna, we may praise and glorify him forever. Amen.

V. The Finding of the Child Jesus in the Temple.

Let us contemplate, in this mystery, how the Blessed Virgin Mary, after having lost (through no fault of hers) her beloved Son in Jerusalem, sought him for the space of three days; and at length found him in the Temple, sitting in the midst of the doctors, hearing them, and asking them questions, being of the age of twelve years.

Our Father. Ten Hail Marys. Glory be to the Father, &c.

Let us pray. O most Blessed Virgin, more than martyr in thy sufferings, and yet the comfort of such as are afflicted; by that unspeakable joy wherewith thy soul was filled, when at length thou didst find thy well-beloved Son in the Temple, teaching in the midst of the doctors; obtain of him that we may so seek him and find him in his holy Catholic Church, as never more to be separated from him. Amen.

Salve Regina, Versicle, and Collect

Hail, Holy Queen, Mother of Mercy, Hail our Life, our Sweetness, and our Hope! To thee do we cry, poor banished children of Eve; to thee do we send up our sighs, mourning and weeping in this vale of tears. Turn, then, most gracious Advocate, thine eyes of mercy towards us; and after this our exile, show unto us the blessed Fruit of thy womb, JESUS, O clement, O loving, O sweet Virgin Mary.

V. Pray for us, O holy Mother of God.
R. That we may be made worthy of the promises of Christ.

Let us pray. *Then is said one of the following collects:*

Hear, O merciful God, the prayer of thy servants; that we who meet together in the society of the most holy Rosary of the Blessed Virgin, Mother of God, may, through her intercession, be delivered by thee from the dangers that continually hang over us; through the merits of our Lord and Saviour Jesus Christ. Amen.

O God, whose only-begotten Son, by his life, death, and resurrection, hath laid open to us the rewards of everlasting life; grant, we beseech thee, that pondering in our heart these Mysteries in the most holy Rosary of the Blessed Virgin Mary, we may imitate what they set forth, and obtain what they promise; through the same our Lord and Saviour Jesus Christ. Amen.

The Five Sorrowful Mysteries

I. The Prayer and Bloody Sweat of our Blessed Saviour in the Garden.

Let us contemplate, in this mystery, how our Lord Jesus was so afflicted for us in the garden of Gethsemani, that his body was bathed in a bloody sweat, which ran down in great drops to the ground.

Our Father. Ten Hail Marys. Glory be to the Father, &c.

Let us pray. O most holy Virgin, more than martyr; by that ardent prayer which our beloved Saviour poured forth to his Heavenly

Father in the garden, vouchsafe to intercede for us, that, our passions being reduced to the obedience of reason, we may always, and in all things, conform and subject ourselves to the holy will of God. Amen.

II. The Scourging of our Blessed Lord at the Pillar.

Let us contemplate, in this mystery, how our Lord Jesus Christ was most cruelly scourged in Pilate's house, the number of stripes they gave him being about five thousand.

Our Father. Ten Hail Marys. Glory be to the Father, &c.

Let us pray. O Mother of God, overflowing fountain of patience; through those stripes thy only and much0-beloved Son vouchsafed to suffer for us, obtain of him for us grace to mortify our rebellious senses, to avoid the occasion of sin, and to be ready to suffer every thing rather than offend God. Amen.

III. The Crowning of our Blessed Saviour with Thorns.

Let us contemplate, in this mystery, how those cruel ministers of Satan plaited a crown of sharp thorns, and cruelly pressed it on the sacred head of our Lord Jesus Christ.

Our Father. Ten Hail Marys. Glory be to the Father, &c.

Let us pray. O Mother of our Eternal Prince, the King of Glory; by those sharp thorns wherewith his sacred head was pierced, we beseech thee obtain, through thy intercession, that we may be delivered from all motions of pride, and escape that shame which our sins deserve at the day of judgment. Amen.

IV. Jesus carrying his Cross.

Let us contemplate, in this mystery, how our Lord Jesus Christ, being sentenced to die, bore with the most amazing patience, the Cross which was laid upon him for his greater torment and ignominy.

Our Father. Ten Hail Marys. Glory be to the Father, &c.

Let us pray. O Holy Virgin, example of patience; by the most painful carrying of the Cross, in which thy Son, our Lord Jesus Christ, bore the heavy weight of our sins, obtain for us of him, through thine intercession, courage and strength to follow his steps, and bear our cross after him to the end of our lives. Amen.

V. The Crucifixion of our Lord Jesus Christ.

Let us contemplate, in this mystery, how our Lord Jesus Christ, being come to Mount Calvary, was stripped of his clothes, and his hands and feet nailed to the Cross, in the presence of his most afflicted Mother.

Our Father. Ten Hail Marys. Glory be to the Father, &c.

Let us pray. O Holy Mary, Mother of God; as the body of thy beloved Son was for us stretched upon the Cross, so may we offer up our souls and bodies to be crucified with him, and our hearts to be pierced with grief at his most bitter Passion; and thou, O most sorrowful Mother, graciously vouchsafe to help us, by thy all-powerful intercession, to accomplish the work of our salvation. Amen.

Salve Regina, Versicle, and Collect

Hail, Holy Queen, Mother of Mercy, Hail our Life, our Sweetness, and our Hope! To thee do we cry, poor banished children of Eve; to thee do we send up our sighs, mourning and weeping in this vale of tears. Turn, then, most gracious Advocate, thine eyes of mercy towards us; and after this our exile, show unto us the blessed Fruit of thy womb, JESUS, O clement, O loving, O sweet Virgin Mary.

V. Pray for us, O holy Mother of God.
R. That we may be made worthy of the promises of Christ.

Let us pray. *Then is said one of the following collects:*

Hear, O merciful God, the prayer of thy servants; that we who meet together in the society of the most holy Rosary of the Blessed Virgin, Mother of God, may, through her intercession, be delivered by thee from the dangers that continually hang over us; through the merits of our Lord and Saviour Jesus Christ. Amen.

O God, whose only-begotten Son, by his life, death, and resurrection, hath laid open to us the rewards of everlasting life; grant, we beseech thee, that pondering in our heart these Mysteries in the most holy Rosary of the Blessed Virgin Mary, we may imitate what they set forth, and obtain what they promise; through the same our Lord and Saviour Jesus Christ. Amen.

The Five Glorious Mysteries

I. The Resurrection of our Lord from the dead.

Let us contemplate, in this mystery, how our Lord Jesus Christ, triumphing gloriously over death, rose again the third day, immortal and impassible.

Our Father. Ten Hail Marys. Glory be to the Father, &c.

Let us pray. O glorious Virgin Mary; by that unspeakable joy thou didst receive in the resurrection of thy Divine Son, we beseech thee obtain for us of him, that our hearts may never go astray after the false joys of this world, but may be forever wholly employed in the pursuit of the only true and solid joys of heaven. Amen.

II. The Ascension of Christ into Heaven.

Let us contemplate, in this mystery, how our Lord Jesus Christ, for forty days after his resurrection, ascended into heaven, attended by angels, in the sight and to the great admiration of his most holy Mother, and his holy Apostles and disciples.

Our Father. Ten Hail Marys. Glory be to the Father, &c.

Let us pray. O Mother of God, comforter of the afflicted; as thy beloved Son, when he ascended into heaven, lifted up his hands and blessed his Apostles, as he was parted from them; so vouchsafe, most holy Mother, to lift up thy pure hands to him on our behalf, that we may enjoy the benefits of his blessing, and of thine, here on earth, and hereafter in heaven. Amen.

III. The Descent of the Holy Ghost on the Apostles.

Let us contemplate, in this mystery, how our Lord Jesus Christ, being seated on the right hand of God, sent, as he had promised, the Holy Ghost upon his Apostles, who, after he was ascended, turning to Jerusalem, continued in prayer and supplication with the Blessed Virgin Mary, expecting the performance of his promise.

Our Father. Ten Hail Marys. Glory be to the Father, &c.

Let us pray. O sacred Virgin, Tabernacle of the Holy Ghost; we beseech thee obtain, by thine intercession, that this most sweet Comforter, whom thy beloved Son sent down upon his Apostles, filling them there with spiritual joy, may teach us in this world the true way of salvation, and make us to walk in the way of virtue and good works. Amen.

IV. The Assumption of the Blessed Virgin Mary into Heaven.

Let us contemplate, in this mystery, how the glorious Virgin, twelve years after the resurrection of her Son, passed out of this world unto him, and was by him assumed into heaven, accompanied by the holy Angels.

Our Father. Ten Hail Marys. Glory be to the Father, &c.

Let us pray. O most prudent Virgin, who, entering the heavenly palaces, didst fill the angels with joy and man with hope; vouchsafe to intercede for us at the hour of our death, that, being delivered from the illusions and temptations of the devil, we may joyfully and securely pass out of this temporal state, to enjoy the happiness of eternal life. Amen.

V. The Coronation of the Blessed Virgin Mary in Heaven.

Let us contemplate, in this mystery, how the glorious Virgin Mary was, to the great jubilee and exultation of the whole court of heaven, and particular glory of all the Saints, crowned by her Son with the brightest diadem of glory.

Our Father. Ten Hail Marys. Glory be to the Father, &c.

Let us pray. O glorious Queen of all the heavenly host; we beseech thee accept this Rosary, which as a crown of roses, we offer at thy feet; and grant, most gracious Lady, that, by thy intercession, our souls may be inflamed with so ardent a desire of seeing thee so gloriously crowned, that it may never die within us, until it shall be changed into the happy fruition of thy blessed sight. Amen.

Salve Regina, Versicle, and Collect

Hail, Holy Queen, Mother of Mercy, Hail our Life, our Sweetness, and our Hope! To thee do we cry, poor banished children of Eve; to thee do we send up our sighs, mourning and weeping in this vale of tears. Turn, then, most gracious Advocate, thine eyes of mercy towards us; and after this our exile, show unto us the blessed Fruit of thy womb, JESUS, O clement, O loving, O sweet Virgin Mary.

V. Pray for us, O holy Mother of God.
R. That we may be made worthy of the promises of Christ.

Let us pray. *Then is said one of the following collects:*

Hear, O merciful God, the prayer of thy servants; that we who meet together in the society of the most holy Rosary of the Blessed Virgin, Mother of God, may, through her intercession, be delivered by thee from the dangers that continually hang over us; through the merits of our Lord and Saviour Jesus Christ. Amen.

O God, whose only-begotten Son, by his life, death, and resurrection, hath laid open to us the rewards of everlasting life; grant, we beseech thee, that pondering in our heart these Mysteries in the most holy Rosary of the Blessed Virgin Mary, we may imitate what they set forth, and obtain what they promise; through the same our Lord and Saviour Jesus Christ. Amen.

A Method of Saying the Rosary, the Second in the *Golden Manual*

With a meditation and an ejaculation to be inserted after the holy name of JESUS in each "Ave;" and a prayer.

The Five Joyful Mysteries

I. The Angelic Salutation.

Let us adore the Son of God hidden within the womb of Mary, the most lowly handmaid of the Lord, *beseeching of him the virtue of humility*.

Our Father. Ten Hail Marys.

Ejaculation. Jesus, whom thou didst conceive, remaining Ever Virgin.

Glory be to the Father, &c.

O Lord, who, when thou didst come down to redeem our nature, didst choose for thyself the most chaste womb of Mary to be the true Tabernacle of God with men; grant, we beseech thee, that, by her holy intercession, our souls may be so filled with thy grace, that we may be made temples of God; who livest and reignest with God the Father in the unity of the Holy Ghost, world without end.

II. The Visitation.

Let us adore the Son of God, inspiring his most holy Mother to visit St. Elisabeth; *beseeching of him the virtue of charity to our neighbor.*

Our Father. Ten Hail Marys.

Ejaculation. Jesus, whom thou didst bear with thee to visit St. Elisabeth.

Glory be to the Father, &c.

O Lord, who, in the visitation of Mary, didst pour forth thy heavenly graces on the house of Zacharias and Elisabeth; sanctify us by thy sacred and most loving presence, as thou didst sanctify thy holy servant John; and give us grace so to instruct others unto righteousness, and to edify men by our holy life, as to escape all danger of pride and vainglory; who livest and reignest with God the Father in the unity of the Holy Ghost, world without end.

III. The Birth of Jesus Christ.

Let us adore the Son of God, born in a poor stable, of a Mother whose only treasure was her Virginal purity; *begging the grace of purity in soul and body.*

Our Father. Ten Hail Marys.

Ejaculation. Jesus, whom thou didst bring forth, remaining Ever Virgin.

Glory be to the Father, &c.

We give thee thanks, most loving Jesus, because for our sake thou didst choose to be born in a poor stable at midnight, and in the midst of winter to be wrapt in swaddling clothes, laid in a manger, and fed at thy Mother's breasts. Grant, dearest Lord, that we may become like little children, humble and poor in spirit. Grant that we may, like the Magi from the East, seek after thee with diligence, and find thee in the cradle of our hearts, and there adore thee, offering up the gold of charity, the incense of devotion, and the myrrh of mortification. Amen.

IV. The Presentation.

Let us adore the Son of God, presented in the Temple to his heavenly Father by the hands of Mary; *begging that our hearts may be set free from the love of all earthly things.*

Our Father. Ten Hail Marys.

Ejaculation. Jesus, by thee presented in the Temple.

Glory be to the Father, &c.

O Lord Jesus Christ, who didst condescend, together with thy holy Mother, for our example, to be obedient to the law for sin; grant us grace never to be ashamed of thy law, but to labor to fulfil thy commandments, to practise penance for our sins, and to approach thy holy altar with those ardent desires with which holy Simeon received thee into his arms. Amen.

V. Mary finds Jesus in the Temple.

Let us adore the Son of God, who left even his own most tender Mother, when the glory of his heavenly Father called him, and was found by Mary in the Temple sitting in the midst of the doctors. *Let us beg of our Lord an ardent zeal to instruct ourselves in our holy faith, and bring others to the knowledge of it.*

Our Father. Ten Hail Marys.

Ejaculation. Jesus, whom thou didst find in the Temple.

Glory be to the Father, &c.

O Lord my God, thou art the only good; thou art the sea of sweetness, and ocean of all perfection. We are confounded when we think how much our souls are moved at the loss of earthly goods, and yet feel so little trouble when we have lost thee by sin. Grant, we beseech thee, that, despising all earthly things, we may sigh only to enjoy the vision of thy glory and beauty in that kingdom, where, together with the Father and the Holy Spirit, thou livest and reignest God, world without end. Amen.

The Five Sorrowful Mysteries

I. The Prayer and Bloody Sweat of our Blessed Saviour in the Garden.

Let us adore our Lord Jesus Christ in the Garden of Olives, accepting all the horrors of his most cruel Passion, whereby the soul of his most tender Mother was so bitterly afflicted; *begging that in all things, however painful and hard, we may seek only the holy will of God.*

Our Father. Ten Hail Marys.

Ejaculation. Jesus, who for us wast bathed in a sweat of Blood.

Glory be to the Father, &c.

O Lord Jesus Christ, who, in the garden of Gethsemani, hast taught us, both by word and example, to overcome temptation by prayer; grant, we beseech thee, that, giving ourselves continually unto prayer, we may obtain its abundant fruit; who livest and reignest with God the Father in the unity of the Holy Ghost, world without end.

II. The Scourging of Jesus Christ.

Let us adore our Lord Jesus Christ, enduring for our sakes that most cruel scourging, by every stroke of which the most tender heat of Mary was torn. *Let us beg of him the spirit of mortification.*

Our Father. Ten Hail Marys.

Ejaculation. Jesus scourged for our sins.

Glory be to the Father, &c.

O Lord Jesus Christ, who, for our sakes, didst take to thee a human nature, and didst suffer in thy flesh for our example; grant, we beseech thee, that, venerating thy sacred Passion, we may imitate thy blessed life of patience and mortification, and attain at last to the glory of thy resurrection; who livest and reignest with God the Father in the unity of the Holy Ghost, world without end.

III. The Crowning with Thorns.

Let us adore Jesus our King, crowned in derision with a crown of thorns; the sight of which increased yet more the grief of Mary. *Let us ask the grace to overcome human respect.*

Our Father. Ten Hail Marys.

Ejaculation. Jesus crowned for us with thorns.

Glory be to the Father, &c.

O Lord Jesus Christ, King immortal and invisible; grant, we beseech thee, that we who venerate thy crown of thorns here upon earth, may receive from thee the crown of eternal glory in the life to come; who livest and reignest with God the Father in the unity of the Holy Ghost, world without end.

IV. Jesus carrying his Cross.

Let us adore our Lord Jesus, bowed down beneath the heavy burden of his cross, in the sight of his most tender Mother, resolved to drink with him the same cup of bitterness. *Let us ask the spirit of meekness and patience.*

Our Father. Ten Hail Marys.

Ejaculation. Jesus, who for us didst bear the cross.

Glory be to the Father, &c.

O Lord Jesus Christ, who hast said, "No man can come to me, except he deny himself, and take up his cross, and follow me;" grant, we beseech thee, that, venerating thy blessed patience in the carrying of the cross, we may bear all the crosses and trials of this valley of tears, that, being purified by suffering, we may be admitted into thy eternal rest; who livest and reignest with God the Father in the unity of the Holy Ghost, world without end.

V. Jesus Crucified.

Let us adore our Lord Jesus, finishing, by his death upon the cross, the great work of our redemption. *Let us ask of him, through the tears of his most sorrowful Mother, the spirit of holy compunction.*

Our Father. Ten Hail Marys.

Ejaculation. Jesus, who died for us upon the cross.

Glory be to the Father, &c.

O Lord Jesus Christ, who, of thy infinite charity, didst become, for the sake of sinful man, the scorn of men and the outcast of the people, and didst die for us upon the cross to obtain our relief from eternal shame; grant us, we beseech thee, by the merits of thy most sorrowful crucifixion, and by the glorious intercession of thy most tender Mother, who stood by thee at the cross, the spirit of perfect contrition for our sins, and of a holy death; who livest and reignest with God the Father in the unity of the Holy Ghost, world without end.

The Five Glorious Mysteries

I. The Resurrection of Jesus Christ.

Let us adore our Divine Saviour, the glorious Conqueror of death; and let us ask of Mary, by the joy which filled her soul at the resurrection of her Son, *to obtain for us the triumph of Jesus and Mary within our hearts.*

Our Father. Ten Hail Marys.

Ejaculation. Jesus, who rose again from the dead.

Glory be to the Father, &c.

O Lord Jesus Christ, who didst descend into hell, and didst rise again the third day from the dead; grant to the souls of the faithful departed thy eternal light and peace; and to us thy servants grace to die each day more and more to ourselves, that we may live wholly unto thee; who livest and reignest with God the Father in the unity of the Holy Ghost, world without end.

II. The Ascension of Jesus Christ.

Let us adore our Divine Saviour, ascending into heaven to prepare a place for us; and let us ask of Mary, who followed Jesus in spirit, to obtain for us *a great desire after our heavenly country.*

Our Father. Ten Hail Marys.

Ejaculation. Jesus, now ascended into heaven.

Glory be to the Father, &c.

O Lord Jesus Christ, who didst descend upon the earth to be our sacrifice, and hast ascended into heaven to be our eternal Priest and Advocate; grant us grace, that, being detached from all earthly things, we may in heart and mind thither ascend, whither thou art gone before, and with thee continually dwell; who livest and reignest with God the Father in the unity of the Holy Ghost, world without end.

III. The Holy Ghost descends upon the Blessed Virgin and the Apostles.

Let us adore our Divine Saviour, sending from above his Holy Spirit; and let us ask of Mary, whom he has appointed to dispense his graces, to obtain *for us all the gifts of the Holy Ghost.*

Our Father. Ten Hail Marys.

Ejaculation. Jesus, who didst send the Holy Ghost.

Glory be to the Father, &c.

O Lord Jesus Christ, to whom is given all power in heaven and on earth; send down upon us the Holy Ghost the Comforter, which may guide, support, and purify the souls of thy servants, and of thy whole Church; who livest and reignest with God the Father in the unity of the Holy Ghost, world without end.

IV. The Assumption of the Blessed Virgin.

Let us adore our Divine Saviour receiving his most gracious Mother into the bosom of his glory, and let us ask her to obtain for us *the desire of perfection*.

Our Father. Ten Hail Marys.

Ejaculation. Jesus, who hath called thee to himself.

Glory be to the Father, &c.

O Lord Jesus Christ, who, when the work of her perfection was accomplished, didst call to thyself the soul of thy most holy Mother, and didst not suffer her body to see corruption; grant us, we beseech thee, the desire of perfection, and daily to purify ourselves more and more from all our faults and imperfection; so that at the hour of death we may be found worthy to pass to the blessed vision of thy glory; who livest and reignest with God the Father in the unity of the Holy Ghost, world without end.

V. The Crowning of the Blessed Virgin Mary.

Let us adore our Divine Saviour crowning the virtues of his most holy Mother in heaven; let us beg her to obtain for *us the grace to love and imitate them*.

Our Father. Ten Hail Marys.

Ejaculation. Jesus, who hath crowned thee in the heavens.

Glory be to the Father, &c.

O Lord Jesus Christ, who hast said, "In my Father's house are many mansions, I go to prepare a place for you;" grant us, we beseech thee, so to copy in our lives the holy virtues of thy blessed Mother, that, through her glorious intercession with thee, we may attain the place prepared for us in thy kingdom from the foundation of the world; who livest and reignest with God the Father in the unity of the Holy Ghost, world without end.

Salve Regina, Versicle, and Collect

Hail, Holy Queen, Mother of Mercy, Hail our Life, our Sweetness, and our Hope! To thee do we cry, poor banished children of Eve; to thee do we send up our sighs, mourning and weeping in this vale of tears. Turn, then, most gracious Advocate, thine eyes of mercy towards us; and after this our exile, show unto us the blessed Fruit of thy womb, JESUS, O clement, O loving, O sweet Virgin Mary.

V. Pray for us, O holy Mother of God.
R. That we may be made worthy of the promises of Christ.

Let us pray. *Then is said one of the following collects:*

Hear, O merciful God, the prayer of thy servants; that we who meet together in the society of the most holy Rosary of the Blessed Virgin, Mother of God, may, through her intercession, be delivered by thee from the dangers that continually hang over us; through the merits of our Lord and Saviour Jesus Christ. Amen.

O God, whose only-begotten Son, by his life, death, and resurrection, hath laid open to us the rewards of everlasting life; grant, we beseech thee, that pondering in our heart these Mysteries in the most holy Rosary of the Blessed Virgin Mary, we may imitate what they set forth, and obtain what they promise; through the same our Lord and Saviour Jesus Christ. Amen.

A Method of Saying the Rosary, the Third in the *Golden Manual*

Adding before each "Ave" one of the ten points into which the meditation is broken up.

The Five Joyful Mysteries

I. The Angelic Salutation.

1. The most Holy Trinity consents to the Incarnation of Jesus Christ.
2. Mary is chosen to be the Mother of the Incarnate Word.
3. The Angel Gabriel announces that happiness to Mary.
4. Mary prays in her holy solitude.
5. The Angel salutes her, saying, "Hail, Mary, full of grace, the Lord is with thee."
6. Mary is troubled at the sight and speech of the Angel.
7. The Angel says, "Fear not, Mary, thou shalt conceive by the power of the Holy Ghost."
8. Mary answers, "Behold the handmaid of the Lord, be it done unto me according to thy word."
9. The Holy Ghost overshadows her.
10. And the Word was made flesh, and dwelt among us.

II. The Visitation.

1. Mary, with great humility and charity, goes to visit her cousin St. Elisabeth.

2. Mary guided by the Holy Ghost, and accompanied by the holy angels.

3. Mary crosses the mountains in haste.

4. Mary is received with great joy by her cousin St. Elisabeth.

5. St. John is sanctified in his mother's womb.

6. St. Elisabeth says, "Blessed is the Fruit of thy womb."

7. Mary replies, "My soul doth magnify the Lord."

8. Elisabeth exclaims, "Whence is this to me, that the mother of my Lord should come to visit me?"

9. The house of Zacharias supremely blessed by the visits of Jesus and Mary.

10. Mary serves her cousin in all humble offices for the space of three months.

III. The Birth of Jesus Christ.

1. Mary gives birth to a Child, and remains a Virgin.

2. Mary gives birth to Jesus, and wraps him in swaddling clothes.

3. Mary contemplates Jesus with love and astonishment.

4. Mary embraces Jesus, and presses him to her heart.

5. Mary feeds Jesus with her Virginal milk.

6. Mary lays Jesus in a manger that Joseph had prepared.

7. Jesus lies in a manger between an ox and an ass.

8. The angels sing, "Glory to God in the highest, on earth peace to men of good will."

9. The shepherds come to visit the Child Jesus.

10. The Magi come to adore the Holy Child, and offer him presents.

IV. The Presentation.

1. Mary goes to the temple to offer her Holy Child.

2. Jesus and Mary submit to the Law.

3. The way from Nazareth to Jerusalem is long and difficult.

4. Mary carries the Child Jesus in her arms.

5. Mary continues her journey, pondering all these things in her heart.

6. Mary offers Jesus in the temple.

7. Mary redeems Jesus at the ransom appointed for the poor.

8. Anna rejoices to see her prophecy fulfilled.

9. The holy hold man, Simeon, embraces Jesus with joy.

10. Simeon says, "Now dost thou dismiss thy servant, Lord, in peace."

V. Mary finds Jesus in the Temple.

1. Mary has lost her beloved Child.

2. Mary deprived of her only treasure.

3. Mary seeks Him with anxiety.

4. Mary seeks Jesus in the streets and roads.

5. Mary finds Jesus again after three days.

6. Mary finds Jesus in the temple.

7. Jesus, twelve years old, teaches the doctors.
8. Mary says, "Son, why hast thou made us sorrowful?"
9. Jesus returns with Mary and Joseph, and is obedient unto them.
10. Mary preserves in her heart the sayings of Jesus.

The Five Sorrowful Mysteries

I. The Prayer and Bloody Sweat of our Blessed Saviour in the Garden.

1. Jesus goes into the Garden of Olives.
2. Jesus prays, lying prostrate on the ground.
3. Jesus perseveres in his prayer.
4. Jesus is sorrowful, even unto death.
5. Jesus is bathed in a sweat of blood.
6. Jesus submits his will to his heavenly Father.
7. Jesus warns his disciples to watch and pray.
8. Jesus betrayed by Judas.
9. Jesus is seized by his own creatures.
10. Jesus cruelly bound, and dragged from one judge to another.

II. The Scourging of Jesus Christ.

1. Jesus is delivered to be scourged.
2. Jesus is falsely accused.
3. Jesus is stripped of his clothes.

4. Jesus is naked in the hands of his executioners.
5. Jesus is fastened to a pillar.
6. Jesus is lashed with scourges.
7. Jesus is bruised with clubs.
8. The flesh of Jesus is torn with points of lead.
9. The blood of Jesus flows down to the ground.
10. They unfasten Jesus; he clothes himself again.

III. The Crowning with Thorns.

1. Jesus brought forth to be crowned with thorns.
2. They prepare a crown of thorns for Jesus.
3. They force the crown of thorns upon the head of Jesus.
4. The head of Jesus is pierced on every side.
5. The blood flows from the head of Jesus.
6. The forehead of Jesus is covered with blood.
7. The eyes of Jesus are bathed in tears.
8. The lips of Jesus are pale as death.
9. Jesus is clothed in a purple garment, through derision.
10. Jesus is cruelly mocked and derided, "Behold the man!"

IV. Jesus carrying his Cross.

1. Jesus condemned to be crucified.
2. Jesus lovingly embraces his cross.

3. Jesus carries his cross on his torn and wounded shoulders.

4. Jesus falls under the weight of his cross for our sins.

5. Jesus, again loaded with his cross, meets his sorrowful Mother.

6. Jesus leaves the impression of his sacred countenance on the veil of St. Veronica.

7. Jesus says, "If these things are done in the green wood, what shall be done in the dry?"

8. None can be found willing to carry the cross for Jesus.

9. Jesus, loaded with his cross, falls at the foot of Calvary.

10. Jesus, again loaded with his cross, ascends the hill of Calvary.

V. Jesus Crucified.

1. Jesus is cruelly stretched upon the cross.

2. His sacred hands and feet are pierced through with nails.

3. Jesus is raised upon the cross, and his blood flows in streams from all his wounds.

4. Jesus prays for his enemies.

5. Jesus promises Paradise to the penitent thief.

6. Jesus recommends St. John to his holy Mother.

7. Jesus in his thirst is offered vinegar and gall.

8. Jesus cries out, "My God, my God, why hast thou forsaken me?"

9. Jesus says, "It is finished!"

10. Jesus gives up his spirit into the hands of God his Father.

The Five Glorious Mysteries

I. The Resurrection of Jesus Christ.

1. Jesus rises again the third day from the dead.
2. Jesus conquers death and hell.
3. Jesus consoles and delivers the holy Fathers.
4. Jesus rises gloriously.
5. Jesus rejoices his holy Mother.
6. Jesus appears to Mary Magdalene.
7. Jesus appears to Peter, and blessed him.
8. The disciples at Emmaus say, "Did not our hearts burn within us, when he spoke to us?"
9. Jesus appears in the midst of his disciples, and gives them his peace.
10. Jesus shows his wounds to St. Thomas.

II. The Ascension of Jesus Christ.

1. The ascension of Jesus Christ.
2. Jesus ascends into heaven by virtue of his own power.
3. Jesus quits his beloved disciples.
4. Jesus promises to remain with them forever.
5. Jesus promises them the Holy Ghost.
6. As Jesus ascends, he blesses his disciples.

7. Jesus opens heaven to us.

8. Jesus is seated at the right hand of God his Father.

9. Jesus displays his five wounds, on our behalf, to his heavenly Father.

10. Jesus is our Mediator in heaven.

III. The Holy Ghost descends upon the Blessed Virgin and the Apostles.

1. Jesus sends the Holy Ghost.

2. Jesus sends the Comforter.

3. Jesus sends fire upon the earth.

4. The Holy Ghost inflames all hearts with his love.

5. The Holy Ghost enlightens their minds.

6. The Holy Ghost strengthens their hearts.

7. The Holy Ghost gives the gift of tongues.

8. The Holy Ghost distributes his gifts.

9. Come, O Holy Ghost, and visit the hearts of thy faithful.

10. Come, Holy Ghost, enlighten our hearts with the fire of thy Divine love.

IV. The Assumption of the Blessed Virgin.

1. Mary is assumed into heaven.

2. God the Father receives his well-beloved daughter.

3. Jesus receives his holy Mother.

4. The Holy Ghost receives his beloved spouse.

5. The Seraphim salute Mary.
6. The Angels serve Mary.
7. Mary rejoices all the heavens.
8. Mary is seated at the right hand of Jesus.
9. Mary is our advocate in heaven.
10. Mary is our Mother and mediatrix in heaven.

V. The Crowning of the Blessed Virgin Mary.

1. Mary gloriously crowned in heaven.
2. Mary crowned through her seraphic love.
3. Mary crowned through her angelical purity.
4. Mary crowned through her profound humility.
5. Mary crowned through her perfect obedience.
6. Mary crowned through her holy prudence.
7. Mary crowned through her admirable patience.
8. Mary crowned through her ardent gratitude.
9. Mary crowned through her holy perseverance.
10. Mary crowned in heaven, above all Saints and Angels, with the honor due to the Mother of God.

Salve Regina, Versicle, and Collect

Hail, Holy Queen, Mother of Mercy, Hail our Life, our Sweetness, and our Hope! To thee do we cry, poor banished children of Eve; to thee do we send up our sighs, mourning and weeping in this vale of tears. Turn, then, most gracious Advocate, thine eyes of mercy towards us; and after this our exile, show unto us the blessed Fruit of thy womb, JESUS, O clement, O loving, O sweet Virgin Mary.

V. Pray for us, O holy Mother of God.
R. That we may be made worthy of the promises of Christ.

Let us pray. *Then is said one of the following collects:*

Hear, O merciful God, the prayer of thy servants; that we who meet together in the society of the most holy Rosary of the Blessed Virgin, Mother of God, may, through her intercession, be delivered by thee from the dangers that continually hang over us; through the merits of our Lord and Saviour Jesus Christ. Amen.

O God, whose only-begotten Son, by his life, death, and resurrection, hath laid open to us the rewards of everlasting life; grant, we beseech thee, that pondering in our heart these Mysteries in the most holy Rosary of the Blessed Virgin Mary, we may imitate what they set forth, and obtain what they promise; through the same our Lord and Saviour Jesus Christ. Amen.

Methods for Saying the Rosary from St. Louis de Montfort

First Method

1. Say the "Come Holy Spirit" and then make this offering of the Rosary: I unite with all the saints in heaven and with all the just on earth; I unite with you, my Jesus, to praise your holy Mother worthily and to praise you in her and by her. I renounce all the distractions that may come to me while I am saying this Rosary. O Blessed Virgin Mary, we offer you this creed to honour the faith you had upon earth and to ask you to permit us to share in that same faith. O Lord, we offer you this Our Father to adore you in your oneness and to acknowledge you as the first cause and the last end of all things. Most Holy Trinity, we offer you these three Hail Marys to thank you for all the graces which you have given to Mary and which you have given to us through her intercession.

Our Father, three Hail Marys, Glory be to the Father....

Offering of the Decades

Joyful Mysteries

2. First decade

We offer you, Lord Jesus, this first decade in honour of your Incarnation. Through this mystery and the intercession of your holy Mother we ask for humility of heart.

Our Father, ten Hail Marys, Glory be to the Father.

May the grace of the mystery of the Incarnation come into me and make me truly humble.

Second decade

We offer you, Lord Jesus, this second decade in honour of the Visitation of your holy Mother to her cousin Saint Elizabeth. Through this mystery and the intercession of Mary we ask for a perfect love of our neighbour.

Our Father, ten Hail Marys, Glory be to the Father.

May the grace of the mystery of the Visitation come into me and make me truly charitable.

Third decade

We offer you, Child Jesus, this third decade in honour of your holy Birth. Through this mystery and the intercession of your blessed Mother we ask for detachment from the things of this world, love of poverty and love of the poor.

Our Father, ten Hail Marys, Glory be to the Father.

May the grace of the Birth of Jesus come into me and make me truly poor in spirit.

Fourth decade

We offer you, O Lord Jesus, this fourth decade in honour of your presentation in the temple by the hands of Mary. Through this mystery and the intercession of your blessed Mother we ask for the gift of wisdom and purity of heart and body.

Our Father, ten Hail Marys, Glory be to the Father.

May the grace of the mystery of the presentation come into me and make me truly wise and pure.

Fifth decade

We offer you, Lord Jesus, this fifth decade to honour Mary's finding you in the temple among the learned men after she had lost you. Through this mystery and the intercession of your blessed Mother we ask you to convert us and all sinners, heretics, schismatics and pagans.

Our Father, ten Hail Marys, Glory be to the Father.

May the grace of the mystery of the Finding of Jesus in the temple come into me that I may be truly converted.

Sorrowful Mysteries

3.Sixth decade

We offer you, Lord Jesus, this sixth decade in honour of your intense agony in the garden of Olives. Through this mystery and the intercession of your holy Mother we ask for perfect sorrow for our sins and perfect conformity to your holy will.

Our Father, ten Hail Marys, Glory be to the Father.

May the grace of the Agony of Jesus come into me and make me truly contrite and perfectly obedient to the will of God.

Seventh decade

We offer you, Lord Jesus, this seventh decade in honour of your cruel Scourging. Through this mystery and the intercession of your holy Mother we ask for the grace to mortify our senses.

Our Father, ten Hail Marys, Glory be to the Father.

May the grace of the Scourging of Jesus come into me and make me truly mortified.

Eighth decade

We offer you, Lord Jesus, this eighth decade in honour of being crowned with Thorns. Through this mystery and the intercession of your holy Mother we ask for a deep contempt of the world.

Our Father, ten Hail Marys, Glory be to the Father.

May the grace of the mystery of Our Lord's Crowning with Thorns come into me and make me truly opposed to the world.

Ninth decade

We offer you, Lord Jesus, this ninth decade in honour of your carrying the Cross. Through this mystery and the intercession of your holy Mother we ask for great patience in carrying our cross after you all the days of our life.

Our Father, ten Hail Marys, Glory be to the Father.

May the grace of the mystery of the carrying of the Cross come into me and make me truly patient.

Tenth decade

We offer you, Lord Jesus, this tenth decade in honour of your Crucifixion on Mount Calvary. Through this mystery and the intercession of your holy Mother we ask for a great horror of sin, a love for the Cross and the grace of a holy death for us and for those who are now in their last agony. Our Father, ten Hail Marys, Glory be to the Father.

May the grace of the Death and Passion of Our Lord and Saviour Jesus Christ come into me and make me truly holy.

Glorious Mysteries

4. Eleventh decade

We offer you, Lord Jesus, this eleventh decade in honour of your triumphant Resurrection. Through this mystery and through the intercession of your holy Mother we ask for a lively faith.

Our Father, ten Hail Marys, Glory be to the Father.

May the grace of the Resurrection come into me and make me truly faithful.

Twelfth decade

We offer you, Lord Jesus, this twelfth decade in honour of your glorious Ascension. Through this mystery and the intercession of your holy Mother we ask for a firm hope and a great longing for heaven.

Our Father, ten Hail Marys, Glory be to the Father.

May the grace of the mystery of the Ascension of Our Lord come into me and prepare me for heaven.

Thirteenth decade

We offer you, O Holy Spirit, this thirteenth decade in honour of the mystery of Pentecost. Through this mystery and the intercession of Mary, your most holy spouse, we ask for your holy wisdom that we may know, taste and practice your truth and share it with everyone.

Our Father, ten Hail Marys, Glory be to the Father.

May the grace of Pentecost come into me and make me truly wise in the eyes of God.

Fourteenth decade

We offer you, Lord Jesus, this fourteenth decade in honour of the Immaculate Conception of your holy Mother and her assumption into heaven body and soul. Through these two mysteries and her intercession we ask for the gift of true devotion to her in order to live a good life and have a happy death.

Our Father, ten Hail Marys, Glory be to the Father.

May the grace of the Immaculate Conception and the Assumption of Mary come into me and make me truly devoted to her.

Fifteenth decade

We offer you, Lord Jesus, this fifteenth and last decade in honour of the Crowning in glory of your holy Mother in heaven. Through this mystery and her intercession we ask for perseverance and an increase in virtue up to the moment of our death and thereafter the eternal crown that is prepared for us. We ask for the same grace for all the just and all our benefactors.

Our Father, ten Hail Marys, Glory be to the Father.

5.We beseech you, Lord Jesus, by the fifteen mysteries of your life, death, passion and glory, and the merits of your holy Mother, to convert sinners, to help the dying, to free the souls in purgatory, and to give all of us your grace so that we may live well and die well. We pray also for the light of glory to see you face to face and love you during all eternity. Amen.

Second, Shorter Method
of Celebrating the life, death and heavenly glory of Jesus and Mary in the Holy Rosary and a method of restraining our imagination and lessening distractions.

6. To do this a word or two is added to each Hail Mary of the decade reminding us of the mystery we are celebrating. This addition follows the name of Jesus in the middle of the Hail Mary:

and blessed is the fruit of thy womb,

Decade 1st "Jesus becoming man"

2nd "Jesus sanctifying"

3rd "Jesus born in poverty"

4th "Jesus sacrificed"

5th "Jesus holy of holies"

6th "Jesus in his agony"

7th "Jesus scourged"

8th "Jesus crowned with thorns"

9th "Jesus carrying his Cross"

10th "Jesus crucified"

11th "Jesus risen from the dead"

12th "Jesus ascending to heaven"

13th "Jesus filling thee with the Holy Spirit"

14th "Jesus raising thee up"

15th "Jesus crowning thee"

At the end of the first five mysteries we say:

May the grace of the joyful mysteries come into our souls and make us really holy.

At the end of the second:

May the grace of the sorrowful mysteries come into our souls and make us truly patient.

At the end of the third:

May the grace of the glorious mysteries come into our souls and make us eternally happy. Amen.

Third Method
of Fr. de Montfort for saying fruitfully the holy Rosary, for the use of the Daughters of Wisdom.

7. I unite with all the saints in heaven, with all the just on earth, and with all the faithful here present. I unite with you, my Jesus, in order to praise your holy Mother worthily and to praise you in her and through her. I renounce all distractions which may arise during this Rosary. I desire to say it with attention and devotion as if it were the last of my life. Amen. We offer you, Lord Jesus, this Creed in honour of all the mysteries of our faith, the Our Father and three Hail Marys in honour of the unity of your being and the Trinity of your persons. We ask of you a lively faith, a firm hope and an ardent charity. Amen.

I believe in God; Our Father; three Hail Marys.

In each mystery, after the word Jesus, add a word to recall and honour the particular mystery. For example: Jesus incarnate, Jesus sanctifying, etc. as it is indicated at each decade.

The Joyful Mysteries

The Incarnation

8. We offer you, Lord Jesus, this first decade in honour of your Incarnation in Mary's womb; through this mystery and her intercession we ask for deep humility. Amen.

Our Father. Hail Mary ten times, adding "Jesus becoming man".

May the grace of the mystery of the Incarnation come into our souls. Amen.

The Visitation

We offer you, Lord Jesus, this second decade in honour of the Visitation of your holy Mother to her cousin Saint Elizabeth and of the sanctification of Saint John the Baptist; through this mystery and the intercession of your holy Mother we ask for charity towards our neighbour. Amen.

Our Father. Hail Mary ten times. "Jesus sanctifying".

May the grace of the Visitation come into our souls. Amen.

The Birth of Jesus

We offer you, Lord Jesus, this third decade in honour of your Birth in the stable at Bethlehem; through this mystery and the intercession of your holy Mother, we ask for detachment from worldly things, contempt of riches and a love of poverty. Amen.

Our Father. Hail Mary ten times. "Jesus being born".

May the grace of the mystery of the Birth of Jesus come into our souls. Amen.

The Presentation in the Temple

We offer you, Lord Jesus, this fourth decade in honour of your presentation in the temple and the purification of Mary; through this mystery and her intercession we ask for purity in body and mind. Amen.

Our Father. Hail Mary ten times. "Jesus sacrificed".

May the grace of the mystery of the Presentation come into our souls. Amen.

The Finding of Jesus

We offer you, Lord Jesus, this fifth decade in honour of your being found in the temple by Mary; through this mystery and her intercession we ask for true wisdom. Amen.

Our Father. Hail Mary ten times. "Jesus Holy of holies".

May the grace of the mystery of the Finding of Jesus come into our souls. Amen.

At the end of this first Rosary the Magnificat is said.

The Sorrowful Mysteries

The Agony

9.We offer you, Lord Jesus, this sixth decade in honour of your Agony in the Garden of Olives; through this mystery and the intercession of your holy Mother we ask for sorrow for our sins. Amen.

Our Father. Hail Mary ten times. "Jesus in Agony".

May the grace of the mystery of the Agony of Jesus come into our souls. Amen.

The Scourging

We offer you, Lord Jesus, this seventh decade in honour of your cruel Scourging; through this mystery and the intercession of your holy Mother we ask for the grace to mortify our senses. Amen.

Our Father. Hail Mary ten times. "Jesus being scourged".

May the grace of the mystery of the Scourging of Jesus come into our souls. Amen.

The Crowning with Thorns

We offer you, Lord Jesus, this eighth decade in honour of your being Crowned with Thorns; through this mystery and the intercession of your holy Mother we ask for contempt of the world. Amen.

Our Father. Hail Mary ten times. "Jesus crowned with thorns".

May the grace of the mystery of the Crowning with Thorns come into our souls. Amen.

The Carrying of the Cross

We offer you, Lord Jesus, this ninth decade in honour of your carrying the Cross; through this mystery and the intercession of your holy Mother we ask for patience in all our crosses. Amen.

Our Father. Hail Mary ten times. "Jesus carrying his Cross".

May the grace of the mystery of the Carrying of the Cross come into our souls. Amen.

The Crucifixion

We offer you, Lord Jesus, this tenth decade in honour of your Crucifixion and shameful Death on Calvary; through this mystery and the intercession of your holy Mother we ask for the conversion of sinners, perseverance for the just and relief for the souls in Purgatory. Amen. Our Father. Hail Mary ten times. "Jesus crucified".

10. In this decade before each Hail Mary we ask God through the intercession of the nine choirs of angels for the graces we stand in need of.

Holy Seraphim, ask God etc. Hail Mary etc.

Holy Cherubim, ask etc.

Holy Thrones, ask etc.

Holy Dominations, ask etc.

Holy Virtues, ask etc.

Holy Powers, ask etc.

Holy Principalities, ask etc.

Holy Archangels, ask etc.

Holy Angels, ask etc.

All the Saints of Paradise, ask etc.

Enchiridion Sanctissimi Rosarii

Glory be to the Father, etc.

May the grace of the mystery of the Crucifixion of Jesus come down into our souls. Amen.

11. At the end of the second rosary the following prayers are said kneeling:

[Prayer composed by Fr. de Montfort asking God for divine Wisdom]

O God of our fathers, Lord of mercy, Spirit of truth, I, a mere worm of the earth, prostrate before your divine Majesty, acknowledging the great need I have of your divine wisdom which I have lost through my sins and trusting in the unfailing promise you have made to all those who ask with confidence, I come before you today to beg this grace of you with all possible earnestness and the greatest humility. Send us, O Lord, this wisdom which sits by your throne to strengthen our weakness, to enlighten our minds, to inflame our hearts, to speak and to act, to work and suffer in union with you, to direct our footsteps and to fill our souls with the virtues of Jesus Christ and the gifts of the Holy Spirit, for only Wisdom can bring us these gifts. O Father of mercy, God of all consolation, we ask you for this infinite treasure of your divine wisdom, through the tender heart of Mary, through the Precious Blood of your dear Son and through the intense desire you have to bestow your gifts on your poor creatures. Hear and grant our prayers. Amen.

12. [Prayer to Saint Joseph]

Hail Joseph the just, Wisdom is with you; blessed are you among all men and blessed is Jesus, the fruit of Mary, your faithful spouse. Holy Joseph, worthy foster-father of Jesus Christ, pray for us sinners and obtain divine Wisdom for us from God, now and at the hour of our death. Amen.

This prayer is said three times.

The Glorious Mysteries

The Resurrection

13. We offer you, Lord Jesus, this eleventh decade in honour of your glorious Resurrection; through this mystery and the intercession of your holy Mother, we ask for love of God and fervour in your service. Amen.

Our Father. Hail Mary ten times. "Jesus risen from the dead".

May the grace of the mystery of the Resurrection come into our souls. Amen.

The Ascension

We offer you, Lord Jesus, this twelfth decade in honour of your triumphant Ascension; through this mystery and the intercession of your holy Mother we ask for an ardent desire for heaven, our true home. Amen.

Our Father. Hail Mary ten times. "Jesus ascending to heaven".

May the grace of the mystery of the Ascension come into our souls. Amen.

The Pentecost

We offer you, Lord Jesus, this thirteenth decade in honour of the mystery of Pentecost; through this mystery and the intercession of your holy Mother we ask that the Holy Spirit may come into our souls. Amen.

Our Father. Hail Mary ten times. "Jesus filling us with the Holy Spirit".

May the grace of the mystery of Pentecost come into our souls. Amen.

The Assumption of the Blessed Virgin

We offer you, Lord Jesus, this fourteenth decade in honour of the Resurrection and triumphant Assumption of your holy Mother into heaven; through this mystery and her intercession we ask for a tender devotion to so good a Mother. Amen.

Our Father. Hail Mary ten times. "Jesus raising thee up".

May the grace of the mystery of the Assumption come into our souls. Amen.

The Coronation of Mary

We offer you, Lord Jesus, this fifteenth and last decade in honour of the Coronation of your holy Mother; through this mystery and her intercession we ask for perseverance in grace and the crown of glory. Amen.

Our Father. Hail Mary ten times. "Jesus crowning thee".

14. In this decade before each Hail Mary we ask God through the intercession of all the saints for the graces we stand in need of.

St. Michael the Archangel and all the holy angels, ask of God etc. Hail Mary etc.

St. Abraham and all the holy Patriarchs, ask of God etc.

St. John Baptist and all the holy Prophets, ask of God etc.

St. Peter and St. Paul and all the holy Apostles, ask of God etc.

St. Stephen, St. Lawrence and all the Martyrs, ask of God etc.

St. Hilary and all the holy Pontiffs, ask of God etc.

St. Joseph and all the holy Confessors, ask of God etc.

St. Catherine, St. Therese and all the holy Virgins, ask of God etc.

St. Anne and all holy Women, ask of God etc.

Glory be to the Father etc.

May the grace of the mystery of the Crowning in glory of Mary come into our souls. Amen.

15. At the end of the third Rosary the following prayer is said:

[Prayer to the Blessed Virgin]

Hail Mary, well-beloved daughter of the eternal Father, admirable Mother of the Son, most faithful spouse of the Holy Spirit, glorious temple of the Blessed Trinity. Hail, sovereign Queen, to whom everyone is subject in heaven and on earth. Hail sure Refuge of sinners, our Lady of mercy, who has never repelled anyone. Sinner as I am, I cast myself at your feet and beg you to obtain from Jesus, your dear Son, contrition and pardon for all my sins and the gift of divine wisdom. I consecrate myself to you with all that I have. I choose you today as my Mother and Mistress; treat me then as the weakest of your children and the most submissive of your servants. Hear, O my Queen, the prayers of a heart that desires to love and serve you faithfully. Let it not be said that of all who have ever had recourse to you, I was the first to be unheeded. O my hope, my life, my faithful and immaculate Virgin Mary, hear me, protect me, strengthen me, instruct me, save me. Amen.

Praised, adored and loved be Jesus in the most holy sacrament of the altar. Forever and ever.

O Jesus, my dear Jesus, O Mary, Mother of Jesus, my beloved Mother, give us your holy blessing. Amen.

Support us in our troubles, hear us when we pray, preserve us from the world and the devil. Amen.

The superior says, "Nos cum prole pia benedicat Virgo Maria. Amen".

Fourth Method
Summary of the life, death and passion and heavenly glory of Jesus and Mary in the holy Rosary.

16. Credo: 1) Faith in the presence of God. 2) Faith in the gospel. 3) Faith and obedience to the pope as Vicar of Jesus Christ.

1 Our Father Unity of one, living and true God.

1 Hail Mary To honour the eternal Father who conceives his Son in contemplating himself.

2 Hail Mary The eternal Word, equal to his Father and who with him produces the Holy Spirit by their mutual love.

3 Hail Mary The Holy Spirit who proceeds from the Father and the Son by the way of love.

2 Our Father Immense charity of God.

The Incarnation

17. 1 Hail Mary To deplore the unhappy state of disobedient Adam; his just condemnation and that of all his descendants.

2 Hail Mary To honour the desires of the patriarchs and prophets who pleaded for the coming of the Messiah.

3 Hail Mary To honour the desires and prayers of the Blessed Virgin Mary to bring forward the coming of the Messiah; and her marriage with Saint Joseph.

4 Hail Mary The love of the eternal Father in giving us his Son.

5 Hail Mary The love of the Son who gave himself up for us.

6 Hail Mary The mission and the greeting of the angel Gabriel.

7 Hail Mary The maidenly fear of Mary.

8 Hail Mary The faith and consent of the Virgin Mary.

9 Hail Mary The creation of the soul and the formation of the body of Jesus in the womb of Mary by the Holy Spirit.

10 Hail Mary The angels adoring the Word Incarnate in the womb of Mary.

3 Our Father The most adorable majesty of God.

The Visitation

18. 1 Hail Mary To honour the joy in the heart of Mary at the Incarnation and the dwelling for nine months of the eternal Word in her womb.

2 Hail Mary The sacrifice of himself that Jesus Christ offered to his Father on coming into the world.

3 Hail Mary The contentment of Jesus Christ in the humble and Virginal womb of Mary and that of Mary in the enjoyment of her God.

4 Hail Mary The doubts of St. Joseph on discovering that Mary was with child.

5 Hail Mary The agreement between Jesus and Mary in her womb on the choice of the elect.

6 Hail Mary The fervour of Mary when visiting her cousin.

7 Hail Mary The greeting of Mary and the sanctification of St. John Baptist and of his mother St. Elizabeth.

8 Hail Mary Mary's thanksgiving to God expressed in her Magnificat.

9 Hail Mary Her charity and humility in the service of her cousin.

10 Hail Mary The mutual dependence of Jesus and Mary and the dependence we should have upon them both.

4   Our Father The infinite richness of God.

The Birth of Jesus

19.   1 Hail Mary To honour the contempt and the rebuffs which Mary and Joseph encountered at Bethlehem.

2 Hail Mary The poverty of the Stable where God came into the world.

3 Hail Mary The deep recollection of the exceeding love of Mary when she was about to give birth to her child.

4 Hail Mary The coming forth of the eternal Word from the womb of Mary without breaking the seal of her Virginity.

5 Hail Mary The adoration and the singing of the angels when Jesus was born.

6 Hail Mary The ravishing beauty of her divine child.

7 Hail Mary The coming of the shepherds into the stable with their humble gifts.

8 Hail Mary The circumcision of Jesus and his suffering accepted in love.

9 Hail Mary The giving of the name of Jesus and the nobility of this name

10 Hail Mary The adoration of the kings and the gifts they brought.

5   Our Father The eternal wisdom of God.

The Purification

20.   1 Hail Mary Obedience of Jesus and Mary to the Law.

2 Hail Mary The sacrifice that Jesus made of his humanity to the Law.

3 Hail Mary The sacrifice of her honour the Virgin Mary made to the Law.

4 Hail Mary The joy and the songs of Simeon and Anne the prophetess.

Enchiridion Sanctissimi Rosarii

5 Hail Mary The ransoming of Jesus by the offering of two turtle doves.

6 Hail Mary The massacre of the Holy Innocents by Herod the Cruel.

7 Hail Mary The flight of Jesus to Egypt through St. Joseph's obedience to the voice of the angel.

8 Hail Mary The mystery of his abode in Egypt.

9 Hail Mary His return to Nazareth

10 Hail Mary His growth in age and wisdom.

6   Our Father The incomprehensible holiness of God.

The Finding of Jesus in the Temple

21. 1 Hail Mary To honour his hidden, hard working and obedient life at Nazareth.

2 Hail Mary His preaching and his being found in the temple among the doctors.

3 Hail Mary His fasting and his temptations in the desert.

4 Hail Mary His baptism by St. John Baptist.

5 Hail Mary His wonderful preaching.

6 Hail Mary His astounding miracles.

7 Hail Mary The choice of the twelve apostles and the powers he gave them.

8 Hail Mary His marvellous transfiguration

9 Hail Mary The washing of the feet of the apostles.

10 Hail Mary The institution of the Holy Eucharist.

7 Our Father The essential happiness of God.

The Agony of Jesus

22. 1 Hail Mary To honour the places of retreat that Jesus Christ chose during his life, especially that of the Garden of Olives.

2 Hail Mary His humble and fervent prayers offered during his life and on the eve of his passion.

3 Hail Mary His patience and gentleness towards his apostles during his life and especially in the Garden of Olives.

4 Hail Mary His weariness of soul during all his life and especially in the Garden of Olives.

5 Hail Mary The outpouring of blood in which his sorrows bathed him.

6 Hail Mary The comfort he consented to receive from an angel in his agony.

7 Hail Mary His conformity to the will of his Father in spite of his natural reluctance.

8 Hail Mary The courage with which he went to meet his executioners and the power of his words with which he crushed them and then uplifted them.

9 Hail Mary His betrayal by Judas and his arrest by the Jews.

10 Hail Mary His desertion by his apostles.

Enchiridion Sanctissimi Rosarii

8   Our Father Wonderful patience of God.

The Scourging

23.   1 Hail Mary To honour the chains and ropes with which Jesus was bound.

2 Hail Mary The blow that he received in the house of Caiphas.

3 Hail Mary The three denials of St. Peter.

4 Hail Mary The shameful treatment he received at the house of Herod when he was dressed in a white robe.

5 Hail Mary His being stripped of all his clothes.

6 Hail Mary The scorn and insults he received from his tormenters because of his nakedness.

7 Hail Mary His being beaten and flayed with rods of thorn and cruel whips.

8 Hail Mary The pillar to which he was bound.

9 Hail Mary The blood he shed and the wounds he received.

10 Hail Mary His collapse through weakness into a pool of his own blood.

9   Our Father Unspeakable beauty of God.

The Crowning with Thorns of Jesus Christ

24.   1 Hail Mary To honour his being stripped a third time.

2 Hail Mary To honour His crown of thorns.

3 Hail Mary The veil with which they blindfolded him.

4 Hail Mary The blows and the spittle rained upon his face.

5 Hail Mary The old robe they put over his shoulders.

6 Hail Mary The reed they put into his hand.

7 Hail Mary The rough stone upon which he was made to sit.

8 Hail Mary The abuse and insults that were hurled at him.

9 Hail Mary The blood which poured from his adorable head.

10 Hail Mary His hair and beard which they tore at.

10   Our Father Limitless omnipotence of God.

The Carrying of the Cross

25.   1 Hail Mary To honour Our Lord being presented to the people at the "Ecce Homo."

2 Hail Mary The preferring of Barabbas to Jesus.

3 Hail Mary The false testimonies given against him.

4 Hail Mary His being condemned to death.

5 Hail Mary The love with which he embraced and kissed the Cross.

6 Hail Mary The dreadful sufferings he endured in carrying it.

7 Hail Mary His falling through weakness under its weight.

8 Hail Mary His sorrow on meeting his Mother.

9 Hail Mary The veil of Veronica on which his face was imprinted.

10 Hail Mary His tears and those of his Mother and the pious women who followed him to Calvary.

11 Our Father Fearful Justice of God.

The Crucifixion of Jesus Christ

26. 1 Hail Mary To honour the five wounds of Jesus Christ and the shedding of his blood on the Cross.

2 Hail Mary His pierced heart and the Cross upon which he was crucified.

3 Hail Mary The nails and the lance which pierced him, the sponge, the gall and the vinegar which he was given to drink.

4 Hail Mary The shame and the ignominy he endured in being crucified naked between two thieves.

5 Hail Mary The compassion of his Blessed Mother.

6 Hail Mary His seven last words.

7 Hail Mary His abandonment and his silence.

8 Hail Mary The distress of the whole universe.

9 Hail Mary His painful and shameful death.

10 Hail Mary His being taken down from the Cross and his burial.

12 Our Father The eternity of God without a beginning.

The Resurrection

27. 1 Hail Mary To honour the descent of the soul of Our Lord into hell.

2 Hail Mary The joy and the release of the ancient fathers who were in limbo.

3 Hail Mary The re-uniting of his body and soul in the tomb.

4 Hail Mary His miraculous emergence from the tomb.

5 Hail Mary His victories over death and sin, the world and the devil.

6 Hail Mary The four qualities of his glorious body.

7 Hail Mary The power that he received from his Father in heaven and on earth.

8 Hail Mary His appearances to his Mother, his apostles and disciples.

9 Hail Mary His discourses on heaven and the meal that he had with his disciples.

10 Hail Mary The peace, the authority and the mission he gave them to go out into the whole world.

13 Our Father The unlimited omnipresence of God.

The Ascension of Jesus Christ

28. 1 Hail Mary To honour the promise that Jesus Christ made to his apostles to send them the Holy Spirit and the command he gave them to prepare to receive him.

2 Hail Mary The gathering of all his disciples on the Mount of Olives.

3 Hail Mary The blessings he gave them as he rose from the earth towards heaven.

4 Hail Mary His glorious ascension by his own power into heaven.

5 Hail Mary The welcome and triumphant acclaim which he received from God, his Father and from all the heavenly court.

6 Hail Mary The triumphant power with which he opened the gates of heaven through which no mortal had passed.

7 Hail Mary His being seated at the right hand of his Father as his beloved Son equal to his Father.

8 Hail Mary The power he received to judge the living and the dead.

9 Hail Mary His last coming upon earth when his power and majesty will appear in all their magnificence.

10 Hail Mary The justice he will mete out at the last judgment when he rewards the just and punishes the wicked for all eternity.

14   Our Father The all-embracing Providence of God.

Pentecost

29.   1 Hail Mary To honour the truth of God the Holy Spirit proceeding from the Father and the Son and who is the love of the Godhead.

2 Hail Mary The sending of the Holy Spirit upon the apostles by the Father and the Son.

3 Hail Mary His descent accompanied by the sound of a great wind which shows his might and power.

4 Hail Mary The tongues of fire he sent to the apostles giving them an understanding of the scriptures and love of God and neighbour

5 Hail Mary The fullness of grace which the heart of Mary, his faithful spouse, was privileged to receive.

6 Hail Mary The marvellous guidance he gave to all the saints and even to the person of Jesus Christ during all his life.

7 Hail Mary The twelve fruits of the Holy Spirit.

8 Hail Mary The seven gifts of the Holy Spirit.

9 Hail Mary To ask especially for the gift of wisdom and the coming of his kingdom into men's hearts.

10 Hail Mary To be victorious over the three evil spirits that are opposed to him, namely the spirit of the flesh, of the world and of the devil.

15 Our Father The unspeakable generosity of God.

The Assumption of Mary

30. 1 Hail Mary To honour the eternal predestination of Mary to be the masterpiece of God's hands.

2 Hail Mary Her Immaculate Conception and her fullness of grace and reason in the very womb of St. Anne.

3 Hail Mary Her birth which gladdened the whole world.

4 Hail Mary Her presentation and her abode in the temple.

5 Hail Mary Her wonderful life and her exemption from all sin.

6 Hail Mary Her fullness of pre-eminent virtue.

7 Hail Mary Her fruitful virginity and her painless childbearing.

8 Hail Mary Her divine Motherhood and her relationship with the three persons of the most holy Trinity.

9 Hail Mary Her precious and loving death.

10 Hail Mary Her resurrection and triumphant Assumption.

16   Our Father The unattainable glory of God.

The Crowning of Mary

31.   1 Hail Mary To honour the triple crown which Mary received from the Holy Trinity.

2 Hail Mary The joy and the added glory that heaven received through her triumphant entry.

3 Hail Mary To acknowledge her as queen of heaven and earth, of angels and men.

4 Hail Mary As treasurer and dispenser of the graces of God, the merits of Jesus Christ and the gifts of the Holy Spirit.

5 Hail Mary Mediatrix and advocate of men.

6 Hail Mary Exterminator and destroyer of the devil and of heresies.

7 Hail Mary Safe refuge of sinners.

8 Hail Mary Nurturing Mother of sinners.

9 Hail Mary The joy and delight of the just.

10 Hail Mary Refuge for all the living, all-powerful relief for the afflicted, for the dying and for the souls in purgatory.

God alone.

Fifth Method
150 Motives Impelling us to say the Rosary

32. Creed: Definition and essence of the Rosary

1 Our Father Eminence of the Rosary

1 Hail Mary the daily Rosary

2 Hail Mary the ordinary Rosary

3 Hail Mary perpetual Rosary

33. 2 Our Father excellence of the holy Rosary as prefigured in the Old Testament and the parables of the New.

1 Hail Mary the strength of the holy Rosary against the world, as prefigured by that small stone, which, thrown by no hand of man, fell upon the statue of Nebuchadnezzar and broke it into pieces.

2 Hail Mary its strength against the devil, as prefigured by the sling of David with which he overcame Goliath.

3 Hail Mary its power against all sorts of enemies of salvation, as prefigured by the power of David which contained innumerable kinds of defensive and offensive arms.

4 Hail Mary its miracles as prefigured in the rod of Moses which caused water to flow from the rock, calmed the waters, divided the seas and performed miracles.

5 Hail Mary its holiness as prefigured by the Ark of the Covenant which contained the law, the manna and the rod and also by the psalter of David which prefigured the Rosary.

6 Hail Mary its light as shown in the columns of fire during the night and the shining cloud during the day which guided the Israelites.

7 Hail Mary its sweetness as shown in the honey found in the mouth of the lion.

8 Hail Mary its fruitfulness as shown in the net that St. Peter by order of Our Lord threw into the sea and which though filled with 153 fish did not break.

9 Hail Mary its marvellous fruitfulness as shown in the parable of the mustard seed which, although so small in appearance, becomes a great tree in which the birds of the air make their nests.

10 Hail Mary its richness as shown in the parable of the treasure hidden in a field for which a wise man must give up all he has to possess it.

34. 3   Our Father It is a gift come down from heaven; a great present that God gives to his most faithful servants.

1 Hail Mary God is the author of the prayers of which it is composed and of the mysteries which it contains.

2 Hail Mary it is the Blessed Virgin who gave the Rosary its form.

3 Hail Mary St. Dominic preached and although he was a saint he converted hardly any sinners.

4 Hail Mary he was accompanied in his missions by several holy bishops and still his efforts were without fruit.

5 Hail Mary by the power of prayer and mortification, he received the holy Rosary in the forest of Toulouse.

6 Hail Mary he entered Toulouse and preached the Rosary and great wonders and great blessings accompanied his preaching.

7 Hail Mary he continued all his life preaching the Rosary with results never seen before.

8 Hail Mary the marvellous effects the Rosary has had wherever it was preached.

9 Hail Mary the decline of the Rosary.

10 Hail Mary the restoration of the Rosary by Blessed Alan de la Roche.

35. 4   Our Father The Rosary is the triple crown that we place on the heads of Jesus and Mary and he who recites it every day will receive the same crown.

1 Hail Mary Mary possesses three kinds of crown.

2 Hail Mary The daily Rosary is her great crown.

3 Hail Mary The reprobate crown themselves with faded roses.

4 Hail Mary The predestinate crown Jesus and Mary with eternal roses.

5 Hail Mary The Jews crown Jesus with piercing crowns.

6 Hail Mary True Christians crown him with fragrant roses.

7 Hail Mary The first is the bridal crown or crown of excellence which we place on Mary's head by the joyful mysteries.

8 Hail Mary The second is the crown of triumph or of power that we give her by the sorrowful mysteries.

9 Hail Mary The third is the royal crown or crown of goodness that we give her by the glorious mysteries.

10 Hail Mary There are three crowns for the one who recites the Holy Rosary every day:

1 crown of graces during life

2 crown of peace at death

3 crown of glory in eternity

36. 5   Our Father The Rosary is a mystical summary of all the most beautiful prayers of the Church.

1 Hail Mary The Creed is a summary of the gospel.

2 Hail Mary It is the prayer of believers.

3 Hail Mary The shield of the soldiers of Jesus Christ.

4 Hail Mary The Our Father - prayer of which Jesus Christ is the sole author.

5 Hail Mary Prayer he used when praying to his Father and through which he obtained what he desired.

6 Hail Mary Prayer which contains a summary of all we must ask of God.

7 Hail Mary Prayer in which are found all our duties towards God.

8 Hail Mary Prayer which contains a summary of all we must ask of God.

9 Hail Mary Prayer whose value is unknown and which is said very badly by the majority of Christians.

10 Hail Mary Paraphrase of the Our Father.

37. 6 Our Father The Rosary contains the angelic greeting which is the most pleasing prayer we can offer our Blessed Lady.

1 Hail Mary The Hail Mary is a divine compliment which wins over the heart of the Blessed Virgin.

2 Hail Mary It is the new song of the New Testament which the faithful sing as they escape from the captivity of the devil.

3 Hail Mary It is the hymn of the angels and saints in heaven.

4 Hail Mary It is the prayer of the predestinate and of Catholics.

5 Hail Mary It is a mysterious rose which is a source of joy to the Blessed Virgin and to the soul.

6 Hail Mary It is a precious stone which embellishes and sanctifies the soul.

7 Hail Mary It is a valuable piece of money with which to purchase heaven.

8 Hail Mary It is the prayer which distinguishes the predestinate from the reprobate.

9 Hail Mary It is the terror of the devil, the blow which crushes him, the nail of Sisera which pierces his head.

10 Hail Mary Paraphrase of the Hail Mary.

38. 7 Our Father The Rosary is a divine Summary of the mysteries of Jesus and Mary in which we proclaim and commemorate their life, passion and glory.

Enchiridion Sanctissimi Rosarii

1 Hail Mary Men's misfortune and ruin come from ignorance and neglect of the mysteries of Jesus Christ.

2 Hail Mary The Rosary provides the knowledge of the mysteries of Jesus and Mary and recalls them to mind in view of applying them to one's life.

3 Hail Mary The greatest desire of Jesus Christ was and still is that we remember him. With this in mind he instituted the sacrifice of the Mass.

4 Hail Mary After holy Mass the Rosary is the holiest action and prayer that we can offer because it is a remembrance and a celebration of what Jesus Christ has done and suffered for us.

5 Hail Mary The Rosary is the prayer of the angels and saints in heaven because they are engaged in celebrating the life, death and glory of Jesus Christ.

6 Hail Mary When we say the Rosary we celebrate in one day or one week all the mysteries that the Church celebrates in a year for the sanctification of her children.

7 Hail Mary Those who say the holy Rosary every day have a share in what the saints are doing in heaven which is the same as they were doing upon earth meritoriously, for they who are on earth are doing what the saints are doing in heaven.

8 Hail Mary The mysteries of the Holy Rosary are like mirrors for the predestinate in which they see their faults and like torches which guide them in this world of darkness.

9 Hail Mary They see springs of living water from the Saviour to whom one may go with joy to draw the saving waters of grace.

10 Hail Mary They are the 15 steps of the temple of Solomon and the 15 rungs of the ladder of Jacob by which the angels descend to them and return to heaven and by which they ascend to heaven.

39. 8   Our Father The Rosary is the tree of life which bears marvellous fruits all the year round.

1 Hail Mary The Rosary enlightens blind and hardened sinners.

2 Hail Mary It brings back obstinate heretics.

3 Hail Mary It sets prisoners free.

4 Hail Mary It heals the incurable.

5 Hail Mary It enriches the poor.

6 Hail Mary It supports the weak.

7 Hail Mary It consoles the afflicted and the dying.

8 Hail Mary It reforms lax religious orders.

9 Hail Mary It checks the effects of God's anger.

10 Hail Mary It makes good people better.

40. 9   Our Father The Rosary is a practice that God has sanctioned by many miracles.

1 Hail Mary Miracles in the conversion of sinners.

2 Hail Mary In the conversion of heretics.

3 Hail Mary In the cure of all sorts of diseases.

4 Hail Mary In favour of the dying brethren.

5 Hail Mary In the sanctification of devout people.

6 Hail Mary In the release of souls from purgatory.

7 Hail Mary In the reception into the Confraternity.

8 Hail Mary For the procession of the holy Rosary and the oil lamp of the holy Rosary.

9 Hail Mary For its devout recitation.

10 Hail Mary To carry it on one's person with devotion.

41. 10 Our Father The holy Rosary is most excellent because it was established for very noble ends which give great glory to God and are very salutary for the soul.

1 Hail Mary By being enrolled in this Confraternity we are strengthened in a wonderful way by joining millions of brothers and sisters.

2 Hail Mary We thus preserve a continuous remembrance of the mysteries of Jesus and Mary.

3 Hail Mary We are able to praise God at every moment of the day and night and in every place on earth, which one could not do on one's own.

4 Hail Mary To thank Our Lord for all the graces he is giving us at every moment.

5 Hail Mary To be ever asking pardon for our daily sins.

6 Hail Mary To make our prayers more powerful by being united with others.

7 Hail Mary For mutual help at the hour of death which is so difficult and so important.

8 Hail Mary To be supported at the hour of judgment by as many intercessors as there are members of the confraternity of the Rosary.

9 Hail Mary To be given relief after death and speedily released from the pains of purgatory by the Masses and prayers which are offered up.

10 Hail Mary To form an army arrayed as for battle to destroy the empire of the devil and establish that of Jesus Christ.

42. 11 Our Father The Rosary is a great store of indulgence accorded by popes outdoing one another.

1 Hail Mary Plenary indulgences of the stations of Rome and Jerusalem by going to Communion on certain days.

2 Hail Mary Plenary indulgence on enrolment in the confraternity.

3 Hail Mary Plenary indulgence at the hour of death.

4 Hail Mary Indulgence for the recitation of the Rosary.

5 Hail Mary Indulgence for those who organize the saying of the Rosary.

6 Hail Mary Indulgence for those who receive communion in the church of the Rosary on the first Sunday of the month.

7 Hail Mary Indulgence on the occasion of the procession.

8 Hail Mary Indulgence for those who say the Mass of the Rosary.

9 Hail Mary Indulgence for certain good works.

Enchiridion Sanctissimi Rosarii

10 Hail Mary Indulgence for those who are unable to visit the church of the Rosary, or receive Communion, or take part in a procession.

43. 12 Our Father The Rosary is sanctioned by the example given to us by the saints.

1 Hail Mary St. Dominic, its origination.

2 Hail Mary Blessed Alan de la Roche who restored it.

3 Hail Mary The saintly Dominicans who propagated it.

4 Hail Mary Among the popes: Pius V, Innocent III, and Boniface VIII who had it embroidered in satin.

5 Hail Mary Among the cardinals: St. Charles Borromeo.

6 Hail Mary Among the bishops: St. Francis de Sales.

7 Hail Mary Among religious: St. Ignatius, St. Philip Neri, St. Felix of Cantalice.

8 Hail Mary Among kings and queens: St. Louis, Philip I, King of Spain, Queen Blanche.

9 Hail Mary Among the learned: Albert the Great, Navarre, etc.

10 Hail Mary Among saintly people: the famous holy women of Rome, Sister Mary of the Incarnation.

44. 13 Our Father The vanquished enemies of the Rosary prove its fame to us.

1 Hail Mary Those who neglect it.

2 Hail Mary Those who say it with indifference and without attention.

3 Hail Mary Those who say it in haste and to get it over with.

4 Hail Mary Those who say it with unrepentant mortal sin.

5 Hail Mary Those who say it out of hypocrisy, lacking any devotion.

6 Hail Mary Critics who strive ingeniously to do away with it.

7 Hail Mary The impious who speak against it.

8 Hail Mary The cowardly who accept it and then abandon it.

9 Hail Mary Heretics who attack it and run it down.

10 Hail Mary The devils who hate it and strive to destroy it by numerous tricks.

45. 14   Our Father The overcoming of objections that heretics, critics, libertines and those who neglect and ignore the Rosary generally make either to do away with it or to avoid saying it.

1 Hail Mary It is a new religious practice.

2 Hail Mary It is an invention of Religious to make money.

3 Hail Mary It is a devotion of ignorant women who do not know how to read.

4 Hail Mary It is superstitious being based on counting prayers.

5 Hail Mary It is preferable to say the penitential psalms.

6 Hail Mary It is preferable to make a meditation.

Enchiridion Sanctissimi Rosarii

7 Hail Mary It is too long and too tiresome a prayer.

8 Hail Mary One cannot be saved without saying the Rosary.

9 Hail Mary We sin if we fail to say it.

10 Hail Mary It is good, but I have not the time to say it.

46. 15 Our Father Manner of saying the Rosary well.

1 Hail Mary It must be said with a pure heart without attachment to grave sin.

2 Hail Mary In a worthy manner with good intentions.

3 Hail Mary With attention avoiding voluntary distractions.

4 Hail Mary Slowly and calmly with pauses in the prayers.

5 Hail Mary Devout whilst meditating on the mysteries.

6 Hail Mary Modestly and in a respectful attitude whether standing or kneeling.

7 Hail Mary Wholeheartedly and every day.

8 Hail Mary Inwardly when it is said alone.

9 Hail Mary Publicly and in two responding groups.

10 Hail Mary Perseveringly until death.

47. 16 Our Father Different methods of saying the holy Rosary.

1 Hail Mary The holy Rosary can be said in a straightforward manner, saying only the Our Fathers and Hail Marys with the intentions of the mysteries.

2 Hail Mary We can add a word to each mystery of the decade.

3 Hail Mary We can make a little offering at each decade.

4 Hail Mary We can make a more important offering at each decade.

5 Hail Mary We can have a special intention for each Hail Mary.

6 Hail Mary We can recite it inwardly without speaking.

7 Hail Mary We can genuflect at each Hail Mary.

8 Hail Mary We can prostrate at each Hail Mary.

9 Hail Mary We can give ourselves a stroke of the discipline.

10 Hail Mary We can commemorate the saints at each decade and blend with one of the above-mentioned methods as the Holy Spirit inspires.

A Scriptural Rosary
with Meditations by Blessed Dom Columba Marmion, O.S.B.

Blessed Columba Marmion, born Joseph Aloysius Marmion (April 1, 1858 – January 30, 1923) was an Irish monk, and the third abbot of Maredsous Abbey in Belgium. Beatified by Pope John Paul II on September 3, 2000, Marmion was one of the most popular and influential Catholic writers of the late 19th and early 20th centuries. His books are considered spiritual classics.

The Joyful Mysteries

Annunciation: Luke 1:31-32

Behold thou shalt conceive in thy womb, and shalt bring forth a son; and thou shalt call his name Jesus. He shall be great, and shall be called the Son of the most High; and the Lord God shall give unto him the throne of David his father; and he shall reign in the house of Jacob for ever.

Meditation

Picture the scene of the Annunciation. God proposes the mystery of the Incarnation which He will accomplish in the Virgin Mary—but not until she has given her consent. The accomplishment of the mystery is held in suspense awaiting the free acceptance of Mary. At this moment Mary represents all of us in her own person; it is as if God is waiting for the response of the humanity to which He longs to unite Himself. What a solemn moment this is! For upon this moment depends the decision of the most vital mystery of Christianity. But see how Mary gives her answer. Full of faith and confidence in the heavenly message and entirely submissive to the Divine Will, the Virgin Mary replies in a spirit of complete and absolute abandonment: "Behold the handmaid of the Lord; be it done to me according to Thy word." This "Fiat" is Mary's consent to the Divine Plan of Redemption. It is like an echo of the "Fiat" of the creation of the world. But this is a new world, a world infinitely superior, a world of grace, which God will cause to arise in consequence of Mary's consent, for at that moment the Divine

Word, the second Person of the Blessed Trinity, becomes Man in Mary: "And the Word was made Flesh and dwelt among us."

Visitation : Luke 1:42-45

And she cried out with a loud voice, and said: Blessed art thou among women, and blessed is the fruit of thy womb. And whence is this to me, that the mother of my Lord should come to me? For behold as soon as the voice of thy salutation sounded in my ears, the infant in my womb leaped for joy. And blessed art thou that hast believed, because those things shall be accomplished that were spoken to thee by the Lord.

Meditation

See how the Holy Spirit greets the Virgin Mary through the mouth of Elizabeth: "Blessed art thou among women and blessed is the fruit of thy womb! And blessed art thou that hast believed, because those things shall be accomplished that were spoke to thee by the Lord." Blessed indeed, for by this faith in the word of God the Virgin Mary became the Mother of Christ. What finite creature has ever received honor such as this from the Infinite Being? Mary gives all the glory to the Lord for the marvelous things which are accomplished in her. From the moment of the Incarnation the Virgin Mother sings in her heart a canticle full of love and gratitude. In the presence of her cousin Elizabeth she allows the most profound sentiments of her heart to break forth in song; she intones the "Magnificat" which, in the course of centuries, her children will repeat with her to praise God for having chosen her among all women: "My soul magnifies the Lord and my spirit rejoices in God my Savior, Because He has regarded the lowliness of His handmaid... Because He Who is mighty has done great things for me And holy is His name."

Nativity: Luke 2:6-7

And it came to pass, that when they were there, her days were accomplished, that she should be delivered. And she brought forth her firstborn son, and wrapped him up in swaddling clothes, and laid him in a manger; because there was no room for them in the inn.

Meditation

The Virgin Mary sees in the Infant that she has given to the world, a child in appearance like all other children, the very Son of God. Mary's soul was filled with an immense faith which welled up in her and surpassed the faith of all the just men of the Old Testament; this is why she recognized her God in her own Son. This faith manifests itself externally by an act of adoration. From her very first glance at Jesus, the Virgin prostrated herself interiorly in a spirit of adoration so profound that we can never fathom its depth. In the heart of Mary are joined in perfect harmony a creature's adoration of her God and a Mother's love for her only Son. How inconceivably great the joy in the soul of Jesus must have been as He experienced this boundless love of His Mother! Between these two souls took place ceaseless exchanges of love which brought them into ever closer unity. O wonderful exchange: to Mary Jesus gives the greatest gifts and graces, and to Jesus Mary gives her fullest cooperation: after the union of the Divine Persons in the Blessed Trinity and the hypostatic union of the divine and human natures in the Incarnation, no more glorious or more profound union can be conceived than the union between Jesus and Mary.

Presentation: Luke 2:22-24

And after the days of her purification, according to the law of Moses, were accomplished, they carried him to Jerusalem, to present him to the Lord: As it is written in the law of the Lord: Every male opening the womb shall be called holy to the Lord: And to offer a sacrifice, according as it is written in the law of the Lord, a pair of turtledoves, or two young pigeons…

Meditation

On the day of the Presentation God received infinitely more glory than He had hitherto received in the temple from all the sacrifices and all the holocausts of the Old Testament. On this day it is His own Son Jesus Who is offered to Him, and Who offers to the Father the infinite homage of adoration, thanksgiving, expiation and supplication. This is indeed a gift worthy of God. And it is from the hands of the Virgin, full of grace, that this offering, so pleasing to God, is received. Mary's faith is perfect. Filled with the wisdom of the Holy Spirit, she has a clear understanding of the value of the offering which she is making to God at this moment; by His inspirations the Holy Spirit brings her soul into harmony with the interior dispositions of the heart of her Divine Son. Just as Mary had given her consent in the name of all humanity when the angel announced to her the mystery of the Incarnation, so also on this day Mary offers Jesus to the Father in the name of the whole human race. For she knows that her Son is "the King of Glory, the new light enkindled before the dawn, the Master of life and death."

Finding in the Temple: Luke 2:46-47

And it came to pass, that, after three days, they found him in the temple, sitting in the midst of the doctors, hearing them, and asking them questions. And all that heard him were astonished at his wisdom and his answers.

Meditation

"How is it that you sought Me? Did you not know that I must be about My Father's business?" This is the answer that Jesus gave to His Mother when, after three days' search she had the joy of finding Him in the Temple. These are the first words coming from the lips of the Word Incarnate to be recorded in the Gospel. In these words Jesus sums up His whole person, His whole life, His whole mission. They reveal His Divine Sonship; they testify to His supernatural mission. Christ's whole life will only be a clarifying and magnificent exposition of the meaning of these words. St. Luke goes on to tell us that Mary "did not understand the word that He spoke." But even if Mary did not grasp the full significance of these words, she did not doubt that Jesus was the Son of God. This is why she submitted in silence to that Divine Will which had demanded such a sacrifice of her love. "Mary kept these words of Jesus carefully in her heart." She kept them in her heart, for there was the tabernacle in which she adored the mystery concealed in the words of he Son, waiting until the full light of understanding would be granted her.

The Sorrowful Mysteries

Agony in the Garden: Matthew 26:36-39

Then Jesus came with them into a country place which is called Gethsemani; and he said to his disciples: Sit you here, till I go yonder and pray. And taking with him Peter and the two sons of Zebedee, he began to grow sorrowful and to be sad. Then he saith to them: My soul is sorrowful even unto death: stay you here, and watch with me. And going a little further, he fell upon his face, praying, and saying: My Father, if it be possible, let this chalice pass from me. Nevertheless not as I will, but as thou wilt.

Meditation

It is for the love of His Father above all else that Jesus willed to undergo His Passion. Behold Jesus Christ in His agony. For three long hours weariness, grief, fear and anguish sweep in upon His soul like a torrent; the pressure of this interior agony is so immense that blood bursts forth from His sacred veins. What an abyss of suffering is reached in this agony! And what does Jesus say to His Father? "Father, if it be possible, let this chalice pass from Me." Can it be that Jesus no longer accepts the Will of His Father? Oh! certainly He does. But this prayer is the cry of the sensitive emotions of poor human nature, crushed by ignominy and suffering. Now is Jesus truly a "Man of Sorrows." Our Savior feels the terrible weight of His agony bearing down upon His shoulders. He wants us to realize this; that is why He utters such a prayer. But listen to what He immediately adds: "Nevertheless, Father, not My will but Thine be done." Here is the triumph of love. Because He loves His Father, He places the Will of His Father above everything else and accepts every possible suffering in order to redeem us.

Scourging at the Pillar: Matthew 27:25-26

And the whole people answering, said: His blood be upon us and our children. Then he released to them Barabbas, and having scourged Jesus, delivered him unto them to be crucified

Meditation

Christ substituted Himself voluntarily for us as a sacrificial victim without blemish in order to pay our debt, and, by the expiation and the satisfaction which He made for us, to restore the Divine life to us. This was the mission which Christ came to fulfill, the course which He had to run. "God has placed upon Him"–a man like unto ourselves, of the race of Adam, but entirely just and innocent and without sin–"the iniquity of us all." Since Christ has become, so to speak, a sharer in our nature and taken upon Himself the debt of our sin, He has merited for us a share in His justice and holiness. In the forceful words of St. Paul, God, "by sending His Son in the likeness of sinful flesh as a sin-offering, has condemned sin in the flesh." And with an impact still more stunning, the Apostle writes: "For our sakes He (God) made Him (Christ) to be sin who knew nothing of sin." How startling this expression is: "made Him to be sin"! The Apostle does not say "sinner," but–what is still more striking–"sin"! Let us never forget that "we have been redeemed at great price by the precious blood of Christ as of a lamb without blemish and without spot."

Crowning with Thorns: Matthew 27:28-29

And stripping him, they put a scarlet cloak about him. And platting a crown of thorns, they put it upon his head, and a reed in his right hand. And bowing the knee before him, they mocked him, saying: Hail, king of the Jews.

Meditation

Christ Jesus becomes an object of derision and insults at the hands of the temple servants. Behold Him, the all-powerful God, struck by sharp blows; His adorable face, the joy of the saints, is covered with spittle; a crown of thorns is forced down upon His head; a purple robe is placed upon His shoulders as a mock of derision; a reed is thrust into His hand; the servants genuflect insolently before Him in mockery. What an abyss of ignominy! What humiliation and disgrace for One before Whom the angels tremble! The cowardly Roman governor imagines that the hatred of the Jews will be satisfied by the sight of Christ in this pitiful state. He shows Him to the crowd: "Ecce Homo–Behold the Man!" Let us contemplate our Divine Master at this moment, plunged into the abyss of suffering and ignominy, and let us realize that the Father also presents Him to us and says to us: "Behold My Son, the splendor of My glory– but bruised for the sins of My people."

Carrying the Cross: John 19:12-18

And from henceforth Pilate sought to release him. But the Jews cried out, saying: If thou release this man, thou art not Caesar's friend. For whosoever maketh himself a king, speaketh against Caesar. Now when Pilate had heard these words, he brought Jesus forth, and sat down in the judgment seat, in the place that is called Lithostrotos, and in Hebrew Gabbatha. And it was the parasceve of the pasch, about the sixth hour, and he saith to the Jews: Behold your king. But they cried out: Away with him; away with him; crucify him. Pilate saith to them: Shall I crucify your king? The chief priests answered: We have no king but Caesar. Then therefore he delivered him to them to be crucified. And they took Jesus, and led him forth. And bearing his own cross, he went forth to that place which is called Calvary, but in Hebrew Golgotha. Where they crucified him, and with him two others, one on each side, and Jesus in the midst.

Meditation

Let us meditate upon Jesus Christ on the way to Calvary laden with His cross. He falls under the weight of this burden. To expiate sin,

He wills to experience in His own flesh the oppression of sin. Fearing that Jesus will not reach the place of crucifixion alive, the Jews force Simon of Cyrene to help Christ to carry His cross, and Jesus accepts this assistance. In this Simon represents all of us. As members of the Mystical Body of Christ, we should all help Jesus to carry His Cross. This is the one sure sign that we belong to Christ–if we carry our cross with Him. But while Jesus carried His cross, He merited for us the strength to bear our trials with generosity. He has placed in His cross a sweetness which makes ours bearable, for when we carry our cross it is really His that we receive. For Christ unites with His own the sufferings, sorrows, pains and burdens which we accept with love from His hand, and by this union He gives them an inestimable value, and they become a source of great merit for us. It is above all His love for His Father which impels Christ to accept the sufferings of His Passion, but it is also the love which He bears us.

Crucifixion & Death: Luke 23:45-46

And the sun was darkened, and the veil of the temple was rent in the midst. And Jesus crying out with a loud voice, said: Father, into thy hands I commend my spirit. And saying this, he gave up the ghost.

Meditation

At the Last Supper, when the hour had come to complete His oblation of self, what did Christ say to His Apostles who were gathered around Him? "Greater love than this no man hath, that a man lay down his life for his friends." And this is the love, surpassing all loves, which Jesus shows us; for, as St. Paul says, "It is for us all that He is delivered up." What greater proof of love could He have given us? None. Hence the Apostle declares without ceasing that "because He loved us, Christ delivered Himself up for us," and "because of the love He bears for me, He gave Himself up for me." "Delivered," "given"–to what extent? Even to the death on the cross! What enhances this love immeasurably is the sovereign liberty with which Christ delivered Himself up: "He offered Himself because He willed it." These words tell us how spontaneously Jesus accepted His Passion. This freedom with which Jesus delivered Himself up to death for us is one of the aspects of His sacrifice which touch our human hearts most profoundly.

The Glorious Mysteries

Resurrection of Our Lord: Matthew 28:5-6

And the angel answering, said to the women: Fear not you; for I know that you seek Jesus who was crucified. He is not here, for he is risen, as he said. Come, and see the place where the Lord was laid.

Meditation

On the day of His Resurrection Jesus Christ left in the tomb the shroud which is the symbol of our infirmities, our weaknesses, our imperfections. Christ comes from the tomb triumphant–completely free of earthly limitation; He is animated with a life that is intense and perfect, and which vibrates in every fibre of His being. In Him everything that is mortal has been absorbed by His glorified life. Here is the first element of the sanctity represented in the risen Christ: the elimination of everything that is corruptible, everything that is earthly and created; freedom from all defects, all infirmities, all capacity for suffering. But there is also another element of sanctity: union with God, self- oblation and consecration to God. Only in heaven shall we be able to understand how completely Jesus lived for His Father during these blessed days. The life of the risen Christ became an infinite source of glory for His Father. Not a single effect of His sufferings was left in Him, for now everything in Him shone with brilliance and beauty and possessed strength and life; every atom of His being sang an unceasing canticle of praise. His holy humanity offered itself in a new manner to the glory of the Father.

Ascension into Heaven: Luke 24:50-51

And he led them out as far as Bethania: and lifting up his hands, he blessed them. And it came to pass, whilst he blessed them, he departed from them, and was carried up to heaven.

Meditation

Our Lord said to His Apostles before He departed from them: "If you loved Me, you would indeed rejoice that I am going to the Father." To us also Christ repeats these words. If we love Him, we shall rejoice in His glorification; we shall rejoice with Him that, after completing His course on earth, He ascends to the right hand of His Father, there to be exalted above all the heavens in infinite glory. But Jesus goes only to precede us; He does not separate Himself from us, nor does He separate us from Himself. If He enters into His glorious kingdom, it is to prepare a place for us there. He promises to return one day to take us with Him so that, as He says, where He is we also may be. True, we are already there in the glory and happiness of Christ, by our title as His heirs; but we shall one day be there in reality. Has not Christ asked this of His Father? "Father, I will that where I am, they also whom Thou hast given Me may be with Me." Let us then say to Christ Jesus: "Draw us into Your triumphal march, O glorious and all-powerful Conqueror! Make us live in heaven by faith and hope and love. Help us to detach ourselves from the fleeting things of earth in order that we may seek the true and lasting goods of heaven!"

The Pentecost: Acts 2:3-4

And there appeared to them parted tongues as it were of fire, and it sat upon every one of them: And they were all filled with the Holy Ghost, and they began to speak with divers tongues, according as the Holy Ghost gave them to speak.

Meditation

The Holy Spirit appeared under the form of tongues of fire in order to fill the Apostles with truth and to prepare them to bear witness to Jesus. He also come to fill their hearts with love. He is the Person of Love in the life of God. He is also like a breath, an aspiration of infinite Love, from which we draw the breath of life. On the day of Pentecost the Divine Spirit communicated such an abundance of life to the whole Church that to symbolize it "there came a sound from heaven, as of a violent wind coming, and it filled the whole house where they (the Apostles) were sitting." But it is also for us that the Holy Spirit has come, for the group in the Cenacle represented the whole Church. The Holy Spirit came to remain with the Church forever. This is the promise of Jesus Himself. He dwells in the Church permanently and unfailingly, performing in it without ceasing, His action of life-giving and sanctification. He establishes the Church infallibly in the truth. It is He Who makes the Church blossom forth with a marvelous supernatural fruitfulness, for He brings to life and full fruition in Virgins, Martyrs, Confessors, those heroic virtues which are one of the marks of true sanctity.

Assumption of Mary: Hebrews 11:5

By faith Henoch was translated, that he should not see death; and he was not found, because God had translated him: for before his translation he had testimony that he pleased God.

Meditation

If Christ Jesus wishes us to love all the members of His Mystical Body, should we not love above all others her who gave Him the very nature by which He became our Head, the same nature which He uses to communicate His grace to us? We cannot doubt but that the love which we show to his Mother is extremely pleasing to Christ. We shall manifest our love by extolling the sublime privileges which Jesus has bestowed on His Mother, among which the Assumption is one of the most glorious. If we wish to please our Lord very much, we shall admire the wonderful gifts with which He has lovingly adorned the soul of His Mother. He wishes that we should sing the praises of the Virgin, who was chosen among all women to give the Savior to the world. "Yes, we shall sing your praises, for you alone have delighted the heart of your

God. May you be blessed, for you have believed the word of God, and in you the eternal promises have been fulfilled."

Coronation of Mary: Apocalypse 11:19-12:1

And the temple of God was opened in heaven: and the ark of his testament was seen in his temple, and there were lightnings, and voices, and an earthquake, and great hail. And a great sign appeared in heaven: A woman clothed with the sun, and the moon under her feet, and on her head a crown of twelve stars…

Meditation

What is the purpose of all the mysteries of Christ? To be the pattern of our supernatural life, the means of our sanctification, the source of all our holiness. To create an eternal and glorious society of brethren who will be like unto Him. For this reason Christ, the new Adam, has associated with Himself Mary, as the new Eve. But she is, much more than Eve, "the Mother of all the living," the Mother of those who live in the grace of her Son. And since here below Mary was associated so intimately with all the mysteries of our salvation, at her Assumption into heaven Jesus crowned her not only with glory but also with power; He has placed His Mother on His right hand and has given her the power, in virtue of her unique title of Mother of God, to distribute the treasures of eternal life. Let us then, full of confidence, pray with the Church: "Show yourself a Mother: Mother of Jesus, by your complete faith in Him, our Mother, by your mercy towards us; ask Christ, Who was born of you, to give us life; and Who willed to be your Son, to receive our prayers through you."

Meditations from The Mystical City of God
A thought for each Hail Mary, taken from the "Mystical City of God," by Sister Mary of Jesus of Agreda.

The Mystical City of God is a book written in the 17th-century by the Franciscan nun, Venerable Mary of Jesus of Ágreda. According to María de Ágreda, the book was to a considerable extent dictated to her by the Blessed Virgin Mary and regarded the life of the Virgin Mary and the divine plan for creation and the salvation of souls.

The Annunciation.

1. The first day: God makes the most holy Mary a participant of his wisdom.

2. The second day: He makes her a participant of the divine omnipotence.

3. The third day: He manifests to her the desire of his divine love to come to the aid of men.

4. The fourth day: He manifests to her the new law of grace.

5. The fifth day: the Princess is instructed in the great mysteries regarding the number of the predestined and the reprobate.

6. The sixth day: The Most High manifests to Mary, our Mistress, additional mysteries and shows her the works of the sixth day of creation.

7. The Most High celebrates a new espousal with the Princess of Heaven, in order to inaugurate the nuptials of the Incarnation.

8. The great Queen pleads for the hastening of the Incarnation.

9. The Most High manifests to her the fabric of the universe, and makes her Sovereign and Queen of all.

10. Mary listens to the message of the holy angel; the mystery of the Incarnation is enacted by the conception of the eternal Word in her womb.

The Visitation.

1. Mary and Joseph journey to Juda: "The Lord be with you, my dearest cousin."

2. The Redeemer justifies the soul of John; Mary says: "May God save thee, my dearest cousin, and may his divine light communicate to thee grace and life."

3. Elizabeth and John see the Word made man, and extol Him and his Mother.

4. Elizabeth and Mary, like two seraphim, discourse on these mysteries.

5. A sweet competition arises between the two cousins.

6. The heavenly Princess converses with her angels.

7. Our Queen obtains pardon and remedy for a servant of the house, and the love of chastity for a woman living in the neighborhood.

8. The Queen receives in her arms the new-born Precursor.

9. St. Elizabeth secures the good counsel and instruction of the Mother of wisdom.

10. Most holy Mary commands the dumbness of Zacharias to leave him.

The Nativity.

1. The ten thousand angels accompany Mary and Joseph, composing new songs in honor of the Lord.

2. The heavenly Lady exercises heroic virtues in return for the in-hospitality of mortals.

3. The Virgin Mother beholds the Godhead itself for over an hour.

4. At the end of the rapture, the most exalted Lady gave to the world the Onlybegotten of the Father.

5. She received her Son in her arms from the hands of the holy an-gels and said: "My sweetest love and light of my eyes, Thou hast arrived in good hour into this world as the Sun of justice, in order to disperse the darkness of sin and death! True God of the true God, save thy servants, and let all flesh see him, who shall draw upon it salvation."

6. The shepherds come to adore the Lord.

7. The most holy name of Jesus is brought from heaven by two cohorts of angels.

8. The divine Infant is circumcised and receives the name Jesus.

9. There is an interchange of caresses between the Infant and His Mother.

10. The three kings of the Orient come to adore the Word made man in Bethlehem.

The Presentation

1. The Holy Family journeys to Jerusalem, accompanied by many angels in visible human forms.

2. Simeon and Anne are enlightened and send the chief procurator to receive the holy Travelers.

3. The great Princess passes the night in divine colloquies.

4. Upon entering the temple, the most blessed Mother is immersed in an intellectual vision of the most holy Trinity.

5. Simeon offers the Infant Jesus up to the Eternal Father and ad-dresses himself to the most holy Mother.

6. The heavenly Lady begins a novena in the temple, and on the fifth day the Divinity reveals itself to her.

7. The angel of the Lord appears to St. Joseph.

8. The ten thousand heavenly courtiers accompany Jesus, Mary and Joseph as they set forth from the portals of the city.

9. An angel proceeds to inform the fortunate and blessed Elizabeth of all these events.

10. Most Holy Mary entertains the poor in Gaza, and interchanges canticles of praise in honor of the infinite essence of God.

The Finding of the Child Jesus in the Temple.

1. The Lord tries the most holy Mary for thirty days.

2. The sweetest Jesus, most pure Mary, and Joseph go up together to the feasts of the unleavened breads, accompanied by ten thousand angels.

3. Jesus and Mary perform heroic works of charity for the benefit of mortals.

4. The afflicted Mother returns to Jerusalem, questioning the ten thousand angels.

5. She searches the byways and hospital of Jerusalem.

6. The most holy Mother and St. Joseph arrive at the temple and she approaches her most loving Son and speaks to him the words recorded by St. Luke.

7. At some distance from Jerusalem, the most prudent Lady kneels before her Son and his soul is revealed to her.

8. Upon arriving at Nazareth, the great Lady responds to the obedience and subjection of her most holy Son by heroic works.

9. The great Queen has a vision of the Divinity, in which she perceives that the holy Trinity decrees that she is to receive the New Testament.

10. The Lord enlightens the most blessed Mother by giving her a knowledge of the whole militant Church, the Sacraments, the doctrines, and all the Scriptures.

The Agony in the Garden.

1. The Lord washes the feet of the disciples.

2. The Lord celebrates the sacramental supper.

3. The Lord's prayer in the garden, and His sorrow at the reprobation of so many.

4. The Eternal Father sends the Archangel Michael.

5. Christ returns to visit the Apostles and weeps over their sloth and negligence.

6. Christ is delivered into the hands of his enemies by the treason of Judas.

7. The Lord spoke to the soldiers: "I am He," and they all fell back-wards to the ground.

8. The apostles flee, and most holy Mary from her retreat sees them and prays for them.

9. Jesus the Savior is dragged to the house of Annas, where the wicked servant strikes Him in the face.

10. Christ is dragged to the house of Caiphas, and proclaims that He is the Son of God.

The Scourging at the Pillar.

1. Frightful insults were heaped upon the Redeemer, during which He established the beatitudes, which He had promised and proposed some time before.

2. The Savior is locked in a dungeon and the ministers of wickedness insult Him again.

3. The council convenes and condemns Christ to death.

4. The executioners bring Christ to the house of Pilate; the Blessed Virgin goes forth to meet Him, and prostrates herself before His sovereign Person.

5. Christ is sent to Herod and mocked.

6. Herod sends the Lord back to Pilate, during which the multitudes trod Him underfoot and kicked Him.

7. Christ is stripped and bound to one of the columns.

8. The first pair of executioners scourged the innocent Savior with thick cords, full of rough knots.

9. The second pair continued the scourging with hardened leather thongs.

10. The third pair of scourgers beat the Lord cruelly with extremely tough rawhides, and they also beat Him in the

face and in the feet and hands, leaving unwounded not a single spot.

The Crowning with Thorns.

1. Jesus is clothed in a purple mantle.
2. A cap of woven thorns is placed on His head.
3. A contemptible reed is placed in His hand.
4. A violet-colored mantle is placed over His shoulders.
5. The soldiers bent their knees and buffeted Him.
6. Then they snatched the cane from His hands and struck Him.
7. They ejected their disgusting spittle.
8. Pilate showed Him to the people and said: "Ecce homo!" Mary fell upon her knees and openly adored Him as the true God-man. The same was also done by saint John and the holy women.
9. Pilate decrees the sentence of death against the author of life.
10. The Redeemer addressed the Cross with a countenance full of extreme joy.

The Carrying of the Cross.

1. The sorrowful Mother feels in soul and body the same torments as her Son.
2. The heavenly Mother hinders Lucifer and his companions.
3. She meets her Son face to face.

4. The sorrow of the most sincere Dove and Virgin Mother was be-yond all human thought while She witnessed with her own eyes her Son carrying the Cross.

5. The sweetest Jesus speaks to the women.

6. Simon of Cyrene carries the Cross.

7. The invincible Mother prays on Mt. Calvary and offers her Son to the Eternal Father as a sacrifice for the redemption of man.

8. The Savior is stripped of the seamless tunic.

9. With inhuman cruelty He is nailed to the Cross.

10. His bones are dislocated.

The Crucifixion.

1. When the Queen of the angels perceived the insults heaped upon her Son, she was inflamed with a new zeal. By virtue of her prayer, all the elements were changed during the crucifixion and the hearts of the bystanders were enlightened.

2. Christ our Lord makes His testament in His prayer to the eternal Father, bestowing on the elect their inheritance, and disinheriting the reprobate.

3. "Father, forgive them, for they know not what they do."

4. "Woman, behold thy son!" "Behold thy Mother!"

5. The side of Christ is opened with a lance.

6. The body of the Lord was taken down from the Cross and placed in the arms of most holy Mary.

7. The sacred body was embalmed with the aromatic ointments, and placed on a bier. The heavenly Queen, accompanied by many angels and by some of the faithful, proceeded to the sepulchre, and therein placed the sacred body of Jesus.

8. She passed the night in the deep consideration of these mysteries.

9. She consoles the Apostles.

10. She contemplates the soul of her Son descend into limbo.

The Resurrection.

1. The Savior arose from the grave, and in the presence of the saints and Patriarchs He promised universal resurrection to all men. The great Queen was aware of this and participated in it from her retreat in the Cenacle.

2. Accompanied by the saints and Patriarchs, our Savior appeared to the most blessed Mary, and she enjoyed briefly the beatific vision.

3. Still remaining in her exalted state, the great Lady turned to the holy Patriarchs and all the just, and spoke to each in succession.

4. The Lord appeared to Mary Magdalen and the holy women. Then they sought the Queen of Heaven to tell Her of the events.

5. The Lord appeared to Cleophas and St. Luke on the road to Emmaus.

6. The Lord appeared to the Apostles and later to St. Thomas. They immediately sought most holy Mary in order to relate to Her what had happened.

7. The Lord appeared at the sea of Tiberias to St. Peter, Thomas, Nathanael, the sons of Zebedee and two other disciples. Most holy Mary had a full intelligence of these mysteries and preserved them within her most prudent and chaste heart.

8. The great Lady persevered in her retirement for the forty days after the Resurrection and there enjoyed the sight of her divine Son and of the angels and saints.

9. Amid all the delights and jubilations of her retreat, the kindest Mother did not forget the misery of the children of Eve, and like a true Mother of mercy, offered for all of them her most fervent prayers.

10. The Eternal Father and the Holy Ghost appeared in the Cenacle upon a throne of ineffable splendor, surrounded by the choirs of angels and saints there present, and they entrusted Mary with the care of the Church and the new law of grace.

The Ascension.

1. On the day of the Ascension, while the Lord was at the table with the eleven Apostles, other disciples and pious women gathered at the Cenacle, and the Lord bade them not to leave Jerusalem until He should send the Holy Spirit.

2. With this little flock Jesus left the Cenacle and conducted them all through the streets of Jerusalem to mount Olivet.

3. Jesus, His countenance beaming forth peace and majesty, joined his hands and, by his own power, began to raise Himself from the earth, drawing after Him also the celestial choirs of the angels and the holy Patriarchs. The most blessed Lady was raised up with her divine Son and placed at his right hand.

4. The entire divine procession arrived at the supreme regions of the empyrean, and the angels repeated the words of David: "Open, ye princes, open your gates eternal; let them be raised and opened up, and receive into his dwelling the great King of glory, the Lord of virtues, the Powerful in battle, the Strong and Invincible, who comes triumphant and victorious over all His enemies."

5. The Eternal Father placed upon the throne of his Divinity at his right hand, the incarnate Word, and in such glory and majesty, that He filled with new admiration and reverential fear all the inhabitants of heaven.

6. The great Queen hovered at the footstool of the royal throne, and prostrate she adored the Father and broke out in new canticles of praise for the glory communicated to His Son.

7. The Redeemer sent down two angels in white and resplendent garments, who appeared to all the disciples to console and encourage them.

8. After having remained in heaven for three days, enjoying in body and soul the glory of the right hand of her Son and true God, the most holy Mary departed with the benediction of the blessed Trinity from the highest empyrean and returned to the earth. She was enveloped in a cloud or globe of most resplendent light, and was borne downward by the seraphim, amid great splendor.

9. The three days in which the great Lady enjoyed the after-effects of glory and while the redundance of its splendors gradually lessened, She spent in most ardent and divine sentiments of love, gratitude and ineffable humility.

10. She began to converse with the faithful, offering prayers for all who in future ages were to receive the grace of the holy Catholic faith.

The Descent of the Holy Ghost.

1. A few days later she spent five hours with the Incarnate Word, enjoying His presence.
2. She instructed and prepared the Apostles and disciples for the advent of the Holy Ghost.
3. Prostrate in the form of a cross, she saw the petition of the Savior to send the Holy Ghost.
4. The Holy Ghost is sent, and the Blessed Virgin enjoys briefly the beatific vision.
5. The Apostles preach, and three thousand are converted.
6. The Blessed Mother speaks words of consolation to the new converts.
7. The catechumens are baptized; St. Peter celebrates the first Mass.
8. From her retirement the great Lady by especial vision saw the martyrdom of saint Stephen and his entrance into heaven.
9. She fasted for forty days, in preparation for the formulation of the Creed.
10. She prayed for the conversion of St. Paul, and witnessed it by an especial vision.

The Assumption.

1. The most blessed Mary takes leave of the holy places and of the Holy Church; she makes her will.
2. Three days before, St. Peter arrives; he speaks to the assembly.

3. The Blessed Virgin kneels before St. Peter and St. John, and takes leave of the entire assembly.

4. The Incarnate Word descends from heaven; the angels sing the canticles.

5. Surrounded by the Apostles, the most blessed Mother dies of love.

6. The assembly sings hymns and psalms; great miracles occur.

7. The Apostles bear her body in procession to the valley of Josaphat and place it in a sepulchre.

8. The soul of Mary is received into glory and placed upon the throne of the most Holy Trinity.

9. Christ descends from heaven, accompanied by many angels and saints; Mary's soul resuscitates her body.

10. The saints and angels formed a solemn procession and ascended into heaven; the most blessed Mary arrived at the throne of the most blessed Trinity and was received by the three divine Persons with an embrace eternally indissoluble.

The Coronation.

1. The most blessed Mary was assigned to the supreme position and state on the throne of the most blessed Trinity.

2. The eternal Father spoke to the angels and saints and said: "Our daughter Mary was chosen according to Our pleasure from among all creatures. We recognize Her dominion by crowning Her as the legitimate and peerless Lady and Sovereign."

3. The Incarnate Word said: "Of all things over which I am King, She too shall be the legitimate and supreme Queen."

4. The Holy Ghost said: "Since She is called my beloved and chosen Spouse, She deserves to be crowned as Queen for all eternity."

5. The three divine Persons then placed upon the head of the most blessed Mary a crown of such new splendor and value, that the like has been seen neither before nor after by any mere creature.

6. At the same time a voice sounded from the throne saying: "My Beloved, chosen among the creatures, our kingdom is Thine; Thou shalt be the Lady and the Sovereign of the seraphim, of all the ministering spirits, the angels and of the entire universe of creatures. Receive now the supreme dignity deserved by Thee and the dominion over all creatures."

7. The Almighty commanded all the courtiers of heaven, angels and men, to recognize Her as their Queen and Lady, and all rendered homage to her, especially saints Joseph, Joachim and Anne, and the thousand angels of her guard.

8. Within her body, over her heart, was visible a small globe or monstrance of singular beauty, in testimony of her having received holy Communion so worthily and holily.

9. St. Peter calls the Apostles and disciples, and decides to remove the stone from the sepulchre; he takes out the tunic and mantle and they sing psalms and hymns in honor of Mary.

10. An angel of the Lord descends from heaven to console the Apostles, and from her throne Mary takes care of them and protects them in their wanderings and at the hour of their martyrdom.

Enchiridion Sanctissimi Rosarii

A Manual of the Most Holy Rosary

54 Day Rosary Novena

Perhaps the most powerful novena is the 54-Day Rosary Novena, a series of six consecutive nine-day novenas. The first three novenas are offered for the intention, while the last three are offered in thanks to God in anticipation of granting the favor.

The Joyful Mysteries

Prayer before the recitation

Sign of the cross. Hail Mary.

In petition

Hail, Queen of the Most Holy Rosary, my Mother Mary, hail! At thy feet I humbly kneel to offer thee a Crown of Roses snow white buds to remind thee of thy joys each bud recalling to thee a holy mystery; each ten bound together with my petition for a particular grace. O Holy Queen, dispenser of God's graces, and Mother of all who invoke thee! thou canst not look upon my gift and fail to see its binding. As thou receivest my gift, so wilt thou receive my petition; from thy bounty thou wilt give me the favor I so earnestly and trustingly seek. I despair of nothing that I ask of thee. Show thyself my Mother!

In thanksgiving

Hail, Queen of the Most Holy Rosary, my Mother Mary, hail! At thy feet I gratefully kneel to offer thee a Crown of Roses snow white buds to remind thee of thy joys each bud recalling to thee a holy mystery; each ten bound together with my petition for a particular grace. O Holy Queen, Dispenser of God's graces. and Mother of all who invoke thee! thou canst not look upon my gift and fail to see its binding. As thou receivest my gift, so wilt thou receive my thanksgiving; from thy bounty thou hast given me the favor I so earnestly and trustingly sought. I despaired not of what I asked of thee, and thou hast truly shown thyself my Mother.

Creed, Our Father, 3 Hail Marys, Glory be to the Father.

The Annunciation

Sweet Mother Mary, meditating on the Mystery of the Annunciation, when the angel Gabriel appeared to thee with the tidings that thou wert to become the Mother of God; greeting thee with that sublime salutation, *"Hail, full of grace! the Lord is with thee!"* and thou didst humbly submit thyself to the will of the Father, responding: *"Behold the handmaid of the Lord. Be it done unto me according to thy word."* I humbly pray:

Our Father, 10 Hail Marys, Glory be to the Father.

I bind these snow white buds with a petition for the virtue of **Humility** and humbly lay this bouquet at thy feet.

The Visitation

Sweet Mother Mary, meditating on the Mystery of the Visitation, when, upon thy visit to thy holy cousin, Elizabeth, she greeted thee with the prophetic utterance, *"Blessed art thou among women, and blessed is the fruit of thy womb!"* and thou didst answer with that canticle of canticles, the Magnificat. I humbly pray:

Our Father, 10 Hail Marys, Glory be to the Father.

I bind these snow white buds with a petition for the virtue of **Charity** and humbly lay this bouquet at thy feet.

The Nativity

Sweet Mother Mary, meditating on the Mystery of the Nativity of Our Lord, when, thy time being completed, thou didst bring forth, O holy Virgin, the Redeemer of the world in a stable at Bethlehem; whereupon choirs of angels filled the heavens with their exultant song of praise *"Glory to God in the highest, and on earth peace to men of good will."* I humbly pray:

Our Father, 10 Hail Marys, Glory be to the Father.

I bind these snow white buds with a petition for the virtue of **Detachment from the world** and humbly lay this bouquet at thy feet.

The Presentation

Sweet Mother Mary, meditating on the Mystery of the Presentation, when, in obedience to the Law of Moses, thou didst present thy Child in the Temple, where the holy prophet Simeon, taking the Child in his arms, offered thanks to God for sparing him to look upon his Saviour and foretold thy sufferings by the words: *"Thy soul also a sword shall pierce . . ."* I humbly pray:

Our Father, 10 Hail Marys, Glory be to the Father.

I bind these snowwhite buds with a petition for the virtue of **Purity** and humbly lay this bouquet at thy feet.

The Finding Of The Child Jesus In The Temple

Sweet Mother Mary, meditating on the Mystery of the Finding of the Child Jesus in the Temple, when, having sought Him for three days, sorrowing, thy heart was gladdened upon finding Him in the

Temple speaking to the doctors; and when, upon thy request, He obediently returned home with thee. I humbly pray:

Our Father, 10 Hail Marys, Glory be to the Father.

I bind these snow white buds with a petition for the virtue of **Obedience to the will of God** and humbly lay this bouquet at thy feet.

Spiritual Communion:

MY JESUS, really present in the most holy Sacrament of the Altar, since I cannot now receive Thee under the sacramental veil, I beseech Thee, with a heart full of love and longing, to come spiritually into my soul through the immaculate heart of Thy most holy Mother, and abide with me forever.

Thou in me,
And I in Thee,
In Time and in Eternity,
In Mary.

In petition

Sweet Mother Mary, I offer thee this Spiritual Communion to bind my bouquets in a wreath to place upon thy brow. O my Mother! look with favor upon my gift, and in thy love obtain for me (specify request) Hail, Mary, etc.

In thanksgiving

Sweet Mother Mary, I offer thee this Spiritual Communion to bind my bouquets in a wreath to place upon thy brow in thanksgiving for (specify request) which thou in thy love hast obtained for me. Hail, Mary, etc.

Prayer

O God! Whose only begotten Son, by His life, death, and resurrection, has purchased for us the reward of eternal life; grant, we beseech Thee, that, meditating upon these mysteries of the Most Holy Rosary of the Blessed Virgin Mary, we may imitate what they contain and obtain what they promise. Through the same Christ our Lord. Amen. May the divine assistance remain always with us. And may the souls of the faithful departed, through the mercy of God, rest in peace. Amen. Holy Virgin, with thy loving Child, thy blessing give to us this day (night). In the name of the Father, and of the Son, and of the Holy Ghost. Amen.

The Sorrowful Mysteries

Prayer before the recitation

Sign of the cross. Hail Mary.

In petition

Hail, Queen of the Most Holy Rosary, my Mother Mary, hail! At thy feet I humbly kneel to offer thee a Crown of Roses blood red roses to remind thee of the passion of thy divine Son, with Whom thou didst so fully partake of its bitterness each rose recalling to thee a holy mystery; each ten bound together with my petition for a particular grace. O Holy Queen, dispenser of God's graces, and Mother of all who invoke thee! Thou canst not look upon my gift and fail to see its binding. As thou receivest my gift, so wilt thou receive my petition; from thy bounty thou wilt give me the favor I so earnestly and trustingly seek. I despair of nothing that I ask of thee. Show thyself my Mother!

In thanksgiving

Hail, Queen of the Most Holy Rosary, my Mother Mary, hail! At thy feet I gratefully kneel to offer thee a Crown of Roses blood red roses to remind thee of the passion of thy divine Son, with Whom thou didst so fully partake of its bitterness each rose recalling to thee a holy mystery; each ten bound together with my petition for a particular grace. O Holy Queen, dispenser of God's graces, and Mother of all who invoke thee! Thou canst not look upon my gift and fail to see its binding. As thou receivest my gift, so wilt thou receive my thanksgiving; from thy bounty thou hast given me the favor I so earnestly and trustingly sought. I despaired not of what I asked of thee, and thou hast truly shown thyself my Mother.

Creed, Our Father, 3 Hail Marys, Glory be to the Father.

The Agony

O most sorrowful Mother Mary, meditating on the Mystery of the Agony of Our Lord in the Garden, when, in the grotto of the Garden of Olives, Jesus saw the sins of the world unfolded before Him by Satan, who sought to dissuade Him from the sacrifice He was about to make; when, His soul shrinking from the sight, and His precious blood flowing from every pore at the vision of the torture and death He was to undergo, thy own sufferings, dear Mother, the future sufferings of His Church, and His own sufferings in the Blessed Sacrament, He cried in anguish, "*Abba! Father! if it be possible, let this chalice pass from Me*"; but, immediately resigning Himself to His Father's will, He prayed, "*Not as I will, but as Thou wilt!*" I humbly pray:

Our Father, 10 Hail Marys, Glory be to the Father.

I bind these blood red roses with a petition for the virtue of **Resignation to the will of God** and humbly lay this bouquet at thy feet.

The Scourging

O most sorrowful Mother Mary, meditating on the Mystery of the Scourging of Our Lord, when, at Pilate's command, thy divine Son, stripped of His garments and bound to a pillar, was lacerated from head to foot with cruel scourges and His flesh torn away until His mortified body could bear no more. 1 humbly pray:

Our Father, 10 Hail Marys, Glory be to the Father.

I bind these blood red roses with a petition for the virtue of **Mortification** and humbly lay this bouquet at thy feet.

The Crowning With Thorns

O most sorrowful Mother Mary, meditating on the Mystery of the Crowning of Our Lord with thorns, when, the soldiers, binding about His head a crown of sharp thorns, showered blows upon it, driving the thorns deeply into His head; then, in mock adoration, knelt before Him, crying, "*Hail, King of the Jews!*" I humbly pray:

Our Father, 10 Hail Marys, Glory be to the Father.

I bind these bloodred roses with a petition for the virtue of **Humility** and humbly lay this bouquet at thy feet.

The Carrying Of The Cross

O most sorrowful Mother Mary, meditating on the Mystery of the Carrying of the Cross, when, with the heavy wood of the cross upon His shoulders, thy divine Son was dragged, weak and suffering, yet patient, through the streets, amidst the revilements of the people, to Calvary; falling often, but urged along by the cruel blows of His executioners. I humbly pray:

Our Father, 10 Hail Marys, Glory be to the Father.

I bind these bloodred roses with a petition for the virtue of **Patience in Adversity** and humbly lay this bouquet at thy feet.

The Crucifixion

O most sorrowful Mother Mary, meditating on the Mystery of the Crucifixion, when, having been stripped of His garments, thy divine Son was nailed to the cross, upon which He died after three hours of indescribable agony, during which time He begged from His Father forgiveness for His enemies. I humbly pray:

Our Father, 10 Hail Marys, Glory be to the Father.

I bind these bloodred roses with a petition for the virtue of **Love of our enemies** and humbly lay this bouquet at thy feet.

Spiritual Communion

MY JESUS, really present in the most holy Sacrament of the Altar, since I cannot now receive Thee under the sacramental veil, I beseech Thee, with a heart full of love and longing, to come spiritually into my soul through the immaculate heart of Thy most holy Mother, and abide with me forever.

Thou in me,
And I in Thee,
In Time and in Eternity,
In Mary.

In petition

Sweet Mother Mary, I offer thee this Spiritual Communion to bind my bouquets in a wreath to place upon thy brow. O my Mother! look with favor upon my gift, and in thy love obtain for me (specify request) Hail, Mary, etc.

In thanksgiving

Sweet Mother Mary, I offer thee this Spiritual Communion to bind my bouquets in a wreath to place upon thy brow in thanksgiving for (specify request) which thou in thy love hast obtained for me. Hail, Mary, etc.

Prayer

O God! Whose only begotten Son, by His life, death, and resurrection, has purchased for us the reward of eternal life; grant, we beseech Thee, that, meditating upon these mysteries of the Most Holy Rosary of the Blessed Virgin Mary, we may imitate what they contain and obtain what they promise. Through the same Christ our Lord. Amen. May the divine assistance remain always with us. And may the souls of the faithful departed, through the mercy of God, rest in peace. Amen. Holy Virgin, with thy loving Child, thy blessing give to us this day (night). In the name of the Father, and of the Son, and of the Holy Ghost. Amen.

The Glorious Mysteries

Prayer before the recitation

Sign of the cross. Hail Mary.

In petition

Hail, Queen of the Most Holy Rosary, my Mother Mary, hail! At thy feet I humbly kneel to offer thee a Crown of Roses full blown white roses, tinged with the red of the passion, to remind thee of thy glories, fruits of the sufferings of thy Son and thee each rose recalling to thee a holy mystery; each ten bound together with my petition for a particular grace. O Holy Queen, dispenser of God's graces, and Mother of all who invoke thee! Thou canst not look upon my gift and fail to see its binding. As thou receivest my gift, so wilt thou receive my petition; from thy bounty thou wilt give me the favor I so earnestly and trustingly seek. I despair of nothing that I ask of thee. Show thyself my Mother!

In thanksgiving

Hail!, Queen of the Most Holy Rosary, my Mother Mary, hail! At thy feet I gratefully kneel to offer thee a Crown of Roses full blown white roses, tinged with the red of the passion, to remind thee of thy glories, fruits of the sufferings of thy Son and thee each rose recalling to thee a holy mystery; each ten bound together with my petition for a particular grace. O Holy Queen, dispenser of God s graces, and Mother of all who invoke thee! thou canst not look upon my gift and fail to see its binding. As thou receivest my gift, so wilt thou receive my thanksgiving; from thy bounty thou hast given me the favor I so earnestly and trustingly sought. I despaired not of what I asked of thee, and thou hast truly shown thyself my Mother.

Creed, Our Father, 3 Hail Marys, Glory be to the Father.

The Resurrection

O glorious Mother Mary, meditating on the Mystery of the Resurrection of Our Lord from the Dead, when, on the morning of the third day after His death and burial. He arose from the dead and appeared to thee, dear Mother, and filled thy heart with unspeakable joy; then appeared to the holy women, and to His disciples, who adored Him as their risen God. I humbly pray:

Our Father, 10 Hail Marys, Glory be to the Father.

I bind these full blown roses with a petition for the virtue of **Faith** and humbly lay this bouquet at thy feet.

The Ascension

O glorious Mother Mary, meditating on the Mystery of the Ascension, when thy divine Son, after forty days on earth, went to Mount Olivet accompanied by His disciples and thee, where all adored Him for the last time, after which He promised to remain with them until the end of the world; then, extending His pierced hands over all in a last blessing, He ascended before their eyes into heaven. I humbly pray:

Our Father, 10 Hail Marys, Glory be to the Father.

I bind these full blown roses with a petition for the virtue of **Hope** and humbly lay this bouquet at thy feet.

The Descent of the Holy Ghost

O glorious Mother Mary, meditating on the Mystery of the Descent of the Holy Ghost, when, the apostles being assembled with thee in a house in Jerusalem, the Holy Ghost descended upon them in the form of fiery tongues, inflaming the hearts of the apostles with the fire of divine love, teaching them all truths, giving to them the gift of tongues, and filling thee with the plenitude of His grace, inspired thee to pray for the apostles and the first Christians. I humbly pray:

Our Father, 10 Hail Marys, Glory be to the Father.

I bind these fullblown roses with a petition for the virtue of **Charity** and humbly lay this bouquet at thy feet.

The Assumption Of Our Blessed Mother Into Heaven

O glorious Mother Mary, meditating on the Mystery of Thy Assumption into Heaven, when, consumed with the desire to be united with thy divine Son in heaven, thy soul departed from thy body and united itself to Him, Who, out of the excessive love He bore for thee, His Mother, whose virginal body was His first tabernacle, took that body into heaven and there, amidst the acclaims of the angels and saints, reinfused into it thy soul. I humbly pray:

Our Father, 10 Hail Marys, Glory be to the Father.

I bind these fullblown roses with a petition for the virtue of **Union with Christ** and humbly lay this bouquet at thy feet.

The Coronation Of Our Blessed Mother In Heaven As Its Queen

O glorious Mother Mary, meditating on the Mystery of Thy Coronation in Heaven, when, upon being taken up to heaven after thy death, thou wert triply crowned as the august Queen of Heaven by God the Father as His beloved Daughter, by God the Son as His dearest Mother, and by God the Holy Ghost as His chosen Spouse; the most perfect adorer of the Blessed Trinity, pleading our cause as our most powerful and merciful Mother, through thee. I humbly pray:

Our Father, 10 Hail Marys, Glory be to the Father.

I bind these full blown roses with a petition for the virtue of **Union with thee** and humbly lay this bouquet at thy feet.

Spiritual Communion

MY JESUS, really present in the most holy Sacrament of the Altar, since I cannot now receive Thee under the sacramental veil, I beseech Thee, with a heart full of love and longing, to come spiritually into my soul through the immaculate heart of Thy most holy Mother, and abide with me forever.

Thou in me,
And I in Thee,
In Time and in Eternity,
In Mary.

In petition

Sweet Mother Mary, I offer thee this Spiritual Communion to bind my bouquets in a wreath to place upon thy brow. O my Mother! look with favor upon my gift, and in thy love obtain for me (specify request) Hail, Mary, etc.

In thanksgiving

Sweet Mother Mary, I offer thee this Spiritual Communion to bind my bouquets in a wreath to place upon thy brow in thanksgiving for (specify request) which thou in thy love hast obtained for me. Hail, Mary, etc.

Prayer

O God! Whose only begotten Son, by His life, death, and resurrection, has purchased for us the reward of eternal life; grant, we beseech Thee, that, meditating upon these mysteries of the Most Holy Rosary of the Blessed Virgin Mary, we may imitate what they contain and obtain what they promise. Through the same Christ our Lord. Amen. May the divine assistance remain always with us. And may the souls of the faithful departed, through the mercy of God, rest in peace. Amen. Holy Virgin, with thy loving Child, thy blessing give to us this day (night). In the name of the Father, and of the Son, and of the Holy Ghost. Amen.

Other Chaplet Prayers

Chaplet of the Twelve Privileges of Our Lady

In the Name of the FATHER and of the SON and of the HOLY GHOST. Amen.

V. O GOD, come to my assistance.
R. O LORD, make haste to help me.

Glory be to the FATHER....

HAIL to thee, purest, holiest Mother of JESUS.

We humbly pray thee, by thy predestination, whereby thou wast even from all eternity elected Mother of GOD; by thy Immaculate Conception, whereby thou wast conceived without stain of original sin; by thy most perfect resignation, whereby thou wast ever conformed to the will of GOD; and, lastly, by thy consummate holiness, whereby throughout thy whole life thou didst never commit one single fault: we pray thee to become our advocate with our LORD, that He may pardon our many sins, which are the cause of his wrath. And thou, O FATHER Almighty, by the merits of these privileges vouchsafed to this thy well-beloved Daughter, hear her supplications for us, and pardon us, her clients.

Spare, O LORD, spare thy people.
PATER once, Ave four times, Gloria once.
By thy holy and Immaculate Conception deliver us, glorious Virgin Mary.

HAIL to thee, purest, holiest Mother of JESUS.

We humbly pray thee, by the most holy Annunciation, when thou didst conceive the Divine Word in thy womb; by thy most happy delivery, in which thou didst experience no pain; by thy perpetual virginity, which thou didst unite with the fruitfulness of a mother; and, lastly, by the bitter martyrdom which thou didst undergo in our SAVIOUR'S death: we pray thee to become our mediatrix, that we may reap the fruit of the Precious Blood of thy Son. And Thou, O Divine Son, by the merit of these privileges granted to thy well-beloved Mother, hear her supplications, and pardon us, her clients.

Spare, O LORD, spare thy people.
PATER once, Ave four times, Gloria once.
By thy holy and Immaculate Conception deliver us, glorious Virgin Mary.

HAIL to thee, purest, holiest Mother of JESUS.

We humbly pray thee, by the joys which thou didst feel in thy heart at the Resurrection and Ascension of JESUS CHRIST; by thy Assumption into Heaven, whereby thou wast exalted above all the Choirs of the Angels; by the glory which GOD has given thee to be Queen of all saints; and, lastly, by that most powerful intercession, where by thou art able to obtain all that thou dost desire: we pray thee, obtain for us true love of GOD. And Thou, O HOLY SPIRIT, by the merits of these privileges of thy well-beloved Spouse, hear her supplications, and pardon us her clients. Amen.

Spare, O LORD, spare thy people.
PATER once, Ave four times, Gloria once.
By thy holy and Immaculate Conception deliver us, glorious Virgin Mary.

Antiphon. Thy Conception, Virgin Mother of GOD, brought joy to the whole world, for of thee was born the Sun of Justice, CHRIST our GOD, who, loosing the curse, bestowed the blessing, and, confounding death, gave unto us eternal life.

V. In thy Conception, Virgin Mary, thou wast Immaculate.
R. Pray to the FATHER for us, whose SON JESUS, conceived by the HOLY GHOST, thou didst bring forth.

Let us pray. GOD of mercy, GOD of pity, GOD of tenderness, who, pitying the affliction of thy people, didst say to the angel smiting them, "Withhold thy hand"; for the love of thy glorious Mother, at whose precious breast thou didst sweetly find an antidote to the venom of our sins, bestow on us the help of thy grace, that we may be freed from all evil, and mercifully protected from every onset of destruction. Who livest and reignest for ever and ever.

R. Amen.

Enchiridion Sanctissimi Rosarii

Rosary of the Seven Dolours

This Chaplet consists of seven divisions, in memory of our Lady's seven sorrows, on which we are to meditate, if we can, saying the *Pater noster* once and the *Ave Maria* seven times at each division, then ending with *Ave* thrice in honour of our Lady's tears.

Way of Saying the Chaplet

Act of Contrition

O MY LORD, Thou who alone art most worthy of my love, behold me standing before thy Divine Presence utterly overwhelmed by the thought of the many grievous injuries I have done Thee. I ask thy pardon for them with my whole heart, repenting of them purely for love of Thee, and at the thought of thy great goodness hating and loathing them above every evil of this life. As I would rather have died a thousand times than have offended Thee, so now I am most firmly resolved to die a thousand deaths rather than offend Thee again. My crucified JESUS, I firmly purpose to cleanse my soul as soon as possible by thy most Precious Blood in the Sacrament of Penance. And thou, most tender Virgin, Mother of mercy and Refuge of sinners, do thou obtain for me by virtue of thy bitter pains, the pardon of sin which I desire; whilst, praying according to the mind of so many holy Pontiffs in order to obtain the Indulgences granted to this thy holy Rosary, I hope thereby to obtain remission of all pains due to my sins.

With this confidence in my heart, I meditate on the *First* Sorrow, when Mary, Virgin Mother of my GOD, presented JESUS her only Son in the Temple, laid Him in the arms of holy and aged Simeon, and heard his prophetic word, *"The sword of grief shall pierce thy soul,"* foretelling thereby the Passion and Death of her Son JESUS. PATER *once*, Ave *seven times*.

The *Second* Sorrow of the Blessed Virgin was when she was obliged to fly into Egypt by reason of the persecution of cruel Herod, who impiously sought to slay her well-beloved Son. PATER *once*, Ave *seven times.*

The *Third* Sorrow of the Blessed Virgin was when, after having gone up to Jerusalem at the Paschal Feast with Joseph her spouse and JESUS her beloved Son, she lost Him on the way back to her poor house, and for three days bewailed the loss of her only Love. PATER *once*, Ave *seven times.*

The *Fourth* Sorrow of the Blessed Virgin was when she met her dear Son JESUS carrying to Mount Calvary on his tender shoulders the heavy Cross whereon He was to be crucified for our salvation. PATER *once*, Ave *seven times.*

The *Fifth* Sorrow of the Blessed Virgin was when she saw her Son JESUS raised upon the hard tree of the Cross, and blood flowing from every part of his sacred Body, and then beheld Him die after three hours agony. PATER *once*, Ave *seven times.*

The *Sixth* Sorrow of the Blessed Virgin was when she saw the lance pierce the sacred Side of JESUS, her beloved Son, the nails withdrawn, and his holy Body laid in her purest bosom. PATER *once*, Ave *seven times.*

The *Seventh* and last Sorrow of the Blessed Virgin, Queen and Advocate of us, her servants, miserable sinners, was when she saw the holy Body of her Son buried in the grave. PATER *once*, Ave *seven times.*

Then say Ave *thrice in veneration of the tears which Mary shed in her sorrows, to obtain thereby true sorrow for sins and the holy Indulgences attached to this pious exercise.*

V. Pray for us, Virgin most sorrowful.
R. That we may be made worthy of the promises of CHRIST.

Let us pray.

GRANT, we beseech Thee, O LORD JESUS CHRIST, that the most blessed Virgin Mary, thy Mother, may intercede for us before the throne of thy mercy, now and at the hour of our death, whose most holy soul was transfixed with the sword of sorrow in the hour of thine own Passion. Through Thee, JESUS CHRIST, SAVIOUR of the world, who livest and reignest, *etc.* Amen.

Chaplet of the Immaculate Conception

In the name of the FATHER and of the SON and of the HOLY GHOST. Amen.

First Set of Beads.
Blessed be the Holy and Immaculate Conception of the most Blessed Virgin Mary.
PATER once, *Ave* four times and *Gloria* once.

Second Set.
Blessed be the Holy and Immaculate Conception of the most Blessed Virgin Mary.
PATER once, *Ave* four times and *Gloria* once.

Third Set.
Blessed be the Holy and Immaculate Conception of the most Blessed Virgin Mary.
PATER once, *Ave* four times and *Gloria* once.

Chaplet of the Immaculate Heart of Mary

V. O GOD, come to our assistance.
R. O LORD, make haste to help us.

V. Glory be to the FATHER, and the SON, and to the HOLY GHOST.
R. As it was in the beginning, is now, and ever shall be, world without end. Amen.

I

IMMACULATE Virgin, who, conceived without sin, didst direct every movement of thy pure heart to GOD, ever the object of thy love, and who wast ever most submissive to his will, obtain for me the grace to hate sin with my whole heart, and to learn of thee to live in perfect resignation to the will of GOD.

PATER *once*, Ave *seven times.*

Heart of Mary, pierced with grief, set my heart on fire with the love of GOD.

II

Mary, I wonder at thy deep humility when thy blessed heart was troubled at the gracious message brought thee by Gabriel the Archangel how that thou wast chosen to be Mother of the SON of GOD Most High and didst still proclaim thyself his humble handmaid; in great confusion at my pride, I ask thee for the grace of a contrite and humble heart, that, knowing my own misery, I may obtain that crown of glory promised to those who are truly humble of heart.

PATER *once*, Ave *seven times.*

Heart of Mary, pierced with grief, set my heart on fire with the love of GOD.

III

Sweetest Heart or Mary, precious treasury, wherein the Blessed Virgin kept the words of JESUS whilst she thought on the high mysteries which she had heard from the lips of her Son, and whereby she learned to live for GOD alone; how does the coldness of my heart confound me! Dearest Mother, obtain for me grace so to meditate within my heart upon the holy law of GOD, that I may strive to follow thee in the fervent practice of every Christian virtue.

PATER *once*, Ave *seven times*.

Heart of Mary, pierced with grief, set my heart on fire with the love of GOD.

IV

Glorious Queen of Martyrs, whose sacred heart was cruelly transfixed in the bitter Passion of thy Son by the sword foretold by the holy old man, Simeon, obtain for my heart true courage and a holy patience to bear well the troubles and adversities of this miserable life, and, by crucifying my flesh with its desires in following the mortification of the Cross, to show myself truly thy son.

PATER *once*, Ave *seven times*.

Heart of Mary, pierced with grief, set my heart on fire with the love of GOD.

V

O Mary, Mystic Rose, whose loving heart, burning with the living fire of charity, accepted us for thy children at the foot of the Cross, whereby thou didst become our most tender Mother; make me feel the sweetness of thy maternal heart, and thy power with JESUS in all the perils of this mortal life, and especially in the terrible hour of death, that so my heart, united with thine own, may love JESUS now and throughout all ages. Amen.

PATER *once*, Ave *seven times*.

Heart of Mary, pierced with grief, set my heart on fire with the love of GOD.

Let us entreat the Most Sacred Heart of JESUS to inflame us with his holy love.

O DIVINE Heart of JESUS, I consecrate myself to Thee, full of deep gratitude for the many blessings I have received, and daily receive, from thy infinite charity. I thank Thee with my whole heart for having also vouchsafed to give me thine own Mother to be my Mother, consigning me to her in the person of the beloved Disciple. Grant unto me that my heart may ever burn with this love of Thee, and so may find in Thee its peace, its refuge and its happiness.

The Franciscan Crown or Seraphic Rosary

The Franciscan Crown (or Seraphic Rosary) is a rosary consisting of seven decades in commemoration of the Seven Joys of the Virgin, namely, the Annunciation, the Visitation, the Nativity of Jesus, the Adoration of the Magi, the Finding in the Temple, the Resurrection of Jesus, and finally, either or both the Assumption of Mary and the Coronation of the Virgin. Devotion to the seven joys of Mary is found in a variety of forms and communities. It is especially popular with the Franciscans, Cistercians, and the Annunciades of St. Joan of France. The devotion was granted many indulgences by different Popes, becoming the most heavily indulgenced devotion in the Church. Whereas other rosaries required blessed beads to be used in order for any associated indulgences to be received it was unnecessary for a Franciscan rosary to have been blessed or even to use beads at all in specific instances.

The Franciscan Crown has variously been called the Franciscan Rosary, the Seraphic Rosary or the Rosary of the Seven Joys of Our Lady. The "Seven Joys" is a devotion that recalls seven joyful episodes in the life of the Blessed Virgin Mary. The practice originated among the Franciscans in early 15th-century Italy. The themes resemble the 12th-century Gaudes, Latin praises that ask Mary to rejoice because God has favored her in various ways.

The Franciscan historian, Father Luke Wadding (1588-1657) dates the origin of the Franciscan Crown to the year 1422. In 1442 an apparition of the Blessed Virgin Mary took place in Assisi, to a Franciscan novice named James. As a child, he had the custom of offering daily the Virgin Mary a crown of roses. When he entered the Friars Minor, he became distressed that he would no longer be able to offer this gift. The Blessed Virgin appeared to him to give him comfort and showed him another daily offering that he might do: to pray every day seven decades of Hail Marys, meditating between each decade on one of the seven joys that she had experienced in her life. Friar James began this devotion, but one day the Director of Novices saw him praying and an angel with him who was weaving a crown of roses, placing a lily of gold between each of the ten roses. When the novice had finished praying, the angel placed the crown upon him. The Director asked Friar James what this vision meant.

Enchiridion Sanctissimi Rosarii

After hearing the explanation, he told the other friars and soon this devotion spread throughout the Franciscan family.

Among the Friars Minor, the promotion of this devotion is attributed to St. Bonaventure, Bl. Cherubin of Spoleto, St. John Capistran, Pelbart of Temesvár, and St. Bernadine of Siena to mention a few. St. Bernadine is also said to have had a vision of the Virgin Mary when he was meditating on the seven joys of Mary.

V. O God, come to my assistance.

R. O Lord, make haste to help me.

Glory be.

First joy of Mary at her Annunciation and Divine Maternity.

Pater, ten Aves, Gloria

Second joy of Mary at her Visit to St. Elizabeth.

Pater, ten Aves, Gloria.

Third joy of Mary at the Birth of Jesus.

Pater, ten Aves, Gloria.

Fourth joy of Mary on the Adoration of the Magi.

Pater, ten Aves, Gloria.

Fifth joy of Mary on finding Jesus in the Temple, after having lost Him, where He was disputing with the doctors.

Pater, ten Aves, Gloria.

Sixth joy of Mary at the glorious Resurrection of her Divine Son.

Pater, ten Aves, Gloria.

Seventh joy of Mary on her Assumption into heaven, in body and soul.

Pater, ten Aves, Gloria.

Two Aves are still further recited; and then a Pater and an Ave for the Sovereign Pontiff.

The Rosary is concluded with the following prayers:

V. In thy Conception, O Virgin Mary, thou wast immaculate.

R. Pray for us to the Father, whose Son thou didst bring forth.

Let us pray. O God, who didst prepare for thy Son a worthy habitation, by the Immaculate Conception of the Blessed Virgin Mary, we beseech Thee that, as Thou didst preserve her from every stain of sin, through the merits of the preordained atonement of Jesus Christ, so Thou wouldst grant that we also may come without spot to Thee. Through the same Christ our Lord. Amen.

Enchiridion Sanctissimi Rosarii

The Rule of the Mother of God of St Seraphim of Sarov

Saint Seraphim of Sarov (1 August 1754 – 14 January 1833), is one of the most renowned Russian monks and mystics in the Orthodox Church. He is generally considered the greatest of the 19th century startsy (elders) and, arguably, the first. He is remembered for extending the monastic teachings of contemplation, theoria and self-denial to the layperson, and taught that the purpose of the Christian life was to acquire the Holy Spirit. Seraphim was glorified (canonized) by the Russian Orthodox Church in 1903. The date of his death is his major feast day. Reverence for him is not limited to the Orthodox; Pope John Paul II referred to him as a saint in his book, <u>Crossing the Threshold of Hope</u>.

St Seraphim of Sarov, prayed the "Rule of the Mother of God". It is similar to the Western Marian Rosary and according to some traditions it even predates the Rosary's introduction to St. Dominic in the 13th Century.

Fr. Zosima, a spiritual son of St. Seraphim, wrote a description of the Rule in a letter:

"...I forgot to give you a piece of advice vital for salvation. Say the O Hail, Mother of God and Virgin one hundred and fifty times, and this prayer will lead you on the way to salvation. This rule was given by the Mother of God herself in about the eighth century, and at one time all Christians fulfilled it. We Orthodox have forgotten about it, and St. Seraphim has reminded me of this Rule. In my hands I have a hand-written book from the cell of St. Seraphim, containing a description of the many miracles which took place through praying to the Mother of God and especially through saying one hundred and fifty times the O Hail, Mother of God and Virgin. If, being unaccustomed to it, it is difficult to master one hundred and fifty repetitions daily, say it fifty times at first. After every ten repetitions say the Our Father

once and 'Open unto us the doors of thy loving-kindness...' Whomever he spoke to about this miracle-working Rule remained grateful to him."

What did the form of this Rule look like? In addition to what is described above it was made up of the "Usual Beginning" of the Trisagion Prayers and the Symbol of the Faith, followed by 150 prayers broken into 15 decades with prayers before and after each decade. Each decade was accompanied by a meditation. These meditations are very similar to the Mysteries of the Western Marian Rosary.

The pre-decade prayers were taught to several disciples, but St Seraphim kept secret his after-decade prayers. The after-decade prayers included here are those of a disciple of the Saint, a holy nun, except for the tenth, thirteenth, fourteenth, and fifteenth, which were incomplete or lost, and have been reconstructed.

In the Name of the Father, the Son, and the Holy Spirit. Amen.

God be merciful to me, a sinner.

Glory to Thee, our God, glory to Thee.

O Heavenly King, Comforter, Spirit of Truth, Who art everywhere present and fillest all things, O Treasury of every good and Bestower of life: come and dwell in us, and cleanse us from every stain, and save our souls, O Good One.

Holy God, Holy Mighty, Holy Immortal, have mercy on us. (Three times.)

Glory to the Father, and to the Son, and to the Holy Spirit, both now and ever and unto the ages of ages. Amen.

O Most Holy Trinity, have mercy on us. O Lord, blot out our sins. O Master, pardon our iniquities. O Holy One, visit and heal our infirmities, for Thy Name's sake.

Lord, have mercy. (Three times.)

Glory to the Father, and to the Son, and to the Holy Spirit, both now and ever and unto the ages of ages. Amen.

Our Father, Who art in heaven, hallowed be Thy Name. Thy kingdom come, Thy will be done on earth as it is in heaven. Give us this day our daily bread, and forgive us our trespasses as we forgive those who trespass against us. And lead us not into temptation, but deliver us from evil.

Lord, have mercy. (Three times.)

Glory to the Father, and to the Son, and to the Holy Spirit, both now and ever and unto the ages of ages. Amen.

O come let us worship God our King. O come, let us worship and fall down before Christ our King and God. O come, let us worship and fall down before Christ Himself, our King and God.

I believe in one God, Father Almighty, Creator of heaven and earth, and of all things visible and invisible. And in one Lord Jesus Christ, the only-begotten Son of God, begotten of the Father before all ages; Light of Light, true God of true God, begotten, not created, of one essence with the Father, through Whom all things were made. Who for us men and for our salvation came down from heaven and was incarnate of the Holy Spirit and the Virgin Mary and became man. He was crucified for us under Pontius Pilate, and suffered and was buried; And He rose on the third day, according to the Scriptures. He ascended into heaven and is seated at the right hand of the Father; And He will come again with glory to judge the living and dead. His kingdom shall have no end. And in the Holy Spirit, the Lord, the Creator of life, Who proceeds from the Father, Who together with the Father and the Son is worshipped and glorified, Who spoke through the prophets. In one, holy, catholic, and apostolic Church. I confess one baptism for the forgiveness of sins. I look for the resurrection of the dead, and the life of the age to come. Amen.

O Lord, open my lips, and my mouth shall proclaim Your praise.

First decade: Let us remember the birth of the Mother of God. Let us pray for mothers, fathers, and children.

Rejoice, O Virgin Mother of God Mary, full of grace, the Lord is with thee. Blessed art thou amongst women and blessed is the fruit of thy womb, for thou hast borne the Savior of our souls. (Ten times)

After: Our Lady, Blessed Mother of God, save and preserve your servants (names of parents, relatives, friends), increase their faith and repentance, and when they die give them rest with the saints in your eternal glory.

Our Father, Who art in heaven, hallowed be Thy Name. Thy kingdom come, Thy will be done on earth as it is in heaven. Give us this day our daily bread, and forgive us our trespasses as we forgive those who trespass against us. And lead us not into temptation, but deliver us from evil.

Open unto us the door of thy loving-kindness, O most blessed Mother of God. As we set our hope in thee, let us not be confounded, but through thee may we be delivered from all adversities. For thou art the salvation of the Christian race.

Second decade: Let us remember the feast of the Presentation of the Blessed Virgin and Mother of God. Let us pray for those who have lost their way and fallen away from the church.

Rejoice, O Virgin Mother of God . . . . (Ten times)

After: Our Lady, Blessed Mother of God, save and preserve and unite or re-unite to the Holy Orthodox Church your servants who have lost their path and fallen away (names).

Our Father.... Open unto us....

Third decade: Let us remember the Annunciation of the Blessed Mother of God. Let us pray for the soothing of sorrows and the consolation of those who grieve.

Rejoice, O Virgin Mother of God.... (Ten times)

After: Our Lady, Blessed Mother of God, soothe our sorrows and send consolation to your servants who are grieving and ill (names).

Our Father.... Open unto us....

Fourth decade: Let us remember the meeting of the Blessed Virgin with the righteous Elizabeth. Let us pray for the reunion of the separated, for those whose dear ones or children are living away from them or missing.

Rejoice, O Virgin Mother of God.... (Ten times)

After: Our Lady, Blessed Mother of God, unite your servants who are separated.

Our Father.... Open unto us....

Fifth decade: Let us remember the Birth of Christ. Let us pray for the rebirth of souls, for new life in Christ.

Rejoice, O Virgin Mother of God.... (Ten times)

After: Our Lady, Blessed Mother of God, grant unto me, who has been baptized in Christ, to be clothed in Christ.

Our Father.... Open unto us....

Sixth decade: Let us remember the Feast of the Purification of the Lord, and the words uttered by St. Simeon: Yea, a sword shall pierce through thy own soul also. Let us pray that the Mother of God will meet our souls at the hour of our death, and will contrive that we receive the Holy Sacrament with our last breath, and will lead our souls through the terrible torments.

Rejoice, O Virgin Mother of God.... (Ten times)

After: Our Lady, Blessed Mother of God, let me receive the Holy Sacrament with my last breath, and lead my soul yourself through the terrible torments.

Our Father.... Open unto us....

Seventh decade: Let us remember the flight of the Mother of God with the God-Child into Egypt. Let us pray that the Mother of God will help us avoid temptation in this life and deliver us from misfortunes.

Rejoice, O Virgin Mother of God.... (Ten times)

After: Our Lady, Blessed Mother of God, help me avoid temptation in this life and deliver me from misfortunes.

Our Father.... Open unto us....

Eighth decade: Let us remember the disappearance of the twelve-year old boy Jesus in Jerusalem and the sorrow of the Mother of God on this account. Let us pray, begging the Mother of God for the constant repetition of the Jesus Prayer.

Rejoice, O Virgin Mother of God.... (Ten times)

After: Our Lady, Blessed Mother of God, grant to me the unceasing Jesus Prayer.

Our Father . . . . Open unto us . . . .

Ninth decade: Let us remember the miracle performed in Cana of Galilee, when the Lord turned water into wine at the words of the Mother of God: They have no wine. Let us ask the Mother of God for help in our affairs and deliverance from need.

Rejoice, O Virgin Mother of God . . . . (Ten times)

After: Our Lady, Blessed Mother of God, help me in all my affairs and deliver me from every need and sorrow.

Our Father . . . . Open unto us . . . .

Tenth decade: Let us remember the Mother of God standing at the Cross of the Lord, when grief pierced through her heart like a sword. Let us pray to the Mother of God for the strengthening of our souls and the banishment of despondency.

Rejoice, O Virgin Mother of God . . . . (Ten times)

After: Our Lady, Blessed Mother of God, strengthen my soul and banish my despair.

Our Father . . . . Open unto us . . . .

Eleventh decade: Let us remember the Resurrection of Christ and ask the Mother of God in prayer to resurrect our souls and give us new courage for spiritual feats.

Rejoice, O Virgin Mother of God . . . . (Ten times)

After: Our Lady, Blessed Mother of God, resurrect my soul and give me constant readiness for spiritual feats.

Our Father.... Open unto us....

Twelfth decade: Let us remember the Ascension of Christ, at which the Mother of God was present. Let us pray and ask the Queen of Heaven to raise up our souls from earthly and worldly amusements and direct them to striving for higher things.

Rejoice, O Virgin Mother of God.... (Ten times)

After: Our Lady, Blessed Mother of God, deliver me from worldly thoughts and give me a mind and heart striving towards the salvation of my soul.

Our Father.... Open unto us....

Thirteenth decade: Let us remember the Upper Room and the descent of the Holy Spirit on the Apostles and the Mother of God.

Let us pray: Create in me a clean heart, O God; and renew a right spirit within me. Cast me not away from thy presence; and take not thy holy spirit from me (Psalm 51).

Rejoice, O Virgin Mother of God.... (Ten times)

After: Our Lady, Blessed Mother of God, make me a clean temple in which God's Holy Spirit will ever dwell.

Our Father.... Open unto us....

Fourteenth decade: Let us remember the Dormition of the Blessed Mother of God, and ask for a peaceful and serene end.

Rejoice, O Virgin Mother of God.... (Ten times)

After: Our Lady, Blessed Mother of God, grant me a peaceful and serene end.

Our Father.... Open unto us....

Fifteenth decade: Let us remember the glory of the Mother of God, with which the Lord crowned her after her removal from earth to heaven. Let us pray to the Queen of Heaven not to abandon the faithful who are on earth but to defend them from every evil, covering them with her honorable and protecting veil.

Rejoice, O Virgin Mother of God.... (Ten times)

After: Our Lady, Blessed Mother of God, preserve me from every evil and cover me with your honorable protecting veil.

Our Father.... Open unto us....

It is truly meet to bless thee, O Theotokos, ever blessed and most pure, and the Mother of God. More honorable than the Cherubim, and beyond compare more glorious than the Seraphim, who without corruption gavest birth to God the Word, the very Theotokos, thee do we magnify.

Glory to the Father, and to the Son, and to the Holy Spirit, both now and ever and unto the ages of ages. Amen.

Lord, have mercy. (Three times.)

O Lord Jesus Christ, Son of God, for the sake of the prayers of Thy most pure Mother, our holy and God-bearing fathers, and all the saints, have mercy on us. Amen.

Enchiridion Sanctissimi Rosarii

A Manual of the Most Holy Rosary

Meditation for the Feast of The Holy Rosary, 5 October 1879
Blessed John Henry Cardinal Newman

Newman had no text for this short sermon. What we have here is the report given in a newspaper and written from notes taken at the time of preaching. It was delivered on Sunday, 5 October 1879. The Cardinal was then 78 years of age, and was speaking "from his heart" to the boys at Oscott College, in the north of Birmingham. As it was the Feast of the Holy Rosary, he preached on the text: "They found Mary and Joseph, and the Infant lying in a manger" (Lk 2,16).

Five months previously, Newman was in Rome to be created Cardinal by Pope Leo XIII.

I am not going to make a long address to you, my dear boys, or say anything that you have not often heard before from your superiors, for I know well in what good hands you are, and I know that their instructions come to you with greater force than any you can have from a stranger. If I speak to you at all, it is because I have lately come from the Holy Father, and am, in some sort, his representative, and so in the years to come you may remember that you saw me today and heard me speak in his name, and remember it to your profit.

You know that today we keep the Feast of the Holy Rosary, and I propose to say to you what occurs to me on this great subject. You know how that devotion came about; how, at a time when heresy was very widespread, and had called in the aid of sophistry, that can so powerfully aid infidelity against religion, God inspired St Dominic to institute and spread this devotion. It seems so simple and easy, but you know God chooses the small things of the world to humble the great (I Cor. 1,27-28).

Of course it was first of all for the poor and simple, but not for them only, for everyone who has practised the devotion knows that there is in it a soothing sweetness that there is in nothing else. It is difficult to know God by your own power, because He is incomprehensible. He is invisible to begin with, and therefore incomprehensible. We can in some way know Him, for even among the heathens there were some who had learned many truths about Him; but even they found it hard to conform their lives to their knowledge of Him. And so in His mercy He has given us a revelation of Himself by coming amongst us, to be one of ourselves, with all the relations and qualities of humanity, to gain us over. He came down from Heaven and dwelt amongst us, and died for us. All these things are in the Creed, which contains the chief things that He has revealed to us about Himself.

Now the great power of the Rosary lies in this, that it makes the Creed into a prayer; of course, the Creed is in some sense a prayer and a great act of homage to God; but the Rosary gives us the great truths of His life and death to meditate upon, and brings them nearer to our hearts. And so we contemplate all the great mysteries of His life and His birth in the manger; and so too the mysteries of His suffering and His glorified life. But even Christians, with all their knowledge of God, have usually more awe than love of Him, and the special virtue of the Rosary lies in the special way in which it looks at these mysteries; for with all our thoughts of Him are mingled thoughts of His Mother, and in the relations between Mother and Son we have set before us the Holy Family, the home in which God lived. Now the family is, even humanly considered, a sacred thing; how much more the family bound together by supernatural ties, and, above all, that in which God dwelt with His Blessed Mother.

This is what I should most wish you to remember in future years. For you will all of you have to go out into the world, and going out into the world means leaving home; and, my dear boys, you don't know what the world is now. You look forward to the time when you will go out into the world, and it seems to you very bright and full of promise. It is not wrong for you to look forward to that time; but most men who know the world find it a world of great trouble, and disappointments, and even misery. If it turns out so to you, seek a home in the Holy Family that you think about in the mysteries of the Rosary. Schoolboys know the difference between school and home. You often hear grown-up people say that the happiest time of their life was that passed at school but when they were at school you know they had a happier time, which was when they went home; that shows there is a good in home which cannot be found elsewhere. So that even if the world should actually prove to be all that you now fancy it, if it should bring you all that you could wish, yet you ought to have in the Holy Family a home with a holiness and sweetness about it that cannot be found elsewhere.

This is, my dear boys, what I most earnestly ask you. I ask you when you go out into the world, as you soon must, to make the Holy Family your home, to which you may turn from all the sorrow and care of the world and find a solace, a compensation, and a refuge. And this I say to you, not as if I should speak to you again, not as if I had of myself any claim upon you, but with the claims of the Holy Father, whose representative I am, and in the hope that in the days to come you will remember that I came amongst you and said it to you. And when I speak of the Holy Family I do not mean Our Lord and Our Lady only, but St Joseph too; for as we cannot separate Our Lord from His Mother, so we cannot separate St Joseph from them both; for who but he was their protector in all the scenes of Our Lord's early life? And with Joseph must be included St Elizabeth and St John, whom we naturally think of as part of the Holy Family; we read of them together and see them in pictures together. May you, my dear boys, throughout your life find a home in the Holy Family; the home of Our Lord and His Blessed Mother, St Joseph, St Elizabeth, and St John.

Enchiridion Sanctissimi Rosarii

A Manual of the Most Holy Rosary

The Secret of the Rosary by St. Louis de Montfort

A White Rose

1. Dear ministers of the most high God, you my fellow priests who preach the truth of God and who teach the gospel to all nations, let me give you this little book as a white rose that I would like you to keep. The truths contained in it are set forth in a very simple and straightforward manner, as you will see.

Please keep them in your heart so that you yourselves may make a practice of the Rosary and taste its fruits.

Please have them always on your lips too, so that you will always preach the Rosary and thus convert others by teaching them the excellence of this holy devotion.

I beg of you to beware of thinking of the Rosary as something of little importance - as do ignorant people, and even several great but proud scholars. Far from being insignificant, the Rosary is a priceless treasure which is inspired by God.

Almighty God has given it to you because he wants you to use it as a means to convert the most hardened sinners and the most obstinate heretics. He has attached to it grace in this life and glory in the next. The saints have said it faithfully and the Popes have endorsed it.

When the Holy Spirit has revealed this secret to a priest and director of souls, how blessed is that priest! For the vast majority of people fail to know this secret or else only know it superficially. If such a priest really understands this secret, he will say the Rosary each day and will encourage others to say it. God and his blessed Mother will pour abundant grace into his soul, so that he may become God's instrument for his glory; and his word, though simple, will do more good in one month than that of other preachers in several years.

2. Therefore, my dear brothers and fellow priests, it will not be enough for us to preach this devotion to others; we must practice it ourselves, for if we firmly believed in the importance of the holy Rosary but never said it ourselves, people could hardly be expected to act upon our advice, since no one can give what he does not have: "Jesus began to do and to teach." We ought to pattern ourselves on our Lord, who began practising what he preached. We ought to emulate St. Paul, who knew and preached nothing but Jesus crucified.

I could tell you at great length of the grace God has given me to know by experience the effectiveness of the preaching of the holy Rosary, and of how I have seen, with my own eyes, the most wonderful conversions it has brought about. I would gladly tell you all these things if I thought that it would move you to preach this beautiful devotion, in spite of the fact that priests are not in the habit of doing so these days. But instead of all this, I think it will be quite enough for this little summary that I am writing if I tell you a few ancient but authentic stories about the holy Rosary. These excerpts really go to prove what I have outlined for the faithful.

A Red Rose

3. Poor men and women who are sinners, I, a greater sinner than you, wish to give you this rose, a crimson one, because the precious blood of our Lord has fallen upon it. Please God that it may bring true fragrance into your lives - but above all, may it save you from the danger that you are in. Every day unbelievers and un-repentant sinners cry, "Let us crown ourselves with roses." But our cry should be, "Let us crown ourselves with the roses of the holy Rosary."

How different are theirs from ours! Their roses are pleasures of the flesh, worldly honours and passing riches which wilt and decay in no time, but ours, which are the Our Father and Hail Mary which we have said devoutly over and over again, and to which we have added good penitential acts, will never wilt or die, and they will be just as exquisite thousands of years from now as they are today.

On the contrary, sinners' roses only look like roses, while in point of fact they are cruel thorns which prick them during life by giving them pangs of conscience, at their death they pierce them with bitter regret and, still worse, in eternity they turn to burning shafts of anger and despair. But if our roses have thorns, they are the thorns of Jesus Christ, who changes them into roses. If our roses prick us, it is only for a short time, and only in order to cure the illness of sin and to save our souls.

4. So by all means we should eagerly crown ourselves with these roses from heaven, and recite the entire Rosary every day, that is to say, three rosaries each of five decades, which are like three little wreaths or crowns of flowers. There are two reasons for doing this: first of all, to honour the three crowns of Jesus and Mary - Jesus' crown of grace at the time of his Incarnation, his crown of thorns during his passion, and his crown of glory in heaven, and of course the three-fold crown which the Blessed Trinity gave Mary in heaven. Secondly, we should do this so that we ourselves may receive three crowns from Jesus and Mary, the first a crown of merit during our lifetime; the second, a crown of peace at our death; and the third, a crown of glory in heaven.

If you say the Rosary faithfully until death, I do assure you that, in spite of the gravity of your sins "you shall receive a never-fading crown of glory." Even if you are on the brink of damnation, even if you have one foot in hell, even if you have sold your soul to the devil as sorcerers do who practice black magic, and even if you are a heretic as obstinate as a devil, sooner or later you will be converted and will amend your life and save your soul, if - and mark well what I say - if you say the Rosary devoutly every day until death for the purpose of knowing the truth and obtaining contrition and pardon for your sins.

In this book there are several stories of great sinners who were converted through the power of the Rosary. Please read and meditate upon them.

A Mystical Rose Tree

5. Good and devout souls, who walk in the light of the Holy Spirit, I do not think you will mind my giving you this little mystical rose tree which comes straight from heaven and which is to be planted in the garden of your soul. It cannot possibly harm the sweet-smelling flowers of your contemplations; for it is a heavenly tree and its scent is very pleasant. It will not in the least interfere with your carefully planned flower-beds; for, being itself all pure and well-ordered, it inclines all to order and purity. If it is carefully watered and properly attended to every day, it will grow to such a marvellous height, and its branches will have such a wide span that, far from hindering your other devotions, it will maintain and perfect them. Of course, you understand what I mean, since you are spiritually minded; this mystical rose tree is Jesus and Mary in life, death and eternity.

6. Its green leaves are the Joyful Mysteries, the thorns the Sorrowful ones, and the flowers the Glorious Mysteries of Jesus and Mary. The buds are the childhood of Jesus and Mary, and the open blooms show us both of them in their sufferings, and the full-blown roses symbolize Jesus and Mary in their triumph and glory.

A rose delights us because of its beauty: so here we have Jesus and Mary in the Joyful Mysteries. Its thorns are sharp, and they prick, which makes us think of them in the Sorrowful Mysteries, and last of all, its perfume is so sweet that everyone loves it, and this fragrance symbolizes their Glorious Mysteries.

So please do not scorn this beautiful and heavenly tree, but plant it with your own hands in the garden of your soul, by making the resolution to say your Rosary every day. By saying it daily and by doing good works you will be tending your tree, watering it, hoeing the earth around it. Eventually you will see that this little seed which I have given you, and which seems so small now, will grow into a tree so great that the birds of heaven, that is, predestinate and contemplative souls, will dwell in it and make their nests there. Its shade will shelter them from the scorching heat of the sun and its height will keep them safe from the wild beasts on the ground. And best of all, they will feed upon the tree's fruit, which is none other than our adorable Jesus, to whom be honour and glory forever and ever. Amen. God Alone

A Rosebud

7. Dear little friends, this beautiful rosebud is for you; it is one of the beads of your Rosary, and it may seem to you to be such a tiny thing. But if you only knew how precious this bead is! This wonderful bud will open out into a gorgeous rose if you say your Hail Mary really well.

Of course it would be too much to expect you to say the whole fifteen mysteries every day, but do say at least five mysteries, and say them properly with love and devotion. This Rosary will be your little wreath of roses, your crown for Jesus and Mary. Please pay attention to every word I have said, and listen carefully to a true story that I want to tell you, and that I would like you to remember.

8. Two little girls, who were sisters, were saying the Rosary very devoutly in front of their house. A beautiful lady suddenly appeared, walked towards the younger girl, who was only about six or seven, took her by the hand, and led her away. Her elder sister was very startled and looked for the little girl everywhere. At last, still not having found her, she went home weeping and told her parents that her sister had been kidnapped. For three whole days the poor father and mother sought the child without success.

At the end of the third day they found her at the front door looking extremely happy and pleased. Naturally they asked her where on earth she had been, and she told them that the lady to whom she had been saying the Rosary had taken her to a lovely place where she had given her delicious things to eat. She said that the lady had also given her a baby boy to hold, that he was very beautiful, and that she had kissed him again and again.

The father and mother, who had been converted to the Catholic faith only a short time before, sent at once for the Jesuit Father who had instructed them for their reception into the Church and who had also taught them devotion to the Rosary. They told him everything that had happened, and it was this priest himself who told me this story. It all took place in Paraguay.

So, dear children, imitate these little girls and say your Rosary every day as they always did. If you do this, you will earn the right to go to heaven to see Jesus and Mary. If it is not their wish that you should see them in this life, at any rate after you die you will see them for all eternity. Amen.

Therefore let all men, the learned and the ignorant, the just and the sinners, the great and the small, praise and honour Jesus and Mary night and day, by saying the holy Rosary. "Greet Mary who has laboured much among you."

FIRST DECADE
The surpassing merit of the Rosary as seen in its origin and name.

First Rose

9. The Rosary is made up of two things: mental prayer and vocal prayer. In the Rosary mental prayer is none other than meditation of the chief mysteries of the life, death and glory of Jesus Christ and of his blessed Mother. Vocal prayer consists in saying fifteen decades of the Hail Mary, each decade headed by an Our Father, while at the same time meditating on and contemplating the fifteen principal virtues which Jesus and Mary practised in the fifteen mysteries of the Rosary.

In the first five decades we must honour the five Joyful Mysteries and meditate on them; in the second five decades, the Sorrowful Mysteries; and in the third group of five, the Glorious Mysteries. So the Rosary is a blessed blending of mental and vocal prayer by which we honour and learn to imitate the mysteries and the virtues of the life, death, passion and glory of Jesus and Mary.

Second Rose

10. Since the Rosary is composed, principally and in substance, of the prayer of Christ and the Angelic Salutation, that is, the Our Father and the Hail Mary, it was without doubt the first prayer and the principal devotion of the faithful and has been in use all through the centuries, from the time of the apostles and disciples down to the present.

11. It was only in the year 1214, however, that the Church received the Rosary in its present form and according to the method we use today. It was given to the Church by St. Dominic, who had

received it from the Blessed Virgin as a means of converting the Albigensians and other sinners.

I will tell you the story of how he received it, which is found in the very well-known book De Dignitate Psalterii, by Blessed Alan de la Roche. Saint Dominic, seeing that the gravity of people's sins was hindering the conversion of the Albigensians, withdrew into a forest near Toulouse, where he prayed continuously for three days and three nights. During this time he did nothing but weep and do harsh penances in order to appease the anger of God. He used his discipline so much that his body was lacerated, and finally he fell into a coma.

At this point our Lady appeared to him, accompanied by three angels, and she said, "Dear Dominic, do you know which weapon the Blessed Trinity wants to use to reform the world?"

"Oh, my Lady," answered Saint Dominic, "you know far better than I do, because next to your Son Jesus Christ you have always been the chief instrument of our salvation."

Then our Lady replied, "I want you to know that, in this kind of warfare, the principal weapon has always been the Angelic Psalter, which is the foundation-stone of the New Testament. Therefore, if you want to reach these hardened souls and win them over to God, preach my Psalter."

So he arose, comforted, and burning with zeal for the conversion of the people in that district, he made straight for the cathedral. At once unseen angels rang the bells to gather the people together, and Saint Dominic began to preach.

At the very beginning of his sermon, an appalling storm broke out, the earth shook, the sun was darkened, and there was so much thunder and lightning that all were very much afraid. Even greater was their fear when, looking at a picture of our Lady exposed in a prominent place, they saw her raise her arms to heaven three times to call down God's vengeance upon them if they failed to be converted, to amend their lives, and seek the protection of the holy Mother of God.

God wished, by means of these supernatural phenomena, to spread the new devotion of the holy Rosary and to make it more widely known.

At last, at the prayer of Saint Dominic, the storm came to an end, and he went on preaching. So fervently and compellingly did he explain the importance and value of the Rosary that almost all the people of Toulouse embraced it and renounced their false beliefs. In a very short time a great improvement was seen in the town; people began leading Christian lives and gave up their former bad habits.

Third Rose

12. The miraculous way in which the devotion to the holy Rosary was established is something of a parallel to the way in which God gave his law to the world on Mount Sinai, and it obviously proves its value and importance.

Inspired by the Holy Spirit, instructed by the Blessed Virgin as well as by his own experience, Saint Dominic preached the Rosary for the rest of his life. He preached it by his example as well as by his sermons, in cities and in country places, to people of high station and low, before scholars and the uneducated, to Catholics and to heretics.

The Rosary, which he said every day, was his preparation for every sermon and his little tryst with our Lady immediately after preaching.

13. One day he had to preach at Notre Dame in Paris, and it happened to be the feast of St. John the Evangelist. He was in a little chapel behind the high altar prayerfully preparing his sermon by saying the Rosary, as he always did, when our Lady appeared to him and said: "Dominic, even though what you have planned to say may be very good, I am bringing you a much better sermon."

Saint Dominic took in his hands the book our Lady proffered, read the sermon carefully and, when he had understood it and meditated on it, he gave thanks to her.

When the time came, he went up into the pulpit and, in spite of the feast day, made no mention of Saint John other than to say that he had been found worthy to be the guardian of the Queen of Heaven. The congregation was made up of theologians and other eminent people, who were used to hearing unusual and polished discourses; but Saint Dominic told them that it was not his desire to give them a learned discourse, wise in the eyes of the world, but that he would speak in the simplicity of the Holy Spirit and with his forcefulness.

So he began preaching the Rosary and explained the Hail Mary word by word as he would to a group of children, and used the very simple illustrations which were in the book given him by our Lady.

14. Carthagena, the great scholar, quoting Blessed Alan de la Roche in De Dignitate Psalterii, describes how this took place.

"Blessed Alan writes that one day Father Dominic said to him in a vision, 'My son, it is good to preach; but there is always a danger of looking for praise rather than the salvation of souls. Listen carefully to what happened to me in Paris, so that you may be on your guard against this kind of mistake. I was to preach in the great church dedicated to the Blessed Virgin and I was particularly anxious to give a fine sermon, not out of pride, but because of the high intellectual stature of the congregation.

"'An hour before the time I had to preach, I was dutifully saying my Rosary - as I always did before giving a sermon - when I fell into ecstasy. I saw my beloved friend, the Mother of God, coming towards me with a book in her hand. "Dominic," she said, "your sermon for today may be very good indeed, but no matter how good it is, I have brought you one that is very much better."

"'Of course I was overjoyed, and I took the book and read every word of it. Just as our Lady had said, I found exactly the right things to say in my sermon, so I thanked her with all my heart.

"'When it was time to begin, I saw that the University of Paris had turned out in full force, as well as a large number of noblemen. They had all seen and heard of the great things that the good Lord had been doing through me.

"'I went up into the pulpit. It was the feast of Saint John the Evangelist but all I said about him was that he had been found worthy to be the guardian of the Queen of Heaven. Then I addressed the congregation:

"'My Lords and illustrious doctors of the University, you are accustomed to hearing learned sermons suited to your refined tastes. Now I do not want to speak to you in the scholarly language of human wisdom but, on the contrary, to show you the Spirit of God and his greatness.'"

Here ends the quotation from Blessed Alan, after which Carthagena goes on to say in his own words, "Then Saint Dominic explained the Angelic Salutation to them, using simple comparisons and examples from everyday life."

15. Blessed Alan, according to Carthagena, mentioned several other occasions when our Lord and our Lady appeared to Saint Dominic to urge him and inspire him to preach the Rosary more and more in order to wipe out sin and convert sinners and heretics.

In another passage Carthagena says, "Blessed Alan said our Lady revealed to him that, after she had appeared to Saint Dominic, her blessed Son appeared to him and said, 'Dominic, I rejoice to see that you are not relying on your own wisdom and that, rather than seek the empty praise of men, you are working with great humility for the salvation of souls.

"'But many priests want to preach thunderously against the worst kinds of sin at the very outset, failing to realize that before a sick person is given bitter medicine, he needs to be prepared by being put into the right frame of mind to really benefit by it.

"'That is why, before doing anything else, priests should try to kindle a love of prayer in people's hearts and especially a love of my Angelic Psalter. If only they would all start saying it and would really persevere, God in his mercy could hardly refuse to give them his grace. So I want you to preach my Rosary.'"

16. In another place Blessed Alan says, "All priests say a Hail Mary with the faithful before preaching, to ask for God's grace.' They do this because of a revelation that Saint Dominic had from our Lady.

'My son,' she said one day, 'do not be surprised that your sermons fail to bear the results you had hoped for. You are trying to cultivate a piece of ground which has not had any rain. Now when God planned to renew the face of the earth, he started by sending down rain from heaven - and this was the Angelic Salutation. In this way God reformed the world.

"'So when you give a sermon, urge people to say my Rosary, and in this way your words will bear much fruit for souls.'

"Saint Dominic lost no time in obeying, and from then on he exerted great influence by his sermons." (This last quotation is from "The Book of Miracles of the Holy Rosary," written in Italian, also found in Justin's works, Sermon 143.)

17. I have been very pleased to quote these well-known authors word for word for the benefit of those who might otherwise have doubts as to the marvellous power of the Rosary.

As long as priests followed Saint Dominic's example and preached devotion to the holy Rosary, piety and fervour thrived throughout the Christian world and in those religious orders which were devoted to the Rosary. But since people have neglected this gift from heaven, all kinds of sin and disorder have spread far and wide.

Fourth Rose

18. All things, even the holiest, are subject to change, especially when they are dependent on man's free will. It is hardly to be wondered at, then, that the Confraternity of the Holy Rosary only retained its first fervour for a century after it was instituted by Saint Dominic. After this it was like a thing buried and forgotten.

Doubtless, too, the wicked scheming and jealousy of the devil were largely responsible for getting people to neglect the Rosary, and thus block the flow of God's grace which it had drawn upon the world.

Thus, in 1349 God punished the whole of Europe with the most terrible plague that had ever been known. Starting in the east, it spread throughout Italy, Germany, France, Poland and Hungary, bringing desolation wherever it went, for out of a hundred men hardly one lived to tell the tale. Big cities, towns, villages and monasteries were almost completely deserted during the three years that the epidemic lasted.

This scourge of God was quickly followed by two others, the heresy of the Flagellants and a tragic schism in 1376.

19. Later on, when these trials were over, thanks to the mercy of God, our Lady told Blessed Alan to revive the former Confraternity of the Holy Rosary. Blessed Alan was one of the Dominican Fathers at the monastery at Dinan, in Brittany. He was an eminent theologian and a famous preacher. Our Lady chose him because, since the Confraternity had originally been started in that province, it was fitting that a Dominican from the same province should have the honour of re-establishing it.

Blessed Alan began this great work in 1460, after a special warning from our Lord. This is how he received that urgent message, as he himself tells it:

One day when he was offering Mass, our Lord, who wished to spur him on to preach the holy Rosary, spoke to him in the Sacred Host. "How can you crucify me again so soon?" Jesus said. "What did you say, Lord?" asked Blessed Alan, horrified. "You crucified me once before by your sins," answered Jesus, "and I would willingly be crucified again rather than have my Father offended by the sins you used to commit. You are crucifying me again now because you have all the learning and understanding that you need to preach my Mother's Rosary, and you are not doing it. If you only did that, you could teach many souls the right path and lead them away from sin. But you are not doing it, and so you yourself are guilty of the sins that they commit."

This terrible reproach made Blessed Alan solemnly resolve to preach the Rosary unceasingly.

20. Our Lady also said to him one day to inspire him to preach the Rosary more and more, "You were a great sinner in your youth, but I obtained the grace of your conversion from my Son. Had such a thing been possible, I would have liked to have gone through all kinds of suffering to save you, because converted sinners are a glory to me. And I would have done that also to make you worthy of preaching my Rosary far and wide."

Saint Dominic appeared to Blessed Alan as well and told him of the great results of his ministry: he had preached the Rosary unceasingly, his sermons had borne great fruit and many people had been converted during his missions.

He said to Blessed Alan, "See what wonderful results I have had through preaching the Rosary. You and all who love our Lady ought to do the same so that, by means of this holy practice of the Rosary, you may draw all people to the real science of the virtues."

Briefly, then, this is the history of how Saint Dominic established the holy Rosary and of how Blessed Alan de la Roche restored it.

Fifth Rose

21. Strictly speaking, there can be only one kind of Confraternity of the Rosary, that is, one whose members agree to say the entire Rosary of 150 Hail Marys every day. However, considering the

fervour of those who say it, we may distinguish three kinds: Ordinary Membership, which entails saying the complete Rosary once a week; Perpetual Membership, which requires it to be said only once a year; Daily Membership, which obliges one to say it all every day, that is, the fifteen decades made up of 150 Hail Marys.

None of these oblige under pain of sin. It is not even a venial sin to fail in this duty because such an undertaking is entirely voluntary and supererogatory. Needless to say, people should not join the Confraternity if they do not intend to fulfil their obligation by saying the Rosary as often as is required, without, however, neglecting the duties of their state in life.

So whenever the Rosary clashes with a duty of one's state in life, holy as the Rosary is, one must give preference to the duty to be performed. Similarly, sick people are not obliged to say the whole Rosary or even part of it if this effort might tire them and make them worse.

If you have been unable to say it because of some duty required by obedience or because you genuinely forgot, or because of some urgent necessity, you have not committed even a venial sin. You will then receive the benefits of the Confraternity just the same, sharing in the graces and merits of your brothers and sisters in the Rosary, who are saying it throughout the world.

And, my dear Catholic people, even if you fail to say your Rosary out of sheer carelessness or laziness, as long as you do not have any formal contempt for it, you do not sin, absolutely speaking, but you forfeit your participation in the prayers, good works and merits of the Confraternity. Moreover, because you have not been faithful in things that are little and of supererogation, almost without knowing it you may fall into the habit of neglecting big things, such as those duties which bind under pain of sin; for "He that scorns small things shall fall little by little."

Sixth Rose

22. From the time Saint Dominic established the devotion to the holy Rosary up to the time when Blessed Alan de la Roche re-established it in 1460, it has always been called the Psalter of Jesus and Mary. This is because it has the same number of Hail Marys as there are psalms in the Book of the Psalms of David. Since simple and uneducated people are not able to say the Psalms of David, the Rosary is held to be just as fruitful for them as David's Psalter is for others.

But the Rosary can be considered to be even more valuable than the latter for three reasons:

1. Firstly, because the Angelic Psalter bears a nobler fruit, that of the Word incarnate, whereas David's Psalter only prophesies his coming;

2. Just as the real thing is more important than its prefiguration and the body surpasses the shadow, so the Psalter of our Lady is greater than David's Psalter, which did no more than prefigure it;

3. Because our Lady's Psalter or the Rosary made up of the Our Father and Hail Mary is the direct work of the Blessed Trinity.

Here is what the learned Carthagena says about it:

The scholarly writer of Aix-la-Chapelle says in his book, The Rose Crown, dedicated to the Emperor Maximilian: "It cannot be maintained that Salutation of Mary is a recent innovation. It spread almost with the Church itself. For at the very beginnings of the Church the more educated members of the faithful celebrated the praises of God in the 150 psalms of David. The ordinary people, who encountered more difficulty in divine service, thus conceived a holy emulation of them.... They considered, which is indeed true, that the heavenly praises of the Rosary contained all the divine secrets of the psalms, for, if the psalms sing of the one who is to come, the Rosary proclaims him as having come.

"That is how they began to call their prayer of 150 Salutations 'The Psalter of Mary,' and to precede each decade with an Our Father, as was done by those who recited the psalms."

23. The Psalter or Rosary of our Lady is divided into three chaplets of five decades each, for the following reasons:

1. to honour the three persons of the Blessed Trinity;

2 to honour the life, death and glory of Jesus Christ;

3. to imitate the Church triumphant, to help the members of the Church militant, and to bring relief to the Church suffering;

4. to imitate the three groups into which the psalms are divided, the first being for the purgative life, the second for the illuminative life, and the third for the unitive life;

5. to give us graces in abundance during life, peace at death, and glory in eternity.

Seventh Rose

24. Ever since Blessed Alan de la Roche re-established this devotion, the voice of the people, which is the voice of God, gave it the name of the Rosary, which means "crown of roses." That is to say that every time people say the Rosary devoutly they place on the heads of Jesus and Mary 153 white roses and sixteen red roses.

Being heavenly flowers, these roses will never fade or lose their beauty.

Our Lady has approved and confirmed this name of the Rosary; she has revealed to several people that each time they say a Hail Mary they are giving her a beautiful rose, and that each complete Rosary makes her a crown of roses.

25. The Jesuit brother, Alphonsus Rodriguez, used to say his Rosary with such fervour that he often saw a red rose come out of his mouth at each Our Father, and a white rose at each Hail Mary, both equal in beauty and differing only in colour.

The chronicles of St. Francis tell of a young friar who had the praiseworthy habit of saying this crown of our Lady every day before dinner. One day, for some reason or other, he did not manage to say it. The refectory bell had already been rung when he asked the Superior to allow him to say it before coming to the table, and, having obtained permission, he withdrew to his cell to pray.

After he had been gone a long time, the Superior sent another friar to fetch him, and he found him in his room bathed in a heavenly light in the presence of our Lady and two angels. Beautiful roses kept issuing from his mouth at each Hail Mary, and the two angels were taking them one by one and placing them on our Lady's head, while she smilingly accepted them. Finally, two other friars who had been sent to find out what had happened to the first two saw the same scene, and our Lady did not leave until the whole Rosary had been said.

So the complete Rosary is a large crown of roses and each chaplet of five decades is a little wreath of flowers or a little crown of heavenly roses which we place on the heads of Jesus and Mary. The rose is the queen of flowers, and so the Rosary is the rose of devotions and the most important one.

Eighth Rose

26. It is scarcely possible for me to put into words how our Lady esteems the Rosary and how she prefers it to all other devotions. Nor can I sufficiently express how wonderfully she rewards those who work to make known the devotion, to establish it and spread it nor, on the other hand, how strictly she punishes those who work against it.

St. Dominic had nothing more at heart during his life than to praise our Lady, to preach her greatness, and to inspire everybody to honour her by saying her Rosary. As a reward he received countless graces from her. This powerful Queen of heaven crowned his labours with many miracles and prodigies. God always granted him what he asked through our Lady. The greatest favour of all was that she helped him to crush the Albigensian heresy and made him the founder and patriarch of a great religious order.

27. As for Blessed Alan de la Roche, who restored the devotion of the Rosary, he received many privileges from our Lady; she graciously appeared to him several times to teach him how to work out his salvation, to become a good priest and perfect religious, and how to pattern himself on our Lord.

He used to be horribly tempted and persecuted by devils, and then a deep sadness would fall upon him and sometimes he would be near to despair. But our Lady always comforted him by her presence, which banished the clouds of darkness from his soul.

She taught him how to say the Rosary, explaining its value and the fruits to be gained by it; and she gave him a great and glorious privilege, which was the honour of being called her new spouse. As a token of her chaste love for him, she placed a ring upon his finger and a necklace made of her own hair about his neck and gave him a Rosary.

Fr. Tritème, the learned Carthagena and Martin of Navarre, as well as others, have spoken of him in terms of highest praise. Blessed Alan died at Zwolle, in Flanders, on September 8th, 1475, after having brought more than a hundred thousand people into the Confraternity.

28. Blessed Thomas of St. John was well known for his sermons on the holy Rosary, and the devil, jealous of his success, tortured him so much that he fell ill and was sick for such a long time that the doctors gave him up. One night, when he really thought he was dying, the devil appeared to him in the most terrible form imaginable. There was a picture of our Lady near his bed; he looked at it and cried with all his heart and soul and strength, "Help me, save me, my dearest Mother." No sooner had he said this than the picture seemed to come alive and our Lady put out her hand, took him by the arm and said, "Do not be afraid, Thomas my son, here I am and I am going to save you; get up now and go on preaching my Rosary as you used to do. I promise to shield you from your enemies."

When our Lady said this, the devil fled and Blessed Thomas got up, finding himself in perfect health. He then thanked our Lady with tears of joy. He resumed his Rosary apostolate, and his sermons were wonderfully successful.

29. Our Lady not only blesses those who preach her Rosary but she highly rewards all those who, by their example, get others to say it.

Alphonsus, King of Leon and Galicia, very much wanted all his servants to honour the Blessed Virgin by saying the Rosary, so he used to hang a large rosary on his belt, though he never said it himself. Nevertheless, his wearing it encouraged his courtiers to say the Rosary devoutly.

One day the King fell seriously ill and when he was given up for dead he found himself, in spirit, before the judgment-seat of our Lord. Many devils were there accusing him of all the sins he had committed, and our Lord was about to condemn him when our Lady came forward to speak in his favour. She called for a pair of scales and had his sins placed in one of the balances, while she put the large rosary which he had always worn on the other scale, together with all the rosaries that had been said through his example. It was found that the Rosaries weighed more than his sins.

Looking at him with great kindness, our Lady said, "As a reward for the little service you did for me in wearing my rosary, I have obtained a great grace for you from my Son. Your life will be spared for a few more years. See that you spend those years wisely, and do penance."

When the King regained consciousness he cried out, "Blessed be the Rosary of the most holy Virgin Mary, by which I have been delivered from eternal damnation."

After he had recovered his health, he spent the rest of his life in spreading devotion to the Rosary, and said it faithfully every day.

People who love the Blessed Virgin ought to follow the example of King Alphonsus and that of the saints whom I have mentioned, so that they too may win other souls for the Confraternity of the Holy

Rosary. They will receive great graces here on earth and finally eternal life. "Those who explain me will have life everlasting."

Ninth Rose

30. It is very wicked indeed and unjust to hinder the progress of the Confraternity of the Holy Rosary. God has severely punished many of those who have been so benighted as to scorn the Confraternity and have sought to destroy it.

Even though God has set his seal of approval on the Rosary by many miracles, and though it has been approved by the Church in many papal bulls, there are only too many people who are against the holy Rosary today. Such are free-thinkers and those who scorn religion, who either condemn the Rosary or try to turn others away from it.

It is easy to see that they have absorbed the poison of hell and that they are inspired by the devil; for no one can condemn devotion to the holy Rosary without condemning all that is most holy in the Catholic faith, such as the Lord's prayer, the Hail Mary and the mysteries of the life, death and glory of Jesus Christ and his holy Mother.

These freethinkers, who cannot bear to have people saying the Rosary, often fall into an heretical state of mind without realizing it and come to hate the Rosary and its mysteries.

To have a loathing for confraternities is to fall away from God and true piety, for our Lord himself has told us that he is always in the midst of those who are gathered together in his name. No good Catholic would neglect the many great indulgences which the Church has granted to confraternities. Finally, to dissuade others from joining the Rosary Confraternity is to be an enemy of souls, because the Rosary is a means of avoiding sin and leading a good life.

St. Bonaventure says in his "Psalter" that whoever neglects our Lady will die in his sins. What, then, must be the punishment in store for those who turn people away from devotion to her?

Tenth Rose

31. While St. Dominic was preaching the Rosary in Carcassone, a heretic made fun of his miracles and the fifteen mysteries of the Rosary, and this prevented other heretics from being converted. As a punishment God allowed fifteen thousand devils to enter the man's body.

His parents took him to Father Dominic to be delivered from the evil spirits. He started to pray and he begged everyone who was there to say the Rosary out loud with him, and at each Hail Mary our Lady drove a hundred devils out of the man, and they came out in the form of red-hot coals.

After he had been delivered, he abjured his former errors, was converted and joined the Rosary Confraternity. Several of his associates did the same, having been greatly moved by his punishment and by the power of the Rosary.

32. The learned Franciscan, Carthagena, as well as several other authors, says that an extraordinary event took place in 1482. The venerable Fr. James Sprenger and the religious of his order were zealously working to re-establish devotion to the Rosary and its Confraternity in the city of Cologne. Unfortunately, two priests who were famous for their preaching ability were jealous of the great influence they were exerting through preaching the Rosary. These two Fathers spoke against this devotion whenever they had a

chance, and as they were very eloquent and had a great reputation, they persuaded many people not to join the Confraternity. One of them, the better to achieve his wicked end, wrote a special sermon against the Rosary and planned to give it the following Sunday. But when the time came for the sermon he did not appear and, after a certain amount of waiting, someone went to fetch him. He was found to be dead, and he had evidently died without anyone to help him.

After persuading himself that this death was due to natural causes, the other priest decided to carry out his friend's plan and give a similar sermon on another day, hoping to put an end to the Confraternity of the Rosary. However, when the day came for him to preach and it was time to give the sermon, God punished him by striking him down with paralysis which deprived him of the use of his limbs and of his power of speech.

At last he admitted his fault and that of his friend and in his heart he silently besought our Lady to help him. He promised that if only she would cure him, he would preach the Rosary with as much zeal as that with which he had formerly fought against it. For this end he implored her to restore his health and his speech, which she did, and finding himself instantaneously cured he rose up like another Saul, a persecutor turned defender of the holy Rosary. He publicly acknowledged his former error and ever afterwards preached the wonders of the Rosary with great zeal and eloquence.

33. I am quite sure that freethinkers and ultra-critical people of today will question the truth of the stories in this little book, as they question most things, but all I have done has been to copy them from very good contemporary authors and, in part, from a book written a short time ago, The Mystical Rose-tree, by Fr. Antonin Thomas, O.P.

Everyone knows that there are three different kinds of faith by which we believe different kinds of stories. To stories from Holy Scripture we owe divine faith; to stories on non-religious subjects which are not against common sense and are written by trustworthy authors, we pay the tribute of human faith; and to stories about holy subjects which are told by good authors and are not in any way contrary to reason, to faith or to morals (even though they may sometimes deal with happenings which are above the ordinary), we pay the tribute of a pious faith.

I agree that we must be neither too credulous nor too critical, and that we should keep a happy medium in all things in order to find just where truth and virtue lie. But on the other hand, I know equally well that charity easily leads us to believe all that is not contrary to faith or morals: "Charity believes all things," in the same way as pride induces us to doubt even well authenticated stories on the plea that they are not to be found in Holy Scripture.

This is one of the devil's traps; heretics of the past who denied tradition have fallen into it, and over-critical people of today are falling into it too, without even realizing it. People of this kind refuse to believe what they do not understand or what is not to their liking, simply because or their own spirit of pride and independence.

SECOND DECADE
The surpassing merit of the Rosary as seen in the prayers which compose it.

Eleventh Rose [The Creed]

34. The Creed or the Symbol of the Apostles, which is said on the crucifix of the rosary, is a holy summary of all the Christian truths. It is a prayer that has great merit, because faith is the root,

foundation and beginning of all Christian virtues, of all eternal virtues, and of all prayers that are pleasing to God. "Anyone who comes to God must believe," and the greater his faith the more merit his prayer will have, the more powerful it will be, and the more it will glorify God.

I shall not take time here to explain the Creed word for word, but I cannot resist saying that the first words, "I believe in God," are wonderfully effective as a means of sanctifying our souls and putting the devils to rout, because these words contain the acts of the three theological virtues of faith, hope and charity.

It was by saying these words that many saints overcame temptations, especially those against faith, hope or charity, either during their lifetime or at the hour of their death. They were also the last words of St. Peter, Martyr. A heretic had cleft his head in two by a blow of his sword, and although St. Peter was at his last gasp, he managed to trace these words in the sand with his finger.

35. The holy Rosary contains many mysteries of Jesus and Mary, and since faith is the only key which opens up these mysteries for us, we must begin the Rosary by saying the Creed very devoutly, and the stronger our faith the more merit our Rosary will have.

This faith must be lively and informed by charity; in other words, to recite the Rosary properly it is necessary to be in God's grace, or at least seeking it. This faith must be strong and constant, that is, one must not be looking for sensible devotion and spiritual consolation in the recitation of the Rosary; nor should one give it up because the mind is flooded with countless involuntary distractions, or because one experiences a strange distaste in the soul or an almost continual and oppressive fatigue of the body. Neither feelings, nor consolation, nor sighs, nor transports, nor the continual attention of the imagination are needed; faith and good intentions are quite enough. Sola fides sufficit.

Twelfth Rose [The Our Father]

36. The Our Father or the Lord's Prayer derives its great value above all from its author, who is neither a man nor an angel, but the King of angels and of men, our Lord Jesus Christ. St. Cyprian says it was necessary that he who came to give us the life of grace as our Saviour should teach us the way to pray as our heavenly Master.

The beautiful order, the tender forcefulness and the clarity of this divine prayer pay tribute to our divine Master's wisdom. It is a short prayer but can teach us so very much, and it is well within the grasp of uneducated people, while scholars find it a continual source of investigation into the mysteries of God.

The Our Father contains all the duties we owe to God, the acts of all the virtues and the petitions for all our spiritual and corporal needs. Tertullian says that the Our Father is a summary of the New Testament. Thomas a Kempis says that it surpasses all the desires of all the saints; that it is a condensation of all the beautiful sayings of all the psalms and canticles; that in it we ask God for everything that we need, that by it we praise him in the very best way; that by it we lift up our souls from earth to heaven and unite them closely to God.

37. St. John Chrysostom says that we cannot be our Master's disciples unless we pray as he did and in the way that he showed us. Moreover, God the Father listens more willingly to the prayer that we have learned from his Son rather than those of our own making, which have all our human limitations.

We should say the Our Father with the certitude that the eternal Father will hear us because it is the prayer of his Son, whom he always hears, and because we are his members. God will surely grant our petitions made through the Lord's Prayer because it is impossible to imagine that such a good Father could refuse a request couched in the language of so worthy a Son, reinforced by his merits, and made at his behest.

St. Augustine assures us that whenever we say the Our Father devoutly our venial sins are forgiven. The just man falls seven times, and in the Lord's Prayer he will find seven petitions which will both help him to avoid lapses and protect him from his spiritual enemies. Our Lord, knowing how weak and helpless we are, and how many difficulties we endure, made his prayer short and easy to say, so that if we say it devoutly and often, we can be sure that God will quickly come to our aid.

38. I have a word for you, devout souls who pay little attention to the prayer that the Son of God gave us himself and asked us all to say: It is high time for you to change your way of thinking. You only esteem prayers that men have written, as though anybody, even the most inspired man in the whole world, could possibly know more about how we ought to pray than Jesus Christ himself! You look for prayers in books written by other men almost as though you were ashamed of saying the prayer that our Lord told us to say.

You have managed to convince yourself that the prayers in those books are for scholars and for the rich, and that the Rosary is only for women and children and the poor people. As if the prayers and praises you have been reading were more beautiful and more pleasing to God than those which are to be found in the Lord's Prayer! It is a very dangerous temptation to lose interest in the prayer that our Lord gave us and to take up prayers that men have written instead.

Not that I disapprove of prayers that saints have written to encourage the faithful to praise God, but it is not to be endured that they should prefer these to the prayer which was uttered by Wisdom incarnate. If they ignore this prayer, it is as though they passed by the spring to go to the brook, and refusing the clear water, they drink instead that which is dirty. For the Rosary, made up of the Lord's Prayer and the Hail Mary, is this clear and ever-flowing water which comes from the fountain of grace, whereas other prayers which they look for in books are nothing but tiny streams which spring from this fountain.

39. People who say the Lord's Prayer carefully, weighing every word and meditating on them, may indeed call themselves blessed, for they find therein everything that they need or can wish for.

When we say this wonderful prayer, we touch God's heart at the very outset by calling him by that sweet name of Father.

"Our Father," he is the dearest of fathers: all-powerful in his creation, wonderful in the way he maintains the world, completely lovable in his divine Providence, all good and infinitely so in the Redemption. We have God for our Father, so we are all brothers, and heaven is our homeland and our heritage. This should be more than enough to teach us to love God and our neighbour, and to be detached from the things of this world.

So we ought to love our heavenly Father and say to him over and over again: "Our Father who art in heaven" -

Thou who dost fill heaven and earth

with the immensity of thy being,

Thou who art present everywhere:

Thou who art in the saints by thy glory,

in the damned by thy justice,

in the good by thy grace,

in sinners by the patience

with which thou dost tolerate them,

grant that we may always remember

that we come from thee;

grant that we may live as thy true children;

that we may direct our course towards thee alone

with all the ardour of our soul.

"Hallowed by thy name." The name of the Lord is holy and to be feared, said the prophet-king David, and heaven, according to Isaiah, echoes with the praises of the seraphim who unceasingly praise the holiness of the Lord, God of hosts.

We ask here that all the world may learn to know and adore the attributes of our God, who is so great and so holy. We ask that he may be known, loved and adored by pagans, Turks, Jews, barbarians and all infidels; that all men may serve and glorify him by a living faith, a staunch hope, a burning charity, and by the renouncing of all erroneous beliefs. In short, we pray that all men may be holy because our God himself is holy.

"Thy kingdom come." That is to say: May you reign in our souls by your grace, during life, so that after death we may be found worthy to reign with thee in thy kingdom, in perfect and unending bliss; that we firmly believe in this happiness to come; we hope for it and we expect it, because God the Father has promised it in his great goodness, and because it was purchased for us by the merits of God the Son; and it has been made known to us by the light of the Holy Spirit.

"Thy will be done on earth as it is in heaven." As Tertullian says, this sentence does not mean in the least that we are afraid of people thwarting God's designs, because nothing whatsoever can happen without divine Providence having foreseen it and having made it fit into his plans beforehand. No obstruction in the whole world can possibly prevent the will of God from being carried out.

Rather, when we say these words, we ask God to make us humbly resigned to all that he has seen fit to send us in this life. We also ask him to help us to do, in all things and at all times, his holy will, made known to us by the commandments, promptly, lovingly and faithfully, as the angels and the blessed do in heaven.

40. "Give us this day our daily bread." Our Lord teaches us to ask God for everything that we need, whether in the spiritual or the temporal order. By asking for our daily bread, we humbly admit our own poverty and insufficiency, and pay tribute to our God, knowing that all temporal goods come from his Providence. When we say bread we ask for that which is necessary to live; and, of course that does not include luxuries.

We ask for this bread today, which means that we are concerned only for the present, leaving the morrow in the hands of Providence.

And when we ask for our daily bread, we recognize that we need God's help every day and that we are entirely dependent upon him for his help and protection.

"Forgive us our trespasses as we forgive those who trespass against us." Every sin, says St. Augustine and Tertullian, is a debt which we contract with God, and he in his justice requires payment down to the last farthing. Unfortunately we all have these sad debts.

No matter how many they may be, we should go to God with all confidence and with true sorrow for our sins, saying, "Our Father who art in heaven, forgive us our sins of thought and those of speech, forgive us our sins of commission and of omission which make us infinitely guilty in the eyes of thy justice.

"We dare to ask this because thou art our loving and merciful Father, and because we have forgiven those who have offended us, out of obedience to you and out of charity.

"Do not permit us, in spite of our infidelity to thy graces, to give in to the temptations of the world, the devil, and the flesh.

"But deliver us from evil." The evil of sin, from the evil of temporal punishment and of everlasting punishment, which we have rightly deserved.

"Amen." This word at the end of the Our Father is very consoling, and St. Jerome says that it is a sort of seal of approbation that God puts at the end of our petitions to assure us that he will grant our requests, as though he himself were answering:

"Amen! May it be as you have asked, for truly you have obtained what you asked for." That is what is meant by this word: Amen.

Thirteenth Rose

41. Each word of the Lord's Prayer is a tribute we pay to the perfections of God. We honour his fecundity by the name of Father.

Father,

thou who throughout eternity

dost beget a Son

who is God like thee,

eternal, consubstantial with thee,

who is of the very same essence as thee;

and is of like power

and goodness

and wisdom

as thou art....

Father and Son,

who, from your mutual love,

produce the Holy Spirit,

who is God like unto you;

three persons

but one God.

Our Father. This means that he is the Father of mankind, because he has created us and continues to sustain us, and because he has redeemed us. He is also the merciful Father of sinners, the Father who is the friend of the just, and the glorious Father of the blessed in heaven.

When we say Who art, we honour by these words the infinity and immensity and fullness of God's essence. God is rightly called "He who is;" that is to say, he exists of necessity, essentially, and eternally, because he is the Being of beings and the cause of all beings. He possesses within himself, in a super-eminent degree, the perfections of all beings, and he is in all of them by his essence, by his presence and by his power, but without being bounded by their limitations. We honour his sublimity and his glory and his majesty by the words Who art in heaven, that is to say, seated as on thy throne, holding sway over all men by thy justice.

When we say Hallowed be thy Name, we worship God's holiness; and we make obeisance to his kingship and bow to the justice of his laws by the words Thy kingdom come, praying that men will obey him on earth as the angels do in heaven.

We show our trust in his Providence by asking for our daily bread, and we appeal to his mercy when we ask for the forgiveness of our sins.

We look to his great power when we beg him not to lead us into temptation, and we show our faith in his goodness by our hope that he will deliver us from evil.

The Son of God has always glorified his Father by his works, and he came into the world to teach men to give glory to him. He showed men how to praise him by this prayer, which he taught us with his own lips. It is our duty, therefore, to say it often, with attention, and in the same spirit as he composed it.

Fourteenth Rose

42. We make as many acts of the noblest Christian virtues as we pronounce words when we recite this divine prayer attentively.

In saying "Our Father, who art in heaven," we make acts of faith, adoration and humility. When we ask that his name be hallowed, we show a burning zeal for his glory. When we ask for the spread of his kingdom, we make an act of hope; by the wish that his will be done on earth as it is in heaven, we show a spirit of perfect obedience. In asking for our daily bread, we practice poverty of spirit and detachment from worldly goods. When we beg him to forgive us our sins, we make an act of sorrow for them. By forgiving those who have trespassed against us, we give proof of the virtue of mercy in its highest degree. Through asking God's help in all our temptations, we make acts of humility, prudence and fortitude. As we wait for him to deliver us from evil, we exercise the virtue of patience.

Finally, while asking for all these things, not only for ourselves but also for our neighbour and for all members of the Church, we are carrying out our duty as true children of God, we are imitating him in his love which embraces all men and we are keeping the commandment of love of our neighbour.

43. If we mean in our hearts what we say with our lips, and if our intentions are not at variance with those expressed in the Lord's Prayer, then, by reciting this prayer, we hate all sin and we observe all of God's laws. For whenever we think that God is in heaven, that is to say, infinitely removed from us by the greatness of his majesty, we place ourselves in his presence filled with

overwhelming reverence. Then the fear of the Lord will chase away all pride and we will bow down before God in utter nothingness.

When we pronounce the name "Father" and remember that we owe our existence to God, by means of our parents, and even the instruction we have received by means of our teachers, who take the place of God and are his living images, we cannot help paying them honour and respect, or, to be more exact, to honour God in them. And nothing would be farther from our thoughts than to be disrespectful to them or hurt them.

When we pray that God's holy name be glorified, we cannot be farther from profaning it. If we really look upon the kingdom of God as our heritage, we cannot possibly be attached to the things of this world.

If we sincerely ask God that our neighbour may have the same blessings that we ourselves stand in need of, it goes without saying that we will give up all hatred, quarrelling and jealousy. And if we ask God for our daily bread, we shall learn to hate gluttony and sensual pleasures which thrive in rich surroundings.

While sincerely asking God to forgive us as we forgive those who trespass against us, we no longer give way to anger and revenge, we return good for evil and we love our enemies.

To ask God to save us from falling into sin when we are tempted is to give proof that we are fighting laziness and that we are genuinely seeking means to root out vicious habits and to work out our salvation.

To pray God to deliver us from evil is to fear his justice, and this will give us true happiness, for the fear of God is the beginning of wisdom. It is through the virtue of the fear of God that men avoid sin.

Fifteenth Rose

44. The Angelic Salutation, or Hail Mary, is so heavenly and so beyond us in its depth of meaning, that Blessed Alan de la Roche held that no mere creature could ever understand it, and that only our Lord Jesus Christ, born of the Virgin Mary, can really explain it.

Its enormous value is due, first of all, to our Lady to whom it was addressed, to the purpose of the Incarnation of the Word, for which reason this prayer was brought from heaven, and also to the archangel Gabriel who was the first ever to say it.

The Angelic Salutation is a most concise summary of all that Catholic theology teaches about the Blessed Virgin. It is divided into two parts, that of praise and that of petition. The first shows all that goes to make up Mary's greatness; and the second, all that we need to ask her for, and all that we may expect to receive through her goodness.

The most Blessed Trinity revealed the first part of it to us; St. Elizabeth, inspired by the Holy Spirit, added the second; and the Church gave us the conclusion in the year 430 when she condemned the Nestorian heresy at the Council of Ephesus and defined that the Blessed Virgin is truly the Mother of God. At this time she ordered us to pray to our Lady under this glorious title by saying, "Holy Mary, Mother of God, pray for us sinners, now and at the hour of our death."

45. The greatest event in the whole history of the world was the Incarnation of the eternal Word by whom the world was redeemed and peace was restored between God and men. Our Lady was

chosen as his instrument for this tremendous event, and it was put into effect when she was greeted with the Angelic Salutation. The archangel Gabriel, one of the leading princes of the heavenly court, was chosen as ambassador to bear these glad tidings.

In the Angelic Salutation can be seen the faith and hope of the patriarchs, the prophets and the apostles. Furthermore, it gives to martyrs their unswerving constancy and strength, it is the wisdom of the doctors of the Church, the perseverance of the holy confessors and the life of all religious (Blessed Alan). It is the new hymn of the law of grace, the joy of angels and men, and the hymn which terrifies devils and puts them to shame.

By the Angelic Salutation God became man, a virgin became the Mother of God, the souls of the just were delivered from Limbo, the empty thrones in heaven have been filled, sin has been pardoned, grace been given to us, the sick been made well, the dead brought back to life, exiles brought home, the Blessed Trinity has been appeased, and men obtained eternal life.

Finally, the Angelic Salutation is the rainbow in the sky, a sign of the mercy and grace which God has given to the world (Blessed Alan).

Sixteenth Rose

46. Even though there is nothing so great as the majesty of God and nothing so low as man in so far as he is a sinner, Almighty God does not despise our poor prayers. On the contrary, he is pleased when we sing his praises.

And the Angel's greeting to our Lady is one of the most beautiful hymns which we could possibly sing to the glory of the Most High. "To you will I sing a new song." This new hymn, which David foretold would be sung at the coming of the Messiah, is none other than the Angelic Salutation.

There is an old hymn and a new hymn: the first is that which the Jews sang out of gratitude to God for creating them and maintaining them in existence, for delivering them from captivity and leading them safely through the Red Sea, for giving them manna to eat, and for all his other blessings.

The new hymn is that which Christians sing in thanksgiving for the graces of the Incarnation and the Redemption. As these marvels were brought about by the Angelic Salutation, so also do we repeat the same salutation to thank the most Blessed Trinity for the immeasurable goodness shown to us.

We praise God the Father because he so loved the world that he gave us his only Son as our Saviour. We bless the Son because he deigned to leave heaven and come down upon earth, because he was made man and redeemed us. We glorify the Holy Spirit because he formed our Lord's pure body in the womb of our Lady, that body which was the victim for our sins. In this spirit of deep thankfulness should we, then, always say the Hail Mary, making acts of faith, hope, love and thanksgiving for the priceless gift of salvation.

47. Although this new hymn is in praise of the Mother of God and is sung directly to her, it is nevertheless most glorious to the Blessed Trinity, for any honour we pay to our Lady returns inevitably to God, the source of all her perfections and virtues. God the Father is glorified when we honour the most perfect of his creatures; God the Son is glorified when we praise his most pure Mother; the Holy Spirit is glorified when we are lost in admiration at the graces with which he has filled his spouse.

When we praise and bless our Lady by saying the Angelic Salutation, she always refers these praises to God in the same way as she did when she was praised by St. Elizabeth. The latter blessed her in her high dignity as Mother of God and our Lady immediately returned these praises to God in her beautiful Magnificat.

48. Just as the Angelic Salutation gave glory to the Blessed Trinity, it is also the very highest praise that we can give to Mary.

One day, when St. Mechtilde was praying and was trying to think of some way in which she could express her love of the Blessed Virgin better than before, she fell into ecstasy. Our Lady appeared to her with the Angelic Salutation written in letters of gold upon her breast and said to her, "My daughter, I want you to know that no one can please me more than by saying the greeting which the most adorable Trinity presented to me and by which I was raised to the dignity of the Mother of God.

"By the word Ave, which is the name of Eve, Eva, I learned that God in his infinite power had preserved me from all sin and its attendant misery which the first woman had been subject to.

"The name Mary, which means 'lady of light,' shows that God has filled me with wisdom and light, like a shining star, to light up heaven and earth.

"The words, full of grace, remind me that the Holy Spirit has showered so many graces upon me that I am able to give these graces in abundance to those who ask for them through my mediation.

"When people say, The Lord is with thee, they renew the indescribable joy that was mine when the eternal Word became incarnate in my womb.

"When you say to me, Blessed art thou among women, I praise the mercy of God who has raised me to this exalted degree of happiness.

"And at the words, Blessed is the fruit of thy womb, Jesus, the whole of heaven rejoices with me to see my Son Jesus adored and glorified for having saved mankind."

Seventeenth Rose

49. Blessed Alan de la Roche, who was so deeply devoted to the Blessed Virgin, had many revelations from her, and we know that he confirmed the truth of these revelations by a solemn oath. Three of them stand out with special emphasis: the first, that if people fail to say the Hail Mary, which has saved the world, out of carelessness, or because they are lukewarm, or because they hate it, this is an indication that they will probably be condemned to eternal punishment.

The second truth is that those who love this divine salutation bear the very special stamp of predestination.

The third is that those to whom God has given this favour of loving our Lady and of serving her out of love must take very great care to continue to love and serve her until the time when she shall have had them placed in heaven by her Son in the degree of glory which they have earned (Blessed Alan)

50. Heretics, all of whom are children of the devil and who clearly bear the sign of God's reprobation, have a horror of the Hail Mary. They still say the Our Father, but never the Hail Mary; they would rather carry a poisonous snake about them than a rosary.

Among Catholics, those who bear the mark of God's reprobation think but little of the Rosary. They either neglect to say it or only say it quickly and in a lukewarm manner.

Even if I did not believe what was revealed to Blessed Alan de la Roche, even then my own experience would be enough to convince me of this terrible but consoling truth. I do not know, nor do I see clearly, how it can be that a devotion which seems to be so small can be the infallible sign of eternal salvation, and how its absence can be the sign of God's eternal displeasure; nevertheless, nothing could be more true.

In our own day we see that people who hold new doctrines that have been condemned by the Church, with all their would-be piety, ignore the devotion to the Rosary and often dissuade their acquaintances from saying it with all sorts of fine pretexts. They are very careful not to condemn the Rosary and the Scapular, as the Calvinists do, but the way they set about attacking them is all the more deadly because it is the more cunning. I shall refer to it again later on.

51. The Hail Mary, the Rosary, is the prayer and the infallible touchstone by which I can tell those who are led by the Spirit of God from those who are deceived by the devil. I have known souls who seemed to soar like eagles to the heights by their sublime contemplation and yet were pitifully led astray by the devil. I only found out how wrong they were when I learned that they scorned the Hail Mary and the Rosary, which they considered as being far beneath them.

The Hail Mary is a blessed dew that falls from heaven upon the souls of the predestinate. It gives them a marvellous spiritual fertility so that they can grow in all virtues. The more the garden of the soul is watered by this prayer, the more enlightened in mind we become, the more zealous in heart, the stronger against all our enemies.

The Hail Mary is a sharp and flaming shaft which, joined to the Word of God, gives the preacher the strength to pierce, move, and convert the most hardened hearts, even if he has little or no natural gift for preaching.

As I have already said, this was the great secret that our Lady taught St. Dominic and Blessed Alan for the conversion of heretics and sinners. Saint Antoninus tells us that that is why many priests acquired the habit of saying a Hail Mary at the beginning of their sermons.

Eighteenth Rose

52. This heavenly salutation draws down upon us the blessings of Jesus and Mary in abundance, for it is an infallible truth that Jesus and Mary reward in a marvellous way those who glorify them. "I love those who love me. I enrich them and fill their treasures." That is what Jesus and Mary say to us. "Those who sow blessings will also reap blessings."

Now if we say the Hail Mary properly, is not that a way to love, bless and glorify Jesus and Mary? In each Hail Mary we bless both Jesus and Mary: "Blessed art thou among women, and blessed is the fruit of thy womb, Jesus."

By each Hail Mary we give our Lady the same honour that God gave her when he sent the archangel Gabriel to greet her for him. How could anyone possibly think that Jesus and Mary, who often do good to those who curse them, could ever curse those who bless and honour them by the Hail Mary?

Both Saint Bernard and Saint Bonaventure say that the Queen of Heaven is certainly no less grateful and good than gracious and well-mannered people of this world. Just as she excels in all other perfections, she surpasses us all in the virtue of gratitude; so she will never let us honour her with respect without repaying us a hundredfold. Saint Bonaventure says that Mary will greet us with grace if we greet her with the Hail Mary.

Who could possibly understand the graces and blessings which the greeting and tender regard of the Virgin Mary effect in us? From the very first instant that Saint Elizabeth heard the greeting given her by the Mother of God, she was filled with the Holy Spirit and the child in her womb leaped for joy. If we make ourselves worthy of the greeting and blessing of our Lady, we shall certainly be filled with graces and a flood of spiritual consolations will flow into our souls.

Nineteenth Rose

53. It is written, "Give, and it shall be given to you." To take Blessed Alan's illustration of this: "Supposing I were to give you a hundred and fifty diamonds every day, even if you were an enemy of mine, would you not forgive me? Would you not treat me as a friend and give me all the graces that you were able to give? If you want to gain the riches of grace and of glory, salute the Blessed Virgin, honour your good Mother."

"He who honours his Mother (the Blessed Virgin) is as one who lays up a treasure." Present her every day with at least fifty Hail Marys, for each one is worth fifteen precious stones, which are more pleasing to her than all the riches of this world put together.

And you can then expect great things from her generosity. She is our Mother and our friend. She is the empress of the universe and loves us more than all the mothers and queens of the world have ever loved any one human being, for, as St. Augustine says, the charity of the Blessed Virgin far surpasses the natural love of all mankind and even of all the angels.

54. One day Saint Gertrude had a vision of our Lord counting gold coins. She summoned the courage to ask him what he was doing, and he answered, "I am counting the Hail Marys that you have said; this is the money with which you purchase heaven."

The holy and learned Jesuit, Father Suarez, was so deeply aware of the value of the Angelic Salutation that he said he would gladly give all his learning for the price of one Hail Mary well said.

55. Blessed Alan de la Roche said, "Let everyone who loves you, O most holy Mary, listen to this and drink it in:

"Whenever I say Hail, Mary, the court of heaven rejoices and earth is lost in wonderment; I despise the world and my heart is filled with the love of God, when I say 'Hail, Mary.' All my fears wilt and die and my passions are quelled, if I say 'Hail, Mary'; devotion grows within me and sorrow for sin awakens, when I say 'Hail, Mary.'

"Hope is made strong in my breast and the dew of consolation falls on my soul more and more, because I say, 'Hail, Mary.' And my spirit rejoices and sorrow fades away, when I say 'Hail, Mary.'

"For the sweetness of this blessed salutation is so great that there are no words to explain it adequately, and even when its wonders have been sung, we still find it so full of mystery and so profound that its depths can never be plumbed. It has but few words but is exceeding rich in mystery; it is sweeter than honey and more precious than gold. We should often meditate on it in our hearts, and have it ever on our lips so as to say it devoutly again and again."

Blessed Alan also relates that a nun who had always had a great devotion to the Rosary appeared after her death to one of her sisters in religion and said to her, "If I were able to return in my body to have the chance of saying just a single Hail Mary, even without great fervour, I would gladly go through the sufferings that I had during my last illness all over again, in order to gain the merit of this prayer" It is to be noted that she had been bedridden and suffered agonizing pains for several years before she died.

56. Michel de Lisle, Bishop of Salubre, who was a disciple and co-worker of Blessed Alan de la Roche in the re-establishment of the holy Rosary, said that the Angelic Salutation is the remedy for all ills that we suffer as long as we say it devoutly in honour of our Lady.

Twentieth Rose: Brief explanation of the Hail Mary

57. Are you in the miserable state of sin? Then call on Mary and say to her, "Ave," which means "I greet thee with the most profound respect, thou who art without sin," and she will deliver you from the evil of your sins.

Are you groping in the darkness of ignorance and error? Go to Mary and say to her, "Hail Mary," which means "Hail, thou who art bathed in the light of the Sun of Justice," and she will give you a share in her light.

Have you strayed from the path leading to heaven? Then call on Mary, for her name means "Star of the Sea, the Polar Star which guides the ships of our souls during the voyage of this life," and she will guide you to the harbour of eternal salvation.

Are you in sorrow? Turn to Mary, for her name means also "Sea of Bitterness which has been filled with bitterness in this world but which is now turned into a sea of purest joy in heaven," and she will turn your sorrow into joy and your affliction into consolation.

Have you lost the state of grace? Praise and honour the numberless graces with which God has filled the Blessed Virgin and say to her, Thou art full of grace and filled with all the gifts of the Holy Spirit, and she will give you some of these graces.

Are you alone, having lost God's protection? Pray to Mary and say, The Lord is with thee, in a nobler and more intimate way than he is with the saints and the just, because thou art one with him. He is thy Son and his flesh is thy flesh; thou art united to the Lord because of thy perfect likeness to him and by your mutual love, for thou art his Mother. And then say to her, "The three persons of the Godhead are with thee because thou art the Temple of the Blessed Trinity," and she will place you once more under the protection and care of God.

Have you become an outcast and been accursed by God? Then say to our Lady, "Blessed art thou above all women and above all nations by thy purity and fertility; thou hast turned God's maledictions into blessings for us." She will bless you.

Do you hunger for the bread of grace and the bread of life? Draw near to her who bore the living Bread which came down from heaven, and say to her, "Blessed be the fruit of thy womb, whom thou hast conceived without the slightest loss to thy virginity, whom thou didst carry without discomfort and brought forth without pain. Blessed be Jesus who redeemed our suffering world when we were in the bondage of sin, who has healed the world of its sickness, who has raised the dead to life, brought home the banished, restored sinners to grace, and saved men from damnation. Without doubt, your soul will be filled with the bread of grace in this life and of eternal glory in the next. Amen."

58. Conclude your prayer with the Church and say, "Holy Mary," holy because of thy incomparable and eternal devotion to the service of God, holy in thy great rank as Mother of God, who has endowed thee with eminent holiness, in keeping with this great dignity.

"Mother of God, and our Mother, our Advocate and Mediatrix, Treasurer and dispenser of God's graces, obtain for us the prompt forgiveness of our sins and grant that we may be reconciled with the divine majesty.

"Pray for us sinners, thou who art always filled with compassion for those in need, who never despise sinners or turn them away, for without them you would never have been Mother of the Redeemer.

"Pray for us now, during this short life, so fraught with sorrow and uncertainty; now, because we can be sure of nothing except the present moment; now that we are surrounded and attacked night and day by powerful and ruthless enemies.

"And at the hour of our death, so terrible and full of danger, when our strength is waning and our spirits are sinking, and our souls and bodies are worn out with fear and pain; at the hour of our death when the devil is working with might and main to ensnare us and cast us into perdition; at that hour when our lot will be decided forever and ever, heaven or hell.

"Come to the help of your poor children, gentle Mother of pity, Advocate and Refuge of sinners, at the hour of our death drive far from us our bitter enemies, the devils, our accusers, whose frightful presence fills us with dread. Light our path through the valley of the shadow of death. Lead us to thy Son's judgment-seat and remain at our side. Intercede for us and ask thy Son to pardon us and receive us into the ranks of thy elect in the realms of everlasting glory. Amen."

59. No one could help admiring the excellence of the holy Rosary, made up as it is of these two divine parts: the Lord's Prayer and the Angelic Salutation. How could there be any prayers more pleasing to God and to the Blessed Virgin, or any that are easier, more precious, or more helpful than these two prayers? We should always have them in our hearts and on our lips to honour the most Blessed Trinity, Jesus Christ our Saviour and his most holy Mother.

In addition, at the end of each decade it is good to add the Gloria Patri, that is: Glory be to the Father, and to the Son, and to the Holy Spirit. As it was in the beginning, is now, and ever shall be, world without end. Amen.

THIRD DECADE
The surpassing merit of the holy Rosary as a meditation on the life and passion of our Lord Jesus Christ

Twenty-first Rose: The Fifteen Mysteries of the Rosary

60. A mystery is a sacred thing which is difficult to understand. The works of our Lord Jesus Christ are all sacred and divine because he is God and man at one and the same time. The works of the Blessed Virgin are very holy because she is the most perfect and the most pure of God's creatures. The works of our Lord and of his blessed Mother can rightly be called mysteries because they are so full of wonders, of all kinds of perfections, and of deep and sublime truths, which the Holy Spirit reveals to the humble and simple souls who honour these mysteries.

The works of Jesus and Mary can also be called wonderful flowers, but their fragrance and beauty can only be appreciated by those who approach them, who breathe in their fragrance, and who discover their beauty by diligent and serious meditation.

61. St. Dominic divided the lives of our Lord and our Lady into fifteen mysteries, which stand for their virtues and their most important actions. These are fifteen pictures whose every detail must rule and inspire our lives. They are fifteen flaming torches to guide our steps throughout this earthly life; fifteen shining mirrors to help us to know Jesus and Mary, to know ourselves and to light the fire of their love in our hearts; fifteen fiery furnaces to consume us completely in their heavenly flames.

Our Lady taught Saint Dominic this excellent method of praying and ordered him to preach it far and wide so as to reawaken the fervour of Christians and to revive in their hearts a love for our Blessed Lord. She also taught it to Blessed Alan de la Roche and said to him in a vision, "When people say 150 Hail Marys, that prayer is very helpful to them and a most pleasing tribute to me. But they will do better still and will please me more if they say these salutations while meditating on the life, death, and passion of Jesus Christ, for this meditation is the soul of this prayer." For the Rosary said without the meditation on the sacred mysteries of our salvation would almost be a body without a soul, excellent matter, but without the form, which is the meditation, and which distinguishes it from other devotions.

62. The first part of the Rosary contains five mysteries: the first, the Annunciation of the archangel Gabriel to our Lady; the second the Visitation of our Lady to Saint Elizabeth; the third, the Nativity of Jesus Christ; the fourth, the Presentation of the Child Jesus in the

Temple and the purification of the Blessed Virgin; the fifth, the Finding of Jesus in the Temple among the doctors.

These are called the Joyful Mysteries because of the joy which they gave to the whole universe. Our Lady and the angels were overwhelmed with joy the moment the Son of God became incarnate. Saint Elizabeth and St. John the Baptist were filled with joy by the visit of Jesus and Mary. Heaven and earth rejoiced at the birth of the Saviour. Holy Simeon felt great consolation and was filled with joy when he took the holy child into his arms. The doctors were lost in admiration and wonderment at the replies which Jesus gave; and who could express the joy of Mary and Joseph when they found Jesus after three days' absence?

63. The second part of the Rosary is also composed of five mysteries, which are called the Sorrowful Mysteries because they show us our Lord weighed down with sadness, covered with wounds, laden with insults, sufferings and torments.

The first of these mysteries is our Lord's prayer and his Agony in the Garden of Olives; the second, his Scourging; the third, his being Crowned with thorns; the fourth, his Carrying of the Cross; the fifth, his Crucifixion and death on Calvary.

64. The third part of the Rosary contains five more mysteries, which are called the Glorious Mysteries, because when we say them we meditate on Jesus and Mary in their triumph and glory. The first is the Resurrection of Jesus; the second, his Ascension into heaven; the third, the Descent of the Holy Spirit upon the apostles; the fourth, our Lady's Assumption in glory; the fifth, her Coronation.

Such are the fifteen fragrant flowers of the mystical Rose-tree, on which devout souls linger, like discerning bees, to gather their nectar and make the honey of a solid devotion.

Twenty-second Rose: The Meditation of the Mysteries makes us resemble Jesus

65. The chief concern of the Christian should be to tend to perfection. "Be faithful imitators of God, as his well-beloved children," the great Apostle tells us. This obligation is included in the eternal decree of our predestination, as the one and only means prescribed by God to attain everlasting glory.

Saint Gregory of Nyssa makes a delightful comparison when he says that we are all artists and that our souls are blank canvasses which we have to fill in. The colours which we use are the Christian virtues, and the original which we have to copy is Jesus Christ, the perfect living image of God the Father. Just as a painter who wants to do a life-like portrait places the model before his eyes and looks at it before making each stroke, so the Christian must always have before his eyes the life and virtues of Jesus Christ, so as never to say, think or do anything which is not in conformity with his model.

66. It was because our Lady wanted to help us in the great task of working out our salvation that she ordered Saint Dominic to teach the faithful to meditate upon the sacred mysteries of the life of Jesus Christ. She did this, not only that they might adore and glorify him, but chiefly that they might pattern their lives and actions on his virtues.

Children copy their parents through watching them and talking to them, and they learn their own language through hearing them speak. An apprentice learns his trade through watching his master at work; in the same way the faithful members of the Confraternity of the Holy Rosary can become like their divine Master if they reverently study and imitate the virtues of Jesus which are shown in the fifteen mysteries of his life. They can do this with the help of his grace and through the intercession of his blessed Mother.

67. Long ago, Moses was inspired by God to command the Jewish people never to forget the graces which had been showered upon them. The Son of God has all the more reason to command us to engrave the mysteries of his life, passion and glory upon our hearts and to have them always before our eyes, since each mystery reminds us of his goodness to us in some special way and it is by these mysteries that he has shown us his overwhelming love and desire for our salvation. "Oh, all you who pass by, pause a while," he says, "and see if there has ever been any sorrow like to the sorrow I have endured for love of you. Be mindful of my poverty and humiliations; think of the gall and wormwood I took for you in my bitter passion."

These words and many others which could be given here should be more than enough to convince us that we must not only say the Rosary with our lips in honour of Jesus and Mary, but also meditate upon the sacred mysteries while we are saying it.

Twenty-third Rose: The Rosary is a Memorial of the Life and Death of Jesus

68. Jesus Christ, the divine spouse of our souls and our very dear friend, wishes us to remember his goodness to us and to prize his gifts above all else. Whenever we meditate devoutly and lovingly upon the sacred mysteries of the Rosary, he receives an added joy, as also do our Lady and all the saints in heaven. His gifts are the most outstanding results of his love for us and the richest presents he could possibly give us, and it is by virtue of such presents that the Blessed Virgin herself and all the saints are glorified in heaven.

One day Blessed Angela of Foligno begged our Lord to let her know by which religious exercise she could honour him best. He appeared to her nailed to his cross and said, "My daughter, look at my wounds." She then realized that nothing pleases our dear Lord more than meditating upon his sufferings. Then he showed her the wounds on his head and revealed still other sufferings and said to her, "I have suffered all this for your salvation. What can you ever do to return my love for you?"

69. The holy sacrifice of the Mass gives infinite honour to the most Blessed Trinity because it represents the passion of Jesus Christ and because through the Mass we offer to God the merits of our Lord's obedience, of his sufferings, and of his precious blood. All the heavenly court also receive an added joy from the Mass. Several doctors of the Church, including St. Thomas, tell us that, for the same reason, all the blessed in heaven rejoice in the communion of the faithful because the Blessed Sacrament is a memorial of the passion and death of Jesus Christ, and that by means of it men share in its fruits and work out their salvation.

Now the holy Rosary, recited with the meditation on the sacred mysteries, is a sacrifice of praise to God for the great gift of our redemption and a holy reminder of the sufferings, death and glory of Jesus Christ. It is therefore true that the Rosary gives glory and added joy to our Lord, our Lady and all the blessed, because they cannot desire anything greater, for the sake of our eternal happiness, than to see us engaged in a practice which is so glorious for our Lord and so salutary for ourselves.

70. The Gospel teaches us that a sinner who is converted and who does penance gives joy to all the angels. If the repentance and conversion of one sinner is enough to make the angels rejoice, how great must be the happiness and jubilation of the whole heavenly

court and what glory for our Blessed Lord himself to see us here on earth meditating devoutly and lovingly on his humiliations and torments and on his cruel and shameful death! Is there anything that could touch our hearts more surely and bring us to sincere repentance?

A Christian who does not meditate on the mysteries of the Rosary is very ungrateful to our Lord and shows how little he cares for all that our divine Saviour has suffered to save the world. This attitude seems to show that he knows little or nothing of the life of Jesus Christ, and that he has never taken the trouble to find out what he has done and what he went through in order to save us. A Christian of that kind ought to fear that, not having known Jesus Christ or having put him out of his mind, Jesus will reject him on the day of judgment with the reproach, "I tell you solemnly, I do not know you."

Let us meditate, then, on the life and sufferings of our Saviour by means of the holy Rosary; let us learn to know him well and to be grateful for all his blessings, so that, on the day of Judgment, he may number us among his children and his friends.

Twenty-fourth Rose: Meditation on the Mysteries of the Rosary is a great means of perfection

71. The saints made our Lord's life the principal object of their study; they meditated on his virtues and his sufferings, and in this way arrived at Christian perfection.

Saint Bernard began with this meditation and he always kept it up. "At the very beginning of my conversion," he said, "I made a bouquet of myrrh fashioned from the sorrows of my Saviour. I placed this bouquet upon my heart, thinking of the lashes, the thorns and the nails of his passion. I applied my whole mind to the meditation on these mysteries every day."

This was also the practice of the holy martyrs; we admire how they triumphed over the most cruel sufferings. Where could this admirable constancy of the martyrs come from, says Saint Bernard, if not from the wounds of Jesus Christ, on which they meditated so frequently? Where was the soul of these generous athletes when their blood gushed forth and their bodies were wracked with cruel torments? Their soul was in the wounds of Christ and those wounds made them invincible."

72. During her whole life, our Saviour's holy Mother was occupied in meditating on the virtues and the sufferings of her Son. When she heard the angels sing their hymn of joy at his birth and saw the shepherds adore him in the stable, her heart was filled with wonder and she meditated on all these marvels. She compared the greatness of the Word incarnate to the way he humbled himself in this lowly fashion; the straw of the crib, to his throne in the heart of his Father; the might of God, to the weakness of a child; his wisdom, to his simplicity.

Our Lady said to Saint Bridget one day, "Whenever I used to contemplate the beauty, modesty, and wisdom of my Son, my heart was filled with joy; and whenever I considered his hands and feet which would be pierced with cruel nails, I wept bitterly and my heart was rent with sorrow and pain."

73. After our Lord's Ascension, our Blessed Lady spent the rest of her life visiting the places that had been hallowed by his presence and by his sufferings. There, she meditated on his boundless love and on his terrible passion.

Saint Mary Magdalene continually performed the same religious exercises during the last thirty years of her life, when she lived at Sainte-Baume.

Saint Jerome tells us that this was the devotion of the faithful in the early centuries of the Church. From all the countries of the world they came to the Holy Land to engrave more deeply on their hearts a great love and remembrance of the Saviour of mankind by seeing the places and things he had made holy by his birth, his work, his sufferings, and his death.

74. All Christians have but one faith and adore one and the same God, and hope for the same happiness in heaven; they know only one mediator, who is Jesus Christ; all must imitate their divine model, and in order to do this they must meditate on the mysteries of his life, of his virtues and of his glory.

It is a great mistake to think that only priests and religious and those who have withdrawn from the turmoil of the world are supposed to meditate upon the truths of our faith and the mysteries of the life of Christ. If priests and religious have an obligation to meditate on the great truths of our holy religion in order to live up to their vocation worthily, the same obligation is just as much incumbent on the laity, because of the fact that every day they meet with spiritual dangers which might cause them to lose their souls. Therefore they should arm themselves with the frequent meditation on the life, virtues, and sufferings of our Blessed Lord, which are presented to us in the fifteen mysteries of the holy Rosary.

Twenty-fifth Rose: The Riches of Holiness contained in the Prayers and Meditations of the Rosary

75. Never will anyone be able to understand the marvellous riches of sanctification which are contained in the prayers and mysteries

of the holy Rosary. This meditation on the mysteries of the life and death of our Lord Jesus Christ is the source of the most wonderful fruits for those who make use of it.

Today people want things that strike and move them, that leave deep impressions on the soul. Now has there ever been anything in the history of the world more moving than the wonderful story of the life, death, and glory of our Saviour which is contained in the holy Rosary? In the fifteen tableaux, the principal scenes or mysteries of his life unfold before our eyes. How could there be any prayers more wonderful and sublime than the Lord's Prayer and the Ave of the angel? All our desires and all our needs are found expressed in these two prayers.

76. The meditation on the mysteries and prayers of the Rosary is the easiest of all prayers, because the diversity of the virtues of our Lord and the different situations of his life which we study, refresh and fortify our mind in a wonderful way and help us to avoid distractions. For the learned, these mysteries are the source of the most profound doctrine, while simple people find in them a means of instruction well within their reach.

We need to learn this easy form of meditation before progressing to the highest state of contemplation. That is the view of Saint Thomas Aquinas, and the advice that he gives when he says that, first of all, one must practice on a battlefield, as it were, by acquiring all the virtues of which we have the perfect model in the mysteries of the Rosary; for, says the learned Cajetan, that is the way we arrive at a really intimate union with God, since without that union contemplation is nothing but an illusion which can lead souls astray.

77. If only the Illuminists or the Quietists of these days had followed this piece of advice, they would never have fallen so low

or caused such scandals among spiritual people. To think that it is possible to say prayers that are finer and more beautiful than the Our Father and the Hail Mary is to fall a prey to a strange illusion of the devil, for these heavenly prayers are the support, the strength and the safeguard of our souls.

I admit it is not always necessary to say them as vocal prayers and that interior prayer is, in a sense, more perfect than vocal. But believe me, it is really dangerous, not to say fatal, to give up saying the Rosary of your own accord under the pretext of seeking a more perfect union with God. Sometimes a soul that is proud in a subtle way and who may have done everything that he can do interiorly to rise to the sublime heights of contemplation that the saints have reached may be deluded by the noonday devil into giving up his former devotions which are good enough for ordinary souls. He turns a deaf ear to the prayers and the greeting of an angel and even to the prayer which God has composed, put into practice, and commanded: Thus shall you pray: Our Father. Having reached this point, such a soul drifts from illusion to illusion, and falls from precipice to precipice.

78. Believe me, dear brother of the Rosary Confraternity, if you genuinely wish to attain a high degree of prayer in all honesty and without falling into the illusions of the devil so common with those who practice mental prayer, say the whole Rosary every day, or at least five decades of it.

If you have already attained, by the grace of God, a high degree of prayer, keep up the practice of saying the holy Rosary if you wish to remain in that state and by it to grow in humility. For never will anyone who says his Rosary every day become a formal heretic or be led astray by the devil. This is a statement which I would sign with my blood.

On the other hand, if God in his infinite mercy draws you to himself as forcibly as he did some of the saints while saying the Rosary, make yourself passive in his hands and let yourself be drawn towards him. Let God work and pray in you and let him say your Rosary in his way, and that will be sufficient for the day.

But if you are still in the state of active contemplation or the ordinary prayer of quietude, of the presence of God, affective prayer, you have even less reason for giving up the Rosary. Far from making you lose ground in mental prayer or stunting your spiritual growth, it will be a wonderful help to you. You will find it a real Jacob's ladder with fifteen rungs by which you will go from virtue to virtue and from light to light. Thus, without danger of being misled, you will easily arrive at the fullness of the age of Jesus Christ.

Twenty-sixth Rose

79. Whatever you do, do not be like a certain pious but self-willed lady in Rome, so often referred to by speakers on the Rosary. She was so devout and fervent that she put to shame by her holy life even the strictest religious in the Church.

Having decided to ask St. Dominic's advice about her spiritual life, she made her confession to him. For penance he gave her one Rosary to say and advised her to say it every day. She excused herself, saying that she had her regular exercises, that she made the Stations of Rome every day, that she wore sack-cloth as well as a hair-shirt, that she gave herself the discipline several times a week, that she often fasted and did other penances. Saint Dominic urged her over and over again to take his advice and say the Rosary, but she would not hear of it. She left the confessional, horrified at the methods of this new spiritual director who had tried so hard to persuade her to take up a devotion for which she had no taste.

Later on, when she was at prayer she fell into ecstasy and had a vision of her soul appearing before the Supreme Judge. Saint Michael put all her penances and other prayers on one side of the scales and all her sins and imperfections on the other. The tray of her good works were greatly outweighed by that of her sins and imperfections.

Filled with alarm, she cried for mercy, imploring the help of the Blessed Virgin, her gracious advocate, who took the one and only Rosary she had said for her penance and dropped it on the tray of her good works. This one Rosary was so heavy that it weighed more than all her sins as well as all her good works. Our Lady then reproved her for having refused to follow the counsel of her servant Dominic and for not saying the Rosary every day.

As soon as she came to herself she rushed and threw herself at the feet of Saint Dominic and told him all that had happened, begged his forgiveness for her unbelief, and promised to say the Rosary faithfully every day. By this means she rose to Christian perfection and finally to the glory of everlasting life.

You who are people of prayer, learn from this the power, the value and the importance of this devotion of the holy Rosary when it is said with meditation on the mysteries.

80. Few saints have reached the same heights of prayer as Saint Mary Magdalene, who was lifted up to heaven by angels each day, and who had the privilege of learning at the feet of Jesus and his holy Mother. Yet one day, when she asked God to show her a sure way of advancing in his love and arriving at the heights of perfection, he sent the archangel St. Michael to tell her, on his behalf, that there was no other way for her to reach perfection than to meditate on our Lord's passion. So he placed a cross in the front of her cave and told her to pray before it, contemplating the

sorrowful mysteries which she had seen take place with her own eyes.

The example of Saint Francis de Sales, the great spiritual director of his time, should spur you on to join the holy confraternity of the Rosary, since, great saint though he was, he bound himself by vow to say the whole Rosary every day for as long as he lived.

Saint Charles Borromeo also said it every day and strongly recommended this devotion to his priests and clerics in seminaries and to all his people.

Blessed Pius V, one of the greatest popes who have ever ruled the Church, used to say the Rosary every day. Saint Thomas of Villanova, Archbishop of Valencia, Saint Ignatius, Saint Francis Xavier, Saint Francis Borgia, Saint Teresa and Saint Philip Neri, as well as many other great men whom I do not mention, were greatly devoted to the Rosary.

Follow their example; your spiritual directors will be very pleased, and if they are aware of the benefits which you can derive from this devotion, they will be the first to urge you to adopt it.

Twenty-seventh Rose

81. To encourage you still more in this devotion practised by so many holy people, I should like to add that the Rosary recited with the meditation of the mysteries brings about the following marvellous results:

1. it gradually brings us a perfect knowledge of Jesus Christ;

2. it purifies our souls from sin;

3 it gives us victory over all our enemies;

4. it makes the practice of virtue easy;

5 it sets us on fire with the love of our Lord;

6. it enriches us with graces and merits;

7 it supplies us with what is needed to pay all our debts to God and to our fellow-men, and finally, it obtains all kinds of graces from God.

82. The knowledge of Jesus Christ is the science of Christians and the science of salvation; it surpasses, says Saint Paul, all human sciences in value and perfection:

1. because of the dignity of its object, which is a God-man, compared to whom the whole universe is but a drop of dew or a grain of sand;

2. because of its utility to us; human sciences only fill us with the wind and emptiness of pride;

3. because of its necessity; for no one can be saved without the knowledge of Jesus Christ, while a person who knows absolutely nothing of any other science will be saved as long as he is enlightened by the knowledge of Jesus Christ.

Blessed is the Rosary which gives us this science and knowledge of our Blessed Lord through our meditations on his life, death, passion and glory.

The Queen of Sheba, lost in admiration at Solomon's wisdom, cried out, "Blessed are your attendants and your servants who are always in your presence and hear your wisdom." But happier still are the faithful who carefully meditate on the life, virtues, sufferings and glory of our Saviour, because by this means they can gain perfect knowledge of him, in which eternal life consists.

83. Our Lady revealed to Blessed Alan that no sooner had Saint Dominic begun preaching the Rosary than hardened sinners were touched and wept bitterly over their grievous sins. Young children performed unbelievable penances, and everywhere he preached the Rosary such fervour was aroused that sinners changed their lives and edified everyone by their penances and the amendment of their lives.

If by chance your conscience is burdened with sin, take your Rosary and say at least a part of it in honour of some of the mysteries of the life, passion, and glory of Jesus Christ, and you can be sure that, while you are meditating on these mysteries and honouring them, he will show his sacred wounds to his Father in heaven. He will plead for you and obtain for you contrition and the forgiveness of your sins. One day our Lord said to Blessed Alan, "If only these poor wretched sinners would say my Rosary often, they would share in the merits of my passion, and I would be their Advocate and would appease the justice of God."

84. This life is a continual war and a series of temptations; we do not have to contend with enemies of flesh and blood, but with the very powers of hell. What better weapon could we possibly use to combat them than the prayer which our great Leader has taught us, than the Angelic Salutation which has put the devils to flight, destroyed sin and renewed the world? What better weapon could we use than meditation on the life and passion of Jesus Christ? For, as Saint Peter tells us, it is with this thought that we must arm ourselves, in order to defend ourselves against the very same enemies whom he has conquered and who molest us every day.

"Ever since the devil was crushed by the humility and the passion of Jesus Christ," says Cardinal Hugues, "he has been practically unable to attack a soul that is armed with meditation on the mysteries of our Lord's life, and, if he does trouble such a soul, he is sure to be shamefully defeated." "Put on the armour of God so as to be able to resist the attacks of the devil."

85. So arm yourself with the arms of God, with the holy Rosary, and you will crush the devil's head and stand firm in the face of all his temptations. That is why even a pair of rosary beads is so terrible to the devil, and why the saints have used them to fetter him and drive him from the bodies of those who were possessed. Such happenings have been recorded more than once.

86. Blessed Alan relates that a man he knew had tried desperately all kinds of devotions to rid himself of the evil spirit which possessed him, but without success. Finally, he thought of wearing his rosary round his neck, which eased him considerably. He discovered that whenever he took it off the devil tormented him cruelly, so he resolved to wear it night and day. This drove the evil spirit away forever because he could not bear such a terrible chain. Blessed Alan also testifies that he delivered a great number of those who were possessed by putting a rosary round their necks.

87. Father Jean Amât, of the Order of St. Dominic, was giving a series of Lenten sermons in the Kingdom of Aragon one year, when a young girl was brought to him who was possessed by the devil. After he had exorcised her several times without success, he put his rosary round her neck. Hardly had he done so when the girl began to scream and cry out in a fearful way, shrieking, "Take it off, take it off; these beads are tormenting me." At last, the priest, filled with pity for the girl, took his rosary off her.

The very next night, when Fr. Amât was in bed, the same devils who had possession of the girl came to him, foaming with rage and tried to seize him. But he had his rosary clasped in his hand and no efforts of theirs could wrench it from him. He beat them with it very well indeed and put them to flight, crying out, "Holy Mary, Our Lady of the Rosary, come to my help."

The next day on his way to the church, he met the poor girl, still possessed; one of the devils within her started to jeer at him, saying, "Well, brother, if you had been without your rosary, we should have made short shrift of you." Then the good Father threw his rosary round the girl's neck without more ado, saying, "By the sacred names of Jesus and Mary his holy Mother, and by the power of the holy Rosary, I command you, evil spirits, to leave the body of this girl at once." They were immediately forced to obey him, and she was delivered from them.

These stories show the power of the holy Rosary in overcoming all sorts of temptations from the evil spirits and all sorts of sins, because these blessed beads of the Rosary put devils to rout.

Twenty-eighth Rose

88. St. Augustine assures us that there is no spiritual exercise more fruitful or more useful than the frequent reflection on the sufferings of our Lord. Blessed Albert the Great, who had St. Thomas Aquinas as his student, learned in a revelation that by simply thinking of or meditating on the passion of Jesus Christ, a Christian gains more merit than if he had fasted on bread and water every Friday for a year, or had beaten himself with the discipline once a week till blood flowed, or had recited the whole Book of Psalms every day. If this is so, then how great must be the merit we can gain from the Rosary, which commemorates the whole life and passion of our Lord?

Our Lady one day revealed to Blessed Alan de la Roche that, after the holy sacrifice of the Mass, which is the first and most living memorial of our Lord's passion, there was indeed no more excellent devotion or one of greater merit than that of the Rosary, which is like a second memorial and representation of the life and passion of Jesus Christ.

89. Fr. Dorland relates that in 1481 our Lady appeared to the Venerable Dominic, a Carthusian devoted to the holy Rosary, who lived at Treves, and said to him:

"Whenever one of the faithful, in a state of grace, says the Rosary while meditating on the mysteries of the life and passion of Christ, he obtains full and entire remission of all his sins."

She also said to Blessed Alan, "I want you to know that, although there are numerous indulgences already attached to the recitation of my Rosary, I shall add many more to every five decades for those who, free from serious sin, say them with devotion, on their knees. And whosoever shall persevere in the devotion of the holy Rosary, with its prayers and meditations, shall be rewarded for it; I shall obtain for him full remission of the penalty and the guilt of all his sins at the end of his life.

"And let this not seem incredible to you; it is easy for me because I am the Mother of the King of heaven, and he calls me full of grace. And being filled with grace, I am able to dispense it freely to my dear children."

90. St. Dominic was so convinced of the efficacy of the Rosary and its great value that, when he heard confessions, he hardly ever gave any other penance, as we have seen in the story I told you of the lady in Rome to whom he gave only a single Rosary. St. Dominic was a great saint and other confessors also ought to walk in his

footsteps by asking their penitents to say the Rosary with meditation on the sacred mysteries, rather than giving them other penances which are less meritorious and less pleasing to God, less likely to help them to advance in virtue, and not as efficacious in helping them to avoid sin. Moreover, while saying the Rosary, people gain numerous indulgences which are not attached to many other devotions.

91. As Abbot Blosius says, "The Rosary, with meditation on the life and passion of Christ, is certainly most pleasing to our Lord and his blessed Mother and is a very successful means of obtaining all graces; we can say it for ourselves as well as for those who have been recommended to our prayers and for the whole Church. Let us turn, then, to the holy Rosary in all our needs, and we shall infallibly obtain the graces we ask for from God to attain our salvation.

Twenty-ninth Rose

92. There is nothing more divine, according to the mind of St. Denis, nothing more noble or agreeable to God than to cooperate in the work of saving souls and to frustrate the devil's plans for ruining them. The Son of God came down to earth for no other reason than to save us. He upset Satan's empire by founding the Church, but the devil rallied his strength and wreaked cruel violence on souls by the Albigensian heresy, by the hatred, dissensions and abominable vices which he spread throughout the world in the eleventh century.

Only severe remedies could possibly cure such terrible disorders and repel Satan's forces. The Blessed Virgin, protectress of the Church, has given us a most powerful means for appeasing her Son's anger, uprooting heresy and reforming Christian morals, in the Confraternity of the Holy Rosary, as events have shown. It has brought back charity and the frequent reception of the sacraments as in the first golden centuries of the Church, and it has reformed Christian morals.

93. Pope Leo X said in his bull that this Confraternity had been founded in honour of God and of the Blessed Virgin as a wall to hold back the evils that were going to break upon the Church. Gregory XIII said that the Rosary was given us from heaven as a means of appeasing God's anger and of imploring the intercession of our Lady.

Julius III said that the Rosary was inspired by God that heaven might be more easily opened to us through the favours of our Lady.

Paul III and Blessed Pius V declared that the Rosary was given to the faithful in order that they might have spiritual peace and consolation more easily. Surely everyone will want to join a confraternity which was founded for such noble purposes.

94. Father Dominic, a Carthusian, who was deeply devoted to the holy Rosary, had a vision in which he saw heaven opened and the whole heavenly court assembled in magnificent array. He heard them sing the Rosary in an enchanting melody, and each decade was in honour of a mystery of the life, passion, or glory of Jesus Christ and his holy Mother. Fr. Dominic noticed that whenever they pronounced the holy name of Mary they bowed their heads, and at the name of Jesus they genuflected and gave thanks to God for the great good he had wrought in heaven and on earth through the holy Rosary. He also saw our Lady and the Saints present to God the Rosaries which the Confraternity members say here on earth. He noticed too that they were praying for those who practice this devotion. He also saw beautiful crowns without number, which were made of sweet-smelling flowers, for those who say the Rosary

devoutly. He learned that by every Rosary that they say they make a crown for themselves which they will be able to wear in heaven.

This holy Carthusian's vision is very much like that which the Beloved Disciple had, in which he saw a great multitude of angels and saints, who continually praised and blessed Jesus Christ for all that he had done and suffered on earth for our salvation. And is not this what the devout members of the Rosary Confraternity do?

95. It must not be imagined that the Rosary is only for women, and for simple and unlearned people; it is also for men and for the greatest of men. As soon as St. Dominic acquainted Pope Innocent III with the fact that he had received a command from heaven to establish the Confraternity of the Holy Rosary, the Holy Father gave it his full approval, urged St. Dominic to preach it, and said that he wished to become a member himself. Even Cardinals embraced the devotion with great fervour, which prompted Lopez to say, "Neither sex nor age nor any other condition has kept anyone from devotion to the Rosary."

Members of this Confraternity have come from all walks of life: dukes, princes, kings, as well as prelates, cardinals and Sovereign Pontiffs. It would take too long to list them in this little book. If you join this Confraternity, dear reader, you will share in their devotion and their graces on earth and their glory in heaven. "Since you are united to them in their devotion, you will share in their dignity."

Thirtieth Rose

96. If privileges, graces and indulgences of a confraternity make God alone it valuable to us, then that of the Rosary is the one to be most recommended, since it is the most favoured and enriched with indulgences, and ever since its inception there has hardly been

a pope who has not opened the treasures of the Church to enrich it with further privileges. And since example is more persuasive than words and favours, the Holy Fathers have found that there was no better way to show their high regard for this holy Confraternity than to join it themselves.

Here is a short summary of the indulgences which they wholeheartedly granted to the Confraternity of the Holy Rosary, and which were confirmed again by our Holy Father Pope Innocent XI on 31st July 1679, and received and made public by the Archbishop of Paris on 25th September of the same year:

1. Members may gain a plenary indulgence on the day of joining the Confraternity;

2. A plenary indulgence at the hour of death;

3 For each rosary of five decades recited: ten years and ten quarantines;

4. Each time that members say the holy names of Jesus and Mary devoutly: seven days' indulgence;

5. For those who assist with devotion at the procession of the holy Rosary: seven years and seven quarantines of indulgence;

6. Members who have made a good confession and are genuinely sorry for their sins may gain a plenary indulgence on certain days by visiting the Rosary Chapel in the church where the Confraternity is established. This may be gained on the first Sunday of every month, and on the feasts of our Lord and our Lady;

7. To those who assist at the Salve Regina: a hundred days' indulgence;

8. To those who openly wear the rosary out of devotion and to set a good example: a hundred days' indulgence;

9. Sick members who are unable to go to church may gain a plenary indulgence by going to confession and Communion and by saying that day the whole Rosary, or at least five decades;

10. The Sovereign Pontiffs have shown their generosity towards members of the Rosary Confraternity by allowing them to gain the indulgences attached to the Stations of the Cross by visiting five altars in the church where the Rosary Confraternity is established, and by saying the Our Father and Hail Mary five times before each altar, for the well-being of the Church. If there are only one or two altars in the Confraternity church, they should say the Our Father and Hail Mary twenty-five times before one of them.

97. This is a wonderful favour granted to Confraternity members, for in the Station Churches in Rome plenary indulgences can be obtained, souls can be delivered from purgatory, and many other important remissions can be gained. and these are available to members without trouble, without expense, and without leaving their own country. And even if the Confraternity is not established in the place where the members live, they can gain the very same indulgences by visiting five altars in any church. This concession was granted by Leo X.

The Sacred Congregation of Indulgences drew up a list of certain definite days on which those outside the city of Rome could gain the indulgences of the Stations of Rome. The Holy Father approved this list on March 7th, 1678, and commanded that it be strictly observed. These indulgences can be gained on the following days:

All the Sundays of Advent; each of the three Ember Days; Christmas Eve, and the Masses of midnight, of the Dawn and of the Day; the feasts of St. Stephen, St. John the Evangelist, the Holy Innocents, the Circumcision and the Epiphany; the Sundays of Septuagesima, Sexagesima, Quinquagesima, and every day from Ash Wednesday to Low Sunday inclusively; each of the three Rogation days; Ascension; the vigil of Pentecost, and every day of its octave; and the three days of the September Ember Days.

Dear brothers and sisters of the Confraternity, there are numerous other indulgences which you can gain. If you want to know about them, read the complete list of indulgences which have been granted to the members of the Confraternity. You will see there the names of the popes, the year in which they granted the indulgence, and many other particulars which I have not been able to include in this little summary.

FOURTH DECADE
The surpassing merit of the holy Rosary as seen in the wonders God has worked through it.

Thirty-first Rose

98. The saintly Blanche of Castille, Queen of France, was deeply grieved because twelve years after her marriage she was still childless. When St. Dominic went to see her he advised her to say the Rosary every day to ask God for the grace of motherhood, and she faithfully carried out his advice. In the year 1213 she gave birth to her eldest child, who was called Philip. But when the child died in infancy, the Queen sought our Lady's help more than ever, and had a large number of rosaries given out to all members of the court and to people in several towns in the Kingdom, asking them to pray to God for a blessing which this time would be complete. This was granted to her, for in 1215 St. Louis was born, the prince

who was to become the glory of France and the model of Christian kings.

99. Alphonsus VIII, King of Aragon and Castille, had been leading a disorderly life and had been punished by God in several ways, and he was forced to take refuge in a town belonging to one of his allies.

St. Dominic happened to be in this town on Christmas Day and he preached on the Rosary as he usually did, and spoke of the graces that we obtain through this devotion. He mentioned, among other things, that those who said the Rosary devoutly would overcome their enemies and regain all they had lost.

The King listened attentively and sent for St. Dominic to ask whether what he had said about the Rosary was really true. The Saint assured him that nothing was more true, and that if only he would practice this devotion and join the Confraternity, he would see for himself. The King resolved to say the Rosary every day and persevered for a year in doing so. The very next Christmas, our Lady appeared to him at the end of his Rosary and said, "Alphonsus, you have served me for a year by saying my Rosary devoutly every day, so I have come to reward you. I have obtained the forgiveness of your sins from my Son. Here is a rosary, which I present to you; wear it, and I promise you that none of your enemies will be able to harm you."

Our Lady vanished, leaving the King overjoyed and greatly encouraged; he immediately went in search of the Queen and told her all about our Lady's gift and the promise that went with it. He touched her eyes with this rosary, for she had lost her sight, and she was cured.

Shortly afterwards the King rallied some troops and with the help of his allies boldly attacked his enemies. He forced them to give back the territory they had taken from him and make reparation for his losses. They were completely routed, and he became so successful in war that soldiers came from all sides to fight under his standard, because it seemed that, whenever he went into battle, the victory was sure to be his.

This is not surprising because he never went into battle without first saying his Rosary on his knees. He made certain that the whole of his court joined the Confraternity of the Rosary and he saw to it that all his officials and servants were devoted to it.

The Queen also joined the Confraternity, and they both persevered in the service of Blessed Virgin and lived very holy lives.

Thirty-second Rose

100. St. Dominic had a cousin named Don Perez or Pedro, who was leading a highly immoral life. When he heard that his cousin was preaching on the wonders of the Rosary and learned that several people had been converted and had amended their lives by means of it, he said, "I had given up all hope of being saved but now I am beginning to take heart again. I really must hear this man of God."

So one day he went to hear one of St. Dominic's sermons. When the latter caught sight of him, he struck out against sin more zealously than ever before, and from the depths of his heart he besought God to enlighten his cousin and let him see what a deplorable state his soul was in.

At first, Don Perez was somewhat alarmed, but he still did not resolve to change his ways. He came once more to hear the Saint preach and his cousin, realizing that a heart as hardened as his could only be moved by something extraordinary, cried out with a loud voice, "Lord Jesus, grant that this whole congregation may see the state of the man who has just come into your house."

Then everyone suddenly saw that Don Perez was completely surrounded by a band of devils in the form of hideous beasts, who were holding him in great iron chains. People fled in all directions in abject terror, and Don Perez himself was even more appalled when he saw how everyone shunned him. St. Dominic told them all to stand still and said to his cousin, "Unhappy man that you are, acknowledge the deplorable state you are in and throw yourself at our Lady's feet. Take this rosary, say it with devotion and with true sorrow for all your sins, and make a resolution to amend your life."

Don Perez knelt down and said the Rosary; he then felt the desire to make his confession, which he did with heartfelt contrition. St. Dominic ordered him to say the Rosary every day; he promised to do this and he entered his own name in the register of the Confraternity. When he left the church his face was no longer horrible to behold but shining like that of an angel. Thereafter he persevered in devotion to the Rosary, led a well-ordered life and died a happy death.

Thirty-third Rose

101. When St. Dominic was preaching the Rosary near Carcassone, an Albigensian was brought to him who was possessed by the devil. The Saint exorcised him in the presence of a great crowd of people; it appears that over twelve thousand had come to hear him speak. The devils who were in possession of this wretched man were forced to answer St. Dominic's questions in spite of themselves. They said:

1. that there were fifteen thousand of them in the body of that poor man, because he had attacked the fifteen mysteries of the Rosary;

2. that by the Rosary which he preached, he put fear and horror into the depths of hell, and that he was the man they hated most throughout the world because of the souls he snatched from them by the devotion of the Rosary.

3. They revealed several other things.

St. Dominic put his rosary round the neck of the possessed man and asked them who, of all the saints in heaven, was the one they feared most, who should therefore be the most loved and revered by men.

At this they let out such unearthly screams that most of the people fell to the ground, seized with fear. Then, using all their cunning so as not to answer, the devils wept and wailed in such a pitiful way that many of the people wept also, out of pure natural pity. The devils, speaking through the mouth of the Albigensian, pleaded in a heart-rending voice, "Dominic, Dominic, have pity on us, we promise you we will never harm you.

"You have always had compassion for sinners and those in distress; have pity on us, for we are in grievous straits. We are suffering so much already, why do you delight in increasing our pains? Can't you be satisfied with the pains we now endure? Have mercy on us, have mercy on us!"

102. St. Dominic was not in the least moved by the pathetic words of those wretched spirits, and told them he would not let them alone until they had answered his question. Then they said they would whisper the answer in such a way that only St. Dominic would be able to hear. The latter firmly insisted upon their

answering clearly and audibly. Then the devils kept quiet and would not say another word, completely disregarding St. Dominic's orders.

So he knelt down and said this prayer to our Lady: "Oh, most glorious Virgin Mary, I implore you by the power of the holy Rosary command these enemies of the human race to answer my question."

No sooner had he said this prayer than a glowing flame leaped out of the ears, nostrils and mouth of the possessed man. Everyone shook with fear, but the fire did not hurt anyone. Then the devils cried, "Dominic, we beseech you, by the passion of Jesus Christ and the merits of his holy Mother and of all the saints, let us leave the body of this man without speaking further; for the angels will answer your question whenever you wish. After all, are we not liars - so why should you want to believe us? Do not torment us any more, have pity on us."

"Woe to you, wretched spirits, who do not deserve to be heard," St. Dominic said, and kneeling down he prayed to the Blessed Virgin: "O most worthy Mother of Wisdom, I am praying for the people assembled here, who have already learned how to say the Angelic Salutation properly. I beg you for the salvation of those here present, compel these adversaries of yours to proclaim the whole truth here and now before the people."

St. Dominic had scarcely finished this prayer when he saw the Blessed Virgin near at hand surrounded by a multitude of angels. She struck the possessed man with a golden rod that she held and said, "Answer my servant Dominic at once." (It must be noted that the people neither saw nor heard our Lady, only St. Dominic.)

103. Then the devils started screaming:

104. "Oh, you who are our enemy, our downfall and our destruction, why have you come from heaven to torture us so grievously? O advocate of sinners, you who snatch them from the very jaws of hell, you who are a most sure path to heaven, must we, in spite of ourselves, tell the whole truth and confess before everyone who it is who is the cause of our shame and our ruin? Oh, woe to us, princes of darkness.

"Then listen, you Christians. This Mother of Jesus is most powerful in saving her servants from falling into hell. She is like the sun which destroys the darkness of our wiles and subtlety. It is she who uncovers our hidden plots, breaks our snares, and makes our temptations useless and ineffective.

"We have to say, however, reluctantly, that no soul who has really persevered in her service has ever been damned with us; one single sigh that she offers to the Blessed Trinity is worth far more than all the prayers, desires, and aspirations of all the saints. We fear her more than all the other saints in heaven together, and we have no success with her faithful servants.

"Many Christians who call on her at the hour of death and who really ought to be damned according to our ordinary standards are saved by her intercession. And if that Marietta (it is thus in their fury they called her) did not counter our plans and our efforts, we should have overcome the Church and destroyed it long before this, and caused all the Orders in the Church to fall into error and infidelity.

"Now that we are forced to speak, we must also tell you that nobody who perseveres in saying the Rosary will be damned, because she obtains for her servants the grace of true contrition for their sins by which they obtain pardon and mercy."

Then St. Dominic had all the people say the Rosary very slowly and with great devotion, and a wonderful thing happened: at each Hail Mary which he and the people said, a large number of devils issued forth from the wretched man's body under the guise of red-hot coals. When the devils had all been expelled and the heretic completely delivered from them, our Lady, although invisible, gave her blessing to the assembled company, and they were filled with joy.

A large number of heretics were converted because of this miracle and joined the Confraternity of the Holy Rosary.

Thirty-fourth Rose

105. It is almost impossible to do credit sufficiently to the victories that Count Simon de Montfort won against the Albigensians under the patronage of Our Lady of the Rosary. They are so famous that the world has never seen anything to match them. One day he defeated ten thousand heretics with a force of five hundred men; on another occasion he overcame three thousand with only thirty men; finally, with eight hundred horsemen and one thousand infantrymen he completely routed the army of the King of Aragon, which was a hundred thousand strong, and this with the loss on his side of only one horseman and eight soldiers.

106. Our Lady also protected Alan de l'Anvallay, a Breton knight, from great perils. He too was fighting for the faith against the Albigensians. One day, when he found himself surrounded by enemies on all sides, our Lady let fall a hundred and fifty rocks upon his enemies and he was delivered from their hands.

Another day, when his ship had foundered and was about to sink, this good Mother caused a hundred and fifty small hills to appear miraculously above the water and by means of them they reached

Brittany in safety. In thanksgiving to our Lady for the miracles she had worked on his behalf in answer to his daily Rosary, he built a monastery at Dinan for the religious of the new Order of St. Dominic and, having become a religious himself, he died a holy death at Orleans.

107. Othère, also a Breton soldier, from Vaucouleurs, often put whole companies of heretics or robbers to flight, wearing his rosary on his arm and on the hilt of his sword. Once when he had beaten his enemies, they admitted that they had seen his sword shining brightly, and another time had noticed a shield on his arm on which our Lord, our Lady and the saints were depicted. This shield made him invisible and gave him the strength to attack well.

Another time he defeated twenty thousand heretics with only ten companies without losing a single man. This so impressed the general of the heretics' army that he sought out Othère, abjured his heresy and declared that he had seen him surrounded by flaming swords during the battle.

Thirty-fifth Rose

108. Blessed Alan relates that a certain Cardinal Pierre, whose titular church was that of St. Mary-beyond-the-Tiber, was a great friend of St. Dominic's and had learned from him to have a great devotion to the holy Rosary. He grew to love it so much that he never ceased singing its praises and encouraging everyone he met to embrace it. Eventually he was sent as legate to the Holy Land to the Christians who were fighting against the Saracens. So successfully did he convince the Christian army of the power of the Rosary that they all started saying it and stormed heaven for help in a battle in which they knew they would be pitifully outnumbered. And in fact, their three thousand triumphed over an enemy of one hundred thousand.

As we have seen, the devils have an overwhelming fear of the Rosary. St. Bernard says that the Angelic Salutation puts them to flight and makes all hell tremble. Blessed Alan assures us that he has seen several people delivered from Satan's bondage after taking up the holy Rosary, even though they had previously sold themselves to him, body and soul, by renouncing their baptismal vows and their allegiance to Jesus Christ.

Thirty-sixth Rose

109. In 1578, a woman of Antwerp had given herself to the devil and signed a contract with her own blood. Shortly afterwards she was stricken with remorse and had an intense desire to make amends for this terrible deed. So she sought out a kind and wise confessor to find out how she could be set free from the power of the devil.

She found a wise and holy priest, who advised her to go to Fr. Henry, director of the Confraternity of the Holy Rosary, at the Dominican Friary, to be enrolled there and to make her confession. Accordingly, she asked to see him but met, not Fr. Henry, but the devil disguised as a friar. He reproved her severely and said she could never hope to receive God's grace, and there was no way of revoking what she had signed. This grieved her greatly but she did not lose hope in God's mercy and sought out Fr. Henry once more, only to find the devil a second time, and to meet with a second rebuff. She came back a third time and then at last, by divine providence, she found Fr. Henry in person, the priest whom she had been looking for, and he treated her with great kindness, urging her to throw herself on the mercy of God and to make a good confession. He then received her into the Confraternity and told her to say the Rosary frequently.

One day, while Fr. Henry was celebrating Mass for her, our Lady forced the devil to give her back the contract she had signed. In this way she was delivered from the devil by the authority of Mary and by devotion to the holy Rosary.

Thirty-seventh Rose

110. A nobleman who had several daughters placed one of them in a lax monastery where the nuns were concerned only with vanity and pleasures. Their confessor, on the other hand, was a zealous priest with a great devotion to the holy Rosary. Wishing to guide this nun into a better way of life, he ordered her to say the Rosary every day in honour of the Blessed Virgin, while meditating on the life, passion and glory of Jesus Christ.

She joyously undertook this devotion, and little by little she grew to have a repugnance for the wayward habits of her sisters in religion. She developed a love of silence and prayer, in spite of the fact that the others despised and ridiculed her and called her a fanatic.

It was at this time that a holy priest, who was making the visitation of the convent, had a strange vision during his meditation: he saw a nun in her room, rapt in prayer, kneeling in front of a Lady of great beauty who was surrounded by angels. The latter had flaming spears with which they repelled a crowd of devils who wanted to come in. These evil spirits then fled to the other nuns' rooms under the guise of vile animals.

By this vision the priest became aware of the lamentable state of that monastery and was so upset that he thought he might die of grief. He sent for the young religious and exhorted her to persevere. As he pondered on the value of the Rosary, he decided to try and reform the Sisters by means of it. He bought a supply of beautiful rosaries and gave one to each nun, imploring them to say it every day and promising them that, if they would only say it faithfully, he would not try to force them to alter their lives. Wonderful and strange though it may seem, the nuns willingly accepted the rosaries and promised to say the prayer on that condition. Little by little they began to give up their empty and worldly pursuits, letting silence and recollection come into their lives. In less than a year they all asked that the monastery be reformed.

The Rosary worked more changes in their hearts than the priest could have done by exhorting and commanding them.

Thirty-eighth Rose

111. A Spanish countess who had been taught the holy Rosary by St. Dominic used to say it faithfully every day, with the result that she was making marvellous progress in her spiritual life. Since her only desire was to attain to perfection, she asked a bishop who was a renowned preacher for some practices that would help her to become perfect. The bishop told her that, before he could give her any advice, she would have to let him know the state of her soul and what her religious exercises were. She answered that her most important exercise was the Rosary, which she said every day, meditating on the Joyful, Sorrowful and Glorious Mysteries, and that she had profited greatly by so doing.

The Bishop was overjoyed to hear her explain what priceless lessons the mysteries contain. "I have been a doctor of theology for twenty years," he exclaimed, "and I have read many excellent books on various devotional practices. But never before have I come across one better than this or more conformed to the Christian life. From now on I shall follow your example, and I shall preach the Rosary."

He did so with such success that in a short while he saw his diocese changed for the better. There was a notable decline in immorality and worldliness of all kinds as well as in gambling. There were several instances of people being brought back to the faith, of sinners making restitution for their crimes, and of others sincerely resolving to give up their lives of vice. Religious fervour and Christian charity began to flourish. These changes were all the more remarkable because this bishop had been striving to reform his diocese for some time but with hardly any results.

To inculcate the devotion of the Rosary all the more, the bishop also wore a beautiful rosary at his side and always showed it to his congregation when he preached. He used to say, "My dear brethren, I am a doctor of theology, and of canon and civil law, but I say to you, as your bishop, that I take more pride in wearing the rosary of the Blessed Virgin than in any of my episcopal regalia or academic robes."

Thirty-ninth Rose

112. A Danish priest used to love to tell how the very same improvement that the Spanish bishop noticed in his diocese had occurred in his own parish. He always told his story with great joy of heart because it gave such glory to God.

"I had," he said, "preached as compellingly as I could, touching on many aspects of our holy Faith, and using every argument I could possibly think of to get people to amend their way of life, but in vain. Finally, I decided to preach the holy Rosary. I told my congregations how precious it was and taught them how to say it, and I affirm that having taught them to appreciate this devotion, I saw a manifest change within six months.

"How true it is that this God-given prayer has a divine power to touch our hearts and inspire them with a horror of sin and a love of virtue!"

One day our Lady said to Blessed Alan, "Just as God chose the Angelic Salutation to bring about the incarnation of his Word and the redemption of mankind, so those who want to bring about moral reforms and regenerate them in Jesus Christ must honour me and greet me with the same salutation. I am the channel by which God came to men, and so, next to Jesus Christ, it is through me that men must obtain grace and virtue."

113. I, who write this, have learnt from my own experience that the Rosary has the power to convert even the most hardened hearts. I have known people who have gone to missions and heard sermons on the most terrifying subjects without being in the least moved; and yet, after they had, on my advice, started to say the Rosary every day. they eventually became converted and gave themselves completely to God.

When I have gone back to parishes where I had given missions, I have seen tremendous differences between them; in those parishes where the people had given up the Rosary, they had generally fallen back into their sinful ways, whereas in places where the Rosary was said faithfully I found the people were persevering in the grace of God and advancing in virtue day by day.

Fortieth Rose

114. Blessed Alan de la Roche, Fr. Jean Dumont, Fr. Thomas, the chronicles of St. Dominic and other writers who have seen these things with their own eyes speak of the marvellous conversions that are brought about by this wonderful devotion. Great sinners, both men and women, have been converted after twenty, thirty or forty

years of sin and unspeakable vice. I will not even relate those which I have seen myself because I do not want to make this book too long; there are several reasons why I would rather not talk about them.

Dear reader, if you practice and preach this devotion, you will learn more, by your own experience, than from spiritual books, and you will have the happiness of being rewarded by our Lady in accordance with the promises she made to St. Dominic, to Blessed Alan de la Roche, and to those who encourage this devotion which is so dear to her. For the Rosary teaches people about the virtues of Jesus and Mary, and leads them to mental prayer, to the imitation of Jesus Christ, to the frequentation of the sacraments, the practice of genuine virtue and of all kinds of good works. It also helps us to gain many wonderful indulgences, which people are unaware of because those who preach this devotion hardly ever mention them and content themselves with giving a popular sermon on the Rosary which very often produces admiration but not instruction.

115. Finally, I shall content myself with saying, in company with Blessed Alan de la Roche, that the Rosary is a source and a storehouse of countless blessings.

1. Sinners obtain pardon;

2 Those who thirst are refreshed;

3. Those who are fettered are set free;

4 Those who weep find joy;

5. Those who are tempted find peace;

6 Those in need find help;

7. Religious are reformed;

8 The ignorant are instructed;

9. The living learn to resist spiritual decline;

10 The dead have their pains eased by suffrages.

Our Lady once said to Blessed Alan, "I want those who are devoted to my Rosary to have my Son's grace and blessing during their lifetime, at death and after their death. I want them to be freed from all slavery so that they will be like kings, with crowns on their heads, sceptres in their hands and to reign in eternal glory. Amen.

FIFTH DECADE
How to say the Rosary worthily

Forty-first Rose

116. It. is not so much the length of a prayer as the fervour with which it is said which pleases God and touches his heart. A single Hail Mary said properly is worth more than a hundred and fifty said badly. Most Catholics say the Rosary, either the whole fifteen mysteries or five of them, or at least a few decades. Why is it then that so few of them give up their sins and make progress in virtue, if not because they are not saying them as they should.

117. It is a good thing to think over how we should pray if we want to please God and become more holy.

1. Firstly, to say the holy Rosary with advantage one must be in a state of grace or at least be fully determined to give up sin, for all our theology teaches us that good works and prayers are dead works if they are done in a state of mortal sin. Therefore, they can neither be pleasing to God nor help us to gain eternal life. As

Scripture says, "Praise is not seemly in the mouth of a sinner" (Ecclus. 15).

The praise and greeting of the angel and the very prayer of Jesus Christ are not pleasing to God when they are said by unrepentant sinners.

"These people honour me with their lips, but their heart is far from me" (Mark 7:6).

Those who join my confraternities (says Jesus Christ), who say the Rosary every day, without any contrition for their sins, offer me lip service only and their hearts are far from me.

2. I have just said that a person must "at least be fully determined to give up sin," 1) because if it were true that God only heard the prayers of those in a state of grace, it would follow that those who are in a state of serious sin should not pray at all. This is an erroneous teaching which has been condemned by the Church, because sinners, of course, need to pray far more than good people. Were this horrible doctrine true, it would be useless and futile to tell a sinner to say the Rosary, because it would never help him; 2) because they join one of our Lady's confraternities, or say the Rosary or some other prayer, without having the slightest intention of giving up sin, they join the ranks of her false devotees. These presumptuous and impenitent devotees, hiding under her mantle, with the scapular round their necks and the rosary in their hands, cry out, "Blessed Virgin, good Mother, Hail Mary," and yet at the same time they are crucifying Jesus Christ and tearing his flesh anew by their sins. It is a great tragedy, but from the ranks of our Lady's most holy confraternities souls are falling into the fires of hell.

118. We earnestly advise everyone to say the Rosary: the virtuous, that they may persevere and grow in the grace of God; sinners, that they may rise from their sins. But God forbid we should ever encourage a sinner to think that our Lady will protect him with her mantle if he continues to love sin, for it will turn into a mantle of damnation which will hide his sins from the public eye. The Rosary, which is a remedy for all ills, would then be turned into a deadly poison. Corruptio optimi pessima.

The learned Cardinal Hugues tells us that one should be as pure as an angel to approach the Blessed Virgin and say the Angelic Salutation. One day, our Lady showed herself to an immoral man who used to say the Rosary regularly every day. She showed him a bowl of beautiful fruit, but the bowl itself was covered with filth. The man was horrified to see this, and our Lady said to him, "This is the way you are honouring me. You are giving me beautiful roses in a dirty bowl. Do you think I can find them pleasing to me?"

Forty-second Rose

119. In order to pray well, it is not enough to give expression to our petitions by means of that most excellent of all prayers, the Rosary, but we must also pray with great attention, for God listens more to the voice of the heart than that of the mouth. To be guilty of wilful distractions during prayer would show a great lack of respect and reverence; it would make our Rosaries unfruitful and make us guilty of sin.

How can we expect God to listen to us if we ourselves do not pay attention to what we are saying? How can we expect him to be pleased if, while in the presence of his tremendous majesty, we give in to distractions, like a child running after a butterfly? People who do that forfeit God's blessing, which is changed into a curse for having treated the things of God disrespectfully: "Cursed be the one who does God's work negligently." Jer. 48:10.

120. Of course, you cannot say your Rosary without having a few involuntary distractions; it is even difficult to say a Hail Mary without your imagination troubling you a little, for it is never still; but you can say it without voluntary distractions, and you must take all sorts of precautions to lessen involuntary distractions and to control your imagination.

To do this, put yourself in the presence of God and imagine that God and his Blessed Mother are watching you, and that your guardian angel is at your right hand, taking your Hail Marys, if they are well said, and using them like roses to make crowns for Jesus and Mary. But remember that at your left hand is the devil, ready to pounce on every Hail Mary that comes his way and to write it down in his book of death, if they are not said with attention, devotion, and reverence. Above all, do not fail to offer up each decade in honour of one of the mysteries, and try to form a picture in your mind of Jesus and Mary in connection with that mystery.

121. We read in the life of Blessed Hermann of the Order of the Premonstratensians, that at one time when he used to say the Rosary attentively and devoutly while meditating on the mysteries, our Lady used to appear to him resplendent in breathtaking majesty and beauty. But, as time went on, his fervour cooled and he fell into the way of saying his Rosary hurriedly and without giving it his full attention. Then one day our Lady appeared to him again, but this time she was far from beautiful, and her face was furrowed and drawn with sadness. Blessed Hermann was appalled at the change in her, and our Lady explained, "This is how I look to you, Hermann, because this is how you are treating me; as a woman to be despised and of no importance. Why do you no longer greet me

with respect and attention while meditating on my mysteries and praising my privileges?"

Forty-third Rose

122. When the Rosary is well said, it gives Jesus and Mary more glory and is more meritorious for the soul than any other prayer. But it is also the hardest prayer to say well and to persevere in, owing especially to the distractions which almost inevitably attend the constant repetition of the same words.

When we say the Little Office of Our Lady, or the Seven Penitential Psalms, or any prayers other than the Rosary, the variety of words and expressions keeps us alert, prevents our imagination from wandering, and so makes it easier for us to say them well. On the contrary, because of the constant repetition of the Our Father and Hail Mary in the same unvarying form, it is difficult, while saying the Rosary, not to become wearied and inclined to sleep, or to turn to other prayers that are more refreshing and less tedious. This shows that one needs much greater devotion to persevere in saying the Rosary than in saying any other prayer, even the psalter of David.

123. Our imagination, which is hardly still a minute, makes our task harder, and then of course there is the devil who never tires of trying to distract us and keep us from praying. To what ends does not the evil one go against us while we are engaged in saying our Rosary against him.

Being human, we easily become tired and slipshod, but the devil makes these difficulties worse when we are saying the Rosary. Before we even begin, he makes us feel bored, distracted, or exhausted; and when we have started praying, he oppresses us from all sides, and when after much difficulty and many distractions, we have finished, he whispers to us, "What you have just said is worthless. It is useless for you to say the Rosary. You had better get on with other things. It is only a waste of time to pray without paying attention to what you are saying; half-an-hour's meditation or some spiritual reading would be much better. Tomorrow, when you are not feeling so sluggish, you'll pray better; leave the rest of your Rosary till then." By tricks of this kind the devil gets us to give up the Rosary altogether or to say it less often, and we keep putting it off or change to some other devotion.

124. Dear friend of the Rosary Confraternity, do not listen to the devil, but be of good heart, even if your imagination has been bothering you throughout your Rosary, filling your mind with all kinds of distracting thoughts, so long as you tried your best to get rid of them as soon as you noticed them. Always remember that the best Rosary is the one with the most merit, and there is more merit in praying when it is hard than when it is easy. Prayer is all the harder when it is, naturally speaking, distasteful to the soul and is filled with those annoying little ants and flies running about in your imagination, against your will, and scarcely allowing you the time to enjoy a little peace and appreciate the beauty of what you are saying.

125. Even if you have to fight distractions all through your whole Rosary, be sure to fight well, arms in hand: that is to say, do not stop saying your Rosary even if it is difficult to say and you have no sensible devotion. It is a terrible battle, but one that is profitable to the faithful soul. If you put down your arms, that is, if you give up the Rosary, you will be admitting defeat and then the devil, having got what he wanted, will leave you in peace, and on the day of judgment will taunt you because of your faithlessness and lack of courage. "He who is faithful in little things will also be faithful in those that are greater." Luke 16:10.

He who is faithful in rejecting the smallest distractions when he says even the smallest prayer, will also be faithful in great things. Nothing is more certain, since the Holy Spirit has told us so.

So all of you, servants and handmaids of Jesus Christ and the Blessed Virgin, who have made up your minds to say the Rosary every day, be of good heart. Do not let the multitude of flies (as I call the distractions that make war on you during prayer) make you abandon the company of Jesus and Mary, in whose holy presence you are when saying the Rosary. In what follows I shall give you suggestions for diminishing distractions in prayer.

Forty-fourth Rose

126. After you have invoked the Holy Spirit, in order to say your Rosary well, place yourself for a moment in the presence of God and make the offering of the decades in the way I will show you later.

Before beginning a decade, pause for a moment or two, depending on how much time you have, and contemplate the mystery that you are about to honour in that decade. Always be sure to ask, by this mystery and through the intercession of the Blessed Virgin, for one of the virtues that shines forth most in this mystery or one of which you are in particular need.

Take great care to avoid the two pitfalls that most people fall into during the Rosary. The first is the danger of not asking for any graces at all, so that if some good people were asked their Rosary intention they would not know what to say. So, whenever you say your Rosary, be sure to ask for some special grace or virtue, or strength to overcome some sin.

The second fault commonly committed in saying the Rosary is to have no intention other than that of getting it over with as quickly as possible. This is because so many look upon the Rosary as a burden, which weighs heavily upon them when it has not been said, especially when we have promised to say it regularly or have been told to say it as a penance more or less against our will.

127. It is sad to see how most people say the Rosary. They say it astonishingly fast, slipping over part of the words. We could not possibly expect anyone, even the most important person, to think that a slipshod address of this kind was a compliment, and yet we imagine that Jesus and Mary will be honoured by it!

Small wonder, then, that the most sacred prayers of our holy religion seem to bear no fruit, and that, after saying thousands of Rosaries, we are still no better than we were before.

Dear friend of the Confraternity, I beg you to restrain your natural precipitation when saying your Rosary, and make some pauses in the middle of the Our Father and Hail Mary, and a smaller one after the words of the Our Father and Hail Mary which I have marked with a cross, as follows:

Our Father who art in heaven, + hallowed by thy name, + thy kingdom come, + thy will be done + on earth as it is in heaven. + Give us this day + our daily bread, + and forgive us our trespasses + as we forgive those who trespass against us, + and lead us not into temptation, + but deliver us from evil. Amen. +

Hail, Mary, full of grace, + the Lord is with thee, + blessed art thou among women, + and blessed is the fruit of thy womb, Jesus. +

Holy Mary, Mother of God, + pray for us sinners, now + and at the hour of our death. Amen. +

A Manual of the Most Holy Rosary

At first, you may find it difficult to make these pauses because of your bad habit of saying prayers in a hurry; but a decade said recollectedly in this way will be worth more than thousands of Rosaries said in a hurry, without pausing or reflecting.

128. Blessed Alan de la Roche and other writers, including Robert Bellarmine, tell the story of how a good priest advised three of his penitents, who happened to be sisters, to say the Rosary every day without fail for a whole year. This was so that they might make a beautiful robe of glory for the Blessed Virgin out of their Rosaries. This was a secret that the priest had received from heaven.

So the three sisters said the Rosary faithfully for a year, and on the feast of the Purification our Lady appeared to them at night when they had retired. St. Catherine and St. Agnes were with her, and she was wearing a dress brilliant with light, on which was written in letters of gold the words "Hail, Mary, full of grace." Our Lady approached the eldest sister and said, "I greet you, my daughter, who have greeted me so often and so well. I want to thank you for the beautiful robes you have made me." The two virgin saints who accompanied our Lady also thanked her and all three disappeared.

An hour later, our Lady, with the same two companions, entered the room again, but this time she was wearing a green dress which had no gold lettering and did not shine. She went to the second sister and thanked her for the robe she had made by saying her Rosary. But since this sister had seen our Lady appear to the eldest sister much more magnificently dressed, she asked the reason why. Our Lady answered, "Your sister made me more beautiful clothes because she has been saying the Rosary better than you."

About an hour after this, she appeared to the youngest of the sisters wearing tattered and dirty rags. "My daughter," she said, "I want to thank you for these clothes you have made me." The young girl, feeling ashamed, cried out, "O my lady, how could I have dressed you so badly! I beg you to forgive me. Please grant me a little more time to make you a beautiful robe by saying my Rosary better." Our Lady and the two saints vanished, leaving the girl heartbroken. She told her confessor everything that had happened and he urged them to say the Rosary for another year and to say it with more devotion than ever.

At the end of this second year, on the same day of the Purification, our Lady, clothed in a magnificent robe, and again attended by St. Catherine and St. Agnes, wearing crowns, appeared to them in the evening. She said to them, "I have come to tell you that you have earned heaven at last, and you will all have the great joy of going there tomorrow." The three of them cried, "Our hearts are ready, dearest Queen, our hearts are ready." Then the vision faded. That same night they became ill and sent for their confessor, and received the last sacraments, after having thanked him for the holy practice he had taught them. After Compline, our Lady appeared with a large company of virgins and had the three sisters clothed in white robes. While angels were singing, "Come, spouses of Jesus Christ, receive the crowns which have been prepared for you for all eternity," they departed from this life.

Some important truths can be learned from this story: 1) How important it is to have a good director who will counsel holy practices, especially that of the holy Rosary; 2) How important it is to say the Rosary with attention and devotion; 3) How kind and merciful is the Blessed Virgin to those who are sorry for the past and are firmly resolved to do better; 4) How generous she is in rewarding us in life, at death, and in eternity for the little services that we render her with fidelity.

Forty-fifth Rose

129. I would like to add that the Rosary ought to be said reverently, that is to say, it ought to be said as much as possible, kneeling, with hands joined, clasping the rosary. However, if you are ill, you can, of course, say it in bed; or if one is travelling it can be said while walking; if, on account of some infirmity, you cannot kneel you can say it standing or sitting. You can even say it while working if your duties do not allow you to leave your job, for work with one's hands is not always incompatible with vocal prayer.

I agree that, since the soul has its limitations and can only do so much, when we are concentrating on manual work we are less attentive to the activities of the spirit, such as prayer. But when we cannot do otherwise, this kind of prayer is not without its value in our Lady's eyes, and she rewards our good- will more than our exterior actions.

130. I advise you to divide up your Rosary into three parts and to say each group of five decades at different times of the day. This is much better than saying the whole fifteen decades at once.

If you cannot find the time to say five decades all together, say a decade here and a decade there; you will thus be able, in spite of your work and the calls upon your time, to complete the whole Rosary before going to bed.

St. Francis de Sales set us a very good example of fidelity in this respect: once when he was extremely tired from the visits he had made during the day and remembered, towards midnight, that he had left a few decades of his Rosary unsaid, he knelt down and said them before going to bed, notwithstanding all the efforts of his secretary, who saw he was tired and begged him to leave the rest of his prayers till the next day.

Imitate also the faithfulness, reverence and devotion of the holy friar, mentioned in the chronicles of St. Francis, who always said five decades of the Rosary with great reverence and attention before dinner. I have mentioned this earlier.

Forty-sixth Rose

131. Of all the ways of saying the holy Rosary, the most glorious to God, most salutary to our souls, and the most terrible to the devil is that of saying or chanting the Rosary publicly in two choirs.

God is very pleased to have people gathered together in prayer. All the angels and the blessed unite to praise him unceasingly. The just on earth, gathered together in various communities, pray in common, night and day. Our Lord expressly recommended this practice to his apostles and disciples, and promised that whenever there would be at least two or three gathered in his name he would be there in the midst of them.

What a wonderful thing to have Jesus Christ in our midst! And all we have to do to have him with us is to come together to say the Rosary. That is why the first Christians met so often to pray together, in spite of the persecutions of the Emperors, who had forbidden them to assemble. They preferred to risk death rather than to miss their gatherings where our Lord was present.

132. This way of praying is of the greatest benefit to us:

1. because our minds are usually more alert during public prayer than when we pray alone;

2. when we pray in common, the prayer of each one belongs to the whole group and make all together but one prayer, so that if one person is not praying well, someone else in the same gathering who is praying better makes up for his deficiency. In the same way,

those who are strong uphold the weak, those who are fervent inspire the lukewarm, the rich enrich the poor, the bad are merged with the good. How can a measure of cockle be sold? This can be done very easily by mixing it with four or five bushels of good wheat.

3. One who says his Rosary alone only gains the merit of one Rosary; but if he says it with thirty other people he gains the merit of thirty Rosaries. This is the law of public prayer. How profitable, how advantageous this is!

4. Urban VIII, who was very pleased to see how the devotion of the holy Rosary had spread to Rome and how it was being said in two groups or choirs, particularly at the convent of Santa Maria sopra Minerva, attached a hundred days' extra indulgence toties quoties, whenever the Rosary was said in two choirs. This is set out in his brief Ad perpetuam rei memoriam, of the year 1626. So every time you say the Rosary in common, you gain a hundred days' indulgence.

5. Public prayer is more powerful than private prayer to appease the anger of God and call down his mercy, and the Church, guided by the Holy Spirit, has always advocated it in times of disasters and general distress.

In his Bull on the Rosary, Pope Gregory XIII declares that we must believe, on pious faith, that the public prayers and processions of the members of the Confraternity of the Holy Rosary were largely responsible for the great victory over the Turkish navy at Lepanto, which God granted to the Christians on the first Sunday of October 1571.

133. When King Louis the Just, of blessed memory, was besieging La Rochelle, where the rebellious heretics had their strongholds, he

wrote to his mother to beg her to have public prayers offered for a victorious outcome. The Queen-Mother decided to have the Rosary recited publicly in Paris in the Dominican church of Faubourg Saint-Honoré, and this was carried out by the Archbishop of Paris. It was begun on May 20th, 1628.

Both the Queen and the Queen-Mother were present, with the Duke of Orleans, Cardinal de la Rochefoucault, Cardinal de Bérulle, and several prelates. The court turned out in full force as well as a great number of the general populace. The Archbishop read the meditations on the mysteries aloud and then began the Our Father and Hail Mary of each decade, while the congregation of religious and lay-folk answered. At the end of the Rosary a statue of the Blessed Virgin was carried solemnly in procession while the Litany of our Lady was sung.

This devotion was continued every Saturday with admirable fervour and resulted in a manifest blessing from heaven, for the King triumphed over the English at the Island of Ré and made his triumphant entry into La Rochelle on All Saints Day of the same year. This shows us the power of public prayer.

134. Finally, when the Rosary is said in common, it is far more formidable to the devil, because in this public prayer it is an army that is attacking him. He can often overcome the prayer of an individual, but if it is joined to that of others, the devil has much more trouble in getting the best of it. It is easy to break a single stick; but if you join it to others to make a bundle, it cannot be broken. Vis unita fit fortior. Soldiers join together in an army to overcome their enemies; immoral people often come together for parties of debauchery and dancing; evil spirits join forces in order to make us lose our souls. Why, then, should not Christians join forces to have Jesus Christ present with them, to appease the anger

of God, to draw down his grace and mercy on us, and to frustrate and overcome the devil more forcefully?

Dear friend of the Confraternity, whether you live in the town or the country, near the parish church or a chapel, go there at least every evening, with the approval of the parish priest, together with all those who want to recite the Rosary in two choirs. If a church or chapel is not available, say the Rosary together in your own or a neighbour's house.

135. This is a holy practice, which God, in his mercy, has set up in places where I have preached missions, in order to safeguard and increase the good brought about by the mission and to prevent further sin. Before the Rosary was established in these little towns and villages, dances and parties of debauchery went on; dissoluteness, wantonness, blasphemy, quarrels and feuds flourished; one heard nothing but evil songs and double-meaning talk. But now nothing is heard but hymns and the chant of the Our Father and Hail Mary. The only gatherings to be seen are those of twenty, thirty or a hundred or more people who, at a fixed time, sing the praises of God as religious do.

There are even places where the Rosary is said in common every day, at three different times of the day. What a blessing from heaven that is! As there are wicked people everywhere, do not expect to find that the place you live in is free of them; there will be people who avoid going to church for the Rosary, who may even make fun of it and do all they can, by what they do and say, to stop you from going. But do not give up. As those wretched people will have to be separated from God and heaven forever, already here on earth they have to be separated from the company of Jesus and his servants.

Forty-seventh Rose

136. People of God, cut yourselves adrift from those who are damning themselves by their impious lives, laziness and lack of devotion without delay, and say the Rosary often with faith, humility, confidence and perseverance.

1. Our Lord told us to pray always, after the example he has given us, because of our endless need of prayer, on account of the darkness of our minds, our ignorance, and weakness, and the number of our enemies. Anyone who really gives heed to this commandment of our Master will surely not be satisfied with saying the Rosary once a year, as the Perpetual Members do, or once a week, like the Ordinary Members, but will say it every day without fail, as a member of the Daily Rosary, even though the only obligation he has is that of his own salvation. "We ought always to pray and not lose heart."

137. These are the eternal words of our Blessed Lord himself. And we must believe his words and abide by them if we do not want to be damned. You can explain them as you wish so long as you do not interpret them as the world does and observe them in a worldly way. Our Lord gave us the true explanation of his words in the examples he left us: "I have given you an example that as I have done to you, so you do also." (Jn. 13:5.) And "he spent the whole night in prayer to God," (Luke 6:12) as if the day was not sufficient for it.

Often he repeated to his Apostles these two words, "Watch and pray." The flesh is weak, temptation is everywhere and always around you. If you do not keep up your prayers, you will fall. And because some of them evidently thought that these words of our Lord constituted only a counsel, they completely missed the point.

A Manual of the Most Holy Rosary

That is why they fell into temptation and sin, even though they were in the company of Jesus Christ.

138. Dear friend of the Confraternity, if you want to lead a fashionable life and belong to the world - by this I mean if you do not mind falling into mortal sin from time to time and then going to confession, and avoiding conspicuous sins which the world considers vile, while keeping up the "respectable" ones - then, of course, there is no need for you to say so many prayers and Rosaries. To be "respectable" you only need to say a little prayer morning and evening, an occasional Rosary given to you for your penance, a few decades said in a casual way, when the fancy takes you - that is quite enough for any good-living person. If you did less, you might be branded as a freethinker or profligate; if you do more, you are becoming an eccentric or a fanatic.

139. But if you want to lead a true Christian life and genuinely want to save your soul and walk in the footsteps of the saints and not fall into serious sin, if you wish to break all the snares of the devil and extinguish all his flaming darts, you must pray always as our Lord taught and commanded you to do.

If you really have this wish at heart, then you should at least say your Rosary every day, or its equivalent.

I repeat "at least," because probably all that you will accomplish through your Rosary will be to avoid mortal sin and temptation. This is because you are exposed to the strong current of the world's wickedness by which many a strong soul is swept away; you are in the midst of the thick, clinging darkness which often blinds even the most enlightened souls; you are surrounded by evil spirits who, being more experienced than ever and knowing that their time is short, are more subtle and more effective in tempting you.

It will indeed be a marvel of grace wrought by the holy Rosary if you manage to keep out of the clutches of the world, the devil and the flesh and sin, and gain eternal life.

140. If you do not want to believe what I say, at least learn from your own experience. I should like to ask you if, when you were in the habit of saying no more prayers than people usually say in the world, and saying them in the way they usually say them, you were able to avoid serious faults and sins that were grievous but seemed of little account to you in your blindness. Now at last you must wake up, and if you want to live and die without sin, at least serious sin, pray always; say your Rosary every day, as all members used to do in the early days of the Confraternity. (See the end of this book for proof of what I say.)

When our Blessed Lady gave the Rosary to St. Dominic, she ordered him to say it every day and to get others to say it daily. St. Dominic never let anyone join the Confraternity unless he were fully determined to say it every day. If nowadays people are allowed to be Ordinary members through saying the Rosary once a week, it is because fervour has dwindled and charity grown cold. You get what you can from one who is poor in prayer. "It was not so in the beginning."

Three things must be noted here.

141. The first is that if you want to be enrolled in the Confraternity of the Daily Rosary and share in the prayers and merits of its members, it is not enough to be enrolled in the Ordinary Rosary or simply to make a resolution to say it every day. In addition, you must give your name to those who have the power of enrolling. It is also a very good thing to go to confession and communion for this intention. The reason for this is that the Ordinary Rosary

membership does not include that of the Daily Rosary, but this latter does include the former.

The second point I want to make is that, absolutely speaking, it is not even a venial sin to fail to say the Rosary every day, or every week, or every year.

The third point is that whenever illness, or obedience to a lawful superior, or necessity, or involuntary forgetfulness has prevented you from saying the Rosary, you do not forfeit your share in the merits and you do not lose your participation in the Rosaries of the other Confraternity members. So it is not absolutely necessary for you to say two Rosaries on the following day to make up for the one you missed, as I suppose, through no fault of your own. If, however, when you are ill, your sickness is such that you are still able to say part of your Rosary, you have to say that part.

"Blessed are those who stand before you always." "Happy those who dwell in your house, O Lord, they praise you continually." Lord Jesus, blessed are the brothers and sisters of the Daily Rosary Confraternity who, day after day, are present in and around your throne in heaven, so that they may meditate and contemplate your joyful, sorrowful and glorious mysteries. How happy they are on earth because of the wonderful graces you bestow on them, and how blessed shall they be in heaven where they will praise you in a special way forever and ever.

142. 2. The Rosary should be said with faith, for our Blessed Lord said, "Believe that you will receive and it will be granted." If you believe that you will receive what you ask from God, he will grant your petitions. He will say to you, "As you have believed, so be it done to you." "If anyone needs wisdom, let him ask God with faith, and without hesitating, and - through his Rosary - it will be given him."

143. 3. Thirdly, we must pray with humility, like the publican; he was kneeling on the ground, on two knees, not on one knee as proud and worldly people do, or one knee on the bench. He was at the back of the church and not in the sanctuary as the Pharisee was; his eyes were cast down, for he dared not look up to heaven; he did not hold his head up and look about him like the Pharisee; he beat his breast, confessing himself a sinner and asking for forgiveness: "Be merciful to me, a sinner," and not like the Pharisee who boasted of his good works, who despised others in their prayers. Do not imitate the prayer of the proud Pharisee which only hardened his heart and increased his guilt; imitate rather the humility of the tax-collector, whose prayer obtained him the remission of his sins.

You must be on your guard against giving yourself to what is extraordinary and asking or even desiring knowledge of extraordinary things, visions, revelations, or other miraculous graces which God has occasionally given to some of the saints while they were saying the Rosary. Sola fides sufficit: Faith alone suffices now that the Gospel and all the devotions and pious practices are sufficiently established.

Even if you suffer from dryness of soul, distaste for prayer and interior discouragement, never give up the least part of your Rosary; this would be a sign of pride and infidelity; but like a brave champion of Jesus and Mary, say your Our Fathers and Hail Marys in your dryness, without seeing, feeling, or appreciating, and concentrating as best you can on the mysteries.

You ought not to look for sweets or jam to eat with your daily bread, as children do; but to imitate Jesus more perfectly in his agony you could say your Rosary more slowly sometimes when you find it particularly hard to say: "Being in agony, he prayed the longer," so that what was said of our Lord when he was in his agony of prayer may be said of you: he prayed all the longer.

144. 4. Pray with great confidence, with confidence based on the goodness and infinite generosity of God and on the promises of Jesus Christ. God is the spring of living water which flows unceasingly into the hearts of those who pray. The eternal Father yearns for nothing so much as to share the life-giving waters of his grace and mercy with us. He entreats us, "All you who thirst, come to the waters," that is, come and drink of my spring through prayer, and when we do not pray to him he sorrowfully says that we are forsaking him, "They have forsaken me, the fountain of living water."

We please our Lord when we ask him for graces, and if we do not ask he makes a loving complaint, "Until now you have not asked anything.... Ask and you will receive, seek and you will find, knock and the door will be opened to you."

Furthermore, to give us more confidence in praying to him, he has bound himself by a promise: that his eternal Father would grant everything we ask in his name.

Forty-eighth Rose

145. As a fifth point, I must add perseverance and prayer. Only he who perseveres in asking, seeking, and knocking, will receive, will find and will enter. It is not enough to ask God for certain graces for a month, a year, ten or twenty years; we must never tire of asking. We must keep on asking until the very moment of death, and even in this prayer, which shows our confidence in God, we must join the thought of death to that of perseverance and say, "Although he should kill me, I will trust in him," will trust him to give me what I ask.

146. Prominent and rich people of the world show their generosity by foreseeing people's wants and ministering to them, even before they are asked for anything. God's munificence, on the other hand, is shown by his making us seek and ask, over a long period of time, for the graces which he wishes to bestow, and the more precious the grace, the longer he takes to grant it:

1. in order to increase the grace still more;

2. in order that the recipient may more deeply appreciate it;

3. in order that the one who receives it may guard against losing it; for people do not appreciate very much what they obtain quickly and at little cost.

So, dear members of the Confraternity, persevere in asking God for all your needs, both spiritual and material, through the holy Rosary; especially should you pray for divine Wisdom, which is "an infinite treasure," and there can be no possible doubt that you will receive it sooner or later, provided you do not give up and do not lose courage in the middle of your journey. "You still have a great way to go."

You have a long way to travel, there will be bad times to weather, many difficulties to overcome, and many enemies to defeat before you will have stored up enough treasures for eternity, enough Our Fathers and Hail Marys with which to buy your way to heaven and win the glorious crown which awaits each faithful brother and sister of the Confraternity.

"Let no one take your crown": take care that your crown is not appropriated by another who has been more faithful than you in saying his Rosary every day. "Your crown": it was yours, God had prepared it for you; it was yours, you had already half obtained it by your Rosaries well said. But because you stopped on the way when you were running so well, another has left you behind and got there first; another who is more diligent and more faithful has paid, by his Rosaries and good works, what was required to obtain that crown.

"You began your race well; who has hindered you?" Who has prevented you from having the crown of the holy Rosary? Alas, none other than the enemies of the Rosary, who are so numerous.

147. Believe me, it is only the violent who take it by force. These crowns are not for the timid who are afraid of this world's taunts and threats, neither are they for the lazy and indolent who only say their Rosary carelessly, or hastily, just for the sake of getting it over with. The same applies to people who say it intermittently, as the spirit moves them. These crowns are not for cowards who lose heart and lay down their arms as soon as they see hell is let loose against their Rosary.

Dear fellow-members, if you want to serve Jesus and Mary by saying the Rosary every day, you must be prepared for temptation: "If you aspire to serve the Lord, prepare yourself for temptation." Heretics, licentious people, the so-called respectable people of the world, persons of superficial piety, and false prophets, hand in glove with your fallen nature and all hell itself - all will wage terrible battles against you in an endeavour to make you give up this holy practice.

148. To help you to be better armed against their onslaught - not so much of acknowledged heretics and profligates as those who are considered "respectable" in the eyes of the world, and even those who are devout but have no use for the Rosary - I am going to tell you simply some of the things these people are always saying and thinking.

"What does this babbler want to say?" "Come, let us attack him, for he is against us." What is he doing, saying so many Rosaries? What is it he is always mumbling? Such laziness! He does nothing but keep on sliding those beads along, he would do much better to work without amusing himself with such foolishness. Oh yes, it's quite true, all you have to do is to say the Rosary and a fortune will fall from heaven into your lap. The Rosary brings you all you need without lifting a finger. But hasn't it been said, "God helps those who help themselves"? Why load yourself with so many prayers? Brevis oratio penetrat coelos; an Our Father and a Hail Mary well said are quite sufficient. God has never commanded us to say the Rosary; of course it's all right, it's not a bad devotion when you've got the time, but don't think for one minute that people who say the Rosary are any more sure of heaven than we are. Just look at the saints who never said it!

Far too many people want everyone to see through their own eyes, people who lack prudence and carry everything to extremes, scrupulous people who see sin almost everywhere, who say that those who do not say the Rosary will be damned.

Oh yes, the Rosary is all right for old women who can't read. But surely the Little Office of our Lady is much more worthwhile, or the seven penitential psalms? Is there anything more beautiful than those psalms which have been inspired by the Holy Spirit?

You say you have undertaken to say the Rosary every day; that's just a flash in the pan, you know it won't last. Wouldn't it be better to undertake less and be more faithful about it? Come, my friend, take my word for it, say your morning and night prayers, work hard during the day and offer it up. God does not ask any more than that. If you didn't have your living to earn, as you have, you could commit yourself to saying your Rosary. But as it is, say your Rosary on Sundays and Holidays when you have plenty of time, but not on days when you have to work.

But really and truly, what are you doing with that enormous pair of beads? I've seen a rosary of only one decade, it's just as good as one of fifteen decades. Why on earth are you wearing it on your belt, fanatic that you are? Why don't you go the whole way and wear it round your neck like the Spaniards? They are great lovers of rosaries; they carry a big rosary in one hand, while in the other they have a dagger to give a treacherous stab. For goodness' sake drop these exterior devotions; true devotion is in the heart. And so on.

149. Similarly, not a few clever people and learned scholars may occasionally try to dissuade you from saying the Rosary, proud and critical people, I mean. They would rather you said the seven penitential psalms or some other prayers. If a good confessor has given you a Rosary for your penance, to be said for a fortnight or a month, all you have to do to get your penance changed to a few other prayers, fasts, alms or Masses, is to go to confession to one of those gentlemen.

If you consult even some people who live lives of prayer in the world, but who have never tried the Rosary, they will not only not encourage it but will turn people away from it to get them to learn contemplation, as if the Rosary and contemplation were incompatible, as if all the saints who have been devoted to the Rosary had not reached the heights of contemplation.

Your closest enemies will attack you all the more cruelly because they are within you. I mean the powers of your soul and your bodily senses, the distractions of the mind, distress and uncertainty of the will, dryness of the heart, exhaustion and illness of the body - all that will combine with the evil spirits to say to you, "Give up your Rosary, that is what is giving you such a headache; give up your Rosary, there is no obligation under pain of sin; at least say only a part of it; the difficulties you are having are a sign that God does not want you to say it; you can say it tomorrow when you are more in the mood." And so on.

150. Finally, my dear brothers and sisters, the daily Rosary has so many enemies that I look upon the grace of persevering in it until death as one of the greatest favours God can give us.

Persevere in it and your fidelity will be rewarded with the wonderful crown which is prepared for you in heaven: "Be faithful until death and I will give you the crown of life."

Forty-ninth Rose

151. This is the time to say a little about the indulgences which have been granted to Rosary Confraternity members, so that you may gain as many as possible.

An indulgence, in general, is a remission or relaxation of temporal punishment due to actual sins, by the application of the superabundant satisfactions of Jesus Christ, of the Blessed Virgin and all the saints, which are contained in the treasury of the Church.

A plenary indulgence is a remission of the whole punishment due to sin; a partial indulgence of, for instance, a hundred or a thousand years can be explained as the remission of as much punishment as could have been expiated during a hundred or a thousand years, if one had been given a corresponding number of the penances prescribed by the Church's ancient Canons.

Now these Canons exacted seven and sometimes ten or fifteen years' penance for a single mortal sin, so that a person who was guilty of twenty mortal sins would probably have had to perform a seven year penance at least twenty times, and so on.

152. Members of the Rosary Confraternity who want to gain the indulgences must:

1. Be truly repentant and go to confession and communion, as the Papal Bull of indulgences states.

2. Be entirely free from affection for venial sin, because if affection for sin remains, the guilt also remains, and if the guilt remains the punishment cannot be lifted.

3. Say the prayers and perform the good works designated by the Bull. If, in accordance with what the Popes have said, one can gain a partial indulgence (for instance, of a hundred years) without gaining a plenary indulgence, it is not always necessary to go to confession and communion in order to gain it. Many such partial indulgences are attached to the Rosary (either of five or fifteen decades), to processions, blessed rosaries, etc. Do not neglect these indulgences.

153. Flammin and a great number of other writers tell the story of a young girl of noble station named Alexandra, who had been miraculously converted and enrolled by St. Dominic in the Confraternity of the Rosary. After her death, she appeared to him and said she had been condemned to seven hundred years in purgatory because of her own sins and those she had caused others to commit by her worldly ways. So she implored him to ease her pains by his prayers and to ask the Confraternity members to pray for the same end. St. Dominic did as she had asked.

Two weeks later she appeared to him, more radiant than the sun, having been quickly delivered from purgatory by the prayers of the Confraternity members. She also told St. Dominic that she had come on behalf of the souls in purgatory to beg him to go on preaching the Rosary and to ask their relations to offer their

Rosaries for them, and that they would reward them abundantly when they entered into glory.

154. To make the recitation of the Rosary easier for you, here are several methods which will help you to say it in a good and holy way, with the meditation on the joyful, sorrowful and glorious mysteries of Jesus and Mary. Choose whichever method pleases you and helps you the most: or you can make up one for yourself, as several holy people have done.

METHODS FOR SAYING THE ROSARY

First Method

1. Say the "Come Holy Spirit" and then make this offering of the Rosary: I unite with all the saints in heaven and with all the just on earth; I unite with you, my Jesus, to praise your holy Mother worthily and to praise you in her and by her. I renounce all the distractions that may come to me while I am saying this Rosary. O Blessed Virgin Mary, we offer you this creed to honour the faith you had upon earth and to ask you to permit us to share in that same faith. O Lord, we offer you this Our Father to adore you in your oneness and to acknowledge you as the first cause and the last end of all things. Most Holy Trinity, we offer you these three Hail Marys to thank you for all the graces which you have given to Mary and which you have given to us through her intercession.

Our Father, three Hail Marys, Glory be to the Father....

Offering of the Decades

Joyful Mysteries

2. First decade

A Manual of the Most Holy Rosary

We offer you, Lord Jesus, this first decade in honour of your Incarnation. Through this mystery and the intercession of your holy Mother we ask for humility of heart.

Our Father, ten Hail Marys, Glory be to the Father.

May the grace of the mystery of the Incarnation come into me and make me truly humble.

Second decade

We offer you, Lord Jesus, this second decade in honour of the Visitation of your holy Mother to her cousin Saint Elizabeth. Through this mystery and the intercession of Mary we ask for a perfect love of our neighbour.

Our Father, ten Hail Marys, Glory be to the Father.

May the grace of the mystery of the Visitation come into me and make me truly charitable.

Third decade

We offer you, Child Jesus, this third decade in honour of your holy Birth. Through this mystery and the intercession of your blessed Mother we ask for detachment from the things of this world, love of poverty and love of the poor.

Our Father, ten Hail Marys, Glory be to the Father.

May the grace of the Birth of Jesus come into me and make me truly poor in spirit.

Fourth decade

We offer you, O Lord Jesus, this fourth decade in honour of your presentation in the temple by the hands of Mary. Through this mystery and the intercession of your blessed Mother we ask for the gift of wisdom and purity of heart and body.

Our Father, ten Hail Marys, Glory be to the Father.

May the grace of the mystery of the presentation come into me and make me truly wise and pure.

Fifth decade

We offer you, Lord Jesus, this fifth decade to honour Mary's finding you in the temple among the learned men after she had lost you. Through this mystery and the intercession of your blessed Mother we ask you to convert us and all sinners, heretics, schismatics and pagans.

Our Father, ten Hail Marys, Glory be to the Father.

May the grace of the mystery of the Finding of Jesus in the temple come into me that I may be truly converted.

Sorrowful Mysteries

3.Sixth decade

We offer you, Lord Jesus, this sixth decade in honour of your intense agony in the garden of Olives. Through this mystery and the intercession of your holy Mother we ask for perfect sorrow for our sins and perfect conformity to your holy will.

Our Father, ten Hail Marys, Glory be to the Father.

May the grace of the Agony of Jesus come into me and make me truly contrite and perfectly obedient to the will of God.

Seventh decade

We offer you, Lord Jesus, this seventh decade in honour of your cruel Scourging. Through this mystery and the intercession of your holy Mother we ask for the grace to mortify our senses.

Our Father, ten Hail Marys, Glory be to the Father.

May the grace of the Scourging of Jesus come into me and make me truly mortified.

Eighth decade

We offer you, Lord Jesus, this eighth decade in honour of being crowned with Thorns. Through this mystery and the intercession of your holy Mother we ask for a deep contempt of the world.

Our Father, ten Hail Marys, Glory be to the Father.

May the grace of the mystery of Our Lord's Crowning with Thorns come into me and make me truly opposed to the world.

Ninth decade

We offer you, Lord Jesus, this ninth decade in honour of your carrying the Cross. Through this mystery and the intercession of your holy Mother we ask for great patience in carrying our cross after you all the days of our life.

Our Father, ten Hail Marys, Glory be to the Father.

May the grace of the mystery of the carrying of the Cross come into me and make me truly patient.

Tenth decade

We offer you, Lord Jesus, this tenth decade in honour of your Crucifixion on Mount Calvary. Through this mystery and the intercession of your holy Mother we ask for a great horror of sin, a love for the Cross and the grace of a holy death for us and for those who are now in their last agony. Our Father, ten Hail Marys, Glory be to the Father.

May the grace of the Death and Passion of Our Lord and Saviour Jesus Christ come into me and make me truly holy.

Glorious Mysteries

4. Eleventh decade

We offer you, Lord Jesus, this eleventh decade in honour of your triumphant Resurrection. Through this mystery and through the intercession of your holy Mother we ask for a lively faith.

Our Father, ten Hail Marys, Glory be to the Father.

May the grace of the Resurrection come into me and make me truly faithful.

Twelfth decade

We offer you, Lord Jesus, this twelfth decade in honour of your glorious Ascension. Through this mystery and the intercession of your holy Mother we ask for a firm hope and a great longing for heaven.

Our Father, ten Hail Marys, Glory be to the Father.

May the grace of the mystery of the Ascension of Our Lord come into me and prepare me for heaven.

Thirteenth decade

We offer you, O Holy Spirit, this thirteenth decade in honour of the mystery of Pentecost. Through this mystery and the intercession of Mary, your most holy spouse, we ask for your holy wisdom that we may know, taste and practice your truth and share it with everyone.

Our Father, ten Hail Marys, Glory be to the Father.

May the grace of Pentecost come into me and make me truly wise in the eyes of God.

Fourteenth decade

We offer you, Lord Jesus, this fourteenth decade in honour of the Immaculate Conception of your holy Mother and her assumption into heaven body and soul. Through these two mysteries and her intercession we ask for the gift of true devotion to her in order to live a good life and have a happy death.

Our Father, ten Hail Marys, Glory be to the Father.

May the grace of the Immaculate Conception and the Assumption of Mary come into me and make me truly devoted to her.

Fifteenth decade

We offer you, Lord Jesus, this fifteenth and last decade in honour of the Crowning in glory of your holy Mother in heaven. Through this mystery and her intercession we ask for perseverance and an increase in virtue up to the moment of our death and thereafter the eternal crown that is prepared for us. We ask for the same grace for all the just and all our benefactors.

Our Father, ten Hail Marys, Glory be to the Father.

Enchiridion Sanctissimi Rosarii

5. We beseech you, Lord Jesus, by the fifteen mysteries of your life, death, passion and glory, and the merits of your holy Mother, to convert sinners, to help the dying, to free the souls in purgatory, and to give all of us your grace so that we may live well and die well. We pray also for the light of glory to see you face to face and love you during all eternity. Amen.

Second, Shorter Method
of Celebrating the life, death and heavenly glory of Jesus and Mary in the Holy Rosary and a method of restraining our imagination and lessening distractions.

6. To do this a word or two is added to each Hail Mary of the decade reminding us of the mystery we are celebrating. This addition follows the name of Jesus in the middle of the Hail Mary:

and blessed is the fruit of thy womb,

Decade 1st "Jesus becoming man"

2nd "Jesus sanctifying"

3rd "Jesus born in poverty"

4th "Jesus sacrificed"

5th "Jesus holy of holies"

6th "Jesus in his agony"

7th "Jesus scourged"

8th "Jesus crowned with thorns"

9th "Jesus carrying his Cross"

10th "Jesus crucified"

11th "Jesus risen from the dead"

12th "Jesus ascending to heaven"

13th "Jesus filling thee with the Holy Spirit"

14th "Jesus raising thee up"

15th "Jesus crowning thee"

At the end of the first five mysteries we say:

May the grace of the joyful mysteries come into our souls and make us really holy.

At the end of the second:

May the grace of the sorrowful mysteries come into our souls and make us truly patient.

At the end of the third:

May the grace of the glorious mysteries come into our souls and make us eternally happy. Amen.

Third Method
of Fr. de Montfort for saying fruitfully the holy Rosary, for the use of the Daughters of Wisdom.

7. I unite with all the saints in heaven, with all the just on earth, and with all the faithful here present. I unite with you, my Jesus, in order to praise your holy Mother worthily and to praise you in her and through her. I renounce all distractions which may arise during this Rosary. I desire to say it with attention and devotion as if it were the last of my life. Amen. We offer you, Lord Jesus, this Creed in honour of all the mysteries of our faith, the Our Father

and three Hail Marys in honour of the unity of your being and the Trinity of your persons. We ask of you a lively faith, a firm hope and an ardent charity. Amen.

I believe in God; Our Father; three Hail Marys.

In each mystery, after the word Jesus, add a word to recall and honour the particular mystery. For example: Jesus incarnate, Jesus sanctifying, etc. as it is indicated at each decade.

The Joyful Mysteries

The Incarnation

8. We offer you, Lord Jesus, this first decade in honour of your Incarnation in Mary's womb; through this mystery and her intercession we ask for deep humility. Amen.

Our Father. Hail Mary ten times, adding "Jesus becoming man".

May the grace of the mystery of the Incarnation come into our souls. Amen.

The Visitation

We offer you, Lord Jesus, this second decade in honour of the Visitation of your holy Mother to her cousin Saint Elizabeth and of the sanctification of Saint John the Baptist; through this mystery and the intercession of your holy Mother we ask for charity towards our neighbour. Amen.

Our Father. Hail Mary ten times. "Jesus sanctifying".

May the grace of the Visitation come into our souls. Amen.

The Birth of Jesus

We offer you, Lord Jesus, this third decade in honour of your Birth in the stable at Bethlehem; through this mystery and the intercession of your holy Mother, we ask for detachment from worldly things, contempt of riches and a love of poverty. Amen.

Our Father. Hail Mary ten times. "Jesus being born".

May the grace of the mystery of the Birth of Jesus come into our souls. Amen.

The Presentation in the Temple

We offer you, Lord Jesus, this fourth decade in honour of your presentation in the temple and the purification of Mary; through this mystery and her intercession we ask for purity in body and mind. Amen.

Our Father. Hail Mary ten times. "Jesus sacrificed".

May the grace of the mystery of the Presentation come into our souls. Amen.

The Finding of Jesus

We offer you, Lord Jesus, this fifth decade in honour of your being found in the temple by Mary; through this mystery and her intercession we ask for true wisdom. Amen.

Our Father. Hail Mary ten times. "Jesus Holy of holies".

May the grace of the mystery of the Finding of Jesus come into our souls. Amen.

At the end of this first Rosary the Magnificat is said.

The Sorrowful Mysteries

Enchiridion Sanctissimi Rosarii

The Agony

9.We offer you, Lord Jesus, this sixth decade in honour of your Agony in the Garden of Olives; through this mystery and the intercession of your holy Mother we ask for sorrow for our sins. Amen.

Our Father. Hail Mary ten times. "Jesus in Agony".

May the grace of the mystery of the Agony of Jesus come into our souls. Amen.

The Scourging

We offer you, Lord Jesus, this seventh decade in honour of your cruel Scourging; through this mystery and the intercession of your holy Mother we ask for the grace to mortify our senses. Amen.

Our Father. Hail Mary ten times. "Jesus being scourged".

May the grace of the mystery of the Scourging of Jesus come into our souls. Amen.

The Crowning with Thorns

We offer you, Lord Jesus, this eighth decade in honour of your being Crowned with Thorns; through this mystery and the intercession of your holy Mother we ask for contempt of the world. Amen.

Our Father. Hail Mary ten times. "Jesus crowned with thorns".

May the grace of the mystery of the Crowning with Thorns come into our souls. Amen.

The Carrying of the Cross

We offer you, Lord Jesus, this ninth decade in honour of your carrying the Cross; through this mystery and the intercession of your holy Mother we ask for patience in all our crosses. Amen.

Our Father. Hail Mary ten times. "Jesus carrying his Cross".

May the grace of the mystery of the Carrying of the Cross come into our souls. Amen.

The Crucifixion

We offer you, Lord Jesus, this tenth decade in honour of your Crucifixion and shameful Death on Calvary; through this mystery and the intercession of your holy Mother we ask for the conversion of sinners, perseverance for the just and relief for the souls in Purgatory. Amen. Our Father. Hail Mary ten times. "Jesus crucified".

10. In this decade before each Hail Mary we ask God through the intercession of the nine choirs of angels for the graces we stand in need of.

Holy Seraphim, ask God etc. Hail Mary etc.

Holy Cherubim, ask etc.

Holy Thrones, ask etc.

Holy Dominations, ask etc.

Holy Virtues, ask etc.

Holy Powers, ask etc.

Holy Principalities, ask etc.

Holy Archangels, ask etc.

Enchiridion Sanctissimi Rosarii

Holy Angels, ask etc.

All the Saints of Paradise, ask etc.

Glory be to the Father, etc.

May the grace of the mystery of the Crucifixion of Jesus come down into our souls. Amen.

11. At the end of the second rosary the following prayers are said kneeling:

[Prayer composed by Fr. de Montfort asking God for divine Wisdom]

O God of our fathers, Lord of mercy, Spirit of truth, I, a mere worm of the earth, prostrate before your divine Majesty, acknowledging the great need I have of your divine wisdom which I have lost through my sins and trusting in the unfailing promise you have made to all those who ask with confidence, I come before you today to beg this grace of you with all possible earnestness and the greatest humility. Send us, O Lord, this wisdom which sits by your throne to strengthen our weakness, to enlighten our minds, to inflame our hearts, to speak and to act, to work and suffer in union with you, to direct our footsteps and to fill our souls with the virtues of Jesus Christ and the gifts of the Holy Spirit, for only Wisdom can bring us these gifts. O Father of mercy, God of all consolation, we ask you for this infinite treasure of your divine wisdom, through the tender heart of Mary, through the Precious Blood of your dear Son and through the intense desire you have to bestow your gifts on your poor creatures. Hear and grant our prayers. Amen.

12. [Prayer to Saint Joseph]

Hail Joseph the just, Wisdom is with you; blessed are you among all men and blessed is Jesus, the fruit of Mary, your faithful spouse. Holy Joseph, worthy foster-father of Jesus Christ, pray for us sinners and obtain divine Wisdom for us from God, now and at the hour of our death. Amen.

This prayer is said three times.

The Glorious Mysteries

The Resurrection

13. We offer you, Lord Jesus, this eleventh decade in honour of your glorious Resurrection; through this mystery and the intercession of your holy Mother, we ask for love of God and fervour in your service. Amen.

Our Father. Hail Mary ten times. "Jesus risen from the dead".

May the grace of the mystery of the Resurrection come into our souls. Amen.

The Ascension

We offer you, Lord Jesus, this twelfth decade in honour of your triumphant Ascension; through this mystery and the intercession of your holy Mother we ask for an ardent desire for heaven, our true home. Amen.

Our Father. Hail Mary ten times. "Jesus ascending to heaven".

May the grace of the mystery of the Ascension come into our souls. Amen.

The Pentecost

We offer you, Lord Jesus, this thirteenth decade in honour of the mystery of Pentecost; through this mystery and the intercession of your holy Mother we ask that the Holy Spirit may come into our souls. Amen.

Our Father. Hail Mary ten times. "Jesus filling us with the Holy Spirit".

May the grace of the mystery of Pentecost come into our souls. Amen.

The Assumption of the Blessed Virgin

We offer you, Lord Jesus, this fourteenth decade in honour of the Resurrection and triumphant Assumption of your holy Mother into heaven; through this mystery and her intercession we ask for a tender devotion to so good a Mother. Amen.

Our Father. Hail Mary ten times. "Jesus raising thee up".

May the grace of the mystery of the Assumption come into our souls. Amen.

The Coronation of Mary

We offer you, Lord Jesus, this fifteenth and last decade in honour of the Coronation of your holy Mother; through this mystery and her intercession we ask for perseverance in grace and the crown of glory. Amen.

Our Father. Hail Mary ten times. "Jesus crowning thee".

14. In this decade before each Hail Mary we ask God through the intercession of all the saints for the graces we stand in need of.

St. Michael the Archangel and all the holy angels, ask of God etc. Hail Mary etc.

St. Abraham and all the holy Patriarchs, ask of God etc.

St. John Baptist and all the holy Prophets, ask of God etc.

St. Peter and St. Paul and all the holy Apostles, ask of God etc.

St. Stephen, St. Lawrence and all the Martyrs, ask of God etc.

St. Hilary and all the holy Pontiffs, ask of God etc.

St. Joseph and all the holy Confessors, ask of God etc.

St. Catherine, St. Therese and all the holy Virgins, ask of God etc.

St. Anne and all holy Women, ask of God etc.

Glory be to the Father etc.

May the grace of the mystery of the Crowning in glory of Mary come into our souls. Amen.

15. At the end of the third Rosary the following prayer is said:

[Prayer to the Blessed Virgin]

Hail Mary, well-beloved daughter of the eternal Father, admirable Mother of the Son, most faithful spouse of the Holy Spirit, glorious temple of the Blessed Trinity. Hail, sovereign Queen, to whom everyone is subject in heaven and on earth. Hail sure Refuge of sinners, our Lady of mercy, who has never repelled anyone. Sinner as I am, I cast myself at your feet and beg you to obtain from Jesus, your dear Son, contrition and pardon for all my sins and the gift of divine wisdom. I consecrate myself to you with all that I have. I choose you today as my Mother and Mistress; treat me then as the weakest of your children and the most submissive of your servants. Hear, O my Queen, the prayers of a heart that desires to love and serve you faithfully. Let it not be said that of all who have ever had recourse to you, I was the first to be unheeded. O my hope, my life, my faithful and immaculate Virgin Mary, hear me, protect me, strengthen me, instruct me, save me. Amen.

Praised, adored and loved be Jesus in the most holy sacrament of the altar. Forever and ever.

O Jesus, my dear Jesus, O Mary, Mother of Jesus, my beloved Mother, give us your holy blessing. Amen.

Support us in our troubles, hear us when we pray, preserve us from the world and the devil. Amen.

The superior says, "Nos cum prole pia benedicat Virgo Maria. Amen".

Fourth Method
Summary of the life, death and passion and heavenly glory of Jesus and Mary in the holy Rosary.

16. Credo: 1) Faith in the presence of God. 2) Faith in the gospel. 3) Faith and obedience to the pope as Vicar of Jesus Christ.

1 Our Father Unity of one, living and true God.

1 Hail Mary To honour the eternal Father who conceives his Son in contemplating himself.

2 Hail Mary The eternal Word, equal to his Father and who with him produces the Holy Spirit by their mutual love.

3 Hail Mary The Holy Spirit who proceeds from the Father and the Son by the way of love.

2 Our Father Immense charity of God.

The Incarnation

17. 1 Hail Mary To deplore the unhappy state of disobedient Adam; his just condemnation and that of all his descendants.

2 Hail Mary To honour the desires of the patriarchs and prophets who pleaded for the coming of the Messiah.

3 Hail Mary To honour the desires and prayers of the Blessed Virgin Mary to bring forward the coming of the Messiah; and her marriage with Saint Joseph.

4 Hail Mary The love of the eternal Father in giving us his Son.

5 Hail Mary The love of the Son who gave himself up for us.

6 Hail Mary The mission and the greeting of the angel Gabriel.

7 Hail Mary The maidenly fear of Mary.

8 Hail Mary The faith and consent of the Virgin Mary.

9 Hail Mary The creation of the soul and the formation of the body of Jesus in the womb of Mary by the Holy Spirit.

10 Hail Mary The angels adoring the Word Incarnate in the womb of Mary.

3 Our Father The most adorable majesty of God.

The Visitation

18. 1 Hail Mary To honour the joy in the heart of Mary at the Incarnation and the dwelling for nine months of the eternal Word in her womb.

2 Hail Mary The sacrifice of himself that Jesus Christ offered to his Father on coming into the world.

3 Hail Mary The contentment of Jesus Christ in the humble and Virginal womb of Mary and that of Mary in the enjoyment of her God.

4 Hail Mary The doubts of St. Joseph on discovering that Mary was with child.

5 Hail Mary The agreement between Jesus and Mary in her womb on the choice of the elect.

6 Hail Mary The fervour of Mary when visiting her cousin.

7 Hail Mary The greeting of Mary and the sanctification of St. John Baptist and of his mother St. Elizabeth.

8 Hail Mary Mary's thanksgiving to God expressed in her Magnificat.

9 Hail Mary Her charity and humility in the service of her cousin.

10 Hail Mary The mutual dependence of Jesus and Mary and the dependence we should have upon them both.

4   Our Father The infinite richness of God.

The Birth of Jesus

19.   1 Hail Mary To honour the contempt and the rebuffs which Mary and Joseph encountered at Bethlehem.

2 Hail Mary The poverty of the Stable where God came into the world.

3 Hail Mary The deep recollection of the exceeding love of Mary when she was about to give birth to her child.

4 Hail Mary The coming forth of the eternal Word from the womb of Mary without breaking the seal of her Virginity.

5 Hail Mary The adoration and the singing of the angels when Jesus was born.

6 Hail Mary The ravishing beauty of her divine child.

7 Hail Mary The coming of the shepherds into the stable with their humble gifts.

8 Hail Mary The circumcision of Jesus and his suffering accepted in love.

9 Hail Mary The giving of the name of Jesus and the nobility of this name

10 Hail Mary The adoration of the kings and the gifts they brought.

5   Our Father The eternal wisdom of God.

The Purification

20. 1 Hail Mary Obedience of Jesus and Mary to the Law.

2 Hail Mary The sacrifice that Jesus made of his humanity to the Law.

3 Hail Mary The sacrifice of her honour the Virgin Mary made to the Law.

4 Hail Mary The joy and the songs of Simeon and Anne the prophetess.

5 Hail Mary The ransoming of Jesus by the offering of two turtle doves.

6 Hail Mary The massacre of the Holy Innocents by Herod the Cruel.

7 Hail Mary The flight of Jesus to Egypt through St. Joseph's obedience to the voice of the angel.

8 Hail Mary The mystery of his abode in Egypt.

9 Hail Mary His return to Nazareth

10 Hail Mary His growth in age and wisdom.

6   Our Father The incomprehensible holiness of God.

The Finding of Jesus in the Temple

21.   1 Hail Mary To honour his hidden, hard working and obedient life at Nazareth.

2 Hail Mary His preaching and his being found in the temple among the doctors.

3 Hail Mary His fasting and his temptations in the desert.

4 Hail Mary His baptism by St. John Baptist.

5 Hail Mary His wonderful preaching.

6 Hail Mary His astounding miracles.

7 Hail Mary The choice of the twelve apostles and the powers he gave them.

8 Hail Mary His marvellous transfiguration

9 Hail Mary The washing of the feet of the apostles.

10 Hail Mary The institution of the Holy Eucharist.

7 Our Father The essential happiness of God.

The Agony of Jesus

22. 1 Hail Mary To honour the places of retreat that Jesus Christ chose during his life, especially that of the Garden of Olives.

2 Hail Mary His humble and fervent prayers offered during his life and on the eve of his passion.

3 Hail Mary His patience and gentleness towards his apostles during his life and especially in the Garden of Olives.

4 Hail Mary His weariness of soul during all his life and especially in the Garden of Olives.

5 Hail Mary The outpouring of blood in which his sorrows bathed him.

6 Hail Mary The comfort he consented to receive from an angel in his agony.

7 Hail Mary His conformity to the will of his Father in spite of his natural reluctance.

8 Hail Mary The courage with which he went to meet his executioners and the power of his words with which he crushed them and then uplifted them.

9 Hail Mary His betrayal by Judas and his arrest by the Jews.

10 Hail Mary His desertion by his apostles.

8   Our Father Wonderful patience of God.

The Scourging

23.   1 Hail Mary To honour the chains and ropes with which Jesus was bound.

2 Hail Mary The blow that he received in the house of Caiphas.

3 Hail Mary The three denials of St. Peter.

4 Hail Mary The shameful treatment he received at the house of Herod when he was dressed in a white robe.

5 Hail Mary His being stripped of all his clothes.

6 Hail Mary The scorn and insults he received from his tormenters because of his nakedness.

7 Hail Mary His being beaten and flayed with rods of thorn and cruel whips.

8 Hail Mary The pillar to which he was bound.

9 Hail Mary The blood he shed and the wounds he received.

10 Hail Mary His collapse through weakness into a pool of his own blood.

9   Our Father Unspeakable beauty of God.

The Crowning with Thorns of Jesus Christ

24.   1 Hail Mary To honour his being stripped a third time.

2 Hail Mary To honour His crown of thorns.

3 Hail Mary The veil with which they blindfolded him.

4 Hail Mary The blows and the spittle rained upon his face.

5 Hail Mary The old robe they put over his shoulders.

6 Hail Mary The reed they put into his hand.

7 Hail Mary The rough stone upon which he was made to sit.

8 Hail Mary The abuse and insults that were hurled at him.

9 Hail Mary The blood which poured from his adorable head.

10 Hail Mary His hair and beard which they tore at.

10   Our Father Limitless omnipotence of God.

The Carrying of the Cross

25.   1 Hail Mary To honour Our Lord being presented to the people at the "Ecce Homo."

2 Hail Mary The preferring of Barabbas to Jesus.

3 Hail Mary The false testimonies given against him.

4 Hail Mary His being condemned to death.

5 Hail Mary The love with which he embraced and kissed the Cross.

6 Hail Mary The dreadful sufferings he endured in carrying it.

7 Hail Mary His falling through weakness under its weight.

8 Hail Mary His sorrow on meeting his Mother.

9 Hail Mary The veil of Veronica on which his face was imprinted.

10 Hail Mary His tears and those of his Mother and the pious women who followed him to Calvary.

11 Our Father Fearful Justice of God.

The Crucifixion of Jesus Christ

26. 1 Hail Mary To honour the five wounds of Jesus Christ and the shedding of his blood on the Cross.

2 Hail Mary His pierced heart and the Cross upon which he was crucified.

3 Hail Mary The nails and the lance which pierced him, the sponge, the gall and the vinegar which he was given to drink.

4 Hail Mary The shame and the ignominy he endured in being crucified naked between two thieves.

5 Hail Mary The compassion of his Blessed Mother.

6 Hail Mary His seven last words.

7 Hail Mary His abandonment and his silence.

8 Hail Mary The distress of the whole universe.

9 Hail Mary His painful and shameful death.

10 Hail Mary His being taken down from the Cross and his burial.

12 Our Father The eternity of God without a beginning.

The Resurrection

27. 1 Hail Mary To honour the descent of the soul of Our Lord into hell.

2 Hail Mary The joy and the release of the ancient fathers who were in limbo.

3 Hail Mary The re-uniting of his body and soul in the tomb.

4 Hail Mary His miraculous emergence from the tomb.

5 Hail Mary His victories over death and sin, the world and the devil.

6 Hail Mary The four qualities of his glorious body.

7 Hail Mary The power that he received from his Father in heaven and on earth.

8 Hail Mary His appearances to his Mother, his apostles and disciples.

9 Hail Mary His discourses on heaven and the meal that he had with his disciples.

10 Hail Mary The peace, the authority and the mission he gave them to go out into the whole world.

13   Our Father The unlimited omnipresence of God.

The Ascension of Jesus Christ

28. 1 Hail Mary To honour the promise that Jesus Christ made to his apostles to send them the Holy Spirit and the command he gave them to prepare to receive him.

2 Hail Mary The gathering of all his disciples on the Mount of Olives.

3 Hail Mary The blessings he gave them as he rose from the earth towards heaven.

4 Hail Mary His glorious ascension by his own power into heaven.

5 Hail Mary The welcome and triumphant acclaim which he received from God, his Father and from all the heavenly court.

6 Hail Mary The triumphant power with which he opened the gates of heaven through which no mortal had passed.

7 Hail Mary His being seated at the right hand of his Father as his beloved Son equal to his Father.

8 Hail Mary The power he received to judge the living and the dead.

9 Hail Mary His last coming upon earth when his power and majesty will appear in all their magnificence.

10 Hail Mary The justice he will mete out at the last judgment when he rewards the just and punishes the wicked for all eternity.

14   Our Father The all-embracing Providence of God.

Pentecost

29.   1 Hail Mary To honour the truth of God the Holy Spirit proceeding from the Father and the Son and who is the love of the Godhead.

2 Hail Mary The sending of the Holy Spirit upon the apostles by the Father and the Son.

3 Hail Mary His descent accompanied by the sound of a great wind which shows his might and power.

4 Hail Mary The tongues of fire he sent to the apostles giving them an understanding of the scriptures and love of God and neighbour

5 Hail Mary The fullness of grace which the heart of Mary, his faithful spouse, was privileged to receive.

6 Hail Mary The marvellous guidance he gave to all the saints and even to the person of Jesus Christ during all his life.

7 Hail Mary The twelve fruits of the Holy Spirit.

8 Hail Mary The seven gifts of the Holy Spirit.

9 Hail Mary To ask especially for the gift of wisdom and the coming of his kingdom into men's hearts.

10 Hail Mary To be victorious over the three evil spirits that are opposed to him, namely the spirit of the flesh, of the world and of the devil.

15   Our Father The unspeakable generosity of God.

The Assumption of Mary

30.   1 Hail Mary To honour the eternal predestination of Mary to be the masterpiece of God's hands.

2 Hail Mary Her Immaculate Conception and her fullness of grace and reason in the very womb of St. Anne.

3 Hail Mary Her birth which gladdened the whole world.

4 Hail Mary Her presentation and her abode in the temple.

5 Hail Mary Her wonderful life and her exemption from all sin.

6 Hail Mary Her fullness of pre-eminent virtue.

7 Hail Mary Her fruitful virginity and her painless childbearing.

8 Hail Mary Her divine Motherhood and her relationship with the three persons of the most holy Trinity.

9 Hail Mary Her precious and loving death.

10 Hail Mary Her resurrection and triumphant Assumption.

16 Our Father The unattainable glory of God.

The Crowning of Mary

31. 1 Hail Mary To honour the triple crown which Mary received from the Holy Trinity.

2 Hail Mary The joy and the added glory that heaven received through her triumphant entry.

3 Hail Mary To acknowledge her as queen of heaven and earth, of angels and men.

4 Hail Mary As treasurer and dispenser of the graces of God, the merits of Jesus Christ and the gifts of the Holy Spirit.

5 Hail Mary Mediatrix and advocate of men.

6 Hail Mary Exterminator and destroyer of the devil and of heresies.

7 Hail Mary Safe refuge of sinners.

8 Hail Mary Nurturing Mother of sinners.

9 Hail Mary The joy and delight of the just.

10 Hail Mary Refuge for all the living, all-powerful relief for the afflicted, for the dying and for the souls in purgatory.

God alone.

Fifth Method
150 Motives Impelling us to say the Rosary

32. Creed: Definition and essence of the Rosary

1 Our Father Eminence of the Rosary

1 Hail Mary the daily Rosary

2 Hail Mary the ordinary Rosary

3 Hail Mary perpetual Rosary

33. 2 Our Father excellence of the holy Rosary as prefigured in the Old Testament and the parables of the New.

1 Hail Mary the strength of the holy Rosary against the world, as prefigured by that small stone, which, thrown by no hand of man, fell upon the statue of Nebuchadnezzar and broke it into pieces.

2 Hail Mary its strength against the devil, as prefigured by the sling of David with which he overcame Goliath.

3 Hail Mary its power against all sorts of enemies of salvation, as prefigured by the power of David which contained innumerable kinds of defensive and offensive arms.

4 Hail Mary its miracles as prefigured in the rod of Moses which caused water to flow from the rock, calmed the waters, divided the seas and performed miracles.

5 Hail Mary its holiness as prefigured by the Ark of the Covenant which contained the law, the manna and the rod and also by the psalter of David which prefigured the Rosary.

6 Hail Mary its light as shown in the columns of fire during the night and the shining cloud during the day which guided the Israelites.

7 Hail Mary its sweetness as shown in the honey found in the mouth of the lion.

8 Hail Mary its fruitfulness as shown in the net that St. Peter by order of Our Lord threw into the sea and which though filled with 153 fish did not break.

9 Hail Mary its marvellous fruitfulness as shown in the parable of the mustard seed which, although so small in appearance, becomes a great tree in which the birds of the air make their nests.

10 Hail Mary its richness as shown in the parable of the treasure hidden in a field for which a wise man must give up all he has to possess it.

34. 3 Our Father It is a gift come down from heaven; a great present that God gives to his most faithful servants.

1 Hail Mary God is the author of the prayers of which it is composed and of the mysteries which it contains.

2 Hail Mary it is the Blessed Virgin who gave the Rosary its form.

3 Hail Mary St. Dominic preached and although he was a saint he converted hardly any sinners.

4 Hail Mary he was accompanied in his missions by several holy bishops and still his efforts were without fruit.

5 Hail Mary by the power of prayer and mortification, he received the holy Rosary in the forest of Toulouse.

6 Hail Mary he entered Toulouse and preached the Rosary and great wonders and great blessings accompanied his preaching.

7 Hail Mary he continued all his life preaching the Rosary with results never seen before.

8 Hail Mary the marvellous effects the Rosary has had wherever it was preached.

9 Hail Mary the decline of the Rosary.

10 Hail Mary the restoration of the Rosary by Blessed Alan de la Roche.

35. 4 Our Father The Rosary is the triple crown that we place on the heads of Jesus and Mary and he who recites it every day will receive the same crown.

1 Hail Mary Mary possesses three kinds of crown.

2 Hail Mary The daily Rosary is her great crown.

3 Hail Mary The reprobate crown themselves with faded roses.

4 Hail Mary The predestinate crown Jesus and Mary with eternal roses.

5 Hail Mary The Jews crown Jesus with piercing crowns.

6 Hail Mary True Christians crown him with fragrant roses.

7 Hail Mary The first is the bridal crown or crown of excellence which we place on Mary's head by the joyful mysteries.

8 Hail Mary The second is the crown of triumph or of power that we give her by the sorrowful mysteries.

9 Hail Mary The third is the royal crown or crown of goodness that we give her by the glorious mysteries.

10 Hail Mary There are three crowns for the one who recites the Holy Rosary every day:

1 crown of graces during life

2 crown of peace at death

3 crown of glory in eternity

36. 5   Our Father The Rosary is a mystical summary of all the most beautiful prayers of the Church.

1 Hail Mary The Creed is a summary of the gospel.

2 Hail Mary It is the prayer of believers.

3 Hail Mary The shield of the soldiers of Jesus Christ.

4 Hail Mary The Our Father - prayer of which Jesus Christ is the sole author.

5 Hail Mary Prayer he used when praying to his Father and through which he obtained what he desired.

6 Hail Mary Prayer which contains a summary of all we must ask of God.

7 Hail Mary Prayer in which are found all our duties towards God.

8 Hail Mary Prayer which contains a summary of all we must ask of God.

9 Hail Mary Prayer whose value is unknown and which is said very badly by the majority of Christians.

10 Hail Mary Paraphrase of the Our Father.

37. 6 Our Father The Rosary contains the angelic greeting which is the most pleasing prayer we can offer our Blessed Lady.

1 Hail Mary The Hail Mary is a divine compliment which wins over the heart of the Blessed Virgin.

2 Hail Mary It is the new song of the New Testament which the faithful sing as they escape from the captivity of the devil.

3 Hail Mary It is the hymn of the angels and saints in heaven.

4 Hail Mary It is the prayer of the predestinate and of Catholics.

5 Hail Mary It is a mysterious rose which is a source of joy to the Blessed Virgin and to the soul.

6 Hail Mary It is a precious stone which embellishes and sanctifies the soul.

7 Hail Mary It is a valuable piece of money with which to purchase heaven.

8 Hail Mary It is the prayer which distinguishes the predestinate from the reprobate.

9 Hail Mary It is the terror of the devil, the blow which crushes him, the nail of Sisera which pierces his head.

10 Hail Mary Paraphrase of the Hail Mary.

38. 7 Our Father The Rosary is a divine Summary of the mysteries of Jesus and Mary in which we proclaim and commemorate their life, passion and glory.

Enchiridion Sanctissimi Rosarii

1 Hail Mary Men's misfortune and ruin come from ignorance and neglect of the mysteries of Jesus Christ.

2 Hail Mary The Rosary provides the knowledge of the mysteries of Jesus and Mary and recalls them to mind in view of applying them to one's life.

3 Hail Mary The greatest desire of Jesus Christ was and still is that we remember him. With this in mind he instituted the sacrifice of the Mass.

4 Hail Mary After holy Mass the Rosary is the holiest action and prayer that we can offer because it is a remembrance and a celebration of what Jesus Christ has done and suffered for us.

5 Hail Mary The Rosary is the prayer of the angels and saints in heaven because they are engaged in celebrating the life, death and glory of Jesus Christ.

6 Hail Mary When we say the Rosary we celebrate in one day or one week all the mysteries that the Church celebrates in a year for the sanctification of her children.

7 Hail Mary Those who say the holy Rosary every day have a share in what the saints are doing in heaven which is the same as they were doing upon earth meritoriously, for they who are on earth are doing what the saints are doing in heaven.

8 Hail Mary The mysteries of the Holy Rosary are like mirrors for the predestinate in which they see their faults and like torches which guide them in this world of darkness.

9 Hail Mary They see springs of living water from the Saviour to whom one may go with joy to draw the saving waters of grace.

10 Hail Mary They are the 15 steps of the temple of Solomon and the 15 rungs of the ladder of Jacob by which the angels descend to them and return to heaven and by which they ascend to heaven.

39. 8   Our Father The Rosary is the tree of life which bears marvellous fruits all the year round.

1 Hail Mary The Rosary enlightens blind and hardened sinners.

2 Hail Mary It brings back obstinate heretics.

3 Hail Mary It sets prisoners free.

4 Hail Mary It heals the incurable.

5 Hail Mary It enriches the poor.

6 Hail Mary It supports the weak.

7 Hail Mary It consoles the afflicted and the dying.

8 Hail Mary It reforms lax religious orders.

9 Hail Mary It checks the effects of God's anger.

10 Hail Mary It makes good people better.

40. 9   Our Father The Rosary is a practice that God has sanctioned by many miracles.

1 Hail Mary Miracles in the conversion of sinners.

2 Hail Mary In the conversion of heretics.

3 Hail Mary In the cure of all sorts of diseases.

4 Hail Mary In favour of the dying brethren.

5 Hail Mary In the sanctification of devout people.

6 Hail Mary In the release of souls from purgatory.

7 Hail Mary In the reception into the Confraternity.

8 Hail Mary For the procession of the holy Rosary and the oil lamp of the holy Rosary.

9 Hail Mary For its devout recitation.

10 Hail Mary To carry it on one's person with devotion.

41. 10   Our Father The holy Rosary is most excellent because it was established for very noble ends which give great glory to God and are very salutary for the soul.

1 Hail Mary By being enrolled in this Confraternity we are strengthened in a wonderful way by joining millions of brothers and sisters.

2 Hail Mary We thus preserve a continuous remembrance of the mysteries of Jesus and Mary.

3 Hail Mary We are able to praise God at every moment of the day and night and in every place on earth, which one could not do on one's own.

4 Hail Mary To thank Our Lord for all the graces he is giving us at every moment.

5 Hail Mary To be ever asking pardon for our daily sins.

6 Hail Mary To make our prayers more powerful by being united with others.

7 Hail Mary For mutual help at the hour of death which is so difficult and so important.

8 Hail Mary To be supported at the hour of judgment by as many intercessors as there are members of the confraternity of the Rosary.

9 Hail Mary To be given relief after death and speedily released from the pains of purgatory by the Masses and prayers which are offered up.

10 Hail Mary To form an army arrayed as for battle to destroy the empire of the devil and establish that of Jesus Christ.

42. 11 Our Father The Rosary is a great store of indulgence accorded by popes outdoing one another.

1 Hail Mary Plenary indulgences of the stations of Rome and Jerusalem by going to Communion on certain days.

2 Hail Mary Plenary indulgence on enrolment in the confraternity.

3 Hail Mary Plenary indulgence at the hour of death.

4 Hail Mary Indulgence for the recitation of the Rosary.

5 Hail Mary Indulgence for those who organize the saying of the Rosary.

6 Hail Mary Indulgence for those who receive communion in the church of the Rosary on the first Sunday of the month.

7 Hail Mary Indulgence on the occasion of the procession.

8 Hail Mary Indulgence for those who say the Mass of the Rosary.

9 Hail Mary Indulgence for certain good works.

10 Hail Mary Indulgence for those who are unable to visit the church of the Rosary, or receive Communion, or take part in a procession.

43. 12 Our Father The Rosary is sanctioned by the example given to us by the saints.

1 Hail Mary St. Dominic, its origination.

2 Hail Mary Blessed Alan de la Roche who restored it.

3 Hail Mary The saintly Dominicans who propagated it.

4 Hail Mary Among the popes: Pius V, Innocent III, and Boniface VIII who had it embroidered in satin.

5 Hail Mary Among the cardinals: St. Charles Borromeo.

6 Hail Mary Among the bishops: St. Francis de Sales.

7 Hail Mary Among religious: St. Ignatius, St. Philip Neri, St. Felix of Cantalice.

8 Hail Mary Among kings and queens: St. Louis, Philip I, King of Spain, Queen Blanche.

9 Hail Mary Among the learned: Albert the Great, Navarre, etc.

10 Hail Mary Among saintly people: the famous holy women of Rome, Sister Mary of the Incarnation.

44. 13 Our Father The vanquished enemies of the Rosary prove its fame to us.

1 Hail Mary Those who neglect it.

2 Hail Mary Those who say it with indifference and without attention.

3 Hail Mary Those who say it in haste and to get it over with.

4 Hail Mary Those who say it with unrepentant mortal sin.

5 Hail Mary Those who say it out of hypocrisy, lacking any devotion.

6 Hail Mary Critics who strive ingeniously to do away with it.

7 Hail Mary The impious who speak against it.

8 Hail Mary The cowardly who accept it and then abandon it.

9 Hail Mary Heretics who attack it and run it down.

10 Hail Mary The devils who hate it and strive to destroy it by numerous tricks.

45. 14 Our Father The overcoming of objections that heretics, critics, libertines and those who neglect and ignore the Rosary generally make either to do away with it or to avoid saying it.

1 Hail Mary It is a new religious practice.

2 Hail Mary It is an invention of Religious to make money.

3 Hail Mary It is a devotion of ignorant women who do not know how to read.

4 Hail Mary It is superstitious being based on counting prayers.

5 Hail Mary It is preferable to say the penitential psalms.

6 Hail Mary It is preferable to make a meditation.

Enchiridion Sanctissimi Rosarii

7 Hail Mary It is too long and too tiresome a prayer.

8 Hail Mary One cannot be saved without saying the Rosary.

9 Hail Mary We sin if we fail to say it.

10 Hail Mary It is good, but I have not the time to say it.

46. 15   Our Father Manner of saying the Rosary well.

1 Hail Mary It must be said with a pure heart without attachment to grave sin.

2 Hail Mary In a worthy manner with good intentions.

3 Hail Mary With attention avoiding voluntary distractions.

4 Hail Mary Slowly and calmly with pauses in the prayers.

5 Hail Mary Devout whilst meditating on the mysteries.

6 Hail Mary Modestly and in a respectful attitude whether standing or kneeling.

7 Hail Mary Wholeheartedly and every day.

8 Hail Mary Inwardly when it is said alone.

9 Hail Mary Publicly and in two responding groups.

10 Hail Mary Perseveringly until death.

47. 16   Our Father Different methods of saying the holy Rosary.

1 Hail Mary The holy Rosary can be said in a straightforward manner, saying only the Our Fathers and Hail Marys with the intentions of the mysteries.

2 Hail Mary We can add a word to each mystery of the decade.

3 Hail Mary We can make a little offering at each decade.

4 Hail Mary We can make a more important offering at each decade.

5 Hail Mary We can have a special intention for each Hail Mary.

6 Hail Mary We can recite it inwardly without speaking.

7 Hail Mary We can genuflect at each Hail Mary.

8 Hail Mary We can prostrate at each Hail Mary.

9 Hail Mary We can give ourselves a stroke of the discipline.

10 Hail Mary We can commemorate the saints at each decade and blend with one of the above-mentioned methods as the Holy Spirit inspires.

Appendix

The Principal Rules Of The Confraternity of the Holy Rosary

48. Members should:

1 Have their names written in the register of the confraternity and, if possible, go to Confession and Communion and say the Rosary on the day they are enrolled.

2 Possess a blessed rosary.

3 Say the Rosary every day or at least once a week.

4 Whenever possible, go to Confession and Communion on the first Sunday of every month and take part in the Rosary processions.

Remember that none of these rules binds under pain of sin.

On the Power and Dignity of the Rosary

49. Through the Rosary, hardened sinners of both sexes became converted and began to lead a holy life, regretting their past sins with genuine tears of sorrow. Even children performed unbelievable penances, and devotion to my Son and to me spread so much that it seemed almost as though angels were living on earth. Faith was increasing and many of the faithful longed to shed their blood for it and fight against heretics....

50. "Thus, through the sermons of my very dear Dominic and through the power of the Rosary the heretical regions became submissive to the Church. Almsgiving became widespread; churches and hospitals were built; people led pure and honourable lives; real wonders were accomplished. Holiness and unworldliness were seen everywhere; the church was seen as honourable; princes were just; people lived at peace with one another and justice and equity reigned in the guilds and in the home. More impressive still, workmen did not take up their tools until after they had greeted me by saying my Rosary and they did not retire at night without again praying to me on their knees. If they remembered in the middle of the night that they had not offered me this tribute, they would immediately rise from their bed and greet me with even greater respect, and with sorrow for their lapse. The Rosary became so well known that people who were devout were considered by others as being obviously confraternity members. If a man lived openly in sin or blasphemed, it was commonly said: "This man cannot possibly be a brother of St. Dominic." I must not fail to mention the signs

and wonders that I have wrought and put in different lands through the holy Rosary.

"I have stopped pestilences and put an end to horrible wars and averted bloodshed, besides strengthening those who said the Rosary in order to avoid sin. When you say the Rosary the angels rejoice in it, the holy Trinity delights in it, my son finds joy in it and I myself am happier than you can possibly imagine. After the holy Sacrifice of the Mass there is nothing that I love so much as the holy Rosary." (Cf. Blessed Alan de la Roche)....

51."Having been strongly urged to do so by St. Dominic, all the brothers and sisters of his Order honoured my Son and me unceasingly and in an indescribably beautiful way by saying this psalter of the Holy Trinity. Every day each one of them said at least one complete Rosary. If anybody failed to say it he felt that the whole of his day was spoiled. The brothers of St. Dominic had so great a love for this holy devotion that it made them hurry to church or choir more willingly. If one of them was seen to carry out his duties carelessly the others would say with assurance, "Dear brother, you must not be saying Mary's psalter any more or else you are saying it badly."

On the Dignity of the Hail Mary

52. The holy angels in heaven salute the most Blessed Virgin with the Hail Mary not audibly but with their angelic mind. For they are fully aware that through it reparation was made for the fallen angels' sin, God became man and the world was renewed" (Blessed Alan). "I myself, knowing the power of this greeting by the Lord, repeated it with great fervour. Indeed, realizing my own human nature, I begged Mary for a share in her divine life of grace and glory" (Blessed Alan). "One night when a woman member of the Confraternity had retired, Our Lady appeared to her and said, 'My

daughter, do not be afraid of me. I am your loving Mother whom you praise so faithfully every day. Be steadfast and persevere. I want you to know that the Hail Mary gives me so much joy that no man could ever really describe it'" (Guillaume Pepin, In Rosario aureo, Sermon 47).

53."This was corroborated by a vision of St. Gertrude. In her revelations, Book IV, chapter XI, we find this story:

"On the morning of the feast of the Annunciation of the Blessed Virgin Mary while the Ave Maria was being sung in Gertrude's monastery, she had a vision in which three streams gushed forth from the Father, the Son and the Holy Spirit and gently flowed into the heart of the Virgin Mary. From this heart these streams flowed back impetuously to their source. From this, Gertrude learned that the Blessed Trinity has allowed Our Lady to be the most powerful after God the Father, the wisest after God the Son and the most loving after God the Holy Spirit. She also learned that every time the Hail Mary is said by the faithful the three mysterious streams surround Our Lady in a mighty current rush to her heart. After they have completely bathed her in happiness they gush back into the bosom of God. The saints and angels share in this abundance of joy, as do the faithful on earth who say this prayer, for the Hail Mary is the source of all good for God's children.

54."Listen to what Our Lady herself said to Saint Mechtilde: 'Never has any man composed anything more beautiful than the Hail Mary. No greeting could be dearer to my heart than those beautiful and dignified words that God the Father addressed to me himself.' Our Lady one day said to Saint Mechtilde, 'All the Hail Marys you have given me are blazoned on my cloak. She then held out a portion of her mantle, saying, 'When this part of my cloak is full of Hail Marys I shall gather you up and take you into the Kingdom of my beloved Son.'" Denis the Carthusian, speaking of a vision of Our Lady to one of her clients, said, "We should greet the Blessed Virgin with our hearts, our lips and our deeds, so that she will not be able to say to us, 'These people honour me with their lips but their hearts are far from me."

55. Richard of St. Laurence lists the reasons why it is good to say a Hail Mary at the beginning of a sermon:

1 The Church militant should follow the example of Saint Gabriel who saluted Mary with great respect saying "Hail Mary," before he told her the joyous news: "Behold you shall conceive and bear a Son...." Thus the Church greets the Virgin before announcing the gospel.

2 The congregation will derive more fruit from a sermon that is prefaced by the Hail Mary. The priest who gives the sermon has the angel's role. But in order that the congregation may give birth to Christ in their souls (by faith) they must first obtain this grace from the Blessed Virgin who gave birth to him the first time, and so together with her, they will become mothers of the Son of God. For without Mary they cannot produce Jesus in their souls.

3 The gospel shows us the effectiveness of the Hail Mary and people will receive help from Our Lady through this prayer.

4 Through the Hail Mary, priests avoid pitfalls in their preaching, for Mary gives enlightenment to preachers.

5 The congregation, following Our Lady's example, listens more attentively and is more apt to remember the Word of God.

6 The devil, who is the enemy of the human race and of the preaching of the gospel, is driven off by the Hail Mary. This is most necessary because, to quote Our Lord's words, there is a danger of

his coming to take the Word of God out of people's hearts, "lest believing they might be saved."

56. In his first sermon on the holy Rosary Clement Losow says: After St. Dominic had gone to heaven, devotion to the Rosary waned and it was nearly extinct, when a terrible pestilence broke out in several parts of the country. The afflicted people sought the advice of a saintly hermit who lived a very austere life in the desert. They besought him to pray to God for them. The holy man called upon the Mother of the Saviour, imploring her as advocate of sinners to come to the aid of the people. Mary appeared and said, 'These people have stopped singing my praises; that is why these misfortunes have come upon them. Let them return to the devotion of the Rosary and they will again enjoy my protection. I shall obtain the graces of salvation for them if they honour me by saying the Rosary for this psalter is very pleasing to me.' So the people did what Mary asked and made themselves rosaries which they said with all their heart."

A Manual of the Most Holy Rosary

Selected Papal Documents on the Rosary

Supremi Apostolatus Officio
On Devotion Of The Rosary

Encyclical of Pope Leo XIII

September 1, 1883

To all the Patriarchs, Primates, Archbishops and Bishops of the Catholic World in the Grace and Communion of the Apostolic See.

Venerable Brethren, Health and the Apostolic Benediction.

The supreme Apostolic office which we discharge and the exceedingly difficult condition of these times, daily warn and almost compel Us to watch carefully over the integrity of the Church, the more that the calamities from which she suffers are greater. While, therefore, we endeavor in every way to preserve the rights of the Church and to obviate or repel present or contingent dangers, We constantly seek for help from Heaven--the sole means of effecting anything--that our labors and our care may obtain their wished for object. We deem that there could be no surer and more efficacious means to this end than by religion and piety to obtain the favor of the great Virgin Mary, the Mother of God, the guardian of our peace and the minister to us of heavenly grace, who is placed on the highest summit of power and glory in Heaven, in order that she may bestow the help of her patronage on men who through so many labors and dangers are striving to reach that eternal city. Now that the anniversary, therefore, of manifold and exceedingly great favors obtained by a Christian people through the devotion of the Rosary is at hand, We desire that that same devotion should be offered by the whole Catholic world with the greatest earnestness to the Blessed Virgin, that by her intercession her Divine Son may be appeased and softened in the evils which afflict us. And therefore We determined, Venerable Brethren, to despatch to you these letters in order that, informed of Our designs, your authority and zeal might excite the piety of your people to conform themselves to them.

2. It has always been the habit of Catholics in danger and in troublous times to fly for refuge to Mary, and to seek for peace in her maternal goodness; showing that the Catholic Church has always, and with justice, put all her hope and trust in the Mother of God. And truly the Immaculate Virgin, chosen to be the Mother of God and thereby associated with Him in the work of man's salvation, has a favor and power with her Son greater than any human or angelic creature has ever obtained, or ever can gain. And, as it is her greatest pleasure to grant her help and comfort to those who seek her, it cannot be doubted that she would deign, and even be anxious, to receive the aspirations of the universal Church.

3. This devotion, so great and so confident, to the august Queen of Heaven, has never shone forth with such brilliancy as when the militant Church of God has seemed to be endangered by the violence of heresy spread abroad, or by an intolerable moral corruption, or by the attacks of powerful enemies. Ancient and modern history and the more sacred annals of the Church bear witness to public and private supplications addressed to the Mother of God, to the help she has granted in return, and to the peace and tranquillity which she had obtained from God. Hence her illustrious titles of helper, consoler, mighty in war, victorious, and peace-giver. And amongst these is specially to be commemorated that familiar title derived from the Rosary by which the signal benefits she has gained for the whole of Christendom have been solemnly perpetuated. There is none among you, venerable brethren, who will not remember how great trouble and grief God's

Holy Church suffered from the Albigensian heretics, who sprung from the sect of the later Manicheans, and who filled the South of France and other portions of the Latin world with their pernicious errors, and carrying everywhere the terror of their arms, strove far and wide to rule by massacre and ruin. Our merciful God, as you know, raised up against these most direful enemies a most holy man, the illustrious parent and founder of the Dominican Order. Great in the integrity of his doctrine, in his example of virtue, and by his apostolic labors, he proceeded undauntedly to attack the enemies of the Catholic Church, not by force of arms, but trusting wholly to that devotion which he was the first to institute under the name of the Holy Rosary, which was disseminated through the length and breadth of the earth by him and his pupils. Guided, in fact, by divine inspiration and grace, he foresaw that this devotion, like a most powerful warlike weapon, would be the means of putting the enemy to flight, and of confounding their audacity and mad impiety. Such was indeed its result. Thanks to this new method of prayer--when adopted and properly carried out as instituted by the Holy Father St. Dominic--piety, faith, and union began to return, and the projects and devices of the heretics to fall to pieces. Many wanderers also returned to the way of salvation, and the wrath of the impious was restrained by the arms of those Catholics who had determined to repel their violence.

4. The efficacy and power of this devotion was also wondrously exhibited in the sixteenth century, when the vast forces of the Turks threatened to impose on nearly the whole of Europe the yoke of superstition and barbarism. At that time the Supreme Pontiff, St. Pius V., after rousing the sentiment of a common defense among all the Christian princes, strove, above all, with the greatest zeal, to obtain for Christendom the favor of the most powerful Mother of God. So noble an example offered to heaven

and earth in those times rallied around him all the minds and hearts of the age. And thus Christ's faithful warriors, prepared to sacrifice their life and blood for the salvation of their faith and their country, proceeded undauntedly to meet their foe near the Gulf of Corinth, while those who were unable to take part formed a pious band of supplicants, who called on Mary, and unitedly saluted her again and again in the words of the Rosary, imploring her to grant the victory to their companions engaged in battle. Our Sovereign Lady did grant her aid; for in the naval battle by the Echinades Islands, the Christian fleet gained a magnificent victory, with no great loss to itself, in which the enemy were routed with great slaughter. And it was to preserve the memory of this great boon thus granted, that the same Most Holy Pontiff desired that a feast in honor of Our Lady of Victories should celebrate the anniversary of so memorable a struggle, the feast which Gregory XIII. dedicated under the title of "The Holy Rosary." Similarly, important successes were in the last century gained over the Turks at Temeswar, in Pannonia, and at Corfu; and in both cases these engagements coincided with feasts of the Blessed Virgin and with the conclusion of public devotions of the Rosary. And this led our predecessor, Clement XI., in his gratitude, to decree that the Blessed Mother of God should every year be especially honored in her Rosary by the whole Church.

5. Since, therefore, it is clearly evident that this form of prayer is particularly pleasing to the Blessed Virgin, and that it is especially suitable as a means of defense for the Church and all Christians, it is in no way wonderful that several others of Our Predecessors have made it their aim to favor and increase its spread by their high recommendations. Thus Urban IV. testified that "every day the Rosary obtained fresh boon for Christianity." Sixtus IV. declared that this method of prayer "redounded to the honor of God and the Blessed Virgin, and was well suited to obviate impending

dangers;" Leo X. that "it was instituted to oppose pernicious heresiarchs and heresies;" while Julius III. called it "the glory of the Church." So also St. Pius V., that "with the spread of this devotion the meditations of the faithful have begun to be more inflamed, their prayers more fervent, and they have suddenly become different men; the darkness of heresy has been dissipated, and the light of Catholic faith has broken forth again." Lastly Gregory XIII. in his turn pronounced that "the Rosary had been instituted by St. Dominic to appease the anger of God and to implore the intercession of the Blessed Virgin Mary."

6. Moved by these thoughts and by the examples of Our Predecessors, We have deemed it most opportune for similar reasons to institute solemn prayers and to endeavor by adopting those addressed to the Blessed Virgin in the recital of the Rosary to obtain from her son Jesus Christ a similar aid against present dangers. You have before your eyes, Venerable Brethren, the trials to which the Church is daily exposed; Christian piety, public morality, nay, even faith itself, the supreme good and beginning of all the other virtues, all are daily menaced with the greatest perils.

7. Nor are you only spectators of the difficulty of the situation, but your charity, like Ours, is keenly wounded; for it is one of the most painful and grievous sights to see so many souls, redeemed by the blood of Christ, snatched from salvation by the whirlwind of an age of error, precipitated into the abyss of eternal death. Our need of divine help is as great today as when the great Dominic introduced the use of the Rosary of Mary as a balm for the wounds of his contemporaries.

8. That great saint indeed, divinely enlightened, perceived that no remedy would be more adapted to the evils of his time than that men should return to Christ, who "is the way, the truth, and the

life," by frequent meditation on the salvation obtained for Us by Him, and should seek the intercession with God of that Virgin, to whom it is given to destroy all heresies. He therefore so composed the Rosary as to recall the mysteries of our salvation in succession, and the subject of meditation is mingled and, as it were, interlaced with the Angelic salutation and with the prayer addressed to God, the Father of Our Lord Jesus Christ. We, who seek a remedy for similar evils, do not doubt therefore that the prayer introduced by that most blessed man with so much advantage to the Catholic world, will have the greatest effect in removing the calamities of our times also. Not only do We earnestly exhort all Christians to give themselves to the recital of the pious devotion of the Rosary publicly, or privately in their own house and family, and that unceasingly, but we also desire that the whole of the month of October in this year should be consecrated to the Holy Queen of the Rosary. We decree and order that in the whole Catholic world, during this year, the devotion of the Rosary shall be solemnly celebrated by special and splendid services. From the first day of next October, therefore, until the second day of the November following, in every parish and, if the ecclesiastical authority deem it opportune and of use, in every chapel dedicated to the Blessed Virgin--let five decades of the Rosary be recited with the addition of the Litany of Loreto. We desire that the people should frequent these pious exercises; and We will that either Mass shall be said at the altar, or that the Blessed Sacrament shall be exposed to the adoration of the faithful, Benediction being afterwards given with the Sacred Host to the pious congregation. We highly approve of the confraternities of the Holy Rosary of the Blessed Virgin going in procession, following ancient custom, through the town, as a public demonstration of their devotion. And in those places where this is not possible, let it be replaced by more assiduous visits to the churches, and let the fervor of piety display itself by a still greater diligence in the exercise of the Christian virtues.

9. In favor of those who shall do as We have above laid down, We are pleased to open the heavenly treasure-house of the Church that they may find therein at once encouragements and rewards for their piety. We therefore grant to all those who, in the prescribed space of time, shall have taken part in the public recital of the Rosary and the Litanies, and shall have prayed for Our intention, seven years and seven times forty days of indulgence, obtainable each time. We will that those also shall share in these favors who are hindered by a lawful cause from joining in these public prayers of which We have spoken, provided that they shall have practiced those devotions in private and shall have prayed to God for Our intention. We remit all punishment and penalties for sins committed, in the form of a Pontifical indulgence, to all who, in the prescribed time, either publicly in the churches or privately at home (when hindered from the former by lawful cause) shall have at least twice practiced these pious exercises; and who shall have, after due confession, approached the holy table. We further grant a plenary indulgence to those who, either on the feast of the Blessed Virgin of the Rosary or within its octave, after having similarly purified their souls by a salutary confession, shall have approached the table of Christ and prayed in some church according to Our intention to God and the Blessed Virgin for the necessities of the Church.

10. And you, Venerable Brethren,--the more you have at heart the honor of Mary, and the welfare of human society, the more diligently apply yourselves to nourish the piety of the people towards the great Virgin, and to increase their confidence in her. We believe it to be part of the designs of Providence that, in these times of trial for the Church, the ancient devotion to the august Virgin should live and flourish amid the greatest part of the

Christian world. May now the Christian nations, excited by Our exhortations, and inflamed by your appeals, seek the protection of Mary with an ardor growing greater day by day; let them cling more and more to the practice of the Rosary, to that devotion which our ancestors were in the habit of practicing, not only as an ever-ready remedy for their misfortunes, but as a whole badge of Christian piety. The heavenly Patroness of the human race will receive with joy these prayers and supplications, and will easily obtain that the good shall grow in virtue, and that the erring should return to salvation and repent; and that God who is the avenger of crime, moved to mercy and pity may deliver Christendom and civil society from all dangers, and restore to them peace so much desired.

11. Encouraged by this hope, We beseech God Himself, with the most earnest desire of Our heart, through her in whom he has placed the fullness of all good, to grant you. Venerable Brethren, every gift of heavenly blessing. As an augury and pledge of which, We lovingly impart to you, to your clergy, and to the people entrusted to your care, the Apostolic Benediction.

Given in Rome, at St. Peter's, the 1st of September, 1883, in the sixth year of Our Pontificate.

Superiore Anno
On The Recitation Of The Rosary
Encyclical of Pope Leo XIII

August 30, 1884

To All Our Venerable Brethren the Patriarchs, Primates, Archbishops, and Bishops of the Catholic World in the Grace and Communion of the Apostolic See.

Venerable Brethren, Health and Apostolic Benediction.

Last year, as each of you is aware, We decreed by an Encyclical Letter that, to win the help of Heaven for the Church in her trials, the great Mother of God should be honored by the means of the most holy Rosary during the whole of the month of October. In this We followed both Our own impulse and the example of Our predecessors, who in times of difficulty were wont to have recourse with increased fervor to the Blessed Virgin, and to seek her aid with special prayers. That wish of Ours has been complied with, with such a willingness and unanimity that it is more than ever apparent how real is the religion and how great is the fervor of the Christian peoples, and how great is the trust everywhere placed in the heavenly patronage of the Virgin Mary. For Us, weighed down with the burden of such and so great trials and evils, We confess that the sight of such intensity of open piety and faith has been a great consolation, and even gives Us new courage for the facing, if that be the wish of God, of still greater trials. Indeed, from the spirit of prayer which is poured out over the house of David and the dwellers in Jerusalem, we have a confident hope that God will at length let Himself be touched and have pity upon the state of His

Church, and give ear to the prayers coming to Him through her whom He has chosen to be the dispenser of all heavenly graces.

2. For these reasons, therefore, with the same causes in existence which impelled Us last year, as We have said, to rouse the piety of all, We have deemed it Our duty to exhort again this year the people of Christendom to persevere in that method and formula of prayer known as the Rosary of Mary, and thereby to merit the powerful patronage of the great Mother of God. In as much as the enemies of Christianity are so stubborn in their aims, its defenders must be equally staunch, especially as the heavenly help and the benefits which are bestowed on us by God are the more usually the fruits of our perseverance. It is good to recall to memory the example of that illustrious widow, Judith--a type of the Blessed Virgin--who curbed the ill-judged impatience of the Jews when they attempted to fix, according to their own judgment, the day appointed by God for the deliverance of His city. The example should also be borne in mind of the Apostles, who awaited the supreme gift promised unto them of the Paraclete, and persevered unanimously in prayer with Mary the Mother of Jesus. For it is indeed, an arduous and exceeding weighty matter that is now in hand: it is to humiliate an old and most subtle enemy in the spread-out array of his power; to win back the freedom of the Church and of her Head; to preserve and secure the fortifications within which should rest in peace the safety and weal of human society. Care must be taken, therefore, that, in these times of mourning for the Church, the most holy devotion of the Rosary of Mary be assiduously and piously observed, the more so that this method of prayer being so arranged as to recall in turn all the mysteries of our salvation, is eminently fitted to foster the spirit of piety.

3. With respect to Italy, it is now most necessary to implore the intercession of the most powerful Virgin through the medium of

the Rosary, since a misfortune, and not an imaginary one, is threatening--nay, rather is among us. The Asiatic cholera, having, under God's will, crossed the boundary within which nature seemed to have confined it, has spread through the crowded shores of a French port, and thence to the neighboring districts of Italian soil.--To Mary, therefore, we must fly--to her whom rightly and justly the Church entitles the dispenser of saving, aiding, and protecting gifts--that she, graciously hearkening to our prayers, may grant us the help they besought, and drive far from us the unclean plague.

4. We have therefore resolved that in this coming month of October, in which the sacred devotions to Our Virgin Lady of the Rosary are solemnized throughout the Catholic world, all the devotions shall again be observed which were commanded by Us this time last year.--We therefore decree and make order that from the 1st of October to the 2nd of November following in all the parish churches (curialibus templis), in all public churches dedicated to the Mother of God, or in such as are appointed by the Ordinary, five decades at least of the Rosary be recited, together with the Litany. If in the morning, the Holy Sacrifice will take place during these prayers; if in the evening, the Blessed Sacrament will be exposed for the adoration of the faithful; after which those present will receive the customary Benediction. We desire that, wherever it be lawful, the local confraternity of the Rosary should make a solemn procession through the streets as a public manifestation of religious devotion.

5. That the heavenly treasures of the Church may be thrown open to all, We hereby renew every Indulgence granted by Us last year. To all those, therefore, who shall have assisted on the prescribed days at the public recital of the Rosary, and have prayed for Our intentions--to all those also who from legitimate causes shall have

been compelled to do so in private--We grant for each occasion an Indulgence of seven years and seven times forty days. To those who, in the prescribed space of time shall have performed these devotions at least ten times--either publicly in the churches or from just causes in the privacy of their homes--and shall have expiated their sins by confession and have received Communion at the altar, We grant from the treasury of the Church a Plenary Indulgence. We also grant this full forgiveness of sins and plenary remission of punishment to all those who, either on the feast day itself of Our Blessed Lady of the Rosary, or on any day within the subsequent eight days, shall have washed the stains from their souls and have holily partaken of the Divine banquet, and shall have also prayed in any church to God and His most holy Mother for Our intentions. As We desire also to consult the interests of those who live in country districts, and are hindered, especially in the month of October, by their agricultural labors, We permit all We have above decreed, and also the holy Indulgences gainable in the month of October, to be postponed to the following months of November or December, according to the prudent decision of the Ordinaries.

6. We doubt not, Venerable Brethren, that rich and abundant fruits will be the result of these efforts, especially if God, by the bestowal of His heavenly graces, bring an added increase to the fields planted by Us and watered by your zeal. We are certain that the faithful of Christendom will hearken to the utterance of Our Apostolic authority with the same fervor of faith and piety of which they gave most ample evidence last year. May our Heavenly Patroness, invoked by us through the Rosary, graciously be with us and obtain that, all disagreements of opinion being removed and Christianity restored throughout the world, we may obtain from God the wished for peace in the Church.--In pledge of that boon, to you,

your clergy, and the flock entrusted to your care, We lovingly bestow the Apostolic Benediction.

Given in Rome, at St. Peter's, the 30th of August, 1884, in the Seventh Year of Our Pontificate.

Quod Auctoritate
Proclaiming An Extraordinary Jubilee

Encyclical of Pope Leo XIII

December 22, 1885

To Our Venerable Brethren the Patriarchs, Primates, Archbishops, Bishops, and other Local Ordinaries, in the Grace and Communion of the Apostolic See.

Venerable Brethren, Health and Apostolic Benediction.

That which We, by the Apostolic authority, have more than once decreed, that an extraordinary year of Jubilee should be kept throughout the whole Christian world, and the treasures of heavenly gifts, the dispensation of which is in Our power, should be thrown open to the faithful--that with the favor of God We have determined to decree for the ensuing year. The advantages of this step will not escape you, Venerable Brethren, who are so familiar with the spirit of the age and the temper of the time, but there is a special reason now which makes Our decision seem more than usually opportune. In view of the fact that in Our recent Encyclical Letter We pointed out how important it is that the States should conform as closely as possible to truth and the Christian ideal, it will easily be understood how fitting it is that We should now use every effort to excite men, or to lead them back to the practice of Christian virtues. For a State is what the lives of the people make it: and just as the excellence of a ship or a house is dependent upon the good quality and the right adjustment of its component parts, so, unless the individual citizens lead good lives, the State cannot keep in the path of virtue, and without offending.

Civil government and those things which constitute the public life of a country come into existence and perish by the act of men; and men almost always succeed in stamping the image of their opinions and their lives upon their public institutions. In order therefore that Our teaching may sink into men's minds, and what is the great thing, actually govern their daily lives, an attempt must be made to bring them to think and act like Christians, not less in public than in private.

2. And in this matter effort is the more needful because perils everywhere abound. The great virtues of our forefathers have in large measure disappeared; the most violent passions have claimed a freer indulgence; the madness of opinion which knows no restraint, or at least no effective restraint, every day extends further; of those whose principles are sound there are many who, through a misplaced timidity, are frightened, and have not the courage even to speak out their opinions boldly, far less to translate them into deeds; everywhere the worst examples are affecting public morals; wicked societies which We ourselves have denounced before now, skilled in all evil arts, are doing their best to lead the people astray, and as far as they are able, to withdraw them from God, their duty, and Christianity.

3. Amid these many and pressing evils, which are the more serious because they are already of long duration, nothing must be left undone by Us which can afford any hope of relief. With this purpose, and in this hope, We proclaim a sacred Jubilee to all those who have their salvation at heart, and need to be reminded and exhorted to raise their thoughts, now busied with worldly matters, to the contemplation of heavenly things. And this with a gain not merely to the individuals themselves, but to the whole future well-being of the commonwealth, because in proportion as individual citizens advance along the path of perfection, there is a

corresponding increase in the general rectitude and probity, in the public life and morals of the nation.

4. But you will observe, Venerable Brethren, that success will largely depend upon your industry and zeal, as it will be needful to prepare the people properly and carefully if they are to reap the fruits which are to be placed before them. We commit it to your judgment and prudence to place this matter in the hands of priests whom you may select, that by discourses fitted to the capacity of the crowd they may instruct them, and above all exhort them to that penance which, according to St. Augustine, consists in "the daily chastisement of the good and the faithful followers of Christ in which we strike our breasts, saying 'forgive us our sins.'" [Ep. 108] With good reason We mention here in the first place that part of penance which consists of the voluntary punishment of the body. You know the temper of the times--how many there are who love to live delicately and shrink from whatever requires manhood and generosity; who, when ailments come, discover in them sufficient reasons for not obeying the salutary laws of the Church, thinking the burden laid upon them more than they can bear, when they are told to abstain from certain kinds of food or to fast during a few days in the year. It is not to be wondered at if, weakened by these habits of indulgence, they gradually give themselves up body and soul to the more imperious passions. It is therefore necessary to recall to the paths of moderation those who have fallen or who are likely to fall through this sort of effeminacy. Therefore those who speak to the people should lay it down persistently and clearly that according not only to the law of the Gospel, but even to the dictates of natural reason, a man is bound to govern himself and keep his passions under strict control, and moreover, that sin cannot be expiated except by penance. That the virtue of which We have spoken may be durable, it will be prudent to put it in some

sort under the safeguard and protection of a stable institution; you know well, venerable brothers, to what We allude; We mean that you should continue each one in his own diocese to protect and propagate the Third Order, called the Secular Order, of the Franciscan Friars. To keep up the spirit of penance in the Christian multitude nothing is more effectual than the example and the grace of the Patriarch Francis of Assisi, who combined with the greatest innocence of life so much zeal for mortification that the image of Jesus Christ crucified was not less visible in his life and conduct than in the signs which were supernaturally impressed upon him. The laws of his Order, which We have modified for the times, are as light to bear as they are effectual for the practice of Christian virtue.

5. In the second place, as every hope of safety lies in the protection and succor of our Heavenly Father in the midst of so great private and public necessities, We would earnestly desire to see confidence united with the revival of an assiduous zeal in prayer. In every great crisis of Christendom, and every time the Church was afflicted by evils within or dangers without, our forefathers, with their eyes lifted to Heaven in supplication, taught us how and when we should seek for the light of our souls, for the strength of virtue, and for help suited to the need. For deeply engraved upon men's minds were these precepts of Jesus Christ: "Ask and it shall be given you;" [Mt vii, 7] "We ought always to pray and not to faint." [Lk xviii, 1] And with this teaching the word of the Apostle corresponds: "Pray without ceasing;" [1 Th v, 17] "I desire, therefore, first of all that supplications, prayers, intercessions, and thanksgivings be made for all men." [1 Tim ii, 1] Upon which subject St. John Chrysostom has left us this saying, not less true than ingenious, in the form of a comparison: "Even as man, who comes into the light of day naked and wanting all things, has been endowed by nature with hands to

procure for himself all the necessaries of life; so in supernatural things, seeing that of himself he can do nothing, he has received from God the faculty of prayer, that he may use it wisely for the obtaining of all that is needful to his salvation."

6. From all this, Venerable Brethren, each one of you may gather how agreeable to Us and how commendable is the zeal with which at Our suggestion you have spread the devotion to the Most Holy Rosary, especially in these last years. Nor can We pass over the popular piety which has almost everywhere been excited by this method of prayer. Now you must watch with the greatest care that this devotion be practiced with even greater and greater fervor, and that it be persevered in without failing. And if We insist upon this exhortation, as We have already done several times, not one of you will be surprised, for you understand how important it is that this habit of the Rosary of Mary should flourish among Christians. And you are perfectly aware that this is a part and a beautiful form of that spirit of prayer of which we speak, and that it is at once admirably suited to our times, easy to practice, and fruitful in results. But as the first and the chief fruit of the Jubilee must be, as We have already pointed out, amendment of life and progress in virtue, We deem especially necessary the avoidance of that evil which We have not neglected to point out in Our past Encyclicals. We allude to those internal, and, as it were, domestic dissensions among some of ourselves; dissensions of which it is hardly possible to say how much they break or relax the bonds of charity, to the great detriment of souls. If We recall this to you once more, Venerable Brethren, who are the guardians of ecclesiastical discipline and of mutual charity, it is that We desire to see your watchfulness and your authority always directed to the prevention of so great an evil. By your warnings, your exhortations, your reproaches, urge all "to keep the unity of spirit in the bond of

peace," induce the authors of the dissensions, if such there be, to return to their duty by the consideration which they should ever keep in mind that the only-begotten Son of God, even at the approach of His last torments, asked nothing more urgently of His Father than the mutual love of those who believed, or should believe, in Him, "that they may all be one, even as Thou, Father, art in Me, and I in Thee, that they also may be one in Us." [Jn xvii, 21]

7. Relying, therefore, on the mercy of the omnipotent God, and the authority of the Blessed Apostles St. Peter and St. Paul, and making use of that power of binding and loosing which our Lord has given to Us, though unworthy of it, We grant under the form of a General Jubilee a plenary indulgence to all the faithful of both sexes upon this condition and subject to this obligation, that during the coming year of 1886 they perform the things mentioned below.

8. The citizens and inhabitants of Rome must pay two visits to the Lateran, the Vatican, and the Liberian Basilicas, and pray there for some time to God according to Our intentions for the well-being and the exaltation of the Church, for the rooting out of all heresy, and for the conversion of all who are in error, and in accordance with Our intentions pour out prayers to God that concord may reign among Christian princes, and that peace and unity may be the lot of all the faithful. They must also fast for two days, only using the food usually allowed in times of penance, in addition to the forty days of Lent and other days set aside by the Church as fast days. They must also, after having properly confessed their sins, receive Holy Communion, and, in accordance with the advice of their confessor, give an alms, each according to his means, to the furthering of some work likely to promote the propagation and increase of the Catholic Church. Each may choose the object he prefers; but We think it well especially to name two, towards which assistance may be given with the greatest advantage; and of these

each is an object which in many places is in need of help and aid, and fruitful in advantage, not less for the State than for the Church, We mean the Primary schools for boys and the Seminaries for the Clergy.

9. Those who reside outside Rome, in whatever part of the world they may live, must pay two visits at prescribed intervals to three churches to be appointed by you, Venerable Brethren, your Vicars or Officials, on your or their command, by those who have the charge of souls; or three visits if there are only two churches, or six visits if there is only one; and also must comply with all the conditions already laid down above. This indulgence may be applied by way of suffrage to the souls who have departed this life joined in charity with God. We give you power to reduce the number of the visits according to your judgment to certain churches in the case of chapters, congregations, as well secular as regular, communities, confraternities, universities, and colleges where the visits are made in procession.

10. Sailors and travelers may obtain the indulgence upon their return home, or their arrival at some fixed station, by visiting six times the principal church, or the parish church of the district, and complying with the other conditions which We have already laid down. In the case of regulars of either sex, and even in the case of persons belonging to enclosed orders, and also in the case of all others, whether ecclesiastical or lay, who are prevented either because they are in prison, or through infirmity, or any other good reason, from fulfilling the above conditions, or some of them, the confessor has power to conmute for other pious works, and also has power to dispense from Communion children who have not yet made their First Communion. Moreover, We grant to all and each of the faithful, both lay and ecclesiastic, secular and regular, of whatever order and institute, and even of those which ought to be

specially named, that they should choose for the purpose of the Jubilee any approved confessor they like; nuns, novices, and other women living in the cloister may avail themselves of this power provided the confessor chosen is approved for nuns. To confessors upon this occasion, and while the time of this Jubilee lasts, We grant all the faculties which were granted by Our Letters Apostolic of February 15th, 1879, beginning with the words Pontifices maximi; always excepting the things which were excepted in those Letters.

11. Finally let all do their best to gain the graces of heaven during this time by a special devotion to the great Mother of God. For We wish this Jubilee to be placed under the patronage of the Most Holy Rosary of the Virgin; and with her assistance We are confident that there will be many whose souls, set free by the cleansing away of the stains of sin, will be renewed by faith and piety and justice, not only to the hope of eternal salvation, but also as an earnest of a more peaceful time.

12. As a pledge of heavenly graces and a witness to Our fatherly goodwill towards you, We give from the bottom of Our heart the Apostolic Benediction to you and your Clergy, and the whole people committed to your care and watchfulness.

Given in Rome, at St. Peter's, on the twenty-second day of December, in the year 1885, the eighth of Our Pontificate.

Vi E Ben Noto
On The Rosary And Public Life
Encyclical of Pope Leo XIII

September 20, 1887

To the Bishops of Italy.

Venerable Brethren,

You know how We place amid present dangers Our confidence in the Glorious Virgin of the Holy Rosary, for the safety and prosperity of Christendom and the peace and tranquillity of the Church. Mindful that in moments of great trial, pastors and people have ever had recourse with entire confidence to the august Mother of God, in whose hands are all graces, certain too, that devotion to Our Lady of the Rosary is most opportune for the needs of these times, We have desired to revive everywhere this devotion, and to spread it far and wide among the faithful of the world. Oftentimes already We, in recommending the pious practice of devoting October to honoring Our Lady, have pointed out Our reasons and hope for so doing, and the forms to be observed; and the entire Church, docile to Our desires, has ever replied by special manifestations of devotion; and now is making ready to pay to Mary, during a whole month, a daily tribute of the devotion so dear to it. In such pious rivalry Italy has not been behind-hand, for devotion to Our Lady is deeply and widely rooted in this land; and We doubt not that this year too, Italy will set a glorious example of love for the august Mother of God, and will give Us fresh reasons for consolation and hope. Nevertheless We cannot do less than address to you, Venerable Brethren, a few words of exhortation, so that with particular and renewed zeal the month dedicated to the Most Holy Virgin of the Rosary may be sanctified in every diocese of Italy.

2. It is easy to imagine what reasons We have for doing this. Since God called Us to govern His Church on earth, We have sought to use every possible means that We deemed suitable, for the sanctification of souls and the extension of the reign of Jesus Christ. We have excepted from Our daily solicitude no nation and no people, mindful that Our Redeemer shed His precious blood on the Cross and opened the reign of grace and of glory for all. None, however, can be surprised that We showed special care for the Italian people, for Our Divine Master Jesus Christ chose, from out all the world, Italy to be the seat of His Vicar on earth, and in His providential designs appointed Rome to be the capital of the Catholic world. On this account the Italian people is called upon to live close to the Father of the whole Christian family, and to share in a special way in his sorrows and his glory. Unfortunately We find in Italy much to sadden Our souls. Faith and Christian morals, the precious inheritance bequeathed by Our ancestors, and in all past times the glory of Our country and of Italy's great ones, are being attacked artfully and in covert ways, or even openly, with cynicism that is revolting, by a handful of men who seek to rob others of that faith and morality they have themselves lost. In this more especially is seen the work of the sects, and of those who are more or less their willing tools. Above all, in this city of Rome, where Christ's Vicar has his See are their efforts concentrated and their diabolical designs displayed with ferocious obstinacy.

3. We need not tell you, Venerable Brethren, with what bitterness Our soul is filled at seeing the danger there is for the salvation of so many of Our beloved children. And Our sorrow is greater because We find it impossible to oppose such great evil with that salutary

efficacy We would desire and that We have the right to use, for you know, Venerable Brethren, and all the world knows, the state to which we are reduced. On this account We feel a still greater desire to call upon the Mother of God and to ask her help. Let all good Italians pray for their misguided brethren, for their common Father the Roman Pontiff, that God, in His infinite mercy, may hear and answer the prayers of a father and his sons. And Our most lively and sure hope is placed in the Queen of the Rosary, who has shown herself, since she has been invoked by that title, so ready to help the Church and Christian peoples in their necessities. Already have We recorded these glories and the great triumphs won over the Albigenses and other powerful enemies, glories and triumphs which have not only profited the Church, afflicted and persecuted, but also the temporal welfare of peoples and nations. Why in this hour of need should We not behold again such marvels of the power and goodness of the august Virgin, for the good of the Church and its Head, and of the whole Christian world, if the faithful only revive, on their part, the magnificent examples of piety given by their forefathers, under similar circumstances? And to make this most powerful Queen more and more propitious, We would honor her more and more in the invocation of the Rosary, and increase this devotion. And to this end We have made a double of the second class for all the Church of the Feast of the Rosary. And for the same purpose We ardently desire the Catholics of Italy, with lively faith, especially during this month of October, to invoke this august Virgin and to do loving violence to her mother's heart, and to pray to her for the triumph of the Church and the Apostolic See, for the liberty of the Vicar of Jesus Christ on earth, and for peace and public prosperity. And, since the effects of such prayers will be proportionate to the dispositions of those offering them, We ardently exhort you, venerable brethren, devote all your care and zeal to kindle among those committed to your charge a strong, living and active faith, and to call on all to return by penance to grace and to the faithful fulfillment of; all their duties. Among such duties, considering the state of the times, must be reckoned as paramount an open and sincere profession of the fait and teaching of Jesus Christ, casting aside all human respect, and considering before all thing the interest of religion and the salvation of souls. It cannot be concealed that, although thanks to the mercy of God religious feeling is strong and widely spread among Italians, nevertheless by the evil influence of men and the times religious indifference is on the increase, and hence there is lessening of that respect and filial love for the Church which was the glory of our ancestors and in which they placed their highest ambition. Let it be your work, venerable brethren, to revive this Christian feeling among your people, an interest in the Catholic cause, a confidence in Our Lady's help, and a spirit of prayer. It is certain that the august Queen, invoked thus well by her man sons, would deign to hear their prayer, console Us in Our sorrow, and crown Our efforts for the Church and for Italy, by granting better times to both. With these desires, We bestow on you venerable brethren, and the clergy and people committed to your care, the Apostolic Benediction as a promise of graces and favors of the highest kind from heaven.

Given at the Vatican this 20th day of September 1887.

Enchiridion Sanctissimi Rosarii

Quamquam Pluries
On Devotion To St. Joseph

Encyclical of Pope Leo XIII

August 15, 1889

To Our Venerable Brethren the Patriarchs, Primates, Archbishops, and other Ordinaries, in Peace and Union With Holy See.

Although We have already many times ordered special prayers to be offered up in the whole world, that the interests of Catholicism might be insistently recommended to God, none will deem it matter for surprise that We consider the present moment an opportune one for again inculcating the same duty. During periods of stress and trial--chiefly when every lawlessness of act seems permitted to the powers of darkness--it has been the custom in the Church to plead with special fervor and perseverance to God, her author and protector, by recourse to the intercession of the saints-- and chiefly of the Blessed Virgin, Mother of God--whose patronage has ever been the most efficacious. The fruit of these pious prayers and of the confidence reposed in the Divine goodness, has always, sooner or later, been made apparent. Now, Venerable Brethren, you know the times in which we live; they are scarcely less deplorable for the Christian religion than the worst days, which in time past were most full of misery to the Church. We see faith, the root of all the Christian virtues, lessening in many souls; we see charity growing cold; the young generation daily growing in depravity of morals and views; the Church of Jesus Christ attacked on every side by open force or by craft; a relentless war waged against the Sovereign Pontiff; and the very foundations of religion undermined with a boldness which waxes daily in intensity. These things are, indeed, so much a matter of notoriety that it is needless for Us to expatiate on the depths to which society has sunk in these days, or on the designs which now agitate the minds of men. In circumstances so unhappy and troublous, human remedies are insufficient, and it becomes necessary, as a sole resource, to beg for assistance from the Divine power.

2. This is the reason why We have considered it necessary to turn to the Christian people and urge them to implore, with increased zeal and constancy, the aid of Almighty God. At this proximity of the month of October, which We have already consecrated to the Virgin Mary, under the title of Our Lady of the Rosary, We earnestly exhort the faithful to perform the exercises of this month with, if possible, even more piety and constancy than heretofore. We know that there is sure help in the maternal goodness of the Virgin, and We are very certain that We shall never vainly place Our trust in her. If, on innumerable occasions. she has displayed her power in aid of the Christian world, why should We doubt that she will now renew the assistance of her power and favor, if humble and constant prayers are offered up on all sides to her? Nay, We rather believe that her intervention will be the more marvelous as she has permitted Us to pray to her, for so long a time, with special appeals. But We entertain another object, which, according to your wont, Venerable Brethren, you will advance with fervor. That God may be more favorable to Our prayers, and that He may come with bounty and promptitude to the aid of His Church, We judge it of deep utility for the Christian people, continually to invoke with great piety and trust, together with the Virgin-Mother of God, her chaste Spouse, the Blessed Joseph; and We regard it as most certain that this will be most pleasing to the Virgin herself. On the subject of this devotion, of which We speak publicly for the first time to-day, We know without doubt that not

only is the people inclined to it, but that it is already established, and is advancing to full growth. We have seen the devotion to St. Joseph, which in past times the Roman Pontiffs have developed and gradually increased, grow into greater proportions in Our time, particularly after Pius IX., of happy memory, Our predecessor, proclaimed, yielding to the request of a large number of bishops, this holy patriarch the patron of the Catholic Church. And as, moreover, it is of high importance that the devotion to St. Joseph should engraft itself upon the daily pious practices of Catholics, We desire that the Christian people should be urged to it above all by Our words and authority.

3. The special motives for which St. Joseph has been proclaimed Patron of the Church, and from which the Church looks for singular benefit from his patronage and protection, are that Joseph was the spouse of Mary and that he was reputed the Father of Jesus Christ. From these sources have sprung his dignity, his holiness, his glory. In truth, the dignity of the Mother of God is so lofty that naught created can rank above it. But as Joseph has been united to the Blessed Virgin by the ties of marriage, it may not be doubted that he approached nearer than any to the eminent dignity by which the Mother of God surpasses so nobly all created natures. For marriage is the most intimate of all unions which from its essence imparts a community of gifts between those that by it are joined together. Thus in giving Joseph the Blessed Virgin as spouse, God appointed him to be not only her life's companion, the witness of her maidenhood, the protector of her honor, but also, by virtue of the conjugal tie, a participator in her sublime dignity. And Joseph shines among all mankind by the most august dignity, since by divine will, he was the guardian of the Son of God and reputed as His father among men. Hence it came about that the Word of God was humbly subject to Joseph, that He obeyed him, and that He

rendered to him all those offices that children are bound to render to their parents. From this two-fold dignity flowed the obligation which nature lays upon the head of families, so that Joseph became the guardian, the administrator, and the legal defender of the divine house whose chief he was. And during the whole course of his life he fulfilled those charges and those duties. He set himself to protect with a mighty love and a daily solicitude his spouse and the Divine Infant; regularly by his work he earned what was necessary for the one and the other for nourishment and clothing; he guarded from death the Child threatened by a monarch's jealousy, and found for Him a refuge; in the miseries of the journey and in the bitternesses of exile he was ever the companion, the assistance, and the upholder of the Virgin and of Jesus. Now the divine house which Joseph ruled with the authority of a father, contained within its limits the scarce-born Church. From the same fact that the most holy Virgin is the mother of Jesus Christ is she the mother of all Christians whom she bore on Mount Calvary amid the supreme throes of the Redemption; Jesus Christ is, in a manner, the first-born of Christians, who by the adoption and Redemption are his brothers. And for such reasons the Blessed Patriarch looks upon the multitude of Christians who make up the Church as confided specially to his trust--this limitless family spread over the earth, over which, because he is the spouse of Mary and the Father of Jesus Christ he holds, as it were, a paternal authority. It is, then, natural and worthy that as the Blessed Joseph ministered to all the needs of the family at Nazareth and girt it about with his protection, he should now cover with the cloak of his heavenly patronage and defend the Church of Jesus Christ.

4. You well understand, Venerable Brethren that these considerations are confirmed by the opinion held by a large number of the Fathers, to which the sacred liturgy gives its

sanction, that the Joseph of ancient times, son of the patriarch Jacob, was the type of St. Joseph, and the former by his glory prefigured the greatness of the future guardian of the Holy Family. And in truth, beyond the fact that the same name--a point the significance of which has never been denied--was given to each, you well know the points of likeness that exist between them; namely, that the first Joseph won the favor and especial goodwill of his master, and that through Joseph's administration his household came to prosperity and wealth; that (still more important) he presided over the kingdom with great power, and, in a time when the harvests failed, he provided for all the needs of the Egyptians with so much wisdom that the King decreed to him the title "Savior of the world." Thus it is that We may prefigure the new in the old patriarch. And as the first caused the prosperity of his master's domestic interests and at the same time rendered great services to the whole kingdom, so the second, destined to be the guardian of the Christian religion, should be regarded as the protector and defender of the Church, which is truly the house of the Lord and the kingdom of God on earth. These are the reasons why men of every rank and country should fly to the trust and guard of the blessed Joseph. Fathers of families find in Joseph the best personification of paternal solicitude and vigilance; spouses a perfect example of love, of peace, and of conjugal fidelity; virgins at the same time find in him the model and protector of virginal integrity. The noble of birth will earn of Joseph how to guard their dignity even in misfortune; the rich will understand, by his lessons, what are the goods most to be desired and won at the price of their labor. As to workmen, artisans, and persons of lesser degree, their recourse to Joseph is a special right, and his example is for their particular imitation. For Joseph, of royal blood, united by marriage to the greatest and holiest of women, reputed the father of the Son of God, passed his life in labor, and won by the toil of the artisan the needful support of his family. It is, then, true that the condition of the lowly has nothing shameful in it, and the work of the laborer is not only not dishonoring, but can, if virtue be joined to it, be singularly ennobled. Joseph, content with his slight possessions, bore the trials consequent on a fortune so slender, with greatness of soul, in imitation of his Son, who having put on the form of a slave, being the Lord of life, subjected himself of his own free-will to the spoliation and loss of everything.

5. Through these considerations, the poor and those who live by the labor of their hands should be of good heart and learn to be just. If they win the right of emerging from poverty and obtaining a better rank by lawful means, reason and justice uphold them in changing the order established, in the first instance, for them by the Providence of God. But recourse to force and struggles by seditious paths to obtain such ends are madnesses which only aggravate the evil which they aim to suppress. Let the poor, then, if they would be wise, trust not to the promises of seditious men, but rather to the example and patronage of the Blessed Joseph, and to the maternal charity of the Church, which each day takes an increasing compassion on their lot.

6. This is the reason why--trusting much to your zeal and episcopal authority, Venerable Brethren, and not doubting that the good and pious faithful will run beyond the mere letter of the law--We prescribe that during the whole month of October, at the recitation of the Rosary, for which We have already legislated, a prayer to St. Joseph be added, the formula of which will be sent with this letter, and that this custom should be repeated every year. To those who recite this prayer, We grant for each time an indulgence of seven years and seven Lents. It is a salutary practice and very praiseworthy, already established in some countries, to consecrate the month of March to the honor of the holy Patriarch by daily

exercises of piety. Where this custom cannot be easily established, it is as least desirable, that before the feast-day, in the principal church of each parish, a "triduo" of prayer be celebrated. In those lands where the 19th of March--the Feast of St. Joseph--is not a Festival of Obligation, We exhort the faithful to sanctify it as far as possible by private pious practices, in honor of their heavenly patron, as though it were a day of Obligation.

7. And in token of heavenly favors, and in witness of Our goodwill, We grant most lovingly in the Lord, to you, Venerable Brethren, to your clergy and to your people, the Apostolic blessing.

Given from the Vatican, August 15th, 1889, the 11th year of Our Pontificate.

Octobri Mense
On The Rosary

Encyclical of Pope Leo XIII

September 22, 1891

To Our Venerable Brethren the Patriarchs, Primates, Archbishops, Bishops, and other Ordinaries having Grace and Communion with the Apostolic See.

Venerable Brethren, Greeting and Apostolic Benediction.

At the coming of the month of October, dedicated and consecrated as it is to the Blessed Virgin of the Rosary, we recall with satisfaction the instant exhortations which in preceding years We addressed to you, venerable brethren, desiring, as We did, that the faithful, urged by your authority and by your zeal, should redouble their piety towards the august Mother of God, the mighty helper of Christians, and should pray to her throughout the month, invoking her by that most holy rite of the Rosary which the Church, especially in the passage of difficult times, has ever used for the accomplishment of all desires. This year once again do We publish Our wishes, once again do We encourage you by the same exhortations. We are persuaded to this in love for the Church, whose sufferings, far from mitigating, increase daily in number and in gravity. Universal and well-known are the evils we deplore: war made upon the sacred dogmas which the Church holds and transmits; derision cast upon the integrity of that Christian morality which she has in keeping; enmity declared, with the impudence of audacity and with criminal malice, against the very Christ, as though the Divine work of Redemption itself were to be destroyed from its foundation--that work which, indeed, no adverse power shall ever utterly abolish or destroy.

2. No new events are these in the career of the Church militant. Jesus foretold them to His disciples. That she may teach men the truth and may guide them to eternal salvation, she must enter upon a daily war; and throughout the course of ages she has fought, even to martyrdom, rejoicing and glorifying herself in nothing more than in the occasion of signing her cause with her Founder's blood, the sure and certain pledge of the victory whereof she holds the promise. Nevertheless we must not conceal the profound sadness with which this necessity of constant war afflicts the righteous. It is indeed a cause of great sorrow that so many should be deterred and led astray by error and enmity to God; that so many should be indifferent to all forms of religion, and should finally become estranged from faith; that so many Catholics should be such in name only, and should pay to religion no honor or worship. And still sadder and more beset with anxieties grows the soul at the thought of the fruitful source of most manifold evils existing in the organization of States that allow no place to the Church, and that oppose her championship of holy virtue. This is truly a terrible manifestation of the just vengeance of God, Who allows blindness of soul to darken upon the nations that forsake Him. These are evils that cry aloud, that cry of themselves with a daily increasing voice. It is absolutely necessary that the Catholic voice should also call to God with unwearied instance, "without ceasing;" [Thes 5.17] that the Faithful should pray not only in their own homes, but in public, gathered together under the sacred roof; that they should beseech urgently the all-foreseeing God to deliver the Church from evil men [2 Thes 3.2] and to bring back the troubled nations to good sense and reason, by the light and love of Christ.

3. Wonderful and beyond hope or belief is this. The world goes on its laborious way, proud of its riches, of its power, of its arms, of its genius; the Church goes onward along the course of ages with an even step, trusting in God only, to Whom, day and night, she lifts her eyes and her suppliant hands. Even though in her prudence she neglects not the human aid which Providence and the times afford her, not in these does she put her trust, which rests in prayer, in supplication, in the invocation of God. Thus it is that she renews her vital breath; the diligence of her prayer has caused her, in her aloofness from worldly things and in her continual union with the Divine will, to live the tranquil and peaceful life of Our very Lord Jesus Christ; being herself the image of Christ, Whose happy and perpetual joy was hardly marred by the horror of the torments He endured for us. This important doctrine of Christian wisdom has been ever believed and practiced by Christians worthy of the name. Their prayers rise to God eagerly and more frequently when the cunning and the violence of the perverse afflict the Church and her supreme Pastor. Of this the faithful of the Church in the East gave an example that should be offered to the imitation of posterity. Peter, Vicar of Jesus Christ, and first Pontiff of the Church, had been cast into prison, loaded with chains by the guilty Herod, and left for certain death. None could carry him help or snatch him from the peril. But there was the certain help that fervent prayer wins from God. The Church, as the sacred story tells us, made prayer without ceasing to God for him; [Acts 12.5] and the greater was the fear of a misfortune, the greater was the fervor of all who prayed to God. After the granting of their desires the miracle stood revealed; and Christians still celebrate with a joyous gratitude the marvel of the deliverance of Peter. Christ has given us a still more memorable instance, a Divine instance, so that the Church might be formed not upon his precepts only, but upon His example also. During His whole life He had given Himself to frequent and

fervent prayer, and in the supreme hours in the Garden of Gethsemane, when His soul was filled with bitterness and sorrow unto death, He prayed to His Father and prayed repeatedly. [Lk 22.44] It was not for Himself that He prayed thus, for He feared nothing and needed nothing, being God; He prayed for us, for His Church, whose prayers and future tears He already then accepted with joy, to give them back in mercies.

4. But since the salvation of our race was accomplished by the mystery of the Cross, and since the Church, dispenser of that salvation after the triumph of Christ, was founded upon earth and instituted, Providence established a new order for a new people. The consideration of the Divine counsels is united to the great sentiment of religion. The Eternal Son of God, about to take upon Him our nature for the saving and ennobling of man, and about to consummate thus a mystical union between Himself and all mankind, did not accomplish His design without adding there the free consent of the elect Mother, who represented in some sort all human kind, according to the illustrious and just opinion of St. Thomas, who says that the Annunciation was effected with the consent of the Virgin standing in the place of humanity. [III. q. xxx, a. 1] With equal truth may it be also affirmed that, by the will of God, Mary is the intermediary through whom is distributed unto us this immense treasure of mercies gathered by God, for mercy and truth were created by Jesus Christ. [Jn 1.17] Thus as no man goeth to the Father but by the Son, so no man goeth to Christ but by His Mother. How great are the goodness and mercy revealed in this design of God! What a correspondence with the frailty of man! We believe in the infinite goodness of the Most High, and we rejoice in it; we believe also in His justice and we fear it. We adore the beloved Savior, lavish of His blood and of His life; we dread the inexorable Judge. Thus do those whose actions have disturbed their

consciences need an intercessor mighty in favor with God, merciful enough not to reject the cause of the desperate, merciful enough to lift up again towards hope in the divine mercy the afflicted and the broken down. Mary is this glorious intermediary; she is the mighty Mother of the Almighty; but-- what is still sweeter--she is gentle, extreme in tenderness, of a limitless loving-kindness. As such God gave her to us. Having chosen her for the Mother of His only begotten Son, He taught her all a mother's feeling that breathes nothing but pardon and love. Such Christ desired she should be, for He consented to be subject to Mary and to obey her as a son a mother. Such He proclaimed her from the cross when he entrusted to her care and love the whole of the race of man in the person of His disciple John. Such, finally, she proves herself by her courage in gathering in the heritage of the enormous labors of her Son, and in accepting the charge of her maternal duties towards us all.

5. The design of this most dear mercy, realized by God in Mary and confirmed by the testament of Christ, was comprehended at the beginning, and accepted with the utmost joy by the Holy Apostles and the earliest believers. It was the counsel and teaching of the venerable Fathers of the Church. All the nations of the Christian age received it with one mind; and even when literature and tradition are silent there is a voice that breaks from every Christian breast and speaks with all eloquence. No other reason is needed that that of a Divine faith which, by a powerful and most pleasant impulse, persuades us towards Mary. Nothing is more natural, nothing more desirable than to seek a refuge in the protection and in the loyalty of her to whom we may confess our designs and our actions, our innocence and our repentance, our torments and our joys, our prayers and our desires--all our affairs. All men, moreover, are filled with the hope and confidence that petitions which might be received with less favor from the lips of unworthy men, God

Enchiridion Sanctissimi Rosarii

will accept when they are recommended by the most Holy Mother, and will grant with all favors. The truth and the sweetness of these thoughts bring to the soul an unspeakable comfort; but they inspire all the more compassion for those who, being without Divine faith, honor not Mary and have her not for their mother; for those also who, holding Christian faith, dare to accuse of excess the devotion to Mary, thereby sorely wounding filial piety.

6. This storm of evils, in the midst of which the Church struggles so strenuously, reveals to all her pious children the holy duty whereto they are bound to pray to God with instance, and the manner in which they may give to their prayers the greater power. Faithful to the religious example of our fathers, let us have recourse to Mary, our holy Sovereign. Let us entreat, let us beseech, with one heart, Mary, the Mother of Jesus Christ, our Mother. "Show thyself to be a mother; cause our prayers to be accepted by Him Who, born for us, consented to be thy Son." [Ex sacr. liturg.]

7. Now, among the several rites and manners of paying honor to the Blessed Mary, some are to be preferred, inasmuch as we know them to be most powerful and most pleasing to our Mother; and for this reason we specially mention by name and recommend the Rosary. The common language has given the name of corona to this manner of prayer, which recalls to our minds the great mysteries of Jesus and Mary united in joys, sorrows, and triumphs. The contemplation of these august mysteries, contemplated in their order, affords to faithful souls a wonderful confirmation of faith, protection against the disease of error, and increase of the strength of the soul. The soul and memory of him who thus prays, enlightened by faith, are drawn towards these mysteries by the sweetest devotion, are absorbed therein and are surprised before the work of the Redemption of mankind, achieved at such a price and by events so great. The soul is filled with gratitude and love

before these proofs of Divine love; its hope becomes enlarged and its desire is increased for those things which Christ has prepared for such as have united themselves to Him in imitation of His example and in participation in His sufferings. The prayer is composed of words proceeding from God Himself, from the Archangel Gabriel, and from the Church; full of praise and of high desires; and it is renewed and continued in an order at once fixed and various; its fruits are ever new and sweet.

8. Moreover, we may well believe that the Queen of Heaven herself has granted an especial efficacy to this mode of supplication, for it was by her command and counsel that the devotion was begun and spread abroad by the holy Patriarch Dominic as a most potent weapon against the enemies of the faith at an epoch not, indeed, unlike our own, of great danger to our holy religion. The heresy of the Albigenses had in effect, one while covertly, another while openly, overrun many countries, and this most vile offspring of the Manicheans, whose deadly errors it reproduced, were the cause in stirring up against the Church the most bitter animosity and a virulent persecution. There seemed to be no human hope of opposing this fanatical and most pernicious sect when timely succor came from on high through the instrument of Mary's Rosary. Thus under the favor of the powerful Virgin, the glorious vanquisher of all heresies, the forces of the wicked were destroyed and dispersed, and faith issued forth unharmed and more shining than before. All manner of similar instances are widely recorded, and both ancient and modern history furnish remarkable proofs of nations saved from perils and winning benedictions therefrom. There is another signal argument in favor of this devotion, inasmuch as from the very moment of its institution it was immediately encouraged and put into most frequent practice by all classes of society. In truth, the piety of the Christian people honors,

by many titles and in multiform ways, the Divine Mother, who, alone most admirable among all creatures, shines resplendent in unspeakable glory. But this title of the Rosary, this mode of prayer which seems to contain, as it were, a final pledge of affection, and to sum up in itself the honor due to Our Lady, has always been highly cherished and widely used in private and in public, in homes and in families, in the meetings of confraternities, at the dedication of shrines, and in solemn processions; for there has seemed to be no better means of conducting sacred solemnities, or of obtaining protection and favors.

9. Nor may we permit to pass unnoticed the especial Providence of God displayed in this devotion; for through the lapse of time religious fervor has sometimes seemed to diminish in certain nations, and even this pious method of prayer has fallen into disuse; but piety and devotion have again flourished and become vigorous in a most marvelous manner, when, either through the grave situation of the commonwealth or through some pressing public necessity, general recourse has been had--more to this than to even other means of obtaining help--to the Rosary, whereby it has been restored to its place of honor on the altars. But there is no need to seek for examples of this power in a past age, since we have in the present a signal instance of it. In these times--so troublous (as we have said before) for the Church, and so heartrending for ourselves--set as We are by the Divine will at the helm, it is still given Us to note with admiration the great zeal and fervor with which Mary's Rosary is honored and recited in every place and nation of the Catholic world. And this circumstance, which assuredly is to be attributed to the Divine action and direction upon men, rather than to the wisdom and efforts of individuals, strengthens and consoles Our heart, filling Us with great hope for

the ultimate and most glorious triumph of the Church under the auspices of Mary.

10. But there are some who, whilst they honestly agree with what We have said, yet because their hopes--especially as regard the peace and tranquillity of the Church--have not yet been fulfilled, nay, rather because troubles seem to augment, have ceased to pray with diligence and fervor, in a fit of discouragement. Let these look into themselves and labor that the prayers they address to God may be made in a proper spirit, according to the precept of our Lord Jesus Christ. And if there be such, let them reflect how unworthy and how wrong it is to wish to assign to Almighty God the time and the manner of giving His assistance, since He owes nothing to us, and when He hearkens to our supplications and crowns our merits, He only crowns His own innumerable benefits; [S. August. Epi CXCIV al 106 Sixtum, c. v., n 19] and when He complies least with our wishes it is as a good father towards his children, having pity on their childishness and consulting their advantage. But as regards the prayers which we join to the suffrages of the heavenly citizens, and offer humbly to God to obtain His mercy for the Church, they are always favorably received and heard, and either obtain for the Church great and imperishable benefits, or their influence is temporarily withheld for a time of greater need. In truth, to these supplications is added an immense weight and grace--the prayers and merits of Christ Our Lord, Who has loved the Church and has delivered Himself up for her to sanctify her . . . so that He should be glorified in her. [Eph 5.25-27] He is her Sovereign Head, holy, innocent, always living to make intercession for us, on whose prayers and supplication we can always by divine authority rely. As for what concerns the exterior and temporal prosperity of the Church, it is evident that she has to cope with most malicious and powerful adversaries. Too often has she

suffered at their hands the abolition of her rights, the diminution and oppression of her liberties, scorn and affronts to her authority, and every conceivable outrage. And if in their wickedness her enemies have not accomplished all the injury they had resolved upon and striven to do, they nevertheless seem to go on unchecked. But, despite them the Church, amidst all these conflicts, will always stand out and increase in greatness and glory. Nor can human reason rightly understand why evil, apparently so dominant, should yet be so restricted as regards its results; whilst the Church, driven into straits, comes forth glorious and triumphant. And she ever remains more steadfast in virtue because she draws men to the acquisition of the ultimate good. And since this is her mission, her prayers must have much power to effect the end and purpose of God's providential and merciful designs towards men. Thus, when men pray with and through the Church, they at length obtain what Almighty God has designed from all eternity to bestow upon mankind. [S. Th. II-II, q LXXXIII, a. 2, ex S. G. reg. M] The subtlety of the human intelligence fails now to grasp the high designs of Providence; but the time will come when, through the goodness of God, causes and effects will be made clear, and the marvelous power and utility of prayer will be shown forth. Then it will be seen how many in the midst of a corrupt age have kept themselves pure and inviolate from all concupiscence of the flesh and the spirit, working out their sanctification in the fear of God; [2 Cor 7.1] how others, when exposed to the danger of temptation, have without delay restrained themselves gaining new strength for virtue from the peril itself; how others, having fallen, have been seized with the ardent desire to be restored to the embraces of a compassionate God.

Therefore, with these reflections before them, We beseech all again and again not to yield to the deceits of the old enemy, nor for any cause whatsoever to cease from the duty of prayer. Let their prayers be persevering, let them pray without intermission; let their first care be to supplicate for the sovereign good--the eternal salvation of the whole world, and the safety of the Church. Then they may ask from God other benefits for the use and comfort of life, returning thanks always, whether their desires are granted or refused, as to a most indulgent father. Finally, may they converse with God with the greatest piety and devotion according to the example of the Saints, and that of our Most Holy Master and Redeemer, with great cries and tears. [Heb 5.7]

11. Our fatherly solicitude urges Us to implore of God, the Giver of all good gifts, not merely the spirit of prayer, but also that of holy penance for all the sons of the Church. And whilst We make this most earnest supplication, We exhort all and each one to the practice with equal fervor of both these virtues combined. Thus prayer fortifies the soul, makes it strong for noble endeavors, leads it up to divine things: penance enables us to overcome ourselves, especially our bodies--most inveterate enemies of reason and the evangelical law. And it is very clear that these virtues unite well with each other, assist each other mutually, and have the same object, namely, to detach man born for heaven from perishable objects, and to raise him up to heavenly commerce with God. On the other hand, the mind that is excited by passions and enervated by pleasure is insensible to the delights of heavenly things, and makes cold and neglectful prayers quite unworthy of being accepted by God. We have before Our eyes examples of the penance of holy men whose prayers and supplications were consequently most pleasing to God, and even obtained miracles. They governed and kept assiduously in subjection their minds and hearts and wills. They accepted with the greatest joy and humility the doctrines of Christ and the teachings of His Church. Their unique desire was to

advance in the science of God; nor had their actions any other object than the increase of His glory. They restrained most severely their passions, treated their bodies rudely and harshly, abstaining from even permitted pleasures through love of virtue. And therefore most deservedly could they have said with the Apostle Paul, our conversation is in Heaven: [Phil. 3.20] hence the potent efficacy of their prayers in appeasing and in supplicating the Divine Majesty. It is clear that not every one is obliged or able to attain to these heights; nevertheless, each one should correct his life and morals in his own measure in satisfaction to the Divine justice: for it is to those who have endured voluntary sufferings in this life that the reward of virtue is vouchsafed. Moreover, when in the mystical body of Christ, which is the Church, all the members are united and flourish, it results, according to St. Paul, that the joy or pain of one member is shared by all the rest, so that if one of the brethren in Christ is suffering in mind or body the others come to his help and succor him as far as in them lies. The members are solicitous in regard of each other, and if one member suffer all the members suffer in sympathy, and if one member rejoice all the others rejoice also. But you are the body of Christ, members of one body. [I Cor 12 25-27] But in this illustration of charity, following the example of Christ, Who in the immensity of His love gave up His life to redeem us from sin, paying Himself the penalties incurred by others, in this is the great bond of perfection by which the faithful are closely united with the heavenly citizens and with God. Above all, acts of holy penance are so numerous and varied and extend over such a wide range, that each one may exercise them frequently with a cheerful and ready will without serious or painful effort.

12. And now, venerable brethren, your remarkable and exalted piety towards the Most Holy Mother of God, and your charity and solicitude for the Christian flock, are full of abundant promise: Our

heart is full of desire for those wondrous fruits which, on many occasions, the devotion of Catholic people to Mary has brought forth; already We enjoy them deeply and abundantly in anticipation. At your exhortation and under your direction, therefore, the faithful, especially during this ensuing month, will assemble around the solemn altars of this august Queen and most benign Mother, and weave and offer to her, like devoted children, the mystic garland so pleasing to her of the Rosary. All the privileges and indulgences We have herein before conceded are confirmed and ratified. [Cf. ep. encycl. "Supremi Apostolatus officio" (September 1, 1893); ep. encycl. "Supreriore anno" (August 30, 1884); decree S. R. C. "Inter plurimos" (August 20, 1885); ep. encycl. "Quamquam pluries" (August 15, 1889)]

13. How grateful and magnificent a spectacle to see in the cities, and towns, and villages, on land and sea--wherever the Catholic faith has penetrated--many hundreds of thousands of pious people uniting their praises and prayers with one voice and heart at every moment of the day, saluting Mary, invoking Mary, hoping everything through Mary. Through her may all the faithful strive to obtain from her Divine Son that the nations plunged in error may return to the Christian teaching and precepts, in which is the foundation of the public safety and the source of peace and true happiness. Through her may they steadfastly endeavor for that most desirable of all blessings, the restoration of the liberty of our Mother, the Church, and the tranquil possession of her rights--rights which have no other object than the careful direction of men's dearest interests, from the exercise of which individuals and nations have never suffered injury, but have derived, in all time, numerous and most precious benefits.

14. And for you, venerable brethren, through the intercession of the Queen of the Most Holy Rosary, We pray Almighty God to

grant you heavenly gifts, and greater and more abundant strength, and aid to accomplish the charge of your pastoral office. As a pledge of which We most lovingly bestow upon you and upon the clergy and people committed to your care, the Apostolic Benediction.

Given at Rome, St. Peter's, the 22nd day of September, 1891, in the fourteenth year of Our Pontificate.

Magnae Dei Matris
On The Rosary

Encyclical of Pope Leo XIII

September 8, 1892

To Our Venerable Brethren, the Patriarchs, Primates, Archbishops, and other Ordinaries in Peace and Communion with the Apostolic See.

As often as the occasion arises to stimulate and intensify the love and veneration of the Christian people for Mary, the great Mother of God, We are filled with wondrous satisfaction and joy, as by a subject which is not only of prime importance in itself and profitable in countless ways, but which also perfectly accords with the inmost sentiments of Our heart. For the holy reverence for Mary which We experienced from Our tenderest years, has grown greater and has taken firmer hold of Our soul with Our advancing age.

2. As time went on, it became more and more evident how deserving of love and honor was she whom God Himself was the first to love, and loved so much more than any other that, after elevating her high above all the rest of His creation and adorning her with His richest gifts, He made her His Mother. The many and splendid proofs of her bounty and beneficence toward us, which We remember with deep gratitude and which move Us to tears, still further encourage and strongly inflame Our filial reverence for her. Throughout the many dreadful events of every kind which the times have brought to pass, always with her have We sought refuge, always to her have We lifted up pleading and confident eyes. And

in all the hopes and fears, the joys and sorrows, that We confided to her, the thought was constantly before Us to ask her to assist Us at all times as Our gracious Mother and to obtain this greatest of favors: that We might be able, in return, to show her the heart of a most devoted son.

3. When, then, it came to pass in the secret design of God's providence that We were chosen to fill this Chair of St. Peter and to take the place of the Person of Christ Himself in the Church, worried by the enormous burden of the office and finding no ground for reliance upon Our own strength, We hastened with fervent zeal to implore the divine aid through the maternal intercession of the ever blessed Virgin. Never has Our hope, We are happy to acknowledge, at any time of Our life but more especially since We began to exercise the Supreme Apostolate, failed in the course of events to bear fruit or bring Us comfort. Thus encouraged, Our hope today mounts more confidently than ever to beseech many more and even greater blessings through her favor and mediation, which will profit alike the salvation of Christ's flock and the happy increase of His Church's glory.

4. It is, therefore, a fitting and opportune time, Venerable Brethren, for Us to induce all Our children--exhorting them through you--to plan on celebrating the coming month of October, consecrated to our Lady as the august Queen of the Rosary, with the fervent and wholehearted devotion which the necessities weighing upon Us demand.

5. It is only too plain how many and of what nature are the corrupting agencies by which the wickedness of the world deceitfully strives to weaken and completely uproot from souls their Christian faith and the respect for God's law on which faith is fed and depends for its effectiveness. Already the fields cultivated

by our Lord are everywhere turning into a wilderness abounding in ignorance of the Faith, in error and vice, as though blown upon by some hideous pest. And to add to the anguish of this thought, so far from putting a check on such insolent and destructive depravity, or imposing the punishment deserved, they who can and should correct matters seem in many cases, by their indifference or open connivance, to increase the spirit of evil.

6. We have good reason to deplore the public institutions in which the teaching of the sciences and arts is purposely so organized that the name of God is passed over in silence or visited with vituperation; to deplore the license--growing more shameless by the day--of the press in publishing whatever it pleases, and the license of speech in addressing any kind of insult to Christ our God and His Church. And We deplore no less the consequent laxity and apathy in the practice of the Catholic religion which if not quite open apostasy from the Faith, is certainly going to prove an easy road to it, since it is a manner of life having nothing in common with faith. Nobody who ponders this disorder and the surrender of the most fundamental principles will be astonished if afflicted nations everywhere are groaning under the heavy hand of God's vengeance and stand anxious and trembling in fear of worse calamities.

7. Now, to appease the might of an outraged God and to bring that health of soul so needed by those who are sorely afflicted, there is nothing better than devout and persevering prayer, provided it be joined with a love for and practice of Christian life. And both of these, the spirit of prayer and the practice of Christian life, are best attained through the devotion of the Rosary of Mary.

8. The well-known origin of the Rosary, illustrated in celebrated monuments of which we have made frequent mention, bears

witness to its remarkable efficacy. For, in the days when the Albigensian sect, posing as the champion of pure faith and morals, but in reality introducing the worst kind of anarchy and corruption, brought many a nation to its utter ruin, the Church fought against it and the other infamous factions associated with it, not with troops and arms, but chiefly with the power of the most holy Rosary, the devotion which the Mother of God taught to our Father Dominic in order that he might propagate it. By this means the Church triumphed magnificently over every obstacle and provided for the salvation of her children not only in that trial but in others like it afterward, always with the same glorious success. For this reason, now, when human affairs have taken the course which We deplore, bringing affection to the Church and ruin to the State, all of us have the duty to unite our voice in prayer, with like devotion, to the holy Mother of God, beseeching her that we too may rejoice, as we ardently desire, in experiencing the same power of her Rosary.

9. When we have recourse to Mary in prayer, we are having recourse to the Mother of mercy, who is so well disposed toward us that, whatever the necessity that presses upon us especially in attaining eternal life, she is instantly at our side of her own accord, even though she has not been invoked. She dispenses grace with a generous hand from that treasure with which from the beginning she was divinely endowed in fullest abundance that she might be worthy to be the Mother of God. By the fullness of grace which confers on her the most illustrious of her many titles, the Blessed Virgin is infinitely superior to all the hierarchies of men and angels, the one creature who is closest of all to Christ. "It is a great thing in any saint to have grace sufficient for the salvation of many souls; but to have enough to suffice for the salvation of everybody in the world. is the greatest of all; and this is found in Christ and in the Blessed Virgin." [St. Thomas Aquinas, Super Salut. Ang.]

10. It is impossible to say how pleasing and gratifying to her it is when we greet her with the Angelic Salutation, "full of grace"; and in repeating it, fashion these words of praise into ritual crowns for her. For every time we say them, we recall the memory of her exalted dignity and of the Redemption of the human race which God began through her. We likewise bring to mind the divine and everlasting bond which links her with the joys and sorrows, the humiliations and triumphs of Christ in directing and helping mankind to eternal life.

11. It pleased Christ to take upon Himself the Son of Man, and to become thereby our Brother, in order that His mercy to us might be shown most openly; for "it behooved him in all things to be made like unto his brethren that he might become a merciful and faithful high priest before God." [Hebr. 2:17] Likewise because Mary was chosen to be the Mother of Christ, our Lord and our Brother, the unique prerogative was given her above all other mothers to show her mercy to us and to pour it out upon us. Besides, as we are indebted to Christ for sharing in some way with us the right, which is peculiarly His own, of calling God our Father and possessing Him as such, we are in like manner indebted to Him for His loving generosity in sharing with us the right to call Mary our Mother and to cherish her as such.

12. While nature itself made the name of mother the sweetest of all names and has made motherhood the very model of tender and solicitous love, no tongue is eloquent enough to put in words what every devout soul feels, namely how intense is the flame of affectionate and active charity which glows in Mary, in her who is truly our mother not in a human way but through Christ. Nobody knows and comprehends so well as she everything that concerns us: what helps we need in life; what dangers, public or private, threaten our welfare; what difficulties and evils surround us; above

all, how fierce is the fight we wage with ruthless enemies of our salvation. In these and in all other troubles of life her power is most far-reaching. Her desire to use it is most ardent to bring consolation, strength, and help of every kind to children who are dear to her.

13. Accordingly, let us approach Mary confidently, wholeheartedly beseeching her by the bonds of her motherhood which unite her so closely to Jesus and at the same time to us. Let us with deepest devotion invoke her constant aid in the prayer which she herself has indicated and which is most acceptable to her. Then with good reason shall we rest with an easy and joyous mind under the protection of the best of mothers.

14. To this commendation of the Rosary which follows from the very nature of the prayer, We may add that the Rosary offers an easy way to present the chief mysteries of the Christian religion and to impress them upon the mind; and this commendation is one of the most beautiful of all. For it is mainly by faith that a man sets out on the straight and sure path to God and learns to revere in mind and heart His supreme majesty, His sovereignty over the whole of creation, His unsounded power, wisdom, and providence. For he who comes to God must believe that God exists and is a rewarder to those who seek Him. Moreover, because God's eternal Son assumed our humanity and shone before us as the Way, the Truth, and the Life, our faith must include the lofty mysteries of the august Trinity of divine Persons and of the Father's only-begotten Son made Man: "This is eternal life: that they may know thee, the only true God, and Jesus Christ, whom thou hast sent." [Jn. 17:3]

15. God gave us a most precious blessing when He gave us faith. By this gift we are not only raised above the level of human things,

to contemplate and share in the divine nature, but are also furnished with the means of meriting the rewards of heaven; and therefore the hope is encouraged and strengthened that we shall one day look upon God, not in the shadowy images of His creatures, but in the fullest light, and shall enjoy Him forever as the Supreme Goodness. But the Christian is kept so busy by the various affairs of life and wanders so easily into matters of little importance, that unless he be helped with frequent reminders, the truths which are of first importance and necessity are little by little forgotten; and then faith begins to grow weak and may even perish.

16. To ward off these exceedingly great dangers of ignorance from her children, the Church, which never relaxes her vigilant and diligent care, has been in the habit of looking for the staunchest support of faith in the Rosary of Mary. And indeed in the Rosary, along with the most beautiful and efficacious prayer arranged in an orderly pattern, the chief mysteries of our religion follow one another, as they are brought before our mind for contemplation: first of all the mysteries in which the Word was made flesh and Mary, the inviolate Virgin and Mother, performed her maternal duties for Him with a holy joy; there come then the sorrows, the agony and death of the suffering Christ, the price at which the salvation of our race was accomplished; then follow the mysteries full of His glory; His triumph over death, the Ascension into heaven, the sending of the Holy Spirit, the resplendent brightness of Mary received among the stars, and finally the everlasting glory of all the saints in heaven united with the glory of the Mother and her Son.

17. This uninterrupted sequence of wonderful events the Rosary frequently and perseveringly recalls to the minds of the faithful and presents almost as though they were unfolding before our eyes: and this, flooding the souls of those who devoutly recite it with a

sweetness of piety that never grows weary, impresses and stirs them as though they were listening to the very voice of the Blessed Mother explaining the mysteries and conversing with them at length about their salvation.

18. It will not, then, seem too much to say that in places, families, and nations in which the Rosary of Mary retains its ancient honor, the loss of faith through ignorance and vicious error need not be feared.

19. There is still another and not lesser advantage which the Church earnestly seeks for her children from the Rosary, and that is the faithful regulation of their lives and their conduct in keeping with the rules and precepts of their holy religion. For if, as we all know from Holy Scripture, "faith without works is dead." [James 2:20] --because faith draws its life from charity and charity flowers forth in a profusion of holy actions--then the Christian will gain nothing for eternal life from his faith unless his life be ordered in accordance with what faith prescribes. "What shall it profit, my brethren, if a man say he hath faith, but hath not works? Shall faith be able to save him?" [James 2:14] A man of this sort will incur a much heavier rebuke from Christ the Judge than those who are, unfortunately, ignorant of Christian faith and its teaching: they, unlike the former, who believes one thing and practices another, have some excuse or at least are less blameworthy, because they lack the light of the Gospel.

20. In order therefore that the faith we profess may the better bring forth a harvest of fruits in keeping with its nature, while the mind is dwelling on mysteries of the Rosary the heart is wonderfully enkindled by them to make virtuous resolutions. What an example we have set before us! This shines forth everywhere in our Lord's work of salvation. Almighty God, in the excess of His love for us,

takes upon Himself the form of lowly man. He dwells in our midst as one of the multitude, converses with us as a friend, instructs and teaches the way of justice to individuals and to multitudes. In His discourse He is the teacher unexcelled; in the authority of His teaching He is God. To all He shows Himself a doer of good; He relieves the sick of the ills of their bodies and, with paternal compassion, heals the most serious sickness of their souls. Those above all whom sorrow troubles or whom the weight of worry crushes, He comforts with the gentle invitation: "Come to me, all you that labor, and are burdened, and I will refresh you." [Mt. 11:28] Then into us, at rest in His embrace, He breathes that mystic fire which He has brought to all men, and benignly imbues us with the meekness and humility of His own heart, with the hope that, by the practice of these virtues, we may share the true and solid peace of which He is the Author: "Learn of me, because I am meek, and humble of heart; and you shall find rest to your souls." [Mt. 11:29] For Himself, in return for that light of heavenly wisdom and that stupendous abundance of blessings which only He could merit for mankind, He suffers the hatred of men and their most atrocious insults; and, nailed to the cross, He pours out His blood and yields up His soul, holding it to be the highest glory to beget life in men by His death.

21. It would be utterly impossible for anyone to meditate on and attentively consider these most precious memorials of our loving Redeemer and not have a heart on fire with gratitude to Him. Such is the power of a faith sincerely practiced that, through the light it brings to man's mind and the vigor with which it moves his heart, he will straightway set out in the footsteps of Christ and follow them through every obstacle, making his own a protestation worthy of a St. Paul: "Who then shall separate us from the love of Christ? Shall tribulation? or distress? or famine? or nakedness? or danger?

or persecution? or the sword?" [Rom. 8:35] "I live, now not I; but Christ liveth in me." [Gal. 2:20]

22. But lest we be dismayed by the consciousness of our native weakness and grow faint when confronted with the unattainable example which Christ, who is Man and at the same time God, has given, along with mysteries which portray Him, we have before our eyes for contemplation the mysteries of His most holy Mother.

23. She was born, it is true, of the royal family of David, but she fell heir to none of the wealth and grandeur of her ancestors. She passed her life in obscurity, in a humble town, in a home humbler still, the more content with her retirement and the poverty of her home because they left her freer to lift up her heart to God and to cling to Him closely as the supreme Goodness for which her heart yearned.

24. The Lord is with her whom He has filled with His grace and made blessed. She is designated by the heavenly messenger sent to her as the Virgin from whom, by the power of the Holy Ghost, the expected Savior of nations is to come forth clothed in our humanity. The more she wonders at the sublime dignity and gives thanks to the power and mercy of God, the more does she, conscious of no merit in herself, grow in humility, promptly proclaiming and consecrating herself the handmaid of God even while she becomes His Mother.

25. Her sacred promise was as sacredly kept with a joyous heart; henceforth she leads a life in perpetual union with her son Jesus, sharing with Him His joys and sorrows. It is thus that she will reach a height of glory granted to no other creature, whether human or angelic, because no one will receive a reward for virtue to be compared with hers; it is thus that the crown of the kingdoms of heaven and of earth will await her because she will be the invincible

Queen of Martyrs. It is thus that she will be seated in the heavenly city of God by the side of her Son, crowned for all eternity, because she will drink with Him the cup overflowing with sorrow faithfully through all her life, most faithfully on Calvary.

26. In Mary we see how a truly good and provident God has established for us a most suitable example of every virtue. As we look upon her and think about her we are not cast down as though stricken by the overpowering splendor of God's power; but, on the contrary, attracted by the closeness of the common nature we share with her, we strive with greater confidence to imitate her. If we, with her powerful help, should dedicate ourselves wholly and entirely to the undertaking, we can portray at least an outline of such great virtue and sanctity, and reproducing that perfect conformity of our lives to all God's designs which she possessed in so marvelous a degree, we shall follow her into heaven.

27. Undaunted and full of courage, let us go on with the pilgrimage we have undertaken even though the way be rough and full of obstacle Amid the vexation and toil let us not cease to hold out suppliant hands to Mary with the words of the Church: "To thee do we send up our sigh mourning and weeping in this valley of tears; turn then, most gracious advocate, thine eyes of mercy toward us. . . Keep our lives all spotless, make our ways secure, till we find in Jesus joys that will endure." [Sacred Liturgy]

28. Although she was never subject to the frailty and perversity of our nature, Mary we knows its condition and is the best and most solicitous of mothers. How willingly will she hasten to our aid when we need her; with what love will she refresh us, and with what strength sustain us. For those of us who follow the journey hallowed by the blood of Christ and by the tears of Mary, our

entrance into their company and the enjoyment of their most blessed glory will be certain and easy.

29. Therefore the Rosary of the Blessed Virgin Mary, combining in a convenient and practical form an unexcelled form of prayer, an instrument well adapted to preserve the faith and an illustrious example of perfect virtue, should be often in the hands of the true Christian and be devoutly recited and meditated upon. We address this commendation especially to the Confraternity of the Holy Family which We recently praised and approved. Since the mystery of the hidden life which Christ our Lord long led within the walls of the house in Nazareth is the reason for the existence of this association, that its members may constantly conform themselves to Christian life on the model of the Holy Family established by God Himself, its intimate connection with the Rosary is plain.

30. Especially is this so in the joyful mysteries, which end with the one in which Jesus, after manifesting His wisdom in the temple, came with Mary and Joseph to Nazareth and was subject to them, preparing, as it were, for the other mysteries which are more closely connected with the instruction and the Redemption of mankind. From this all the members may understand that it is their duty to be devotees of the Rosary themselves and to be diligent in propagating devotion to it among others.

31. For Our part, We confirm and ratify the grants of sacred indulgences made in years past in favor of the faithful who spend the month of October in the manner We have prescribed. Because of your authority and zeal, Venerable Brethren, We know that the Catholic people will be fired with devotion and holy emulation in venerating through the Rosary, the Blessed Virgin, Help of Christians.

32. And now let Us bring Our exhortation to a close in the way it began, proclaiming once more and even more openly the devotion we cherish toward the great Mother of God, a devotion both mindful of past blessings and full of joyous hope. We ask the prayers of the Christian people in devout supplication before her altars on behalf of the Church, tormented by such adverse and turbulent times, and on behalf of Ourself as well. Advanced in age, worn out with labors, fettered by distressingly difficult events with no human help to rely upon, We must yet carry on the government of the Church. Our hope in Mary, powerful and benign Mother, is daily more confirmed and more sweetly consoling. To her intercession We attribute the many and remarkable gifts We have obtained from God; with thanks still more profuse do we attribute the fact that it has been given Us to reach the fiftieth anniversary of Our episcopal consecration.

33. It is, indeed, a great comfort to us, looking back over the long years of Our pastoral charge, troubled as they have been by daily worry, that We are still engaged in ruling the whole Christian flock. During that time We have had, as happens in men's lives and as the mysteries of Christ and Mary illustrate, reasons for joy mixed with reasons for many and bitter sorrows, as well as occasions to glory in gains won for Christ. All of this We, with a mind submissive to God and with a grateful heart, have tried to turn to the good and the honor of the Church. And now--for the rest of Our life will run a course not unlike the past--should new joys come to gladden Our heart, or sorrow to threaten Us, or honors to glory in, We, steadfast in the same heart and mind, yearning only for the heavenly glory which God confers, say with David: "Blessed be the name of the Lord"; [Ps. 112:2] Not to us, but to thy name give glory." [Ps. 113:1]

34. From Our devoted children, whose filial and affectionate concern for us We know burns bright, We look for heartfelt thanks to God, prayers, and holy aspirations, rather than for congratulations and honors. It will be a special joy to Us if they ask for Us this grace, that all the strength and life that remain to Us, all the authority and grace with which We are invested, may profit the Church, and in the first place bring back into her fold her enemies and those who have wandered from the right way, to whom our voice has this long time been appealing for reconciliation.

35. Upon all of Our dearly beloved children may there flow, from the happiness and joy of Our coming Jubilee, God granting, gifts of justice, peace, prosperity, holiness, and all good things. This, with paternal love, We beg God; this do We exhort in the words of His Holy Scriptures: "Hear me. . . and bud forth as the rose planted by the brooks of waters: Give ye a sweet odor as frankincense. . . Send forth flowers, as the lily, and yield a smell, and bring forth leaves in grace and praise with canticles and bless the Lord in his works. Magnify his name, and give glory to him with the voice of your lips, and with the canticles of your mouths. and with harps. . . With the whole heart and mouth praise ye him, and bless the name of the Lord." [Ecclus. 39:17-20, 41]

36. If these plans, so ardently desired, be scoffed at by the wicked who blaspheme that of which they are ignorant, may God mercifully spare them. But that He may give Our hopes His propitious aid through the prayers of the Queen of the Most Holy Rosary, take as a token of divine favor and at the same time as a pledge of Our affection, Venerable Brethren, the Apostolic Benediction, which We, lovingly in the Lord, bestow on each of you, on your clergy, and on your people.

A Manual of the Most Holy Rosary

Given at Rome, at St. Peter's, the eighth of September, 1892, in the fifteenth year of Our Pontificate.

Enchiridion Sanctissimi Rosarii

Laetittiae Sanctae
Commending Devotion To The Rosary

Encyclical of Pope Leo XIII

September 8, 1893

To Our Venerable Brethren the Patriarchs, Primates, Archbishops, Bishops, and other Ordinaries, having Peace and Communion with the Apostolic See.

Venerable Brethren, Greeting and Apostolic Benediction.

The sacred joy which it has been given to Us to feel in attaining the fiftieth anniversary of Our Episcopal Consecration has been deepened by the knowledge that it was shared by the people of the whole Catholic world, and that as a father in the midst of his children We have been consoled by the touching testimonies of their loyalty and love. We gratefully accept it and record it as a fresh proof of God's special providence, and one which is markedly full of bounty to Ourselves, and of blessing to the Church.

2. At the same time We love to offer Our thanks for this signal benefit to the august Mother of God, whose powerful intercession We feel to have been exercised in Our behalf. For hers is the loving kindness which, during the length of years and the vicissitudes of life, has never failed Us, and which day by day seems to draw nearer to Us than ever, filling Our soul with gladness, and strengthening Us with a confidence of which the surety is higher than the things of time. It is as if the voice of the heavenly Queen made itself heard to Us, at one moment graciously consoling Us in the midst of trials; at another guiding Us by her counsel in directing the great work of the salvation of souls; at another, urging Us to

admonish the Christian people to advance in piety and in the practice of every virtue. For Us it is once more a joy as well as a duty to respond to her inspirations. Amongst the happy results which have already rewarded Our exhortations which were due to her prompting, We have to reckon the remarkable impulse given to the Devotion of the Most Holy Rosary. This awakening has made itself felt in the increased number of Confraternities instituted for the purpose, the voluminous literature of pious and learned works written upon the subject, and the manifold tributes which Christian art has not failed to bring to its service. And now, as if for yet another time, listening to the voice of the same zealous Mother, who calls upon Us to "cry out and cease not," We rejoice once more to address you, Venerable Brethren, upon the subject of the Rosary, standing as We do upon the eve of that month of October which, by the award of special Indulgences, We have deemed it well to dedicate to this most popular devotion. Our appeal to you, however, will not be directed so much to add any further recommendation of a method of prayer so praiseworthy in itself, nor yet to press upon the faithful the necessity of practicing it still more fervently, but rather to point out how we may draw from this devotion certain advantages which are especially valuable and needful at the present day.

3. For We are convinced that the Rosary, if devoutly used, is bound to benefit not only the individual but society at large. No one will do Us the injustice to deny that in the discharge of the duties of the Supreme Apostolate We have labored--as, God helping, We shall ever continue to labor--to promote the civil prosperity of mankind. Repeatedly have We admonished those who are invested with sovereign power that they should neither make nor execute laws except in conformity with the equity of the Divine mind. On the other hand, we have constantly besought citizens who were

conspicuous by genius, industry, family, or fortune, to join together in common counsel and action to safeguard and to promote whatever would tend to the strength and well-being of the community. Only too many causes are at work, in the present condition of things, to loosen the bonds of public order, and to withdraw the people from sound principles of life and conduct.

4. There are three influences which appear to Us to have the chief place in effecting this downgrade movement of society. These are-- first, the distaste for a simple and laborious life; secondly, repugnance to suffering of any kind; thirdly, the forgetfulness of the future life.

5. We deplore--and those who judge of all things merely by the light and according to the standard of nature join with Us in deploring-that society is threatened with a serious danger in the growing contempt of those homely duties and virtues which make up the beauty of humble life. To this cause we may trace in the home, the readiness of children to withdraw themselves from the natural obligation of obedience to the parents, and their impatience of any form of treatment which is not of the indulgent and effeminate kind. In the workman, it evinces itself in a tendency to desert his trade, to shrink from toil, to become discontented with his lot, to fix his gaze on things that are above him, and to look forward with unthinking hopefulness to some future equalization of property. We may observe the same temper permeating the masses in the eagerness to exchange the life of the rural districts for the excitements and pleasures of the town. Thus the equilibrium between the classes of the community is being destroyed, everything becomes unsettled, men's minds become a prey to jealousy and heart-burnings, rights are openly trampled under foot, and, finally, the people, betrayed in their expectations, attack public

order, and place themselves in conflict with those who are charged to maintain it.

6. For evils such as these let us seek a remedy in the Rosary, which consists in a fixed order of prayer combined with devout meditation on the life of Christ and His Blessed Mother. Here, if the joyful mysteries be but clearly brought home to the minds of the people, an object lesson of the chief virtues is placed before their eyes. Each one will thus be able to see for himself how easy, how abundant, how sweetly attractive are the lessons to be found therein for the leading of an honest life. Let us take our stand in front of that earthly and divine home of holiness, the House of Nazareth. How much we have to learn from the daily life which was led within its walls! What an all-perfect model of domestic society! Here we behold simplicity and purity of conduct, perfect agreement and unbroken harmony, mutual respect and love--not of the false and fleeting kind--but that which finds both its life and its charm in devotedness of service. Here is the patient industry which provides what is required for food and raiment; which does so "in the sweat of the brow," which is contented with little, and which seeks rather to diminish the number of its wants than to multiply the sources of its wealth. Better than all, we find there that supreme peace of mind and gladness of soul which never fail to accompany the possession of a tranquil conscience. These are precious examples of goodness, of modesty, of humility, of hard-working endurance, of kindness to others, of diligence in the small duties of daily life, and of other virtues, and once they have made their influence felt they gradually take root in the soul, and in course of time fail not to bring about a happy change of mind and conduct. Then will each one begin to feel his work to be no longer lowly and irksome, but grateful and lightsome, and clothed with a certain joyousness by his sense of duty in discharging it conscientiously.

Then will gentler manners everywhere prevail; home-life will be loved and esteemed, and the relations of man with man will be loved and esteemed, and the relations of man with man will be hallowed by a larger infusion of respect and charity. And if this betterment should go forth from the individual to the family and to the communities, and thence to the people at large so that human life should be lifted up to this standard, no one will fail to feel how great and lasting indeed would be the gain which would be achieved for society.

7. A second evil, one which is specially pernicious, and one which, owing to the increasing mischief which it works among souls, we can never sufficiently deplore, is to be found in repugnance to suffering and eagerness to escape whatever is hard or painful to endure. The greater number are thus robbed of that peace and freedom of mind which remains the reward of those who do what is right undismayed by the perils or troubles to be met with in doing so. Rather do they dream of a chimeric civilization in which all that is unpleasant shall be removed, and all that is pleasant shall be supplied. By this passionate and unbridled desire of living a life of pleasure, the minds of men are weakened, and if they do not entirely succumb, they become demoralized and miserably cower and sink under the hardships of the battle of life.

8. In such a contest example is everything, and a powerful means of renewing our courage will undoubtedly be found in the Holy Rosary, if from our earliest years our minds have been trained to dwell upon the sorrowful mysteries of Our Lord's life, and to drink in their meaning by sweet and silent meditation. In them we shall learn how Christ, "the Author and Finisher of Our faith," began "to do and teach," in order that we might see written in His example all the lessons that He Himself had taught us for the bearing of our burden of labor-- and sorrow, and mark how the sufferings which

were hardest to bear were those which He embraced with the greatest measure of generosity and good will. We behold Him overwhelmed with sadness, so that drops of blood ooze like sweat from His veins. We see Him bound like a malefactor, subjected to the judgment of the unrighteous, laden with insults, covered with shame, assailed with false accusations, torn with scourges, crowned with thorns, nailed to the cross, accounted unworthy to live, and condemned by the voice of the multitude as deserving of death. Here, too, we contemplate the grief of the most Holy Mother, whose soul was not merely wounded but "pierced" by the sword of sorrow, so that she might be named and become in truth "the Mother of Sorrows." Witnessing these examples of fortitude, not with sight but by faith, who is there who will not feel his heart grow warm with the desire of imitating them?

9. Then, be it that the "earth is accursed" and brings forth "thistles and thorns,"--be it that the soul is saddened with grief and the body with sickness; even so, there will be no evil which the envy of man or the rage of devils can invent, nor calamity which can fall upon the individual or the community, over which we shall not triumph by the patience of suffering. For this reason it has been truly said that "it belongs to the Christian to do and to endure great things," for he who deserves to be called a Christian must not shrink from following in the footsteps of Christ. But by this patience, We do not mean that empty stoicism in the enduring of pain which was the ideal of some of the philosophers of old, but rather do We mean that patience which is learned from the example of Him, who "having joy set before Him, endured the cross, despising the shame" (Heb. xvi., 2). It is the patience which is obtained by the help of His grace; which shirks not a trial because it is painful, but which accepts it and esteems it as a gain, however hard it may be to undergo. The Catholic Church has always had, and happily still has,

multitudes of men and women, in every rank and condition of life, who are glorious disciples of this teaching, and who, following faithfully in the path of Christ, suffer injury and hardship for the cause of virtue and religion. They re- echo, not with their lips, but with their life, the words of St. Thomas: "Let us also go, that we may die with him" (John xi., 16).

10. May such types of admirable constancy be more and more splendidly multiplied in our midst to the weal of society and to the glory and edification of the Church of God!

11. The third evil for which a remedy is needed is one which is chiefly characteristic of the times in which we live. Men in former ages, although they loved the world, and loved it far too well, did not usually aggravate their sinful attachment to the things of earth by a contempt of the things of heaven. Even the right-thinking portion of the pagan world recognized that this life was not a home but a dwelling-place, not our destination, but a stage in the journey. But men of our day, albeit they have had the advantages of Christian instruction, pursue the false goods of this world in such wise that the thought of their true Fatherland of enduring happiness is not only set aside, but, to their shame be it said, banished and entirely erased from their memory, notwithstanding the warning of St. Paul, "We have not here a lasting city, but we seek one which is to come" (Heb. xiii., 4).

12. When We seek out the causes of this forgetfulness, We are met in the first place by the fact that many allow themselves to believe that the thought of a future life goes in some way to sap the love of our country, and thus militates against the prosperity of the commonwealth. No illusion could be more foolish or hateful. Our future hope is not of a kind which so monopolizes the minds of men as to withdraw their attention from the interests of this life.

Christ commands us, it is true, to seek the Kingdom of God, and in the first place, but not in such a manner as to neglect all things else. For, the use of the goods of the present life, and the righteous enjoyment which they furnish, may serve both to strengthen virtue and to reward it. The splendor and beauty of our earthly habitation, by which human society is ennobled, may mirror the splendor and beauty of our dwelling which is above. Therein we see nothing that is not worthy of the reason of man and of the wisdom of God. For the same God who is the Author of Nature is the Author of Grace, and He willed not that one should collide or conflict with the other, but that they should act in friendly alliance, so that under the leadership of both we may the more easily arrive at that immortal happiness for which we mortal men were created.

13. But men of carnal mind, who love nothing but themselves, allow their thoughts to grovel upon things of earth until they are unable to lift them to that which is higher. For, far from using the goods of time as a help towards securing those which are eternal, they lose sight altogether of the world which is to come, and sink to the lowest depths of degradation. We may doubt if God could inflict upon man a more terrible punishment than to allow him to waste his whole life in the pursuit of earthly pleasures, and in forgetfulness of the happiness which alone lasts for ever.

14. It is from this danger that they will be happily rescued, who, in the pious practice of the Rosary, are wont, by frequent and fervent prayer, to keep before their minds the glorious mysteries. These mysteries are the means by which in the soul of a Christian a most clear light is shed upon the good things, hidden to sense, but visible to faith, "which God has prepared for those who love Him." From them we learn that death is not an annihilation which ends all things, but merely a migration and passage from life to life. By them we are taught that the path to Heaven lies open to all men,

and as we behold Christ ascending thither, we recall the sweet words of His promise, "I go to prepare a place for you." By them we are reminded that a time will come when "God will wipe away every tear from our eyes," and that "neither mourning, nor crying, nor sorrow, shall be any more," and that "We shall be always with the Lord," and "like to the Lord, for we shall see Him as He is," and "drink of the torrent of His delight," as "fellow-citizens of the saints," in the blessed companionship of our glorious Queen and Mother. Dwelling upon such a prospect, our hearts are kindled with desire, and we exclaim, in the words of a great saint, "How vile grows the earth when I look up to heaven!" Then, too, shall we feel the solace of the assurance "that which is at present momentary and light of our tribulation worketh for us above measure exceedingly an eternal weight of glory" (2 Cor. iv., 17).

15. Here alone we discover the true relation between time and eternity, between our life on earth and our life in heaven; and it is thus alone that are formed strong and noble characters. When such characters can be counted in large numbers, the dignity and well-being of society are assured. All that is beautiful, good, and true will flourish in the measure of its conformity to Him who is of all beauty, goodness, and truth the first Principle and the Eternal Source.

16. These considerations will explain what We have already laid down concerning the fruitful advantages which are to be derived from the use of the Rosary, and the healing power which this devotion possesses for the evils of the age and the fatal sores of society. These advantages, as we may readily conceive, will be secured in a higher and fuller measure by those who band themselves together in the sacred Confraternity of the Rosary, and who are thus more than others united by a special and brotherly bond of devotion to the Most Holy Virgin. In this Confraternity,

approved by the Roman Pontiffs, and enriched by them with indulgences and privileges, they possess their own rule and government, hold their meetings at stated times, and are provided with ample means of leading a holy life and of laboring for the good of the community. They are, are so to speak, the battalions who fight the battle of Christ, armed with His Sacred Mysteries, and under the banner and guidance of the Heavenly Queen. How faithfully her intercession is exercised in response to their prayers, processions, and solemnities is written in the whole experience of the Church not less than in the splendor of the victory of Lepanto.

17. It is, therefore, to be desired that renewed zeal should be called forth in the founding, enlarging, and directing of these confraternities, and that not only by the sons of St. Dominic, to whom by virtue of their Order a leading part in this Apostolate belongs, but by all who are charged with the care of souls, and notable in those places in which the Confraternity has not yet been canonically established. We have it especially at heart that those who are engaged in the sacred field of the missions, whether in carrying the Gospel to barbarous nations abroad, or in spreading it amongst the Christian nations at home, should look upon this work as especially their own. If they will make it the subject of their preaching, We cannot doubt that there will be large numbers of the faithful of Christ who will readily enroll themselves in the Confraternity, and who will earnestly endeavor to avail themselves of those spiritual advantages of which We have spoken, and in which consist the very meaning and motive of the Rosary. From the Confraternities, the rest of the faithful will receive the example of greater esteem and reverence for the practice of the Rosary, and they will be thus encouraged to reap from it, as We heartily desire that they may, the same abundant fruits for their souls' salvation.

18. This then is the hope, which, amid the manifold evils which beset society, brightens, consoles, and supports Us. May Mary, the Mother of God and of men, herself the authoress and teacher of the Rosary, procure for Us its happy fulfillment. It will be your part, Venerable Brethren, to provide that by your efforts Our words and Our wishes may go forth on their mission of good for the prosperity of families and the peace of peoples.

19. And as a pledge of the Divine favor, and of Our own affection, We lovingly bestow upon you, your clergy, and your people, the Apostolic Benediction.

Given at St. Peter's, Rome, this 8th day of September, in the year of Our Lord 1893, and the 16th of Our Pontificate.

A Manual of the Most Holy Rosary

Iucunda Semper Expectatione
On The Rosary

Encyclical of Pope Leo XIII

September 8, 1894

To the Partiarchs, Primates, Archbishops, Bishops, and other Ordinaries in Peace and Communion with the Apostolic See.

Venerable Brethren, Greeting and Apostolic Benediction.

It is always with joyful expectation and inspired hope that We look forward to the return of the month of October. At Our exhortation and by Our express order this month has been consecrated to the Blessed Virgin, during which for some years now the devotion of her Rosary has been practiced by Catholic nations throughout the world with sedulous earnestness. Our reasons for making this exhortation We have made known more than once. For as the disastrous condition of the Church and of Society proved to Us the extreme necessity for signal aid from God, it was manifest to Us that that aid should be sought through the intercession of His Mother, and by the express means of the Rosary, which Christians have ever found to be of marvelous avail. This indeed has been well proved since the very institution of the devotion, both in the vindication of Holy Faith against the furious attacks of heresy, and in restoring to honor the virtues, which by reason of the Age's corruption, required to be rekindled and sustained. And this same proof was continued in all succeeding ages, by a never failing series of private and public benefits, whereof the illustrious remembrance is everywhere perpetuated and immortalized by monuments and existing institutions. Likewise in Our age, afflicted with that tempest of various evils, it is a joy to Our soul to relate the beneficent influence of the Rosary. Notwithstanding all this, you yourselves, Venerable Brethren, behold with your own eyes the persistence--nay, the increase--of the reasons for renewing again this year Our summons to the Faithful to turn with increased ardor in prayer to Mary, the Queen of Heaven. Besides, the more We fix Our thoughts upon the character of the Rosary, the clearer its excellence and power appear to Us. Hence, while Our wish increases that it may flourish, Our hope grows also that through Our recommendation it may come to be more greatly prized, its holy use become more extended and flourish abundantly. But We shall not now return to the various instructions which in past years We have given upon this subject. We shall take instead the opportunity of pointing out the particular ruling and designs of Providence which ordains that the Rosary should have new power to instill confidence into the hearts of those who pray, and new influence to move the compassionate heart of Our Mother to comfort and succor Us with the utmost bounty.

2. The recourse we have to Mary in prayer follows upon the office she continuously fills by the side of the throne of God as Mediatrix of Divine grace; being by worthiness and by merit most acceptable to Him, and, therefore, surpassing in power all the angels and saints in Heaven. Now, this merciful office of hers, perhaps, appears in no other form of prayer so manifestly as it does in the Rosary. For in the Rosary all the part that Mary took as our co-Redemptress comes to us, as it were, set forth, and in such wise as though the facts were even then taking place; and this with much profit to our piety, whether in the contemplation of the succeeding sacred mysteries, or in the prayers which we speak and repeat with the lips. First come the Joyful Mysteries. The Eternal Son of God stoops to mankind, putting on its nature; but with the assent of Mary, who

conceives Him by the Holy Ghost. Then St. John the Baptist, by a singular privilege, is sanctified in his mother's womb and favored with special graces that he might prepare the way of the Lord; and this comes to pass by the greeting of Mary who had been inspired to visit her cousin. At last the expected of nations comes to light, Christ the Savior. The Virgin bears Him. And when the Shepherds and the wise men, first-fruits of the Christian faith, come with longing to His cradle, they find there the young Child, with Mary, His Mother. Then, that He might before men offer Himself as a victim to His Heavenly Father, He desires to be taken to the Temple; and by the hands of Mary He is there presented to the Lord. It is Mary who, in the mysterious losing of her Son, seeks Him sorrowing, and finds Him again with joy. And the same truth is told again in the sorrowful mysteries.

3. In the Garden of Gethsemane, where Jesus is in an agony; in the judgment-hall, where He is scourged, crowned with thorns, condemned to death, not there do we find Mary. But she knew beforehand all these agonies; she knew and saw them. When she professed herself the handmaid of the Lord for the mother's office, and when, at the foot of the altar, she offered up her whole self with her Child Jesus--then and thereafter she took her part in the laborious expiation made by her Son for the sins of the world. It is certain, therefore, that she suffered in the very depths of her soul with His most bitter sufferings and with His torments. Moreover, it was before the eyes of Mary that was to be finished the Divine Sacrifice for which she had borne and brought up the Victim. As we contemplate Him in the last and most piteous of those Mysteries, there stood by the Cross of Jesus His Mother, who, in a miracle of charity, so that she might receive us as her sons, offered generously to Divine Justice her own Son, and died in her heart with Him, stabbed with the sword of sorrow.

4. Thence the Rosary takes us on to the Glorious Mysteries, wherein likewise is revealed the mediation of the great Virgin, still more abundant in fruitfulness. She rejoices in heart over the glory of her Son triumphant over death, and follows Him with a mother's love in His Ascension to His eternal kingdom; but, though worthy of Heaven, she abides a while on earth, so that the infant Church may be directed and comforted by her "who penetrated, beyond all belief, into the deep secrets of Divine wisdom" (St. Bernard). Nevertheless, for the fulfillment of the task of human redemption there remains still the coming of the Holy Ghost, promised by Christ. And behold, Mary is in the room, and there, praying with the Apostles and entreating for them with sobs and tears, she hastens for the Church the coming of the Spirit, the Comforter, the supreme gift of Christ, the treasure that will never fail. And later, without measure and without end will she be able to plead our cause, passing upon a day to the life immortal. Therefore we behold her taken up from this valley of tears into the heavenly Jerusalem, amid choirs of Angels. And we honor her, glorified above all the Saints, crowned with stars by her Divine Son and seated at His side the sovereign Queen of the universe.

5. If in all this series of Mysteries, Venerable Brethren, are developed the counsels of God in regard to us--"counsels of wisdom and of tenderness" (St. Bernard)--not less apparent is the greatness of the benefits for which we are debtors to the Virgin Mother. No man can meditate upon these without feeling a new awakening in his heart of confidence that he will certainly obtain through Mary the fullness of the mercies of God. And to this end vocal prayer chimes well with the Mysteries. First, as is meet and right, comes the Lord's Prayer, addressed to Our Father in Heaven: and having, with the elect petitions dictated by Our Divine Master, called upon the Father, from the throne of His Majesty we turn our

prayerful voices to Mary. Thus is confirmed that law of merciful meditation of which We have spoken, and which St. Bernardine of Siena thus expresses: "Every grace granted to man has three degrees in order; for by God it is communicated to Christ, from Christ it passes to the Virgin, and from the Virgin it descends to us." And we, by the very form of the Rosary, do linger longest, and, as it were, by preference upon the last and lowest of these steps, repeating by decades the Angelic Salutation, so that with greater confidence we may thence attain to the higher degrees--that is, may rise, by means of Christ, to the Divine Father. For if thus we again and again greet Mary, it is precisely that our failing and defective prayers may be strengthened with the necessary confidence; as though we pledged her to pray for us, and as it were in our name, to God.

6. Nor can our prayers fail to ascend to Him as a sweet savor, commended by the prayers of the Virgin. And He it is who, all-benign, invites her: "Let thy voice sound in My ears, for thy voice is sweet." For this cause do we repeatedly celebrate those glorious titles of her ministry as Mediatrix. Her do we greet who found favor with God, and who was in a signal manner filled with grace by Him so that the superabundance thereof might overflow upon all men; her, united with the Lord by the most intimate of all conjunction; her who was blessed among women, and who "alone took away the curse and bore the blessing" (St. Thomas)--that fruit of her womb, that happy fruit, in which all the nations of the earth are blessed. Her do we invoke, finally, as Mother of God; and in virtue of a dignity so sublime what graces from her may we not promise to ourselves, sinners, in life and in the agonies of the end?

7. A soul that shall devoutly repeat these prayers, that shall ponder with faith these mysteries, will, without doubt, be filled with wonder at the Divine purposes in this great Virgin and in the work

of the restoration of mankind. Doubtless, this soul, moved by the warmth of love for her and of confidence, will desire to take refuge upon her breast, as was the sweet feeling of St. Bernard: "Remember, O most pious Virgin Mary, that never was it heard that any who fled to thy protection, called upon thy help, and sought thy intercession, was left forsaken." But the fruits of the Rosary appear likewise, and with equal greatness, in the turning with mercy of the heart of the Mother of God towards us. How sweet a happiness must it be for her to see us all intent upon the task of weaving crowns for her of righteous prayers and lovely praises! And if, indeed, by those prayers we desire to render to God the glory which is His due; if we protest that we seek nothing whatsoever except the fulfillment in us of His holy will; if we magnify His goodness and graciousness; if we call Him Our Father; if we, being most unworthy, yet entreat of Him His best blessings-- Oh, how shall Mary in all these things rejoice! How shall she magnify the Lord! There is no language so fit to lead us to the majesty of God as the language of the Lord's Prayer. Furthermore, to each of these things for which we pray, things that are righteous and are ordered, and are in harmony with Christian faith, hope, and charity, is added a special joy for the Blessed Virgin. With our voices she seems to hear also the voice of her Divine Son, Who with His own mouth taught us this prayer, and by His own authority commanded it, saying: "You shall pray thus." And seeing how we observe that command, saying our Rosary, she will bend towards us with the more loving solicitude; and the mystical crowns we offer her will be to her welcome, and to us fruitful of graces. And of this generosity of Mary to our supplications we have no slight pledge in the very nature of a practice that has the power to help us in praying well. In many ways, indeed, is man apt, by his frailty, to allow his thoughts to wander from God and to let his purpose go astray. But the Rosary, if rightly considered, will be found to have in itself special virtues, whether for producing and continuing a state of recollection, or for touching the conscience for its healing, or for lifting up the soul. As all men know, it is composed of two parts, distinct but inseparable--the meditation of the Mysteries and the recitation of the prayers. It is thus a kind of prayer that requires not only some raising of the soul to God, but also a particular and explicit attention, so that by reflection upon the things to be contemplated, impulses and resolutions may follow for the reformation and sanctification of life.

8. Those same things are, in fact, the most important and the most admirable of Christianity, the things through which the world was renewed and filled with the fruits of truth, justice, and peace. And it is remarkable how well adapted to every kind of mind, however unskilled, is the manner in which these things are proposed to us in the Rosary. They are proposed less as truths or doctrines to be speculated upon than as present facts to be seen and perceived. Thus presented, with the circumstances of place, time, and persons, these Mysteries produce the most living effect; and this without the slightest effort of imagination; for they are treated as things learnt and engraven in the heart from infancy. Thus, hardly is a Mystery named but the pious soul goes through it with ease of thought and quickness of feeling, and gathers therefrom, by the gift of Mary, abundance of the food of Heaven. And yet another title of joy and of acceptation in her eyes do our crowns of prayer acquire. For every time that we look once more with devotional remembrance upon these Mysteries we give her a sign of the gratitude of our hearts; we prove to her that we cannot often enough call to mind the blessings of her unwearied charity in the work of our salvation. At such recollections, practiced by us with the frequency of love in her presence, who may express, who may even conceive, what ever-new joys overflow her ever-blessed soul, and what tender affections

arise therein, of mercy and of a mother's love! Besides these recollections, moreover, as the sacred Mysteries pass by they cause our prayers to be transformed into impulses of entreaty that have an indescribable power over the heart of Mary. Yes, we fly to thee, we miserable children of Eve, O holy Mother of God. To thee we lift our prayers, for thou art the Mediatrix, powerful at once and pitiful, of our salvation. Oh, by the sweetness of the joys that came to thee from thy Son Jesus, by thy participation in His ineffable sorrows, by the splendors of His glory shining in thee, we instantly beseech thee, listen, be pitiful, hear us, unworthy though we be!

9. Thus the excellence of the Rosary; considered under the double aspect We have here set forth, will convince you, Venerable Brethren, of the reasons We have for an incessant eagerness to commend and to promote it. At the present day--and on this We have already touched--there is a signal necessity of special help from Heaven, particularly manifest in the many tribulations suffered by the Church as to her liberties and her rights, as also in the perils whereby the prosperity and peace of Christian society are fundamentally threatened. So it is that it belongs to Our office to assert once again that We place the best of Our hopes in the holy Rosary, inasmuch as more than any other means it can impetrate from God the succor which We need. It is Our ardent wish that this devotion shall be restored to the place of honor; in the city and in the village, in the family and in the workshop, in the noble's house and in the peasant's; that it should be to all a dear devotion and a noble sign of their faith; that it may be a sure way to the gaining of the favor of pardon. To this end it is indispensable that zeal should be redoubled, while impiety daily redoubles its efforts and labors to move the justice of God and to provoke, for the general ruin, His terrible vengeance. Amongst so many causes of grief to all good men, and to Ourself, not the least is this, that in

the very midst of Catholic nations there exist persons who are ever ready to rejoice in that which insults and outrages our august religion; and that they themselves, with incredible effrontery and with all publicity, seize every opportunity of teaching the multitude to hold reverend things in contempt and of persuading them from their old confidence in the intercession of the Blessed Virgin. During the last months the very person of Our Divine Redeemer has not been spared. Such a depth of shameless indignity has been reached that Jesus Christ Himself has been dragged upon the stage of a theater often contaminated with corruptions, and has been represented there discrowned of that Divinity upon which rests the whole work of human salvation. And the last touch of shame was added in an attempt to rescue from the execration of ages the guilty name of him who was the very sign of perfidy, the betrayer of Christ. At the consummation of such excesses in the cities of Italy there arose a general cry of indignation, and energetic protest against the violation and trampling under foot of the inviolable rights of religion, and this in a nation that has for its greatest and most righteous boast that it is Catholic. The Bishops rose at once, on fire with holy zeal. And first they made their vigorous appeal to those whose sacred duty it is to safeguard the decorum of the religion of the country. Next, they informed their people of the gravity of the scandal, and exhorted them to special acts of reparation towards our most loving Savior exposed to such slanders.

10. We have pleasure, however, in rendering praise to the free and fruitful faith manifested by men of good will; and this has brought Us comfort in the bitterness inflicted upon the very quick of Our heart. And having regard to the duties of Our supreme ministry, We take this occasion to lift up Our voice and to unite Our complaints and protests to those of the Bishops and of their

people, authenticated by Our Apostolic authority. And with a like ardor to that wherewith we condemned this sacrilegious offense, do We preach faith to all Catholics, and particularly to the Italians. Let them with jealous care guard this inestimable inheritance received from their fathers, let them defend it with courage, let them not cease from magnifying it with good actions of which their faith is the inspiring motive. This is a motive the more for the enkindling, in private and in common prayer, throughout the coming month of October, of a holy emulation in celebrating and honoring the Mother of God, the mighty succorer of the Christian people, the most glorious Queen of Heaven. For Our own part, We confirm with all Our heart the favors and indulgences We have already awarded upon this point.

11. Now may God, "Who in His most merciful Providence gave us this Mediatrix." and "decreed that all good should come to us by the hands of Mary" (St. Bernard), receive propitiously our common prayers and fulfill our common hopes. May you receive a pledge thereof in the Apostolic Benediction which We give to you, to your clergy, and to your people, with all affection in Our Lord.

Given in Rome at St. Peter's, on September 8, 1894, in the seventeenth year of our Pontificate.

Adiutricem Populi
On the Rosary

Encyclical of Pope Leo XIII

September 5, 1895

To Our Venerable Brethren the Patriarchs, Primates, Archbishops, Bishops, and other Ordinaries in Peace and Communion with the Apostolic See.

The mightiest helper of the Christian people, and the most merciful, is the Virgin Mother of God. How fitting it is to accord her honors ever increasing in splendor, and call upon her aid with a confidence daily growing more ardent. The abundant blessings, infinitely varied and constantly multiplying, which flow from her all over the whole world for the common benefit of mankind, add fresh motives for invoking and honoring her.

2. For such magnanimous favors, Catholics on their part have not failed to return to her the tender devotion of grateful hearts; because, if ever there was a time when love and veneration of the Blessed Virgin were awakened to new life and inflaming every class of society, it is in these days so bitterly anti-religious. The clearest evidence of this fact lies in the sodalities which have everywhere been restored and multiplied under her patronage; in the magnificent temples erected to her august name; in the pilgrimages undertaken by throngs of devout souls to her most venerated shrines; in the congresses whose deliberations are devoted to the increase of her glory; in other things of a like nature which are praiseworthy in themselves and augur well for the future.

3. It is specially deserving of notice, and it gives Us the greatest pleasure to recall, that of all the forms of devotion to the Blessed Virgin, that most excellent method of prayer, Mary's Rosary, is establishing itself most widely in popular esteem and practice. This, We repeat, is a source of great joy to Us. If We have spent so large a share of our activities, in promoting the Rosary devotion, We can easily see with what benevolence the Queen of Heaven has come to Our aid when We prayed to her; and We express the confident conviction that she will continue to stand at Our side to lighten the burdens and the afflictions which the days to come will bring.

4. It is mainly to expand the kingdom of Christ that We look to the Rosary for the most effective help. On many occasions We have declared that the object which at the present time engrosses Our most earnest attention, is the reconciliation to the Church of nations which have become separated from her. We recognize, at the same time, that the realization of Our hopes must be sought chiefly in prayer and supplication addressed to almighty God. This conviction We again affirmed not long ago, when We recommended that special prayers be offered for this intention to the Holy Ghost during the solemnities of Pentecost; a recommendation that was adopted everywhere with the greatest good will.

5. But in view of the importance and the difficulty of such an undertaking, and the necessity of perseverance in the practice of any virtue, it is well to recall the Apostle's apt counsel: "Be instant in prayer"[Col. 4:2]--counsel all the more to the point because an auspicious beginning of the enterprise will supply the best inducement to perseverance in prayer. Next October, therefore, if you and your people devoutly spend the whole month with Us in praying assiduously to the Virgin Mother of God through her Rosary and the other customary devotions, nothing could do more

to further this project or be more pleasing to Us. We have the best reasons for entrusting Our plans and Our aspirations to her protection and the highest hopes of seeing them realized.

6. The mystery of Christ's immense love for us is revealed with dazzling brilliance in the fact that the dying Saviour bequeathed His Mother to His disciple John in the memorable testament: "Behold thy son." Now in John, as the Church has constantly taught, Christ designated the whole human race, and in the first rank are they who are joined with Him by faith. It is in this sense that St. Anselm of Canterbury says: "What dignity, O Virgin, could be more highly prized than to be the Mother of those to whom Christ deigned to be Father and Brother!"[St. Anselm, Orat, 47] With a generous heart Mary undertook and discharged the duties of her high but laborious office, the beginnings of which were consecrated in the Cenacle. With wonderful care she nurtured the first Christians by her holy example, her authoritative counsel, her sweet consolation, her fruitful prayers. She was, in very truth, the Mother of the Church, the Teacher and Queen of the Apostles, to whom, besides, she confided no small part of the divine mysteries which she kept in her heart.

7. It is impossible to measure the power and scope of her offices since the day she was taken up to that height of heavenly glory in the company of her Son, to which the dignity and luster of her merits entitle her. From her heavenly abode she began, by God's decree, to watch over the Church, to assist and befriend us as our Mother; so that she who was so intimately associated with the mystery of human salvation is just as closely associated with the distribution of the graces which for all time will flow from the Redemption.

Enchiridion Sanctissimi Rosarii

8. The power thus put into her hands is all but unlimited. How unerringly right, then, are Christian souls when they turn to Mary for help as though impelled by an instinct of nature, confidently sharing with her their future hopes and past achievements, their sorrows and joys, commending themselves like children to the care of a bountiful mother. How rightly, too, has every nation and every liturgy without exception acclaimed her great renown, which has grown greater with the voice of each succeeding century. Among her many other titles we find her hailed as "our Lady, our Mediatrix,"[St. Bernard, Serm.II in Adv.] "the Reparatrix of the whole world,"[St. Tharasius, Orat. in Praesentatione] "the Dispenser of all heavenly gifts."[On Off. Graec., 8 Dec]

9. Since faith is the foundation, the source, of the gifts of God by which man is raised above the order of nature and is endowed with the dispositions requisite for life eternal, we are in justice bound to recognize the hidden influence of Mary in obtaining the gift of faith and its salutary cultivation-of Mary who brought the "author of faith"[Hebr. 12:1] into this world and who, because of her own great faith, was called "blessed." "O Virgin most holy, none abounds in the knowledge of God except through thee; none, O Mother of God, attains salvation except through thee; none receives a gift from the throne of mercy except through thee."[St. Germ. Constantinop., Orat. 11, in Dortnitione B.M.V.]

10. It is no exaggeration to say that it is due chiefly to her leadership and help that the wisdom and teachings of the Gospel spread so rapidly to all the nations of the world in spite of the most obstinate difficulties and most cruel persecutions, and brought everywhere in their train a new reign of justice and peace. This it was that stirred the soul of St. Cyril of Alexandria to the following prayerful address to the Blessed Virgin: "Through you the Apostles have preached salvation to the nations. . . through you the priceless

Cross is everywhere honored and venerated; through you the demons have been put to rout and mankind has been summoned back to Heaven; through you every misguided creature held in the thrall of idols is led to recognize the truth; through you have the faithful been brought to the laver of holy Baptism and churches been founded among every people."[St. Cyril Alex., Homil. contra Nestor]

11. Nay she has even, as this same Doctor claims, upheld and given strength to the "sceptre of the orthodox faith."[Ibid] It has been her unremitting concern to see to it that the Catholic Faith stands firmly lodged in the midst of the people, there to thrive in its fertile and undivided unity. Many and well known are the proofs of her solicitude, manifested from time to time even in a miraculous manner. In the times and places in which, to the Church's grief, faith languished in lethargic indifference or was tormented by the baneful scourge of heresy, our great and gracious Lady in her kindness was ever ready with her aid and comfort.

12. Under her inspiration, strong with her might, great men were raised up-illustrious for their sanctity no less than for their apostolic spirit-to beat off the attacks of wicked adversaries and to lead souls back into the virtuous ways of Christian life, firing them with a consuming love of the things of God. One such man, an army in himself, was Dominic Guzman. Putting all his trust in our Lady's Rosary, he set himself fearlessly to the accomplishment of both these tasks with happy results.

13. No one will fail to remark how much the merits of the venerable Fathers and Doctors of the Church, who spent their lives in the defense and explanation of the Catholic Faith, redound to the Virgin Mother of God. For from her, the Seat of Divine Wisdom, as they themselves gratefully tell us, a strong current of

the most sublime wisdom has coursed through their writings. And they were quick to acknowledge that not by themselves but by her have iniquitous errors been overcome. Finally, princes as well as Pontiffs, the guardians and defenders of the faith-the former by waging holy wars, the latter by the solemn decrees which they have issued- have not hesitated to call upon the name of the Mother of our God, and have found her answer powerful and propitious.

14. Hence it is that the Church and the Fathers have given expression to their joy in Mary in words whose beauty equals their truth: "Hail, voice of the Apostles forever eloquent, solid foundation of the faith, unshakable prop of the Church."[Ex hymno Graecorum] "Hail, thou through whom we have been enrolled as citizens of the One, Holy, Catholic and Apostolic Church."[St. John Damasc., in Annuntiatione Deigenitricis, n. 9.] "Hail, thou fountain springing forth by God's design, whose rivers flowing over in pure and unsullied waves of orthodoxy put to flight the hosts of error."[St. German. Constantinop., Orat. in Praesentatione B.M.V.] "Rejoice, because thou alone hast destroyed all the heresies in the world."[In Officio B.M.V.]

15. The unexampled part which the Virgin most admirably played and still plays in the progress, the battles, and the triumphs of the Catholic Faith, makes it evident what God has planned for her to do. It should fill the hearts of all good people with a firm hope of obtaining those things which are now the object of our common desire. Trust Mary, implore her aid.

16. That the one self same profession of faith may unite the minds of Christian nations in peace and harmony, that the one and only bond of perfect charity may gather their hearts within its embrace- such is our prayerful hope! And may Mary, by her powerful help, bring this ardently desired gift into our possession! And

remembering that her only begotten Son prayed so earnestly to His heavenly Father for the closest union among the nations whom He has called by the one Baptism to the one inheritance of salvation bought for an infinite price, will she not, for that reason, see to it that all in His marvelous light will strive as with one mind for unity? And will it not be her wish to employ her goodness and providence to console the Spouse of Christ, the Church, through her long-sustained efforts in this enterprise, as well as to bring to full perfection the boon of unity among the members of the Christian family, which is the illustrious fruit of her motherhood?

17. A token that the fulfillment of these hopes may soon be a reality is to be seen in the conviction and the confidence which warms the hearts of the devout. Mary will be the happy bond to draw together, with strong yet gentle constraint, all who love Christ, no matter where they may be, to form a nation of brothers yielding obedience to the Vicar of Christ on earth, the Roman Pontiff, their common Father.

18. Here our mind, almost of its own accord, looks back through the annals of the Church to the illustrious examples of her ancient unity, and dwells with affectionate regard on the memory of the great Council of Ephesus. The absolute unity of faith, the participation in identical worship, which in those days linked East with West, manifested itself in the Council with a strength unparalleled, and shone beyond it with a radiant beauty when, after the Fathers had emphasized the dogma that the Blessed Virgin is the Mother of God, the news of their procedure-spread abroad from the exultant populace of that most devout of cities-filled all Christendom with transports of universal joy.

19. Every motive which bolsters and increases confidence in the power of our mighty and kindhearted Virgin Mother to obtain the

things we ask for, should act as a powerful incentive generating in us that fiery zeal to pray to her-a zeal We would incite in every Catholic heart. Let each one weigh for himself, moreover, how fitting is this practice and how fruitful to himself; and how acceptable and pleasing to the Blessed Virgin it is bound to be. For, possessing as they do unity of faith, Catholics thus make clear not only that they value this precious gift at its true worth, but also that they intend to hold to it with jealous tenacity. No better way is afforded of proving a fraternal feeling toward their separated brethren than to aid them by every means within their power to recover this, the greatest of all gifts.

20. Such brotherly affection, truly Christian and practiced as long as the Church can remember, has traditionally sought a special efficacy from the Mother of God, since she has been the foremost promoter of peace and unity. St. Germain of Constantinople addresses this prayer to her: "Be mindful of Christians who are thy servants; commend the prayers of all; help all to realize their hopes; strengthen the faith; keep the Church in unity."'[Orat. hist. in Dormitione Deiparae] And to this day the Greeks beseech her in this manner: "O Virgin most pure, whose privilege it is to approach thy Son without fear of rebuff! Beseech Him, O Virgin most holy, to grant peace to the world and to breathe into the churches of Christendom one mind and one heart; and we shall all magnify thee."[Men., 5 maii, Theotokion]

21. There is another special reason why Mary will be favorably disposed to grant our united prayers in behalf of the nations cut off from communion with the Church: namely, the prodigious things they have done for her honor in the past, especially in the East. To them is due much of the credit for propagating and increasing devotion to her. From them have come some of the best-remembered heralds and champions of her dignity, who have

wielded a mighty influence by their authority or by their writings- eulogists famed for the ardor and the charm of their eloquence; "empresses well beloved of God,"[St. Cyril Alex., De fide, Ad Pulcheriam] who imitated the Virgin most pure in the example of their lives, and paid honor to her with lavish generosity; temples and basilicas built to her glory with regal splendor.

22. And We may here add a detail not foreign to Our subject and reflecting further glory upon the Mother of God. It is common knowledge that, under the changing fortunes of time, great numbers of venerable images of our Lady have been brought from the East to the West, most of them finding their way to Italy and to Rome.

23. Our forebears received them with deepest respect and venerated them with magnificent honors; and their descendants, emulating their piety, continue to cherish these images as highly sacred treasures. It is a delight for the mind to discover in this fact the approval and the favor of a mother wholly devoted to her children. For it seems to indicate that these images have been left in our midst as witness of the ages when the entire Christian family was held together by ties of absolute unity, and as so many precious pledges of our common inheritance. The very sight of them must needs invite souls, as though the Virgin herself were bidding them, to keep in devout remembrance those whom the Catholic Church calls with loving care back to the peace and the gladness which they formerly enjoyed, within her embrace.

24. And so, in Mary, God has given us the most zealous guardian of Christian unity. There are, of course, more ways than one to win her protection by prayer, but as for Us, We think that the best and most effective way to her favor lies in the Rosary. We have elsewhere brought it to the attention of the devout Christian and

not least among the advantages of the Rosary is the ready and easy means it puts in his hands to nurture his faith, and to keep him from ignorance of his religion and the danger of error.

25. The very origin of the Rosary makes that plain. When such faith is exercised by vocally repeating the Our Father and Hail Mary of the Rosary prayers, or better still in the contemplation of the mysteries, it is evident how close we are brought to Mary. For every time we devoutly say the Rosary in supplication before her, we are once more brought face to face with the marvel of our salvation; we watch the mysteries of our Redemption as though they were unfolding before our eyes; and as one follows another, Mary stands revealed at once as God's Mother and our Mother.

26. The sublimity of that double dignity, the fruits of her twofold ministry, appear in vivid light when in devout meditation we think of Mary's share in the joyful, the sorrowful, the glorious mysteries of her Son. The heart is inflamed by these reflections with a feeling of grateful love toward her and, esteeming everything beneath her as so much worthless chaff, strives with manful purpose to prove worthy of such a Mother and the gifts she bestows. Meditation on the mysteries of the Rosary, often repeated in the spirit of faith, cannot help but please her and move her, the fondest of mothers, to show mercy to her children.

27. For that reason We say that the Rosary is by far the best prayer by which to plead before her the cause of our separated brethren. To grant a favorable hearing belongs properly to her office of spiritual Mother. For Mary has not brought forth-nor could she-those who are of Christ except in the one same Faith and in the one same love; for "Can Christ be divided?"[I Cor. 1:13] All must live the life of Christ in an organic unity in order to "bring forth fruit to God"[Rom. 7:4] in the one same body. Every one of the

multitudes, therefore, whom the mischief of calamitous events has stolen away from that unity, must be born again to Christ of that same Mother whom God has endowed with a never failing fertility to bring forth a holy people. And this Mary, for her part, longs to do. Adorned by us with garlands of her favorite prayer, she will obtain by her entreaties help in abundance from the Spirit that quickeneth. God grant that they refuse not to comply with the burning desire of their merciful Mother but, on the contrary, give ear, like men of good will, with a proper regard for their eternal salvation, to the voice, gently persuasive, which calls to them: "My little children, of whom I am in labor again, until Christ be formed in you."[Gal. 4:19]

28. Knowing what power our Lady's Rosary possesses, not a few of Our Predecessors took special care to spread the devotion throughout the countries of the East-in particular Eugene IV in the Constitution "Advesperascente" issued in 1439, and later Innocent XII and Clement XI. By their authority, privileges of wide extent were granted to the Order of Preachers in favor of this project. The hoped-for results were forthcoming, thanks to the energetic activity of the brethren of that Order, result to which many a bright record bears witness, although time and adversity have since raised great obstacles in the way of further progress. Yet even today the same zeal for the Rosary devotion which We cited at the beginning of this Letter still fills the hearts of great numbers in those lands-a fact which, We trust, will be as useful in the realization of Our hopes as it was in raising them.

29. Along with this hope, there is the joyful fact, of equal importance to the East and the West, and in keeping with the longing We have expressed: namely the plan, Venerable Brethren, which took form at the celebrated Eucharistic Congress held in Jerusalem, to build a shrine in honor of the Queen of the Most

Holy Rosary at Patras in Achaia, not far from places where at one time Christianity, under her patronage, shone brilliantly. For, as We have with great pleasure learned from the committee which was organized with Our approval to advance the project and take charge of the work, most of you have already sent in contributions collected for this purpose and have promised to continue your help until the project has been completed.

30. On the strength of this it has been decided to begin work on a scale proportioned to the size of the undertaking, and We have granted permission for the laying of the first stone of the shrine at an early date with solemn ceremonies. The temple will stand as a monument of ever lasting thanksgiving erected in the name of the Christian people to their heavenly Helper and Mother. There she will be invoked unceasingly in the Greek and the Latin rites that, ever more propitious, she will continue to heap new favors upon the ancient blessings.

31. And now, Venerable Brethren, Our exhortation returns to the point from which it began. Well may all, shepherds and flocks alike, fly with fullest confidence to the protection of the great Virgin, especially next month. Let them not fail to call upon her name, with one voice beseeching her as God's Mother, publicly and in private, by praise, by prayer, by the ardor of their desire: "Show thyself our Mother." May her motherly compassion keep her whole family safe from every danger, lead them in the path of genuine prosperity, above all establish them in holy unity. She looks upon Catholics of every nation with a kindly eye. Where the bond of charity joins them together she makes them more ready, more and more determined, to uphold the honor of religion which, at the same time, brings upon the state the greatest blessings. May she look with utmost compassion upon those great and illustrious

nations which are cut off from the Church and upon the noble souls who have not forgotten their Christian duty.

32. May she aspire in them most salutary desires, foster their holy aspirations, and bring them to happy completion. In the East, may that widespread devotion to her which the dissident nations profess, as well as the countless glorious acts of their ancestors in her honor, effectively aid them. In the West, may the memory of her beneficent patronage stand its dissidents in good stead; with surpassing kindness she has, through many ages, manifested her approval of, and has rewarded, the admirable devotion shown her among every class.

33. May the peoples of the East and West, and all the others wherever they may be, profit by the suppliant voice of Catholics united in prayer, and by our voice which will cry to Our last breath: <Show thyself a Mother.>

Given at Rome, at St. Peter's, the fifth day of September, in the eighteenth year of Our Pontificate.

Enchiridion Sanctissimi Rosarii

Fidentem Piumque Animum
On the Rosary

Encyclical of Pope Leo XIII

September 20, 1896

To Our Venerable Brethren, The Patriarchs, Primates, Bishops, and other Local Ordinaries Enjoying Peace and Communion with the Apostolic See.

Venerable Brethren, Health and the Apostolic Blessing.

We have already had the opportunity on several occasions during Our Pontificate of bearing public testimony to that confidence and devotion towards the Blessed Virgin which We imbibed in Our tenderest years, and have endeavoured to cherish and develop all our life long. For, having fallen upon times of calamity for Christendom and perils for the nations, We have realised how prudent it is to warmly recommend this means of safe-guarding happiness and peace which God has most mercifully granted to Mankind in His August Mother, and which hath ever been celebrated in the annals of the Church. The manifold zeal of Christian people has responded to Our desires and exhortations, most particularly in exciting a devotion to the Rosary; and a plentiful harvest of excellent fruits has not been wanting. Still we can never be satisfied with celebrating the Divine Mother, who is in truth <worthy of all praise>, and in urging love and affection towards her who is also the mother of mankind, who is <full of mercy, full of grace>. Yea, Our soul, wearied with the cares of the Apostolate, the nearer it feels the time of Our departure to be at hand, with the more earnest confidence looks up to her from whom, as from a blessed dawn, arose the Day of happiness and joy that was never to set. It is pleasant to us to remember, Venerable Brethren, that We have in other letters issued from time to time extolled the devotion of the Rosary; for it is in many ways most pleasing to her in whose honour it is employed, and most advantageous to those who properly use it. But it is equally pleasant to be able now to insist upon and confirm the same fact. Herein we have an excellent opportunity to paternally exhort men's minds and hearts to an increase of religion, and to stimulate within them the hope of eternal reward.

2. The form of prayer We refer to has obtained the special name of "Rosary," as though it represented by its arrangement the sweetness of roses and the charm of a garland. This is most fitting for a method of venerating the Virgin, who is rightly styled the <Mystical Rose> of Paradise, and who, as Queen of the universe, shines therein with a crown of stars. So that by its very name it appears to foreshadow and be an augury of the joys and garlands of Heaven offered by her to those who are devoted to her. This appears clearly if we consider the nature of the Rosary of Our Lady. There is no duty which Christ and His Apostles more emphatically urged by both precept and example than that of prayer and supplication to Almighty God. The Fathers and Doctors in subsequent times have taught that this is a matter of such grave necessity, that if men neglect it they hope in vain for eternal salvation. Every one who prays finds the door open to impetration, both from the very nature of prayer and from the promises of Christ. And we all know that prayer derives its chief efficacy from two principal circumstances: perseverance, and the union of many for one end. The former is signified in those invitations of Christ so full of goodness: <ask, seek, knock> (Matt. vii., 7), just as a kind father desires to indulge the wishes of his children, but who also

requires to be continually asked by them and as it were wearied by their prayers, in order to attach their hearts more closely to himself. The second condition Our Lord has born witness to more than once: <If two of you shall consent upon earth concerning anything whatsoever they shall ask, it shall be done to them by My Father who is in heaven. For where there are two or three gathered in My name, there am I in the midst of them> (Matt. xviii. 19, 20). Hence that pregnant saying of Tertullian: <Let us gather into an assembly and congregation that we may, as it were, make up a band and solicit God (Apologet. c. xxxix): such violence

is pleasing to God>; and the memorable words of Aquinas: <It is impossible that the prayers of many should not be heard, if one prayer is made up as it were out of many supplications.> (In Evang. Matt. c. xvii). Both of these qualities are conspicuous in the Rosary. For, to be brief, by repeating the same prayers we strenuously implore from Our Heavenly Father the Kingdom of His grace and glory; we again and again beseech the Virgin Mother to aid us sinners by her prayers, both during our whole life and especially at that last moment which is the stepping-stone to eternity. The formula of the Rosary, too, is excellently adapted to prayer in common, so that it has been styled, not without reason, "The Psalter of Mary." And that old custom of our forefathers ought to be preserved or else restored, according to which Christian families, whether in town or country, were religiously wont at close of day, when their labours were at an end, to assemble before a figure of Our Lady and alternately recite the Rosary. She, delighted at this faithful and unanimous homage, was ever near them like a loving mother surrounded by her children, distributing to them the blessings of domestic peace, the foretaste of the peace of heaven. Considering the efficacy of public prayer, We, among other decrees which we have from time to time issued concerning the Rosary, have spoken thus: "It is Our desire that in the principal church of each diocese it should be recited every day, and in parish churches on every feast-day (Apostolic Letter <Salutaris Ille>, 24th December, 1883). <Let this be constantly and devoutly carried out. We also see with joy the custom extended on other solemn occasions of public devotion and in pilgrimages to venerated shrines, the growing frequency of which is to be commended. This association of prayer and praise to Mary is both delightful and salutary for souls. We ourselves have most strongly experienced this--and Our heart rejoices to recall it - when at certain times in Our Pontificate We have been present in the Vatican basilica, surrounded by great crowds of all classes, who united with Us in mind, voice, and hope, earnestly invoked by the mysteries and prayers of the Rosary, her who is the most powerful patroness of the Catholic name.>

3. And who could think or say that the confidence so strongly felt in the patronage and protection of the Blessed Virgin is excessive? Undoubtedly the name and attributes of the absolute Mediator belong to no other than to Christ, for being one person, and yet both man and God, He restored the human race to the favour of the Heavenly Father: <One Mediator of God and men, the man Christ Jesus, who gave Himself a redemption for all> (1 Tim. ii. 5, 6). And yet, as the Angelic Doctor teaches, <there is no reason why certain others should not be called in a certain way mediators between God and man, that is to say, in so far as they cooperate by predisposing and ministering in the union of man with God> (Summa, p. 111., q. xxvi., articles 1, 2). Such are the angels and saints, the prophets and priests of both Testaments; but especially has the Blessed Virgin a claim to the glory of this title. For no single individual can even be imagined who has ever contributed or ever will contribute so much towards reconciling man with God.

She offered to mankind. hastening to eternal ruin, a Saviour, at that moment when she received the announcement of the mystery of peace brought to this earth by the Angel, with that admirable act of consent <in the name of the whole human race> (Summa. p. III., q. xxx., art. 1). She it is <from whom is born Jesus>; she is therefore truly His mother, and for this reason a worthy and acceptable "Mediatrix to the Mediator." As the various mysteries present themselves one after the other in the formula of the Rosary for the meditation and contemplation of men's minds, they also elucidate what we owe to Mary for our reconciliation and salvation. No one can fail to be sweetly affected when considering her who appeared in the house of Elizabeth as the minister of the divine gifts, and who presented her Son to the Shepherds, to the kings, and to Simeon. Moreover, one must remember that the Blood of Christ shed for our sake and those members in which He offers to His Father the wounds He received, <the price of our liberty>, are no other than the flesh and blood of the virgin, <since the flesh of Jesus is the flesh of Mary, and however much it was exalted in the glory of His resurrection, nevertheless the nature of His flesh derived from Mary remained and still remains the same> (<de Assumpt. B. V. M., c. v.>, among the <Opera S. Aug>).

4. Yet another excellent fruit follows from the Rosary, exceedingly opportune to the character of our times. This we have referred to elsewhere. It is that, whilst the virtue of Divine Faith is daily exposed to so many dangers and attacks, the Christian may here derive nourishment and strength for his faith. Holy writ calls Christ the <Author and finisher of faith> (Heb. vii. 2), the <Author>, because He taught men many things which they had to believe, especially about Himself in whim <dwelleth all the fullness of the Godhead> (Colos. ii., 9), and also because He mercifully gives the power of believing by the grace and, as it were, the function of the

Holy Ghost; the Finisher, because in Heaven, where He will change the habit of faith into the splendour of glory, He openly discloses to them those things which they have seen in this mortal life as through a veil. Now Christ stands forth clearly in the Rosary. We behold in meditation His life, whether His hidden life in joy, or His public life in excessive toil and sufferings unto death, or His glorious life from His triumphant resurrection to His eternal enthronement at the right hand of the Father. And since faith, to be full and sufficient, must display itself, - for with the heart we believe unto justice, but <with the mouth confession is made unto salvation> (Rom. x., 10), - so have we also in the Rosary an excellent means unto this, for by those vocal prayers with which it is intermingled, we are enabled to express and profess our faith in God, our most watchful Father; in the future life, the forgiveness of sins; in the mysteries of the august Trinity, the Incarnation of the Word, the Divine Maternity, and others. All know the value and merit of faith. For faith is just like a most precious gem, producing now the blossoms of all virtue by which we are pleasing to God, and hereafter to bring forth fruits that will last for ever: <for to know Thee is perfect justice, and to know Thy justice and Thy power is the root of immortality> (Wisdom xv., 3). It is here the place to add a remark respecting the duties of those virtues which faith rightly postulates. Among them is the virtue of penance, and one part of this is abstinence, which for more reasons than one is necessary and salutary. It is true the Church is growing more indulgent towards her children in this matter, but they must understand they are bound to take all care to make up for this maternal indulgence by other good works. We rejoice for this reason also to propose particularly the use of the rosary, which is capable of producing worthy fruits of penance, especially by the remembrance of the sufferings of Christ and His Mother.

5. To those therefore who are striving after supreme happiness this means of the Rosary has been most providentially offered, and it is one unsurpassed for facility and convenience. For any person, even moderately instructed in his religion can make use of it with fruit, and the time it occupies cannot delay any man's business. Sacred history abounds with striking and evident examples. It is well known that there have been many persons occupied in most weighty functions or absorbed in laborious cares who have never omitted for a single day this pious practice. Combined with this advantage is that inward sentiment of devotion which attracts minds to the Rosary, so that they love it as the intimate companion and faithful protector of life; and in their last agony they embrace and hold fast to it as the dear pledge of the <unfading Crown of glory>. Such a pledge is greatly enhanced by the benefits of <sacred indulgences>, if properly employed; for the devotion of the Rosary has been richly endowed with such indulgences by both our Predecessors and Ourselves. These favours will certainly prove most efficacious to both the dying and the departed, being bestowed as it were by the hands of the merciful Virgin, in order that they may the sooner enjoy the eternal peace and light they have desired.

6. These considerations, Venerable Brethren, move us incessantly to extol and recommend to Catholic peoples this excellent and most salutary form of devotion. Yet another very urgent reason, of which we have often spoken both in Letters and Allocutions, encourages us to do this. For that earnest desire, which We have learnt from the Divine Heart of Jesus, of fostering the work of reconciliation among those who are separated from Us daily urges Us more pressingly to action; and we are convinced that this most excellent Re-union cannot be better prepared and strengthened than by the power of prayer. The example of Christ is before us,

for in order that His disciples <might be one> in faith and charity, he poured forth prayer and supplication to His Father. And concerning the efficacious prayer of His most holy Mother for the same end, there is a striking testimony in the Acts of the Apostles. Therein is described the first assembly of the Disciples, expecting with earnest hope and prayer the promised fullness of the Holy Spirit. And the presence of Mary united with them in prayer is specially indicated: <All these were persevering with one mind in prayer with Mary the Mother of Jesus> (Acts i., 14). Wherefore as the nascent church rightly joined itself in prayer with her as the patroness and most excellent custodian of Unity, so in these times is it most opportune to do the same all over the Catholic World, particularly during the whole month of October, which we have long ago decreed to be dedicated and consecrated, by the solemn devotion of the Rosary, to the Divine Mother, in order to implore her for the afflicted Church. Let then the zeal for this prayer everywhere be re-kindled, particularly for the end of Holy Unity. Nothing will be more agreeable and acceptable to Mary; for, as she is most closely united with Christ she especially wishes and desires that they who have received the same Baptism with Him may be united with Him and with one another in the same faith and perfect charity. So may the sublime mysteries of this same faith by means of the Rosary devotion be more deeply impressed in men's minds, with the happy result that "we may imitate what they contain and obtain what they promise."

7. Meanwhile, as a pledge of the Divine Favours and Our affection, We most lovingly impart to You, your clergy and People, the Apostolic Benediction.

Given at St. Peter's in Rome, September 20, 1896, in the 19th year of Our Pontificate.

Enchiridion Sanctissimi Rosarii

Augustissimae Virginis Mariae
On The Confraternity Of The Holy Rosary

Encyclical of Pope Leo XIII

September 12, 1897

To Our Venerable Brethren, The Patriarchs, Primates, Archbishops, Bishops, and other Local Ordinaries having Peace and Communion with the Apostolic See.

Venerable Brethren, Health and the Apostolic Blessing.

Whoever considers the height of dignity and glory to which God has raised the Most August Virgin Mary, will easily perceive how important it is, both for public and for private benefit, that devotion to her should be assiduously practised, and daily promoted more and more.

Mary's Place in the Incarnation and Redemption

2. God predestined her from all eternity to be the Mother of the Incarnate Word, and for that reason so highly distinguished her among all His most beautiful works in the triple order of nature, grace and glory, that the Church justly applies to her these words: "I came out of the mouth of the Most High, the first-born before all creatures" (Ecclus. xxiv., 5). And when, in the first ages, the parents of mankind fell into sin, involving their posterity in the same ruin, she was set up as a pledge of the restoration of peace and salvation. The Only-begotten Son of God ever paid to His Most Holy Mother indubitable marks of honour. During His private life on earth He associated her with Himself in each of His first two miracles: the miracle of grace, when, at the salutation of

Mary, the infant leaped in the womb of Elizabeth; the miracle of nature, when He turned water into wine at the marriage-feast of Cana. And, at the supreme moment of His public life, when sealing the New Testament in His precious Blood, He committed her to his beloved Apostle in those sweet words, "Behold, thy Mother!" John xix.,27).

3. We, therefore, who, though unworthy, hold the place of Vicar of Christ upon earth, shall never cease to promote the glory of so great a Mother, as long as life endures. And since, as old age draws on apace, We feel that life cannot now last much longer, We are constrained to repeat to each and all of our beloved children in Christ those last words of His upon the Cross, left to us as a testament, "Behold, thy Mother!" Greatly rewarded indeed shall We be, if Our exhortations succeed in making even one of the faithful hold nothing dearer than devotion to Mary; so that those words which St. John wrote about himself may be applied to each, "the disciple took her to his own" [Ibid.].

4. As the month of October again approaches, Venerable Brethren, We would not willingly leave you without Our letters this year, also once more urging you with all possible earnestness to strive by the recitation of the Rosary to aid both yourselves individually, and the Church in her need. This form of prayer appears, under the guidance of Divine Providence, to have been wonderfully developed at the close of the century, for the purpose of stimulating the lagging piety of the faithful. This is witnessed by the splendid churches and much-frequented sanctuaries of the Mother of God. To this Divine Mother we have offered the flowers of the month of May; to her we would have also fruit-bearing October dedicated with especial tenderness of devotion. It is fitting that both parts of the year should be consecrated to her who said: "My flowers are the fruit of honour and riches" (Ecclus. xxiv., 23).

5. The natural tendency of man to association has never been stronger, or more earnestly and generally followed, than in our own age. This is not at all to be reprehended, unless when so excellent a natural tendency is perverted to evil purposes, and wicked men, banding together in various forms of societies, conspire "against the Lord and against His Christ" (Ps ii., 2). It is, however, most gratifying to observe that pious associations are becoming more and more popular among Catholics also. They are frequently formed; indeed, all Catholics are so closely drawn together and united by the bonds of charity, as members of one household, that they both may be and are truly styled brethren. But if the charity of Christ be absent, none may glory in the name and fellowship of brethren. So wrote Tertullian long ago in pungent words: "We are your brethren by right of a common mother, nature, yet are ye less than men, because unnatural brothers. How much more justly are they called and esteemed as brethren who acknowledge one and the same Father, God; who have drunk in one and the same spirit of charity; who have been borne from one and the same womb of ignorance into the one light of truth?" [Apolog. c. xxxix.]

6. There are many reasons for Catholics joining useful associations of this kind. We include in these clubs, popular savings-banks, recreative classes, associations for the care of youth, sodalities, and many other organizations for excellent purposes. All these, though from their name, constitution, and special ends, apparently of modern invention, are in reality of great antiquity. Traces of societies of this kind are to be found even in the earliest ages of Christianity. In later ages they were legally approved, distinguished by special emblems, enriched with privileges, associated with divine worship in the Churches, or devoted to works of spiritual or corporal mercy, and at different epochs known under different names. Their numbers increased to such an extent, especially in

Italy, that no city or town, nay scarcely any parish, was without one or more of them.

7. We do not hesitate to assign a pre-eminent place among these societies to that known as the Society of the Holy Rosary. If we regard its origin, we find it distinguished by its antiquity, for St. Dominic himself is said to have been its founder. If we estimate its privileges, we see it enriched with a vast number of them granted by the munificence of our predecessors. The form of the association, its very soul, is the Rosary of Our Lady, of the excellence of which We have elsewhere spoken at length. Still the virtue and efficacy of the Rosary appear all the greater when considered as the special office of the Sodality which bears its name. Everyone knows how necessary prayer is for all men; not that God's decrees can be changed, but, as St. Gregory says, "that men by asking may merit to receive what Almighty God hath decreed from eternity to grant them" [Dialog., lib. i., c. 8]. And St. Augustine says, "He who knoweth how to pray aright, knoweth how to live aright" [In Ps. cxviii]. But prayers acquire their greatest efficacy in obtaining God's assistance when offered publicly, by large numbers, constantly, and unanimously, so as to form as it were a single chorus of supplication; as those words of the Acts of the Apostles clearly declare wherein the disciples of Christ, awaiting the coming of the Holy Ghost, are said to have been "persevering with one mind in prayer" (Acts i., 14). Those who practice this manner of prayer will never fail to obtain certain fruit. Such is certainly the case with members of the Rosary Sodality. Just as by the recitation of the Divine Office, priests offer a public, constant, and most efficacious supplication; so the supplication offered by the members of this Sodality in the recitation of the Rosary, or "Psalter of Our Lady," as it has been styled by some of the Popes, is also in a way public, constant, and universal.

8. Since, as We have said, public prayers are much more excellent and more efficacious than private ones, so ecclesiastical writers have given to the Rosary Sodality the title of "the army of prayer, enrolled by St. Dominic, under the banner of the Mother of God,"--of her, whom sacred literature and the history of the Church salute as the conqueror of the Evil One and of all errors. The Rosary unites together all who join the Sodality in a common bond of paternal or military comradeship; so that a mighty host is thereby formed, duly marshalled and arrayed, to repel the assaults of the enemy, both from within and without. Wherefore may the members of this pious society take to themselves the words of St. Cyprian: "Our prayer is public and in common; and when we pray, we pray not for one, but for the whole people, for we, the entire people, are one" [De Orat. Domin.]. The history of the Church bears testimony to the power and efficacy of this form of prayer, recording as it does the rout of the Turkish forces at the naval battle of Lepanto, and the victories gained over the same in the last century at Temesvar in Hungary and in the island of Corfu. Our predecessor, Gregory XIII., in order to perpetuate the memory of the first-named victory, established the feast of Our Lady of Victories, which later on Clement XI. distinguished by the title of Rosary Sunday and commanded to be celebrated throughout the universal Church.

9. From the fact that this warfare of prayer is "enrolled under the name of the Mother of God," fresh efficacy and fresh honour are thereby added to it. Hence the frequent repetition in the Rosary of the "Hail Mary" after each "Our Father." So far from this derogating in any way from the honour due to God, as though it indicated that we placed greater confidence in Mary's patronage than in God's power, it is rather this which especially moves God, and wins His mercy for us. We are taught by the Catholic faith that

we may pray not only to God himself, but also to the Blessed in heaven [Conc. Trid. Sess. xxv.], though in different manner; because we ask from God as from the Source of all good, but from the Saints as from intercessors. "Prayer," says St. Thomas, "is offered to a person in two ways--one as though to be granted by himself; another, as to be obtained through him. In the first way we pray to God alone, because all our prayers ought to be directed to obtaining grace and glory, which God alone gives, according to those words of Psalm lxxxiii., 12, "The Lord will give grace and glory." But in the second way we pray to holy angels and men, not that God may learn our petition through them, but that by their prayers and merits our prayers may be efficacious. Wherefore, it is said in the Apocalypse (viii., 4): "The smoke of the incense of the prayers of the Saints ascended up before God from the hand of the angel" [Summa Theol. 2a 2ae, q. lxxxiii. a. iv.]. Now, of all the blessed in heaven, who can compare with the august Mother of God in obtaining grace? Who seeth more clearly in the Eternal Word what troubles oppress us, what are our needs? Who is allowed more power in moving God? Who can compare with her in maternal affection? We do not pray to the Blessed in the same way as to God; for we ask the Holy Trinity to have mercy on us, but we ask all the Saints to pray for us [Ibid.]. Yet our manner of praying to the Blessed Virgin has something in common with our worship of God, so that the Church even addresses to her the words with which we pray to God: "Have mercy on sinners." The members of the Rosary Sodality, therefore, do exceedingly well in weaving together, as in a crown, so many salutations and prayers to Mary. For, so great is her dignity, so great her favour before God, that whosoever in his need will not have recourse to her is trying to fly without wings.

10. We must not omit to mention another excellence of this Sodality. As often as, in reciting the Rosary, we meditate upon the mysteries of our Redemption, so often do we in a manner emulate the sacred duties once committed to the Angelic hosts. The Angels revealed each of these mysteries in its due time; they played a great part in them; they were constantly present at them, with countenances indicative now of joy, now of sorrow, now of triumphant exultation. Gabriel was sent to announce the Incarnation of the Eternal Word to the Virgin. In the cave of Bethlehem, Angels sang the glory of the new-born Saviour. The Angel gave Joseph command to fly with the Child into Egypt. An Angel consoled, with his loving words, Jesus in His bloody sweat in the garden. Angels announced His resurrection, after He had triumphed over death, to the women. Angels carried Him up into Heaven; and foretold His second coming, surrounded by Angelic hosts, unto whom He will associate the souls of the elect, and carry them aloft with Him to the heavenly choirs, "above whom the Holy Mother of God is exalted." To those, therefore, who make use of the pious prayers of the Rosary in this Sodality, may be well applied the words with which St. Paul addressed the new Christians: "You are come to Mount Sion, and to the city of the living God, the Heavenly Jerusalem, and to the company of many thousands of Angels" (Heb. xii., 22). What more divine, what more delightful, than to meditate and pray with the Angels? With what confidence may we not hope that those who on earth have united with the Angels in this ministry will one day enjoy their blessed company in Heaven?

11. For these reasons the Roman Pontiffs have ever given the highest praise to this Sodality of Our Lady. Innocent VIII. calls it "a most devout confraternity" [Splendor Paternae Gloriae, Feb. 26, 1491.] Pius V declares that by its virtue "Christians began suddenly

to be transformed into other men, the darkness of heresy to be dispelled, and the light of Catholic faith to shine forth" [Consueverunt Romani Pontifices], September 17, 1569). Sixtus V, noting how fruitful for religion this Sodality was, professed himself most devoted to it. Many others, too, enriched it with numerous and very special indulgences, or took it under their particular patronage, enrolling themselves in it and giving it many testimonies of their goodwill.

12. We also, Venerable Brethren, moved by the example of Our predecessors, earnestly exhort and conjure you, as We have so often done, to devote special care to this sacred warfare, so that by your efforts fresh forces may be daily enrolled on every side. Through you and those of your clergy who have care of souls, let the people know and duly appreciate the efficacy of this Sodality and its usefulness for man's salvation. This We beg all the more earnestly as of late that beautiful devotion to our Blessed Mother, called "the living Rosary," has once more become popular. We have gladly blessed this devotion, and We earnestly desire that you would sedulously and strenuously encourage its growth. We cherish the strongest hope that these prayers and praises, rising incessantly from the lips and hearts of so great a multitude, will be most efficacious. Alternately rising by night and by day, throughout the different countries of the earth, they combine a harmony of vocal prayer with meditation upon the divine mysteries. In ages long past this perennial stream of praise and prayer was foretold in those inspired words with which Ozias in his song addressed Judith: "Blessed art thou, O daughter, by the Lord, the Most High God, above all women upon the earth ... because He hath so magnified thy name this day that thy praise shall not depart out of the mouth of man." And all the people of Israel acclaimed him in these words: "So be it, so be it!" (Judith xiii., 23, 24, 26).

13. Meanwhile, as a pledge of heavenly blessings, and a testimony of Our paternal affection, We lovingly impart to You, in the name of the Lord, Venerable Brethren, and to all the clergy and people committed to your faithful care, the Apostolic Benediction.

Given at St. Peter's, in Rome, on the 12th day of September, 1897, in the 20th year of Our Pontificate.

A Manual of the Most Holy Rosary

Fausto Appetente Die
On St. Dominic

Encyclical of Pope Benedict XV

June 29, 1921

To the Patriarchs, Primates, Archbishops, Bishops, and other Ordinaries in Peace and Communion with the Apostolic See.

Venerable Brethren, Health and The Apostolic Benediction.

The seventh centenary approaches of the day when that light of holiness, Dominic, passed from these miseries to the seat of the Blessed. We for long have been most interested in his clients, especially since We assumed the government of the Church of Bologna, which with the greater devotion preserves his remains. We, therefore, are pleased to be able from this Apostolic See to exhort the Christian people to celebrate the memory of such a great man. In this We not only consult Our own piety but fulfil a duty of gratitude towards the father and lawgiver and towards the distinguished Order he founded.

2. This man of God and true Dominicus was fully given up to Holy Church, which had in him an invincible champion of the Faith. The Order of Preachers, too, founded by him, has ever been the stout defense of the Roman Church. And so not only did he strengthen the temple in his time, but he provided for the continuance of the defense. The words of Honorius III in approving the Order seem prophetical: ". . . looking to the brethren of thy Order as the future champions of the Faith and the true lights of the world."

3. Indeed, as all know, for the spread of God's kingdom Jesus Christ used no other weapon than the preaching of the Gospel,

that is, the living voice of His heralds, who diffused everywhere the celestial doctrine. "Teach," he said, "all nations." "Preach the Gospel to every creature." Accordingly, from the preaching of the Apostles, and especially of St. Paul, it came to pass, that preaching being followed up with the doctrine and discipline of the Fathers and afterwards of the Doctors, men's minds were enlightened with the light of truth and conceived a love for all the virtues. Following the same lines in his work for the salvation of souls. Dominic proposed to himself and to all his followers "to hand to others what they had contemplated." For this reason, in addition to the duty of cultivating poverty, innocence of life, and religious discipline, he commanded his Order in a strict and solemn manner to be zealous in the study of Christian doctrine and the preaching of the truth.

4. In the Dominican preaching three qualities shine forth: great solidity of doctrine, the fullness of fidelity towards the Apostolic See, piety towards the Virgin Mother. For although Dominic felt himself mature for preaching, yet he did not undertake that office until he had worked hard in the Palentine Athenaeum of philosophy and theology. Long familiar with the Fathers, under their guidance and teaching, he first, as it were, received into his blood and marrow the riches of Sacred Scripture, and especially of Paul.

5. The value of this knowledge of Divine things not long after was to be seen in his disputations against the heretics. They were armed with all arts and fallacies to attack the dogmas of Faith; yet with wonderful success he confounded and refuted them. This appeared especially at Toulouse, the head and center of the heresies, where the most learned of the adversaries had come together. It is recorded that he, with his first companions, powerful in word and work, invincibly withstood the insolence of the heretics. Indeed,

not only did he withstand their strength, but he so softened their spirits by his eloquence and charity that he recalled an immense number to the bosom of the Church. God Himself was ever at hand to aid him in his battle for the Faith. Thus, having accepted the challenge of the heretics that each should consign his book to the flames, his book alone remained untouched by the fire. Thus by the valor of Dominic Europe was freed from the danger of the Albigensian heresy.

6. With this quality of solid doctrine he ordered his children to be adorned. For, soon after the approbation of his Order by the Apostolic See and the confirmation of the noble title of Preachers, he arranged for houses to be founded as near as possible to the celebrated universities that his brethren might the more easily exercise themselves in every branch of culture, and get followers from the ranks of university students. Accordingly, the Dominican institute from the beginning was famed for its learning. Its special mission was always to care for the various wounds of error and to diffuse the light of the Christian Faith, seeing that nothing is such a hindrance to eternal salvation as the ignorance of the truth and perversity of doctrine. It was not strange, then, that the eyes and hearts of all should be turned towards this new apostolate which was based upon the Gospel and the teachings of the Fathers and commended by the abundance of all branches of knowledge.

7. The very wisdom of God seemed to speak through the Dominicans when there rose up among them such heralds and defenders of Christian wisdom as Hyacinth Polonus, Peter the Martyr, Vincent Ferrer, and such miracles of genius and erudition as Albert the Great, Raymond de Penafort, Thomas Aquinas, in whom especially, a follower of Dominic, God "deigned to enlighten his Church." This Order, therefore, always in honor as the teacher of truth, acquired new luster when the Church declared the

teaching of Thomas to be her own and that Doctor, honored with the special praises of the Pontiffs, the master and patron of Catholic schools.

8. Joined to this zeal in retaining and defending the Faith there was in Dominic a supreme reverence for the Apostolic See. It is recorded that, prostrate at the feet of Innocent III, he vowed himself to the defense of the Roman Pontificate, and that the same predecessor of ours the following night saw him in vision sustain on his courageous shoulder the tottering pile of the Lateran Basilica. History tells, too, how when he was training his first followers to Christian perfection, Dominic thought of gathering from pious and devout lay people a certain sacred militia which would defend the rights of the Church and resist heresy with vigor. Hence arose the Third Order of the Dominicans which, spreading among lay people the institute of a more perfect life, was to be a truly great ornament and defense to the Church.

9. Handed down by their Father and Lawgiver, the heritage of such devotion to this See passed to the children. As often, therefore, as, through the infatuated minds of men, the Church had to suffer from popular movements or the tyranny of princes, this Apostolic See had in the Dominicans, the defenders of truth and justice, a most opportune help in the preservation and honor of its authority. Who does not know the glorious deeds in that connection of the Dominican Virgin, Catherine of Sienna? Urged by the charity of Jesus Christ she persuaded the Roman Pontiff, what no one else had been able to do, to return to his Roman See after an interval of seventy years. Afterwards, while the Western Church was torn by a dire schism, she kept a great number of Christians in loyal obedience to the legitimate Pontiff.

10. And, to pass over other things, We cannot but recall that four great Roman Pontiffs came from the Dominican ranks. Of these, the last, St. Pius V, won undying gratitude from Christianity and civil society. He joined together, after unceasing efforts, the arms of the Catholic princes, and under the patronage of the Virgin Mother of God, whom, therefore, he ordered to be saluted in future as Help to Christians, destroyed forever at Lepanto the power of the Turks.

11. In this is amply shown the third quality We have noted in Dominican preaching: a most zealous piety towards the Mother of God. It is said that the Pontiff knew by Divine revelation of the victory of Lepanto achieved at that very moment when through the Catholic world the pious sodalities of the Holy Rosary implored the aid of Mary in that formula initiated by the Founder of the Friar Preachers and diffused far and wide by his followers. Loving the Blessed Virgin as a Mother, confiding chiefly in her patronage, Dominic started his battle for the Faith. The Albigenses, among other dogmas, attacked both the Divine maternity and the virginity of Mary. He, attacked by them with every insult, defending to the utmost of his strength the sanctity of these dogmas, he invoked the help of the Virgin Mother herself, frequently using these words: "Make me worthy to praise thee, Sacred Virgin; give me strength against thine enemies." How pleased was the Heavenly Queen with her pious servant may be easily gathered from this, that she used his ministry to teach the Most Holy Rosary to the Church, the Spouse of her Son; that prayer which, being both vocal and mental, in the contemplation especially of the mysteries of religion, while the Lord's Prayer is fifteen times repeated together with as many decades of the Hail Mary, is most adapted to fostering widely piety and every virtue. Rightly, then, did Dominic order his followers, in preaching to the people, to inculcate frequently this manner of

prayer, the utility of which he had experienced. He knew, on the one hand, Mary's authority with her Son to be such that whatever graces he confers on men she has their distribution and apportionment. On the other hand, he knew that she is of a nature so kind and merciful that, seeing that it is her custom to succor the miserable of her own accord, it is impossible she should refuse the petitions of those who pray to her. Accordingly the Church, which is wont to salute her "the Mother of Grace and the Mother of Mercy," has so found her always, but especially in answer to the Rosary. Wherefore the Roman Pontiffs have let pass no occasion of commending the Rosary and have enriched it with Apostolic Indulgences.

12. Now the Dominican institutes, as you yourself understand, Venerable Brethren, are not less opportune at present than in the time of their Founder. How many today, destitute of the bread of life, that is, celestial doctrine, are, as it were, in a state of starvation. How many, deceived by the appearance of truth, are turned away from the Faith by a variety of errors. That priests may minister fittingly to the necessities of all these by the Word of God, how zealous must they be for the salvation of others and how grounded in solid knowledge. How many, too, ungrateful and forgetful children of the Church, are turned away from the Vicar of Jesus Christ by ignorance of facts or by a perverse will whom it is necessary to lead to the common bosom. For the healing of these and every other ill how much do we need the maternal patronage!

13. The Dominicans have, therefore, an almost boundless field in which to labor for the common welfare. Wherefore to all of them We wish that in these centenary celebrations they renew their devotion to the holy example of their founder, and make themselves daily more worthy of such a father. In this let a fitting lead be taken by his children of the First Order, and let them be

ever more zealous in preaching the Divine Word, such as may give men a reverence for the successor of St. Peter and a devotion to the Virgin Mother, and may spread and defend the truth. But from the Dominican Tertiaries, too, the Church looks for much, if they study to conform themselves to the spirit of their patriarch, in the instruction of the rude and unskilled in Christian doctrine and morality. In this We hope they will be assiduous, as it is a matter of great consequence for the good of souls. Finally, We wish this to be a special care of the Dominicans-the spread and frequent use of the Rosary among Christian people. We make this exhortation in these troublous times, following our predecessor, Leo XIII, and should it bear fruit this centenary celebration will not have been in vain.

Meanwhile, as an augury of the Divine gifts and a proof of Our benevolence, We impart the Apostolic Blessing, Venerable Brethren, to you, your clergy, and your people.

Given at Rome, at St. Peter's, June 29, Feast of the Prince of the Apostles, 1921, the seventh year of Our Pontificate.

Enchiridion Sanctissimi Rosarii

Ingravescentibus Malis
On The Rosary

Encyclical of Pope Pius XI

September 29, 1937

To the Venerable Brethren, Patriarchs, Primates, Archbishops, Bishops, and other Ordinaries in Peace and Communion with the Holy See.

More than once have We asserted--and We recently repeated this in the Encyclical Letter Divini Redemptoris (Acta Ap. Sedis, 1937, Vol. XXIX, p. 65)--that there is no remedy for the ever-growing evils of our times except a return to Our Lord Jesus Christ and to His most holy precepts. Truly, only He "hath the words of eternal life" (Cf. John, vi, 69), and individuals and society can only fall into immediate and miserable ruin if they ignore the majesty of God and repudiate His Law.

2. However, anyone who studies with diligence the records of the Catholic Church will easily recognize that the true patronage of the Virgin Mother of God is linked with all the annals of the Christian name. When, in fact, errors everywhere diffused were bent upon rending the seamless robe of the Church and upon throwing the Catholic world into confusion, our fathers turned with confident soul to her "alone who destroys all heresies in the world" (Roman Breviary), and the victory won through her brought the return of tranquillity.

3. When the impious Mohammedan power, trusting in its powerful fleet and war-hardened armies, threatened the peoples of Europe with ruin and slavery, then--upon the suggestion of the Sovereign

Pontiff--the protection of the heavenly Mother was fervently implored and the enemy was defeated and his ships sunk. Thus the Faithful of every age, both in public misfortune and in private need, turn in supplication to Mary, the benignant, so that she may come to their aid and grant help and remedy against sorrows of body and soul. And never was her most powerful aid hoped for in vain by those who besought it with pious and trustful prayer.

4. But also in our day, dangers no less grave than in the past beset civil and religious society. In fact, because the supreme and eternal authority of God, which commands and forbids, is despised and completely repudiated by men, the result is that the consciousness of Christian duty is weakened, and that faith becomes tepid in souls or entirely lost, and his afterward affects and ruins the very basis of human society.

5. Thus on the one hand are seen citizens intent on an atrocious struggle among themselves because some are provided with abundant riches and others must gain bread for themselves and their dear ones by the sweat of their brows. Indeed, as we all know, in some regions the evil had reached such a pitch that it seeks to destroy all private right of property, so that everything might be shared in common.

6. On the other hand, there are not lacking men who declare that they honor and exalt, above all, the power of the State. They say they must use every means to assure civil order and enforce authority, and pretend that only thus are they able totally to repulse the execrable theories of the Communists. However, they despise the light of evangelic wisdom and endeavor to revive the errors of the pagans and their way of life.

7. To this is added the clever and lamentable sect of those who, denying and hating God, declare themselves the enemies of the

Eternal, and who insinuate themselves everywhere. They discredit and uproot all religious belief from souls. Finally, they trample on every human and Divine right. And while they cast scorn on the hope of heavenly reward, they incite men to seek, even by illicit means, false earthly happiness, and therefore drive them with brazen temerity to the dissolution of the social order, causing disorder, cruel rebellions and even the conflagration of civil war.

8. Nevertheless, Venerable Brethren, though such great and numerous evils hang over us, and others still greater are to be feared for the future, we must not lose heart nor let the confident hope that rests solely on God become fainter. He who "made the nations of the earth for health" (Cf. Wisdom i, 14) without doubt will not let those perish whom He has redeemed with His Precious Blood, nor will He abandon His Church. But rather, as We said in the beginning, shall We beseech God through the mediation of the Blessed Virgin, so acceptable to Him, since, to use the words of St. Bernard: "Such is the will of God, who has wished that we should have all things through Mary." (Sermon on the Nativity of the Blessed Virgin Mary.)

9. Among the various supplications with which we successfully appeal to the Virgin Mother of God, the Holy Rosary without doubt occupies a special and distinct place. This prayer, which some call the Psalter of the Virgin or Breviary of the Gospel and of Christian life, was described and recommended by Our Predecessor of happy memory, Leo XIII, with these vigorous passages: "Very admirable is this crown interwoven with the angelic salutation which is interposed in the Sunday prayer, and unites with it the obligation of interior meditation. It is an excellent manner of prayer . . . and very useful for the attainment of immortal life" (Acta Leonis, 1898, Vol. XVIII, pp. 154, 155).

10. And this can well be deduced from the very flowers that form this mystic garland. What prayers in fact can be found more adaptable and holy? This first is that which our Divine Redeemer Himself pronounced when His disciples asked Him: "Lord, teach us to pray" (Luke xi, 1); a very holy supplication which both offers us the way--as far as it is possible for us--to render glory to God, and also takes into account all the necessities of our body and soul. How can the Eternal Father, when prayed to with the very words of His Son, refuse to come to our aid?

11. The other prayer is the Angelic Salutation, which begins with the eulogies of the Archangel Gabriel and of St. Elizabeth, and ends with that very pious supplication by which we beg the help of the Blessed Virgin now and at the hour of our death. To these invocations, said aloud, is added the contemplation of the sacred mysteries, through which they place, as it were, under our eyes the joys, sorrows and triumphs of Jesus Christ and of His Mother, so that we receive relief and comfort in our sorrows. Following those most holy examples, we ascend to the happiness of the heavenly country by steps of ever higher virtue.

12. This practice of piety, Venerable Brethren, admirably diffused by St. Dominic, not without the heavenly suggestion and inspiration of the Virgin Mother of God, is without doubt easy for all, even for the ignorant and the simple. But those wander from the path of truth who consider this devotion merely an annoying formula repeated with monotonous singsong intonation, and refuse it as good only for children and silly women!

13. In this regard, it is to be noted that both piety and love, though always renewing the same words, do not always repeat the same thing but always express something new issuing from the intimate sentiment of devotion. And besides, this mode of prayer has the

perfume of evangelic simplicity and requires humility of spirit; and, if we disdain humility, as the Divine Redeemer teaches, it will be impossible for us to enter the heavenly kingdom: "Amen, I say to you, unless you become as little children you shall not enter the kingdom of heaven" (Matt. xviii, 3).

14. Nevertheless, if men in our century, with its derisive pride, refuse the Holy Rosary, there is an innumerable multitude of holy men of every age and every condition who have always held it dear. They have recited it with great devotion, and in every moment they have used it as a powerful weapon to put the demons to flight, to preserve the integrity of life, to acquire virtue more easily, and in a word to attain real peace among men.

15. Nor are there lacking men famous as to doctrine and wisdom who, although intensely occupied in scientific study and researches, never even for a day fail to pray fervently on bended knee, before the image of the Virgin, in this most pious form. Thus kings and princes, however burdened with most urgent occupations and affairs, made it their duty to recite the Rosary.

16. This mystic crown, then, not only is found in and glides through the hands of the poor, but it also is honored by citizens of every social rank. And We do not wish here to pass over in silence the fact that the Blessed Virgin herself, even in our times, has solicitously recommended this manner of prayer, when she appeared and taught it to the innocent girl in the Grotto of Lourdes.

17. Therefore why should We not hope for every grace if We supplicate Our Heavenly Mother in this manner with due disposition and holiness? We desire very earnestly, Venerable Brethren, that the Holy Rosary should be recited in a special

manner in the month of October and with increased devotion both in the churches and in homes.

18. And so much the more must it be done since the enemies of the Divine Name--that is, those who have rebelled against and denied and scorned the Eternal God--spread snares for the Catholic Faith and the liberty due to the Church, and finally rebel with insane efforts against divine and human rights, to send mankind to ruin and perdition. Through efficacious recourse to the Virgin Mother of God, they may be finally bent and led to penance and return to the straight path, trusting to the care and protection of Mary.

19. The Holy Virgin who once victoriously drove the terrible sect of the Albigenses from Christian countries, now suppliantly invoked by us, will turn aside the new errors, especially those of Communism, which reminds us in many ways, in its motives and misdeeds, of the ancient ones.

20. And as in the times of the Crusades, in all Europe there was raised one voice of the people, one supplication; so today, in all the world, the cities, and even the smallest villages, united with courage and strength, with filial and constant insistence, the people seek to obtain from the great Mother of God the defeat of the enemies of Christian and human civilization, to the end that true peace may shine again over tired and erring men.

21. If, then, all will do this with due disposition, with great faith and with fervent piety, it is right to hope that as in the past, so in our day, the Blessed Virgin will obtain from her divine Son that the waves of the present tempests be calmed and that a brilliant victory crown this rivalry of Christians in prayer.

22. The Holy Rosary, besides, not only serves admirably to overcome the enemies of God and Religion, but is also a stimulus and spur to the practice of evangelic virtues which it injects and cultivates in our souls. Above all, it nourishes the Catholic Faith, which flourishes again by due meditation on the sacred mysteries, and raises minds to the truth revealed to us by God.

23. Every one can understand how salutary it is, especially in our times wherein sometimes a certain annoyance of the things of the spirit is felt even among the Faithful, and a dislike, as it were, for the Christian doctrine. Therefore, revive the hope of immortal welfare, while the triumph of Jesus Christ and of His Mother, meditated on by us in the last part of the Rosary, shows us Heaven open and invites us to the conquest of the Eternal Country.

24. Thus while an unbridled longing for the things of this earth has penetrated into the hearts of mortals and each one more ardently longs for the short-lived riches and ephemeral pleasures, all feel a fruitful call back to the heavenly treasures "where thieves do not break in and neither rust nor moth doth consume" (Matt. xii, 33), and to the wealth that will never perish.

25. And the charity which has been weakened and cooled in many, how can it fail to be rekindled into love in the souls of those who recall with a full heart the tortures and death of our Redeemer and the afflictions of His Sorrowful Mother? From this charity towards God, then, there cannot but rise a more intense love of one's neighbor if one dwells on the labors and sorrows that Our Lord suffered for all, reinstating the lost inheritance of the children of God.

26. Therefore see to it, Venerable Brethren, that such a fruitful practice shall be more diffused, more highly esteemed by all, and that common piety be increased. Through your work and that of

the priests who help you in the care of souls, its praises and advantages shall be preached and repeated to the Faithful of every social class.

27. From it, the young will draw fresh energy with which to control the rebellious tendencies to evil and to preserve intact the stainless purity of the soul; also in it, the old will again find repose, relief and peace from their anxious cares. To those who devote themselves to Catholic Action may it be a spur to impel them to a more fervent and active work of apostolate; and to all those who suffer in any way, especially the dying, may it bring comfort and increase the hope of eternal happiness.

28. The fathers and mothers of families particularly must give an example to their children, especially when, at sunset, they gather together after the day's work, within the domestic walls, and recite the Holy Rosary on bended knees before the image of the Virgin, together fusing voice, faith and sentiment. This is a beautiful and salutary custom, from which certainly there cannot but be derived tranquillity and abundance of heavenly gifts for the household.

29. When very frequently We receive newly married couples in audience and address paternal words to them, We give them rosaries, We recommend these to them earnestly, and We exhort them, citing Our own example, not to let even one day pass without saying the Rosary, no matter how burdened they may be with many cares and labors.

30. For these reasons, Venerable Brethren, We have thought fit earnestly to exhort you, and through you, all the Faithful, to carry out this pious practice. Nor do We doubt that you, listening, with your usual response to Our paternal invitation will bring about abundant fruits once more.

31. And in addressing this Encyclical to you, another motive impels Us. We wish that, together with Us, Our many children in Jesus shall unite and render thanks to the Mother of God for the better health We have happily regained.

32. This grace, as We have had occasion to write (Cf. Letter to Cardinal E. Pacelli, Osservatore Romano, September 5, 1937), We attribute to the special intercession of the virgin of Lisieux, St. Therese of the Child Jesus. But We know, though, that everything comes to us from Almighty God through the hands of Our Lady.

33. And lastly, as there has been launched in the public press with rash insolence, a very grave injury to the Blessed Virgin, We cannot do less than profit by this occasion to offer, together with the Episcopate and the people of that nation which venerates Mary as "Queen of the Kingdom of Poland," and with the homage of our piety, due reparation to the august Queen, and denounce to the whole world this sacrilege committed with impunity, as a painful and unworthy thing.

34. Meanwhile, with a full heart We impart to you, Venerable Brethren, and to the flock entrusted to the care of each of you, the Apostolic Blessing as an augury of heavenly graces and in token to Our Paternal benevolence.

Given at Castel Gandolfo, near Rome, on the 29th day of the month of September, on the Feast of the Dedication of St. Michael the Archangel, in the year 1937, the sixteenth of Our Pontificate.

Ingruentium Malorum
On Reciting The Rosary

Encyclical of Pope Pius XII

September 15, 1951

To Our Venerable Brethren, Patriarchs, Primates, Archbishops, Bishops, and other Ordinaries having Peace and Communion with the Apostolic See.

Venerable Brethren, Greetings and Apostolic Benediction.

Ever since We were raised, by the design of Divine Providence, to the supreme Chair of Peter, We have never ceased, in the face of approaching evils, to entrust to the most powerful protection of the Mother of God the destiny of the human family, and, to this end, as you know, We have from time to time written letters of exhortation.

2. You know, Venerable Brethren, with what zeal and with what spontaneous and unanimous approval the Christian people everywhere have answered Our invitation. It has been magnificently testified many times by the great demonstration of faith and love towards the august Queen of Heaven, and above all, by that manifestation of universal joy which, last year, Our eyes had the pleasure to behold, when, in St. Peter's Square, surrounded by an immense multitude of the faithful, We solemnly proclaimed the Assumption into Heaven of the Virgin Mary, body and soul.

3. The recollection of these things comes back pleasantly to Us and encourages Us to trust firmly in Divine Mercy. However, at present, We do not lack reasons for profound sorrow which torment and sadden Our paternal heart.

4. You know well, Venerable Brethren, the calamitous conditions of our times. Fraternal harmony among nations, shattered for so long a time, has not yet been re-established everywhere. On the contrary, here and there, we see souls upset by hatred and rivalry, while threats of new bloody conflicts still hover over the peoples. To this, one must add the violent storm of persecution, which in many parts of the world, has been unleashed against the Church, depriving it of its liberty, saddening it very cruelly with calumnies and miseries of all kinds, and making the blood of martyrs flow again and again.

5. To what and to how many snares are the souls of so many of Our sons submitted in those areas to make them reject the Faith of their fathers, and to make them break, most wretchedly, the bond of union which links them to this Apostolic See! Nor can We pass over in silence a new crime to which, with utmost sorrow, We want earnestly to draw not only your attention, but the attention of the clergy, of parents, and even of public authorities. We refer to the iniquitous campaign that the impious lead everywhere to harm the shining souls of children. Not even the age of innocence has been spared, for, alas, there are not lacking those who boldly dare to snatch from the mystical garden of the Church even the most beautiful flowers, which constitute the hope of religion and society. Considering this, one cannot be surprised if peoples groan under the weight of the Divine punishment, and live under the fear of even greater calamities.

6. However, consideration of a situation so pregnant with dangers must not depress your souls, Venerable Brethren. Instead, mindful of that Divine teaching: "Ask and it shall be given to you; seek and you shall find; knock, and it shall be opened to you" (Luke 11, 9), fly with greater confidence to the Mother of God. There, the Christian people have always sought chief refuge in the hour of

danger, because "she has been constituted the cause of salvation for the whole human race" (St. Irenaeus).

7. Therefore, we look forward with joyful expectation and revived hope to the coming month of October, during which the faithful are accustomed to flock in larger numbers to the churches to raise their supplications to Mary by means of the Holy Rosary.

8. O Venerable Brethren, We desire that, this year, this prayer should be offered with such greater fervor of heart as is demanded by the increased urgency of the need. We well know the Rosary's powerful efficacy to obtain the maternal aid of the Virgin. By no means is there only one way to pray to obtain this aid. However, We consider the Holy Rosary the most convenient and most fruitful means, as is clearly suggested by the very origin of this practice, heavenly rather than human, and by its nature. What prayers are better adapted and more beautiful than the Lord's prayer and the angelic salutation, which are the flowers with which this mystical crown is formed? With meditation of the Sacred Mysteries added to the vocal prayers, there emerges another very great advantage, so that all, even the most simple and least educated, have in this a prompt and easy way to nourish and preserve their own faith.

9. And truly, from the frequent meditation on the Mysteries, the soul little by little and imperceptibly draws and absorbs the virtues they contain, and is wondrously enkindled with a longing for things immortal, and becomes strongly and easily impelled to follow the path which Christ Himself and His Mother have followed. The recitation of identical formulas repeated so many times, rather than rendering the prayer sterile and boring, has on the contrary the admirable quality of infusing confidence in him who prays and brings to bear a gentle compulsion on the motherly Heart of Mary.

10. Let it be your particular care, O Venerable Brethren, that the faithful, on the occasion of the coming month of October, should use this most fruitful form of prayer with the utmost possible zeal, and that it become always more esteemed and more diligently recited.

11. Through your efforts, the Christian people should be led to understand the dignity, the power, and the excellence of the Rosary.

12. But it is above all in the bosom of the family that We desire the custom of the Holy Rosary to be everywhere adopted, religiously preserved, and ever more intensely practiced. In vain is a remedy sought for the wavering fate of civil life, if the family, the principle and foundation of the human community, is not fashioned after the pattern of the Gospel.

13. To undertake such a difficult duty, We affirm that the custom of the family recitation of the Holy Rosary is a most efficacious means. What a sweet sight--most pleasing to God-- when, at eventide, the Christian home resounds with the frequent repetition of praises in honor of the august Queen of Heaven! Then the Rosary, recited in common, assembles before the image of the Virgin, in an admirable union of hearts, the parents and their children, who come back from their daily work. It unites them piously with those absent and those dead. It links all more tightly in a sweet bond of love, with the most Holy Virgin, who, like a loving mother, in the circle of her children, will be there bestowing upon them an abundance of the gifts of concord and family peace.

14. Then the home of the Christian family, like that of Nazareth, will become an earthly abode of sanctity, and, so to speak, a sacred temple, where the Holy Rosary will not only be the particular prayer which every day rises to heaven in an odor of sweetness, but will also form the most efficacious school of Christian discipline

and Christian virtue. This meditation on the Divine Mysteries of the Redemption will teach the adults to live, admiring daily the shining examples of Jesus and Mary, and to draw from these examples comfort in adversity, striving towards those heavenly treasures "where neither thief draws near, nor moth destroys" (Luke 12, 33). This meditation will bring to the knowledge of the little ones the main truths of the Christian Faith, making love for the Redeemer blossom almost spontaneously in their innocent hearts, while, seeing, their parents kneeling before the majesty of God, they will learn from their very early years how great before the throne of God is the value of prayers said in common.

15. We do not hesitate to affirm again publicly that We put great confidence in the Holy Rosary for the healing of evils which afflict our times. Not with force, not with arms, not with human power, but with Divine help obtained through the means of this prayer, strong like David with his sling, the Church undaunted shall be able to confront the infernal enemy, repeating to him the words of the young shepherd: "Thou comest to me with a sword, and a spear, and with a shield; but I come to thee in the name of the Lord of Hosts, the God of armies . . . and all this assembly shall know that the Lord saveth not with sword and spear, for this is his battle, and he will deliver you into our hands" (I Kings 17, 45-47)

16. For this reason, We earnestly desire, Venerable Brethren, that all the faithful, following your example and your exhortation should respond solicitously to Our paternal exhortation, uniting their hearts and their voices with the same ardor of charity. If the evils and the assaults of the wicked increase, so likewise must the piety of all good people increase and become ever more vigorous. Let them strive to obtain from our most loving Mother, especially through this form of prayer, that better times may quickly return for the Church and society.

17. May the very powerful Mother of God, moved by the prayers of so many of her sons, obtain from her only Son--let us all beseech her-- that those who have miserably wandered from the path of truth and virtue may, with new fervor, find it again; that hatred and rivalry, which are the sources of discord and every kind of mishap, may be put aside, and that a true, just, and genuine peace may shine again upon individuals, families, peoples, and nations. And, finally, may she obtain that, after the rights of the Church have been secured in accord with justice, its beneficent influence may penetrate without obstacle the hearts of men, the social classes, and the avenues of public life so as to join people among themselves in brotherhood and lead them to that prosperity which regulates, preserves, and coordinates the rights and duties of all without harming anyone and which daily makes for greater and greater mutual friendship and collaboration.

18. Venerable Brethren and beloved sons, while you entwine new flowers of supplication by reciting your Rosary, do not forget those who languish miserably in prison camps, jails, and concentration camps. There are among them, as you know, also Bishops dismissed from their Sees solely for having heroically defended the sacred rights of God and the Church. There are sons, fathers and mothers, wrested from their homes and compelled to lead unhappy lives far away in unknown lands and strange climates.

19. Just as We love them with a special charity and embrace them with the love of a father, so must you, with a brotherly love which the Christian religion nourishes and enkindles, join with us before the altar of the Virgin Mother of God and recommend them to her motherly heart. She doubtlessly will, with exquisite sweetness, revive in their hearts the hope of eternal reward and, We firmly believe, will not fail to hasten the end of so much sorrow.

20. We do not doubt that you, O Venerable Brethren, with your usual burning zeal, will bring to the knowledge of your clergy and people these Our paternal exhortations in a way which will appear most appropriate to you.

21. Feeling certain that Our sons throughout the world will respond willingly and generously to this Our invitation, We impart, from the fullness of Our heart and as an evidence of Our favor and an augury of heavenly graces, to each and every one of you, to the flock entrusted to each of you and particularly to those who, especially during the month of October, will devoutly recite the holy Rosary according to Our intentions, Our Apostolic Blessing.

Given in Rome, at St. Peter's, the 15th day of September, the Feast of the Seven Sorrows of the Virgin Mary, in the Year 1951, the 13th of Our pontificate.

Enchiridion Sanctissimi Rosarii

Grata Recordatio
On The Rosary

Encyclical of Pope John XXIII

September 26, 1959

To the Venerable Brethren, the Patriarchs, Primates, Archbishops, Bishops, and other Local Ordinaries in Peace and Communion with the Apostolic See. Venerable Brethren, Greetings and Apostolic Benediction.

Among the pleasant recollections of Our younger days are the Encyclicals which Pope Leo XIII used to write to the whole Catholic world as the month of October drew near, in order to urge the faithful to devout recitation of Mary's rosary during that month in particular. [Cf. the following encyclical epistles in "Acta Leonis XIII," in the volumes indicated: Supremi Apostolatus," III, 280 ff.; "Superiore anno," IV, 123 ff., "Quamquam pluries," IX, 175 ff., "Octobri mense," XI, 299 ff.; "Magnae Dei Matris," XII, 221 ff.; "Laetitiae sanctae," XIII, 283 ff.; "Iucunda semper," XIV, 30s ff., "Adiutricem populi," XV, 300 ff., "Fidentem piumque," XVI, 278 ff.; "Augustissimae Virginis," XVII, 285 ff; "Diuturni temporis," XVIII, 153 ff]

2. These Encyclicals had varied contents, but they were all very wise, vibrant with fresh inspiration, and directly relevant to the practice of the Christian life. In strong and persuasive terms they exhorted Catholics to pray to God in a spirit of faith through the intercession of Mary, His Virgin Mother, by reciting the holy rosary. For the rosary is a very commendable form of prayer and meditation. In saying it we weave a mystic garland of Ave Maria's, Pater Noster's, and Gloria Patri's. And as we recite these vocal

prayers, we meditate upon the principal mysteries of our religion; the Incarnation of Jesus Christ and the Redemption of the human race are proposed, one event after another, for our consideration.

3. These pleasant memories of Our younger days have not faded or vanished as the years of Our life have passed. On the contrary, We want to declare in complete frankness and simplicity that the years have made Mary's rosary all the dearer to Us. We never fail to recite it each day in its entirety and We intend to recite it with particular devotion during the coming month.

4. During Our first year as pope--a year which is almost over--We have several times had occasion to urge the clergy and laity to public and private prayer. But today We make this same request with even greater emphasis and earnestness, for reasons which this Encyclical will set out very briefly.

5. This coming October will mark the end of the first year since the saintly departure of Our predecessor, Pius XII, from this mortal life in which he had distinguished himself by so many glorious achievements.

6. Twenty days after his death, We, though all unworthy, were raised to the Sovereign Pontificate in accord with God's mysterious designs.

7. One pope bequeathed, as it were, to another pope, as a sacred legacy, the care of the whole Christian flock; with the same pastoral concern each of them declared his paternal love for all mankind.

8. These two events--the one full of sorrow, the other full of joy-- attest clearly to the world that while all things human gradually decline and decay, the Roman Pontificate withstands the rush of centuries, even though the visible Heads of the Church must, one

Enchiridion Sanctissimi Rosarii

after another, leave this mortal exile as they complete the span of days which God in His providence has set for them.

9. But all Christians should turn their thoughts to the late Pope Pius XII and to his lowly successor, in whom Blessed Peter continues his eternal mission as supreme pastor, and they should address this prayer to God: "To preserve in holy religion the Pope, and all clerics in holy orders, we beg Thee hear us." [Litany of the Saints]

10. And now it is a pleasure also to recall that this same Predecessor of Ours urged all the faithful to pious recitation of the rosary during October in the Encyclical Ingruentium malorum. [On September 15, 1951: AAS 43 (1951) 577 ff] We would like to repeat one admonition ["Ibid.," 578-579] from that Encyclical: "Turn in spirit with ever greater confidence to the Virgin Mother of God, the constant refuge of Christians in adversity, since she 'has been made a source of salvation for the human race.'" [St. Irenaeus, "Adv. haer." III, 22 Migne, PG VII, 959]

11. On October 11, 1959, We shall have the great pleasure of presenting mission crucifixes to a large group of Catholic missionaries who are about to leave their beloved homes and undertake the heavy responsibility of bringing the light of Christianity to distant people. [A precis of the talk given on this occasion appears in TPS, v. 6 (1959) 46] On the same day, in the afternoon, We are scheduled to visit the North American College on the Janiculum and there joyously celebrate with its superiors, faculty, and seminarians the completion of that college's first century. [A translation of the talk given on this occasion appears in TPS, v. 6 (1959), 37-42]

12. Although these two celebrations fall only by coincidence on the same day, they have the same meaning and importance: in all that

she does the Catholic Church is motivated by heaven's inspiration and drawn on by the principles and precepts of eternal truth; all of her children contribute with a selfless and dynamic will to mutual respect, the fraternal union of mankind, and solid peace.

13. These young men present such a wonderful spectacle that We must be optimistic for the future. They have overcome many obstacles and inconveniences and given themselves to God that other men might gain Christ, [Cf. Phil. 3:8] whether in foreign lands as yet untouched by the light of truth or in those immense, noisy, and busy cities in which the pace of daily activity, rapid as a whirlwind, sometimes makes souls wither and become content with earthly goods. From the lips of their elders, who have labored long in the same cause, comes the ardent prayer of the Prince of the Apostles: "Grant to thy servants to speak thy word with all boldness." [Cf. Acts 4:29]

14. We trust that the apostolic labors of these young men will be commended to the Virgin Mary in your devout prayers through the month of October.

15. There is another matter also which compels Us to ask that the Sacred College of Cardinals, you, Venerable Brethren, all priests and nuns, the sick and disabled, our innocent children, and all Christians address earnest and suppliant prayers to Jesus Christ and His most loving Mother. It is this: that those who, in great measure, hold the future of nations in their hands consider attentively the dangerous pass to which our age has come. Be these nations large or small, their legitimate rights and their inheritance of spiritual riches are sacred and must be safeguarded.

16. Therefore We pray God that their rulers may carefully weigh and consider the causes of dissension and endeavor in good faith to remove them. They must, above all, realize that war (God keep it

from us!) can have only one result, vast ruins everywhere, and thus cannot be the object of anyone's reliance. They must adapt to the needs of men of today the laws which regulate the state and society and which bind together nations and classes of society. They must be mindful of the eternal laws which come from God and are the bases and pivots of all government. Finally, they must be ever aware that the individual souls of men are created by God and destined to possess and enjoy Him.

17. It must also be remarked that there are current today certain schools of thought and philosophy and certain attitudes toward the practical conduct of life which cannot possibly be reconciled with the teachings of Christianity. This impossibility We shall never cease from asserting in firm and unambiguous, though also calm terms. But God wishes the welfare of men and of nations! [Cf. Wisd. 1, 14]

18. And so We hope that men will set aside those sterile postulates and assumptions, hard as rock and just as inflexible, which rise from a way of thinking and acting that is infected with laicism and materialism, and that they will find a complete cure in that sound doctrine which experience makes more certain with every day that passes. We mean that doctrine which attests that God is the author of life and its laws, that He is guarantor of the rights and dignity of the human person. God then is "our refuge and our Redemption." [Sacred Liturgy]

19. Our thoughts turn to all the lands of this earth. We see all mankind striving for a better future; We see the awakening of a mysterious force, and this permits Us to hope that men will be drawn by a right conscience and a sense of duty to advance the real interests of human society. That this goal may be realized in the fullest sense--that is, with the triumph of the kingdom of truth,

justice, peace, and charity--We exhort all Our children in Christ to be "of one heart and one soul" [Acts 4:32] and to pour out ardent prayers in October to our Queen in heaven and our loving Mother, reflecting upon the words of the Apostle: "In all things we suffer tribulation, but we are not distressed; we are sore pressed, but we are not destitute; we endure persecution, but we are not forsaken; we are cast down, but we do not perish; always bearing about in our body the dying of Jesus, so that the life also of Jesus may be made manifest in our bodily frame." [2 Cor. 4:8-10]

20. Before We conclude this Encyclical We also wish to ask you, Venerable Brethren, to recite Mary's rosary through the month of October with particular devotion, and to entreat the Virgin Mother of God in suppliant prayer, for another intention which is dear to Our heart: that the Roman Synod may bring many blessings and benefits upon this city; that the forthcoming Ecumenical Council, in which you will participate by your presence and your advice, will add wondrous growth to the universal Church; and that the renewed vigor of all the Christian virtues which We hope this Council will produce will also serve as an invitation and incentive to reunion for Our Brethren and children who are separated from this Apostolic See.

21. In this fond hope, We lovingly impart the Apostolic Blessing to each and every one of you, Venerable Brethren, to the flocks entrusted to your care, and to those individuals especially who will respond to Our entreaties in a devout and zealous spirit.

22. Given at Rome, in St. Peter's, on the 26th day of September, in the year 1959, the first of Our Pontificate.

Christi Matri
On Praying the Rosary During the Month of October

Encyclical of Pope Paul VI

September 15, 1966

To Our Venerable Brothers the Patriarchs, Primates, Archbishops, Bishops and other Local Ordinaries in Peace and Communion with the Apostolic See.

Venerable Brothers, Health and Apostolic Benediction.

It is a solemn custom of the faithful during the month of October to weave the prayers of the Rosary into mystical garlands for the Mother of Christ. Following in the footsteps of Our predecessors, We heartily approve this, and We call upon all the sons of the church to offer special devotions to the Most Blessed Virgin this year. For the danger of a more serious and extensive calamity hangs over the human family and has increased, especially in parts of eastern Asia where a bloody and hard-fought war is raging. So We feel most urgently that We must once again do what We can to safeguard peace. We are also disturbed by what We know to be going on in other areas, such as the growing nuclear armaments race, the senseless nationalism, the racism, the obsession for revolution, the separations imposed upon citizens, the nefarious plots, the slaughter of innocent people. All of these can furnish material for the greatest calamity.

2. Like Our immediate predecessors, We seem to have received a special task from God in His providence to work patiently and constantly to preserve and strengthen peace. This task, as is evident, arises from the fact that We have been entrusted with the

governing of the whole Church, which, as a "sign lifted up to the nations,"[Cf.Is 11. 12] does not serve political ends but rather must bring the truth and grace of Jesus Christ, its divine Founder, to mankind.

3. Indeed, from the very beginning of Our apostolic ministry, We have omitted no effort to further the cause of peace in the world through prayers, entreaties and exhortations. As you well remember, last year We flew to North America to speak about the most desirable blessing of peace at the General Assembly of the United Nations, before a very distinguished audience representing almost every nation.[Cf. TPS XI, 47-57] We warned against allowing some to be inferior to others, and against allowing some to attack others. Instead, all should devote their efforts and zeal to the establishment of peace. Even afterwards, moved by apostolic concern, We did not stop urging those upon whom this great matter depends to ward off from mankind the frightful disaster that might result.

4. Now once again We raise Our voice "with a loud cry and with tears,"[Heb 5.7] urgently beseeching those who rule over nations to do everything they can to see to it that the conflagration spreads no farther but rather is completely extinguished. We do not doubt that all men who want what is right and honorable--whatever their race, color, religion and social class--feel the same as We do.

5. Therefore, let all those responsible bring about the necessary conditions for the laying down of arms before the possibility of doing so is taken away by the pressure of events. Those in whose hands rests the safety of the human race should realize that in this day and age they have a very grave obligation in conscience. Mindful of their own nation, of the world, of God and history, let them examine their own consciences. Let them realize that in the

future their names will be blessed if they wisely succeed in complying with this exhortation.

6. In the name of the Lord We cry out to them to stop. Men must come together and get down to sincere negotiations. Things must be settled now, even at the cost of some loss of inconvenience, for later they may have to be settled at the cost of immense harm and enormous slaughter that cannot even be imagined now. But this peace must be based on justice and freedom for mankind, and must take into account the rights of individuals and communities. Otherwise it will be fluid and unstable.

7. As We say all this with deep emotion and an anxious heart, it is only right for Us to do as Our supreme pastoral care urges, and ask for help from heaven. Peace, which "is such a great good that even among earthly, mortal things, there is nothing more pleasant to hear, nothing more ardently desired, and finally nothing better to be found,"[St. Augustine, The City of God, 19. 11: PL 41. 637] has to be sought from Him who is the Prince of Peace.[Is 9. 6] But since the Church, in uncertain and anxious times, has been accustomed to have recourse to that most ready intercessor, her Mother Mary, We have good reason to direct Our own attention and yours, venerable brethren, and that of all the Christian faithful, to her. For as St. Irenaeus says, she "has become the cause of 180 salvation for the whole human race."[Adversus Haereses 3. 22: PG 7. 959]

8. Nothing seems more appropriate and valuable to Us than to have the prayers of the whole Christian family rise to the Mother of God, who is invoked as the Queen of Peace, begging her to pour forth abundant gifts of her maternal goodness in midst of so many great trials and hardships. We want constant and devout prayers to be offered to her whom We declared Mother of the Church, its

spiritual parent, during the celebration of the Second Vatican Council, thereby winning the applause of the Fathers and of the Catholic world, and confirming a point of traditional doctrine. For the Mother of the Savior is, as St. Augustine teaches, "surely the mother of His members,"[De Sanct. virg. 6: PL 40. 399] and St. Anselm, to mention only one other, agrees with him in these words: "What could ever be deemed more suitable than for you to be the mother of those whose father and brother Christ deigned to become?"[Or. 47: PL 158. 945] She was called "most truly the mother of the Church" by Our predecessor Leo XIII.[Encyc. Letter Adjutricem populi christiani, Sept. 5, 1895: Acta Leon. 15, 1896, p. 302] Hence We have good reason to place our trust in her in the midst of this terrible disorder.

9. If evils increase, the devotion of the People of God should also increase. And so, venerable brothers, We want you to take the lead in urging and encouraging people to pray ardently to our most merciful mother Mary by saying the Rosary during the month of October, as We have already indicated. This prayer is well-suited to the devotion of the People of God, most pleasing to the Mother of God and most effective in gaining heaven's blessings. The Second Vatican Council recommended use of the Rosary to all the sons of the Church, not in express words but in unmistakable fashion in this phrase: "Let them value highly the pious practices and exercises directed to the Blessed Virgin and approved over the centuries by the magisterium."[Dogmatic Constitution on the Church, no. 67 [cf. TPS X, 399]]

10. As the history of the Church makes clear, this very fruitful way of praying is not only efficacious in warding off evils and preventing calamities, but is also of great help in fostering Christian life. "It nourishes the Catholic faith which readily takes on new life from a timely commentary on the sacred mysteries, and it turns

minds toward the truths that have been taught us by God."[Pius XI, Encyc. Letter Ingravescentibus malis, Sept. 29, 1937: AAS 29 (1937), 378]

11. And so during the month of October, dedicated to Our Lady of the Rosary, prayers and petitions should be increased, so that through her intercession the dawn of true peace may shine forth to men. This means true religious peace too, for unfortunately, not everyone is allowed to profess his religion freely in this age. In particular, We want October 4th--the day on which, as We mentioned earlier, We went last year to the United Nations for the sake of peace--to be celebrated throughout the whole Catholic world this year as a Day of Prayer for Peace. It will be up to you, venerable brethren, in the light of your own commendable devotion and on the basis of the obvious importance of this matter, to prescribe sacred ceremonies in which priests, religious and the faithful--especially boys and girls in the flower of their innocence, and the sick and others who are suffering--can all ask the help of the Mother of God and of the Church.

12. On that day We Ourself will go to St. Peter's Basilica, to the tomb of the Prince of the Apostles, to offer special prayers to the Virgin Mother of God, protector of Christians and mediator for peace. In this way heaven will be moved, in a sense, by the one voice of the Church resounding from all the continents on the earth. For as St. Augustine says, "Amid the various languages of men, the faith of the heart speaks one tongue.[Enarr. in Ps. 54. 11: PL 36. 636]

13. Look down with maternal clemency, Most Blessed Virgin, upon all your children. Consider the anxiety of bishops who fear that their flocks will be tormented by a terrible storm of evils. Heed the anguish of so many people, fathers and mothers of families who are

uncertain about their future and beset by hardships and cares. Soothe the minds of those at war and inspire them with "thoughts of peace." Through your intercession, may God, the avenger of injuries, turn to mercy. May He give back to nations the tranquillity they seek and bring them to a lasting age of genuine prosperity.

14. With confidence that the exalted Mother of God will graciously hear Our humble prayer, We lovingly impart the apostolic blessing to you, venerable brethren, and to the clergy and people committed to your care.

Given at St. Peter's, Rome, on the 15th day of September, in the year 1966, the fourth of Our pontificate.

Enchiridion Sanctissimi Rosarii

Marialis Cultus
Apostolic Exhortation For The Right Ordering And Development Of Devotion To The Blessed Virgin Mary

Encyclical of Pope Paul VI

February 2, 1974

To All Bishops in Peace and Communion with the Apostolic See Venerable Brothers: Health and the Apostolic Blessing: From the moment when we were called to the See of Peter, we have constantly striven to enhance devotion to the Blessed Virgin Mary, not only with the intention of interpreting the sentiments of the Church and our own personal inclination but also because, as is well known, this devotion forms a very noble part of the whole sphere of that sacred worship in which there intermingle the highest expressions of wisdom and of religion[1] and which is therefore the primary task of the People of God.

1) Cf. Lactantius, Divinae Institutiones IV, 3, 6-10: CSEL 19, p. 279.

Precisely with a view to this task, we have always favored and encouraged the great work of liturgical reform promoted by the Second Vatican Ecumenical Council; and it has certainly come about not without a particular design of divine Providence that the first conciliar document which together with the venerable Fathers we approved and signed in Spiritu Sancto was the Constitution Sacrosanctum concilium. The purpose of this document was precisely to restore and enhance the liturgy and to make more fruitful the participation of the faithful in the sacred mysteries.[2] From that time onwards, many acts of our pontificate have been directed towards the improvement of divine worship, as is demonstrated by the fact that we have promulgated in these recent years numerous books of the Roman Rite, restored according to the principles and norms of the same Council. For this we profoundly thank the Lord, the giver of all good things, and we are grateful to the episcopal conferences and individual bishops who in various ways have collaborated with us in the preparation of these books.

2) Cf. II Vatican Council, Constitution on the Sacred Liturgy, Sacrosanctum Concilium, 1-3, 11, 21, 48: AAS 56 (1964), pp. 97-98, 102-103, 105-106, 113.

We contemplate with joy and gratitude the work so far accomplished and the first positive results of the liturgical renewal, destined as they are to increase as this renewal comes to be understood in its basic purposes and correctly applied. At the same time we do not cease with vigilant solicitude to concern ourself with whatever can give orderly fulfillment to the renewal of the worship with which the Church in spirit and truth (cf. Jn. 4:24) adores the Father and the Son and the Holy Spirit, "venerates with special love Mary the most holy Mother of God"[3] and honors with religious devotion the memory of the martyrs and the other saints.

3) II Vatican Council, Constitution on the Sacred Liturgy, Sacrosanctum Concilium, 103: AAS 56 (1964), p. 125.

The development, desired by us, of devotion to the Blessed Virgin Mary is an indication of the Church's genuine piety. This devotion fits--as we have indicated above--into the only worship that is rightly called "Christian," because it takes its origin and effectiveness from Christ, finds its complete expression in Christ, and leads through Christ in the Spirit to the Father. In the sphere of worship this devotion necessarily reflects God's redemptive plan, in which a special form of veneration is appropriate to the singular place which Mary occupies in that plan.[4] Indeed every authentic development of Christian worship is necessarily followed by a fitting increase of veneration for the Mother of the Lord. Moreover, the history of piety shows how "the various forms of devotion towards the Mother of God that the Church has approved within the limits of wholesome and orthodox doctrine"[5] have developed in harmonious subordination to the worship of Christ, and have gravitated towards this worship as to their natural and necessary point of reference. The same is happening in our own time. The Church's reflection today on the mystery of Christ and on her own nature has led her to find at the root of the former and as a culmination of the latter the same figure of a woman: the Virgin Mary, the Mother of Christ and the Mother of the Church. And the increased knowledge of Mary's mission has become joyful veneration of her and adoring respect for the wise plan of God, who has placed within His family (the Church), as in every home, the figure of a Woman, who in a hidden manner and in a spirit of service watches over that family "and carefully looks after it until the glorious day of the Lord."[6]

4) Cf. II Vatican Council, Dogmatic Constitution on the Church, Lumen Gentium, 66: AAS 57 (1965), p. 65.5) Ibid.6) Votive Mass of the Blessed Virgin Mary, Mother of the Church, Preface.

In our time, the changes that have occurred in social behavior, people's sensibilities, manners of expression in art and letters and in the forms of social communication have also influenced the manifestations of religious sentiment. Certain practices of piety that not long ago seemed suitable for expressing the religious sentiment of individuals and of Christian communities seem today inadequate or unsuitable because they are linked with social and cultural patterns of the past. On the other hand, in many places people are seeking new ways of expressing the unchangeable relationship of creatures with their Creator, of children with their Father. In some people this may cause temporary confusion. But anyone who with trust in God reflects upon these phenomena discovers that many tendencies of modern piety (for example, the interiorization of religious sentiment) are meant to play their part in the development of Christian piety in general and devotion to the Blessed Virgin in particular. Thus our own time, faithfully attentive to tradition and to the progress of theology and the sciences, will make its contribution of praise to her whom, according to her own prophetical words, all generations will call blessed (cf. Lk. 1:48).We therefore judge it in keeping with our apostolic service, venerable Brothers, to deal, in a sort of dialogue, with a number of themes connected with the place that the Blessed Virgin occupies in the Church's worship. These themes have already been partly touched upon by the Second Vatican Council[7] and also by ourself,[8] but it is useful to return to them in order to remove doubts and, especially, to help the development of that devotion to the Blessed Virgin which in the Church is motivated by the Word of God and practiced in the Spirit of Christ.

7) Cf. II Vatican Council, Dogmatic Constitution of the Church, Lumen Gentium, 66-67: AAS 57 (1965), pp. 65-66, Constitution on the Sacred Liturgy, Sacrosanctum Concilium, 103: AAS 56 (1964), p. 125.8) Apostolic Exhortation, Signum Magnum: AAS 59 (1967), pp. 465-475.

We therefore wish to dwell upon a number of questions concerning the relationship between the sacred liturgy and devotion to the Blessed Virgin (I), to offer considerations and directives suitable for favoring the development of that devotion (II) and finally to put forward a number of reflections intended to encourage the restoration, in a dynamic and more informed manner, of the recitation of the Rosary, the practice of which was so strongly recommended by our predecessors and is so widely diffused among the Christian people (III).1. As we prepare to discuss the place which the Blessed Virgin Mary occupies in Christian worship, we must first turn our attention to the sacred liturgy. In addition to its rich doctrinal content, the liturgy has an incomparable pastoral effectiveness and a recognized exemplary value for the other forms of worship. We would have liked to take into consideration the various liturgies of the East and the West, but for the purpose of this document we shall dwell almost exclusively on the books of the Roman Rite. In fact, in accordance with the practical norms issued by the Second Vatican Council,[9] it is this Rite alone which has been the object of profound renewal. This is true also in regard to expressions of veneration for Mary. This Rite therefore deserves to be carefully considered and evaluated.

9) Cf. II Vatican Council, Constitution on the Sacred Liturgy, Sacrosanctum Concilium, 3: AAS 56 (I[964]), p. 98.

2. The reform of the Roman liturgy presupposed a careful restoration of its General Calendar. This Calendar is arranged in such a way as to give fitting prominence to the celebration on appropriate days of the work of salvation. It distributes throughout the year the whole mystery of Christ, from the Incarnation to the expectation of His return in glory,[10] and thus makes it possible in a more organic and closely-knit fashion to include the commemoration of Christ's Mother in the annual cycle of the mysteries of her Son.

10) Cf. II Vatican Council, ibid., 102: AAS 56 (1964), p. 125.

3. For example, during Advent there are many liturgical references to Mary besides the Solemnity of December 8, which is a joint

celebration of the Immaculate Conception of Mary, of the basic preparation (cf. Is. 11:1, 10) for the coming of the Savior and of the happy beginning of the Church without spot or wrinkle.[11] Such liturgical references are found especially on the days from December 17 to 24, and more particularly on the Sunday before Christmas, which recalls the ancient prophecies concerning the Virgin Mother and the Messiah[12] and includes readings from the Gospel concerning the imminent birth of Christ and His precursor.[13]

11) Cf. Roman Missal restored by Decree of the Sacred Ecumenical II Vatican Council, promulgated by authority of Pope Paul VI typical edition, MCMLXX, 8 December, Preface.12) Roman Missal, restored by Decree of the Sacred Ecumenical II Vatican Council promulgated by authority of Pope Paul VI, Orio Lectionum Missae. typical edition MCMLXIX, p. 8, First Reading (Year A: Is 7:10-14: "Behold a Virgin shall conceive"; Year B: 2 Sam 7:1-15: 8b-11. 16: "The throne of David shall be established for ever before the face of the Lord"; Year C: Mic 5:2-5a [Heb 1-4a]: "Out of you will be born for me the one who is to rule over Israel").13) Ibid., p. 8, Gospel (Year A: Mt 1:18-24: "Jesus is born of Mary who was espoused to Joseph. the son of David"; Year B: Lk 1:26-38: "You are to conceive and bear a son"; Year C: Lk 1:39-45: "Why should I be honoured with a visit from the Mother of my Lord?").

4. In this way the faithful, living in the liturgy the spirit of Advent, by thinking about the inexpressible love with which the Virgin Mother awaited her Son,[14] are invited to take her as a model and to prepare themselves to meet the Savior who is to come. They must be "vigilant in prayer and joyful in...praise."[15] We would also remark that the Advent liturgy, by linking the awaiting of the Messiah and the awaiting of the glorious return of Christ with the admirable commemoration of His Mother, presents a happy

balance in worship. This balance can be taken as a norm for preventing any tendency (as has happened at times in certain forms of popular piety) to separate devotion to the Blessed Virgin from its necessary point of reference--Christ. It also ensures that this season, as liturgy experts have noted, should be considered as a time particularly suited to devotion to the Mother of the Lord. This is an orientation that we confirm and which we hope to see accepted and followed everywhere.

14) Cf. Roman Missal, Advent Preface, II.15) Roman Missal, ibid.

5. The Christmas season is a prolonged commemoration of the divine, virginal and salvific motherhood of her whose "inviolate virginity brought the Savior into the world."[16] In fact, on the Solemnity of the Birth of Christ the Church both adores the Savior and venerates His glorious Mother. On the Epiphany, when she celebrates the universal call to salvation, the Church contemplates the Blessed Virgin, the true Seat of Wisdom and true Mother of the King, who presents to the Wise Men, for their adoration, the Redeemer of all peoples (cf. Mt. 2:11). On the Feast of the Holy Family of Jesus, Mary and Joseph (the Sunday within the octave of Christmas) the Church meditates with profound reverence upon the holy life led in the house at Nazareth by Jesus, the Son of God and Son of Man, Mary His Mother, and Joseph the just man (cf. Mt. 1:19).

16) Roman Missal, Eucharistic Prayer I, Communicantes for Christmas and its octave.

In the revised ordering of the Christmas period it seems to us that the attention of all should be directed towards the restored Solemnity of Mary the holy Mother of God. This celebration, placed on January 1 in conformity with the ancient indication of the liturgy of the City of Rome, is meant to commemorate the part played by Mary in this mystery of salvation. It is meant also to exalt the singular dignity which this mystery brings to the "holy Mother...through whom we were found worthy to receive the Author of life."[17] It is likewise a fitting occasion for renewing adoration of the newborn Prince of Peace, for listening once more to the glad tidings of the angels (cf. Lk. 2:14), and for imploring from God, through the Queen of Peace, the supreme gift of peace. It is for this reason that, in the happy concurrence of the Octave of Christmas and the first day of the year, we have instituted the World Day of Peace, an occasion that is gaining increasing support and already bringing forth fruits of peace in the hearts of many.

17) Roman Missal, 1 January, Entry antiphon and Collect.

6. To the two solemnities already mentioned (the Immaculate Conception and the Divine Motherhood) should be added the ancient and venerable celebrations of March 25 and August 15. For the Solemnity of the Incarnation of the Word, in the Roman Calendar the ancient title--the Annunciation of the Lord--has been deliberately restored, but the feast was and is a joint one of Christ and of the Blessed Virgin: of the Word, who becomes "Son of Mary" (Mk. 6:3), and of the Virgin, who becomes Mother of God. With regard to Christ, the East and the West, in the inexhaustible riches of their liturgies, celebrate this solemnity as the commemoration of the salvific "fiat" of the Incarnate Word, who, entering the world, said: "God, here I am! I am coming to obey Your will" (cf. Heb. 10:7; Ps. 39:8-9). They commemorate it as the beginning of the redemption and of the indissoluble and wedded union of the divine nature with human nature in the one Person of the Word. With regard to Mary, these liturgies celebrate it as a feast of the new Eve, the obedient and faithful virgin, who with her generous "fiat" (cf. Lk. 1:38) became through the working of the Spirit the Mother of God, but also the true Mother of the living,

and, by receiving into her womb the one Mediator (cf: 1 Tm. 2:5), became the true Ark of the Covenant and true Temple of God. These liturgies celebrate it as a culminating moment in the salvific dialogue between God and man, and as a commemoration of the Blessed Virgin's free consent and cooperation in the plan of redemption. The solemnity of August 15 celebrates the glorious Assumption of Mary into heaven. It is a feast of her destiny of fullness and blessedness, of the glorification of her immaculate soul and of her virginal body, of her perfect configuration to the Risen Christ, a feast that sets before the eyes of the Church and of all mankind the image and the consoling proof of the fulfillment of their final hope, namely, that this full glorification is the destiny of all those whom Christ has made His brothers, having "flesh and blood in common with them" (Heb. 2:14; cf. Gal. 4:4). The Solemnity of the Assumption is prolonged in the celebration of the Queenship of the Blessed Virgin Mary, which occurs seven days later. On this occasion we contemplate her who, seated beside the King of ages, shines forth as Queen and intercedes as Mother.[18] These four solemnities, therefore, mark with the highest liturgical rank the main dogmatic truths concerning the handmaid of the Lord.

18) Cf. Roman Missal, 22 August, Collect.

7. After the solemnities just mentioned, particular consideration must be given to those celebrations that commemorate salvific events in which the Blessed Virgin was closely associated with her Son. Such are the feasts of the Nativity of Our Lady (September 8), "the hope of the entire world and the dawn of salvation"[19]; and the Visitation (May 31), in which the liturgy recalls the "Blessed Virgin Mary carrying her Son within her,"[20] and visiting Elizabeth to offer charitable assistance and to proclaim the mercy of God the Savior.[21] Then there is the commemoration of Our Lady of

Sorrows (September 15), a fitting occasion for reliving a decisive moment in the history of salvation and for venerating, together with the Son "lifted up on the cross, His suffering Mother."[22]

19) Roman Missal, 8 September, Prayer after Communion .20) Roman Missal, 31 May, Collect.21) Cf. ibid., Collect and Prayer over the gifts.22) Cf. Roman Missal, 15 September, Collect.

The feast of February 2, which has been given back its ancient name, the Presentation of the Lord, should also be considered as a joint commemoration of the Son and of the Mother, if we are fully to appreciate its rich content. It is the celebration of a mystery of salvation accomplished by Christ, a mystery with which the Blessed Virgin was intimately associated as the Mother of the Suffering Servant of Yahweh, as the one who performs a mission belonging to ancient Israel, and as the model for the new People of God, which is ever being tested in its faith and hope by suffering and persecution (cf. Lk. 2:21-35).8. The restored Roman Calendar gives particular prominence to the celebrations listed above, but it also includes other kinds of commemorations connected with local devotions and which have acquired a wider popularity and interest (e.g., February 11, Our Lady of Lourdes; August 5, the Dedication of the Basilica of St. Mary Major). Then there are others, originally celebrated by particular religious families but which today, by reason of the popularity they have gained, can truly be considered ecclesial (e.g., July 16, Our Lady of Mount Carmel; October 7, Our Lady of the Rosary). There are still others which, apart from their apocryphal content, present lofty and exemplary values and carry on venerable traditions having their origin especially in the East (e.g., the Immaculate Heart of the Blessed Virgin, celebrated on the Saturday following the second Sunday after Pentecost).9. Nor must one forget that the General Roman Calendar does not include all celebrations in honor of the Blessed Virgin. Rather, it is for individual Calendars to include, with fidelity to liturgical norms but with sincere endorsement, the Marian feasts proper to the different local Churches. Lastly, it should be noted that frequent commemorations of the Blessed Virgin are possible through the use of the Saturday Masses of our Lady. This is an ancient and simple commemoration and one that is made very adaptable and varied by the flexibility of the modern Calendar and the number of formulas provided by the Missal.10. In this Apostolic Exhortation we do not intend to examine the whole content of the new Roman Missal. But by reason of the work of evaluation that we have undertaken to carry out in regard to the revised books of the Roman Rite,[23] we would like to mention some of the aspects and themes of the Missal. In the first place, we are pleased to note how the Eucharistic Prayers of the Missal, in admirable harmony with the Eastern liturgies,[24] contain a significant commemoration of the Blessed Virgin. For example, the ancient Roman Canon, which commemorates the Mother of the Lord in terms full of doctrine and devotional inspiration: "In union with the whole Church we honor Mary, the ever-virgin Mother of Jesus Christ our Lord and God." In a similar way the recent Eucharistic Prayer III expresses with intense supplication the desire of those praying to share with the Mother the inheritance of sons: "May he make us an everlasting gift to you [the Father] and enable us to share in the inheritance of your saints, with Mary, the Virgin Mother of God." This daily commemoration, by reason of its place at the heart of the divine Sacrifice, should be considered a particularly expressive form of the veneration that the Church pays to the "Blessed of the Most High" (cf. Lk. 1:28).

23) Cf. 1, p. 15.24) From among the many anaphoras cf. the following which are held in special honour by the Eastern rites: Anaphora Marci Evangelistae: Prex Eucharistica, ed. A. Hanggi-l.

Pahl, Fribourg, Editions Universitaires, 1968, p. 107; Anaphora Iacobi fratris Domini graeca ibid., p. 257; Anaphora Iannis Chrysostomi, ibid., p. 229.

11. As we examine the texts of the revised Missal we see how the great Marian themes of the Roman prayerbook have been accepted in perfect doctrinal continuity with the past. Thus, for example, we have the themes of Mary's Immaculate Conception and fullness of grace, the divine motherhood, the unblemished and fruitful virginity, the Temple of the Holy Spirit, Mary's cooperation in the work of her Son, her exemplary sanctity, merciful intercession, Assumption into heaven, maternal Queenship and many other themes. We also see how other themes, in a certain sense new ones, have been introduced in equally perfect harmony with the theological developments of the present day. Thus, for example, we have the theme of Mary and the Church, which has been inserted into the texts of the Missal in a variety of aspects, a variety that matches the many and varied relations that exist between the Mother of Christ and the Church. For example, in the celebration of the Immaculate Conception which texts recognize the beginning of the Church, the spotless Bride of Christ.[25] In the Assumption they recognize the beginning that has already been made and the image of what, for the whole Church, must still come to pass.[26] In the mystery of Mary's motherhood they confess that she is the Mother of the Head and of the members--the holy Mother of God and therefore the provident Mother of the Church.[27]

25) Cf. Roman Missal, 8 December, Preface.26) Cf. Roman Missal, 15 August, Preface.27) Cf. Roman Missal, 1 January, Prayer after Communion.

When the liturgy turns its gaze either to the primitive Church or to the Church of our own days it always finds Mary. In the primitive

Church she is seen praying with the apostles[28]; in our own day she is actively present, and the Church desires to live the mystery of Christ with her: "Grant that your Church which with Mary shared Christ's passion may be worthy to share also in his resurrection."[29] She is also seen represented as a voice of praise in unison with which the Church wishes to give glory to God: "...with her [Mary] may we always praise you."[30] And since the liturgy is worship that requires a way of living consistent with it, it asks that devotion to the Blessed Virgin should become a concrete and deeply-felt love for the Church, as is wonderfully expressed in the prayer after Communion in the Mass of September 15: "...that as we recall the sufferings shared by the Blessed Virgin Mary, we may with the Church fulfill in ourselves what is lacking in the sufferings of Christ."

28) Cf. Roman Missal, Common of the Blessed Virgin Mary, 6, Paschaltide, Collect.29) Roman Missal, 15 September, Collect.30) Roman Missal, 31 May Collect. On the same lines is the Preface of the Blessed Virgin Mary, II: "We doe well... in celebrating the memory of the Virgin Mary... to glorify your love for us in the words of her song of thanksgiving."

12. The Lectionary is one of the books of the Roman Rite that has greatly benefited from the post-conciliar reform, by reason both of its added texts and of the intrinsic value of these texts, which contain the ever-living and efficacious word of God (cf. Heb. 4:12). This rich collection of biblical texts has made it possible to arrange the whole history of salvation in an orderly three-year cycle and to set forth more completely the mystery of Christ. The logical consequence has been that the Lectionary contains a larger number of Old and New Testament readings concerning the Blessed Virgin. This numerical increase has not however been based on random choice: only those readings have been accepted which in different

ways and degrees can be considered Marian, either from the evidence of their content or from the results of careful exegesis, supported by the teachings of the magisterium or by solid Tradition. It is also right to observe that these readings occur not only on feasts of the Blessed Virgin but are read on many other occasions, for example on certain Sundays during the liturgical year,[31] in the celebration of rites that deeply concern the Christian's sacramental life and the choices confronting him,[32] as also in the joyful or sad experiences of his life on earth.[33]

31) Cf. Lectionary, III Sunday of Advent (Year C: Zeph 3:14-18a): IV Sunday of Advent (cf. above footnote 12); Sunday within the octave of Christmas (Year A, Mt 2:13-15; 19-23; Year B: Lk 2:22-40; Year C: Lk 2:41-52) II Sunday after Christmas (Jn 1:1-18) VII Sunday after Easter (Year A: Acts 1:12-14); II Sunday of the Year C: Jn 1:1-12); X Sunday of the Year (Year B: Gen 3:9-15); XIV Sunday of the Year (Year B: Mk 6:1-6).32) Cf. Lectionary, the catechumenate and baptism of adults the Lord's Prayer (Second Reading, 2, Gal 4:4-7); Christian initiation outside the Easter Vigil (Gospel, 7, Jn 1:1-5; 9-14; 16-18); Nuptial Mass (Gospel, 7, Jn 2:1-11); Consecration of Virgins and religious profession (First Reading 7, Is 61:9-11; Gospel, 6, Mk 3:31-35; Lk 1:26-38 [cf. Ordo Consecrationis Virginum, 130; Ordo professionis religiosae, Pars altera, 145]).33) Cf. Lectionary, For refugees and exiles (Gospel, 1, Mt 2:13-15, 19-23); In thanksgiving (First Reading, 4, Zeph 3:14-15).

13. The Liturgy of the Hours, the revised book of the Office, also contains outstanding examples of devotion to the Mother of the Lord. These are to be found in the hymns--which include several masterpieces of universal literature, such as Dante's sublime prayer to the Blessed Virgin[34]--and in the antiphons that complete the daily Office. To these lyrical invocations there has been added the

well-known prayer Sub tuum praesidium, venerable for its antiquity and admirable for its content. Other examples occur in the prayers of intercession at Lauds and Vespers, prayers which frequently express trusting recourse to the Mother of mercy. Finally there are selections from the vast treasury of writings on our Lady composed by authors of the first Christian centuries, of the Middle Ages and of modern times.

34) Cf. La Divina Commedia, Paradiso XXXIII, 1-9, cf. Liturgy of the Hours, remembrance of Our Lady on Saturdays, Office of Reading, Hymn.

14. The commemoration of the Blessed Virgin occurs often in the Missal, the Lectionary and the Liturgy of the Hours--the hinges of the liturgical prayer of the Roman Rite. In the other revised liturgical books also expressions of love and suppliant veneration addressed to the Theotokos are not lacking. Thus the Church invokes her, the Mother of grace, before immersing candidates in the saving waters of baptism[35]; the Church invokes her intercession for mothers who, full of gratitude for the gift of motherhood, come to church to express their joy[36]; the Church holds her up as a model to those who follow Christ by embracing the religious life[37] or who receive the Consecration of Virgins.[38] For these people the Church asks Mary's motherly assistance.[39] The Church prays fervently to Mary on behalf of her children who have come to the hour of their death.[40] The Church asks Mary's intercession for those who have closed their eyes to the light of this world and appeared before Christ, the eternal Light[41]; and the Church, through Mary's prayers, invokes comfort upon those who in sorrow mourn with faith the departure of their loved ones.[42]

35) Ordo baptismi parvulorum, 48: Ordo initiationis christianae adultorum, 214.36) Cf. Rituale Romanum, Tit. Vll, cap. III, De benedictione mulieris post partum.37) Cf. Ordo professionis religiosae, Pars Prior, 57 and 67.38) Cf. Ordo consecrationis virginum, 16.39) Cf. Ordo professionis religiosae, Pars Prior, 62 and 142; Pars Altera, 67 and 158; Ordo consecrationis virginum, 18 and 20.40) Cf. Ordo unctionis infirmorum eorumque pastoralis curae, 143, 146, 147, 15041) Cf. Roman Missal, Masses for the Dead, For dead brothers and sisters, relations and benefactors, Collect.42) Cf. Ordo exsequiarum, 226.

15. The examination of the revised liturgical books leads us to the comforting observation that the postconciliar renewal has, as was previously desired by the liturgical movement, properly considered the Blessed Virgin in the mystery of Christ, and, in harmony with tradition, has recognized the singular place that belongs to her in Christian worship as the holy Mother of God and the worthy Associate of the Redeemer. It could not have been otherwise. If one studies the history of Christian worship, in fact, one notes that both in the East and in the West the highest and purest expressions of devotion to the Blessed Virgin have sprung from the liturgy or have been incorporated into it. We wish to emphasize the fact that the veneration which the universal Church today accords to blessed Mary is a derivation from and an extension and unceasing increase of the devotion that the Church of every age has paid to her, with careful attention to truth and with an ever watchful nobility of expression. From perennial Tradition kept alive by reason of the uninterrupted presence of the Spirit and continual attention to the Word, the Church of our time draws motives, arguments and incentives for the veneration that she pays to the Blessed Virgin. And the liturgy, which receives approval and strength from the magisterium, is a most lofty expression and an evident proof of this

living Tradition.16. In accordance with some of the guidelines of the Council's teaching on Mary and the Church, we now wish to examine more closely a particular aspect of the relationship between Mary and the liturgy--namely, Mary as a model of the spiritual attitude with which the Church celebrates and lives the divine mysteries. That the Blessed Virgin is an exemplar in this field derives from the fact that she is recognized as a most excellent exemplar of the. Church in the order of faith, charity and perfect union with Christ,[43] that is, of that interior disposition with which the Church, the beloved spouse, closely associated with her Lord, invokes Christ and through Him worships the eternal Father.[44]

43) Cf. II Vatican Council, Dogmatic Constitution on the Church, Lumen Gentium, 63: AAS 57 (1965), p. 64.44) Cf. II Vatican Council, Constitution on the Sacred Liturgy, Sacrosanctum Concilium, 7: AAS 56 (1964), pp. 100; 101.

17. Mary is the attentive Virgin, who receives the word of God with faith, that faith which in her case was the gateway and path to divine motherhood, for, as Saint Augustine realized, "Blessed Mary by believing conceived Him [Jesus] whom believing she brought forth."[45] In fact, when she received from the angel the answer to her doubt (cf. Lk. 1:34-37), "full of faith, and conceiving Christ in her mind before conceiving Him in her womb, she said, 'I am the handmaid of the Lord, let what you have said be done to me' (Lk. 1:38)."[46] It was faith that was for her the cause of blessedness and certainty in the fulfillment of the promise: "Blessed is she who believed that the promise made her by the Lord would be fulfilled" (Lk. 1:45). Similarly, it was faith with which she, who played a part in the Incarnation and was a unique witness to it, thinking back on the events of the infancy of Christ, meditated upon these events in her heart (cf. Lk. 2:19, 51). The Church also acts in this way,

especially in the liturgy, when with faith she listens, accepts, proclaims and venerates the word of God, distributes it to the faithful as the bread of life[47] and in the light of that word examines the signs of the times and interprets and lives the events of history.

45) Sermo 215, 4: PL 38, 1074.46) Ibid.47) Cf. II Vatican Council, Dogmatic Constitution on Divine Revelation, Dei Verbum, 21: AAS 58 (1966), pp. 827-828.

18. Mary is also the Virgin in prayer. She appears as such in the visit to the mother of the precursor, when she pours out her soul in expressions glorifying God, and expressions of humility, faith and hope. This prayer is the Magnificat (cf. Lk. 1:46-55), Mary's prayer par excellence, the song of the messianic times in which there mingles the joy of the ancient and the new Israel. As St. Irenaeus seems to suggest, it is in Mary's canticle that there was heard once more the rejoicing of Abraham who foresaw the Messiah (cf. Jn. 8:56)[48] and there rang out in prophetic anticipation the voice of the Church: "In her exultation Mary prophetically declared in the name of the Church: 'My soul proclaims the glory of the Lord....'"[49] And in fact Mary's hymn has spread far and wide and has become the prayer of the whole Church in all ages.

48) Cf. Adversus Haereses IV, 7, 1: PG 7, 1, 990-991; S. Ch. 100, t. II, pp. 454-458.49) Cf. Adversus Haereses III, 10, 2: PG 7, 1, 873; S. Ch. 34, p. 164.

At Cana, Mary appears once more as the Virgin in prayer: when she tactfully told her Son of a temporal need, she also obtained an effect of grace, namely, that Jesus, in working the first of His "signs," confirmed His disciples' faith in Him (cf. Jn. 2:1-12).Likewise, the last description of Mary's life presents her as praying. The apostles "joined in continuous prayer, together with several women, including Mary the mother of Jesus, and with his brothers" (Acts 1:14). We have here the prayerful presence of Mary in the early Church and in the Church throughout all ages, for, having been assumed into heaven, she has not abandoned her mission of intercession and salvation.[50] The title Virgin in prayer also fits the Church, which day by day presents to the Father the needs of her children, "praises the Lord unceasingly and intercedes for the salvation of the world."[51]

50) Cf. II Vatican Council, Dogmatic Constitution on the Church, Lumen Gentium, 62: AAS 57 (1965), p. 63.51) II Vatican Council, Constitution on the Sacred Liturgy, Sacrosanctum Concilium, 83: AAS 56 (1964), p. 121.

19. Mary is also the Virgin-Mother--she who "believing and obeying...brought forth on earth the Father's Son. This she did, not knowing man but overshadowed by the Holy Spirit."[52] This was a miraculous motherhood, set up by God as the type and exemplar of the fruitfulness of the Virgin-Church, which "becomes herself a mother.... For by her preaching and by baptism she brings forth to a new and immortal life children who are conceived by the power of the Holy Spirit and born of God."[53] The ancient Fathers rightly taught that the Church prolongs in the sacrament of Baptism the virginal motherhood of Mary. Among such references we like to recall that of our illustrious predecessor, Saint Leo the Great, who in a Christmas homily says: "The origin which [Christ] took in the womb of the Virgin He has given to the baptismal font: He has given to water what He had given to His Mother--the power of the Most High and the overshadowing of the Holy Spirit (cf. Lk. 1:35), which was responsible for Mary's bringing forth the Savior, has the same effect, so that water may regenerate the believer."[54] If we wished to go to liturgical sources, we could quote the beautiful Illatio of the Mozarabic liturgy: "The former

[Mary] carried Life in her womb; the latter [the Church] bears Life in the waters of baptism. In Mary's members Christ was formed; in the waters of the Church Christ is put on."[55]

52) II Vatican Council, Dogmatic Constitution on the Church, Lumen Gentium, 63: AAS 57 (1965), p. 64.53) Ibid., 64: AAS 57 (1965), p. 64.54) Tractatus XXV (In Nativitate Domini), 5: CCL 138, p. 123; S. Ch. 22 bis, p. 132; cf. also Tractatus XXIX (In Nativitate Domini), I: CCL ibid., p. 147; S. Ch ibid., p. 178; Tractatus LXIII (De Passione Domini) 6: CCL ibid., p. 386; S. Ch. 74, p. 82.55) M. Ferotin, Le Liber Mozarabicus Sacramentorum", col. 56.

20. Mary is, finally, the Virgin presenting offerings. In the episode of the Presentation of Jesus in the Temple (cf. Lk. 2:22-35), the Church, guided by the Spirit, has detected, over and above the fulfillment of the laws regarding the offering of the firstborn (cf. Ex. 13:11-16) and the purification of the mother (cf. Lv. 12:6-8), a mystery of salvation related to the history of salvation. That is, she has noted the continuity of the fundamental offering that the Incarnate Word made to the Father when He entered the world (cf. Heb. 15:5-7). The Church has seen the universal nature of salvation proclaimed, for Simeon, greeting in the Child the light to enlighten the peoples and the glory of the people Israel (cf. Lk. 2:32), recognized in Him the Messiah, the Savior of all. The Church has understood the prophetic reference to the Passion of Christ: the fact that Simeon's words, which linked in one prophecy the Son as "the sign of contradiction" (Lk. 2:34) and the Mother, whose soul would be pierced by a sword (cf. Lk. 2:35), came true on Calvary. A mystery of salvation, therefore, that in its various aspects orients the episode of the Presentation in the Temple to the salvific event of the cross. But the Church herself, in particular from the Middle Ages onwards, has detected in the heart of the Virgin taking her

Son to Jerusalem to present Him to the Lord (cf. Lk. 2:22) a desire to make an offering, a desire that exceeds the ordinary meaning of the rite. A witness to this intuition is found in the loving prayer of Saint Bernard: "Offer your Son, holy Virgin, and present to the Lord the blessed fruit of your womb. Offer for the reconciliation of us all the holy Victim which is pleasing to God."[56]

56) In Purificatione B. Mariae, Sermo III, 2: PL 183, 370; Sancti Bernardi Opera, ed. J. Leclercq-H. Rochais, vol. IV, Rome 1966, p. 342.

This union of the Mother and the Son in the work of redemption[57] reaches its climax on Calvary, where Christ "offered himself as the perfect sacrifice to God" (Heb. 9:14) and where Mary stood by the cross (cf. Jn. 19:25), "suffering grievously with her only-begotten Son. There she united herself with a maternal heart to His sacrifice, and lovingly consented to the immolation of this victim which she herself had brought forth"[58] and also was offering to the eternal Father.[59] To perpetuate down the centuries the Sacrifice of the Cross, the divine Savior instituted the Eucharistic Sacrifice, the memorial of His death and resurrection, and entrusted it to His spouse the Church,[60] which, especially on Sundays, calls the faithful together to celebrate the Passover of the Lord until He comes again.[61] This the Church does in union with the saints in heaven and in particular with the Blessed Virgin,[62] whose burning charity and unshakeable faith she imitates.

57) Cf. II Vatican Council, Dogmatic Constitution on the Church, Lumen Gentium, 57: AAS 57 (1965), p. 61.58) Ibid., 58: AAS 57 (1965), p. 61.59) Cf. Pius XII, Encyclical Letter Mystici Corporis: AAS 35 (1943), p. 247.60) Cf. II Vatican Council, Constitution on the Sacred Liturgy, Sacrosanctum Concilium, 47: AAS 56 (1964), p.

113.61) Ibid., 102, 106: AAS 56 (1964), pp. 125, 126.62) "...deign to remember all who have been pleasing to you throughout the ages the holy Father, Patriarchs. Prophets. Apostles... and the holy and glorious Mother of God and all the saints... may they remember our misery and poverty, and together with us may they offer you this great and unbloody sacrifice": Anaphora Iacobi fratris Domini syriaca: Prex Eucharistica ed. A. Hanggi-l. Pahl, Fribourg, Editions Universitaires, 1968, p. 274.

21. Mary is not only an example for the whole Church in the exercise of divine worship but is also, clearly, a teacher of the spiritual life for individual Christians. The faithful at a very early date began to look to Mary and to imitate her in making their lives an act of worship of God and making their worship a commitment of their lives. As early as the fourth century, St. Ambrose, speaking to the people, expressed the hope that each of them would have the spirit of Mary in order to glorify God: "May the heart of Mary be in each Christian to proclaim the greatness of the Lord; may her spirit be in everyone to exult in God."[63] But Mary is above all the example of that worship that consists in making one's life an offering to God. This is an ancient and ever new doctrine that each individual can hear again by heeding the Church's teaching, but also by heeding the very voice of the Virgin as she, anticipating in herself the wonderful petition of the Lord's Prayer--"Your will be done" (Mt. 6:10)--replied to God's messenger: "I am the handmaid of the Lord. Let what you have said be done to me" (Lk. 1:38). And Mary's "yes" is for all Christians a lesson and example of obedience to the will of the Father, which is the way and means of one's own sanctification.

63) Expositio Evangelii secundum Lucam, 11, 26: CSEL 32, IV, p. 55; S. Ch. 45, pp. 83-84.

22. It is also important to note how the Church expresses in various effective attitudes of devotion the many relationships that bind her to Mary: in profound veneration, when she reflects on the singular dignity of the Virgin who, through the action of the Holy Spirit, has become Mother of the Incarnate Word, in burning love, when she considers the spiritual motherhood of Mary towards all members of the Mystical Body; in trusting invocation, when she experiences the intercession of her advocate and helper[64]; in loving service, when she sees in the humble handmaid of the Lord the queen of mercy and the mother of grace; in zealous imitation, when she contemplates the holiness and virtues of her who is "full of grace" (Lk. 1:28); in profound wonder, when she sees in her, "as in a faultless model, that which she herself wholly desires and hopes to be"[65]; in attentive study, when she recognizes in the associate of the Redeemer, who already shares fully in the fruits of the Paschal Mystery, the prophetic fulfillment of her own future, until the day on which, when she has been purified of every spot and wrinkle (cf. Eph. 5:27), she will become like a bride arrayed for the bridegroom, Jesus Christ (cf. Rev. 21:2).

64) Cf. II Vatican Council, Dogmatic Constitution on the Church, Lumen Gentium, 62: AAS 57 (1965), p. 63.65) II Vatican Council, Constitution on the Sacred Liturgy Sacrosanctum Concilium, 103: AAS 56 (1964), p. 125.

23. Therefore, venerable Brothers, as we consider the piety that the liturgical Tradition of the universal Church and the renewed Roman Rite expresses towards the holy Mother of God, and as we remember that the liturgy through its pre-eminent value as worship constitutes the golden norm for Christian piety, and finally as we observe how the Church when she celebrates the sacred mysteries assumes an attitude of faith and love similar to that of the Virgin, we realize the rightness of the exhortation that the Second Vatican

Council addresses to all the children of the Church, namely "that the cult, especially the liturgical cult, of the Blessed Virgin be generously fostered."[66] This is an exhortation that we would like to see accepted everywhere without reservation and put into zealous practice.

66) II Vatican Council, Dogmatic Constitution on the Church, Lumen Gentium, 67: AAS 57 (1965), pp. 65-66.

24. The Second Vatican Council also exhorts us to promote other forms of piety side by side with liturgical worship, especially those recommended by the magisterium.[67] However, as is well known, the piety of the faithful and their veneration of the Mother of God has taken on many forms according to circumstances of time and place the different sensibilities of peoples and their different cultural traditions. Hence it is that the forms in which this devotion is expressed, being subject to the ravages of time, show the need for a renewal that will permit them to substitute elements that are transient, to emphasize the elements that are ever new and to incorporate the doctrinal data obtained from theological reflection and the proposals of the Church's magisterium. This shows the need for episcopal conferences, local churches, religious families and communities of the faithful to promote a genuine creative activity and at the same time to proceed to a careful revision of expressions and exercises of piety directed towards the Blessed Virgin. We would like this revision to be respectful of wholesome tradition and open to the legitimate requests of the people of our time. It seems fitting therefore, venerable Brothers, to put forward some principles for action in this field.

67) Cf. ibid.

25. In the first place it is supremely fitting that exercises of piety directed towards the Virgin Mary should clearly express the

Trinitarian and Christological note that is intrinsic and essential to them. Christian worship in fact is of itself worship offered to the Father and to the Son and to the Holy Spirit, or, as the liturgy puts it, to the Father through Christ in the Spirit. From this point of view worship is rightly extended, though in a substantially different way, first and foremost and in a special manner, to the Mother of the Lord and then to the saints, in whom the Church proclaims the Paschal Mystery, for they have suffered with Christ and have been glorified with Him.[68] In the Virgin Mary everything is relative to Christ and dependent upon Him. It was with a view to Christ that God the Father from all eternity chose her to be the all-holy Mother and adorned her with gifts of the Spirit granted to no one else. Certainly genuine Christian piety has never failed to highlight the indissoluble link and essential relationship of the Virgin to the divine Savior.[69] Yet it seems to us particularly in conformity with the spiritual orientation of our time, which is dominated and absorbed by the "question of Christ,"[70] that in the expressions of devotion to the Virgin the Christological aspect should have particular prominence. It likewise seems to us fitting that these expressions of devotion should reflect God's plan, which laid down "with one single decree the origin of Mary and the Incarnation of the divine Wisdom."[71] This will without doubt contribute to making piety towards the Mother of Jesus more solid, and to making it an effective instrument for attaining to full "knowledge of the Son of God, until we become the perfect man, fully mature with the fullness of Christ himself" (Eph. 4:13). It will also contribute to increasing the worship due to Christ Himself, since, according to the perennial mind of the Church authoritatively repeated in our own day,[72] "what is given to the handmaid is referred to the Lord; thus what is given to the Mother redounds to the Son; ...and thus what is given as humble tribute to the Queen becomes honor rendered to the King."[73]

68) Cf. II Vatican Council, Constitution on the Sacred Liturgy, Sacrosanctum Concilium, 104: AAS 56 (1964), pp. 125-126.69) Cf. II Vatican Council, Dogmatic Constitution on the Church, Lumen Gentium, 66: AAS 57 (1965), p. 65.70) Cf. Paul VI, Talk of 24 April 1970, in the church of Our Lady of Bonaria in Cagliari: AAS 62 (1970), p. 300.71) Pius IX, Apostolic Letter Ineffabilis Deus: Pii IX Pontificis Maximi Acta I, 1 Rome 1854, p. 599. Cf. also V. Sardi, La solenne definizione del dogma dell'Immacolato concepimento di Maria Sanctissima. Atti e documenti... Rome 1904-1905, vol. II, p. 302.72) Cf. II Vatican Council, Dogmatic Constitution on the Church, Lumen Gentium, 66: AAS 57 (1965), p. 65.73) S. Ildephonsus, De virginitate perpetua sanctae Mariae, chapter XII: PL 96, 108.

26. It seems to us useful to add to this mention of the Christological orientation of devotion to the Blessed Virgin a reminder of the fittingness of giving prominence in this devotion to one of the essential facts of the Faith: the Person and work of the Holy Spirit. Theological reflection and the liturgy have in fact noted how the sanctifying intervention of the Spirit in the Virgin of Nazareth was a culminating moment of the Spirit's action in the history of salvation. Thus, for example, some Fathers and writers of the Church attributed to the work of the Spirit the original holiness of Mary, who was as it were "fashioned by the Holy Spirit into a kind of new substance and new creature."[74] Reflecting on the Gospel texts--"The Holy Spirit will come upon you and the power of the Most High will cover you with his shadow" (Lk. 1:35) and "[Mary] was found to be with child through the Holy Spirit.... She has conceived what is in her by the Holy Spirit" (Mt. 1:18, 20)--they saw in the Spirit's intervention an action that consecrated and made fruitful Mary's virginity[75] and transformed her into the "Abode of the King" or "Bridal Chamber of the Word,"[76] the "Temple" or

"Tabernacle of the Lord,"[77] the "Ark of the Covenant" or "the Ark of Holiness,"[78] titles rich in biblical echoes. Examining more deeply still the mystery of the Incarnation, they saw in the mysterious relationship between the Spirit and Mary an aspect redolent of marriage, poetically portrayed by Prudentius: "The unwed Virgin espoused the Spirit,"[79] and they called her the "Temple of the Holy Spirit,"[80] an expression that emphasizes the sacred character of the Virgin, now the permanent dwelling of the Spirit of God. Delving deeply into the doctrine of the Paraclete, they saw that from Him as from a spring there flowed forth the fullness of grace (cf. Lk. 1:28) and the abundance of gifts that adorned her. Thus they attributed to the Spirit the faith, hope and charity that animated the Virgin's heart, the strength that sustained her acceptance of the will of God, and the vigor that upheld her in her suffering at the foot of the cross.[81] In Mary's prophetic canticle (cf. Lk. 1:46-55) they saw a special working of the Spirit who had spoken through the mouths of the prophets.[82] Considering, finally, the presence of the Mother of Jesus in the Upper Room, where the Spirit came down upon the infant Church (cf. Acts 1:12-14; 2:1-4), they enriched with new developments the ancient theme of Mary and the Church.[83] Above all they had recourse to the Virgin's intercession in order to obtain from the Spirit the capacity for engendering Christ in their own soul, as is attested to by Saint Ildephonsus in a prayer of supplication, amazing in its doctrine and prayerful power: "I beg you, holy Virgin, that I may have Jesus from the Holy Spirit, by whom you brought Jesus forth. May my soul receive Jesus through the Holy Spirit by whom your flesh conceived Jesus.... May I love Jesus in the Holy Spirit in whom you adore Jesus as Lord and gaze upon Him as your Son."[84]

74) Cf. II Vatican Council, Dogmatic Constitution on the Church, Lumen Gentium, 56: AAS 57 (1965), p. 60 and the authors mentioned in note 176 of the document.75) Cf. St. Ambrose, De Spiritu Sancto II, 37-38; CSEL 79 pp. 100-101; Cassian, De incarnatione Domini II, chapter II: CSEL 17, pp. 247-249; St. Bede, Homilia I, 3: CCL 122, p. 18 and p. 20.76) Cf. St. Ambrose, De institutione virginis, chapter XII, 79: PL 16 (ed. 1880), 339; Epistula 30, 3 and Epistula 42, 7: ibid., 1107 and 1175 Expositio evangelii secundum Lucam X, 132 S. Ch. 52 p. 200; S. Proctus of Constantinople, Oratio I, 1 and Oratio V, 3: PG 65, 681 and 720: St. Basil of Seleucia, Oratio XXXIX, 3: PG 85, 433; St. Andrew of Crete, Oratio IV: PG 97, 868; St. Germanus of Constantinople, Oratio III, 15: PG 98, 305.77) Cf. St. Jerome, Adversus Iovinianum I, 33: PL 23, 267; St. Ambrose, Epistula 63, 33: PL 16 (ed. 1880), 1249; De institutione virginis, chapter XVII, 105: ibid. 346; De Spiritu Sancto III, 79-80: CSEL 79, pp. 182-183; Sedulius, Hymn "A solis ortus cardine", verses 13-14: CSEL 10, p. 164; Hymnus Acathistos, Str. 23; ed. 1. B. Pitra, Analecta Sacra I, p. 261; St. Proctus of Constantinople, Oratio I, 3: PG 65, 648: Oratio II, 6: Ibid., 700; St. Basil of Seleucia, Oratio IV, In Nativitatem B. Mariae: PG 97, 868; St. John Damascene, Oratio IV, 10: PG 96, 677.78) Cf. Severus of Anthioch, Homilia 57; PO 8, pp. 357-358; Hesychius of Jerusalem, Homilia de sancta Maria Deipara, PG 93, 1464; Chrysippus of Jerusalem, Oratio in sanctam Mariam Deiparam, 2 PO 19, p. 338; St. Andrew of Crete, Oratio V: PG 97, 896: St. John Damascene, Oratio VI, 6: PG 96, 972.79) Liber Apotheosis, verses 571-572: CCL 126, p. 97.80) Cf. S. Isidore, De ortu et obitu Patrum, chapter LXVII, 111: PL 83, 148; St. Ildephonsus, De virginitate perpetua sanctae Mariae, chapter X: PL 96, 95; St. Bernard, In Assumptione B. Virginis Mariae: Sermo IV, 4: PL 183, 428; In Nativitate B. Virginis Mariae: II, Oratio ad Deum Filium: PL 145, 921; Antiphon "Beata Dei Genetrix Maria":

Corpus antiphonalium officii, ed. R. J. Hesbert, Rome 1970, vol. IV, n. 6314, p. 80.81) Cf. Paulus Diaconus, Homilia I, In Assumptione B. Mariae Virginis: PL 95, 1567; De Assumptione sanctae Mariae Virginis: Paschasio Radherto trib., 31, 42, 57, 83: ed. A. Ripberger, in "Spicilegium Friburgense", 9, 1962, pp. 72, 76, 84, 96-97; Eadmer of Canterbury, De excellentia Virginis Mariae, chapters IV-V: PL 159, 562-567: St. Bernard, In laudibus Virginis Matris, Homilia IV, 3: Sancti Bernardi Opera, ed. J. Leclercq-H. Rochais, IV Rome 1966, pp. 49-50.82) Cf. Origen, In Lucam Homilia VII, 3: PG 13, 1817; S. Ch. 87, p. 156; St. Cyril of Alexandria, Commentarius in Aggacum prophetam, chapter XIX: PG 71, 1060; St. Ambrose, De fide IV 9, 113-114: CSEL 78, pp. 197-198: Expositio evangelii secundum; Lucam II, 23 and 27-28: CSEL 32, IV, pp. 53-54 and 55-56; Severianus Galbalensis, In mundi creationem, Oratio VI, 10: PG 56, 497-498; Antipater of Bostra, Homilia in Sanctissimae Deiparae Annuntiationem, 16: PG 85, 1785.83) Cf. Eadmer of Canterbury, De excellentia Virginis Mariae, chapter VII: PL 159, 571: St. Amedeus of Lausanne, De Maria Virginea Matre, Homilia VII: PL 188, 1337; S. Ch. 72, p. 184.84) De virginitate perpetua sanctae mariae, chapter XII: PL 96, 106.

27. It is sometimes said that many spiritual writings today do not sufficiently reflect the whole doctrine concerning the Holy Spirit. It is the task of specialists to verify and weigh the truth of this assertion, but it is our task to exhort everyone, especially those in the pastoral ministry and also theologians, to meditate more deeply on the working of the Holy Spirit in the history of salvation, and to ensure that Christian spiritual writings give due prominence to His life-giving action. Such a study will bring out in particular the hidden relationship between the Spirit of God and the Virgin of Nazareth, and show the influence they exert on the Church. From a

more profound meditation on the truths of the Faith will flow a more vital piety.28. It is also necessary that exercises of piety with which the faithful honor the Mother of the Lord should clearly show the place she occupies in the Church: "the highest place and the closest to us after Christ."[85] The liturgical buildings of Byzantine rite, both in the architectural structure itself and in the use of images, show clearly Mary's place in the Church. On the central door of the iconostasis there is a representation of the Annunciation and in the apse an image of the glorious Theotokos. In this way one perceives how through the assent of the humble handmaid of the Lord mankind begins its return to God and sees in the glory of the all-holy Virgin the goal towards which it is journeying. The symbolism by which a church building demonstrates Mary's place in the mystery of the Church is full of significance and gives grounds for hoping that the different forms of devotion to the Blessed Virgin may everywhere be open to ecclesial perspectives.

85) II Vatican Council, Dogmatic Constitution on the Church, Lumen Gentium, 54: AAS 57 (1965), p. 59. Cf. Paulus VI, Allocutio ad Patres Conciliares habita, altera exacta Concilii Oecumenici Vaticani Secundi Sessione, 4 December 1963: AAS 56 (1964), p. 57.

The faithful will be able to appreciate more easily Mary's mission in the mystery of the Church and her preeminent place in the communion of saints if attention is drawn to the Second Vatican Council's references to the fundamental concepts of the nature of the Church as the Family of God, the People of God, the Kingdom of God and the Mystical Body of Christ.[86] This will also bring the faithful to a deeper realization of the brotherhood which unites all of them as sons and daughters of the Virgin Mary, "who with a mother's love has cooperated in their rebirth and spiritual formation,"[87] and as sons and daughters of the Church, since "we are born from the Church's womb we are nurtured by the Church's milk, we are given life by the Church's Spirit."[88] They will also realize that both the Church and Mary collaborate to give birth to the Mystical Body of Christ since "both of them are the Mother of Christ, but neither brings forth the whole [body] independently of the other."[89] Similarly the faithful will appreciate more clearly that the action of the Church in the world can be likened to an extension of Mary's concern. The active love she showed at Nazareth, in the house of Elizabeth, at Cana and on Golgotha--all salvific episodes having vast ecclesial importance--finds its extension in the Church's maternal concern that all men should come to knowledge of the truth (cf. 1 Tm. 2:4), in the Church's concern for people in lowly circumstances and for the poor and weak, and in her constant commitment to peace and social harmony, as well as in her untiring efforts to ensure that all men will share in the salvation which was merited for them by Christ's death. Thus love for the Church will become love for Mary, and vice versa, since the one cannot exist without the other, as St. Chromatius of Aquileia observed with keen discernment: "The Church was united... in the Upper Room with Mary the Mother of Jesus and with His brethren. The Church therefore cannot be referred to as such unless it includes Mary the Mother of our Lord, together with His brethren."[90] In conclusion, therefore, we repeat that devotion to the Blessed Virgin must explicitly show its intrinsic and ecclesiological content: thus it will be enabled to revise its forms and texts in a fitting way.

86) Cf. II Vatican Council, Dogmatic Constitution of the Church, Lumen Gentium, 6, 7-8. 9-11: AAS 57 (1965), pp. 8-9, 9-12, 12-21.87) Ibid., 63: AAS 57 (1965), p. 64.88) St. Cyprian, De Catholicae Ecclesiae unitate, 5: CSEL 3, p. 214.89) Isaac de Stella,

Sermo LI, In Assumptione B. Mariae: PL 194, 1863.90) Sermo XXX, 1: S. Ch. 164, p. 134.

29. The above considerations spring from an examination of the Virgin Mary's relationship with God--the Father and the Son and the Holy Spirit--and with the Church. Following the path traced by conciliar teaching,[91] we wish to add some further guidelines from Scripture, liturgy, ecumenism and anthropology. These are to be borne in mind in any revision of exercises of piety or in the creation of new ones, in order to emphasize and accentuate the bond which unites us to her who is the Mother of Christ and our Mother in the communion of saints.

91) Cf. II Vatican Council, Dogmatic Constitution on the Church, Lumen Gentium, 66-69: AAS 57 (1965), pp. 65-67.

30. Today it is recognized as a general need of Christian piety that every form of worship should have a biblical imprint. The progress made in biblical studies, the increasing dissemination of the Sacred Scriptures, and above all the example of Tradition and the interior action of the Holy Spirit are tending to cause the modern Christian to use the Bible ever increasingly as the basic prayerbook, and to draw from it genuine inspiration and unsurpassable examples. Devotion to the Blessed Virgin cannot be exempt from this general orientation of Christian piety[92]; indeed it should draw inspiration in a special way from this orientation in order to gain new vigor and sure help. In its wonderful presentation of God's plan for man's salvation, the Bible is replete with the mystery of the Savior, and from Genesis to the Book of Revelation, also contains clear references to her who was the Mother and associate of the Savior. We would not, however, wish this biblical imprint to be merely a diligent use of texts and symbols skillfully selected from the Sacred Scriptures. More than this is necessary. What is needed is that texts

of prayers and chants should draw their inspiration and their wording from the Bible, and above all that devotion to the Virgin should be imbued with the great themes of the Christian message. This will ensure that, as they venerate the Seat of Wisdom, the faithful in their turn will be enlightened by the divine word, and be inspired to live their lives in accordance with the precepts of Incarnate Wisdom.

92) Cf. II Vatican Council, Dogmatic Constitution on Divine Revelation, Dei Verbum, 25: AAS 58 (1966), pp. 829-830.

31. We have already spoken of the veneration which the Church gives to the Mother of God in the celebration of the sacred liturgy. However, speaking of the other forms of devotion and of the criteria on which they should be based we wish to recall the norm laid down in the Constitution Sacrosanctum concilium. This document, while wholeheartedly approving of the practices of piety of the Christian people, goes on to say: "...it is necessary however that such devotions with consideration for the liturgical seasons should be so arranged as to be in harmony with the sacred liturgy. They should somehow derive their inspiration from it, and because of its pre-eminence they should orient the Christian people towards it."[93] Although this is a wise and clear rule, its application is not an easy matter, especially in regard to Marian devotions, which are so varied in their formal expressions. What is needed on the part of the leaders of the local communities is effort, pastoral sensitivity and perseverance, while the faithful on their part must show a willingness to accept guidelines and ideas drawn from the true nature of Christian worship; this sometimes makes it necessary to change long-standing customs wherein the real nature of this Christian worship has become somewhat obscured.

93) Op cit., 13: AAS 50 (1964), p. 103.

A Manual of the Most Holy Rosary

In this context we wish to mention two attitudes which in pastoral practice could nullify the norm of the Second Vatican Council. In the first place there are certain persons concerned with the care of souls who scorn, a priori, devotions of piety which, in their correct forms, have been recommended by the magisterium, who leave them aside and in this way create a vacuum which they do not fill. They forget that the Council has said that devotions of piety should harmonize with the liturgy, not be suppressed. Secondly there are those who, without wholesome liturgical and pastoral criteria, mix practices of piety and liturgical acts in hybrid celebrations. It sometimes happens that novenas or similar practices of piety are inserted into the very celebration of the Eucharistic Sacrifice. This creates the danger that the Lord's Memorial Rite, instead of being the culmination of the meeting of the Christian community, becomes the occasion, as it were, for devotional practices. For those who act in this way we wish to recall the rule laid down by the Council prescribing that exercises of piety should be harmonized with the liturgy, not merged into it. Wise pastoral action should, on the one hand, point out and emphasize the proper nature of the liturgical acts, while on the other hand it should enhance the value of practices of piety in order to adapt them to the needs of individual communities in the Church and to make them valuable aids to the liturgy.32. Because of its ecclesial character, devotion to the Blessed Virgin reflects the preoccupations of the Church herself. Among these especially in our day is her anxiety for the re-establishment of Christian unity. In this way devotion to the Mother of the Lord is in accord with the deep desires and aims of the ecumenical movement, that is, it acquires an ecumenical aspect. This is so for a number of reasons. In the first place, in venerating with particular love the glorious Theotokos and in acclaiming her as the "Hope of Christians,"[94] Catholics unite themselves with their brethren of the Orthodox

Churches, in which devotion to the Blessed Virgin finds its expression in a beautiful lyricism and in solid doctrine. Catholics are also united with Anglicans, whose classical theologians have already drawn attention to the sound scriptural basis for devotion to the Mother of our Lord, while those of the present day increasingly underline the importance of Mary's place in the Christian life. Praising God with the very words of the Virgin (cf. Lk. 1:46-55), they are united, too, with their brethren in the Churches of the Reform, where love for the Sacred Scriptures flourishes.

94) Cf. Officum magni canonis paracletici, Magnum Orologion, Athens 1963, p. 558; passim in liturgical canons and prayers: cf. Sophronius Eustradiadou, Theotokarion, Chennevieres, sur Marne 1931, pp. 9, 19.

For Catholics, devotion to the Mother of Christ and Mother of Christians is also a natural and frequent opportunity for seeking her intercession with her Son in order to obtain the union of all the baptized within a single People of God.[95] Yet again, the ecumenical aspect of Marian devotion is shown in the Catholic Church's desire that, without in any way detracting from the unique character of this devotion,[96] every care should be taken to avoid any exaggeration which could mislead other Christian brethren about the true doctrine of the Catholic Church.[97] Similarly, the Church desires that any manifestation of cult which is opposed to correct Catholic practice should be eliminated.

95) Cf. II Vatican Council, Dogmatic Constitution on the Church, Lumen Gentium, 69: AAS 57 (1965), pp. 66-6796) Cf. ibid., 66: AAS 57 (1965), p. 65; Constitution on the Sacred Liturgy, Sacrosanctum Concilium, 103: AAS 56 (1964), p. 125.97) Cf. II

Vatican Council, Dogmatic Constitution on the Church, Lumen Gentium, 67: AAS 57 (1965), pp. 65-66.

Finally, since it is natural that in true devotion to the Blessed Virgin "the Son should be duly known, loved and glorified...when the Mother is honored,"[98] such devotion is an approach to Christ, the source and center of ecclesiastical communion, in which all who openly confess that He is God and Lord, Savior and sole Mediator (cf. 1 Tm. 2:5) are called to be one, with one another, with Christ and with the Father in the unity of the Holy Spirit.[99]

98) Ibid., 66: AAS 57 (1965), p. 65.99) Cf. Paul VI, Address in the Vatican Basilica to the Fathers of the Council, 21 November 1964: AAS 56 (1964), p. 1017.

33. We realize that there exist important differences between the thought of many of our brethren in other Churches and ecclesial communities and the Catholic doctrine on "Mary's role in the work of salvation."[100] In consequence there are likewise differences of opinion on the devotion which should be shown to her. Nevertheless, since it is the same power of the Most High which overshadowed the Virgin of Nazareth (cf. Lk. 1:35) and which today is at work within the ecumenical movement and making it fruitful, we wish to express our confidence that devotion to the humble handmaid of the Lord, in whom the Almighty has done great things (cf. Lk. 1:49), will become, even if only slowly, not an obstacle but a path and a rallying point for the union of all who believe in Christ. We are glad to see that, in fact, a better understanding of Mary's place in the mystery of Christ and of the Church on the part also of our separated brethren is smoothing the path to union. Just as at Cana the Blessed Virgin's intervention resulted in Christ's performing His first miracle (cf. Jn. 2:1-12), so today her intercession can help to bring to realization the time

when the disciples of Christ will again find full communion in faith. This hope of ours is strengthened by a remark of our predecessor Leo XIII, who wrote that the cause of Christian unity "properly pertains to the role of Mary's spiritual motherhood. For Mary did not and cannot engender those who belong to Christ, except in one faith and one love: for 'Is Christ divided?' (1 Cor. 1:13) We must all live together the life of Christ, so that in one and the same body 'we may bear fruit for God' (Rom. 7:4).[101]

100)Cf. II Vatican Council, Decree on Ecumenism, Unitatis Redintegratio, 20: AAS 57 (1965), p. 105.101) Encyclical Letter, Adiutricem Populi: ASS 28 (1895-1896), p. 135.

34. Devotion to the Blessed Virgin must also pay close attention to certain findings of the human sciences. This will help to eliminate one of the causes of the difficulties experienced in devotion to the Mother of the Lord, namely, the discrepancy existing between some aspects of this devotion and modern anthropological discoveries and the profound changes which have occurred in the psycho-sociological field in which modern man lives and works. The picture of the Blessed Virgin presented in a certain type of devotional literature cannot easily be reconciled with today's life-style, especially the way women live today. In the home, woman's equality and co-responsibility with man in the running of the family are being justly recognized by laws and the evolution of customs. In the sphere of politics women have in many countries gained a position in public life equal to that of men. In the social field women are at work in a whole range of different employments, getting further away every day from the restricted surroundings of the home. In the cultural field new possibilities are opening up for women in scientific research and intellectual activities. In consequence of these phenomena some people are becoming disenchanted with devotion to the Blessed Virgin and finding it

difficult to take as an example Mary of Nazareth because the horizons of her life, so they say, seem rather restricted in comparison with the vast spheres of activity open to mankind today. In this regard we exhort theologians, those responsible for the local Christian communities and the faithful themselves to examine these difficulties with due care. At the same time we wish to take the opportunity of offering our own contribution to their solution by making a few observations.35. First, the Virgin Mary has always been proposed to the faithful by the Church as an example to be imitated, not precisely in the type of life she led, and much less for the socio-cultural background in which she lived and which today scarcely exists anywhere. She is held up as an example to the faithful rather for the way in which, in her own particular life, she fully and responsibly accepted the will of God (cf. Lk. 1:38), because she heard the word of God and acted on it, and because charity and a spirit of service were the driving force of her actions. She is worthy of imitation because she was the first and the most perfect of Christ's disciples. All of this has a permanent and universal exemplary value.36. Secondly, we would like to point out that the difficulties alluded to above are closely related to certain aspects of the image of Mary found in popular writings. They are not connected with the Gospel image of Mary nor with the doctrinal data which have been made explicit through a slow and conscientious process of drawing from Revelation. It should be considered quite normal for succeeding generations of Christians in differing socio-cultural contexts to have expressed their sentiments about the Mother of Jesus in a way and manner which reflected their own age. In contemplating Mary and her mission these different generations of Christians, looking on her as the New Woman and perfect Christian, found in her as a virgin, wife and mother the outstanding type of womanhood and the pre-eminent exemplar of life lived in accordance with the Gospels and summing up the most characteristic situations in the life of a woman. When the Church considers the long history of Marian devotion she rejoices at the continuity of the element of cult which it shows, but she does not bind herself to any particular expression of an individual cultural epoch or to the particular anthropological ideas underlying such expressions. The Church understands that certain outward religious expressions, while perfectly valid in themselves, may be less suitable to men and women of different ages and cultures.37. Finally, we wish to point out that our own time, no less than former times, is called upon to verify its knowledge of reality with the word of God, and, keeping to the matter at present under consideration, to compare its anthropological ideas and the problems springing therefrom with the figure of the Virgin Mary as presented by the Gospel. The reading of the divine Scriptures, carried out under the guidance of the Holy Spirit, and with the discoveries of the human sciences and the different situations in the world today being taken into account, will help us to see how Mary can be considered a mirror of the expectations of the men and women of our time. Thus, the modern woman, anxious to participate with decision-making power in the affairs of the community, will contemplate with intimate joy Mary who, taken into dialogue with God, gives her active and responsible consent,[102] not to the solution of a contingent problem, but to that "event of world importance," as the Incarnation of the Word has been rightly called.[103] The modern woman will appreciate that Mary's choice of the state of virginity, which in God's plan prepared her for the mystery of the Incarnation, was not a rejection of any of the values of the married state but a courageous choice which she made in order to consecrate herself totally to the love of God. The modern woman will note with pleasant surprise that Mary of Nazareth, while completely devoted to the will of God, was far from being a timidly submissive woman or one whose piety was repellent to others; on the contrary, she was a woman who did not hesitate to proclaim that God vindicates the humble and the oppressed, and removes the powerful people of this world from their privileged positions (cf. Lk. 1:51-53). The modern woman will recognize in Mary, who "stands out among the poor and humble of the Lord,"[104] a woman of strength, who experienced poverty and suffering, flight and exile (cf. Mt. 2:13-23). These are situations that cannot escape the attention of those who wish to support, with the Gospel spirit, the liberating energies of man and of society. And Mary will appear not as a Mother exclusively concerned with her own divine Son, but rather as a woman whose action helped to strengthen the apostolic community's faith in Christ (cf. Jn. 2:1-12), and whose maternal role was extended and became universal on Calvary.[105] These are but examples, but examples which show clearly that the figure of the Blessed Virgin does not disillusion any of the profound expectations of the men and women of our time but offers them the perfect model of the disciple of the Lord: the disciple who builds up the earthly and temporal city while being a diligent pilgrim towards the heavenly and eternal city; the disciple who works for that justice which sets free the oppressed and for that charity which assists the needy; but above all, the disciple who is the active witness of that love which builds up Christ in people's hearts.

102) Cf. II Vatican Council, Dogmatic Constitution on the Church, Lumen Gentium, 56: AAS 57 (1965), p. 60.103) Cf. St. Peter Chrysologus, Sermo CXLIII: PL 52, 583.104) II Vatican Council, Dogmatic Constitution on the Church, Lumen Gentium, 55: AAS 57 (1965), pp. 59-60.105) Cf. Paul VI, Apostolic Constitution, Signum Magnum, I: AAS 59 (1967), pp. 467-468: Roman Missal, 15 September, Prayer over the gifts.

38. Having offered these directives, which are intended to favor the harmonious development of devotion to the Mother of the Lord, we consider it opportune to draw attention to certain attitudes of piety which are incorrect. The Second Vatican Council has already authoritatively denounced both the exaggeration of content and form which even falsifies doctrine and likewise the small-mindedness which obscures the figure and mission of Mary. The Council has also denounced certain devotional deviations, such as vain credulity, which substitutes reliance on merely external practices for serious commitment. Another deviation is sterile and ephemeral sentimentality, so alien to the spirit of the Gospel that demands persevering and practical action.[106] We reaffirm the Council's reprobation of such attitudes and practices. They are not in harmony with the Catholic Faith and therefore they must have no place in Catholic worship. Careful defense against these errors and deviations will render devotion to the Blessed Virgin more vigorous and more authentic. It will make this devotion solidly based, with the consequence that study of the sources of Revelation and attention to the documents of the magisterium will prevail over the exaggerated search for novelties or extraordinary phenomena. It will ensure that this devotion is objective in its historical setting, and for this reason everything that is obviously legendary or false must be eliminated. It will ensure that this devotion matches its doctrinal content--hence the necessity of avoiding a one-sided presentation of the figure of Mary, which by overstressing one element compromises the overall picture given by the Gospel. It will make this devotion clear in its motivation; hence every unworthy self-interest is to be carefully banned from the area of what is sacred.

106) Cf. Dogmatic Constitution on the Church, Lumen Gentium, 67: AAS 57 (1965), pp. 65-66.

39. Finally, insofar as it may be necessary we would like to repeat that the ultimate purpose of devotion to the Blessed Virgin is to glorify God and to lead Christians to commit themselves to a life which is in absolute conformity with His will. When the children of the Church unite their voices with the voice of the unknown woman in the Gospel and glorify the Mother of Jesus by saying to Him: "Blessed is the womb that bore you and the breasts that you sucked" (Lk. 11:27), they will be led to ponder the Divine Master's serious reply: "Blessed rather are those who hear the word of God and keep it!" (Lk. 11:28) While it is true that this reply is in itself lively praise of Mary, as various Fathers of the Church interpreted it[107] and the Second Vatican Council has confirmed,[108] it is also an admonition to us to live our lives in accordance with God's commandments. It is also an echo of other words of the Savior: "Not every one who says to me 'Lord, Lord,' will enter the kingdom of heaven, but he who does the will of my Father who is in heaven" (Mt. 7:21); and again: "You are my friends if you do what I command you" (Jn. 15:14).

107) St. Augustine, In Johannis Evangelium Tractatus X, 3: CCL 36, pp. 101-102; Epistula 243, Ad Laetum, 9: CSEL 57, pp. 575-576; St. Bede, In Lucae Evangelium expositio, IV, XI, 28: CCL 120, p. 237; Homilia I, 4: CCL 122, pp. 26-27.108) Cf. II Vatican Council, Dogmatic Constitution on the Church, Lumen Gentium, 58: AAS 57 (1965), p. 61.

40. We have indicated a number of principles which can help to give fresh vigor to devotion to the Mother of the Lord. It is now up to episcopal conferences, to those in charge of local communities and to the various religious congregations prudently to revise practices and exercises of piety in honor of the Blessed Virgin, and to encourage the creative impulse of those who through genuine religious inspiration or pastoral sensitivity wish to establish

new forms of piety. For different reasons we nevertheless feel it is opportune to consider here two practices which are widespread in the West, and with which this Apostolic See has concerned itself on various occasions: the Angelus and the Rosary.41. What we have to say about the Angelus is meant to be only a simple but earnest exhortation to continue its traditional recitation wherever and whenever possible. The Angelus does not need to be revised, because of its simple structure, its biblical character, its historical origin which links it to the prayer for peace and safety, and its quasi-liturgical rhythm which sanctifies different moments during the day, and because it reminds us of the Paschal Mystery, in which recalling the Incarnation of the Son of God we pray that we may be led "through his passion and cross to the glory of his resurrection."[109] These factors ensure that the Angelus despite the passing of centuries retains an unaltered value and an intact freshness. It is true that certain customs traditionally linked with the recitation of the Angelus have disappeared or can continue only with difficulty in modern life. But these are marginal elements. The value of contemplation on the mystery of the Incarnation of the Word, of the greeting to the Virgin, and of recourse to her merciful intercession remains unchanged. And despite the changed conditions of the times, for the majority of people there remain unaltered the characteristic periods of the day--morning, noon and evening--which mark the periods of their activity and constitute an invitation to pause in prayer.

109) Roman Missal, IV Sunday of Advent, Collect. Similarly the Collect of 25 March, which may be used in place of the previous one in the recitation of the Angelus.

42. We wish now, venerable Brothers, to dwell for a moment on the renewal of the pious practice which has been called "the compendium of the entire Gospel"[110]: the Rosary. To this our

predecessors have devoted close attention and care. On many occasions they have recommended its frequent recitation, encouraged its diffusion, explained its nature, recognized its suitability for fostering contemplative prayer--prayer of both praise and petition--and recalled its intrinsic effectiveness for promoting Christian life and apostolic commitment.

110) Pius XII, Letter to the Archbishop of Manila, "Philippinas Insulas": AAS 38 (1946), p. 419.

We, too, from the first general audience of our pontificate on July 13, 1963, have shown our great esteem for the pious practice of the Rosary.[111] Since that time we have underlined its value on many different occasions, some ordinary, some grave. Thus, at a moment of anguish and uncertainty, we published the Letter Christi Matri (September 15, 1966), in order to obtain prayers to Our Lady of the Rosary and to implore from God the supreme benefit of peace.[112] We renewed this appeal in our Apostolic Exhortation Recurrens mensis October (October 7, 1969), in which we also commemorated the fourth centenary of the Apostolic Letter Consueverunt Romani pontifices of our predecessor Saint Pius V, who in that document explained and in a certain sense established the traditional form of the Rosary.[113]

111) Discourse to the participants in the III Dominican International Rosary Congress: Insegnamenti di Paolo VI, 1, (1963) pp. 463-464.112) In AAS 58 (1966), pp. 745-749.113) In AAS 61 (1969), pp. 649-654.113) ?

43. Our assiduous and affectionate interest in the Rosary has led us to follow very attentively the numerous meetings which in recent years have been devoted to the pastoral role of the Rosary in the modern world, meetings arranged by associations and individuals profoundly attached to the Rosary and attended by bishops, priests,

religious and lay people of proven experience and recognized ecclesial awareness. Among these people special mention should be made of the sons of Saint Dominic, by tradition the guardians and promoters of this very salutary practice. Parallel with such meetings has been the research work of historians, work aimed not at defining in a sort of archaeological fashion the primitive form of the Rosary but at uncovering the original inspiration and driving force behind it and its essential structure. The fundamental characteristics of the Rosary, its essential elements and their mutual relationship have all emerged more clearly from these congresses and from the research carried out.44. Thus, for instance, the Gospel inspiration of the Rosary has appeared more clearly: the Rosary draws from the Gospel the presentation of the mysteries and its main formulas. As it moves from the angel's joyful greeting and the Virgin's pious assent, the Rosary takes its inspiration from the Gospel to suggest the attitude with which the faithful should recite it. In the harmonious succession of Hail Mary's the Rosary puts before us once more a fundamental mystery of the Gospel-- the Incarnation of the Word, contemplated at the decisive moment of the Annunciation to Mary. The Rosary is thus a Gospel prayer, as pastors and scholars like to define it, more today perhaps than in the past.45. It has also been more easily seen how the orderly and gradual unfolding of the Rosary reflects the very way in which the Word of God, mercifully entering into human affairs, brought about the Redemption. The Rosary considers in harmonious succession the principal salvific events accomplished in Christ, from His virginal conception and the mysteries of His childhood to the culminating moments of the Passover--the blessed passion and the glorious resurrection--and to the effects of this on the infant Church on the day of Pentecost, and on the Virgin Mary when at the end of her earthly life she was assumed body and soul into her heavenly home. It has also been observed that the division of the mysteries of the Rosary into three parts not only adheres strictly to the chronological order of the facts but above all reflects the plan of the original proclamation of the Faith and sets forth once more the mystery of Christ in the very way in which it is seen by Saint Paul in the celebrated "hymn" of the Letter to the Philippians-- kenosis, death and exaltation (cf. 2:6-11).46. As a Gospel prayer, centered on the mystery of the redemptive Incarnation, the Rosary is therefore a prayer with a clearly Christological orientation. Its most characteristic element, in fact, the litany-like succession of Hail Mary's, becomes in itself an unceasing praise of Christ, who is the ultimate object both of the angel's announcement and of the greeting of the mother of John the Baptist: "Blessed is the fruit of your womb" (Lk. 1:42). We would go further and say that the succession of Hail Mary's constitutes the warp on which is woven the contemplation of the mysteries. The Jesus that each Hail Mary recalls is the same Jesus whom the succession of the mysteries proposes to us--now as the Son of God, now as the Son of the Virgin--at His birth in a stable at Bethlehem, at His presentation by His Mother in the Temple, as a youth full of zeal for His Father's affairs, as the Redeemer in agony in the garden, scourged and crowned with thorns, carrying the cross and dying on Calvary; risen from the dead and ascended to the glory of the Father to send forth the gift of the Spirit. As is well known, at one time there was a custom, still preserved in certain places, of adding to the name of Jesus in each Hail Mary a reference to the mystery being contemplated. And this was done precisely in order to help contemplation and to make the mind and the voice act in unison.47. There has also been felt with greater urgency the need to point out once more the importance of a further essential element in the Rosary, in addition to the value of the elements of praise and petition, namely the element of contemplation. Without this the Rosary is a body without a soul, and its recitation is in danger of becoming a mechanical repetition of formulas and of going counter to the warning of Christ: "And in praying do not heap up empty phrases as the Gentiles do; for they think that they will be heard for their many words" (Mt. 6:7). By its nature the recitation of the Rosary calls for a quiet rhythm and a lingering pace, helping the individual to meditate on the mysteries of the Lord's life as seen through the eyes of her who was closest to the Lord. In this way the unfathomable riches of these mysteries are unfolded.48. Finally, as a result of modern reflection the relationships between the liturgy and the Rosary have been more clearly understood. On the one hand it has been emphasized that the Rosary is, as it were, a branch sprung from the ancient trunk of the Christian liturgy, the Psalter of the Blessed Virgin, whereby the humble were associated in the Church's hymn of praise and universal intercession. On the other hand it has been noted that this development occurred at a time--the last period of the Middle Ages--when the liturgical spirit was in decline and the faithful were turning from the liturgy towards a devotion to Christ's humanity and to the Blessed Virgin Mary, a devotion favoring a certain external sentiment of piety. Not many years ago some people began to express the desire to see the Rosary included among the rites of the liturgy, while other people, anxious to avoid repetition of former pastoral mistakes, unjustifiably disregarded the Rosary. Today the problem can easily be solved in the light of the principles of the Constitution Sacrosanctum concilium. Liturgical celebrations and the pious practice of the Rosary must be neither set in opposition to one another nor considered as being identical.[114] The more an expression of prayer preserves its own true nature and individual characteristics the more fruitful it becomes. Once the pre-eminent value of liturgical rites has been reaffirmed it will not be difficult to appreciate the fact that the Rosary is a practice of piety which easily harmonizes with the liturgy. In fact, like the liturgy, it is of a community nature, draws its inspiration from Sacred Scripture and is oriented towards the mystery of Christ. The commemoration in the liturgy and the contemplative remembrance proper to the Rosary, although existing on essentially different planes of reality, have as their object the same salvific events wrought by Christ. The former presents anew, under the veil of signs and operative in a hidden way, the great mysteries of our Redemption. The latter, by means of devout contemplation, recalls these same mysteries to the mind of the person praying and stimulates the will to draw from them the norms of living. Once this substantial difference has been established, it is not difficult to understand that the Rosary is an exercise of piety that draws its motivating force from the liturgy and leads naturally back to it, if practiced in conformity with its original inspiration. It does not, however, become part of the liturgy. In fact, meditation on the mysteries of the Rosary, by familiarizing the hearts and minds of the faithful with the mysteries of Christ, can be an excellent preparation for the celebration of those same mysteries in the liturgical action and can also become a continuing echo thereof. However, it is a mistake to recite the Rosary during the celebration of the liturgy, though unfortunately this practice still persists here and there.

114) Cf. 13: AAS 56 (1964), p. 103.

49. The Rosary of the Blessed Virgin Mary, according to the tradition accepted by our predecessor St. Pius V and authoritatively taught by him, consists of various elements disposed in an organic fashion:

a) Contemplation in communion with Mary, of a series of mysteries of salvation, wisely distributed into three cycles. These mysteries express the joy of the messianic times, the salvific suffering of Christ and the glory of the Risen Lord which fills the Church. This contemplation by its very nature encourages practical reflection and provides stimulating norms for living. b) The Lord's Prayer, or Our Father, which by reason of its immense value is at the basis of Christian prayer and ennobles that prayer in its various expressions. c) The litany-like succession of the Hail Mary, which is made up of the angel's greeting to the Virgin (cf. Lk. 1:28), and of Elizabeth's greeting (cf. Lk. 1:42), followed by the ecclesial supplication, Holy Mary. The continued series of Hail Mary's is the special characteristic of the Rosary, and their number, in the full and typical number of one hundred and fifty, presents a certain analogy with the Psalter and is an element that goes back to the very origin of the exercise of piety. But this number, divided, according to a well-tried custom, into decades attached to the individual mysteries, is distributed in the three cycles already mentioned, thus giving rise to the Rosary of fifty Hail Mary's as we know it. This latter has entered into use as the normal measure of the pious exercise and as such has been adopted by popular piety and approved by papal authority, which also enriched it with numerous indulgences. d) The doxology Glory be to the Father which, in conformity with an orientation common to Christian piety, concludes the prayer with the glorifying of God who is one and three, from whom, through whom and in whom all things have their being (cf. Rom. 11:36).

50. These are the elements of the Rosary. Each has its own particular character which, wisely understood and appreciated, should be reflected in the recitation in order that the Rosary may express all its richness and variety. Thus the recitation will be grave and suppliant during the Lord's Prayer, lyrical and full of praise during the tranquil succession of Hail Mary's, contemplative in the recollected meditation on the mysteries and full of adoration during the doxology. This applies to all the ways in which the Rosary is

usually recited: privately, in intimate recollection with the Lord; in community, in the family or in groups of the faithful gathered together to ensure the special presence of the Lord (cf. Mt. 18:20); or publicly, in assemblies to which the ecclesial community is invited.51. In recent times certain exercises of piety have been created which take their inspiration from the Rosary. Among such exercises we wish to draw attention to and recommend those which insert into the ordinary celebration of the word of God some elements of the Rosary, such as meditation on the mysteries and litany-like repetition of the angel's greeting to Mary. In this way these elements gain in importance, since they are found in the context of Bible readings, illustrated with a homily, accompanied by silent pauses and emphasized with song. We are happy to know that such practices have helped to promote a more complete understanding of the spiritual riches of the Rosary itself and have served to restore esteem for its recitation among youth associations and movements.52. We now desire, as a continuation of the thought of our predecessors, to recommend strongly the recitation of the family Rosary. The Second Vatican Council has pointed out how the family, the primary and vital cell of society, "shows itself to be the domestic sanctuary of the Church through the mutual affection of its members and the common prayer they offer to God."[115] The Christian family is thus seen to be a domestic Church[116] if its members, each according to his proper place and tasks, all together promote justice, practice works of mercy, devote themselves to helping their brethren, take part in the apostolate of the wider local community and play their part in its liturgical worship.[117] This will be all the more true if together they offer up prayers to God. If this element of common prayer were missing, the family would lack its very character as a domestic Church. Thus there must logically follow a concrete effort to reinstate communal prayer in family life if there is to be a restoration of the theological concept of the family as the domestic Church.

115) Decree on the Lay Apostolate, Apostolicam Actuositatem, II: AAS 58 (1966), p. 848.116) Cf. II Vatican Council, Dogmatic Constitution on the Church, Lumen Gentium, 11: AAS 57 (1965), p. 16.117) Cf. II Vatican Council, Decree on the Lay Apostolate, Apostolicam Actuositatem, 11: AAS 58 (1966), p. 848.

53. In accordance with the directives of the Council the Institutio Generalis de Liturgia Horarum rightly numbers the family among the groups in which the Divine Office can suitably be celebrated in community: "It is fitting...that the family, as a domestic sanctuary of the Church, should not only offer prayers to God in common, but also, according to circumstances, should recite parts of the Liturgy of the Hours, in order to be more intimately linked with the Church."[118] No avenue should be left unexplored to ensure that this clear and practical recommendation finds within Christian families growing and joyful acceptance.

118) Op cit., 27.

54. But there is no doubt that, after the celebration of the Liturgy of the Hours, the high point which family prayer can reach, the Rosary should be considered as one of the best and most efficacious prayers in common that the Christian family is invited to recite. We like to think, and sincerely hope, that when the family gathering becomes a time of prayer, the Rosary is a frequent and favored manner of praying. We are well aware that the changed conditions of life today do not make family gatherings easy, and that even when such a gathering is possible many circumstances make it difficult to turn it into an occasion of prayer. There is no doubt of the difficulty. But it is characteristic of the Christian in his manner of life not to give in to circumstances but to overcome

them, not to succumb but to make an effort. Families which want to live in full measure the vocation and spirituality proper to the Christian family must therefore devote all their energies to overcoming the pressures that hinder family gatherings and prayer in common.55. In concluding these observations, which give proof of the concern and esteem which the Apostolic See has for the Rosary of the Blessed Virgin, we desire at the same time to recommend that this very worthy devotion should not be propagated in a way that is too one-sided or exclusive. The Rosary is an excellent prayer, but the faithful should feel serenely free in its regard. They should be drawn to its calm recitation by its intrinsic appeal.56. Venerable Brothers, as we come to the end of this our Apostolic Exhortation we wish to sum up and emphasize the theological value of devotion to the Blessed Virgin and to recall briefly its pastoral effectiveness for renewing the Christian way of life.The Church's devotion to the Blessed Virgin is an intrinsic element of Christian worship. The honor which the Church has always and everywhere shown to the Mother of the Lord, from the blessing with which Elizabeth greeted Mary (cf. Lk. 1:42-45) right up to the expressions of praise and petition used today, is a very strong witness to the Church's norm of prayer and an invitation to become more deeply conscious of her norm of faith. And the converse is likewise true. The Church's norm of faith requires that her norm of prayer should everywhere blossom forth with regard to the Mother of Christ. Such devotion to the Blessed Virgin is firmly rooted in the revealed word and has solid dogmatic foundations. It is based on the singular dignity of Mary, "Mother of the Son of God, and therefore beloved daughter of the Father and Temple of the Holy Spirit--Mary, who, because of this extraordinary grace, is far greater than any other creature on earth or in heaven."[119] This devotion takes into account the part she played at decisive moments in the history of the salvation which her Son accomplished, and her holiness, already full at her Immaculate Conception yet increasing all the time as she obeyed the will of the Father and accepted the path of suffering (cf. Lk. 2:34-35, 41-52; Jn. 19:25-27), growing constantly in faith, hope and charity. Devotion to Mary recalls too her mission and the special position she holds within the People of God, of which she is the preeminent member, a shining example and the loving Mother; it recalls her unceasing and efficacious intercession which, although she is assumed into heaven, draws her close to those who ask her help, including those who do not realize that they are her children. It recalls Mary's glory which ennobles the whole of mankind, as the outstanding phrase of Dante recalls: "You have so ennobled human nature that its very Creator did not disdain to share in it."[120] Mary, in fact, is one of our race, a true daughter of Eve--though free of that mother's sin--and truly our sister, who as a poor and humble woman fully shared our lot.

119) II Vatican Council, Dogmatic Constitution on the Church, Lumen Gentium, 53: AAS 57 (1965), pp. 58-59.120) La Divina Commedia, Paradiso XXXIII, 4-6.

We would add further that devotion to the Blessed Virgin finds its ultimate justification in the unfathomable and free will of God who, being eternal and divine charity (cf. 1 Jn. 4:7-8, 16), accomplishes all things according to a loving design. He loved her and did great things for her (cf. Lk. 1:49). He loved her for His own sake, and He loved her for our sake, too; He gave her to Himself and He gave her also to us.57. Christ is the only way to the Father (cf. Jn. 14:4-11), and the ultimate example to whom the disciple must conform his own conduct (cf. Jn. 13:15), to the extent of sharing Christ's sentiments (cf. Phil. 2:5), living His life and possessing His Spirit (cf. Gal. 2:20; Rom. 8:10-11). The Church has always taught this and nothing in pastoral activity should obscure this doctrine. But the Church, taught by the Holy Spirit and benefiting from centuries of experience, recognizes that devotion to the Blessed Virgin, subordinated to worship of the divine Savior and in connection with it, also has a great pastoral effectiveness and constitutes a force for renewing Christian living. It is easy to see the reason for this effectiveness. Mary's many-sided mission to the People of God is a supernatural reality which operates and bears fruit within the body of the Church. One finds cause for joy in considering the different aspects of this mission, and seeing how each of these aspects with its individual effectiveness is directed towards the same end, namely, producing in the children the spiritual characteristics of the first-born Son. The Virgin's maternal intercession, her exemplary holiness and the divine grace which is in her become for the human race a reason for divine hope. The Blessed Virgin's role as Mother leads the People of God to turn with filial confidence to her who is ever ready to listen with a mother's affection and efficacious assistance.[121] Thus the People of God have learned to call on her as the Consoler of the afflicted, the Health of the sick, and the Refuge of sinners, that they may find comfort in tribulation, relief in sickness and liberating strength in guilt. For she, who is free from sin, leads her children to combat sin with energy and resoluteness.[122] This liberation from sin and evil (cf. Mt. 6:13)--it must be repeated--is the necessary premise for any renewal of Christian living.

121) Cf. II Vatican Council, Dogmatic Constitution on the Church, Lumen Gentium, 60-63; AAS 57 (1965), pp. 62-64.122) Cf. ibid., 65: AAS 57 (1965), pp. 64-65.

The Blessed Virgin's exemplary holiness encourages the faithful to "raise their eyes to Mary who shines forth before the whole community of the elect as a model of the virtues."[123] It is a question of solid, evangelical virtues: faith and the docile acceptance of the Word of God (cf. Lk. 1:26-38, 1:45, 11:27-28, Jn. 2:5); generous obedience (cf. Lk. 1:38); genuine humility (cf. Lk. 1:48); solicitous charity (cf. Lk. 1:39-56); profound wisdom (cf. Lk. 1:29, 34; 2:19, 33:51); worship of God manifested in alacrity in the fulfillment of religious duties (cf. Lk. 2:2141), in gratitude for gifts received (cf. Lk. 1:46-49), in her offering in the Temple (cf. Lk. 2:22-24) and in her prayer in the midst of the apostolic community (cf. Acts 1:12-14); her fortitude in exile (cf. Mt. 2:13-23) and in suffering (cf. Lk. 2:34-35, 49; Jn. 19:25); her poverty reflecting dignity and trust in God (cf. Lk. 1:48, 2:24); her attentive care for her Son, from His humble birth to the ignominy of the cross (cf. Lk. 2:1-7; Jn. 19:25-27); her delicate forethought (cf. Jn. 2:1-11); her virginal purity (cf. Mt. 1:18-25; Lk. 1:26-38); her strong and chaste married love. These virtues of the Mother will also adorn her children who steadfastly study her example in order to reflect it in their own lives. And this progress in virtue will appear as the consequence and the already mature fruit of that pastoral zeal which springs from devotion to the Blessed Virgin.

123) Ibid., 65: AAS 57 (1965), p. 64.

Devotion to the Mother of the Lord becomes for the faithful an opportunity for growing in divine grace, and this is the ultimate aim of all pastoral activity. For it is impossible to honor her who is "full of grace" (Lk. 1:28) without thereby honoring in oneself the state of grace, which is friendship with God, communion with Him and the indwelling of the Holy Spirit. It is this divine grace which takes possession of the whole man and conforms him to the image of the Son of God (cf. Rom. 8:29; Col. 1:18). The Catholic Church, endowed with centuries of experience, recognizes in devotion to the Blessed Virgin a powerful aid for man as he strives for fulfillment. Mary, the New Woman, stands at the side of Christ, the New Man, within whose mystery the mystery of man[124] alone finds true light; she is given to us as a pledge and guarantee that God's plan in Christ for the salvation of the whole man has already achieved realization in a creature: in her. Contemplated in the episodes of the Gospels and in the reality which she already possesses in the City of God, the Blessed Virgin Mary offers a calm vision and a reassuring word to modern man, torn as he often is between anguish and hope, defeated by the sense of his own limitations and assailed by limitless aspirations, troubled in his mind and divided in his heart, uncertain before the riddle of death, oppressed by loneliness while yearning for fellowship, a prey to boredom and disgust. She shows forth the victory of hope over anguish, of fellowship over solitude, of peace over anxiety, of joy and beauty over boredom and disgust, of eternal visions over earthly ones, of life over death.

124) Cf. II Vatican Council, Pastoral Constitution on the Church in the Modern World, Gaudium et Spes, 22: AAS 58 (1966), pp. 1042-1044.

Let the very words that she spoke to the servants at the marriage feast of Cana, "Do whatever he tells you" (Jn. 2:5), be a seal on our Exhortation and a further reason in favor of the pastoral value of devotion to the Blessed Virgin as a means of leading men to Christ. Those words, which at first sight were limited to the desire to remedy an embarrassment at the feast, are seen in the context of Saint John's Gospel to re-echo the words used by the people of Israel to give approval to the Covenant at Sinai (cf. Ex. 19:8, 24:3, 7; Dt. 5:27) and to renew their commitments (cf. Jos. 24:24; Ezr. 10:12; Neh. 5:12). And they are words which harmonize wonderfully with those spoken by the Father at the theophany on Mount Tabor: "Listen to him" (Mt. 17:5).58. Venerable Brothers, we have dealt at length with an integral element of Christian worship: devotion to the Mother of the Lord. This has been called for by the nature of the subject, one which in these recent years has been the object of study and revision and at times the cause of some perplexity. We are consoled to think that the work done by this Apostolic See and by yourselves in order to carry out the norms of the Council--particularly the liturgical reform--is a stepping-stone to an ever more lively and adoring worship of God, the Father and the Son and the Holy Spirit, and to an increase of the Christian life of the faithful. We are filled with confidence when we note that the renewed Roman liturgy, also taken as a whole, is a splendid illustration of the Church's devotion to the Blessed Virgin. We are upheld by the hope that the directives issued in order to render this devotion ever more pure and vigorous will be applied with sincerity. We rejoice that the Lord has given us the opportunity of putting forward some points for reflection in order to renew and confirm esteem for the practice of the rosary. Comfort, confidence, hope and joy are the sentiments which we wish to transform into fervent praise and thanksgiving to the Lord as we unite our voice with that of the Blessed Virgin in accordance with the prayer of the Roman Liturgy.[125]

125) Cf. Roman Missal, 31 May, Collect.

Dear Brothers, while we express the hope that, thanks to your generous commitment, there will be among the clergy and among the people entrusted to your care a salutary increase of devotion to Mary with undoubted profit for the Church and for society, we cordially impart our special apostolic blessing to yourselves and to all the faithful people to whom you devote your pastoral zeal. Given in Rome, at Saint Peter's, on the second day of February, the Feast of the Presentation of the Lord, in the year 1974, the eleventh of our Pontificate.

A Manual of the Most Holy Rosary

Redemptoris Mater
On The Blessed Virgin Mary In The Life Of The Pilgrim Church

Encyclical of Pope John Paul II

March 25, 1987

Venerable Brothers and dear Sons and Daughters,
Health and the Apostolic Blessing.

INTRODUCTION

1. The Mother of the Redeemer has a precise place in the plan of salvation, for "when the time had fully come, God sent forth his Son, born of woman, born under the law, to redeem those who were under the law, so that we might receive adoption as sons. And because you are sons, God has sent the Spirit of his Son into our hearts, crying, 'Abba! Father!'" (Gal. 4:4-6)

With these words of the Apostle Paul, which the Second Vatican Council takes up at the beginning of its treatment of the Blessed Virgin Mary,(1) I too wish to begin my reflection on the role of Mary in the mystery of Christ and on her active and exemplary presence in the life of the Church. For they are words which celebrate together the love of the Father, the mission of the Son, the gift of the Spirit, the role of the woman from whom the Redeemer was born, and our own divine filiation, in the mystery of the "fullness of time."(2)

[1] Cf. Second Vatican Ecumenical Council, Dogmatic Constitution on the Church Lumen Gentium, 52 and the whole of Chapter VIII, entitled "The Role of the Blessed Virgin Mary, Mother of God, in the Mystery of Christ and the Church."

[2] The expression "fullness of time" (pleroma tou chronou) is parallel with similar expressions of Judaism, both Biblical (cf. Gen. 29:21; 1 Sam. 7:12; Tob. 14:5) and extra-Biblical, and especially of the New Testament (cf. Mk. 1:15; Lk. 21:24; Jn. 7:8; Eph. 1:10). From the point of view of form, it means not only the conclusion of a chronological process but also and especially the coming to maturity or completion of a particularly important period, one directed towards the fulfillment of an expectation, a coming to completion which thus takes on an eschatological dimension. According to Gal. 4:4 and its context, it is the coming of the Son of God that reveals that time has, so to speak, reached its limit. That is to say, the period marked by the promise made to Abraham and by the Law mediated by Moses has now reached its climax, in the sense that Christ fulfills the divine promise and supersedes the old law.

This "fullness" indicates the moment fixed from all eternity when the Father sent his Son "that whoever believes in him should not perish but have eternal life" (Jn. 3:16). It denotes the blessed moment when the Word that "was with God...became flesh and dwelt among us" (Jn. 1:1, 14), and made himself our brother. It marks the moment when the Holy Spirit, who had already infused the fullness of grace into Mary of Nazareth, formed in her virginal womb the human nature of Christ. This "fullness" marks the moment when, with the entrance of the eternal into time, time itself is redeemed, and being filled with the mystery of Christ becomes definitively "salvation time." Finally, this "fullness" designates the hidden beginning of the Church's journey. In the liturgy the Church salutes Mary of Nazareth as the Church's own beginning,(3) for in the event of the Immaculate Conception the Church sees projected, and anticipated in her most noble member, the saving grace of Easter. And above all, in the Incarnation she encounters Christ and

Mary indissolubly joined: he who is the Church's Lord and Head and she who, uttering the first fiat of the New Covenant, prefigures the Church's condition as spouse and mother.

[3] Cf. Roman Missal, Preface of 8 December, Immaculate Conception of the Blessed Virgin Mary; Saint Ambrose, De Institutione Virginis, XV, 93-94: PL 16, 342; Second Vatican Ecumenical Council, Dogmatic Constitution on the Church Lumen Gentium, 68.

2. Strengthened by the presence of Christ (cf. Mt. 28:20), the Church journeys through time towards the consummation of the ages and goes to meet the Lord who comes. But on this journey-and I wish to make this point straightaway-she proceeds along the path already trodden by the Virgin Mary, who "advanced in her pilgrimage of faith, and loyally persevered in her union with her Son unto the cross."(4)

[4] Second Vatican Ecumenical Council, Dogmatic Constitution on the Church Lumen Gentium, 58.

I take these very rich and evocative words from the Constitution Lumen Gentium, which in its concluding part offers a clear summary of the Church's doctrine on the Mother of Christ, whom she venerates as her beloved Mother and as her model in faith hope and charity.

Shortly after the Council, my great predecessor Paul VI decided to speak further of the Blessed Virgin. In the Encyclical Epistle Christi Matri and subsequently in the Apostolic Exhortations Signum Magnum and Marialis Cultus(5) he expounded the foundations and criteria of the special veneration which the Mother of Christ receives in the Church, as well as the various forms of

Marian devotion- liturgical, popular and private-which respond to the spirit of faith.

[5] Pope Paul VI, Encyclical Epistle Christi Matri (15 September 1966): AAS 58 (1966) 745-749, Apostolic Exhortation Signum Magnum (13 May 1967): AAS 59 (1967) 465:475; Apostolic Exhortation Marialis Cultus (2 February 1974): AAS 66 (1974) 113-168.

3. The circumstance which now moves me to take up this subject once more is the prospect of the year 2000, now drawing near, in which the Bimillennial Jubilee of the birth of Jesus Christ at the same time directs our gaze towards his Mother. In recent years, various opinions have been voiced suggesting that it would be fitting to precede that anniversary by a similar Jubilee in celebration of the birth of Mary.

In fact, even though it is not possible to establish an exact chronological point for identifying the date of Mary's birth, the Church has constantly been aware that Mary appeared on the horizon of salvation history before Christ.(6) It is a fact that when "the fullness of time" was definitively drawing near-the saving advent of Emmanuel- he who was from eternity destined to be his Mother already existed on earth. The fact that she "preceded" the coming of Christ is reflected every year in the liturgy of Advent. Therefore, if to that ancient historical expectation of the Savior we compare these years which are bringing us closer to the end of the second Millennium after Christ and to the beginning of the third, it becomes fully comprehensible that in this present period we wish to turn in a special way to her, the one who in the "night" of the Advent expectation began to shine like a true "Morning Star" (Stella Matutina). For just as this star, together with the "dawn," precedes the rising of the sun, so Mary from the time of her

Immaculate Conception preceded the coming of the Savior, the rising of the "Sun of Justice" in the history of the human race.(7)

[6] The Old Testament foretold in many different ways the mystery of Mary: cf. Saint John Damascene, Hom. in Dormitionem 1, 8-9: S. Ch. 80, 103-107.

[7] Cf. Insegnamenti di Giovanni Paolo II, VI/2 (1983) 225f.; Pope Pius IX, Apostolic Letter Ineffabilis Deus (8 December 1854): Pii IX P. M. Acta, pars I, 597-599.

Her presence in the midst of Israel-a presence so discreet as to pass almost unnoticed by the eyes of her contemporaries-shone very clearly before the Eternal One, who had associated this hidden "daughter of Sion" (cf. Zeph. 3:14; Zeph. 2:10) with the plan of salvation embracing the whole history of humanity. With good reason, then, at the end of this Millennium, we Christians who know that the providential plan of the Most Holy Trinity is the central reality of Revelation and of faith feel the need to emphasize the unique presence of the Mother of Christ in history, especially during these last years leading up to the year 2000.

4. The Second Vatican Council prepares us for this by presenting in its teaching the Mother of God in the mystery of Christ and of the Church. If it is true, as the Council itself proclaims,(8) that "only in the mystery of the Incarnate Word does the mystery of man take on light," then this principle must be applied in a very particular way to that exceptional "daughter of the human race," that extraordinary "woman" who became the Mother of Christ. Only in the mystery of Christ is her mystery fully made clear. Thus has the Church sought to interpret it from the very beginning: the mystery of the Incarnation has enabled her to penetrate and to make ever clearer the mystery of the Mother of the Incarnate Word. The Council of Ephesus (431) was of decisive importance in clarifying

this, for during that Council, to the great joy of Christians, the truth of the divine motherhood of Mary was solemnly confirmed as a truth of the Church's faith. Mary is the Mother of God (= Theotókos), since by the power of the Holy Spirit she conceived in her virginal womb and brought into the world Jesus Christ, the Son of God, who is of one being with the Father.(9) "The Son of God...born of the Virgin Mary...has truly been made one of us,"(10) has been made man. Thus, through the mystery of Christ, on the horizon of the Church's faith there shines in its fullness the mystery of his Mother. In turn, the dogma of the divine motherhood of Mary was for the Council of Ephesus and is for the Church like a seal upon the dogma of the Incarnation, in which the Word truly assumes human nature into the unity of his person, without cancelling out that nature.

[8] Cf. Pastoral Constitution on the Church in the Modern World Gaudium et Spes, 22.

[9] Ecumenical Council of Ephesus, in Conciliorum Oecumenicorum Decreta, Bologna 1973, 41-44; 59-61: DS 250-264; cf. Ecumenical Council of Chalcedon, o. c. 84-87: DS 300-303.

[10] Second Vatican Ecumenical Council, Pastoral Constitution on the Church in the Modern World Gaudium et Spes, 22.

5. The Second Vatican Council, by presenting Mary in the mystery of Christ, also finds the path to a deeper understanding of the mystery of the Church. Mary, as the Mother of Christ, is in a particular way united with the Church, "which the Lord established as his own body."(11) It is significant that the conciliar text places this truth about the Church as the Body of Christ (according to the teaching of the Pauline Letters) in close proximity to the truth that the Son of God "through the power of the Holy Spirit was born of the Virgin Mary." The reality of the Incarnation finds a sort of

extension in the mystery of the Church-the Body of Christ. And one cannot think of the reality of the Incarnation without referring to Mary, the Mother of the Incarnate Word.

[11] Dogmatic Constitution on the Church Lumen Gentium, 52.

In these reflections, however, I wish to consider primarily that "pilgrimage of faith" in which "the Blessed Virgin advanced," faithfully preserving her union with Christ.(12) In this way the "twofold bond" which unites the Mother of God with Christ and with the Church takes on historical significance. Nor is it just a question of the Virgin Mother's life-story, of her personal journey of faith and "the better part" which is hers in the mystery of salvation; it is also a question of the history of the whole People of God, of all those who take part in the same "pilgrimage of faith."

[12] Cf. ibid., 58.

The Council expresses this when it states in another passage that Mary "has gone before," becoming "a model of the Church in the matter of faith, charity and perfect union with Christ."(13) This "going before" as a figure or model is in reference to the intimate mystery of the Church, as she actuates and accomplishes her own saving mission by uniting in herself-as Mary did-the qualities of mother and virgin. She is a virgin who "keeps whole and pure the fidelity she has pledged to her Spouse" and "becomes herself a mother," for "she brings forth to a new and immortal life children who are conceived of the Holy Spirit and born of God."(14)

[13] Ibid., 63, cf. Saint Ambrose, Expos. Evang. sec. Lucam, II, 7: CSEL 32/4, 45; De Institutione Virginis, XIV, 88-89: PL 16, 341.

[14] Cf. Dogmatic Constitution on the Church Lumen Gentium, 64.

6. All this is accomplished in a great historical process, comparable "to a journey." The pilgrimage of faith indicates the interior history, that is, the story of souls. But it is also the story of all human beings, subject here on earth to transitoriness, and part of the historical dimension. In the following reflections we wish to concentrate first of all on the present, which in itself is not yet history, but which nevertheless is constantly forming it, also in the sense of the history of salvation. Here there opens up a broad prospect, within which the Blessed Virgin Mary continues to "go before" the People of God. Her exceptional pilgrimage of faith represents a constant point of reference for the Church, for individuals and for communities, for peoples and nations and, in a sense, for all humanity. It is indeed difficult to encompass and measure its range.

The Council emphasizes that the Mother of God is already the eschatological fulfillment of the Church: "In the most holy Virgin the Church has already reached that perfection whereby she exists without spot or wrinkle (cf. Eph. 5:27)"; and at the same time the Council says that "the followers of Christ still strive to increase in holiness by conquering sin, and so they raise their eyes to Mary, who shines forth to the whole community of the elect as a model of the virtues."(15) The pilgrimage of faith no longer belongs to the Mother of the Son of God: glorified at the side of her Son in heaven, Mary has already crossed the threshold between faith and that vision which is "face to face" (1 Cor. 13:12). At the same time, however, in this eschatological fulfillment, Mary does not cease to be the "Star of the Sea" (Maris Stella) (16) for all those who are still on the journey of faith. If they lift their eyes to her from their earthly existence, they do so because "the Son whom she brought forth is he whom God placed as the first-born among many brethren (Rom. 8:29),"(17) and also because "in the birth and development" of these brothers and sisters "she cooperates with a maternal love."(18)

[15] Ibid., 65.

[16] "Take away this star of the sun which illuminates the world: where does the day go? Take away Mary, this star of the sea, of the great and boundless sea: what is left but a vast obscurity and the shadow of death and deepest darkness?": Saint Bernard, In Navitate B. Mariae Sermo-De aquaeductu, 6: S. Bernardi Opera, V, 1968, 279; cf. In laudibus Virginis Matris Homilia II, 17: ed. cit., IV, 1966, 34f.

[17] Dogmatic Constitution on the Church Lumen Gentium, 63.

[18] Ibid., 63.

PART I

Mary In The Mystery Of Christ

1. Full of Grace

7. "Blessed be the God and Father of our Lord Jesus Christ, who has blessed us in Christ with every spiritual blessing in the heavenly places" (Eph. 1:3). These words of the Letter to the Ephesians reveal the eternal design of God the Father, his plan of man's salvation in Christ. It is a universal plan, which concerns all men and women created in the image and likeness of God (cf. Gen. 1:26). Just as all are included in the creative work of God "in the beginning," so all are eternally included in the divine plan of salvation, which is to be completely revealed, in the "fullness of time," with the final coming of Christ. In fact, the God who is the "Father of our Lord Jesus Christ"-these are the next words of the same Letter-"chose us in him before the foundation of the world,

that we should be holy and blameless before him. He destined us in love to be his sons through Jesus Christ, according to the purpose of his will, to the praise of his glorious grace, which he freely bestowed on us in the Beloved. In him we have redemption through his blood, the forgiveness of our trespasses, according to the riches of his grace" (Eph. 1:4-7).

The divine plan of salvation-which was fully revealed to us with the coming of Christ-is eternal. And according to the teaching contained in the Letter just quoted and in other Pauline Letters (cf. Col. 1:12- 14; Rom. 3:24; Gal. 3:13; 2 Cor. 5:18-29), it is also eternally linked to Christ. It includes everyone, but it reserves a special place for the "woman" who is the Mother of him to whom the Father has entrusted the work of salvation.(19) As the Second Vatican Council says, "she is already prophetically foreshadowed in that promise made to our first parents after their fall into sin"- according to the Book of Genesis (cf. 3:15). "Likewise she is the Virgin who is to conceive and bear a son, whose name will be called Emmanuel"- according to the words of Isaiah (cf. 7:14).(20) In this way the Old Testament prepares that "fullness of time" when God "sent forth his Son, born of woman...so that we might receive adoption as sons." The coming into the world of the Son of God is an event recorded in the first chapters of the Gospels according to Luke and Matthew.

[19] Concerning the predestination of Mary, cf. Saint John Damascene, Hom. in Nativitatem, 7, 10: S. Ch. 80, 65; 73; Hom. in Dormitionem 1, 3: S. Ch. 80, 85: "For it is she, who, chosen from the ancient generations, by virtue of the predestination and benevolence of the God and Father who generated you (the Word of God) outside time without coming out of himself or suffering change, it is she who gave you birth, nourished of her flesh, in the last time...."

[20] Dogmatic Constitution on the Church Lumen Gentium, 55.

8. Mary is definitively introduced into the mystery of Christ through this event: the Annunciation by the angel. This takes place at Nazareth, within the concrete circumstances of the history of Israel, the people which first received God's promises. The divine messenger says to the Virgin: "Hail, full of grace, the Lord is with you" (Lk. 1:28). Mary "was greatly troubled at the saying, and considered in her mind what sort of greeting this might be" (Lk. 1:29): what could those extraordinary words mean, and in particular the expression "full of grace" (kecharitoméne).(21)

[21] In Patristic tradition there is a wide and varied interpretation of this expression: cf. Origen, In Lucam homiliae, VI, 7: S. Ch. 87, 148; Severianus of Gabala, In mundi creationem, Oratio VI, 10: PG 56, 497f.; Saint John Chrysostom (Pseudo), In Annunhationem Deiparae et contra Arium impium, PG 62, 765f.; Basil of Seleucia, Oratio 39, In Sanctissimae Deiparae Annuntiationem, 5: PG 85, 441-46; Antipater of Bosra, Hom. II, In Sanctissimae DeiparaeAnnuntiationem, 3-11: PG 85, 1777-1783; Saint Sophronius of Jerusalem, Oratio 11, In Sanctissimae Deiparae Annuntiationem, 17-19: PG 87/3, 3235-3240; Saint John Damascene Hom. in Dormitionem, 1, 70: S. Ch. 80, 96-101; Saint Jerome, Epistola 65, 9: PL 22, 628, Saint Ambrose, Expos. Evang. sec. Lucam, II, 9: CSEL 32/4, 45f.; Saint Augustine, Sermo 291, 4-6: PL 38, 131 8f.; Enchiridion, 36, 11: PL 40, 250; Saint Peter Chrysologus, Sermo 142: PL 52, 579f.; Sermo 143: PL 52, 583; Saint Fulgentius of Ruspe, Epistola 17, VI 12: PL 65 458; Saint Bernard, In laudibus Virginis Matris, Homilia III, 2-3: S. Bernardi Opera, IV, 1966, 36-38.

If we wish to meditate together with Mary on these words, and especially on the expression "full of grace," we can find a significant echo in the very passage from the Letter to the Ephesians quoted above. And if after the announcement of the heavenly messenger the Virgin of Nazareth is also called "blessed among women" (cf. Lk. 1:42), it is because of that blessing with which "God the Father" has filled us "in the heavenly places, in Christ." It is a spiritual blessing which is meant for all people and which bears in itself fullness and universality ("every blessing"). It flows from that love which, in the Holy Spirit, unites the consubstantial Son to the Father. At the same time, it is a blessing poured out through Jesus Christ upon human history until the end: upon all people. This blessing, however, refers to Mary in a special and exceptional degree: for she was greeted by Elizabeth as "blessed among women."

The double greeting is due to the fact that in the soul of this "daughter of Sion" there is manifested, in a sense, all the "glory of grace," that grace which "the Father...has given us in his beloved Son." For the messenger greets Mary as "full of grace"; he calls her thus as if it were her real name. He does not call her by her proper earthly name: Miryam (= Mary), but by this new name: "full of grace." What does this name mean? Why does the archangel address the Virgin of Nazareth in this way?

In the language of the Bible "grace" means a special gift, which according to the New Testament has its source precisely in the Trinitarian life of God himself, God who is love (cf. 1 Jn. 4:8). The fruit of this love is "the election" of which the Letter to the Ephesians speaks. On the part of God, this election is the eternal desire to save man through a sharing in his own life (cf. 2 Pt. 1:4) in Christ: it is salvation through a sharing in supernatural life. The effect of this eternal gift, of this grace of man's election by God, is like a seed of holiness, or a spring which rises in the soul as a gift from God himself, who through grace gives life and holiness to those who are chosen. In this way there is fulfilled, that is to say there comes about, that "blessing" of man "with every spiritual blessing," that "being his adopted sons and daughters...in Christ," in him who is eternally the "beloved Son" of the Father.

When we read that the messenger addresses Mary as "full of grace," the Gospel context, which mingles revelations and ancient promises, enables us to understand that among all the "spiritual blessings in Christ" this is a special "blessing." In the mystery of Christ she is present even "before the creation of the world," as the one whom the Father "has chosen" as Mother of his Son in the Incarnation. And, what is more, together with the Father, the Son has chosen her, entrusting her eternally to the Spirit of holiness. In an entirely special and exceptional way Mary is united to Christ, and similarly she is eternally loved in this "beloved Son," this Son who is of one being with the Father, in whom is concentrated all the "glory of grace." At the same time, she is and remains perfectly open to this "gift from above" (cf. Jas. 1:17). As the Council teaches, Mary "stands out among the poor and humble of the Lord, who confidently await and receive salvation from him."(22)

[22] Dogmatic Constitution on the Church Lumen Gentium, 55.

9. If the greeting and the name "full of grace" say all this, in the context of the angel's announcement they refer first of all to the election of Mary as Mother of the Son of God. But at the same time the "fullness of grace" indicates all the supernatural munificence from which Mary benefits by being chosen and destined to be the Mother of Christ. If this election is fundamental for the accomplishment of God's salvific designs for humanity, and if the eternal choice in Christ and the vocation to the dignity of adopted children is the destiny of everyone, then the election of

Mary is wholly exceptional and unique. Hence also the singularity and uniqueness of her place in the mystery of Christ.

The divine messenger says to her: "Do not be afraid, Mary, for you have found favor with God. And behold, you will conceive in your womb and bear a son, and you shall call his name Jesus. He will be great, and will be called the Son of the Most High" (Lk. 1:30-32). And when the Virgin, disturbed by that extraordinary greeting, asks: "How shall this be, since I have no husband?" she receives from the angel the confirmation and explanation of the preceding words. Gabriel says to her: "The Holy Spirit will come upon you, and the power of the Most High will overshadow you; therefore the child to be born will be called holy, the Son of God" (Lk. 1:35).

The Annunciation, therefore, is the revelation of the mystery of the Incarnation at the very beginning of its fulfillment on earth. God's salvific giving of himself and his life, in some way to all creation but directly to man, reaches one of its high points in the mystery of the Incarnation. This is indeed a high point among all the gifts of grace conferred in the history of man and of the universe: Mary is "full of grace," because it is precisely in her that the Incarnation of the Word, the hypostatic union of the Son of God with human nature, is accomplished and fulfilled. As the Council says, Mary is "the Mother of the Son of God. As a result she is also the favorite daughter of the Father and the temple of the Holy Spirit. Because of this gift of sublime grace, she far surpasses all other creatures, both in heaven and on earth."(23)

[23] Ibid., 53.

10. The Letter to the Ephesians, speaking of the "glory of grace" that "God, the Father...has bestowed on us in his beloved Son," adds: "In him we have redemption through his blood" (Eph. 1:7). According to the belief formulated in solemn documents of the

Church, this "glory of grace" is manifested in the Mother of God through the fact that she has been "redeemed in a more sublime manner."(24) By virtue of the richness of the grace of the beloved Son, by reason of the redemptive merits of him who willed to become her Son, Mary was preserved from the inheritance of original sin.(25) In this way, from the first moment of her conception- which is to say of her existence-she belonged to Christ, sharing in the salvific and sanctifying grace and in that love which has its beginning in the "Beloved," the Son of the Eternal Father, who through the Incarnation became her own Son. Consequently, through the power of the Holy Spirit, in the order of grace, which is a participation in the divine nature, Mary receives life from him to whom she herself, in the order of earthly generation, gave life as a mother. The liturgy does not hesitate to call her "mother of her Creator"(26) and to hail her with the words which Dante Alighieri places on the lips of St. Bernard: "daughter of your Son."(27) And since Mary receives this "new life" with a fullness corresponding to the Son's love for the Mother, and thus corresponding to the dignity of the divine motherhood, the angel at the Annunciation calls her "full of grace."

[24] Cf. Pope Pius XI, Apostolic Letter Ineffabilis Deus (8 December 1854): Pii IX P.M. Acta, pars I, 616; Second Vatican Ecumenical Council, Dogmatic Constitution on the Church Lumen Gentium, 53.

[25] Cf. Saint Germanus of Constantinople, In Annuntiationem SS. Deiparae Hom.: PG 98, 327f.; Saint Andrew of Crete, Canon in B. Mariae Natalem, 4. PG 97, 1321f., In Nativitatem B. Mariae, I: PG 97, 81 1f. Hom. in Dormitionem S. Mariae I: PG 97, 1067f.

[26] Liturgy of the Hours of 15 August, Assumption of the Blessed Virgin Mary, Hymn at First and Second Vespers; Saint Peter Damian, Carmina et preces, XLVII: PL 145, 934.

[27] Divina Commedia, Paradiso, XXXIII, 1; cf. Liturgy of the Hours, Memomial of the Blessed Virgin Mary on Saturday, Hymn II in the Office of Readings.

11. In the salvific design of the Most Holy Trinity, the mystery of the Incarnation constitutes the superabundant fulfillment of the promise made by God to man after original sin, after that first sin whose effects oppress the whole earthly history of man (cf. Gen. 3:15). And so, there comes into the world a Son, "the seed of the woman" who will crush the evil of sin in its very origins: "he will crush the head of the serpent." As we see from the words of the Protogospel, the victory of the woman's Son will not take place without a hard struggle, a struggle that is to extend through the whole of human history. The "enmity," foretold at the beginning, is confirmed in the Apocalypse (the book of the final events of the Church and the world), in which there recurs the sign of the "woman," this time "clothed with the sun" (Rev. 12:1).

Mary, Mother of the Incarnate Word, is placed at the very center of that enmity, that struggle which accompanies the history of humanity on earth and the history of salvation itself. In this central place, she who belongs to the "weak and poor of the Lord" bears in herself, like no other member of the human race, that "glory of grace" which the Father "has bestowed on us in his beloved Son," and this grace determines the extraordinary greatness and beauty of her whole being. Mary thus remains before God, and also before the whole of humanity, as the unchangeable and inviolable sign of God's election, spoken of in Paul's letter: "in Christ…he chose us…before the foundation of the world,…he destined us…to be his sons" (Eph. 1:4, 5). This election is more powerful than any experience of evil and sin, than all that "enmity" which marks the history of man. In this history Mary remains a sign of sure hope.

2. Blessed is she who believed

12. Immediately after the narration of the Annunciation, the Evangelist Luke guides us in the footsteps of the Virgin of Nazareth towards "a city of Judah" (Lk. 1:39). According to scholars this city would be the modern Ain Karim, situated in the mountains, not far from Jerusalem. Mary arrived there "in haste," to visit Elizabeth her kinswoman. The reason for her visit is also to be found in the fact that at the Annunciation Gabriel had made special mention of Elizabeth, who in her old age had conceived a son by her husband Zechariah, through the power of God: "your kins woman Elizabeth in her old age has also conceived a Son; and this is the sixth month with her who was called barren. For with God nothing will be impossible" (Lk. 1:36-37). The divine messenger had spoken of what had been accomplished in Elizabeth in order to answer Mary's question. "How shall this be, since I have no husband?" (Lk. 1:34) It is to come to pass precisely through the "power of the Most High," just as it happened in the case of Elizabeth, and even more so.

Moved by charity, therefore, Mary goes to the house of her kinswoman. When Mary enters, Elizabeth replies to her greeting and feels the child leap in her womb, and being "filled with the Holy Spirit" she greets Mary with a loud cry: "Blessed are you among women, and blessed is the fruit of your womb!" (cf. Lk. 1:40-42) Elizabeth's exclamation or acclamation was subsequently to become part of the Hail Mary, as a continuation of the angel's greeting, thus becoming one of the Church's most frequently used prayers. But still more significant are the words of Elizabeth in the question which follows: "And why is this granted me, that the mother of my Lord should come to me?" (Lk. 1:43) Elizabeth bears witness to Mary: she recognizes and proclaims that before her stands the Mother of the Lord, the Mother of the Messiah. The son whom Elizabeth is carrying in her womb also shares in this witness: "The babe in my womb leaped for joy" (Lk. 1:44). This child is the future John the Baptist, who at the Jordan will point out Jesus as the Messiah.

While every word of Elizabeth's greeting is filled with meaning, her final words would seem to have fundamental importance: "And blessed is she who believed that there would be a fulfillment of what was spoken to her from the Lord" (Lk. 1:45).(28) These words can be linked with the little "full of grace" of the angel's greeting. Both of these texts reveal an essential Mariological content, namely the truth about Mary, who has become really present in the mystery of Christ precisely because she "has believed." The fullness of grace announced by the angel means the gift of God himself. Mary's faith, proclaimed by Elizabeth at the Visitation, indicates how the Virgin of Nazareth responded to this gift.

[28] Cf. Saint Augustine, De Sancta Virginitate, III, 3: PL 40, 398; Sermo 25, 7: PL 46,

13. As the Council teaches, "'The obedience of faith' (Rom. 16:26; cf. Rom. 1:5; 2 Cor. 10:5-6) must be given to God who reveals, an obedience by which man entrusts his whole self freely to God."(29) This description of faith found perfect realization in Mary. The "decisive" moment was the Annunciation, and the very words of Elizabeth: "And blessed is she who believed" refer primarily to that very moment.(30)

[29] Dogmatic Constitution on Divine Revelation Dei Verbum, 5

[30] This is a classic theme, already expounded by Saint Irenaeus: "And, as by the action of the disobedient virgin, man was afflicted and, being cast down, died, so also by the action of the Virgin who obeyed the word of God, man being regenerated received, through life, life.... For it was meet and Just...that Eve should be "recapitulated" in Mary, so that the Virgin, becoming the advocate of the virgin, should dissolve and destroy the virginal disobedience by means of virginal obedience": Expositio doctrinae apostolicae, 33: S.Ch. 62, 83-86; cf. also Adversus Haereses, V, 19, 1: 5. Ch. 153, 248-250.

Indeed, at the Annunciation Mary entrusted herself to God completely, with the "full submission of intellect and will," manifesting "the obedience of faith" to him who spoke to her through his messenger.(31) She responded, therefore, with all her human and feminine "I," and this response of faith included both perfect cooperation with "the grace of God that precedes and assists" and perfect openness to the action of the Holy Spirit, who "constantly brings faith to completion by his gifts."(32)

[31] Second Vatican Ecumenical Council, Dogmatic Constitution on Divine Revelation Dei Verbum, 5.

[32] Ibid., 5, cf. Dogmatic Constitution on the Church Lumen Gentium, 56.

The word of the living God, announced to Mary by the angel, referred to her: "And behold, you will conceive in your womb and bear a son" (Lk. 1:31). By accepting this announcement, Mary was to become the "Mother of the Lord," and the divine mystery of the Incarnation was to be accomplished in her: "The Father of mercies willed that the consent of the predestined Mother should precede the Incarnation."(33) And Mary gives this consent, after she has heard everything the messenger has to say. She says: "Behold, I am the handmaid of the Lord; let it be to me according to your word" (Lk. 1:38). This fiat of Mary-"let it be to me"-was decisive, on the human level, for the accomplishment of the divine mystery. There is a complete harmony with the words of the Son, who, according to the Letter to the Hebrews, says to the Father as he comes into the world: "Sacrifices and offering you have not desired, but a body you have prepared for me.... Lo, I have come to do your will, O God" (Heb. 10:5-7). The mystery of the Incarnation was accomplished when Mary uttered her fiat: "Let it be to me according to your word," which made possible, as far as it depended upon her in the divine plan, the granting of her Son's desire.

[33] Second Vatican Ecumenical Council, Dogmatic Constitution on the Church Lumen Gentium, 56.

Mary uttered this fiat in faith. In faith she entrusted herself to God without reserve and "devoted herself totally as the handmaid of the Lord to the person and work of her Son."(34) And as the Fathers of the Church teach-she conceived this Son in her mind before she conceived him in her womb: precisely in faith!(35) Rightly therefore does Elizabeth praise Mary: "And blessed is she who believed that there would be a fulfillment of what was spoken to her from the Lord." These words have already been fulfilled: Mary of Nazareth presents herself at the threshold of Elizabeth and Zechariah's house as the Mother of the Son of God. This is Elizabeth's joyful discovery: "The mother of my Lord comes to me"!

[34] Ibid., 56.

[35] Cf. ibid., 53; Saint Augustine, De Sancta Virginitate, III, 3: PL 40, 398; Sermo 215, 4; PL 38, 1074; Sermo 196, I: PL 38, 1019; De peccatorum meritis et remissione, I, 29, 57: PL 44, 142; Sermo 25,

7: PL 46, 937-938; Saint Leo the Great, Tractatus 21, de natale Domini, I: CCL 138, 86.

14. Mary's faith can also be compared to that of Abraham, whom St. Paul calls "our father in faith" (cf. Rom. 4:12). In the salvific economy of God's revelation, Abraham's faith constitutes the beginning of the Old Covenant; Mary's faith at the Annunciation inaugurates the New Covenant. Just as Abraham "in hope believed against hope, that he should become the father of many nations" (cf. Rom. 4:18), so Mary, at the Annunciation, having professed her virginity ("How shall this be, since I have no husband?") believed that through the power of the Most High, by the power of the Holy Spirit, she would become the Mother of God's Son in accordance with the angel's revelation: "The child to be born will be called holy, the Son of God" (Lk. 1:35).

However, Elizabeth's words "And blessed is she who believed" do not apply only to that particular moment of the Annunciation. Certainly the Annunciation is the culminating moment of Mary's faith in her awaiting of Christ, but it is also the point of departure from which her whole "journey towards God" begins, her whole pilgrimage of faith. And on this road, in an eminent and truly heroic manner- indeed with an ever greater heroism of faith-the "obedience" which she professes to the word of divine revelation will be fulfilled. Mary's "obedience of faith" during the whole of her pilgrimage will show surprising similarities to the faith of Abraham. Just like the Patriarch of the People of God, so too Mary, during the pilgrimage of her filial and maternal fiat, "in hope believed against hope." Especially during certain stages of this journey the blessing granted to her "who believed" will be revealed with particular vividness. To believe means "to abandon oneself" to the truth of the word of the living God, knowing and humbly recognizing "how unsearchable are his judgments and how inscrutable his ways" (Rom. 11:33). Mary, who by the eternal will of the Most High stands, one may say, at the very center of those "inscrutable ways" and "unsearchable judgments" of God, conforms herself to them in the dim light of faith, accepting fully and with a ready heart everything that is decreed in the divine plan.

15. When at the Annunciation Mary hears of the Son whose Mother she is to become and to whom "she will give the name Jesus" (= Savior), she also learns that "the Lord God will give to him the throne of his father David," and that "he will reign over the house of Jacob for ever and of his kingdom there will be no end" (Lk. 1:32- 33). The hope of the whole of Israel was directed towards this. The promised Messiah is to be "great," and the heavenly messenger also announces that "he will be great"-great both by bearing the name of Son of the Most High and by the fact that he is to assume the inheritance of David. He is therefore to be a king, he is to reign "over the house of Jacob." Mary had grown up in the midst of these expectations of her people: could she guess, at the moment of the Annunciation, the vital significance of the angel's words? And how is one to understand that "kingdom" which "will have no end"?

Although through faith she may have perceived in that instant the was the mother of the "Messiah King," nevertheless she replied: "Behold, I am the handmaid of the Lord; let it be to me according to your word" (Lk. 1:38). From the first moment Mary professed above all the "obedience of faith," abandoning herself to the meaning which was given to the words of the Annunciation by him from whom they proceeded: God himself.

16. Later, a little further along this way of the "obedience of faith," Mary hears other words: those uttered by Simeon in the Temple of Jerusalem. It was now forty days after the birth of Jesus when, in

accordance with the precepts of the Law of Moses, Mary and Joseph "brought him up to Jerusalem to present him to the Lord" (Lk. 2:22). The birth had taken place in conditions of extreme poverty. We know from Luke that when, on the occasion of the census ordered by the Roman authorities, Mary went with Joseph to Bethlehem, having found "no place in the inn," she gave birth to her Son in a stable and "laid him in a manger" (cf. Lk. 2:7).

A just and God-fearing man, called Simeon, appears at this beginning of Mary's "journey" of faith. His words, suggested by the Holy Spirit (cf. Lk. 2:25-27), confirm the truth of the Annunciation. For we read that he took up in his arms the child to whom-in accordance with the angel's command-the name Jesus was given (cf. Lk. 2:21). Simeon's words match the meaning of this name, which is Savior: "God is salvation." Turning to the Lord, he says: "For my eyes have seen your salvation which you have prepared in the presence of all peoples, a light for revelation to the Gentiles, and for glory to your people Israel" (Lk. 2:30-32). At the same time, however, Simeon addresses Mary with the following words: "Behold, this child is set for the fall and rising of many in Israel, and for a sign that is spoken against, that thoughts out of many hearts may be revealed"; and he adds with direct reference to her: "and a sword will pierce through your own soul also" (cf. Lk. 2:34-35). Simeon's words cast new light on the announcement which Mary had heard from the angel: Jesus is the Savior, he is "a light for revelation" to mankind. Is not this what was manifested in a way on Christmas night, when the shepherds come to the stable (cf. Lk. 2:8-20)? Is not this what was to be manifested even more clearly in the coming of the Magi from the East (cf. Mt. 2:1-12)? But at the same time, at the very beginning of his life, the Son of Mary, and his Mother with him, will experience in themselves the truth of those other words of Simeon: "a sign that is spoken against" (Lk.

2:34). Simeon's words seem like a second Annunciation to Mary, for they tell her of the actual historical situation in which the Son is to accomplish his mission, namely, in misunderstanding and sorrow. While this announcement on the one hand confirms her faith in the accomplishment of the divine promises of salvation, on the other hand it also reveals to her that she will have to live her obedience of faith in suffering, at the side of the suffering Savior, and that her motherhood will be mysterious and sorrowful. Thus, after the visit of the Magi who came from the East, after their homage ("they fell down and worshipped him") and after they had offered gifts (cf. Mt. 2:11), Mary together with the child has to flee into Egypt in the protective care of Joseph, for "Herod is about to search for the child, to destroy him" (cf. Mt. 2:13). And until the death of Herod they will have to remain in Egypt (cf. Mt. 2:15).

17. When the Holy Family returns to Nazareth after Herod's death, there begins the long period of the hidden life. She "who believed that there would be a fulfillment of what was spoken to her from the Lord" (Lk. 1:45) lives the reality of these words day by day. And daily at her side is the Son to whom "she gave the name Jesus"; therefore in contact with him she certainly uses this name, a fact which would have surprised no one, since the name had long been in use in Israel. Nevertheless, Mary knows that he who bears the name Jesus has been called by the angel "the Son of the Most High" (cf. Lk. 1:32). Mary knows she has conceived and given birth to him "without having a husband," by the power of the Holy Spirit, by the power of the Most High who overshadowed her (cf. Lk. 1:35), just as at the time of Moses and the Patriarchs the cloud covered the presence of God (cf. Ex. 24:16; 40:34-35; I Kings 8:10-12). Therefore Mary knows that the Son to whom she gave birth in a virginal manner is precisely that "Holy One," the Son of God, of whom the angel spoke to her.

During the years of Jesus' hidden life in the house at Nazareth, Mary's life too is "hid with Christ in God" (cf. Col. 3:3) through faith. For faith is contact with the mystery of God. Every day Mary is in constant contact with the ineffable mystery of God made man, a mystery that surpasses everything revealed in the Old Covenant. From the moment of the Annunciation, the mind of the Virgin-Mother has been initiated into the radical "newness" of God's self-revelation and has been made aware of the mystery. She is the first of those "little ones" of whom Jesus will say one day: "Father, ...you have hidden these things from the wise and understanding and revealed them to babes" (Mt. 11:25). For "no one knows the Son except the Father" (Mt. 11:27). If this is the case, how can Mary "know the Son"? Of course she does not know him as the Father does; and yet she is the first of those to whom the Father "has chosen to reveal him" (cf. Mt. 11:26-27; 1 Cor. 2:11). If though, from the moment of the Annunciation, the Son-whom only the Father knows completely, as the one who begets him in the eternal "today" (cf. Ps. 2:7) was revealed to Mary, she, his Mother, is in contact with the truth about her Son only in faith and through faith! She is therefore blessed, because "she has believed," and continues to believe day after day amidst all the trials and the adversities of Jesus' infancy and then during the years of the hidden life at Nazareth, where he "was obedient to them" (Lk. 2:51). He was obedient both to Mary and also to Joseph, since Joseph took the place of his father in people's eyes; for this reason, the Son of Mary was regarded by the people as "the carpenter's son" (Mt. 13:55).

The Mother of that Son, therefore, mindful of what has been told her at the Annunciation and in subsequent events, bears within herself the radical "newness" of faith: the beginning of the New Covenant. This is the beginning of the Gospel, the joyful Good

News. However, it is not difficult to see in that beginning a particular heaviness of heart, linked with a sort of night of faith"-to use the words of St. John of the Cross-a kind of "veil" through which one has to draw near to the Invisible One and to live in intimacy with the mystery.(36) And this is the way that Mary, for many years, lived in intimacy with the mystery of her Son, and went forward in her "pilgrimage of faith," while Jesus "increased in wisdom...and in favor with God and man" (Lk. 2:52). God's predilection for him was manifested ever more clearly to people's eyes. The first human creature thus permitted to discover Christ was Mary, who lived with Joseph in the same house at Nazareth.

[36] Ascent of Mount Carmel, 1. II, Ch. 3, 4-6.

However, when he had been found in the Temple, and his Mother asked him, "Son, why have you treated us so?" the twelve-year-old Jesus answered: "Did you not know that I must be in my Father's house?" And the Evangelist adds: "And they (Joseph and Mary) did not understand the saying which he spoke to them" (Lk. 2:48-50). Jesus was aware that "no one knows the Son except the Father" (cf. Mt. 11:27); thus even his Mother, to whom had been revealed most completely the mystery of his divine sonship, lived in intimacy with this mystery only through faith! Living side by side with her Son under the same roof, and faithfully persevering "in her union with her Son," she "advanced in her pilgrimage of faith," as the Council emphasizes.(37) And so it was during Christ's public life too (cf. Mk. 3:21-35) that day by day there was fulfilled in her the blessing uttered by Elizabeth at the Visitation: "Blessed is she who believed."

[37] Cf. Dogmatic Constitution on the Church Lumen Gentium, 58.

18. This blessing reaches its full meaning when Mary stands beneath the Cross of her Son (cf. Jn. 19:25). The Council says that this happened "not without a divine plan": by "suffering deeply with her only-begotten Son and joining herself with her maternal spirit to his sacrifice, lovingly consenting to the immolation of the victim to whom she had given birth," in this way Mary "faithfully preserved her union with her Son even to the Cross."(38) It is a union through faith- the same faith with which she had received the angel's revelation at the Annunciation. At that moment she had also heard the words: "He will be great...and the Lord God will give to him the throne of his father David, and he will reign over the house of Jacob for ever; and of his kingdom there will be no end" (Lk. 1:32-33).

[38] Ibid., 58.

And now, standing at the foot of the Cross, Mary is the witness, humanly speaking, of the complete negation of these words. On that wood of the Cross her Son hangs in agony as one condemned. "He was despised and rejected by men; a man of sorrows...he was despised, and we esteemed him not": as one destroyed (cf. Is. 53:3-5). How great, how heroic then is the obedience of faith shown by Mary in the face of God's "unsearchable judgments"! How completely she "abandons herself to God" without reserve, offering the full assent of the intellect and the will"(39) to him whose "ways are inscrutable" (cf. Rom. 11:33)! And how powerful too is the action of grace in her soul, how all-pervading is the influence of the Holy Spirit and of his light and power!

[39] Cf. Second Vatican Ecumenical Council, Dogmatic Constitution on Divine Revelation Dei Verbum, 5.

Through this faith Mary is perfectly united with Christ in his self-emptying. For "Christ Jesus, who, though he was in the form of

God, did not count equality with God a thing to be grasped, but emptied himself, taking the form of a servant, being born in the likeness of men": precisely on Golgotha "humbled himself and became obedient unto death, even death on a cross" (cf. Phil. 2:5-8). At the foot of the Cross Mary shares through faith in the shocking mystery of this self-emptying. This is perhaps the deepest "kenosis" of faith in human history. Through faith the Mother shares in the death of her Son, in his redeeming death; but in contrast with the faith of the disciples who fled, hers was far more enlightened. On Golgotha, Jesus through the Cross definitively confirmed that he was the "sign of contradiction" foretold by Simeon. At the same time, there were also fulfilled on Golgotha the words which Simeon had addressed to Mary: "and a sword will pierce through your own soul also."(40)

[40] Concerning Mary's participation or "compassion" in the death of Christ, cf. Saint Bernard, In Dominica infra octavam Assumptionis Sermo, 14: S. Bernardi Opera, V, 1968, 273.

19. Yes, truly "blessed is she who believed"! These words, spoken by Elizabeth after the Annunciation, here at the foot of the Cross seem to re-echo with supreme eloquence, and the power contained within them becomes something penetrating. From the Cross, that is to say from the very heart of the mystery of Redemption, there radiates and spreads out the prospect of that blessing of faith It goes right hack to "the beginning." and as a sharing in the sacrifice of Christ-the new Adam-it becomes in a certain sense the counterpoise to the disobedience and disbelief embodied in the sin of our first parents. Thus teach the Fathers of the Church and especially St. Irenaeus, quoted by the Constitution Lumen Gentium: "The knot of Eve's disobedience was untied by Mary's obedience; what the virgin Eve bound through her unbelief, the Virgin Mary loosened by her faith."(41) In the light of this

comparison with Eve, the Fathers of the Church-as the Council also says-call Mary the "mother of the liing" and often speak of "death through Eve, life through Mary."(42)

[41] Saint Irenaeus, Adversus Haereses III, 22, 4: S. Ch. 211, 438-444; cf. Dogmatic Constitution on the Church Lumen Gentium, 56, Note 6.

[42] Cf. Dogmatic Constitution on the Church Lumen Gentium, 56, and the Fathers quoted there in Notes 8 and 9.

In the expression "Blessed is she who believed," we can therefore rightly find a kind of "key" which unlocks for us the innermost reality of Mary, whom the angel hailed as "full of grace." If as "full of grace" she has been eternally present in the mystery of Christ, through faith she became a sharer in that mystery in every extension of her earthly journey. She "advanced in her pilgrimage of faith" and at the same time, in a discreet yet direct and effective way, she made present to humanity the mystery of Christ. And she still continues to do so. Through the mystery of Christ, she too is present within mankind. Thus through the mystery of the Son the mystery of the Mother is also made clear.

3. Behold your mother

20. The Gospel of Luke records the moment when "a woman in the crowd raised her voice" and said to Jesus: "Blessed is the womb that bore you, and the breasts that you sucked!" (Lk. 11:27) These words were an expression of praise of Mary as Jesus' mother according to the flesh. Probably the Mother of Jesus was not personally known to this woman; in fact, when Jesus began his messianic activity Mary did not accompany him but continued to remain at Nazareth. One could say that the words of that unknown woman in a way brought Mary out of her hiddenness.

Through these words, there flashed out in the midst of the crowd, at least for an instant, the gospel of Jesus' infancy. This is the gospel in which Mary is present as the mother who conceives Jesus in her womb, gives him birth and nurses him: the nursing mother referred to by the woman in the crowd. Thanks to this motherhood, Jesus, the Son of the Most High (cf. Lk. 1:32), is a true son of man. He is "flesh," like every other man: he is "the Word (who) became flesh" (cf. Jn. 1:14). He is of the flesh and blood of Mary!(43)

[43] "Christ is truth, Christ is flesh: Christ truth in the mind of Mary, Christ flesh in the womb of Mary": Saint Augustine, Sermo 25 (Sermones inediti), 7: PL 46, 938.

But to the blessing uttered by that woman upon her who was his mother according to the flesh, Jesus replies in a significant way: "Blessed rather are those who hear the word of God and keep it" (Lk. 11:28). He wishes to divert attention from motherhood understood only as a fleshly bond, in order to direct it towards those mysterious bonds of the spirit which develop from hearing and keeping God's word.

This same shift into the sphere of spiritual values is seen even more clearly in another response of Jesus reported by all the Synoptics. When Jesus is told that "his mother and brothers are standing outside and wish to see him," he replies: "My mother and my brothers are those who hear the word of God and do it" (cf. Lk. 8:20-21). This he said "looking around on those who sat about him," as we read in Mark (3:34) or, according to Matthew (12:49), "stretching out his hand towards his disciples."

These statements seem to fit in with the reply which the twelve-year-old Jesus gave to Mary and Joseph when he was found after three days in the Temple at Jerusalem.

Now, when Jesus left Nazareth and began his public life throughout Palestine, he was completely and exclusively "concerned with his Father's business" (cf. Lk. 2:49). He announced the Kingdom: the "Kingdom of God" and "his Father's business," which add a new dimension and meaning to everything human, and therefore to every human bond, insofar as these things relate to the goals and tasks assigned to every human being. Within this new dimension, also a bond such as that of "brotherhood" means something different from "brotherhood according to the flesh" deriving from a common origin from the same set of parents. "Motherhood," too, in the dimension of the Kingdom of God and in the radius of the fatherhood of God himself, takes on another meaning. In the words reported by Luke, Jesus teaches precisely this new meaning of motherhood.

Is Jesus thereby distancing himself from his mother according to the flesh? Does he perhaps wish to leave her in the hidden obscurity which she herself has chosen? If this seems to be the case from the tone of those words, one must nevertheless note that the new and different motherhood which Jesus speaks of to his disciples refers precisely to Mary in a very special way. Is not Mary the first of "those who hear the word of God and do it"? And therefore does not the blessing uttered by Jesus in response to the woman in the crowd refer primarily to her? Without any doubt, Mary is worthy of blessing by the very fact that she became the mother of Jesus according to the flesh ("Blessed is the womb that bore you, and the breasts that you sucked"), but also and especially because already at the Annunciation she accepted the word of God, because she believed it, because she was obedient to God, and because she "kept" the word and "pondered it in her heart" (cf. Lk. 1:38, 45; 2:19, 51) and by means of her whole life accomplished it. Thus we can say that the blessing proclaimed by Jesus is not in opposition, despite appearances, to the blessing uttered by the unknown woman, but rather coincides with that blessing in the person of this Virgin Mother, who called herself only "the handmaid of the Lord" (Lk. 1:38). If it is true that "all generations will call her blessed" (cf. Lk. 1:48), then it can be said that the unnamed woman was the first to confirm unwittingly that prophetic phrase of Mary's Magnificat and to begin the Magnificat of the ages.

If through faith Mary became the bearer of the Son given to her by the Father through the power of the Holy Spirit, while preserving her virginity intact, in that same faith she discovered and accepted the other dimension of motherhood revealed by Jesus during his messianic mission. One can say that this dimension of motherhood belonged to Mary from the beginning, that is to say from the moment of the conception and birth of her Son. From that time she was "the one who believed." But as the messianic mission of her Son grew clearer to her eyes and spirit, she herself as a mother became ever more open to that new dimension of motherhood which was to constitute her "part" beside her Son. Had she not said from the very beginning: "Behold, I am the handmaid of the Lord; let it be to me according to your word" (Lk. 1:38)? Through faith Mary continued to hear and to ponder that word, in which there became ever clearer, in a way "which surpasses knowledge" (Eph. 3:19), the self-revelation of the living God. Thus in a sense Mary as Mother became the first "disciple" of her Son, the first to whom he seemed to say: "Follow me," even before he addressed this call to the Apostles or to anyone else (cf. Jn. 1:43).

21. From this point of view, particularly eloquent is the passage in the Gospel of John which presents Mary at the wedding feast of Cana. She appears there as the Mother of Jesus at the beginning of his public life: "There was a marriage at Cana in Galilee, and the

mother of Jesus was there; Jesus also was invited to the marriage, with his disciples" (Jn. 2:1-2). From the text it appears that Jesus and his disciples were invited together with Mary, as if by reason of her presence at the celebration: the Son seems to have been invited because of his mother. We are familiar with the sequence of events which resulted from that invitation, that "beginning of the signs" wrought by Jesus-the water changed into wine-which prompts the Evangelist to say that Jesus "manifested his glory; and his disciples believed in him" (Jn. 2:11).

Mary is present at Cana in Galilee as the Mother of Jesus, and in a significant way she contributes to that "beginning of the signs" which reveal the messianic power of her Son. We read: "When the wine gave out, the mother of Jesus said to him, 'They have no wine.' And Jesus said to her, 'O woman, what have you to do with me? My hour has not yet come'" (Jn. 2:3-4). In John's Gospel that "hour" means the time appointed by the Father when the Son accomplishes his task and is to be glorified (cf. Jn. 7:30; 8:20; 12:23, 27; 13:1; 17:1; 19:27). Even though Jesus' reply to his mother sounds like a refusal (especially if we consider the blunt statement "My hour has not yet come" rather than the question), Mary nevertheless turns to the servants and says to them: "Do whatever he tells you" (Jn. 2:5). Then Jesus orders the servants to fill the stone jars with water, and the water becomes wine, better than the wine which has previously been served to the wedding guests.

What deep understanding existed between Jesus and his mother? How can we probe the mystery of their intimate spiritual union? But the fact speaks for itself. It is certain that that event already quite clearly outlines the new dimension, the new meaning of Mary's motherhood. Her motherhood has a significance which is not exclusively contained in the words of Jesus and in the various episodes reported by the Synoptics (Lk. 11:27-28 and Lk. 8:19-21;

Mt. 12:46-50; Mk. 3:31-35). In these texts Jesus means above all to contrast the motherhood resulting from the fact of birth with what this "motherhood" (and also "brotherhood") is to be in the dimension of the Kingdom of God, in the salvific radius of God's fatherhood. In John's text on the other hand, the description of the Cana event outlines what is actually manifested as a new kind of motherhood according to the spirit and not just according to the flesh, that is to say Mary's solicitude for human beings, her coming to them in the wide variety of their wants and needs. At Cana in Galilee there is shown only one concrete aspect of human need, apparently a small one of little importance ("They have no wine"). But it has a symbolic value: this coming to the aid of human needs means, at the same time, bringing those needs within the radius of Christ's messianic mission and salvific power. Thus there is a mediation: Mary places herself between her Son and mankind in the reality of their wants, needs and sufferings. She puts herself "in the middle," that is to say she acts as a mediatrix not as an outsider, but in her position as mother. She knows that as such she can point out to her Son the needs of mankind, and in fact, she "has the right" to do so. Her mediation is thus in the nature of intercession: Mary "intercedes" for mankind. And that is not all. As a mother she also wishes the messianic power of her Son to be manifested, that salvific power of his which is meant to help man in his misfortunes, to free him from the evil which in various forms and degrees weighs heavily upon his life. Precisely as the Prophet Isaiah had foretold about the Messiah in the famous passage which Jesus quoted before his fellow townsfolk in Nazareth: "To preach good news to the poor...to proclaim release to the captives and recovering of sight to the blind..." (cf. Lk. 4:18).

Another essential element of Mary's maternal task is found in her words to the servants: "Do whatever he tells you." The Mother of

Christ presents herself as the spokeswoman of her Son's will, pointing out those things which must be done so that the salvific power of the Messiah may be manifested. At Cana, thanks to the intercession of Mary and the obedience of the servants, Jesus begins "his hour." At Cana Mary appears as believing in Jesus. Her faith evokes his first "sign" and helps to kindle the faith of the disciples.

22. We can therefore say that in this passage of John's Gospel we find as it were a first manifestation of the truth concerning Mary's maternal care. This truth has also found expression in the teaching of the Second Vatican Council. It is important to note how the Council illustrates Mary's maternal role as it relates to the mediation of Christ. Thus we read: "Mary's maternal function towards mankind in no way obscures or diminishes the unique mediation of Christ, but rather shows its efficacy," because "there is one mediator between God and men, the man Christ Jesus" (1 Tim. 2:5). This maternal role of Mary flows, according to God's good pleasure, "from the superabundance of the merits of Christ; it is founded on his mediation, absolutely depends on it, and draws all its efficacy from it."(44) It is precisely in this sense that the episode at Cana in Galilee offers us a sort of first announcement of Mary's mediation, wholly oriented towards Christ and tending to the revelation of his salvific power.

[44] Dogmatic Constitution on the Church Lumen Gentium, 60.

From the text of John it is evident that it is a mediation which is maternal. As the Council proclaims: Mary became "a mother to us in the order of grace." This motherhood in the order of grace flows from her divine motherhood. Because she was, by the design of divine Providence, the mother who nourished the divine Redeemer, Mary became "an associate of unique nobility, and the Lord's humble handmaid," who "cooperated by her obedience, faith, hope and burning charity in the Savior's work of restoring supernatural life to souls."(45) And "this maternity of Mary in the order of grace. . .will last without interruption until the eternal fulfillment of all the elect." (46)

[45] Ibid., 61.

[46] Ibid., 62.

23. If John's description of the event at Cana presents Mary's caring motherhood at the beginning of Christ's messianic activity, another passage from the same Gospel confirms this motherhood in the salvific economy of grace at its crowning moment, namely when Christ's sacrifice on the Cross, his Paschal Mystery, is accomplished. John's description is concise: "Standing by the cross of Jesus were his mother, and his mother's sister, Mary the wife of Clopas, and Mary Magdalene. When Jesus saw his mother, and the disciple whom he loved standing near, he said to his mother: 'Woman, behold your son!' Then he said to the disciple, 'Behold, your mother!' And from that hour the disciple took her to his own home" (Jn. 19:25-27).

Undoubtedly, we find here an expression of the Son's particular solicitude for his Mother, whom he is leaving in such great sorrow. And yet the "testament of Christ's Cross" says more. Jesus highlights a new relationship between Mother and Son, the whole truth and reality of which he solemnly confirms. One can say that if Mary's motherhood of the human race had already been outlined, now it is clearly stated and established. It emerges from the definitive accomplishment of the Redeemer's Paschal Mystery. The Mother of Christ, who stands at the very center of this mystery-a mystery which embraces each individual and all humanity-is given as mother to every single individual and all mankind. The man at the foot of the Cross is John, "the disciple whom he loved."(47) But it is not he alone. Following tradition, the Council does not hesitate to call Mary "the Mother of Christ and mother of mankind": since she "belongs to the offspring of Adam she is one with all human beings.... Indeed she is 'clearly the mother of the members of Christ...since she cooperated out of love so that there might be born in the Church the faithful.'"(48)

[47] There is a well-known passage of Origen on the presence of Mary and John on Calvary: "The Gospels are the first fruits of all Scripture and the Gospel of John is the first of the Gospels: no one can grasp its meaning without having leaned his head on Jesus' breast and having received from Jesus Mary as Mother": Comm. in Ioan., I, 6: PG 14, 31; cf. Saint Ambrose, Expos. Evang. sec. Lucam, X, 129-131: CSEL 32/4, 504f.

[48] Dogmatic Constitution on the Church Lumen Gentium, 54 and 53; the latter text quotes Saint Augustine, De Sancta Virginitate, VI, 6: PL 40, 399.

And so this "new motherhood of Mary," generated by faith, is the fruit of the "new" love which came to definitive maturity in her at the foot of the Cross, through her sharing in the redemptive love of her Son.

24. Thus we find ourselves at the very center of the fulfillment of the promise contained in the Proto-gospel: the "seed of the woman...will crush the head of the serpent" (cf. Gen. 3:15). By his redemptive death Jesus Christ conquers the evil of sin and death at its very roots. It is significant that, as he speaks to his mother from the Cross, he calls her "woman" and says to her: "Woman, behold your son!" Moreover, he had addressed her by the same term at Cana too (cf. Jn. 2:4). How can one doubt that especially now, on Golgotha, this expression goes to the very heart of the mystery of

Mary, and indicates the unique place which she occupies in the whole economy of salvation? As the Council teaches, in Mary "the exalted Daughter of Sion, and after a long expectation of the promise, the times were at length fulfilled and the new dispensation established. All this occurred when the Son of God took a human nature from her, that he might in the mysteries of his flesh free man from sin."(49)

[49] Dogmatic Constitution on the Church Lumen Gentium, 55.

The words uttered by Jesus from the Cross signify that the motherhood of her who bore Christ finds a "new" continuation in the Church and through the Church, symbolized and represented by John. In this way, she who as the one "full of grace" was brought into the mystery of Christ in order to be his Mother and thus the Holy Mother of God, through the Church remains in that mystery as "the woman" spoken of by the Book of Genesis (3:15) at the beginning and by the Apocalypse (12:1) at the end of the history of salvation. In accordance with the eternal plan of Providence, Mary's divine motherhood is to be poured out upon the Church, as indicated by statements of Tradition, according to which Mary's "motherhood" of the Church is the reflection and extension of her motherhood of the Son of God.(50)

[50] Cf. Saint Leo the Great, Tractatus 26, de natale Domini, 2: CCL 138, 126.

According to the Council the very moment of the Church's birth and full manifestation to the world enables us to glimpse this continuity of Mary's motherhood: "Since it pleased God not to manifest solemnly the mystery of the salvation of the human race until he poured forth the Spirit promised by Christ, we see the Apostles before the day of Pentecost 'continuing with one mind in prayer with the women and Mary the mother of Jesus, and with his brethren' (Acts 1:14). We see Mary prayerfully imploring the gift of the Spirit, who had already overshadowed her in the Annunciation."(51)

[51] Dogmatic Constitution on the Church Lumen Gentium, 59.

And so, in the redemptive economy of grace, brought about through the action of the Holy Spirit, there is a unique correspondence between the moment of the Incarnation of the Word and the moment of the birth of the Church. The person who links these two moments is Mary: Mary at Nazareth and Mary in the Upper Room at Jerusalem. In both cases her discreet yet essential presence indicates the path of "birth from the Holy Spirit." Thus she who is present in the mystery of Christ as Mother becomes-by the will of the Son and the power of the Holy Spirit-present in the mystery of the Church. In the Church too she continues to be a maternal presence, as is shown by the words spoken from the Cross: "Woman, behold your son!"; "Behold, your mother."

PART II

The Mother Of God At The Center Of The Pilgrim Church

1. The Church, the People of God present in all the nations of the earth

25. "The Church `like a pilgrim in a foreign land, presses forward amid the persecutions of the world and the consolations of God,'(52) announcing the Cross and Death of the Lord until he comes (cf. 1 Cor. 11:26)."(53) "Israel according to the flesh, which wandered as an exile in the desert, was already called the Church of God (cf. 2 Esd. 13:1; Num. 20:4; Dt. 23:1ff.). Likewise the new Israel...is also called the Church of Christ (cf Mt 16:18). For he has

bought it for himself with his blood (Acts 20:28), has filled it with his Spirit, and provided it with those means which befit it as a visible and social unity. God has gathered together as one all those who in faith look upon Jesus as the author of salvation and the source of unity and peace, and has established them as Church, that for each and all she may be the visible sacrament of this saving unity."(54)

[52] Saint Augustine, De civitate Dei, XVIII, 51: CCL 48, 650.

[53] Second Vatican Ecumenical Council, Dogmatic Constitution on the Church Lumen Gentium, 8.

[54] Ibid., 9.

The Second Vatican Council speaks of the pilgrim Church, establishing an analogy with the Israel of the Old Covenant journeying through the desert. The journey also has an external character, visible in the time and space in which it historically takes place. For the Church "is destined to extend to all regions of the earth and so to enter into the history of mankind," but at the same time "she transcends all limits of time and of space."(55) And yet the essential character of her pilgrimage is interior: it is a question of a pilgrimage through faith, by "the power of the Risen Lord,"(56) a pilgrimage in the Holy Spirit, given to the Church as the invisible Comforter (parakletos) (cf. Jn. 14:26; 15:26; 16:7): "Moving forward through trial and tribulation, the Church is strengthened by the power of God's grace promised to her by the Lord, so that...moved by the Holy Spirit, she may never cease to renew herself, until through the Cross she arrives at the light which knows no setting."(57)

[55] Ibid., 9.

[56] Ibid., 8.

[57] Ibid., 9.

It is precisely in this ecclesial journey or pilgrimage through space and time, and even more through the history of souls, that Mary is present, as the one who is "blessed because she believed," as the one who advanced on the pilgrimage of faith, sharing unlike any other creature in the mystery of Christ. The Council further says that "Mary figured profoundly in the history of salvation and in a certain way unites and mirrors within herself the central truths of the faith."(58) Among all believers she is like a "mirror" in which are reflected in the most profound and limpid way "the mighty works of God" (Acts 2:11).

[58] Ibid., 65.

26. Built by Christ upon the Apostles, the Church became fully aware of these mighty works of God on the day of Pentecost, when those gathered together in the Upper Room "were all filled with the Holy Spirit and began to speak in other tongues, as the Spirit gave them utterance" (Acts 2:4). From that moment there also begins that journey of faith, the Church's pilgrimage through the history of individuals and peoples. We know that at the beginning of this journey Mary is present. We see her in the midst of the Apostles in the Upper Room, "prayerfully imploring the gift of the Spirit."(59)

[59] Ibid., 59.

In a sense her journey of faith is longer. The Holy Spirit had already come down upon her, and she became his faithful spouse at the Annunciation, welcoming the Word of the true God, offering "the full submission of intellect and will...and freely assenting to the truth revealed by him," indeed abandoning herself totally to God through "the obedience of faith,"(60) whereby she replied to the angel: "Behold, I am the handmaid of the Lord; let it be to me according to your word." The journey of faith made by Mary, whom we see praying in the Upper Room, is thus longer than that of the others gathered there: Mary "goes before them," "leads the way" for them.(61) The moment of Pentecost in Jerusalem had been prepared for by the moment of the Annunciation in Nazareth, as well as by the Cross. In the Upper Room Mary's journey meets the Church's journey of faith. In what way?

[60] Cf. Second Vatican Ecumenical Council, Dogmatic Constitution on Divine Revelation Dei Verbum, 5.

[61] Cf. Second Vatican Ecumenical Council, Dogmatic Constitution on the Church Lumen Gentium, 63.

Among those who devoted themselves to prayer in the Upper Room, preparing to go "into the whole world" after receiving the Spirit, some had been called by Jesus gradually from the beginning of his mission in Israel. Eleven of them had been made Apostles, and to them Jesus had passed on the mission which he himself had received from the Father. "As the Father has sent me, even so I send you" (Jn. 20:21), he had said to the Apostles after the Resurrection. And forty days later, before returning to the Father, he had added: "when the Holy Spirit has come upon you...you shall be my witnesses...to the end of the earth" (cf. Acts 1:8). This mission of the Apostles began the moment they left the Upper Room in Jerusalem. The Church is born and then grows through the testimony that Peter and the Apostles bear to the Crucified and Risen Christ (cf. Acts 2:31-34; 3:15-18; 4:10-12; 5:30-32).

Mary did not directly receive this apostolic mission. She was not among those whom Jesus sent "to the whole world to teach all nations" (cf. Mt. 28:19) when he conferred this mission on them.

But she was in the Upper Room, where the Apostles were preparing to take up this mission with the coming of the Spirit of Truth: she was present with them. In their midst Mary was "devoted to prayer" as the "mother of Jesus" (cf. Acts 1:13-14), of the Crucified and Risen Christ. And that first group of those who in faith looked "upon Jesus as the author of salvation,"(62) knew that Jesus was the Son of Mary, and that she was his Mother, and that as such she was from the moment of his conception and birth a unique witness to the mystery of Jesus, that mystery which before their eyes had been disclosed and confirmed in the Cross and Resurrection. Thus, from the very first moment, the Church "looked at" Mary through Jesus, just as she "looked at" Jesus through Mary. For the Church of that time and of every time Mary is a singular witness to the years of Jesus' infancy and hidden life at Nazareth, when she "kept all these things, pondering them in her heart" (Lk. 2:19; cf. Lk. 2:51).

[62] Cf. ibid., 9.

But above all, in the Church of that time and of every time Mary was and is the one who is "blessed because she believed"; she was the first to believe. From the moment of the Annunciation and conception, from the moment of his birth in the stable at Bethlehem, Mary followed Jesus step by step in her maternal pilgrimage of faith. She followed him during the years of his hidden life at Nazareth; she followed him also during the time after he left home, when he began "to do and to teach" (cf. Acts 1:1) in the midst of Israel. Above all she followed him in the tragic experience of Golgotha. Now, while Mary was with the Apostles in the Upper Room in Jerusalem at the dawn of the Church, her faith, born from the words of the Annunciation, found confirmation. The angel had said to her then: "You will conceive in your womb and bear a son, and you shall call his name Jesus. He will be great...and he will reign over the house of Jacob for ever; and of his kingdom there will be no end." The recent events on Calvary had shrouded that promise in darkness, yet not even beneath the Cross did Mary's faith fail. She had still remained the one who, like Abraham, "in hope believed against hope" (Rom. 4:18). But it is only after the Resurrection that hope had shown its true face and the promise had begun to be transformed into reality. For Jesus, before returning to the Father, had said to the Apostles: "Go therefore and make disciples of all nations . . . lo, I am with you always, to the close of the age" (cf. Mt. 28:19-20). Thus had spoken the one who by his Resurrection had revealed himself as the conqueror of death, as the one who possessed the kingdom of which, as the angel said, "there will be no end."

27. Now, at the first dawn of the Church, at the beginning of the long journey through faith which began at Pentecost in Jerusalem, Mary was with all those who were the seed of the "new Israel." She was present among them as an exceptional witness to the mystery of Christ. And the Church was assiduous in prayer together with her, and at the same time "contemplated her in the light of the Word made man." It was always to be so. For when the Church "enters more intimately into the supreme mystery of the Incarnation," she thinks of the Mother of Christ with profound reverence and devotion.(63) Mary belongs indissolubly to the mystery of Christ, and she belongs also to the mystery of the Church from the beginning, from the day of the Church's birth. At the basis of what the Church has been from the beginning, and of what she must continually become from generation to generation, in the midst of all the nations of the earth, we find the one "who believed that there would be a fulfillment of what was spoken to her from the Lord" (Lk. 1:45). It is precisely Mary's faith which marks the beginning of the new and eternal Covenant of God with

man in Jesus Christ; this heroic faith of hers "precedes" the apostolic witness of the Church, and ever remains in the Church's heart hidden like a special heritage of God's revelation. All those who from generation to generation accept the apostolic witness of the Church share in that mysterious inheritance, and in a sense share in Mary's faith.

[63] Cf. ibid., 65.

Elizabeth's words "Blessed is she who believed" continue to accompany the Virgin also at Pentecost; they accompany her from age to age, wherever knowledge of Christ's salvific mystery spreads, through the Church's apostolic witness and service. Thus is fulfilled the prophecy of the Magnificat: "All generations will call me blessed; for he who is mighty has done great things for me, and holy is his name" (Lk. 1:48-49). For knowledge of the mystery of Christ leads us to bless his Mother, in the form of special veneration for the Theotokos. But this veneration always includes a blessing of her faith, for the Virgin of Nazareth became blessed above all through this faith, in accordance with Elizabeth's words. Those who from generation to generation among the different peoples and nations of the earth accept with faith the mystery of Christ, the Incarnate Word and Redeemer of the world, not only turn with veneration to Mary and confidently have recourse to her as his Mother, but also seek in her faith support for their own. And it is precisely this lively sharing in Mary's faith that determines her special place in the Church's pilgrimage as the new People of God throughout the earth.

28. As the Council says, "Mary figured profoundly in the history of salvation.... Hence when she is being preached and venerated, she summons the faithful to her Son and his sacrifice, and to love for the Father."(64) For this reason, Mary's faith, according to the

Church's apostolic witness, in some way continues to become the faith of the pilgrim People of God: the faith of individuals and communities, of places and gatherings, and of the various groups existing in the Church. It is a faith that is passed on simultaneously through both the mind and the heart. It is gained or regained continually through prayer. Therefore, "the Church in her apostolic work also rightly looks to her who brought forth Christ, conceived by the Holy Spirit and born of the Virgin, so that through the Church Christ may be born and increase in the hearts of the faithful also."(65)

[64] Ibid., 65.

[65] Ibid., 65.

Today, as on this pilgrimage of faith we draw near to the end of the second Christian Millennium, the Church, through the teaching of the Second Vatican Council, calls our attention to her vision of herself, as the "one People of God...among all the nations of the earth." And she reminds us of that truth according to which all the faithful, though "scattered throughout the world, are in communion with each other in the Holy Spirit."(66) We can therefore say that in this union the mystery of Pentecost is continually being accomplished. At the same time, the Lord's apostles and disciples, in all the nations of the earth, "devote themselves to prayer together with Mary, the mother of Jesus" (Acts 1:14). As they constitute from generation to generation the "sign of the Kingdom" which is not of his world,(67) they are also aware that in the midst of this world they must gather around that King to whom the nations have been given in heritage (cf. Ps. 2:8), to whom the Father has given "the throne of David his father," so that he "will reign over the house of Jacob for ever, and of his kingdom there will be no end."

[66] Cf. ibid., 13.

[67] Cf. ibid., 13.

During this time of vigil, Mary, through the same faith which made her blessed, especially from the moment of the Annunciation, is present in the Church's mission, present in the Church's work of introducing into the world the Kingdom of her Son.(68)

[68] Cf. ibid., 13.

This presence of Mary finds many different expressions in our day, just as it did throughout the Church's history. It also has a wide field of action. Through the faith and piety of individual believers; through the traditions of Christian families or "domestic churches," of parish and missionary communities, religious institutes and dioceses; through the radiance and attraction of the great shrines where not only individuals or local groups, but sometimes whole nations and societies, even whole continents, seek to meet the Mother of the Lord, the one who is blessed because she believed is the first among believers and therefore became the Mother of Emmanuel. This is the message of the Land of Palestine, the spiritual homeland of all Christians because it was the homeland of the Savior of the world and of his Mother. This is the message of the many churches in Rome and throughout the world which have been raised up in the course of the centuries by the faith of Christians. This is the message of centers like Guadalupe, Lourdes, Fatima and the others situated in the various countries. Among them how could I fail to mention the one in my own native land, Jasna Gora? One could perhaps speak of a specific "geography" of faith and Marian devotion, which includes all these special places of pilgrimage where the People of God seek to meet the Mother of God in order to find, within the radius of the maternal presence of her "who believed," a strengthening of their own faith. For in

Mary's faith, first at the Annunciation and then fully at the foot of the Cross, an interior space was reopened within humanity which the eternal Father can fill "with every spiritual blessing." It is the space "of the new and eternal Covenant,"(69) and it continues to exist in the Church, which in Christ is "a kind of sacrament or sign of intimate union with God, and of the unity of all mankind."(70)

[69] Cf. Roman Missal, formula of the Consecration of the Chalice in the Eucharistic Prayers.

[70] Second Vatican Ecumenical Council, Dogmatic Constitution on the Church Lumen Gentium, 1.

In the faith which Mary professed at the Annunciation as the "handmaid of the Lord" and in which she constantly "precedes" the pilgrim People of God throughout the earth, the Church "strives energetically and constantly to bring all humanity...back to Christ its Head in the unity of his Spirit."(71)

[71] Ibid., 13.

2. The Church's journey and the unity of all Christians

29. "In all of Christ's disciples the Spirit arouses the desire to be peacefully united, in the manner determined by Christ, as one flock under one shepherd."(72) The journey of the Church, especially in our own time, is marked by the sign of ecumenism: Christians are seeking ways to restore that unity which Christ implored from the Father for his disciples on the day before his Passion: "That they may all be one; even as you, Father, are in me, and I in you that they also may be in us, so that the world may believe that you have sent me" (Jn. 17:21). The unity of Christ's disciples, therefore, is a great sign given in order to kindle faith in the world while their division constitutes a scandal.(73)

[72] Ibid., 15.

[73] Cf. Second Vatican Ecumenical Council, Decree on Ecumenism Unitatis Redintegratio, 1.

The ecumenical movement, on the basis of a clearer and more widespread awareness of the urgent need to achieve the unity of all Christians, has found on the part of the Catholic Church its culminating expression in the work of the Second Vatican Council: Christians must deepen in themselves and each of their communities that "obedience of faith" of which Mary is the first and brightest example. And since she "shines forth on earth,...as a sign of sure hope and solace for the pilgrim People of God," "it gives great joy and comfort to this most holy Synod that among the divided brethren, too, there are those who live due honor to the Mother of our Lord and Savior. This is especially so among the Easterners."(74)

[74] Dogmatic Constitution on the Church Lumen Gentium, 68, 69. On Mary Most Holy, promoter of Christian unity, and on the cult of Mary in the East, cf. Leo XIII, Encyclical Epistle Adiutricem Populi (5 September 1985): Acta Leonis XV, 300-312.

30. Christians know that their unity will be truly rediscovered only if it is based on the unity of their faith. They must resolve considerable discrepancies of doctrine concerning the mystery and ministry of the Church, and sometimes also concerning the role of Mary in the work of salvation.(75) The dialogues begun by the Catholic Church with the Churches and Ecclesial Communities of the West(76) are steadily converging upon these two inseparable aspects of the same mystery of salvation. If the mystery of the Word made flesh enables us to glimpse the mystery of the divine motherhood and is, in turn, contemplation of the Mother of God brings us to a more profound understanding of the mystery of the

Incarnation, then the same must be said for the mystery of the Church and Mary's role in the work of salvation. By a more profound study of both Mary and the Church, clarifying each by the light of the other, Christians who are eager to do what Jesus tells them-as their Mother recommends (cf. Jn. 2:5)- will be able to go forward together on this "pilgrimage of faith." Mary, who is still the model of this pilgrimage, is to lead them to the unity which is willed by their one Lord and so much desired by those who are attentively listening to what "the Spirit is saying to the Churches" today (Rev. 2:7, 11, 17).

[75] Cf. Second Vatican Ecumenical Council, Decree on Ecumenism Unitatis Redintegratio, 20.

[76] Cf. ibid., 19.

Meanwhile, it is a hopeful sign that these Churches and Ecclesial Communities are finding agreement with the Catholic Church on fundamental points of Christian belief, including matters relating to the Virgin Mary. For they recognize her as the Mother of the Lord and hold that this forms part of our faith in Christ, true God and true man. They look to her who at the foot of the Cross accepts as her son the beloved disciple, the one who in his turn accepts her as his mother.

Therefore, why should we not all together look to her as our common Mother, who prays for the unity of God's family and who "precedes" us all at the head of the long line of witnesses of faith in the one Lord, the Son of God, who was conceived in her virginal womb by the power of the Holy Spirit?

31. On the other hand, I wish to emphasize how profoundly the Catholic Church, the Orthodox Church and the ancient Churches of the East feel united by love and praise of the Theotokos. Not

A Manual of the Most Holy Rosary

only "basic dogmas of the Christian faith concerning the Trinity and God's Word made flesh of the Virgin Mary were defined in Ecumenical Councils held in the East,"(77) but also in their liturgical worship "the Orientals pay high tribute, in very beautiful hymns, to Mary ever Virgin...God's Most Holy Mother."(78)

[77] Ibid., 14.

[78] Ibid., 15.

The brethren of these Churches have experienced a complex history, but it is one that has always been marked by an intense desire for Christian commitment and apostolic activity, despite frequent persecution, even to the point of bloodshed. It is a history of fidelity to the Lord, an authentic "pilgrimage of faith" in space and time, during which Eastern Christians have always looked with boundless trust to the Mother of the Lord, celebrated her with praise and invoked her with unceasing prayer. In the difficult moments of their troubled Christian existence, "they have taken refuge under her protection,"(79) conscious of having in her a powerful aid. The Churches which profess the doctrine of Ephesus proclaim the Virgin as "true Mother of God," since "our Lord Jesus Christ, born of the Father before time began according to his divinity, in the last days, for our sake and for our salvation, was himself begotten of Mary, the Virgin Mother of God according to his humanity."(80) The Greek Fathers and the Byzantine tradition contemplating the Virgin in the light of the Word made flesh, have sought to penetrate the depth of that bond which unites Mary, as the Mother of God, to Christ and the Church: the Virgin is a permanent presence in the whole reality of the salvific mystery.

[79] Second Vatican Ecumenical Council, Dogmatic Constitution on the Church Lumen Gentium, 66.

[80] Ecumenical Council of Chalcedon, Definitio fidei: Conciliorum Oecumenicorum Decreta, Bologna 1973, 86 (DS 301).

The Coptic and Ethiopian traditions were introduced to this contemplation of the mystery of Mary by St. Cyril of Alexandria, and in their turn they have celebrated it with a profuse poetic blossoming.(81) The poetic genius of St. Ephrem the Syrian, called "the lyre of the Holy Spirit," tirelessly sang of Mary, leaving a still living mark on the whole tradition of the Syriac Church.(82) In his panegyric of the Theotókos, St. Gregory of Narek, one of the outstanding glories of Armenia, with powerful poetic inspiration ponders the different aspects of the mystery of the Incarnation, and each of them is for him an occasion to sing and extol the extraordinary dignity and magnificent beauty of the Virgin Mary, Mother of the Word made flesh.(83)

[81] Cf. the Weddase Maryam (Praises of Mary), which follows the Ethiopian Psalter and contains hymns and prayers to Mary for each day of the week. Cf. also the Matshafa Kidana Mehrat (Book of the Pact of Mercy); the importance given to Mary in the Ethiopian hymnology and liturgy deserves to be emphasized.

[82] Cf. Saint Ephrem, Hymn. de Nativitate: Scriptores Syri, 82, CSCO, 186.

[83] Cf. Saint Gregory of Narek, Le livre de prieres: S. Ch. 78, 160-163; 428-432.

It does not surprise us therefore that Mary occupies a privileged place in the worship or the ancient Oriental Churches with an incomparable abundance of feasts and hymns.

32. In the Byzantine liturgy, in all the hours of the Divine Office, praise of the Mother is linked with praise of her Son and with the

praise which, through the Son, is offered up to the Father in the Holy Spirit. In the Anaphora or Eucharistic Prayer of St. John Chrysostom, immediately after the epiclesis the assembled community sings in honor of the Mother of God: "It is truly just to proclaim you blessed, O Mother of God, who are most blessed, all pure and Mother of our God. We magnify you who are more honorable than the Cherubim and incomparably more glorious than the Seraphim. You who, without losing your virginity, gave birth to the Word of God. You who are truly the Mother of God."

These praises, which in every celebration of the Eucharistic Liturgy are offered to Mary, have moulded the faith, piety and prayer of the faithful. In the course of the centuries they have permeated their whole spiritual outlook, fostering in them a profound devotion to the "All Holy Mother of God."

33. This year there occurs the twelfth centenary of the Second Ecumenical Council of Nicaea (787). Putting an end to the wellknown controversy about the cult of sacred images, this Council defined that, according to the teaching of the holy Fathers and the universal tradition of the Church, there could be exposed for the veneration of the faithful, together with the Cross, also images of the Mother of God, of the angels and of the saints, in churches and houses and at the roadside.(84) This custom has been maintained in the whole of the East and also in the West. Images of the Virgin have a place of honor in churches and houses. In them Mary is represented in a number of ways: as the throne of God carrying the Lord and giving him to humanity (Theotokos); as the way that leads to Christ and manifests him (Hodegetria); as a praying figure in an attitude of intercession and as a sign of the divine presence on the journey of the faithful until the day of the Lord (Deesis); as the protectress who stretches out her mantle over the peoples (Pokrov), or as the merciful Virgin of tenderness

(Eleousa). She is usually represented with her Son, the child Jesus, in her arms: it is the relationship with the Son which glorifies the Mother. Sometimes she embraces him with tenderness (Glykophilousa); at other times she is a hieratic figure, apparently rapt in contemplation of him who is the Lord of history (cf. Rev. 5:9-14).(85)

[84] Second Ecumenical Council of Nicaea: Conciliorurn Oecumenicorum Decreta, Bologna 19733, 135-138 (DS 600-609).

[85] Cf. Second Vatican Ecumenical Council, Dogmatic Constitution on the Church Lumen Gentium, 59.

It is also appropriate to mention the icon of Our Lady of Vladimir, which continually accompanied the pilgrimage of faith of the peoples of ancient Rus'. The first Millennium of the conversion of those noble lands to Christianity is approaching: lands of humble folk, of thinkers and of saints. The Icons are still venerated in the Ukraine, in Byelorussia and in Russia under various titles. They are images which witness to the faith and spirit of prayer of that people, who sense the presence and protection of the Mother of God. In these Icons the Virgin shines as the image of divine beauty, the abode of Eternal Wisdom, the figure of the one who prays, the prototype of contemplation, the image of glory: she who even in her earthly life possessed the spiritual knowledge inaccessible to human reasoning and who attained through faith the most sublime knowledge. I also recall the Icon of the Virgin of the Cenacle, praying with the Apostles as they awaited the Holy Spirit: could she not become the sign of hope for all those who, in fraternal dialogue, wish to deepen their obedience of faith?

34. Such a wealth of praise, built up by the different forms of the Church's great tradition, could help us to hasten the day when the Church can begin once more to breathe fully with her "two lungs,"

the East and the West. As I have often said, this is more than ever necessary today. It would be an effective aid in furthering the progress of the dialogue already taking place between the Catholic Church and the Churches and Ecclesial Communities of the West.(86) It would also be the way for the pilgrim Church to sing and to live more perfectly her "Magnificat."

[86] Cf. Second Vatican Ecumenical Council, Decree on Ecumenism Unitatis Redintegratio, 19.

3. The "Magnificat" of the pilgrim Church

35. At the present stage of her journey, therefore, the Church seeks to rediscover the unity of all who profess their faith in Christ, in order to show obedience to her Lord, who prayed for this unity before his Passion. "Like a pilgrim in a foreign land, the Church presses forward amid the persecutions of the world and the consolations of God, announcing the Cross and Death of the Lord until he comes."(87) "Moving forward through trial and tribulation, the Church is strengthened by the power of God's grace promised to her by the Lord, so that in the weakness of the flesh she may not waver from perfect fidelity, but remain a bride worthy of her Lord; that moved by the Holy Spirit she may never cease to renew herself, until through the Cross she arrives at the light which knows no setting."(88)

[87] Second Vatican Ecumenical Council, Dogmatic Constitution on the Church Lumen Gentium, 8.

[88] Ibid., 9.

The Virgin Mother is constantly present on this journey of faith of the People of God towards the light. This is shown in a special way by the canticle of the "Magnificat," which, having welled up from the depths of Mary's faith at the Visitation, ceaselessly re-echoes in the heart of the Church down the centuries. This is proved by its daily recitation in the liturgy of Vespers and at many other moments of both personal and communal devotion.

"My soul magnifies the Lord,
and my spirit rejoices in God my Savior,
for he has looked on his servant in her lowliness.
For behold, henceforth all generations
will call me blessed;
for he who is mighty has done great things for me,
and holy is his name:
and his mercy is from age to age
on those who fear him.
He has shown strength with his arm,
he has scattered the proud-hearted,
he has cast down the mighty from their thrones,
and lifted up the lowly;
he has filled the hungry with good things,
sent the rich away empty.
He has helped his servant Israel,
remembering his mercy,
as he spoke to our fathers,
to Abraham and to his posterity for ever." (Lk.1 :46-55)

36. When Elizabeth greeted her young kinswoman coming from Nazareth, Mary replied with the Magnificat. In her greeting, Elizabeth first called Mary "blessed" because of "the fruit of her womb," and then she called her "blessed" because of her faith (cf. Lk. 1:42, 45). These two blessings referred directly to the Annunciation. Now, at the Visitation, when Elizabeth's greeting bears witness to that culminating moment, Mary's faith acquires a new consciousness and a new expression. That which remained

hidden in the depths of the "obedience of faith" at the Annunciation can now be said to spring forth like a clear and life-giving flame of the spirit. The words used by Mary on the threshold of Elizabeth's house are an inspired profession of her faith, in which her response to the revealed word is expressed with the religious and poetical exultation of her whole being towards God. In these sublime words, which are simultaneously very simple and wholly inspired by the sacred texts of the people of Israel,(89) Mary's personal experience, the ecstasy of her heart, shines forth. In them shines a ray of the mystery of God, the glory of his ineffable holiness, the eternal love which, as an irrevocable gift, enters into human history.

[89] As is well-known, the words of the Magnificat contain or echo numerous passages of the Old Testament.

Mary is the first to share in this new revelation of God and, within the same, in this new "self-giving" of God. Therefore she proclaims: "For he who is mighty has done great things for me, and holy is his name." Her words reflect a joy of spirit which is difficult to express: "My spirit rejoices in God my Savior." Indeed, "the deepest truth about God and the salvation of man is made clear to us in Christ, who is at the same time the mediator and the fullness of all revelation."(90) In her exultation Mary confesses that she finds herself in the very heart of this fullness of Christ. She is conscious that the promise made to the fathers, first of all "to Abraham and to his posterity for ever," is being fulfilled in herself. She is thus aware that concentrated within herself as the mother of Christ is the whole salvific economy, in which "from age to age" is manifested he who as the God of the Covenant, "remembers his mercy."

[90] Second Vatican Ecumenical Council, Dogmatic Constitution on Divine Revelation Dei Verbum, 2.

37. The Church, which from the beginning has modelled her earthly journey on that of the Mother of God, constantly repeats after her the words of the Magnificat. From the depths of the Virgin's faith at the Annunciation and the Visitation, the Church derives the truth about the God of the Covenant: the God who is Almighty and does "great things" for man: "holy is his name." In the Magnificat the Church sees uprooted that sin which is found at the outset of the earthly history of man and woman, the sin of disbelief and of "little faith" in God. In contrast with the "suspicion" which the "father of lies" sowed in the heart of Eve the first woman, Mary, whom tradition is wont to call the "new Eve"(91) and the true "Mother of the living,"(92) boldly proclaims the undimmed truth about God: the holy and almighty God, who from the beginning is the source of all gifts, he who "has done great things" in her, as well as in the whole universe. In the act of creation God gives existence to all that is. In creating man, God gives him the dignity of the image and likeness of himself in a special way as compared with all earthly creatures. Moreover, in his desire to give God gives himself in the Son, notwithstanding man's sin: "He so loved the world that he gave his only Son" (Jn. 3:16). Mary is the first witness of this marvelous truth, which will be fully accomplished through "the works and words" (cf. Acts 1:1) of her Son and definitively through his Cross and Resurrection.

[91] Cf. for example Saint Justin, Dialogus cum Tryphone Iudaeo, 100: Otto II, 358; Saint Irenaeus, Adversus Haereses III, 22, 4: S. Ch. 211, 439-445; Tertullian, De carne Christi, 17, 4-6: CCL 2, 904f.

[92] Cf. Saint Epiphanius, Panarion, III, 2; Haer. 78, 18: PG 42, 727-730.

A Manual of the Most Holy Rosary

The Church, which even "amid trials and tribulations" does not cease repeating with Mary the words of the Magnificat, is sustained by the power of God's truth, proclaimed on that occasion with such extraordinary simplicity. At the same time, by means of this truth about God, the Church desires to shed light upon the difficult and sometimes tangled paths of man's earthly existence. The Church's journey, therefore, near the end of the second Christian Millennium, involves a renewed commitment to her mission. Following him who said of himself: "(God) has anointed me to preach good news to the poor" (cf. Lk. 4:18), the Church has sought from generation to generation and still seeks today to accomplish that same mission.

The Church's love of preference for the poor is wonderfully inscribed in Mary's Magnificat. The God of the Covenant, celebrated in the exultation of her spirit by the Virgin of Nazareth, is also he who "has cast down the mighty from their thrones, and lifted up the lowly, ...filled the hungry with good things, sent the rich away empty, ...scattered the proud-hearted...and his mercy is from age to age on those who fear him." Mary is deeply imbued with the spirit of the "poor of Yahweh," who in the prayer of the Psalms awaited from God their salvation, placing all their trust in him (cf. Pss. 25; 31; 35; 55). Mary truly proclaims the coming of the "Messiah of the poor" (cf. Is. 11:4; 61:1). Drawing from Mary's heart, from the depth of her faith expressed in the words of the Magnificat, the Church renews ever more effectively in herself the awareness that the truth about God who saves, the truth about God who is the source of every gift, cannot be separated from the manifestation of his love of preference for the poor and humble, that love which, celebrated in the Magnificat, is later expressed in the words and works of Jesus.

The Church is thus aware-and at the present time this awareness is particularly vivid-not only that these two elements of the message contained in the Magnificat cannot be separated, but also that there is a duty to safeguard carefully the importance of "the poor" and of "the option in favor of the poor" in the word of the living God. These are matters and questions intimately connected with the Christian meaning of freedom and liberation. "Mary is totally dependent upon God and completely directed towards him, and at the side of her Son, she is the most perfect image of freedom and of the liberation of humanity and of the universe. It is to her as Mother and Model that the Church must look in order to understand in its completeness the meaning of her own mission."(93)

[93] Congregation for the Doctrine of the Faith, Instruction on Christian Freedom and Liberation (22 March 1986), 97.

PART III

Maternal Mediation

1. Mary, the Handmaid of the Lord

38. The Church knows and teaches with Saint Paul that there is only one mediator: "For there is one God, and there is one mediator between God and men, the man Christ Jesus, who gave himself as a ransom for all" (1 Tim. 2:5-6). "The maternal role of Mary towards people in no way obscures or diminishes the unique mediation of Christ, but rather shows its power":(94) it is mediation in Christ.

[94] Second Vatican Ecumenical Council, Dogmatic Constitution on the Church Lumen Gentium, 60.

The Church knows and teaches that "all the saving influences of the Blessed Virgin on mankind originate...from the divine pleasure. They flow forth from the superabundance of the merits of Christ, rest on his mediation, depend entirely on it, and draw all their power from it. In no way do they impede the immediate union of the faithful with Christ. Rather, they foster this union."(95) This saving influence is sustained by the Holy Spirit, who, just as he overshadowed the Virgin Mary when he began in her the divine motherhood, in a similar way constantly sustains her solicitude for the brothers and sisters of her Son.

[95] Ibid., 60.

In effect, Mary's mediation is intimately linked with her motherhood. It possesses a specifically maternal character, which distinguishes it from the mediation of the other creatures who in various and always subordinate ways share in the one mediation of Christ, although her own mediation is also a shared mediation.(96) In fact, while it is true that "no creature could ever be classed with the Incarnate Word and Redeemer," at the same time "the unique mediation of the Redeemer does not exclude but rather gives rise among creatures to a manifold cooperation which is but a sharing in this unique source." And thus "the one goodness of God is in reality communicated diversely to his creatures."(97)

[96] Cf. the formula of mediatrix "ad Mediatorem" of Saint Bernard, In Dominica infra oct. Assumptionis Sermo, 2: S. Bernardi Opera, V, 1968, 263. Mary as a pure mirror sends back to her Son all the glory and honor which she receives: Id., In Nativitate B. Mariae Sermo-De Aquaeductu, 12: ed. cit., 283.

[97] Second Vatican Ecumenical Council, Dogmatic Constitution on the Church Lumen Gentium, 62.

The teaching of the Second Vatican Council presents the truth of Mary's mediation as "a sharing in the one unique source that is the mediation of Christ himself." Thus we read: "The Church does not hesitate to profess this subordinate role of Mary. She experiences it continuously and commends it to the hearts of the faithful, so that, encouraged by this maternal help, they may more closely adhere to the Mediator and Redeemer."(98) This role is at the same time special and extraordinary. It flows from her divine motherhood and can be understood and lived in faith only on the basis of the full truth of this motherhood. Since by virtue of divine election Mary is the earthly Mother of the Father's consubstantial Son and his "generous companion" in the work of redemption "she is a mother to us in the order of grace."(99) This role constitutes a real dimension of her presence in the saving mystery of Christ and the Church.

[98] Ibid., 62.

[99] Ibid., 61.

39. From this point of view we must consider once more the fundamental event in the economy of salvation, namely the Incarnation of the Word at the moment of the Annunciation. It is significant that Mary, recognizing in the words of the divine messenger the will of the Most High and submitting to his power, says: "Behold, I am the handmaid of the Lord; let it be to me according to your word" (Lk. 1:38). The first moment of submission to the one mediation "between God and men"-the mediation of Jesus Christ-is the Virgin of Nazareth's acceptance of motherhood. Mary consents to God's choice, in order to become through the power of the Holy Spirit the Mother of the Son of God. It can be said that a consent to motherhood is above all a result of her total selfgiving to God in virginity. Mary accepted her

election as Mother of the Son of God, guided by spousal love, the love which totally "consecrates" a human being to God. By virtue of this love, Mary wished to be always and in all things "given to God," living in virginity. The words "Behold, I am the handmaid of the Lord" express the fact that from the outset she accepted and understood her own motherhood as a total gift of self, a gift of her person to the service of the saving plans of the Most High. And to the very end she lived her entire maternal sharing in the life of Jesus Christ, her Son, in a way that matched her vocation to virginity.

Mary's motherhood, completely pervaded by her spousal attitude as the "handmaid of the Lord," constitutes the first and fundamental dimension of that mediation which the Church confesses and proclaims in her regard(100) and continually "commends to the hearts of the faithful," since the Church has great trust in her. For it must be recognized that before anyone else it was God himself, the Eternal Father, who entrusted himself to the Virgin of Nazareth, giving her his own Son in the mystery of the Incarnation. Her election to the supreme office and dignity of Mother of the Son of God refers, on the ontological level, to the very reality of the union of the two natures in the person of the Word (hypostatic union). This basic fact of being the Mother of the Son of God is from the very beginning a complete openness to the person of Christ, to his whole work, to his whole mission. The words "Behold, I am the handmaid of the Lord" testify to Mary's openness of spirit: she perfectly unites in herself the love proper to virginity and the love characteristic of motherhood, which are joined and, as it were, fused together.

[100] Ibid., 62.

For this reason Mary became not only the "nursing mother" of the Son of Man but also the "associate of unique nobility"(101) of the

Messiah and Redeemer. As I have already said, she advanced in her pilgrimage of faith, and in this pilgrimage to the foot of the Cross there was simultaneously accomplished her maternal cooperation with the Savior's whole mission through her actions and sufferings. Along the path of this collaboration with the work of her Son, the Redeemer, Mary's motherhood itself underwent a singular transformation, becoming ever more imbued with "burning charity" towards all those to whom Christ's mission was directed. Through this "burning charity," which sought to achieve, in union with Christ, the restoration of "supernatural life to souls,"(102) Mary entered, in a way all her own, into the one mediation "between God and men" which is the mediation of the man Christ Jesus. If she was the first to experience within herself the supernatural consequences of this one mediation-in the Annunciation she had been greeted as "full of grace"-then we must say that through this fullness of grace and supernatural life she was especially predisposed to cooperation with Christ, the one Mediator of human salvation. And such cooperation is precisely this mediation subordinated to the mediation of Christ.

[101] Ibid., 61.

[102] Ibid., 61.

In Mary's case we have a special and exceptional mediation, based upon her "fullness of grace," which was expressed in the complete willingness of the "handmaid of the Lord." In response to this interior willingness of his Mother, Jesus Christ prepared her ever more completely to become for all people their "mother in the order of grace." This is indicated, at least indirectly, by certain details noted by the Synoptics (cf. Lk. 11:28; 8:20-21; Mk. 3:32-35; Mt. 12:47-50) and still more so by the Gospel of John (cf. 2:1-12; 19:25-27), which I have already mentioned. Particularly eloquent in this regard are the words spoken by Jesus on the Cross to Mary and John.

40. After the events of the Resurrection and Ascension Mary entered the Upper Room together with the Apostles to await Pentecost, and was present there as the Mother of the glorified Lord. She was not only the one who "advanced in her pilgrimage of faith" and loyally persevered in her union with her Son "unto the Cross," but she was also the "handmaid of the Lord," left by her Son as Mother in the midst of the infant Church: "Behold your mother." Thus there began to develop a special bond between this Mother and the Church. For the infant Church was the fruit of the Cross and Resurrection of her Son. Mary, who from the beginning had given herself without reserve to the person and work of her Son, could not but pour out upon the Church, from the very beginning, her maternal self-giving. After her Son's departure, her motherhood remains in the Church as maternal mediation: interceding for all her children, the Mother cooperates in the saving work of her Son, the Redeemer of the world. In fact the Council teaches that the "motherhood of Mary in the order of grace...will last without interruption until the eternal fulfillment of all the elect."(103) With the redeeming death of her Son, the maternal mediation of the handmaid of the Lord took on a universal dimension, for the work of redemption embraces the whole of humanity. Thus there is manifested in a singular way the efficacy of the one and universal mediation of Christ "between God and men" Mary's cooperation shares, in its subordinate character, in the universality of the mediation of the Redeemer, the one Mediator. This is clearly indicated by the Council in the words quoted above.

[103] Ibid., 62.

"For," the text goes on, "taken up to heaven, she did not lay aside this saving role, but by her manifold acts of intercession continues to win for us gifts of eternal salvation."(104) With this character of "intercession," first manifested at Cana in Galilee, Mary's mediation continues in the history of the Church and the world. We read that Mary "by her maternal charity, cares for the brethren of her Son who still journey on earth surrounded by dangers and difficulties, until they are led to their happy homeland."(105) In this way Mary's motherhood continues unceasingly in the Church as the mediation which intercedes, and the Church expresses her faith in this truth by invoking Mary "under the titles of Advocate, Auxiliatrix, Adjutrix and Mediatrix."(106)

[104] Ibid., 62.

[105] Ibid., 62; in her prayer too the Church recognizes and celebrates Mary's "maternal role": it is a role "of intercession and forgiveness, petition and grace, reconciliation and peace" (cf. Preface of the Mass of the Blessed Virgin Mary, Mother and Mediatrix of Grace, in Collectio Missarum de Beata Maria Virgine, ed. typ. 1987, I, 120).

[106] Ibid., 62.

41. Through her mediation, subordinate to that of the Redeemer, Mary contributes in a special way to the union of the pilgrim Church on earth with the eschatological and heavenly reality of the Communion of Saints, since she has already been "assumed into heaven."(107) The truth of the Assumption, defined by Pius XII, is reaffirmed by the Second Vatican Council, which thus expresses the Church's faith: "Preserved free from all guilt of original sin, the Immaculate Virgin was taken up body and soul into heavenly glory upon the completion of her earthly sojourn. She was exalted by the Lord as Queen of the Universe, in order that she might be the

more thoroughly conformed to her Son, the Lord of lords (cf. Rev. 19:16) and the conqueror of sin and death."(108) In this teaching Pius XII was in continuity with Tradition, which has found many different expressions in the history of the Church, both in the East and in the West.

[107] Ibid., 62; cf. Saint John Damascene, Hom. in Dormitionem, I, 11; II, 2, 14; III, 2: S. Ch. 80, 111f.; 127-131; 157-161; 181-185; Saint Bernard, In Assumptione Beatae Mariae Sermo, 1-2: S. Bernardi Opera, V, 1968, 228-238.

[108] Dogmatic Constitution on the Church Lumen Gentium, 59; cf. Pope Pius XII, Apostolic Constitution Munificentissimus Deus (1 November 1950): AAS 42 (1950) 769-771; Saint Bernard presents Mary immersed in the splendor of the Son's glory: In Dominica infra oct. Assumptionis Sermo, 3; S. Bernardi Opera, V, 1968, 263f.

By the mystery of the Assumption into heaven there were definitively accomplished in Mary all the effects of the one mediation of Christ the Redeemer of the world and Risen Lord: "In Christ shall all be made alive. But each in his own order: Christ the first fruits, then at his coming those who belong to Christ" (1 Cor. 15:22-23). In the mystery of the Assumption is expressed the faith of the Church, according to which Mary is "united by a close and indissoluble bond" to Christ, for, if as Virgin and Mother she was singularly united with him in his first coming, so through her continued collaboration with him she will also be united with him in expectation of the second; "redeemed in an especially sublime manner by reason of the merits of her Son,"(109) she also has that specifically maternal role of mediatrix of mercy at his final coming, when all those who belong to Christ "shall be made alive," when "the last enemy to be destroyed is death" (1 Cor. 15:26)."(110)

[109] Dogmatic Constitution on the Church Lumen Gentium, 53.

[110] On this particular aspect of Mary's mediation as implorer of clemency from the "Son as Judge," cf. Saint Bernard, In Dominica infra oct. Assumptionis Sermo, 1-2: S. Bernardi Opera, V, 1968, 262f; Pope Leo XIII, Encyclical Epistle Octobri Mense (22 September 1891): Acta Leonis, XI, 299-315.

Connected with this exaltation of the noble "Daughter of Sion"(111) through her Assumption into heaven is the mystery of her eternal glory. For the Mother of Christ is glorified as "Queen of the Universe."(112) She who at the Annunciation called herself the "handmaid of the Lord" remained throughout her earthly life faithful to what this name expresses. In this she confirmed that she was a true "disciple" of Christ, who strongly emphasized that his mission was one of service: the Son of Man came not to be served but to serve, and to give his life as a ransom for many" (Mt. 20:28). In this way Mary became the first of those who, "serving Christ also in others, with humility and patience lead their brothers and sisters to that King whom to serve is to reign,"(113) and she fully obtained that "state of royal freedom" proper to Christ's disciples: to serve means to reign!

[111] Second Vatican Ecumenical Council, Dogmatic Constitution on the Church Lumen Gentium, 55.

[112] Ibid., 59.

[113] Ibid., 36.

"Christ obeyed even at the cost of death, and was therefore raised up by the Father (cf. Phil. 2:8-9). Thus he entered into the glory of his kingdom. To him all things are made subject until he subjects himself and all created things to the Father, that God may be all in all (cf. 1 Cor. 15:27-28)."(114) Mary, the handmaid of the Lord, has a share in this Kingdom of the Son.(115) The glory of serving does not cease to be her royal exaltation: assumed into heaven, she does not cease her saving service, which expresses her maternal mediation "until the eternal fulfillment of all the elect."(116) Thus, she who here on earth "loyally preserved in her union with her Son unto the Cross," continues to remain united with him, while now "all things are subjected to him, until he subjects to the Father himself and all things." Thus in her Assumption into heaven, Mary is as it were clothed by the whole reality of the Communion of Saints, and her very union with the Son in glory is wholly oriented towards the definitive fullness of the Kingdom, when "God will be all in all."

[114] Ibid., 36.

[115] With regard to Mary as Queen, cf. Saint John Damascene, Hom. in Nativitatem, 6; 12; Hom. in Dormitionem, 1, 2, 12, 14; II, 11;III, 4: S. Ch. 80, 59f.; 77f.; 83f.; 113f.; 117; 151f.; 189-193.

[116] Second Vatican Ecumenical Council. Dogmatic Constitution on the Church Lumen Gentium, 62.

In this phase too Mary's maternal mediation does not cease to be subordinate to him who is the one Mediator, until the final realization of "the fullness of time," that is to say until "all things are united in Christ" (cf. Eph. 1:10).

2. Mary in the life of the Church and of every Christian

42. Linking itself with Tradition, the Second Vatican Council brought new light to bear on the role of the Mother of Christ in the life of the Church. "Through the gift...of divine motherhood, Mary is united with her Son, the Redeemer, and with his singular graces

and offices. By these, the Blessed Virgin is also intimately united with the Church: the Mother of God is a figure of the Church in the matter of faith, charity and perfect union with Christ."(117) We have already noted how, from the beginning, Mary remains with the Apostles in expectation of Pentecost and how, as "the blessed one who believed," she is present in the midst of the pilgrim Church from generation to generation through faith and as the model of the hope which does not disappoint (cf. Rom. 5:5).

[117] Ibid., 63.

Mary believed in the fulfillment of what had been said to her by the Lord. As Virgin, she believed that she would conceive and bear a son: the "Holy One," who bears the name of "Son of God," the name "Jesus" (= God who saves). As handmaid of the Lord, she remained in perfect fidelity to the person and mission of this Son. As Mother, "believing and obeying...she brought forth on earth the Father's Son. This she did, knowing not man but overshadowed by the Holy Spirit."(118)

[118] Ibid., 63.

For these reasons Mary is honored in the Church "with special reverence. Indeed, from most ancient times the Blessed Virgin Mary has been venerated under the title of 'God-bearer.' In all perils and needs, the faithful have fled prayerfully to her protection."(119) This cult is altogether special: it bears in itself and expresses the profound link which exists between the Mother of Christ and the Church.(120) As Virgin and Mother, Mary remains for the Church a "permanent model." It can therefore be said that especially under this aspect, namely as a model, or rather as a "figure," Mary, present in the mystery of Christ, remains constantly present also in the mystery of the Church. For the Church too is "called mother and virgin," and these names have a profound biblical and theological justification.(121)

[119] Ibid., 66.

[120] Cf. Saint Ambrose, De Institutione Virginis, XIV, 88-89: PL 16, 341, Saint Augustine, Sermo 215, 4: PL 38, 1074; De Sancta Virginitate, II, 2; V, 5; VI, 6: PL 40, 397-398f.; 399; Sermo 191, II, 3: PL 38, 1010f.

[121] Cf. Second Vatican Ecumenical Council, Dogmatic Constitution on the Church Lumen Centium, 63.

43. The Church "becomes herself a mother by accepting God's word with fidelity."(122) Like Mary, who first believed by accepting the word of God revealed to her at the Annunciation and by remaining faithful to that word in all her trials even unto the Cross, so too the Church becomes a mother when, accepting with fidelity the word of God, "by her preaching and by baptism she brings forth to a new and immortal life children who are conceived of the Holy Spirit and born of God."(123) This "maternal" characteristic of the Church was expressed in a particularly vivid way by the Apostle to the Gentiles when he wrote: "My little children, with whom I am again in travail until Christ be formed in you!" (Gal. 4:19) These words of Saint Paul contain an interesting sign of the early Church's awareness of her own motherhood, linked to her apostolic service to mankind. This awareness enabled and still enables the Church to see the mystery of her life and mission modelled upon the example of the Mother of the Son, who is "the first-born among many brethren" (Rom. 8:29).

[122] Ibid., 64.

[123] Ibid., 64.

It can be said that from Mary the Church also learns her own motherhood: she recognizes the maternal dimension of her vocation, which is essentially bound to her sacramental nature, in "contemplating Mary's mysterious sanctity, imitating her charity and faithfully fulfilling the Father's will."(124) If the Church is the sign and instrument of intimate union with God, she is so by reason of her motherhood, because, receiving life from the Spirit, she "generates" sons and daughters of the human race to a new life in Christ. For, just as Mary is at the service of the mystery of the Incarnation, so the Church is always at the service of the mystery of adoption to sonship through grace.

[124] Ibid., 64.

Likewise, following the example of Mary, the Church remains the virgin faithful to her spouse: The Church herself is a virgin who keeps whole and pure the fidelity she has pledged to her Spouse."(125) For the Church is the spouse of Christ, as is clear from the Pauline Letters (cf. Eph. 5:21-33; 2 Cor. 11:2), and from the title found in John: "bride of the Lamb" (Rev. 21:9). If the Church as spouse "keeps the fidelity she has pledged to Christ," this fidelity, even though in the Apostle's teaching it has become an image of marriage (cf. Eph. 5:23-33), also has value as a model of total self-giving to God in celibacy "for the kingdom of heaven," in virginity consecrated to God (cf. Mt. 19:11-12; 2 Cor. 11:2). Precisely such virginity, after the example of the Virgin of Nazareth, is the source of a special spiritual fruitfulness: it is the source of motherhood in the Holy Spirit.

[125] Ibid., 64.

But the Church also preserves the faith received from Christ. Following the example of Mary, who kept and pondered in her heart everything relating to her divine Son (cf. Lk. 2:19, 51), the

Church is committed to preserving the word of God and investigating its riches with discernment and prudence, in order to bear faithful witness to it before all mankind in every age.(126)

[126] Cf. Second Vatican Ecumenical Council, Dogmatic Constitution on Divine Revelation Dei Verbum, 8; Saint Bonaventure, Comment. in Evang. Lucae, Ad Claras Aquas, VII, 53, No. 40, 68, No. 109.

44. Given Mary's relationship to the Church as an exemplar, the Church is close to her and seeks to become like her: "Imitating the Mother of her Lord, and by the power of the Holy Spirit, she preserves with virginal purity an integral faith, a firm hope, and a sincere charity."(127) Mary is thus present in the mystery of the Church as a model. But the Church's mystery also consists in generating people to a new and immortal life: this is her motherhood in the Holy Spirit. And here Mary is not only the model and figure of the Church; she is much more. For, "with maternal love she cooperates in the birth and development" of the sons and daughters of Mother Church. The Church's motherhood is accomplished not only according to the model and figure of the Mother of God but also with her "cooperation." The Church draws abundantly from this cooperation, that is to say from the maternal mediation which is characteristic of Mary, insofar as already on earth she cooperated in the rebirth and development of the Church's sons and daughters, as the Mother of that Son whom the Father "placed as the first-born among many brethren."(128)

[127] Second Vatican Ecumenical Council, Dogmatic Constitution on the Church Lumen Gentium, 64.

[128] Ibid., 63.

She cooperated, as the Second Vatican Council teaches, with a maternal love.(129) Here we perceive the real value of the words spoken by Jesus to his Mother at the hour of the Cross: "Woman, behold your son" and to the disciple: "Behold your mother" (Jn. 19:26-27). They are words which determine Mary's place in the life of Christ's disciples and they express-as I have already said-the new motherhood of the Mother of the Redeemer: a spiritual motherhood, born from the heart of the Paschal Mystery of the Redeemer of the world. It is a motherhood in the order of grace, for it implores the gift of the Spirit, who raises up the new children of God, redeems through the sacrifice of Christ that Spirit whom Mary too, together with the Church, received on the day of Pentecost.

[129] Cf. ibid., 63.

Her motherhood is particularly noted and experienced by the Christian people at the Sacred Banquet-the liturgical celebration of the mystery of the Redemption-at which Christ, his true body born of the Virgin Mary, becomes present.

The piety of the Christian people has always very rightly sensed a profound link between devotion to the Blessed Virgin and worship of the Eucharist: this is a fact that can be seen in the liturgy of both the West and the East, in the traditions of the Religious Families, in the modern movements of spirituality, including those for youth, and in the pastoral practice of the Marian Shrines. Mary guides the faithful to the Eucharist.

45. Of the essence of motherhood is the fact that it concerns the person. Motherhood always establishes a unique and unrepeatable relationship between two people: between mother and child and between child and mother. Even when the same woman is the mother of many children, her personal relationship with each one

of them is of the very essence of motherhood. For each child is generated in a unique and unrepeatable way, and this is true both for the mother and for the child. Each child is surrounded in the same way by that maternal love on which are based the child's development and coming to maturity as a human being.

It can be said that motherhood "in the order of grace" preserves the analogy with what "in the order of nature" characterizes the union between mother and child. In the light of this fact it becomes easier to understand why in Christ's testament on Golgotha his Mother's new motherhood is expressed in the singular, in reference to one man: "Behold your son."

lit can also be said that these same words fully show the reason for the Marian dimension of the life of Christ's disciples. This is true not only of John, who at that hour stood at the foot of the Cross together with his Master's Mother, but it is also true of every disciple of Christ, of every Christian. The Redeemer entrusts his mother to the disciple, and at the same time he gives her to him as his mother. Mary's motherhood, which becomes man's inheritance, is a gift: a gift which Christ himself makes personally to every individual. The Redeemer entrusts Mary to John because he entrusts John to Mary. At the foot of the Cross there begins that special entrusting of humanity to the Mother of Christ, which in the history of the Church has been practiced and expressed in different ways. The same Apostle and Evangelist, after reporting the words addressed by Jesus on the Cross to his Mother and to himself, adds: "And from that hour the disciple took her to his own home" (Jn. 19:27). This statement certainly means that the role of son was attributed to the disciple and that he assumed responsibility for the Mother of his beloved Master. And since Mary was given as a mother to him personally, the statement indicates, even though indirectly, everything expressed by the intimate relationship of a child with its mother. And all of this can be included in the word "entrusting." Such entrusting is the response to a person's love, and in particular to the love of a mother.

The Marian dimension of the life of a disciple of Christ is expressed in a special way precisely through this filial entrusting to the Mother of Christ, which began with the testament of the Redeemer on Golgotha. Entrusting himself to Mary in a filial manner, the Christian, like the Apostle John, "welcomes" the Mother of Christ "into his own home"(130) and brings her into everything that makes up his inner life, that is to say into his human and Christian "I": he "took her to his own home." Thus the Christian seeks to be taken into that "maternal charity" with which the Redeemer's Mother "cares for the brethren of her Son,"(131) "in whose birth and development she cooperates"(132) in the measure of the gift proper to each one through the power of Christ's Spirit. Thus also is exercised that motherhood in the Spirit which became Mary's role at the foot of the Cross and in the Upper Room.

[130] Clearly, in the Greek text the expression "eis ta idia" goes beyond the mere acceptance of Mary by the disciple in the sense of material lodging and hospitality in his house; it indicates rather a communion of life established between the two as a result of the words of the dying Christ: cf. Saint Augustine, In Ioan. Evang. tract. 119, 3: CCL 36, 659: "He took her to himself, not into his own property, for he possessed nothing of his own, but among his own duties, which he attended to with dedication."

[131] Second Vatican Ecumenical Council, Dogmatic Constitution on the Church Lumen Gentium, 62.

[132] Ibid., 63.

46. This filial relationship, this self-entrusting of a child to its mother, not only has its beginning in Christ but can also be said to be definitively directed towards him. Mary can be said to continue to say to each individual the words which she spoke at Cana in Galilee: "Do whatever he tells you." For he, Christ, is the one Mediator between God and mankind; he is "the way, and the truth, and the life" (Jn. 14:6); it is he whom the Father has given to the world, so that man "should not perish but have eternal life" (Jn. 3:16). The Virgin of Nazareth became the first "witness" of this saving love of the Father, and she also wishes to remain its humble handmaid always and everywhere. For every Christian, for every human being, Mary is the one who first "believed," and precisely with her faith as Spouse and Mother she wishes to act upon all those who entrust themselves to her as her children. And it is well known that the more her children persevere and progress in this attitude, the nearer Mary leads them to the "unsearchable riches of Christ"(Eph. 3:8). And to the same degree they recognize more and more clearly the dignity of man in all its fullness and the definitive meaning of his vocation, for "Christ...fully reveals man to man himself."(133)

[133] Second Vatican Ecumenical Council, Pastoral Constitution on the Church in the Modern World Gaudium et Spes, 22.

This Marian dimension of Christian life takes on special importance in relation to women and their status. In fact, femininity has a unique relationship with the Mother of the Redeemer, a subject which can be studied in greater depth elsewhere. Here I simply wish to note that the figure of Mary of Nazareth sheds light on womanhood as such by the very fact that God, in the sublime event of the Incarnation of his Son, entrusted himself to the ministry, the free and active ministry of a woman. It can thus be said that women, by looking to Mary, find in her the secret of living their femininity with dignity and of achieving their own true advancement. In the light of Mary, the Church sees in the face of women the reflection of a beauty which mirrors the loftiest sentiments of which the human heart is capable: the self-offering totality of love; the strength that is capable of bearing the greatest sorrows; limitless fidelity and tireless devotion to work; the ability to combine penetrating intuition with words of support and encouragement.

47. At the Council Paul VI solemnly proclaimed that Mary is the Mother of the Church, "that is, Mother of the entire Christian people, both faithful and pastors."(134) Later, in 1968, in the Profession of faith known as the "Credo of the People of God." he restated this truth in an even more forceful way in these words: "We believe that the Most Holy Mother of God, the new Eve, the Mother of the Church, carries on in heaven her maternal role with regard to the members of Christ, cooperating in the birth and development of divine life in the souls of the redeemed."(135)

[134] Cf. Pope Paul VI, Discourse of 21 November 1964: AAS 56 (1964) 1015.

[135] Pope Paul VI, Solemn Profession of Faith (30 June 1968), 15: AAS 60 (1968) 438f.

The Council's teaching emphasized that the truth concerning the Blessed Virgin, Mother of Christ, is an effective aid in exploring more deeply the truth concerning the Church. When speaking of the Constitution Lumen Gentium, which had just been approved by the Council, Paul VI said: "Knowledge of the true Catholic doctrine regarding the Blessed Virgin Mary will always be a key to the exact understanding of the mystery of Christ and of the Church."(136) Mary is present in the Church as the Mother of Christ, and at the same time as that Mother whom Christ, in the mystery of the Redemption, gave to humanity in the person of the Apostle John. Thus, in her new motherhood in the Spirit, Mary embraces each and every one in the Church, and embraces each and every one through the Church. In this sense Mary, Mother of the Church, is also the Church's model. Indeed, as Paul VI hopes and asks, the Church must draw "from the Virgin Mother of God the most authentic form of perfect imitation of Christ."(137)

[136] Pope Paul VI, Discourse of 21 November 1964: AAS 56 (1964) 1015.

[137] Ibid., 1016.

Thanks to this special bond linking the Mother of Christ with the Church, there is further clarified the mystery of that "woman" who, from the first chapters of the Book of Genesis until the Book of Revelation, accompanies the revelation of God's salvific plan for humanity. For Mary, present in the Church as the Mother of the Redeemer, takes part, as a mother, in that monumental struggle; against the powers of darkness"(138) which continues throughout human history. And by her ecclesial identification as the "woman clothed with the sun" (Rev. 12:1),(139) it can be said that "in the Most Holy Virgin the Church has already reached that perfection whereby she exists without spot or wrinkle." Hence, as Christians raise their eyes with faith to Mary in the course of their earthly pilgrimage, they "strive to increase in holiness."(140) Mary, the exalted Daughter of Sion, helps all her children, wherever they may be and whatever their condition, to find in Christ the path to the Father's house.

[138] Cf. Second Vatican Ecumenical Council, Pastoral Constitution on the Church in the Modern World Gaudium et Spes, 37.

[139] Cf. Saint Bernard, In Dominica infra oct. Assumptionis Sermo: S. Bernardi Opera V, 1968, 262-274.

[140] Second Vatican Ecumenical Council, Dogmatic Constitution on the Church Lumen Gentium, 65.

Thus, throughout her life, the Church maintains with the Mother of God a link which embraces, in the saving mystery, the past, the present and the future, and venerates her as the spiritual mother of humanity and the advocate of grace.

3. The meaning of the Marian Year

48. It is precisely the special bond between humanity and this Mother which has led me to proclaim a Marian Year in the Church, in this period before the end of the Second Millennium since Christ's birth, a similar initiative was taken in the past. when Pius XII proclaimed 1954 as a Marian Year, in order to highlight the exceptional holiness of the Mother of Christ as expressed in the mysteries of her Immaculate Conception (defined exactly a century before) and of her Assumption into heaven.(141)

[141] Cf. Encyclical Letter Fulgens Corona (8 September 1953): AAS 45 (1953) 577-592. Pius X with his Encyclical Letter Ad Diem Illum (2 February 1904), on the occasion of the 50th anniversary of the dogmatic definition of the Immaculate Conception of the Blessed Virgin Mary, had proclaimed an Extraordinary jubilee of a few months; Pii X P. M. Acta, I, 147-166.

Now, following the line of the Second Vatican Council, I wish to emphasize the special presence of the Mother of God in the mystery of Christ and his Church. For this is a fundamental dimension emerging from the Mariology of the Council, the end of which is now more than twenty years behind us. The Extraordinary

Synod of Bishops held in 1985 exhorted everyone to follow faithfully the teaching and guidelines of the Council We can say that these two events-the Council and the synod-embody what the Holy Spirit himself wishes "to say to the Church" in the present phase of history.

In this context, the Marian Year is meant to promote a new and more careful reading of what the Council said about the Blessed Virgin Mary, Mother of God, in the mystery of Christ and of the Church, the topic to which the contents of this Encyclical are devoted. Here we speak not only of the doctrine of faith but also of the life of faith, and thus of authentic "Marian spirituality," seen in the light of Tradition, and especially the spirituality to which the Council exhorts us.(142) Furthermore, Marian spirituality, like its corresponding devotion, finds a very rich source in the historical experience of individuals and of the various Christian communities present among the different peoples and nations of the world. In this regard, I would like to recall, among the many witnesses and teachers of this spirituality, the figure of Saint Louis Marie Grignion de Montfort,(143) who proposes consecration to Christ through the hands of Mary, as an effective means for Christians to live faithfully their baptismal commitments. I am pleased to note that in our own time too new manifestations of this spirituality and devotion are not lacking.

[142] Cf. Dogmatic Constitution on the Church Lumen Gentium, 66-67.

[143] Saint Louis Marie Grignion de Montfort, Traite de la varie devotion a la sainte Vierge. This saint can rightly be linked with the figure of Saint Alfonso Maria de' Liguori, the second centenary of whose death occurs this year; cf. among his works Le glorie di Maria.

There thus exist solid points of reference to look to and follow in the context of this Marian Year.

49. This Marian Year will begin on the Solemnity of Pentecost, on June 7 next. For it is a question not only of recalling that Mary "preceded" the entry of Christ the Lord into the history of the human family, but also of emphasizing, in the light of Mary, that from the moment when the mystery of the Incarnation was accomplished, human history entered "the fullness of time," and that the Church is the sign of this fullness. As the People of God, the Church makes her pilgrim way towards eternity through faith, in the midst of all the peoples and nations, beginning from the day of Pentecost. Christ's Mother-who was present at the beginning of "the time of the Church," when in expectation of the coming of the Holy Spirit she devoted herself to prayer in the midst of the Apostles and her Son's disciples-constantly "precedes" the Church in her journey through human history. She is also the one who, precisely as the "handmaid of the Lord," cooperates unceasingly with the work of salvation accomplished by Christ, her Son.

Thus by means of this Marian Year the Church is called not only to remember everything in her past that testifies to the special maternal cooperation of the Mother of God in the work of salvation in Christ the lord, but also, on her own part, to prepare for the future the paths of this cooperation. For the end of the second Christian Millennium opens up as a new prospect.

50. As has already been mentioned, also among our divided brethren many honor and celebrate the Mother of the Lord, especially among the Orientals. It is a Marian light cast upon ecumenism. In particular, I wish to mention once more that during the Marian Year there will occur the Millennium of the Baptism of Saint Vladimir, Grand Duke of Kiev [988]. This marked the

beginning of Christianity in the territories of what was then called Rus', and subsequently in other territories of Eastern Europe. In this way, through the work of evangelization, Christianity spread beyond Europe, as far as the northern territories of the Asian continent. We would therefore like, especially during this Year, to join in prayer with all those who are celebrating the Millennium of this Baptism, both Orthodox and Catholics, repeating and confirming with the Council those sentiments of joy and comfort that "the Easterners...with ardent emotion and devout mind concur in reverencing the Mother of God, ever Virgin."(144) Even though we are still experiencing the painful effects of the separation which took place some decades later [1054], we can say that in the presence of the Mother of Christ we feel that we are true brothers and sisters within that messianic People, which is called to be the one family of God on earth. As I announced at the beginning of the New Year "We desire to reconfirm this universal inheritance of all the Sons and daughters of this earth."(145)

[144] Dogmatic Constitution on the Church Lumen Gentium, 69.

[145] Homily on 1 January 1987.

In announcing the Year of Mary, I also indicated that it will end next year on the Solemnity of the Assumption of the Blessed Virgin into heaven, in order to emphasize the "great sign in heaven" spoken of by the Apocalypse. In this way we also wish to respond to the exhortation of the Council, which looks to Mary as "a sign of sure hope and solace for the pilgrim People of God." And the Council expresses this exhortation in the following words: "Let the entire body of the faithful pour forth persevering prayer to the Mother of God and Mother of mankind. Let them implore that she who aided the beginning of the Church by her prayers may now, exalted as she is in heaven above all the saints and angels, intercede with her Son in the fellowship of all the saints. May she do so until all the peoples of the human family, whether they are honored with the name of Christian or whether they still do not know their Savior, are happily gathered together in peace and harmony into the one People of God, for the glory of the Most Holy and Undivided Trinity."(146)

[146] Dogmatic Constitution on the Church Lumen Gentium, 69.

CONCLUSION

51. At the end of the daily Liturgy of the Hours, among the invocations addressed to Mary by the Church is the following:

"Loving Mother of the Redeemer, gate of heaven, star of the sea, assist your people who have fallen yet strive to rise again.
To the wonderment of nature you bore your Creator!"

"To the wonderment of nature"! These words of the antiphon express that wonderment of faith which accompanies the mystery of Mary's divine motherhood. In a sense, it does so in the heart of the whole of creation, and, directly, in the heart of the whole People of God, in the heart of the Church. How wonderfully far God has gone, the Creator and Lord of all things, in the "revelation of himself" to man!(147) How clearly he has bridged all the spaces of that infinite "distance" which separates the Creator from the creature! If in himself he remains ineffable and unsearchable, still more ineffable and unsearchable is he in the reality of the Incarnation of the Word, who became man through the Virgin of Nazareth.

[147] Cf. Second Vatican Ecumenical Council, Dogmatic Constitution on Divine Revelation Dei Verbum, 2: "Through this revelation...the invisible God...out of the abundance of his love

speaks to men as friends...and lives among them..., so that he may invite and take them into fellowship with himself."

If he has eternally willed to call man to share in the divine nature (cf. 2 Pt. 1:4), it can be said that he has matched the "divinization" of man to humanity's historical conditions, so that even after sin he is ready to restore at a great price the eternal plan of his love through the "humanization" of his Son, who is of the same being as himself. The whole of creation, and more directly man himself, cannot fail to be amazed at this gift in which he has become a sharer, in the Holy Spirit: "God so loved the world that he gave his only Son" (Jn. 3:16).

At the center of this mystery, in the midst of this wonderment of faith, stands Mary. As the loving Mother of the Redeemer, she was the first to experience it: "To the wonderment of nature you bore your Creator"!

52. The words of this liturgical antiphon also express the truth of the "great transformation" which the mystery of the Incarnation establishes for man. It is a transformation which belongs to his entire history, from that beginning which is revealed to us in the first chapters of Genesis until the final end, in the perspective of the end of the world, of which Jesus has revealed to us "neither the day nor the hour" (Mt. 25:13). It is an unending and continuous transformation between falling and rising again, between the man of sin and the man of grace and justice. The Advent liturgy in particular is at the very heart of this transformation and captures its unceasing "here and now" when it exclaims: "Assist your people who have fallen yet strive to rise again"!

These words apply to every individual, every community, to nations and peoples, and to the generations and epochs of human history, to our own epoch, to these years of the Millennium which is drawing to a close: "Assist, yes assist, your people who have fallen"!

This is the invocation addressed to Mary, the "loving Mother of the Redeemer," the invocation addressed to Christ, who through Mary entered human history. Year after year the antiphon rises to Mary, evoking that moment which saw the accomplishment of this essential historical transformation, which irreversibly continues: the transformation from "falling" to "rising."

Mankind has made wonderful discoveries and achieved extraordinary results in the fields of science and technology. It has made great advances along the path of progress and civilization, and in recent times one could say that it has succeeded in speeding up the pace of history. But the fundamental transformation, the one which can be called "original," constantly accompanies man's journey, and through all the events of history accompanies each and every individual. It is the transformation from "falling" to "rising," from death to life. It is also a constant challenge to people's consciences, a challenge to man's whole historical awareness: the challenge to follow the path of "not falling" in ways that are ever old and ever new, and of "rising again" if a fall has occurred.

As she goes forward with the whole of humanity towards the frontier between the two Millennia, the Church, for her part, with the whole community of believers and in union with all men and women of good will, takes up the great challenge contained in these words of the Marian antiphon: "the people who have fallen yet strive to rise again," and she addresses both the Redeemer and his Mother with the plea: "Assist us." For, as this prayer attests, the Church sees the Blessed Mother of God in the saving mystery of Christ and in her own mystery. She sees Mary deeply rooted in humanity's history, in man's eternal vocation according to the providential plan which God has made for him from eternity She sees Mary maternally present and sharing in the many complicated problems which today beset the lives of individuals, families and nations; she sees her helping the Christian people in the constant struggle between good and evil, to ensure that it "does not fall," or, if it has fallen, that it "rises again."

I hope with all my heart that the reflections contained in the present Encyclical will also serve to renew this vision in the hearts of all believers.

As Bishop of Rome, I send to all those to whom these thoughts are addressed the kiss of peace, my greeting and my blessing in our Lord Jesus Christ. Amen.

Given in Rome, at Saint Peter's, on March 25, the Solemnity of the Annunciation of the Lord, in the year 1987, the ninth of my Pontificate.

Enchiridion Sanctissimi Rosarii

Rosarium Virginis Mariae
On the Most Holy Rosary

Apolostic Letter of Pope John Paul II

October 16, 2002

TO THE BISHOPS, CLERGY AND FAITHFUL
ON THE MOST HOLY ROSARY

INTRODUCTION

1. The Rosary of the Virgin Mary, which gradually took form in the second millennium under the guidance of the Spirit of God, is a prayer loved by countless Saints and encouraged by the Magisterium. Simple yet profound, it still remains, at the dawn of this third millennium, a prayer of great significance, destined to bring forth a harvest of holiness. It blends easily into the spiritual journey of the Christian life, which, after two thousand years, has lost none of the freshness of its beginnings and feels drawn by the Spirit of God to "set out into the deep" (duc in altum!) in order once more to proclaim, and even cry out, before the world that Jesus Christ is Lord and Saviour, "the way, and the truth and the life" (Jn 14:6), "the goal of human history and the point on which the desires of history and civilization turn".[1]

[1] Pastoral Constitution on the Church in the Modern World Gaudium et Spes, 45.

The Rosary, though clearly Marian in character, is at heart a Christocentric prayer. In the sobriety of its elements, it has all the depth of the Gospel message in its entirety, of which it can be said to be a compendium.[2] It is an echo of the prayer of Mary, her perennial Magnificat for the work of the redemptive Incarnation which began in her virginal womb. With the Rosary, the Christian people sits at the school of Mary and is led to contemplate the beauty on the face of Christ and to experience the depths of his love. Through the Rosary the faithful receive abundant grace, as though from the very hands of the Mother of the Redeemer.

[2] Pope Paul VI, Apostolic Exhortation Marialis Cultus (2 February 1974), 42: AAS 66 (1974), 153.

The Popes and the Rosary

2. Numerous predecessors of mine attributed great importance to this prayer. Worthy of special note in this regard is Pope Leo XIII who on 1 September 1883 promulgated the Encyclical Supremi Apostolatus Officio,[3] a document of great worth, the first of his many statements about this prayer, in which he proposed the Rosary as an effective spiritual weapon against the evils afflicting society. Among the more recent Popes who, from the time of the Second Vatican Council, have distinguished themselves in promoting the Rosary I would mention Blessed John XXIII[4] and above all Pope Paul VI, who in his Apostolic Exhortation Marialis Cultus emphasized, in the spirit of the Second Vatican Council, the Rosary's evangelical character and its Christocentric inspiration. I myself have often encouraged the frequent recitation of the Rosary. From my youthful years this prayer has held an important place in my spiritual life. I was powerfully reminded of this during my recent visit to Poland, and in particular at the Shrine of Kalwaria. The Rosary has accompanied me in moments of joy and in moments of difficulty. To it I have entrusted any number of concerns; in it I have always found comfort. Twenty-four years ago, on 29 October 1978, scarcely two weeks after my election to the See of Peter, I frankly admitted: "The Rosary is my favourite

prayer. A marvellous prayer! Marvellous in its simplicity and its depth. [...]. It can be said that the Rosary is, in some sense, a prayer-commentary on the final chapter of the Vatican II Constitution Lumen Gentium, a chapter which discusses the wondrous presence of the Mother of God in the mystery of Christ and the Church. Against the background of the words Ave Maria the principal events of the life of Jesus Christ pass before the eyes of the soul. They take shape in the complete series of the joyful, sorrowful and glorious mysteries, and they put us in living communion with Jesus through -- we might say -- the heart of his Mother. At the same time our heart can embrace in the decades of the Rosary all the events that make up the lives of individuals, families, nations, the Church, and all mankind. Our personal concerns and those of our neighbour, especially those who are closest to us, who are dearest to us. Thus the simple prayer of the Rosary marks the rhythm of human life".[5]

[3] Cf. Acta Leonis XIII, 3 (1884), 280-289.

[4] Particularly worthy of note is his Apostolic Epistle on the Rosary Il religioso convegno (29 September 1961): AAS 53 (1961), 641-647.

[5] Angelus: Insegnamenti di Giovanni Paolo II, I (1978): 75-76.

With these words, dear brothers and sisters, I set the first year of my Pontificate within the daily rhythm of the Rosary. Today, as I begin the twenty-fifth year of my service as the Successor of Peter, I wish to do the same. How many graces have I received in these years from the Blessed Virgin through the Rosary: Magnificat anima mea Dominum! I wish to lift up my thanks to the Lord in the words of his Most Holy Mother, under whose protection I have placed my Petrine ministry: Totus Tuus!

A Manual of the Most Holy Rosary

October 2002 -- October 2003: The Year of the Rosary

3. Therefore, in continuity with my reflection in the Apostolic Letter Novo Millennio Ineunte, in which, after the experience of the Jubilee, I invited the people of God to "start afresh from Christ",[6] I have felt drawn to offer a reflection on the Rosary, as a kind of Marian complement to that Letter and an exhortation to contemplate the face of Christ in union with, and at the school of, his Most Holy Mother. To recite the Rosary is nothing other than to contemplate with Mary the face of Christ. As a way of highlighting this invitation, prompted by the forthcoming 120th anniversary of the aforementioned Encyclical of Leo XIII, I desire that during the course of this year the Rosary should be especially emphasized and promoted in the various Christian communities. I therefore proclaim the year from October 2002 to October 2003 the Year of the Rosary.

[6] 6 AAS 93 (2001), 285.

I leave this pastoral proposal to the initiative of each ecclesial community. It is not my intention to encumber but rather to complete and consolidate pastoral programmes of the Particular Churches. I am confident that the proposal will find a ready and generous reception. The Rosary, reclaimed in its full meaning, goes to the very heart of Christian life; it offers a familiar yet fruitful spiritual and educational opportunity for personal contemplation, the formation of the People of God, and the new evangelization. I am pleased to reaffirm this also in the joyful remembrance of another anniversary: the fortieth anniversary of the opening of the Second Vatican Ecumenical Council on October 11, 1962, the "great grace" disposed by the Spirit of God for the Church in our time.[7]

[7] During the years of preparation for the Council, Pope John XXIII did not fail to encourage the Christian community to recite the Rosary for the success of this ecclesial event: cf. Letter to the Cardinal Vicar (28 September 1960): AAS 52 (1960), 814-816.

Objections to the Rosary

4. The timeliness of this proposal is evident from a number of considerations. First, the urgent need to counter a certain crisis of the Rosary, which in the present historical and theological context can risk being wrongly devalued, and therefore no longer taught to the younger generation. There are some who think that the centrality of the Liturgy, rightly stressed by the Second Vatican Ecumenical Council, necessarily entails giving lesser importance to the Rosary. Yet, as Pope Paul VI made clear, not only does this prayer not conflict with the Liturgy, it sustains it, since it serves as an excellent introduction and a faithful echo of the Liturgy, enabling people to participate fully and interiorly in it and to reap its fruits in their daily lives.

Perhaps too, there are some who fear that the Rosary is somehow unecumenical because of its distinctly Marian character. Yet the Rosary clearly belongs to the kind of veneration of the Mother of God described by the Council: a devotion directed to the Christological centre of the Christian faith, in such a way that "when the Mother is honoured, the Son ... is duly known, loved and glorified".[8] If properly revitalized, the Rosary is an aid and certainly not a hindrance to ecumenism!

[8] Dogmatic Constitution on the Church Lumen Gentium, 66.

A path of contemplation

5. But the most important reason for strongly encouraging the practice of the Rosary is that it represents a most effective means of fostering among the faithful that commitment to the contemplation of the Christian mystery which I have proposed in the Apostolic Letter Novo Millennio Ineunte as a genuine "training in holiness": "What is needed is a Christian life distinguished above all in the art of prayer".[9] Inasmuch as contemporary culture, even amid so many indications to the contrary, has witnessed the flowering of a new call for spirituality, due also to the influence of other religions, it is more urgent than ever that our Christian communities should become "genuine schools of prayer".[10]

[9] No. 32: AAS 93 (2001), 288.

[10] Ibid., 33: loc. cit., 289.

The Rosary belongs among the finest and most praiseworthy traditions of Christian contemplation. Developed in the West, it is a typically meditative prayer, corresponding in some way to the "prayer of the heart" or "Jesus prayer" which took root in the soil of the Christian East.

Prayer for peace and for the family

6. A number of historical circumstances also make a revival of the Rosary quite timely. First of all, the need to implore from God the gift of peace. The Rosary has many times been proposed by my predecessors and myself as a prayer for peace. At the start of a millennium which began with the terrifying attacks of 11 September 2001, a millennium which witnesses every day innumerous parts of the world fresh scenes of bloodshed and violence, to rediscover the Rosary means to immerse oneself in contemplation of the mystery of Christ who "is our peace", since he made "the two of us one, and broke down the dividing wall of

hostility" (Eph 2:14). Consequently, one cannot recite the Rosary without feeling caught up in a clear commitment to advancing peace, especially in the land of Jesus, still so sorely afflicted and so close to the heart of every Christian.

A similar need for commitment and prayer arises in relation to another critical contemporary issue: the family, the primary cell of society, increasingly menaced by forces of disintegration on both the ideological and practical planes, so as to make us fear for the future of this fundamental and indispensable institution and, with it, for the future of society as a whole. The revival of the Rosary in Christian families, within the context of a broader pastoral ministry to the family, will be an effective aid to countering the devastating effects of this crisis typical of our age.

"Behold, your Mother!" (Jn 19:27)

7. Many signs indicate that still today the Blessed Virgin desires to exercise through this same prayer that maternal concern to which the dying Redeemer entrusted, in the person of the beloved disciple, all the sons and daughters of the Church: "Woman, behold your son!" (Jn19:26). Well-known are the occasions in the nineteenth and the twentieth centuries on which the Mother of Christ made her presence felt and her voice heard, in order to exhort the People of God to this form of contemplative prayer. I would mention in particular, on account of their great influence on the lives of Christians and the authoritative recognition they have received from the Church, the apparitions of Lourdes and of Fatima;[11] these shrines continue to be visited by great numbers of pilgrims seeking comfort and hope.

[11] It is well-known and bears repeating that private revelations are not the same as public revelation, which is binding on the whole Church. It is the task of the Magisterium to discern and recognize

the authenticity and value of private revelations for the piety of the faithful.

Following the witnesses

8. It would be impossible to name all the many Saints who discovered in the Rosary a genuine path to growth in holiness. We need but mention Saint Louis Marie Grignion de Montfort, the author of an excellent work on the Rosary,[12] and, closer to ourselves, Padre Pio of Pietrelcina, whom I recently had the joy of canonizing. As a true apostle of the Rosary, Blessed Bartolo Longo had a special charism. His path to holiness rested on an inspiration heard in the depths of his heart: "Whoever spreads the Rosary is saved!".[13] As a result, he felt called to build a Church dedicated to Our Lady of the Holy Rosary in Pompei, against the background of the ruins of the ancient city, which scarcely heard the proclamation of Christ before being buried in 79 A.D. during an eruption of Mount Vesuvius, only to emerge centuries later from its ashes as a witness to the lights and shadows of classical civilization. By his whole life's work and especially by the practice of the "Fifteen Saturdays", Bartolo Longo promoted the Christocentric and contemplative heart of the Rosary, and received great encouragement and support from Leo XIII, the "Pope of the Rosary".

[12] The Secret of the Rosary.

[13] Blessed Bartolo Longo, Storia del Santuario di Pompei, Pompei, 1990, 59.

CHAPTER I
CONTEMPLATING CHRIST WITH MARY

A face radiant as the sun

9. "And he was transfigured before them, and his face shone like the sun" (Mt 17:2). The Gospel scene of Christ's transfiguration, in which the three Apostles Peter, James and John appear entranced by the beauty of the Redeemer, can be seen as an icon of Christian contemplation. To look upon the face of Christ, to recognize its mystery amid the daily events and the sufferings of his human life, and then to grasp the divine splendour definitively revealed in the Risen Lord, seated in glory at the right hand of the Father: this is the task of every follower of Christ and therefore the task of each one of us. In contemplating Christ's face we become open to receiving the mystery of Trinitarian life, experiencing ever anew the love of the Father and delighting in the joy of the Holy Spirit. Saint Paul's words can then be applied to us: "Beholding the glory of the Lord, we are being changed into his likeness, from one degree of glory to another; for this comes from the Lord who is the Spirit" (2Cor 3:18).

Mary, model of contemplation

10. The contemplation of Christ has an incomparable model in Mary. In a unique way the face of the Son belongs to Mary. It was in her womb that Christ was formed, receiving from her a human resemblance which points to an even greater spiritual closeness. No one has ever devoted himself to the contemplation of the face of Christ as faithfully as Mary. The eyes of her heart already turned to him at the Annunciation, when she conceived him by the power of the Holy Spirit. In the months that followed she began to sense his presence and to picture his features. When at last she gave birth to him in Bethlehem, her eyes were able to gaze tenderly on the face of her Son, as she "wrapped him in swaddling cloths, and laid him in a manger" (Lk2:7).

Thereafter Mary's gaze, ever filled with adoration and wonder, would never leave him. At times it would be a questioning look, as in the episode of the finding in the Temple: "Son, why have you treated us so?" (Lk 2:48); it would always be a penetrating gaze, one capable of deeply understanding Jesus, even to the point of perceiving his hidden feelings and anticipating his decisions, as at Cana (cf. Jn 2:5). At other times it would be a look of sorrow, especially beneath the Cross, where her vision would still be that of a mother giving birth, for Mary not only shared the passion and death of her Son, she also received the new son given to her in the beloved disciple (cf. Jn 19:26-27). On the morning of Easter hers would be a gaze radiant with the joy of the Resurrection, and finally, on the day of Pentecost, a gaze afire with the outpouring of the Spirit (cf. Acts 1:14).

Mary's memories

11. Mary lived with her eyes fixed on Christ, treasuring his every word: "She kept all these things, pondering them in her heart" (Lk 2:19; cf. 2:51). The memories of Jesus, impressed upon her heart, were always with her, leading her to reflect on the various moments of her life at her Son's side. In a way those memories were to be the "rosary" which she recited uninterruptedly throughout her earthly life.

Even now, amid the joyful songs of the heavenly Jerusalem, the reasons for her thanksgiving and praise remain unchanged. They inspire her maternal concern for the pilgrim Church, in which she continues to relate her personal account of the Gospel. Mary constantly sets before the faithful the "mysteries" of her Son, with the desire that the contemplation of those mysteries will release all their saving power. In the recitation of the Rosary, the Christian community enters into contact with the memories and the contemplative gaze of Mary.

The Rosary, a contemplative prayer

12. The Rosary, precisely because it starts with Mary's own experience, is an exquisitely contemplative prayer. Without this contemplative dimension, it would lose its meaning, as Pope Paul VI clearly pointed out: "Without contemplation, the Rosary is a body without a soul, and its recitation runs the risk of becoming a mechanical repetition of formulas, in violation of the admonition of Christ: 'In praying do not heap up empty phrases as the Gentiles do; for they think they will be heard for their many words' (Mt 6:7). By its nature the recitation of the Rosary calls for a quiet rhythm and a lingering pace, helping the individual to meditate on the mysteries of the Lord's life as seen through the eyes of her who was closest to the Lord. In this way the unfathomable riches of these mysteries are disclosed".[14]

[14] Apostolic Exhortation Marialis Cultus (2 February 1974), 47: AAS (1974), 156.

It is worth pausing to consider this profound insight of Paul VI, in order to bring out certain aspects of the Rosary which show that it is really a form of Christocentric contemplation.

Remembering Christ with Mary

13. Mary's contemplation is above all a remembering. We need to understand this word in the biblical sense of remembrance (zakar) as a making present of the works brought about by God in the history of salvation. The Bible is an account of saving events culminating in Christ himself. These events not only belong to "yesterday"; they are also part of the "today" of salvation. This

making present comes about above all in the Liturgy: what God accomplished centuries ago did not only affect the direct witnesses of those events; it continues to affect people in every age with its gift of grace. To some extent this is also true of every other devout approach to those events: to "remember" them in a spirit of faith and love is to be open to the grace which Christ won for us by the mysteries of his life, death and resurrection.

Consequently, while it must be reaffirmed with the Second Vatican Council that the Liturgy, as the exercise of the priestly office of Christ and an act of public worship, is "the summit to which the activity of the Church is directed and the font from which all its power flows",[15] it is also necessary to recall that the spiritual life "is not limited solely to participation in the liturgy. Christians, while they are called to prayer in common, must also go to their own rooms to pray to their Father in secret (cf. Mt 6:6); indeed, according to the teaching of the Apostle, they must pray without ceasing (cf.1Thes 5:17)".[16] The Rosary, in its own particular way, is part of this varied panorama of "ceaseless" prayer. If the Liturgy, as the activity of Christ and the Church, is a saving action par excellence, the Rosary too, as a "meditation" with Mary on Christ, is a salutary contemplation. By immersing us in the mysteries of the Redeemer's life, it ensures that what he has done and what the liturgy makes present is profoundly assimilated and shapes our existence.

[15] Constitution on the Sacred Liturgy Sacrosanctum Concilium, 10.

[16] Ibid., 12.

Learning Christ from Mary

14. Christ is the supreme Teacher, the revealer and the one revealed. It is not just a question of learning what he taught but of "learning him". In this regard could we have any better teacher than Mary? From the divine standpoint, the Spirit is the interior teacher who leads us to the full truth of Christ (cf. Jn 14:26; 15:26; 16:13). But among creatures no one knows Christ better than Mary; no one can introduce us to a profound knowledge of his mystery better than his Mother.

The first of the "signs" worked by Jesus -- the changing of water into wine at the marriage in Cana -- clearly presents Mary in the guise of a teacher, as she urges the servants to do what Jesus commands (cf. Jn 2:5). We can imagine that she would have done likewise for the disciples after Jesus' Ascension, when she joined them in awaiting the Holy Spirit and supported them in their first mission. Contemplating the scenes of the Rosary in union with Mary is a means of learning from her to "read" Christ, to discover his secrets and to understand his message.

This school of Mary is all the more effective if we consider that she teaches by obtaining for us in abundance the gifts of the Holy Spirit, even as she offers us the incomparable example of her own "pilgrimage of faith".[17] As we contemplate each mystery of her Son's life, she invites us to do as she did at the Annunciation: to ask humbly the questions which open us to the light, in order to end with the obedience of faith: "Behold I am the handmaid of the Lord; be it done to me according to your word" (Lk 1:38).

[17] Second Vatican Ecumenical Council, Dogmatic Constitution on the Church Lumen Gentium, 58.

Being conformed to Christ with Mary

15. Christian spirituality is distinguished by the disciple's commitment to become conformed ever more fully to his Master (cf. Rom 8:29; Phil 3:10,12). The outpouring of the Holy Spirit in Baptism grafts the believer like a branch onto the vine which is Christ (cf. Jn 15:5) and makes him a member of Christ's mystical Body (cf.1Cor 12:12; Rom 12:5). This initial unity, however, calls for a growing assimilation which will increasingly shape the conduct of the disciple in accordance with the "mind" of Christ: "Have this mind among yourselves, which was in Christ Jesus" (Phil 2:5). In the words of the Apostle, we are called "to put on the Lord Jesus Christ" (cf. Rom 13:14; Gal 3:27).

In the spiritual journey of the Rosary, based on the constant contemplation -- in Mary's company -- of the face of Christ, this demanding ideal of being conformed to him is pursued through an association which could be described in terms of friendship. We are thereby enabled to enter naturally into Christ's life and as it were to share his deepest feelings. In this regard Blessed Bartolo Longo has written: "Just as two friends, frequently in each other's company, tend to develop similar habits, so too, by holding familiar converse with Jesus and the Blessed Virgin, by meditating on the mysteries of the Rosary and by living the same life in Holy Communion, we can become, to the extent of our lowliness, similar to them and can learn from these supreme models a life of humility, poverty, hiddenness, patience and perfection".[18]

[18] I Quindici Sabati del Santissimo Rosario, 27th ed., Pompei, 1916, 27.

In this process of being conformed to Christ in the Rosary, we entrust ourselves in a special way to the maternal care of the Blessed Virgin. She who is both the Mother of Christ and a member of the Church, indeed her "pre-eminent and altogether singular member",[19] is at the same time the "Mother of the Church". As such, she continually brings to birth children for the mystical Body of her Son. She does so through her intercession, imploring upon them the inexhaustible outpouring of the Spirit. Mary is the perfect icon of the motherhood of the Church.

[19] Second Vatican Ecumenical Council, Dogmatic Constitution on the Church Lumen Gentium, 53.

The Rosary mystically transports us to Mary's side as she is busy watching over the human growth of Christ in the home of Nazareth. This enables her to train us and to mold us with the same care, until Christ is "fully formed" in us (cf. Gal 4:19). This role of Mary, totally grounded in that of Christ and radically subordinated to it, "in no way obscures or diminishes the unique mediation of Christ, but rather shows its power".[20] This is the luminous principle expressed by the Second Vatican Council which I have so powerfully experienced in my own life and have made the basis of my episcopal motto: Totus Tuus.[21] The motto is of course inspired by the teaching of Saint Louis Marie Grignion de Montfort, who explained in the following words Mary's role in the process of our configuration to Christ: "Our entire perfection consists in being conformed, united and consecrated to Jesus Christ. Hence the most perfect of all devotions is undoubtedly that which conforms, unites and consecrates us most perfectly to Jesus Christ. Now, since Mary is of all creatures the one most conformed to Jesus Christ, it follows that among all devotions that which most consecrates and conforms a soul to our Lord is devotion to Mary, his Holy Mother, and that the more a soul is consecrated to her the more will it be consecrated to Jesus Christ".[22] Never as in the Rosary do the life of Jesus and that of Mary appear so deeply joined. Mary lives only in Christ and for Christ!

[20] Ibid., 60.

[21] Cf. First Radio Address Urbi et Orbi (17 October 1978): AAS 70 (1978), 927.

[22] Treatise on True Devotion to the Blessed Virgin Mary.

Praying to Christ with Mary

16. Jesus invited us to turn to God with insistence and the confidence that we will be heard: "Ask, and it will be given to you; seek, and you will find; knock, and it will be opened to you" (Mt 7:7). The basis for this power of prayer is the goodness of the Father, but also the mediation of Christ himself (cf. 1Jn 2:1) and the working of the Holy Spirit who "intercedes for us" according to the will of God (cf. Rom 8:26-27). For "we do not know how to pray as we ought" (Rom 8:26), and at times we are not heard "because we ask wrongly" (cf. Jas 4:2-3).

In support of the prayer which Christ and the Spirit cause to rise in our hearts, Mary intervenes with her maternal intercession. "The prayer of the Church is sustained by the prayer of Mary".[23] If Jesus, the one Mediator, is the Way of our prayer, then Mary, his purest and most transparent reflection, shows us the Way. "Beginning with Mary's unique cooperation with the working of the Holy Spirit, the Churches developed their prayer to the Holy Mother of God, centering it on the person of Christ manifested in his mysteries".[24] At the wedding of Cana the Gospel clearly shows the power of Mary's intercession as she makes known to Jesus the needs of others: "They have no wine" (Jn 2:3).

[23] Catechism of the Catholic Church, 2679.

[24] Ibid., 2675.

The Rosary is both meditation and supplication. Insistent prayer to the Mother of God is based on confidence that her maternal intercession can obtain all things from the heart of her Son. She is "all-powerful by grace", to use the bold expression, which needs to be properly understood, of Blessed Bartolo Longo in his Supplication to Our Lady.[25] This is a conviction which, beginning with the Gospel, has grown ever more firm in the experience of the Christian people. The supreme poet Dante expresses it marvellously in the lines sung by Saint Bernard: "Lady, thou art so great and so powerful, that whoever desires grace yet does not turn to thee, would have his desire fly without wings".[26] When in the Rosary we plead with Mary, the sanctuary of the Holy Spirit (cf. Lk 1:35), she intercedes for us before the Father who filled her with grace and before the Son born of her womb, praying with us and for us.

[25] The Supplication to the Queen of the Holy Rosary was composed by Blessed Bartolo Longo in 1883 in response to the appeal of Pope Leo XIII, made in his first Encyclical on the Rosary, for the spiritual commitment of all Catholics in combating social ills. It is solemnly recited twice yearly, in May and October.

[26] Divina Commedia, Paradiso XXXIII, 13-15.

Proclaiming Christ with Mary

17. The Rosary is also a path of proclamation and increasing knowledge, in which the mystery of Christ is presented again and again at different levels of the Christian experience. Its form is that of a prayerful and contemplative presentation, capable of forming Christians according to the heart of Christ. When the recitation of the Rosary combines all the elements needed for an effective meditation, especially in its communal celebration in parishes and shrines, it can present a significant catechetical opportunity which

pastors should use to advantage. In this way too Our Lady of the Rosary continues her work of proclaiming Christ. The history of the Rosary shows how this prayer was used in particular by the Dominicans at a difficult time for the Church due to the spread of heresy. Today we are facing new challenges. Why should we not once more have recourse to the Rosary, with the same faith as those who have gone before us? The Rosary retains all its power and continues to be a valuable pastoral resource for every good evangelizer.

CHAPTER II
MYSTERIES OF CHRIST -- MYSTERIES OF HIS MOTHER

The Rosary, "a compendium of the Gospel"

18. The only way to approach the contemplation of Christ's face is by listening in the Spirit to the Father's voice, since "no one knows the Son except the Father" (Mt 11:27). In the region of Caesarea Philippi, Jesus responded to Peter's confession of faith by indicating the source of that clear intuition of his identity: "Flesh and blood has not revealed this to you, but my Father who is in heaven" (Mt 16:17). What is needed, then, is a revelation from above. In order to receive that revelation, attentive listening is indispensable: "Only the experience of silence and prayer offers the proper setting for the growth and development of a true, faithful and consistent knowledge of that mystery".[27]

[27] John Paul II, Apostolic Letter Novo Millennio Ineunte (6 January 2001), 20: AAS 93 (2001), 279.

The Rosary is one of the traditional paths of Christian prayer directed to the contemplation of Christ's face. Pope Paul VI described it in these words: "As a Gospel prayer, centred on the mystery of the redemptive Incarnation, the Rosary is a prayer with a clearly Christological orientation. Its most characteristic element, in fact, the litany- like succession of Hail Marys, becomes in itself an unceasing praise of Christ, who is the ultimate object both of the Angel's announcement and of the greeting of the Mother of John the Baptist: 'Blessed is the fruit of your womb' (Lk 1:42). We would go further and say that the succession of Hail Marys constitutes the warp on which is woven the contemplation of the mysteries. The Jesus that each Hail Mary recalls is the same Jesus whom the succession of mysteries proposes to us now as the Son of God, now as the Son of the Virgin".[28]

[28] Apostolic Exhortation Marialis Cultus (2 February 1974), 46: AAS 6 (1974), 155.

A proposed addition to the traditional pattern

19. Of the many mysteries of Christ's life, only a few are indicated by the Rosary in the form that has become generally established with the seal of the Church's approval. The selection was determined by the origin of the prayer, which was based on the number 150, the number of the Psalms in the Psalter.

I believe, however, that to bring out fully the Christological depth of the Rosary it would be suitable to make an addition to the traditional pattern which, while left to the freedom of individuals and communities, could broaden it to include the mysteries of Christ's public ministry between his Baptism and his Passion. In the course of those mysteries we contemplate important aspects of the person of Christ as the definitive revelation of God. Declared the beloved Son of the Father at the Baptism in the Jordan, Christ is the one who announces the coming of the Kingdom, bears witness to it in his works and proclaims its demands. It is during the years of his public ministry that the mystery of Christ is most evidently a mystery of light: "While I am in the world, I am the light of the world" (Jn 9:5).

Consequently, for the Rosary to become more fully a "compendium of the Gospel", it is fitting to add, following reflection on the Incarnation and the hidden life of Christ (the joyful mysteries) and before focusing on the sufferings of his Passion (the sorrowful mysteries) and the triumph of his Resurrection (the glorious mysteries), a meditation on certain particularly significant moments in his public ministry (the mysteries of light). This addition of these new mysteries, without prejudice to any essential aspect of the prayer's traditional format, is meant to give it fresh life and to enkindle renewed interest in the Rosary's place within Christian spirituality as a true doorway to the depths of the Heart of Christ, ocean of joy and of light, of suffering and of glory.

The Joyful Mysteries

20. The first five decades, the "joyful mysteries", are marked by the joy radiating from the event of the Incarnation. This is clear from the very first mystery, the Annunciation, where Gabriel's greeting to the Virgin of Nazareth is linked to an invitation to messianic joy: "Rejoice, Mary". The whole of salvation history, in some sense the entire history of the world, has led up to this greeting. If it is the Father's plan to unite all things in Christ (cf. Eph 1:10), then the whole of the universe is in some way touched by the divine favour with which the Father looks upon Mary and makes her the Mother of his Son. The whole of humanity, in turn, is embraced by the fiat with which she readily agrees to the will of God.

Exultation is the keynote of the encounter with Elizabeth, where the sound of Mary's voice and the presence of Christ in her womb cause John to "leap for joy" (cf. Lk 1:44). Gladness also fills the scene in Bethlehem, when the birth of the divine Child, the Saviour of the world, is announced by the song of the angels and proclaimed to the shepherds as "news of great joy" (Lk 2:10).

The final two mysteries, while preserving this climate of joy, already point to the drama yet to come. The Presentation in the Temple not only expresses the joy of the Child's consecration and the ecstasy of the aged Simeon; it also records the prophecy that Christ will be a "sign of contradiction" for Israel and that a sword will pierce his mother's heart (cf Lk 2:34-35). Joy mixed with drama marks the fifth mystery, the finding of the twelve-year-old Jesus in the Temple. Here he appears in his divine wisdom as he listens and raises questions, already in effect one who "teaches". The revelation of his mystery as the Son wholly dedicated to his Father's affairs proclaims the radical nature of the Gospel, in which even the closest of human relationships are challenged by the absolute demands of the Kingdom. Mary and Joseph, fearful and anxious, "did not understand" his words (Lk 2:50).

To meditate upon the "joyful" mysteries, then, is to enter into the ultimate causes and the deepest meaning of Christian joy. It is to focus on the realism of the mystery of the Incarnation and on the obscure foreshadowing of the mystery of the saving Passion. Mary leads us to discover the secret of Christian joy, reminding us that Christianity is, first and foremost, euangelion, "good news", which has as its heart and its whole content the person of Jesus Christ, the Word made flesh, the one Saviour of the world.

The Mysteries of Light

21. Moving on from the infancy and the hidden life in Nazareth to the public life of Jesus, our contemplation brings us to those mysteries which may be called in a special way "mysteries of light".

Certainly the whole mystery of Christ is a mystery of light. He is the "light of the world" (Jn 8:12). Yet this truth emerges in a special way during the years of his public life, when he proclaims the Gospel of the Kingdom. In proposing to the Christian community five significant moments -- "luminous" mysteries -- during this phase of Christ's life, I think that the following can be fittingly singled out: (1) his Baptism in the Jordan, (2) his self-manifestation at the wedding of Cana, (3) his proclamation of the Kingdom of God, with his call to conversion, (4) his Transfiguration, and finally, (5) his institution of the Eucharist, as the sacramental expression of the Paschal Mystery.

Each of these mysteries is a revelation of the Kingdom now present in the very person of Jesus. The Baptism in the Jordan is first of all a mystery of light. Here, as Christ descends into the waters, the innocent one who became "sin" for our sake (cf. 2Cor 5:21), the heavens open wide and the voice of the Father declares him the beloved Son (cf. Mt 3:17 and parallels), while the Spirit descends on him to invest him with the mission which he is to carry out. Another mystery of light is the first of the signs, given at Cana (cf. Jn 2:1- 12), when Christ changes water into wine and opens the hearts of the disciples to faith, thanks to the intervention of Mary, the first among believers. Another mystery of light is the preaching by which Jesus proclaims the coming of the Kingdom of God, calls to conversion (cf. Mk 1:15) and forgives the sins of all who draw near to him in humble trust (cf. Mk 2:3-13; Lk 7:47- 48): the inauguration of that ministry of mercy which he continues to exercise until the end of the world, particularly through the Sacrament of Reconciliation which he has entrusted to his Church (cf. Jn 20:22-23). The mystery of light par excellence is the Transfiguration, traditionally believed to have taken place on Mount Tabor. The glory of the Godhead shines forth from the face of Christ as the Father commands the astonished Apostles to "listen to him" (cf. Lk 9:35 and parallels) and to prepare to experience with him the agony of the Passion, so as to come with him to the joy of the Resurrection and a life transfigured by the Holy Spirit. A final mystery of light is the institution of the Eucharist, in which Christ offers his body and blood as food under the signs of bread and wine, and testifies "to the end" his love for humanity (Jn 13:1), for whose salvation he will offer himself in sacrifice.

In these mysteries, apart from the miracle at Cana, the presence of Mary remains in the background. The Gospels make only the briefest reference to her occasional presence at one moment or other during the preaching of Jesus (cf. Mk 3:31-5; Jn 2:12), and they give no indication that she was present at the Last Supper and the institution of the Eucharist. Yet the role she assumed at Cana in some way accompanies Christ throughout his ministry. The revelation made directly by the Father at the Baptism in the Jordan and echoed by John the Baptist is placed upon Mary's lips at Cana, and it becomes the great maternal counsel which Mary addresses to the Church of every age: "Do whatever he tells you" (Jn 2:5). This counsel is a fitting introduction to the words and signs of Christ's public ministry and it forms the Marian foundation of all the "mysteries of light".

The Sorrowful Mysteries

22. The Gospels give great prominence to the sorrowful mysteries of Christ. From the beginning Christian piety, especially during the Lenten devotion of the Way of the Cross, has focused on the individual moments of the Passion, realizing that here is found the culmination of the revelation of God's love and the source of our salvation. The Rosary selects certain moments from the Passion,

inviting the faithful to contemplate them in their hearts and to relive them. The sequence of meditations begins with Gethsemane, where Christ experiences a moment of great anguish before the will of the Father, against which the weakness of the flesh would be tempted to rebel. There Jesus encounters all the temptations and confronts all the sins of humanity, in order to say to the Father: "Not my will but yours be done" (Lk 22:42 and parallels). This "Yes" of Christ reverses the "No" of our first parents in the Garden of Eden. And the cost of this faithfulness to the Father's will is made clear in the following mysteries; by his scourging, his crowning with thorns, his carrying the Cross and his death on the Cross, the Lord is cast into the most abject suffering: Ecce homo!

This abject suffering reveals not only the love of God but also the meaning of man himself.

Ecce homo: the meaning, origin and fulfilment of man is to be found in Christ, the God who humbles himself out of love "even unto death, death on a cross" (Phil 2:8). The sorrowful mysteries help the believer to relive the death of Jesus, to stand at the foot of the Cross beside Mary, to enter with her into the depths of God's love for man and to experience all its life-giving power.

The Glorious Mysteries

23. "The contemplation of Christ's face cannot stop at the image of the Crucified One. He is the Risen One!"[29] The Rosary has always expressed this knowledge born of faith and invited the believer to pass beyond the darkness of the Passion in order to gaze upon Christ's glory in the Resurrection and Ascension. Contemplating the Risen One, Christians rediscover the reasons for their own faith (cf. 1Cor 15:14) and relive the joy not only of those to whom Christ appeared -- the Apostles, Mary Magdalene and the disciples on the road to Emmaus -- but also the joy of Mary, who

must have had an equally intense experience of the new life of her glorified Son. In the Ascension, Christ was raised in glory to the right hand of the Father, while Mary herself would be raised to that same glory in the Assumption, enjoying beforehand, by a unique privilege, the destiny reserved for all the just at the resurrection of the dead. Crowned in glory -- as she appears in the last glorious mystery -- Mary shines forth as Queen of the Angels and Saints, the anticipation and the supreme realization of the eschatological state of the Church.

[29] John Paul II, Apostolic Letter Novo Millennio Ineunte (6 January 2001), 28: AAS 93 (2001), 284.

At the centre of this unfolding sequence of the glory of the Son and the Mother, the Rosary sets before us the third glorious mystery, Pentecost, which reveals the face of the Church as a family gathered together with Mary, enlivened by the powerful outpouring of the Spirit and ready for the mission of evangelization. The contemplation of this scene, like that of the other glorious mysteries, ought to lead the faithful to an ever greater appreciation of their new life in Christ, lived in the heart of the Church, a life of which the scene of Pentecost itself is the great "icon". The glorious mysteries thus lead the faithful to greater hope for the eschatological goal towards which they journey as members of the pilgrim People of God in history. This can only impel them to bear courageous witness to that "good news" which gives meaning to their entire existence.

From "mysteries" to the "Mystery": Mary's way

24. The cycles of meditation proposed by the Holy Rosary are by no means exhaustive, but they do bring to mind what is essential and they awaken in the soul a thirst for a knowledge of Christ continually nourished by the pure source of the Gospel. Every

individual event in the life of Christ, as narrated by the Evangelists, is resplendent with the Mystery that surpasses all understanding (cf. Eph 3:19): the Mystery of the Word made flesh, in whom "all the fullness of God dwells bodily" (Col 2:9). For this reason the Catechism of the Catholic Church places great emphasis on the mysteries of Christ, pointing out that "everything in the life of Jesus is a sign of his Mystery".[30] The "duc in altum" of the Church of the third millennium will be determined by the ability of Christians to enter into the "perfect knowledge of God's mystery, of Christ, in whom are hidden all the treasures of wisdom and knowledge" (Col 2:2-3). The Letter to the Ephesians makes this heartfelt prayer for all the baptized: "May Christ dwell in your hearts through faith, so that you, being rooted and grounded in love, may have power... to know the love of Christ which surpasses knowledge, that you may be filled with all the fullness of God" (3:17-19).

[30] No. 515.

The Rosary is at the service of this ideal; it offers the "secret" which leads easily to a profound and inward knowledge of Christ. We might call it Mary's way. It is the way of the example of the Virgin of Nazareth, a woman of faith, of silence, of attentive listening. It is also the way of a Marian devotion inspired by knowledge of the inseparable bond between Christ and his Blessed Mother: the mysteries of Christ are also in some sense the mysteries of his Mother, even when they do not involve her directly, for she lives from him and through him. By making our own the words of the Angel Gabriel and Saint Elizabeth contained in the Hail Mary, we find ourselves constantly drawn to seek out afresh in Mary, in her arms and in her heart, the "blessed fruit of her womb" (cf Lk 1:42).

Mystery of Christ, mystery of man

25. In my testimony of 1978 mentioned above, where I described the Rosary as my favourite prayer, I used an idea to which I would like to return. I said then that "the simple prayer of the Rosary marks the rhythm of human life".[31]

[31] Angelus Message of 29 October 1978 : Insegnamenti, I (1978), 76.

In the light of what has been said so far on the mysteries of Christ, it is not difficult to go deeper into this anthropological significance of the Rosary, which is far deeper than may appear at first sight. Anyone who contemplates Christ through the various stages of his life cannot fail to perceive in him the truth about man. This is the great affirmation of the Second Vatican Council which I have so often discussed in my own teaching since the Encyclical Letter Redemptor Hominis: "it is only in the mystery of the Word made flesh that the mystery of man is seen in its true light".[32] The Rosary helps to open up the way to this light. Following in the path of Christ, in whom man's path is "recapitulated",[33] revealed and redeemed, believers come face to face with the image of the true man. Contemplating Christ's birth, they learn of the sanctity of life; seeing the household of Nazareth, they learn the original truth of the family according to God's plan; listening to the Master in the mysteries of his public ministry, they find the light which leads them to enter the Kingdom of God; and following him on the way to Calvary, they learn the meaning of salvific suffering. Finally, contemplating Christ and his Blessed Mother in glory, they see the goal towards which each of us is called, if we allow ourselves to be healed and transformed by the Holy Spirit. It could be said that each mystery of the Rosary, carefully meditated, sheds light on the mystery of man.

[32] Second Vatican Ecumenical Council, Pastoral Constitution on the Church in the Modern World Gaudium et Spes, 22.

[33] Cf. Saint Irenaeus of Lyons, Adversus Haereses, III, 18, 1: PG 7, 932.

At the same time, it becomes natural to bring to this encounter with the sacred humanity of the Redeemer all the problems, anxieties, labours and endeavours which go to make up our lives. "Cast your burden on the Lord and he will sustain you" (Ps 55:23). To pray the Rosary is to hand over our burdens to the merciful hearts of Christ and his Mother. Twenty-five years later, thinking back over the difficulties which have also been part of my exercise of the Petrine ministry, I feel the need to say once more, as a warm invitation to everyone to experience it personally: the Rosary does indeed "mark the rhythm of human life", bringing it into harmony with the "rhythm" of God's own life, in the joyful communion of the Holy Trinity, our life's destiny and deepest longing.

CHAPTER III
"FOR ME, TO LIVE IS CHRIST"

The Rosary, a way of assimilating the mystery

26. Meditation on the mysteries of Christ is proposed in the Rosary by means of a method designed to assist in their assimilation. It is a method based on repetition. This applies above all to the Hail Mary, repeated ten times in each mystery. If this repetition is considered superficially, there could be a temptation to see the Rosary as a dry and boring exercise. It is quite another thing, however, when the Rosary is thought of as an outpouring of that love which tirelessly returns to the person loved with expressions

similar in their content but ever fresh in terms of the feeling pervading them.

In Christ, God has truly assumed a "heart of flesh". Not only does God have a divine heart, rich in mercy and in forgiveness, but also a human heart, capable of all the stirrings of affection. If we needed evidence for this from the Gospel, we could easily find it in the touching dialogue between Christ and Peter after the Resurrection: "Simon, son of John, do you love me?" Three times this question is put to Peter, and three times he gives the reply: "Lord, you know that I love you" (cf. Jn 21:15-17). Over and above the specific meaning of this passage, so important for Peter's mission, none can fail to recognize the beauty of this triple repetition, in which the insistent request and the corresponding reply are expressed in terms familiar from the universal experience of human love. To understand the Rosary, one has to enter into the psychological dynamic proper to love.

One thing is clear: although the repeated Hail Mary is addressed directly to Mary, it is to Jesus that the act of love is ultimately directed, with her and through her. The repetition is nourished by the desire to be conformed ever more completely to Christ, the true programme of the Christian life. Saint Paul expressed this project with words of fire: "For me to live is Christ and to die is gain" (Phil 1:21). And again: "It is no longer I that live, but Christ lives in me" (Gal 2:20). The Rosary helps us to be conformed ever more closely to Christ until we attain true holiness.

A valid method...

27. We should not be surprised that our relationship with Christ makes use of a method. God communicates himself to us respecting our human nature and its vital rhythms. Hence, while Christian spirituality is familiar with the most sublime forms of

mystical silence in which images, words and gestures are all, so to speak, superseded by an intense and ineffable union with God, it normally engages the whole person in all his complex psychological, physical and relational reality.

This becomes apparent in the Liturgy. Sacraments and sacramentals are structured as a series of rites which bring into play all the dimensions of the person. The same applies to non-liturgical prayer. This is confirmed by the fact that, in the East, the most characteristic prayer of Christological meditation, centred on the words "Lord Jesus Christ, Son of God, have mercy on me, a sinner"[34] is traditionally linked to the rhythm of breathing; while this practice favours perseverance in the prayer, it also in some way embodies the desire for Christ to become the breath, the soul and the "all" of one's life.

... which can nevertheless be improved

[34] Catechism of the Catholic Church, 2616.

28. I mentioned in my Apostolic Letter Novo Millennio Ineunte that the West is now experiencing a renewed demand for meditation, which at times leads to a keen interest in aspects of other religions.[35] Some Christians, limited in their knowledge of the Christian contemplative tradition, are attracted by those forms of prayer. While the latter contain many elements which are positive and at times compatible with Christian experience, they are often based on ultimately unacceptable premises. Much in vogue among these approaches are methods aimed at attaining a high level of spiritual concentration by using techniques of a psychophysical, repetitive and symbolic nature. The Rosary is situated within this broad gamut of religious phenomena, but it is distinguished by characteristics of its own which correspond to specifically Christian requirements.

[35] Cf. No. 33: AAS 93 (2001), 289.

In effect, the Rosary is simply a method of contemplation. As a method, it serves as a means to an end and cannot become an end in itself. All the same, as the fruit of centuries of experience, this method should not be undervalued. In its favour one could cite the experience of countless Saints. This is not to say, however, that the method cannot be improved. Such is the intent of the addition of the new series of mysteria lucis to the overall cycle of mysteries and of the few suggestions which I am proposing in this Letter regarding its manner of recitation. These suggestions, while respecting the well-established structure of this prayer, are intended to help the faithful to understand it in the richness of its symbolism and in harmony with the demands of daily life. Otherwise there is a risk that the Rosary would not only fail to produce the intended spiritual effects, but even that the beads, with which it is usually said, could come to be regarded as some kind of amulet or magic object, thereby radically distorting their meaning and function.

Announcing each mystery

29. Announcing each mystery, and perhaps even using a suitable icon to portray it, is as it were to open up a scenario on which to focus our attention. The words direct the imagination and the mind towards a particular episode or moment in the life of Christ. In the Church's traditional spirituality, the veneration of icons and the many devotions appealing to the senses, as well as the method of prayer proposed by Saint Ignatius of Loyola in the Spiritual Exercises, make use of visual and imaginative elements (the compositio loci), judged to be of great help in concentrating the mind on the particular mystery. This is a methodology, moreover, which corresponds to the inner logic of the Incarnation: in Jesus,

God wanted to take on human features. It is through his bodily reality that we are led into contact with the mystery of his divinity.

This need for concreteness finds further expression in the announcement of the various mysteries of the Rosary. Obviously these mysteries neither replace the Gospel nor exhaust its content. The Rosary, therefore, is no substitute for lectio divina; on the contrary, it presupposes and promotes it. Yet, even though the mysteries contemplated in the Rosary, even with the addition of the mysteria lucis, do no more than outline the fundamental elements of the life of Christ, they easily draw the mind to a more expansive reflection on the rest of the Gospel, especially when the Rosary is prayed in a setting of prolonged recollection.

Listening to the word of God

30. In order to supply a Biblical foundation and greater depth to our meditation, it is helpful to follow the announcement of the mystery with the proclamation of a related Biblical passage, long or short, depending on the circumstances. No other words can ever match the efficacy of the inspired word. As we listen, we are certain that this is the word of God, spoken for today and spoken "for me".

If received in this way, the word of God can become part of the Rosary's methodology of repetition without giving rise to the ennui derived from the simple recollection of something already well known. It is not a matter of recalling information but of allowing God to speak. In certain solemn communal celebrations, this word can be appropriately illustrated by a brief commentary.

Silence

31. Listening and meditation are nourished by silence. After the announcement of the mystery and the proclamation of the word, it is fitting to pause and focus one's attention for a suitable period of time on the mystery concerned, before moving into vocal prayer. A discovery of the importance of silence is one of the secrets of practicing contemplation and meditation. One drawback of a society dominated by technology and the mass media is the fact that silence becomes increasingly difficult to achieve. Just as moments of silence are recommended in the Liturgy, so too in the recitation of the Rosary it is fitting to pause briefly after listening to the word of God, while the mind focuses on the content of a particular mystery.

The "Our Father"

32. After listening to the word and focusing on the mystery, it is natural for the mind to be lifted up towards the Father. In each of his mysteries, Jesus always leads us to the Father, for as he rests in the Father's bosom (cf. Jn 1:18) he is continually turned towards him. He wants us to share in his intimacy with the Father, so that we can say with him: "Abba, Father" (Rom 8:15; Gal 4:6). By virtue of his relationship to the Father he makes us brothers and sisters of himself and of one another, communicating to us the Spirit which is both his and the Father's. Acting as a kind of foundation for the Christological and Marian meditation which unfolds in the repetition of the Hail Mary, the Our Father makes meditation upon the mystery, even when carried out in solitude, an ecclesial experience.

The ten "Hail Marys"

33. This is the most substantial element in the Rosary and also the one which makes it a Marian prayer par excellence. Yet when the Hail Mary is properly understood, we come to see clearly that its

A Manual of the Most Holy Rosary

Marian character is not opposed to its Christological character, but that it actually emphasizes and increases it. The first part of the Hail Mary, drawn from the words spoken to Mary by the Angel Gabriel and by Saint Elizabeth, is a contemplation in adoration of the mystery accomplished in the Virgin of Nazareth. These words express, so to speak, the wonder of heaven and earth; they could be said to give us a glimpse of God's own wonderment as he contemplates his "masterpiece" -- the Incarnation of the Son in the womb of the Virgin Mary. If we recall how, in the Book of Genesis, God "saw all that he had made" (Gen 1:31), we can find here an echo of that "pathos with which God, at the dawn of creation, looked upon the work of his hands".[36] The repetition of the Hail Mary in the Rosary gives us a share in God's own wonder and pleasure: in jubilant amazement we acknowledge the greatest miracle of history. Mary's prophecy here finds its fulfilment: "Henceforth all generations will call me blessed" (Lk 1:48).

[36] John Paul II, Letter to Artists (4 April 1999), 1: AAS 91 (1999), 1155.

The centre of gravity in the Hail Mary, the hinge as it were which joins its two parts, is the name of Jesus. Sometimes, in hurried recitation, this centre of gravity can be overlooked, and with it the connection to the mystery of Christ being contemplated. Yet it is precisely the emphasis given to the name of Jesus and to his mystery that is the sign of a meaningful and fruitful recitation of the Rosary. Pope Paul VI drew attention, in his Apostolic Exhortation Marialis Cultus, to the custom in certain regions of highlighting the name of Christ by the addition of a clause referring to the mystery being contemplated.[37] This is a praiseworthy custom, especially during public recitation. It gives forceful expression to our faith in Christ, directed to the different moments of the Redeemer's life. It is at once a profession of faith and an aid in concentrating our meditation, since it facilitates the process of assimilation to the mystery of Christ inherent in the repetition of the Hail Mary. When we repeat the name of Jesus -- the only name given to us by which we may hope for salvation (cf. Acts 4:12) -- in close association with the name of his Blessed Mother, almost as if it were done at her suggestion, we set out on a path of assimilation meant to help us enter more deeply into the life of Christ.

[37] Cf. No. 46: AAS 66 (1974), 155. This custom has also been recently praised by the Congregation for Divine Worship and for the Discipline of the Sacraments in its Direttorio su pietà popolare e liturgia. Principi e orientamenti (17 December 2001), 201, Vatican City, 2002, 165.

From Mary's uniquely privileged relationship with Christ, which makes her the Mother of God, Theotókos, derives the forcefulness of the appeal we make to her in the second half of the prayer, as we entrust to her maternal intercession our lives and the hour of our death.

The "Gloria"

34. Trinitarian doxology is the goal of all Christian contemplation. For Christ is the way that leads us to the Father in the Spirit. If we travel this way to the end, we repeatedly encounter the mystery of the three divine Persons, to whom all praise, worship and thanksgiving are due. It is important that the Gloria, the high-point of contemplation, be given due prominence in the Rosary. In public recitation it could be sung, as a way of giving proper emphasis to the essentially Trinitarian structure of all Christian prayer.

To the extent that meditation on the mystery is attentive and profound, and to the extent that it is enlivened -- from one Hail

Mary to another -- by love for Christ and for Mary, the glorification of the Trinity at the end of each decade, far from being a perfunctory conclusion, takes on its proper contemplative tone, raising the mind as it were to the heights of heaven and enabling us in some way to relive the experience of Tabor, a foretaste of the contemplation yet to come: "It is good for us to be here!" (Lk 9:33).

The concluding short prayer

35. In current practice, the Trinitarian doxology is followed by a brief concluding prayer which varies according to local custom. Without in any way diminishing the value of such invocations, it is worthwhile to note that the contemplation of the mysteries could better express their full spiritual fruitfulness if an effort were made to conclude each mystery with a prayer for the fruits specific to that particular mystery. In this way the Rosary would better express its connection with the Christian life. One fine liturgical prayer suggests as much, inviting us to pray that, by meditation on the mysteries of the Rosary, we may come to "imitate what they contain and obtain what they promise".[38]

[38] "...concede, quaesumus, ut haec mysteria sacratissimo beatae Mariae Virginis Rosario recolentes, et imitemur quod continent, et quod promittunt assequamur". Missale Romanum 1960, in festo B.M. Virginis a Rosario.

Such a final prayer could take on a legitimate variety of forms, as indeed it already does. In this way the Rosary can be better adapted to different spiritual traditions and different Christian communities. It is to be hoped, then, that appropriate formulas will be widely circulated, after due pastoral discernment and possibly after experimental use in centres and shrines particularly devoted to the Rosary, so that the People of God may benefit from an abundance of authentic spiritual riches and find nourishment for their personal contemplation.

The Rosary beads

36. The traditional aid used for the recitation of the Rosary is the set of beads. At the most superficial level, the beads often become a simple counting mechanism to mark the succession of Hail Marys. Yet they can also take on a symbolism which can give added depth to contemplation.

Here the first thing to note is the way the beads converge upon the Crucifix, which both opens and closes the unfolding sequence of prayer. The life and prayer of believers is centred upon Christ. Everything begins from him, everything leads towards him, everything, through him, in the Holy Spirit, attains to the Father.

As a counting mechanism, marking the progress of the prayer, the beads evoke the unending path of contemplation and of Christian perfection. Blessed Bartolo Longo saw them also as a "chain" which links us to God. A chain, yes, but a sweet chain; for sweet indeed is the bond to God who is also our Father. A "filial" chain which puts us in tune with Mary, the "handmaid of the Lord" (Lk 1:38) and, most of all, with Christ himself, who, though he was in the form of God, made himself a "servant" out of love for us (Phil 2:7).

A fine way to expand the symbolism of the beads is to let them remind us of our many relationships, of the bond of communion and fraternity which unites us all in Christ.

The opening and closing

37. At present, in different parts of the Church, there are many ways to introduce the Rosary. In some places, it is customary to begin

with the opening words of Psalm 70: "O God, come to my aid; O Lord, make haste to help me", as if to nourish in those who are praying a humble awareness of their own insufficiency. In other places, the Rosary begins with the recitation of the Creed, as if to make the profession of faith the basis of the contemplative journey about to be undertaken. These and similar customs, to the extent that they prepare the mind for contemplation, are all equally legitimate. The Rosary is then ended with a prayer for the intentions of the Pope, as if to expand the vision of the one praying to embrace all the needs of the Church. It is precisely in order to encourage this ecclesial dimension of the Rosary that the Church has seen fit to grant indulgences to those who recite it with the required dispositions.

If prayed in this way, the Rosary truly becomes a spiritual itinerary in which Mary acts as Mother, Teacher and Guide, sustaining the faithful by her powerful intercession. Is it any wonder, then, that the soul feels the need, after saying this prayer and experiencing so profoundly the motherhood of Mary, to burst forth in praise of the Blessed Virgin, either in that splendid prayer the Salve Regina or in the Litany of Loreto? This is the crowning moment of an inner journey which has brought the faithful into living contact with the mystery of Christ and his Blessed Mother.

Distribution over time

38. The Rosary can be recited in full every day, and there are those who most laudably do so. In this way it fills with prayer the days of many a contemplative, or keeps company with the sick and the elderly who have abundant time at their disposal. Yet it is clear -- and this applies all the more if the new series of mysteria lucis is included -- that many people will not be able to recite more than a part of the Rosary, according to a certain weekly pattern. This

weekly distribution has the effect of giving the different days of the week a certain spiritual "colour", by analogy with the way in which the Liturgy colours the different seasons of the liturgical year.

According to current practice, Monday and Thursday are dedicated to the "joyful mysteries", Tuesday and Friday to the "sorrowful mysteries", and Wednesday, Saturday and Sunday to the "glorious mysteries". Where might the "mysteries of light" be inserted? If we consider that the "glorious mysteries" are said on both Saturday and Sunday, and that Saturday has always had a special Marian flavour, the second weekly meditation on the "joyful mysteries", mysteries in which Mary's presence is especially pronounced, could be moved to Saturday. Thursday would then be free for meditating on the "mysteries of light".

This indication is not intended to limit a rightful freedom in personal and community prayer, where account needs to be taken of spiritual and pastoral needs and of the occurrence of particular liturgical celebrations which might call for suitable adaptations. What is really important is that the Rosary should always be seen and experienced as a path of contemplation. In the Rosary, in a way similar to what takes place in the Liturgy, the Christian week, centred on Sunday, the day of Resurrection, becomes a journey through the mysteries of the life of Christ, and he is revealed in the lives of his disciples as the Lord of time and of history.

CONCLUSION

"Blessed Rosary of Mary, sweet chain linking us to God"

39. What has been said so far makes abundantly clear the richness of this traditional prayer, which has the simplicity of a popular devotion but also the theological depth of a prayer suited to those who feel the need for deeper contemplation.

A Manual of the Most Holy Rosary

The Church has always attributed particular efficacy to this prayer, entrusting to the Rosary, to its choral recitation and to its constant practice, the most difficult problems. At times when Christianity itself seemed under threat, its deliverance was attributed to the power of this prayer, and Our Lady of the Rosary was acclaimed as the one whose intercession brought salvation.

Today I willingly entrust to the power of this prayer -- as I mentioned at the beginning -- the cause of peace in the world and the cause of the family.

Peace

40. The grave challenges confronting the world at the start of this new Millennium lead us to think that only an intervention from on high, capable of guiding the hearts of those living in situations of conflict and those governing the destinies of nations, can give reason to hope for a brighter future.

The Rosary is by its nature a prayer for peace, since it consists in the contemplation of Christ, the Prince of Peace, the one who is "our peace" (Eph 2:14). Anyone who assimilates the mystery of Christ -- and this is clearly the goal of the Rosary -- learns the secret of peace and makes it his life's project. Moreover, by virtue of its meditative character, with the tranquil succession of Hail Marys, the Rosary has a peaceful effect on those who pray it, disposing them to receive and experience in their innermost depths, and to spread around them, that true peace which is the special gift of the Risen Lord (cf. Jn 14:27; 20.21).

The Rosary is also a prayer for peace because of the fruits of charity which it produces. When prayed well in a truly meditative way, the Rosary leads to an encounter with Christ in his mysteries and so cannot fail to draw attention to the face of Christ in others, especially in the most afflicted. How could one possibly contemplate the mystery of the Child of Bethlehem, in the joyful mysteries, without experiencing the desire to welcome, defend and promote life, and to shoulder the burdens of suffering children all over the world? How could one possibly follow in the footsteps of Christ the Revealer, in the mysteries of light, without resolving to bear witness to his "Beatitudes" in daily life? And how could one contemplate Christ carrying the Cross and Christ Crucified, without feeling the need to act as a "Simon of Cyrene" for our brothers and sisters weighed down by grief or crushed by despair? Finally, how could one possibly gaze upon the glory of the Risen Christ or of Mary Queen of Heaven, without yearning to make this world more beautiful, more just, more closely conformed to God's plan?

In a word, by focusing our eyes on Christ, the Rosary also makes us peacemakers in the world. By its nature as an insistent choral petition in harmony with Christ's invitation to "pray ceaselessly" (Lk 18:1), the Rosary allows us to hope that, even today, the difficult "battle" for peace can be won. Far from offering an escape from the problems of the world, the Rosary obliges us to see them with responsible and generous eyes, and obtains for us the strength to face them with the certainty of God's help and the firm intention of bearing witness in every situation to "love, which binds everything together in perfect harmony" (Col 3:14).

The family: parents...

41. As a prayer for peace, the Rosary is also, and always has been, a prayer of and for the family. At one time this prayer was particularly dear to Christian families, and it certainly brought them closer together. It is important not to lose this precious inheritance. We need to return to the practice of family prayer and prayer for families, continuing to use the Rosary.

In my Apostolic Letter Novo Millennio Ineunte I encouraged the celebration of the Liturgy of the Hours by the lay faithful in the ordinary life of parish communities and Christian groups;[39] I now wish to do the same for the Rosary. These two paths of Christian contemplation are not mutually exclusive; they complement one another. I would therefore ask those who devote themselves to the pastoral care of families to recommend heartily the recitation of the Rosary.

[39] Cf. No. 34: AAS 93 (2001), 290.

The family that prays together stays together. The Holy Rosary, by age-old tradition, has shown itself particularly effective as a prayer which brings the family together. Individual family members, in turning their eyes towards Jesus, also regain the ability to look one another in the eye, to communicate, to show solidarity, to forgive one another and to see their covenant of love renewed in the Spirit of God.

Many of the problems facing contemporary families, especially in economically developed societies, result from their increasing difficulty in communicating. Families seldom manage to come together, and the rare occasions when they do are often taken up with watching television. To return to the recitation of the family Rosary means filling daily life with very different images, images of the mystery of salvation: the image of the Redeemer, the image of his most Blessed Mother. The family that recites the Rosary together reproduces something of the atmosphere of the household of Nazareth: its members place Jesus at the centre, they share his joys and sorrows, they place their needs and their plans in his hands, they draw from him the hope and the strength to go on.

... and children

42. It is also beautiful and fruitful to entrust to this prayer the growth and development of children. Does the Rosary not follow the life of Christ, from his conception to his death, and then to his Resurrection and his glory? Parents are finding it ever more difficult to follow the lives of their children as they grow to maturity. In a society of advanced technology, of mass communications and globalization, everything has become hurried, and the cultural distance between generations is growing ever greater. The most diverse messages and the most unpredictable experiences rapidly make their way into the lives of children and adolescents, and parents can become quite anxious about the dangers their children face. At times parents suffer acute disappointment at the failure of their children to resist the seductions of the drug culture, the lure of an unbridled hedonism, the temptation to violence, and the manifold expressions of meaninglessness and despair.

To pray the Rosary for children, and even more, with children, training them from their earliest years to experience this daily "pause for prayer" with the family, is admittedly not the solution to every problem, but it is a spiritual aid which should not be underestimated. It could be objected that the Rosary seems hardly suited to the taste of children and young people of today. But perhaps the objection is directed to an impoverished method of praying it. Furthermore, without prejudice to the Rosary's basic structure, there is nothing to stop children and young people from praying it -- either within the family or in groups -- with appropriate symbolic and practical aids to understanding and appreciation. Why not try it? With God's help, a pastoral approach to youth which is positive, impassioned and creative -- as shown by the World Youth Days! -- is capable of achieving quite remarkable results. If the Rosary is well presented, I am sure that young people will once more surprise adults by the way they make this prayer their own and recite it with the enthusiasm typical of their age group.

The Rosary, a treasure to be rediscovered

43. Dear brothers and sisters! A prayer so easy and yet so rich truly deserves to be rediscovered by the Christian community. Let us do so, especially this year, as a means of confirming the direction outlined in my Apostolic Letter Novo Millennio Ineunte, from which the pastoral plans of so many particular Churches have drawn inspiration as they look to the immediate future.

I turn particularly to you, my dear Brother Bishops, priests and deacons, and to you, pastoral agents in your different ministries: through your own personal experience of the beauty of the Rosary, may you come to promote it with conviction.

I also place my trust in you, theologians: by your sage and rigorous reflection, rooted in the word of God and sensitive to the lived experience of the Christian people, may you help them to discover the Biblical foundations, the spiritual riches and the pastoral value of this traditional prayer.

I count on you, consecrated men and women, called in a particular way to contemplate the face of Christ at the school of Mary.

I look to all of you, brothers and sisters of every state of life, to you, Christian families, to you, the sick and elderly, and to you, young people: confidently take up the Rosary once again. Rediscover the Rosary in the light of Scripture, in harmony with the Liturgy, and in the context of your daily lives.

May this appeal of mine not go unheard! At the start of the twenty-fifth year of my Pontificate, I entrust this Apostolic Letter to the loving hands of the Virgin Mary, prostrating myself in spirit before her image in the splendid Shrine built for her by Blessed Bartolo Longo, the apostle of the Rosary. I willingly make my own the touching words with which he concluded his well-known Supplication to the Queen of the Holy Rosary: "O Blessed Rosary of Mary, sweet chain which unites us to God, bond of love which unites us to the angels, tower of salvation against the assaults of Hell, safe port in our universal shipwreck, we will never abandon you. You will be our comfort in the hour of death: yours our final kiss as life ebbs away. And the last word from our lips will be your sweet name, O Queen of the Rosary of Pompei, O dearest Mother, O Refuge of Sinners, O Sovereign Consoler of the Afflicted. May you be everywhere blessed, today and always, on earth and in heaven".

From the Vatican, on the 16th day of October in the year 2002, the beginning of the twenty-fifth year of my Pontificate.

Printed in Great Britain
by Amazon

RAW FEEDING

The trend towards feeding healthy and natural food does not stop at us humans. More and more owners are trying to feed their dogs as naturally as they can – meaning as closely to the way of the wolf as possible.

The raw feeding method was introduced by the Australian vet, Ian Billinghurst, who has been promoting the use of raw feeding for dogs since 1993. The raw feeding method is known by some as BARF which is short for "bone and raw food".

Specifically, this means that feeding your Labrador would consist exclusively of raw meat, offal, bones and fish. Added to this are fresh fruit, vegetables and nuts which are meant to imitate the stomach contents of the dog's prey.

The biggest advantage of raw feeding from my point of view is that you know exactly what your Labrador is getting to eat and you can ensure yourself of its quality. With normal commercially processed foods, you only see compressed pellets which do not give you any insight as to what they contain, meaning that you have to take the word of the manufacturer.

A further, often overlooked, advantage is that dogs are occupied much longer with their feeding. In most cases it is not possible to devour their food at speed, as with processed foods, because the meat is given in large pieces or whole bones. The dog needs to work to get his food, which may take him some time and this leads to some very active dogs being calmer and more balanced. At this point I would like to discourage you from taking commercial BARF mixtures as they are often already cut into small pieces, which partly diminishes the benefits of the method.

In most cases, BARF food is easier for dogs to digest, particularly those with sensitive digestion or some food sensitivities.

It is not scientifically proven, but many owners believe that the following side effects could be considered positive:

- Better immune system
- Less parasites
- Stronger bones
- Shinier fur

Labrador Training

Vol 3

Taking care of your Labrador

Nutrition, common diseases and general care of your Labrador

©2021, Claudia Kaiser

Published by Expertengruppe Verlag

The contents of this book have been written with great care. However, we cannot guarantee the accuracy, comprehensiveness and topicality of the subject matter. The contents of the book represent the personal experiences and opinions of the author. No legal responsibility or liability will be accepted for damages caused by counter-productive practices or errors of the reader. There is also no guarantee of success. The author, therefore, does not accept responsibility for lack of success, using the methods described in this book.

All information contained herein is purely for information purposes. It does not represent a recommendation or application of the methods mentioned within. This book does not purport to be complete, nor can the topicality and accuracy of the book be guaranteed. This book in no way replaces the competent recommendations of, or care given by a dog school. The author and publisher do not take responsibility for inconvenience or damages caused by use of the information contained herein.

Labrador Training

Vol 3

Taking care of your Labrador

Nutrition, common diseases and general care of your Labrador

Published by Expertengruppe Verlag

TABLE OF CONTENTS

About the Author 7

Preface 9

What you need to know about your Labrador 13

Fundamentals of nutrition 18

    Basic rules for feeding 19

    When to let your Labrador make decisions 26

    What goes into the food bowl? 29

        Commercially processed food 31

        Raw feeding 37

        Home-cooked food 42

        Vegetarianism and Veganism 46

        What you need to consider when feeding your Labrador 49

    Regulating your Labrador's water supply 51

        Regulating the water requirement of your Labrador 52

        How to encourage your Labrador to drink 56

Basics of grooming 60

Eye care 65

Skin and fur care 69

Ear care 76

Tooth care 80

Paw care 84

What you need to pay particular attention to with your Labrador 91

Checklist: Regular care 93

Checklist: Care utensils 94

Common illnesses 95

Parasite infestation 97

    Mites 99

    Ticks 103

    Fleas 111

Gastro-intestinal disorders 118

    Gastric dilatation volvulus 119

    Diarrhoea 121

    Worms 124

    Poisonous substances and other problematic things 127

Cancers 131

Fever 135

Vaccinations 139

Castration 142

Diseases typical for your breed 149

Checklist: For a healthy dog life 151

Checklist: Dog first aid kit 153

Special chapter: Making your own dog food 154

Recipe 1: Apple and carrot crackers 155

Recipe 2: Wild potato cookies 157

Recipe 3: Lung with rice 158

Recipe 4: Chicken with millet and egg 159

Recipe 5: Rice meatballs 160

Recipe 6: Beef mix 161

Recipe 7: Wild turkey (BARF) 162

Recipe 8: Italian turkey 163

Recipe 9: Dog ice-cream with banana and apple 164

Recipe 10: Dog ice-cream with liver sausage and oat flakes 165

Conclusion 166

Book recommendation for you 168

Did you enjoy my book? 172

Space for your notes 174

References 178

Disclaimer 181

ABOUT THE AUTHOR

Claudia Kaiser lives with her husband and dogs Danny (2 years old) and Daika (8 years old), in an old farmhouse in beautiful Rhineland, Germany.

At first only as a dog owner, but later and after 20 years actively training dogs, she has gained a lot of experience, helping other people to train their Labradors. She formed the idea of writing this book in order to reach more people, than she could have in the local dog training schools and the small circle of dog owners to whom she gave personal coaching.

The publishing of this guide book is the fruit of considerable research, writing and editing. It is designed to be a guide for all budding Labrador owners, to help them get the difficult task of training right the first time, and to avoid those mistakes, which Claudia herself made at the beginning. She worked through her own bad experiences over the years, so that the reader does not have to.

Those who follow the tips and tricks covered in this guidebook are sure to have many years of pleasure from these unusual and wonderful companions.

PREFACE

Congratulations! You are lucky enough to share your life with a Labrador, or you are close to making that choice. This beautiful and memorable breed will fulfil your days and soon you will not be able to imagine life without your four-legged friend.

It has been scientifically proven that taking care of dogs has a positive effect on humans. You will notice it yourself when you automatically begin to light up and be happy when your Labrador greets you, tail wagging, after a long day at work. Does it not help you to relax when your dog lies snoring in front of the couch while you watch a film?

Dogs are real stress killers for us people. Their honest love for us makes us feel better and happier, besides the incentive that every dog owner has to go out into the fresh air and ideally move around much more than those who do not own dogs. Even those who are chronically ill have confirmed that they feel better having a dog. Your four-legged friend is therefore a real bonus for your health.

It is exactly for that reason it is important you take care of the health of your Labrador. Hence the German saying "If the dog is healthy, the human is happy". It is particularly important for you to take care of him because your dog is often unable to do it for himself.

Unfortunately, these days many dogs are overbred, which itself is the cause of many diseases and other problems which can overwhelm an unexpecting owner. I recommend strongly that you take care when choosing your dog.

Look at his parents and ask the breeder about diseases which have occurred in the litters up to then. If a puppy is already in poor health when you buy it, you will probably have a lot of problems with him later on. In order to avoid this, you should take care before making your choice and, if necessary, speak to a veterinary surgeon for his advice.

Apart from breeding-related problems, there are also a number of challenges which present themselves due to modern processes and developments which did not exist at the time of their ancestor, the wolf. Therefore, it is often necessary to take certain precautions which may cause those who are not familiar with dogs to shake their heads, using the argument: "A wolf would not need that".

If someone says that to you, I would suggest you ignore him. After all, it is about the well-being of your dog.

With this guide I want to give you the necessary knowledge and self-assurance to keep a watchful eye on your Labrador so that you know how to react if something is wrong. If this would happen to you, you would probably react as I did and try everything within my power to take the pain away, but I did not know what to do.

It is not possible to prevent your dog from getting sick, even with this guide. However, what you can do is to ensure that these problems are either noticed early enough or you are able to use your knowledge to prevent them in the first place.

In conclusion, it is important for me to emphasise that this book contains tips and recommendations which I have collected through my own experiences and during general dog training sessions. This guide cannot replace a visit to the veterinary surgeon. It is purely intended to give you some knowledge and recommendations along the way. If your Labrador is suffering from acute or long-term problems, you should take him to the vet without delay.

I wish you and your Labrador all the best for the future and, above all, good health!

- Chapter 1 -

WHAT YOU NEED TO KNOW ABOUT YOUR LABRADOR

Did you know that, according to the World Canine Association (FCI), there are officially more than 350 canine breeds recognised today?

Your Labrador is only one of many different breeds. Naturally, many have things in common. After all, every dog is a descendent, one way or another, from his remote ancestor, the wolf. You can see it more in some breeds than in others.

In this chapter I would like to give you a brief summary about this fascinating breed, so that you know what you are letting yourself in for when you choose a Labrador.

When you decided on your Labrador, you chose a well-balanced, bright and friendly creature. Even though the Labrador Retriever was bred for the hunt, as the name "Retriever" suggests, he is just as well-known for being a family dog.

Many dog experts appreciate the Labrador, not least because of his will to please humans. For this reason, he is easy to teach, reacts quickly and is not difficult for beginners to train. If your Labrador is your first dog, you do not need to worry too much about his training. You have chosen a breed, which will not make it difficult for you.

As you have chosen a classical hunting dog, you should be aware of what living with him will mean for you. Your four-legged friend is a total bundle of energy. He is often used in the hunt to collect shot game. As these often land in the water, your new friend will be fixated on water. He will love jumping in and having a swim in any kind of water.

The Labrador does not have much of an instinct to follow wild animals or cats. This is because, during the hunt, they have to wait until the game has been shot before they get the command to retrieve. It is no surprise then that, in addition to water, your Labrador also loves fetching. throwing a ball will become one of your main activities.

The Labrador Retriever is naturally good-natured and supremely loyal, which makes him a good family dog.

It is important that he is trained with much patience, a large portion of sensitivity and loving consistency. Dogs should never be kept in a cage or kennel or trained using pressure and punishment. Unfortunately, many people believe, erroneously, that this type of training is suitable for a Labrador Retriever.

The Labrador is well balanced and has strong nerves, which makes him very good with children, a fact which I can confirm from my own experiences as a young girl. He likes company, loves to be part of the family and socialises well with all breeds and even cats.

Now you can see what a wonderful breed you have chosen! On the following pages you can find a short portrait of the breed, according to the FCI standard.

These pages are not enough to give you a full picture of this magnificent animal. However, I hope I have been able to draw you a picture of what it is like to own a Labrador. Of course, there are always dogs which do not conform to this description and some have much stronger or weaker characteristics, but I hope that you are able to recognise your Labrador in this description.[1]

---

[1] If you would like to find out more about the upbringing and training of your Labrador, I recommend that you read the first two books in this series. You can find more information about those books at the end of this one.

Short breed portrait according to the FCI:

Country of Origin	Great Britain
Character	Good-tempered, very agile, excellent nose, keen lover of water, adaptable, devoted, intelligent, keen
Height at withers	Males: 56 - 57 cm Females: 54 - 56 cm
Weight	Males: 29 - 36kg Females: 25 - 32 kg
General Appearance	Strongly built, short-coupled, very active, broad in skull
Eyes	Medium size, expressing intelligence and good temper, brown or hazel
Ears	Not large or heavy, hanging close to head
Fur and Fur Colour	Short, dense, without wave or feathering, weather-resistant undercoat Colour: Wholly black, yellow or liver/chocolate
FCI-Classification	Group 8: Retrievers, Flushing dogs, Water dogs Section 1: Retrievers
Utilization	Retriever

- Chapter 2 -

FUNDAMENTALS OF NUTRITION

In this chapter you will discover what you need to know about feeding your dog. Firstly, I will explain some recommendations for healthy eating and then go on to explore the various types of food available today, such as commercially processed food, raw feeding, home-cooked food, vegetarianism and veganism. After that we will look into what you need to know regarding the feeding of your Labrador.

In conclusion, we will touch on a subject which is underrated by many: The water consumption of your Labrador. Only too often, owners fail to provide enough fluids for their dogs. I will give you some tips on how you can encourage your dog to drink more.

BASIC RULES FOR FEEDING

It may sound a bit surprising at first, but it is not so important what you feed your dog, but how. For this reason, you will discover in this chapter how you should be feeding him. There are many details which dog owners do not know about and because of that they often harm their dog's health or make their training much more difficult.

It is important to emphasise at this point that these tips are the result of my own training and experience, extensive research and many conversations with other dog trainers. If you have concerns about the methods, I recommend that you speak about them with your vet.

One of the most common questions which I am asked, and which is generally discussed intensively, is how often to feed your Labrador. My initial answer is always: It depends!

Depends on what?

It depends on the age of your dog, as an example. A puppy would need to be fed about six times a day, slowly reducing the frequency as he gets older.

I recommend that a fully-grown Labrador should be fed twice a day. That of course depends on your daily routine and the health of your dog. Feeding healthy dogs once a day should not cause any problems.

You do not need to worry that your dog will get too hungry. It is a mistake to think they are like us humans. A dog does not need to eat several times a day. Once a day is enough. Of course, that does not mean that you cannot give him some treats in-between. On the contrary, you should continue to give him treats during his daily training sessions, but remember to count the amount that you use as part of his daily food intake. On days where you feed a lot of treats you should reduce the amount he gets in his main meals and vice versa. Failure to do so will result in him putting on more pounds than are good for him.

If you do not feel comfortable with feeding one to two times a day, you can feed your dog more often than he needs if you like, as long as you do not change the amount of food you give him.

It is not unusual, particularly with working dogs, for them to have regular fasting days. This is in compliance with the feeding habits of your dog's ancestors and at the same time ensures that he uses up surplus reserves. I do this with my dogs. Think about it!

A further tip that I have for you is that feeding can be an indirect way of pulling rank. What do I mean by that? Not only with wolves, but also in every pack of dogs, there are specific rules and processes which show, to those who understand them, which dog has which rank among them. Understanding these subtleties will make the training of your dog much easier.

Always give your dog his food last. All the other "pack members" should be finished before he gets his food.

It is important that your Labrador does not tuck straight into his food but waits for the command to do so. The best way to do that is for him to take up a sitting position while you calmly put his bowl on the ground, wait a few seconds (or later a little longer) until you give him the command "eat".[2]

It may seem strange to many people, but using this indirect rank pulling, you will rise in rank in the mind of your dog. In addition, you will avoid your Labrador

---

[2] You will discover how to give these commands and many more in my guide "Labrador Training – Dog Training for your Labrador puppy". You will find more information on this subject at the end of the book.

trying to defend his food from you. Often, owners find themselves being growled at if they come close to the dog's full bowl. You can avoid this by practising this exercise every day and showing that you are the boss over his food.

A further and underrated aspect of feeding is the place. Unfortunately, some owners believe that their dogs should be fed in a quiet and secluded spot where it will not be disturbed. Of course, it is important that your Labrador is left in peace to eat his food. During this time, children should not be allowed to pester him or urge him to play. However, wolves also never eat completely alone. They are always in sight and calling distance of their pack. Choose a place where he can eat undisturbed but where he is in contact with the rest of the family. In this way, he is involved in family life but learns that it is not a problem when people are close him or walk past him while he is eating. As surprisingly as it may seem, dogs who are used to eating alone can become aggressive if someone suddenly gets close to them. Follow my tip from the very start and you will avoid that.

Once your dog has finished eating, I recommend taking away his bowl immediately, no matter whether there is something in it or not. Why is this tip so helpful? On the one hand, you get your dog used to eating all his food. This is useful if you are in a hurry. On the other hand, this is also an indirect form of pulling rank. This way, you teach him that he can only eat when you (the pack leader) allow it. If you allow your dog to finish his food in his own time, you undermine your own position.

I suggest giving him a quiet time after feeding. Your Labrador should not be running around or jumping for at least an hour after he has eaten. A quiet walk, to allow him to relieve himself is quite safe but jumping and running should be avoided at all costs. Why? Your dog's stomach is obviously full after feeding and when he moves around quickly, this can cause a gastric torsion (also known as a twisted stomach), which in 15 to 45 percent of cases can be deadly. You can read about how to recognise a twisted stomach and what to do about it in Chapter 4 – Common Diseases.

In conclusion, I would also advise you not to change the food your dog is eating. Every change can lead to gastrointestinal disorders. This not only applies to changing from dry to wet food but also to the brand or type of food you give your dog. A change of flavour in your dog's feed, however, is not considered to be problematic. Do not worry that you dog may become bored with eating the same food every day. He will not! It is much more challenging for him to get used to new foods on a regular basis. You should carry out any changes on an incremental basis. This means you should start very slowly and change only a small amount of the new food in place of the old. You can increase the amount slowly until, after about 3 to 4 weeks, you have completely replaced the feed.

If your Labrador is a poor eater, I recommend checking the temperature of the feed. If the wet food is too cold, for example, because you have just taken it out of the fridge or the dry food is soaked in cold water, it could be unpleasant to eat. Take care to ensure that the food you give him is always at room temperature. I suggest soaking dry food for at least 10 minutes beforehand to enable it to develop its flavour and is not so difficult to eat.

On the following page, I have summarised the points which are most important to consider when feeding your Labrador.

Checklist of Feeding Rules:

- ☐ Feeding your dog 1 or 2 times a day is quite sufficient.
- ☐ Your Labrador should receive his food last of the family.
- ☐ Before you feed your Labrador, you should make him sit and only start eating when you allow it.
- ☐ During feeding, your dog should not be disturbed but should not be too far away from the family.
- ☐ Put the bowl away after feeding is finished, whether or not there is still food in it.
- ☐ Adhere to the quiet time after feeding (at least 1 hour).
- ☐ Do not change the brand or type of food unnecessarily. If it becomes unavoidable, you should introduce him to the new food slowly.
- ☐ Pay attention to the temperature of the food – if it is too cold, it becomes unpleasant for many dogs.

WHEN TO LET YOUR LABRADOR MAKE DECISIONS

As mentioned previously on several occasions, your Labrador is descended from the wolf. It is important that you understand his descent so that you know what the important things are to consider and how to feed your dog in a consistent manner. As a direct descendent of the wolf, he only differs from his ancestor by 0.1 to 0.3 percent! Did you know that?

What does that mean for you?

The wolf normally only eats unprocessed meat (including offal, bones, fur etc.) and only seldom, when forced to through circumstances, plant-based foods. His teeth are designed for tearing meat and coarsely separating it into pieces. His teeth are not designed to eat ground food (for example grain-based) and the same applies to a typical pet dog of today.

Look carefully into the mouth of your Labrador! It differs considerably from your own, which is less designed for tearing and more for grinding and chewing. Your dog seldom chews or grinds his food.

More often he devours smaller pieces without thinking of chewing them.

If you were to ask your Labrador, he would instinctively (and genetically triggered) choose unprocessed meat which he could tear apart – quite happily with bone, fur and offal. This is particularly the case with this original breed, which has not yet been overbred and kept very naturally.

Labradors enjoy working at their food. The tearing off of pieces of meat or chewing the bone is a real joy and not annoying for your dog, as we humans would perhaps imagine it to be.

However, not everything has remained unchanged with today's pets. As wolves do not know when they will get their next meal, their stomachs can stretch to become extremely big. A fully-grown wolf can eat up to 3 kg of food at once. In comparison, this would be almost 16 kg for an average-sized man of 80 kg! Modern dogs have largely lost this ability, although many dogs tend to eat as much as they possibly can. If you give your Labrador as much to eat as he would like, he would become overweight. It is your job to give him just the amount of food that he really needs.

The classical pet dog has become omnivorous (eating all kinds of foods) due to its century-long cohabitation with humans, although he should be given mostly meaty food. Many studies suggest that the nutrition which a modern pet needs differs considerably from that of the wolf. Through centuries of cohabitation with humans, a certain amount of plant-based nutrition has been added to their diet as well as the feeding of dry food or cooked food, which is not thought to be harmful for your pet dog (in contrast to the wolf). It can be seen that not only his behaviour but also his feeding habits have evolved through living with humans, so it is not quite correct to believe that a dog can eat the same as his wolf ancestor. In the next chapter you can read about what could go into his food bowl.

WHAT GOES INTO THE FOOD BOWL?

There are many varying opinions regarding the correct feeding of the modern pet often leading to heated discussions. There are forceful voices supporting every possible method of feeding, which do not allow for contradictions or other opinions.

There are very vocal advocates for all types of nutriation, who are not interested in listening to other opinions.

Jürgen Zentek - Director of the Institute for Animal Nutrition, in Berlin – has a definite opinion on this question:

> "It is basically of no consequence whether the dog is fed cooked food, raw food (including meat and vegetables) or dry food."

This is a statement which may surprise many animal owners. According to Zentek, it does not matter what you feed your dog. More importantly, it should cover his nutritional and energy needs, and ensure that he gets enough minerals, trace elements and vitamins. How he gets them is not important.

On the following pages, I will introduce you to the most common methods of feeding. These will include commercially processed foods, raw foods and home-cooked food. We will also talk about vegetarianism and veganism.

You will discover the pros and cons of feeding processed foods and what you need to be careful of.

In the last sub-section, we will look into what you need to consider when feeding your Labrador, compared to other breeds.

COMMERCIALLY PROCESSED FOOD

Although processed foods are often demonised, I think I am not sticking my neck out too far to suggest that it is one of the most common types of pet food used today. In Germany alone, 435 million Euros was spent on dry food, only surpassed by the 473 million Euros spent on wet food during 2018. A further 538 million Euros were also spent on snacks. All of the above belong in the category of commercially processed foods. In total, the sum of 1.4 billion Euros passed over the cashiers' counters.

There are a number of reasons for the enormous popularity of processed foods. These include:

- Its general availability.

- Its simplicity in storage and speed in preparation.

- Its simplicity for working out how much to feed.

- Preparation is carefully state controlled and conforms to the highest standards.

- Experts in the field have calculated the correct amount of vitamins, minerals and trace elements that your dog needs so there is no danger of under or over feeding those.

In short: Commercially processed food is practical! The owner does not need to worry much about anything. However, few people know that we separate processed foods into three separate categories:

- Straight feed material: This is food which consists of a single component and is not meant for feeding on its own. An example of this is the non-mineralised meat tin.

- Supplementary feed material: This is food which consists of at least two components, neither of which are designed to provide all the nutrition a dog needs. Dog biscuits are an example of this, or non-mineralised meat tins with vegetables. With a little experience, the dog owner can make a balanced diet from a mixture of straight and supplementary feed.

- Complete feed material: As the name suggests, this food supplies enough nutrition on its own to cover the needs of your dog.

Unfortunately, there are some processed feed manufacturers who use the latitude of the existing laws to their own advantage and who put their own profits before the well-being of the dog.

If you decide on feeding processed food, it is advisable to check carefully if you are buying a "good" product. I will explain here how you can do that. Take a packet of your dog's food so that you can see what is in it.

Check which type of food you are using. See if it is straight, supplementary or complete. If it is designed as straight or supplementary food, it is possible that your Labrador is not receiving all the nutrition he needs.

Next, you should look at the list of ingredients. Interestingly, the law does not require all ingredients to be laid down in writing. If you cannot clearly see the ingredients it is a possible (although not definite) sign that they are not using the best ingredients. Perhaps you need to reconsider your choice of food. Do you not want to know exactly what your dog is eating? And why do the manufacturers not want to tell you what it contains?

Often, manufacturers use descriptions like "chicken flavoured" on their packaging. Have you ever asked yourself how much chicken needs to be present in the food? Here is a short summary:

- "With chicken flavour": In this case, the food must contain more than 0% but less than 4% chicken.

- "Rich in chicken", "extra chicken" or "with extra chicken": These descriptions mean that they must contain at least 14% chicken.

- "Chicken dinner": This means that at least 26% chicken should be present in the food.

The other analytical data mentioned on the packaging is less important in my opinion. The crude protein includes both animal and plant proteins, which differ considerably in both quality and digestibility. In reality, your Labrador needs more animal protein, but it is not possible to see how much of it he is getting in this example.

The amount of crude fibre in the package, on the other hand, is important information and something which is underestimated by many. Crude fibre (plant fibre which is difficult to digest or completely indigestible) influences your Labrador's stool consistency. It stimulates the digestive system and assists it in its work. I have had very good personal experience with a fibre value of between 1.5 and 2 percent. This value should not be too high as that could be harmful.

The crude fat values on the packaging seem to be as meaningless as the crude protein value as you cannot see which types of fats it includes.

If the crude ash value lies above 5 percent, this could be a sign that it is produced using a lot of feathers and bones. Of course, a wolf eats that and it can provide useful minerals and trace elements. However, I find it hard to believe that these would be present in significant amounts, but they serve as a cheap alternative to valuable lean meat. I would treat feed made from offal, which is advertised as premium quality with caution as it should also contain a sufficient amount of lean meat.

The above was a rough summary of what you should look out for when browsing over the contents of the processed food packaging. It is important that you keep exactly to the recommendations on the packaging. If you only use dry complete feed, you should never add tinned dog food to that. This would cause a surplus to his needs. Keep exactly to the amounts which the manufacturer recommends.

If you are feeding a mixture of straight and supplementary food, I recommend using exactly the amount recommended by animal nutrition experts which can be calculated specifically for your Labrador.

RAW FEEDING

The trend towards feeding healthy and natural food does not stop at us humans. More and more owners are trying to feed their dogs as naturally as they can – meaning as closely to the way of the wolf as possible.

The raw feeding method was introduced by the Australian vet, Ian Billinghurst, who has been promoting the use of raw feeding for dogs since 1993. The raw feeding method is known by some as BARF which is short for "bone and raw food".

Specifically, this means that feeding your Labrador would consist exclusively of raw meat, offal, bones and fish. Added to this are fresh fruit, vegetables and nuts which are meant to imitate the stomach contents of the dog's prey.

The biggest advantage of raw feeding from my point of view is that you know exactly what your Labrador is getting to eat and you can ensure yourself of its quality. With normal commercially processed foods, you only see compressed pellets which do not give you any insight as to what they contain, meaning that you have to take the word of the manufacturer.

A further, often overlooked, advantage is that dogs are occupied much longer with their feeding. In most cases it is not possible to devour their food at speed, as with processed foods, because the meat is given in large pieces or whole bones. The dog needs to work to get his food, which may take him some time and this leads to some very active dogs being calmer and more balanced. At this point I would like to discourage you from taking commercial BARF mixtures as they are often already cut into small pieces, which partly diminishes the benefits of the method.

In most cases, BARF food is easier for dogs to digest, particularly those with sensitive digestion or some food sensitivities.

It is not scientifically proven, but many owners believe that the following side effects could be considered positive:

- Better immune system
- Less parasites
- Stronger bones
- Shinier fur

However, despite the advantages of BARF feeding, there are also disadvantages, which can be serious for your Labrador. Naturally, the idea of feeding your dog naturally is great, but there could also be dangerous bacteria in the food, parasites in raw meat or it could lead to an under or over supply of nutrients.

Salmonella has often been found in commercial BARF packets. Although dogs with healthy immune systems do not get sick with them, they can pass an infection on through their excrement to their owners or other animals.

To ensure that no parasites are present in raw feed, I recommend buying your meat fresh from the butcher or alternatively freezing it by -20°C so that most parasites are killed off.

Preparing a healthy and balanced diet for your Labrador is not easy and probably would not be carried out correctly by the layman. Often there would be insufficient calcium and too much phosphorus, as an example. Also, often the feed does not contain enough vitamin D and iodine. In addition, the ingestion of too much lean meat can be harmful to dogs, causing damage to the kidneys.

If someone were to ask me if I would recommend BARF food, my answer would always be: It depends!

You, as a Labrador owner, need to be clear that this method of nutrition takes up a lot more time than feeding processed foods and the costs are usually much higher.

I believe it is absolutely necessary not to feed BARF until you have consulted a vet who is specialised in animal nutrition. You will find a large number of recipes on the internet but few would receive the OK from an expert. No one who has not seen or examined your dog could give you a recipe which contained all the nutrients, minerals and vitamins that he needs at his particular stage of life. Do not allow yourself to be convinced by any online guru.

BARF food yes, but only fed correctly and after consultation with an expert who will examine your dog regularly. I could not, in all honesty, recommend a half-baked solution with pre-prepared BARF feed from a commercial supplier.

To give you an idea of what BARF food looks like, I give below an example for feeding a 30 kg dog. Please do not use this on your dog for any length of time if you have not previously consulted an expert.

- 480 g beef head meat
- 240 g boiled potatoes
- 60 g shredded carrots
- 6 g finely crushed eggshells
- 1,5 g Ascophyllum seaweed powder

This recipe needs to be swapped with a different recipe during the week because there is not enough Vitamin D, E and B1 in it to balance your dog's needs.

HOME-COOKED FOOD

The same principle applies to home-cooked food as previously mentioned with BARF food. You, as the owner, have full control over what the dog is given to eat and for that reason, it is important that you speak about the composition of the feed with an expert in dog nutrition.

In contrast to BARF food, however, you would feed your dog little or no raw meat, but would prepare his feed much as you would with a human. An important difference is that your Labrador should not be given human meals under any circumstances.

One reason for this is that certain foods are very harmful to your dog and can even be fatal. Another reason is that dog food should not be seasoned or spiced. If you observe these aspects, you can feed your Labrador cooked foods without concern.

Normally, dog food consists of the same components as human food, meat, vegetables and a satiating portion, except that the distribution of those components varies. Home-cooked foods for your dog would include:

- **Meat:**
Beef, poultry, lamb and almost any other types of meat are suitable for dogs to eat. However, with pork you will need to ensure that it is cooked through. Offal is rich in vitamins and trace elements but should not be given too often.

- **Fish:**
Almost all kinds of fish are suitable for your dog and he will love them too. Please be careful that you remove all bones or they would lead to the same problems as we humans have.

- **Eggs:**
Eggs are high in protein and make for shiny fur. A small amount of the shells can also be used.

- **Milk/Dairy products:**
Many dogs are intolerant to dairy products, there are only a few which are suitable. These include curd, sour milk and cottage cheese.

- **Grain:**
    Rice, oatmeal, pasta and bread are very well digested by most dogs and can be mixed in with the home-made feed.

- **Pulses:**
    These can only be fed cooked and if possible chopped, then they can be added to the feed.

- **Fruit/Vegetables:**
    Both fruit and vegetables are well liked by many dogs. The best way to add them to the feed is shredded or pureed.

At this point I would like to add that some foods which can be eaten by humans without problems are harmful to our four-legged friends and can even be fatal. A list of these poisonous foods can be found in Chapter 4 under "Poisonous and other problematic substances".

I personally use home-made food for two very different reasons. The first is that the food can be made very bland. If my beloved companion is suffering from a gastrointestinal problem, I would only give him bland foods for a couple of days, as I later describe. Since I am cooking his food, I can cater for what my dog's already weakened digestive system will be able to deal with.

In addition, I like to prepare snacks and treats myself. You can make them in large amounts in advance and use them as you need them.

The second reason I like to make my own dog food is so that I can pamper them. When I cook the food myself, I believe I am doing something which my dogs will enjoy. I have detailed the 10 recipes, which my dogs seem to like best, at the end of this book. I hope you will have as much enjoyment from trying them out as I do.

VEGETARIANISM AND VEGANISM

For staunch vegetarians and vegans, dealing with meat is not easy. For this reason, many people decide to feed their dogs vegetarian food (without meat) or even vegan food (purely plant-based). There is a lot of heated discussion as to whether this form of feeding is at all appropriate for dogs.

If owners decide to feed their dogs vegetarian food, this seldom has anything to do with the health of the dogs but is mostly based on ethical or religious grounds. For some owners, who build a close relationship with their animals, the thought of intensive animal farming or slaughter is simple unacceptable and is the reason why they want to give their dog a vegetarian diet.

The argument that this form of nutrition is not natural is weakened by the fact that this also goes for tinned foods. Even the Animal Protection Association PETA supports feeding vegetarian foods. In the meantime, there are countless studies, many in favour and just as many against it. As I already mentioned at the beginning of this book, dogs are not purely meat eaters but they eat many varied things, although their digestive systems are developed to deal predominantly with meat.

What can you do if you do not wish to feed your dog meat?

On the one hand, I would ask you to consider if you have chosen the right kind of pet for yourself. The question whether meat is necessary for your dog or not is not yet scientifically resolved. There are many animals which prefer vegetarian foods and eat them voluntarily and happily. I would recommend any staunch vegetarian not to choose a dog as a pet. I believe that a wholly plant-based diet does not cover the important amino acids that your dog needs on a regular basis.

However, should you be firmly of the opinion that you want to have a dog, I would recommend that you do this in consultation with a dog nutrition expert. It is your responsibility to ensure that he gets all the minerals, trace elements and vitamins he needs. Create a feeding plan with the expert and make sure that your Labrador's blood values are regularly checked.

I do not see any problem with occasionally feeding your dog only on plant-based foods. My dog, Daika, for example loves cucumber above everything and she often gets it as a snack. Sometimes, I leave out the meat component in the homemade meals, but not in all meals and certainly not the majority of the time.

As an alternative to vegetarian food and tinned food, you can buy your dog's feed from controlled, organic, non-laboratory tested animal sources, for use in the previously mentioned BARF or homecooked methods. Having all these alternatives means that you can rest assured that what your dog is eating is not the result of intensive farming or animal cruelty.

I am completely opposed to the sole feeding of vegetarian meals for dogs and I do not want to go into further detail about it here. I can only repeat my suggestion that, in future, owners choose another animal, rather than a Labrador as a pet.

WHAT YOU NEED TO CONSIDER WHEN FEEDING YOUR LABRADOR

The good news to start with: Unlike other breeds, the Labrador does not demonstrate any breed-typical intolerances or deficits. For that reason, you do not need to concern yourself about anything in principle when feeding your dog, which cannot be said for some breeds.

Many Labradors tend to have almost insatiable appetites – they eat everything they can get their "paws" on. For this reason, it is particularly important that you, as his owner, watch what and especially how much he eats. Studies show that an overweight Labrador dies two years earlier on average than his slim counterpart. This can make a great deal of difference with a life expectancy of 10 to 12 years.

Should your sweetheart have a few too many pounds on his ribs, you could try reducing the meat and grain portion of his feed and increasing the vegetable portion.

But how can you, as a layperson, recognise if your Labrador is being fed correctly?

A healthy Labrador should have a flat, sinewy belly, and strong limbs, which do not have a fatty layer. His fur should shine, his eyes should be watchful and attentive and he should always be ready to move. Laziness is not normal behaviour for a Labrador and could be a sign of incorrect feeding.

Labradors particularly like dry and wet foods, rather than other kinds, which makes the preparation and storage considerably easier. Of course, BARF foods and home-cooked foods are also suitable for your Labrador. However, do not be surprised if your dog is less than enthusiastic about these alternatives at the beginning if he is used to processed foods. The high amount of flavourings in the processed foods make natural food seem too insipid. However, if you stick with it, you will notice that he begins to devour the new food with enthusiasm.

It is important with all feeding alternatives to ensure the quality and the origin of the food. If it covers the nutritional needs of your dog and if he tolerates it well, any type of food is suitable.

REGULATING YOUR LABRADOR'S WATER SUPPLY

There has been much discussion about the right amount, quality and type of food for your dog, but there is something which he needs more urgently than food: Water!

If necessary, your dog could live for a long time without food if he had to, but he could only exist for a few days without water. On the following pages, you will discover how much water your Labrador needs and how you can convince him to drink, if he is not drinking enough.

REGULATING THE WATER REQUIREMENT OF YOUR LABRADOR.

Your Labrador cannot live for long without sufficient water, as he needs it for many of his physiological functions. For example, he needs water to break down the components of food in his digestive system, in order to extract the nutrients into the bloodstream and then into the tissues where it can transport toxic substances out through the kidneys or regulate his body temperature.

You can see how many physiological processes are dependent upon drinking enough water. Normally, this can be achieved in three different ways:

1. **By actively drinking:** This is how your dog satisfies most of his water requirement and is the most obvious method.

2. **Through his food:** Even while eating, your dog can take in fluids. Naturally, there is a great difference depending on whether he is given wet or dry food. Dogs fed with BARF food can obtain most of their daily requirement through the fresh food.

3. **Through his metabolism:** As strange as it may seem, your dog is able to cover some of his water requirement through his metabolic processes.

It is important to keep your Labrador's water intake at a constant level in order that his physiological functions can work properly. It is not good if your dog can only quench his thirst once a day. It can cause deficiency symptoms and he will probably be very thirsty. In order to avoid that, you should ensure that he always has access to water.

The water you set down for him should always be clean and, if it is given in a bowl, I recommend cleaning it regularly – at least once a week – with dishwashing liquid or vinegar essence. Remember to rinse off remnants of your cleaning liquid carefully so that it does not enter his system. I suggest you take water with you when you exercise your Labrador. Of course, he can also drink from puddles and ponds, but water can easily be contaminated with germs, if it is standing. Some ponds are breeding grounds for bacteria. Your dog should be able to drink flowing water, which seems clean in most countries, without worries.

Tap water is quite safe to drink in Germany. However, if it is highly chlorinated, some dogs will refuse to drink it because of its taste. For a few weeks I would suggest giving him still mineral water. Fizzy water is not necessarily harmful for your dog but it could cause stomach problems and flatulence. Take care to give him his water at room temperature. If it is too cold, it can also cause irritation of the stomach, vomiting or diarrhoea. Alternatively, dogs often refuse to drink water which is too warm.

A healthy Labrador loses fluids through various ways during the day. It can be lost through his stools, in his urine, through his breath, skin and by lactating dogs, through the teats. Many factors dictate how much water your dog needs. These include his weight, how much fluid he has lost through the above-mentioned methods, the air temperature, the amount of physical activity he has had, or through his food. Three quarters of his requirement can be satisfied using wet food.

You can use this rule of thumb to give you an idea how much water your Labrador needs each day:

A fully-grown Labrador who is fed with dry food, at a normal air temperature of about 20°C, moving an average amount, needs about 40 to 100 ml of water per kilogram body weight. A dog of 30 kg would need 1,200 to 3,000 ml. If he is fed wet food, that amount reduces by about 20 to 50 ml per kilogram body weight. This would be 600 to 1,500 ml for an average-sized Labrador.

If your dog is exercising more or if the air temperature rises, the water requirement will increase accordingly. The same applies to particularly salty food. As with us humans, that can also lead to an increased requirement of water. I have given you the rule of thumb, but as you can see, there is a lot of leeway upwards and downwards. If he is drinking much more or less than that, you should consult with your dog's veterinary surgeon, as it could be sign of a disease of some kind.

If your Labrador is drinking roughly the amounts mentioned above, everything would seem to be alright. Once you have watched your dog's water intake for a few weeks, you will see how much he normally needs and how more exercise or higher temperature affects his thirst. As always, you should make adjustments according to the specific needs of your dog.

HOW TO ENCOURAGE YOUR LABRADOR TO DRINK

Normally, a healthy dog will drink enough water, provided it is available to him, as dogs listen to their bodies carefully, which cannot be said for humans.

However, even a healthy dog may not drink enough. One reason could be the high temperatures in summer when your dog needs to drink more than he is used to. It could also be caused by a stress situation. As with us humans, a dog can also refuse to eat and drink when stressed. Particularly with male dogs, it can happen if they see a bitch on heat.

Here are a few tips from me to ensure that your dog is drinking enough:

- Give him more water than usual. You could exchange some of his dry food for wet food, which automatically increases his intake. You would not normally add water to wet food but, in this case, I would suggest you do.

- Give him water with flavour. Bouillon, liver sausage or sausage water are good examples, but ensure that the water is not too salty.

- Add fruit to the water, such as cranberries or bilberries. This way, you can make the drink more interesting and many dogs try to fish the fruit out of the water, just for fun. At the same time, they are automatically swallowing water.
- Think about buying a water dispenser. Some dogs drink much better if you give them running water to drink.

If your dog is still refusing to drink, or drinking less than would be considered normal, even after trying all the above, I suggest you consult your vet. It is possible that he has an illness that you need to check out.

On the following pages you will find a checklist which covers all the main points regarding the drinking behaviour of your Labrador.

Checklist of Drinking Behaviour:

- ☐ Always provide enough water for your Labrador.

- ☐ Ensure that the water is room temperature and is not sparkling so as to avoid problems with his stomach.

- ☐ Clean his water bowl regularly.

- ☐ Do not let him drink from still waters while he is out, take fresh water with you for your dog.

- ☐ Increase the amount of water you give him if he has been very active or if the outside temperatures are high.

- ☐ Add bouillon, liver sausage or sausage water to his drink, to awaken his interest.

- ☐ Soften dry food in plenty of water and optionally add some wet food to his meal.

- ☐ Add some fruit to the water to make a playful way of awakening his interest to drink.

- ☐ Consult a vet if, despite trying all of the above, your dog is still not drinking, appears tired and lacking in motivation.

- Chapter 3 -

BASICS OF GROOMING

We humans take for granted that we take care of our bodies. However, what is normal for us is not always true for our dogs. I would even go so far as to say that most dog owners assume that they do not need to take care of their dog's grooming, as he would do what is necessary himself.

In principle, this assumption is not completely wrong. However, certain breeds need much more care than others.

With your Labrador, you have chosen a breed which needs significantly less grooming than others, such as a Yorkshire Terrier. However, there are things which you need to take care of, even with a Labrador.

If your Labrador is not used to having his fur checked over and groomed, I suggest starting with it cautiously. Do not start straight away with the full programme that you will find in this book. It is better to begin with short periods of checking him over and repeating the process several times a day, so that he can get used to it. Try to make the examination and the grooming as pleasurable as possible for him and sweeten it with treats, strokes and praise if your Labrador stays still and behaves as you would like him to.

The most important thing is that you stay calm. Even if your dog is wriggling around, you need to stay calm and composed. If you react to his behaviour and become irritated or even angry, you will only achieve the opposite. The tension in your dog will only increase and he will begin to hate the examinations. This will set the tone for many years of stress and regular conflict. So, stay calm, no matter what your Labrador does!

Again, I recommend the following: Begin with small steps and do not overstress your Labrador. Every step, which is carried out confidently, is much more valuable than an over-hasty big step which is carried out with uncertainty.

I am often asked why it is necessary to make such a big thing about grooming, even though your dog descended from the wolf and that the wolf never had anyone looking after it. This argument seems sensible at first, but does not withstand closer examination.

In comparison to the wolf, which can reproduce freely, today's pet dogs are bred purposefully to show specific characteristics, which, according to Darwin's theory, would not have established themselves in the wild. Humans have influenced greatly how the various breeds have developed and how certain characteristics have been fostered, which need receive special attention. For example: The lop ears of a Labrador.

In addition, the life of a pet dog is vastly different from that of a wolf. Living with humans has made dogs dependent on us, which is most noticeable by the amount of care they need.

There are also simple aspects which come into play, such as being able to keep your home cleaner if you regularly brush your Labrador. Instead of him losing his long hair little by little, as happens with the wolf, brushing him will help to loosen his fur quicker and at the same time minimise the hair flying around in your home.

As I already mentioned, choosing a Labrador you have luckily chosen a breed which needs relatively low maintenance. Therefore, I have explained in the following pages how you can regularly check the eyes, skin, fur, ears, teeth and paws of your Labrador. If you stick to this regime, it will ensure that you are able to notice signs of sickness in the early stages and you and your dog will feel much better.

The tips on the following pages are based on the opinions of doctors, advisors and other experts. If you follow the procedure exactly, you will soon be spending many hours checking and grooming your dog. It is probable that you will suspect illness and danger everywhere with your four-legged friend at first – I do not want to burden you with that. Here, you will read about many problems which could affect your Labrador. However, it is important that you understand that the word "could" does not mean that problems "will" occur and certainly not all at once.

As with all things, it is important that you listen to your common sense. If your dog has already had problems with his eyes, you need to look after them more than you would with a dog which has always had healthy eyes. If your dog is showing no sign of abnormalities, do not wear him out with unnecessary inspections and special care programmes. Just do what is necessary correctly and leave anything which is not necessary.

At the end of each chapter I will give a recommendation, based on what I consider to be necessary for my dogs and what I think can be ignored. Please do not follow my recommendations blindly but take care of the needs of your own dog in particular. Every dog is different and his needs are different, but with the help of my recommendations, I want to give you a feeling for the appropriate care which your dog needs specifically.

EYE CARE

The sweet, heart-warming look that your dog gives you is part of your relationship with him. In order to keep it that way, it is important that you inspect his eyes regularly. Experts and vets recommend checking your dog's eyes every day.

The eyes of a healthy dog should be clear and shiny. The eye lids should be close to his eye ball and be clean. There should be no mucus or incrustation. If your dog shows a dryness in his eyes just after waking up, that is quite normal and is similar the rheum or sleep dust which we humans often get in our eyes.

If you want to inspect his eyes, hold his head gently in your hands and, if necessary, stroke the hair to the side.

If you notice that your dog often has that rheum in his eyes, you could wipe his eyes gently every morning with a damp cloth to clean it away. Take care that the cloth you use is not fluffy or you could end up getting some in his eyes. You should use a separate cloth for each eye, so that any bacteria are not transferred from one eye to the other.

If your dog often has problems with his eyes, you could exchange the plain water on the cloth with a warm saline solution or camomile tea. The water to be used in any case should be filtered to ensure that there is no residue which can transfer to your dog's eye.

If your Labrador tends to have long hair around his eyes, it is a good idea to have it cut regularly. This way, no hair impurities will transfer into your dog's eyes and his hair itself will not irritate them.

The following symptoms could be a clue that there is something wrong with your dog's eyes and you should call the vet:

- Above average light sensitivity
- Touching his eyes with his paw
- Sensitivity to the touch
- Thick discharge coming from the eye
- Heavy, bloodshot eyes
- Enlarged pupils
- Any changes in the eye

In addition, I advise you to protect your dog from getting too much dust or pollen in his eyes. Even though the Labrador is not a small breed which is so close to the ground and that he would particularly suffer from that, you still need to be aware of the possibility.

Do not let him walk through flowery meadows or over very dusty fields. The small particles can get into his eyes very quickly and cause conjunctivitis. If you cannot avoid taking him to places with large amounts of pollen or dust, I suggest you rinse his eyes after his walk with a mild cleaning agent without additives. Such cleaning agents can be obtained from most drugstores or pet shops.

As well as pollen and dust, you should avoid dry air in the home. Just like we humans, a dog can suffer from dry, heated air, which can cause burning or runny eyes. However, unlike humans, the dogs do not know why and so do not avoid being close to fireplaces and heaters. If you notice that your Labrador often suffers from runny eyes or blinks often, particularly in the wintertime, it would be helpful to increase the humidity in the room. This will not only improve the symptoms in your dog's eyes, but also in your own.

Just as dogs do not recognise dry, heated air, they also do not recognise draughts. In fact, many dogs deliberately lie with their heads in the draught. Try to prevent your dog from doing that too often because it can also lead to conjunctivitis.

My recommendations for you:

If your dog is not suffering from problems with his eyes, you will not need to examine them specifically each day. Some dogs never need to have the discharge removed from their eyes. That does not mean that your dog does not have any, but that up to that point it has cleared up by itself. If I notice anything, I would keep my eye on it and, as long as it does not get any worse, I would not take any action.

The tips with the draught and dry, heated air need to be taken seriously. It does not take long to fix and it will save your dog a lot of suffering.

SKIN AND FUR CARE

Generally, a dog's fur is seen as the mirror to his health. If his fur is shiny, full and robust, you can assume that your Labrador is healthy. However, as soon as this changes and the fur becomes dull and brittle, or if it is excessively matted, or your dog is losing a lot of fur, there may be a problem. The problem could lie deeper – often fur problems can be caused by irritations. Other problems could be nutritional deficiencies or parasites.

The skin is not only your dog's largest organ, it also carries out some very important tasks:

- **It protects your dog from pathogens.** It serves as an immunological barrier and deters bacteria, fungi and other harmful substances from entering the inner organs.

- **It regulates the temperature of your dog.** By widening or tightening the blood vessels, it protects your dog from the heat or cold.

- **It supports your dog through communication.** Tiny muscles in the skin enable the fur to stand up on end. In addition, smells and hormones can be emitted through the skin.

- **It helps to detoxify.** Waste products from the metabolic processes and other harmful substances are discharged through the skin.

- **It is responsible for replenishing the fur.** The hair follicles which form the fur on your dog, are found in the skin. The skin replaces the fur twice a year.

To ensure that your dog has not only healthy skin but also beautiful fur, you need more than regular grooming; you need to give him a balanced diet. Many dog owners do not know that nutritional deficiencies first show themselves on the skin and fur.

You may be asking yourself what healthy skin looks like on your Labrador. Usually, your dog will present with white to grey-coloured skin. If the skin is reddened, dry or scaly, or your dog seems to be scratching a lot, this could be a symptom of a skin disorder. The same can be said for dull or oily fur and hair loss.

Experts recommend grooming the skin and fur daily while at the same time carrying out your examination.

It does not have to be a boring routine. It could become a cherished ritual which could strengthen your relationship with each other.

Daily brushing and massaging takes less time than you would imagine, as it ensures that much less hair and skin particles will be shed than if you do it only once a week. Through daily brushing I also remove dirt particles remaining from his walks before they spread all over the house and I can also notice tics, fleas and other parasites much quicker.

If a Labrador is not used to daily brushing and reacts anxiously or even aggressively to it, I offer the same advice as with his eye care. Take it slowly and using a lot of treats and strokes. Try to make his daily brushing as pleasant an experience as possible so that he looks forward to it. Start with giving him a lot of attention before you reach for a soft brush. Wait until your dog is relaxed with that before you change to a harder brush or even to an undercoat brush

You are lucky that your Labrador, like his ancestor the wolf, has a full upper coat and thick undercoat. His fur is very robust, natural and needs little grooming – at least on the part of your dog as it does not bother him if there are dog hair everywhere in your home – you probably think differently about that.

You should not really bath your Labrador except to get rid of any dirt which you think necessary. Intensive bathing and particularly shampooing destroy the natural protection and oil layer of the fur and skin. This can lead to skin irritation and itchiness. Only bathe your dog in exceptional circumstances and only use shampoo if it is absolutely necessary.

Never use human shampoo as your Labrador has a different pH-value and therefore his skin does not react well to it. You can find dog shampoo in all normal pet shops.

In preparation for bathing, I suggest putting down a non-slip pad in the shower or bath tub. Make sure that the water is warm but never hot.

The first time you bathe him be very gentle and take it slowly. Shower your dog down very carefully, beginning with each individual paw. If your Labrador remains quiet and relaxed, then go on to shower his legs. Slowly work towards the front, starting with the tail, continuing down his flanks and back.

Only shower over his head when your dog is used to bathing or is completely relaxed. If he is not, I suggest using a damp cloth instead. Do not use the shampoo on his head to avoid soap getting into his eyes, ears, muzzle or nose. Be just as careful when hosing down with fresh water.

If your Labrador begins to panic, stop what you are doing straight away. He needs to feel good about it and you cannot achieve that with pressure. Try giving him treats and petting him to get him to relax. The main thing is that you remain calm and do not get angry, annoyed or show that you are stressed.

When you are finished with bathing, your Labrador will probably want to give himself a good shake. Try drying him as well as you can in the shower or bath tub. Do not rub too hard. Many dogs do not like the hairdryer. You can test it if you like but if your dog does not like it, then it is better to stop. In winter you need to ensure that the environment around your dog is warmuntil he is completely dry. In the summer, when it is warm, you can leave the towelling down and hair-drying completely as your dog will enjoy his cool, wet fur very much.

Care products, such as sprays can be used but are not really necessary. If your dog is receiving a balanced, nutritional diet, his fur will shine without using them.

You do not need to plan regular visits to the grooming salon with your Labrador. In contrast to other breeds, he does not need to be trimmed or cut. However, if you put a lot of value on the optics of your dog, I recommend choosing your grooming salon well, as there are black sheep in this industry too. Make sure he prepares your dog slowly for the procedure and does not overstress him. Look for good advice. Many mistakes can be made, particularly on dogs with thick undercoats, such as your Labrador. Therefore, I am not a great fan of trimming or shearing. I prefer carefully removing any dead hair in the undercoat.

My recommendation for you:

I do not undertake a special inspection of his fur or skin as this is not necessary. We have a tradition at home that our dogs get a lot of petting in the evenings. I use this time to have a closer look at their fur.

I am quite flexible with brushing. In principle I brush my beloved dogs once a week. However, if he is beginning to moult, I brush him every day. I also brush him thoroughly after a long, rainy walk when his fur is very dirty. I usually wait until he is dry before I brush him, to get the dirt out of his fur, so that I do not have to bathe him. Sometimes I do not get all the dirt out the first time, so the next day I repeat the brushing - several times if necessary. Especially in the warmer months, I try to make it as easy for my dog as possible, by regularly removing the dead hair in the undercoat and brushing him to give him some relief.

If your dog has acute or chronic problems with his skin, or his fur, this procedure may suit you.

EAR CARE

I do not need to stress how important the ears are for your Labrador. They serve not only for him to hear, but are important for his balance and communication with his fellow creatures. Regular, daily inspection of the ears is therefore recommended by experts.

The dog's ear consists of three parts:
- The outer ear
- The middle ear
- The inner ear

He can hear much better than you or I and recognises additional frequencies which are higher or lower than those which we can hear. In order to keep it that way, you need to inspect your dog's ears regularly.

Ideally, you will not find anything, because a healthy dog's ear is well supplied with blood and clean. Your dog's body is able to produce its own cleaning mechanisms. For example, it is able to produce enough wax to get rid of impurities, fine protective hair prevents dust particles and other such foreign bodies from entering the inner ear, and good ventilation prevents bacteria from multiplying in the warm, damp climate.

The most common problem in dogs' ears affects the outer ear and outer ear canal. The following symptoms could mean that something is not quite right:

- There is a strange, unpleasant smell coming out of his ear.
- His ear passage is very dirty or sticky (e.g. a black substance or ear wax).
- You notice small black spots in his ear (it could be parasites).
- His ear is red or even discharging (be careful, this could be an infection).
- You see a fresh wound or bleeding of some kind.
- You notice that your Labrador is often scratching his ears, or shaking his head, or perhaps not holding his head straight.

I would suggest calling a vet if any of these symptoms appear. However, if his outer ear is only slightly soiled, you can try to clean it yourself.

Use a damp, fuzz-free cloth, which you can wrap around your index finger and carefully clean the ear shell. It is important not to wet the cloth too much and that no moisture gets into his middle ear. Make sure to dry his outer ear well, as the moisture can cause the bacteria to multiply around the area. If you prefer, you can use camomile tea instead of water as this also acts as an anti-inflammation agent. Ensure that the liquid you use is at room temperature.

If the ear is badly soiled, you can get a cleaning agent and drops from a specialist shop. I suggest applying it outside as your dog will want to shake his head violently afterwards. If the symptoms do not improve, you should consider taking your dog to the vet.

Under no circumstances should you use ear cotton swabs to clean his ears. The danger of pushing germs, wax or other dirt further into the ear is very great and you could cause bad injuries. In addition, if your dog makes a sudden movement, it could result in his eardrum being irreparably damaged.

Finally, I want to mention: Similar to the eye and skin care, I recommend getting your dog used to his ear care very early on in his life. Start slowly and carefully and link the examination and possible cleaning of his ears with lots of petting and one or two treats right from the beginning.

My recommendation for you:

As your Labrador does not have standing ears like a German Shepherd for example, they are more prone to having ear problems. I have a look at my dogs' ears every evening during cuddle time. That way I can see early on if there is any soiling to worry about. Up to now I have had very few problems with the ears of my dogs.

TOOTH CARE

We humans take care of our teeth as a matter of course, but many owners do not think it is necessary to do the same for their dogs. That is wrong. Your dog's teeth are used for communication, as a hunting weapon and as an eating tool. For these reasons it is important that they remain in good condition. You will find out how to do that in this chapter.

Just like us, your Labrador first cuts his milk teeth. These fall out after the third to sixth month, which sometimes leads to your puppy chewing everything in sight. He does that, by the way, to speed up the painful process of transitioning from baby to permanent teeth. An adult dog possesses 42 teeth which he needs to grab, hold onto, tear, kill and eat.

Get your dog used to you examining his teeth and gums on a regular basis. If you notice that the teeth are slightly discoloured yellow-brown or the gums have brown edges, you should see that as an alarm signal. It is probably plaque or a bacterial infection. If, in addition, your dog has an unpleasant smell on his breath, this is also a strong sign that he has tooth problems or gum inflammation. You may also notice bloody or very red-looking gums.

I strongly recommend not waiting until these symptoms occur but being proactive in providing good toothcare to reduce the chances of that happening. Statistically, 85% of all dogs over three years old suffer from tooth problems – a stunningly high number – which proves how important prevention is.

The main cause of plaque is being given the wrong food or leftovers, which stick between the teeth, causing bacteria to collect. The minerals in the saliva will turn the plaque into tartar which only the vet can get rid of.

Tooth care for your dog always begins with the food. Dogs which are only given softened dry food or wet food never have to chew. They swallow the small, soft pieces whole. Dogs which are given fresh, lean meat have to chew a lot more and that is exactly where natural tooth care begins.

Chewing automatically cleans the surface of your Labrador's teeth and avoids plaque and later tartar to form. The increased saliva flow while chewing will assist in the cleaning. This is even more effective when your dog is given bones as well as meat. However, it is important that the bone is always fresh (i.e. not cooked) and not pork or chicken. In addition, it should be big enough that he cannot swallow it in one go, which is particularly important with puppies.

Chew toys or other special chewing items from the pet shop are a good substitute for the natural tooth care. There is also the possibility of giving your Labrador a thorough tooth clean with special dog toothbrushes and toothpaste.

Did you know that active dogs have significantly less problems with their teeth? Scientific studies have shown that dogs produce more saliva during sporting activities, which helps the tooth-cleaning process.

My recommendation for you:

I personally recommend only physically cleaning your dog's teeth if he has had problems with them in the past or if specific genetic characteristics are present.

It should be sufficient to give your Labrador chewing items or bones if he is healthy. Ensure that your dog is only given unsugared food. Feeding too many treats in between meals can also increase plaque formation.

If your dog is not suffering from illness, you do not need to look at your dog's teeth and gums every day. Once a week should be enough. If your dog is refusing his food, or has a strong mouth odour, I suggest taking a look at his teeth. Sometimes that can be the reason.

Just like us humans, the same applies to dogs: The older the dog, the more vulnerable the teeth and gums will become. You will probably not find any abnormalities or notice any disorders in a young, healthy dog during the first few years. The older your Labrador becomes, the more probable it will be that he will develop plaque. For this reason, you will need to adjust your inspection frequencies to his age.

PAW CARE

Many people think that pedicures for dogs are extravagant – but I and many experts see it differently.

Perhaps you have noticed that your Labrador has been licking his paws or chewing on his claws. If he has, he urgently needs a pedicure. It is not strictly a cosmetic treatment as it is also important care which can prevent serious health problems.

But why is it necessary at all? After all, the wolf even nowadays does not need a pedicure as nature takes care of his important paw care. For the most part, the wolf walks over hard ground, rocks and stones from being a puppy, causing the claws and hair on his paws to be rubbed off regularly.

It is different with modern dogs. They walk mostly on soft ground and are only out in their natural surroundings for a few hours per day. Life with us humans has caused additional burdens on our dogs which were unknown to the wolf, such as de-icing salt.

How do you know if your Labrador needs some paw care?

- If his claws touch the ground (your dog's feet make clicking noises when he walks over tiles).
- If your dog is licking or chewing on his feet.
- If your dog stumbles a lot
- If your dog sets his paws at an unusual angle while walking

If you notice any of these signs, you should take a closer look at your dog's paws. In addition, many experts recommend inspecting the paws at least once a week or after a long walk.

Look closely if dirt has become lodged between the pads or under the claws. If so, you should remove it. If the hair between the pads is so long that it protrudes out of them, you should cut it shorter. Dirt and small stones can gather in the hair which can become painful. Also, the hair can become matted, with the result that your dog has less grip, particularly on slippery surfaces, and can slip and stumble. I suggest buying a pair of special scissors with rounded ends. If the paws are badly soiled, a lukewarm footbath could help.

If you notice cracks, cuts or even in-growing claws, you should consult your vet. You can use an oily cream or

Vaseline (particularly with cracked pads) but I suggest getting them looked at by your vet, particularly if the problem continues over a longer period of time or happens often. In both cases, using camomile in the footbath can be quite effective.

In the winter, your dog's paws need particular care. Grit, ice and salt can place a lot of strain on them. During the cold months, you should try to avoid gritted roads as much as you can and check his paws after every walk. I put Vaseline on my dogs' feet after each walk. If your dog is already suffering from wounds and split pads in the warmer months, you could think about buying special dog shoes for him. You will need to make sure that they fit well, are of good quality and also that your dog can not take them off by himself.

Now we come to claw care: If the claws are too long, your Labrador is not able to walk putting his pads down first but steps directly onto his claws (which is what causes the clicking sound). During the rolling motion, the claws are pushed into the claw bed which can cause painful pressure on the pads. If the pressure becomes too strong, your dog will try to avoid this by putting his paw down on the side. In turn, this can lead to long-term muscle hardening, joint damage and deformity of his musculoskeletal system.

If you are not sure if your dog's claws are too long, try the following: Let your Labrador stand in front of you. Make sure that his weight is evenly distributed on all four paws. Try sliding a piece of paper under the claws towards the pads. If you are not able to do that, his claws are too long, they should be about 2mm above the ground.

Clipping claws can really be done by anyone. However, I suggest that you let your vet show you how to do it the first time, as there is a part of the claw which contained nerves and blood vessels, which we call the "quick". You should never cut into the quick because that is very painful for your dog and the claw can bleed profusely.

Never rely on the spacer on your claw clippers when deciding how far to clip, you should always monitor it yourself. I suggest staying well away from the quick. If you look carefully, you can usually see where the quick starts. Sometimes it is useful to use a torch under the claw to be able to see it better.

It is very important that your dog is lying quietly while you are clipping his claws so that he does not suddenly try to pull his foot away. I always try to tire out my Labrador before I start because that increases the chances of him staying still. Do not hold the paw too loosely. Remember though, that you want to make his claw clip as pleasant as possible. Use a lot of treats and strokes here.

Only cut the horny part of the claw with the clippers. You should stop before you reach the part which is not hardened. Hold the clippers horizontally and ensure that you clip at a right angle to the claw's growth direction. Do not cut any more than a few millimetres at a time, so that you do not cut too much. Do not forget the so-called wolf's claw at the end. That is the fifth claw on the back leg which is rounded in appearance and does not touch the ground, but it has to be clipped.

Stay calm during the procedure and keep him well grounded. Do not overtax him and praise him well once you are finished.

You also need to remain calm if you happen to damage the quick. It will look worse than it is because of the heavy bleeding. Hold a gauze pad or compress against the injury and wait for a few minutes. Normally, the bleeding will have stopped by then. If it has not, you can try an old household remedy by mixing some flour and water to a thick mass. Place the mass onto a gauze pad and press onto the wound again for a few minutes. The mass will form a clump and act as a kind of plug on the wound.

If the bleeding has not stopped after about 20 minutes, you should call your vet. If it has stopped, it would be best to lightly bandage the wound and then put a clean, old sock over the hole paw. You can stick it into place with sticky tape so that your Labrador does cannot bite or pull it off. The sock should ensure that the fresh wound does not become soiled and you should keep it on for about a week. Check it daily to ensure that it does not become infected. If your dog behaves normally, in my opinion it is probably not necessary to call a vet.

If you want to file the claw after you have cut it, so that there are no sharp edges, you should ensure that you are only filing in one direction. If you file backwards and forwards, this could cause your Labrador some pain. In addition, it is not good for the structure of his claw – by the way, the same applies to finger nails.

As I said before, looking after your dog's claws is not difficult but you need to be watchful, have a sure hand and lots of patience. As it is difficult for a beginner to know where the quick begins, it is a good idea to ask a professional – such as your vet – to show you. If you feel able to, you can do it from then onwards.

My recommendation for you:

I tend not to check my dog's paws very often except during the winter months. The salt, road grit and ice can often cause cracks in them, which I treat with Vaseline. My four-legged friends also have to wear the previously mentioned dog shoes from time to time, if necessary.

I do not need to check the length of my dogs' claws because I can hear when they get too long. Since I accidentally injured one of my dog's claws during clipping, I prefer to let the vet do it.

WHAT YOU NEED TO PAY PARTICULAR ATTENTION TO WITH YOUR LABRADOR

As I mentioned at the beginning of this chapter, you have less things to worry about with your Labrador, as he is a really low maintenance breed compared to many others.

He was originally bred as a hunting dog, who spent a lot of time alone in the wild. Because of this it was necessary to breed into him so that he would not need much grooming.

In order to promote and maintain the well-being and health of your Labrador, I urge you not to forego the routine examinations which I have mentioned previously. Of course, there are many Labradors who life long and happy lives without any of the care mentioned above. However, there are still many who suffer silently and no one notices their suffering. In the interest of your dog's well-being, you should invest the little time it takes in taking care of him.

The good part is: Not only the health of your Labrador will be increased, but also your relationship with him. Through intensive care a high level of trust will develop between you and your relationship with your dog will become even closer.

CHECKLIST: REGULAR CARE

- ☐ The eyes are clear and shiny. They are not reddened, there is no mucus or other changes.

- ☐ The skin is white to grey, not reddened, not dry or flaky.

- ☐ The fur is shiny and dense. There is no hair loss except for normal moulting.

- ☐ The ears are not dirty, nor showing signs of redness or dark spots and your dog is not shaking his head often or scratching his ears.

- ☐ The teeth are not showing a yellow-brown coating and the gums are not reddened or bleeding. There is no unpleasant breath.

- ☐ The paws are not cracked or sore, nor is there any distinguishable dirt between the pads.

- ☐ The claws are not touching the ground when your Labrador is standing normally.

CHECKLIST: CARE UTENSILS

- ☐ Claw clippers
- ☐ Tick tweezers
- ☐ Dog shampoo
- ☐ Brush (curry comb if necessary)
- ☐ Comb (coarse and fine-toothed, perhaps also a flea comb)
- ☐ Lotion or drops for cleaning the ears
- ☐ Fuzz-free cloths
- ☐ Camomile tea
- ☐ Chewing items (e.g. Chew toys or fresh beef bones)

- Chapter 4 -

COMMON ILLNESSES

For some owners, the health of their dog is almost more important than their own health. If the dog is not feeling well, neither is the person.

Luckily, we are living in times when we have a good health system for our animals. There are sufficient medicines, good vets and even clinics where our four-legged friends can receive excellent treatment.

Just like we humans, our dogs can suffer from all kinds of illnesses. Some of them are easy to treat, some are less easy. In some cases, we owners are able to help and in others there is no other choice but to visit the animal clinic.

In this chapter I will give you a brief summary of the most common illnesses, which can be caused by parasites and the gastro-intestinal conditions which occur most often. I will give you tips as to how to recognise them and what to do. At this point, it is important for me to emphasise that any serious conditions need to be treated by your vet. All these tips which I am listing below are meant for mild conditions.

In addition, I will give you a lot of helpful information on fever, vaccinations and castrating your Labrador, as well as those conditions which are typical for specific breeds.

The chapter ends with two checklists as to how you can recognise a healthy dog and what you need to have in your first-aid kit.

PARASITE INFESTATION

Many owners fear parasite infestations and not without good reason. These little insects can cause a lot of harm to our four-legged friends and some can also be transmitted to humans.

For this reason, I am outlining the three most common parasites – mites, ticks and fleas – in greater detail. You will discover how they get there, what they do and what you can do to get rid of them.

As with all parasites, it is important to detect them early on, then you can avoid greater harm. If you discover them late – meaning there is already a heavy infestation – it is much more difficult to remove them.

The best way to detect them early on is to follow the care inspection tips which I gave you in the previous chapter. Inspect your dog's fur regularly, particularly after a long walk on meadows and fields, then you will probably detect them early, which is the aim of the exercise.

In addition, there are a few things you can do to prevent infestation in the first place, but I will tell you that later in the individual sub-paragraphs in this chapter.

MITES

Mites belong to the spider family, but because of their size they are often only recognisable under a microscope. There are basically three types of mite, which differ by their mouth parts.

Chewing mites are at home in the ear passages of your dog and mainly feed on skin flakes. They cause skin infections and itchiness. Scratching, in turn, causes increased irritation which can lead to secondary infections and wounds.

Sucking mites have a trunk-like mouth with which they can suck blood and the lymphatic liquids of their host. This causes the danger of pathogens transferring to the host.

The last type is the *digging mite*. These "dig" through the outer skin layer, causing strong irritation which may lead to your dog injuring himself. In dogs we speak of "mange", in humans we say "scabies".

Probably the biggest danger facing your Labrador is the so-called grass mite, which belongs to the blood-sucking mite group. As the name suggests, these mites lurk in the grass, waiting for passing hosts.

Grass mites are only 0.3 millimetres in size and can be seen well because of their orange-coloured bodies. If you notice these creatures in your lawn at home, you can put out a white or light cloth on your grass during the summer. After a very short while, there will be a lot of orange spots collecting on the cloth to take a sunbathe.

They mostly attack places where they come directly in contact with your dog, such as the paws (often between the pads), the head (mostly on the bridge of the nose), the ears, the belly and the chest. They try to break into small cracks in the thinner parts of the skin and inject their saliva.

It is that saliva which causes intense irritation and, in some cases, a so-called mite allergy. The grass mites are not interested in your dog's blood but in the lymphatic fluid. You can see the affected areas because there is an orange colouring on the skin. In addition, if you go through his coat with a flea comb, you would probably notice small red spots in the fur. If not, then tap the comb onto a white cloth, where they will be more visible.

Unfortunately, there is no reliable preventative treatment against the attack of mites. There are some combi-treatments which are supposed to work against fleas, ticks and mites, but their success is dubious and questioned by many experts.

However, you are not completely helpless against them. There are a few things which you can do:

- Inspect your grass at home. If you can see grass mites, mow your lawn with greater frequency and treat it with stinging nettle compound. This successfully kills the larvae. It is important that you do not leave the cut grass on the lawn but remove it quickly.
- Examine your dog regularly after he has been playing in the meadows. The sooner you notice mite infestation, the better. If you do notice something, comb him thoroughly with a flea comb and give him a full bath. I suggest using an unscented ivory soap mixture, or in particularly acute cases, a mixture of olive oil, apple vinegar and salt water together with a mild, alcohol-based solution. Ensure that you only use lukewarm water and that you rinse your Labrador thoroughly afterwards. Both of

these suggested remedies will work against the skin irritation.
- Clean the floors of your home thoroughly too, and wash all the dog blankets. Vacuum other areas where you dog may have lain, such as the sofa.
- If your dog often suffers from heavy mite infestation, you should ask your vet for his advice on which suitable (chemical) product it would be best to use.

TICKS

As soon as the winter has passed and it starts to get warm, that is the time that the ticks get busy. Ticks also belong to the sucking group of the spider family as you had probably guessed. But contrary to grass mites, which are interested in the lymphatic liquids of their hosts, ticks are only interested in blood.

At the beginning, ticks are only as big as the head of a pin and can be difficult to spot or feel. But once they have found a host, and have nourished themselves on his blood for several days, the females in particular can grow up to 3 cm in size.

Ticks are mostly found on the edges of forests, in clearings, in grassland or parks. They climb on to high blades of grass or bushes and wait for their next victim. They have a particularly good sense of smell which helps them to prepare for the arrival of their host, i.e. they perceive the smell of sweat. They are also acutely aware of vibrations and changes in the CO_2 content of the air. Once the tick has sensed a victim, it falls onto them and searches for a suitable place. Suitable places are mostly on thin-skinned areas but those well-circulating with blood, such as the head, haunches, ears or belly.

Most ticks prefer a particular kind of host. This is because they have usually specialised themselves on a particular host type by assimilating the anaesthetic part of their saliva secretion to them.

About 20 of the 900 tick species known world-wide, can be found in Germany. Your dog will probably only be attacked by three of them: The wood tick, the alluvial forest tick and the brown dog tick.

The fear that many people have for the tick is justified, as there are no other parasites which can transmit as many diseases. Ticks transmit bacteria in their saliva which can, for example, cause Borrelioses and other viruses which fall into the category of early-summer meningoencephalitis (ESME). It can also carry other parasites such as the Babesiosis which transmit toxins.

Not all such diseases are fatal but they can severely affect the health of your dog. For this reason, it is important to try and avoid tick bites and if your dog does get one, to recognise it quickly and remove it safely.

But what happens exactly when a tick bites?

Once it has found a suitable place, it cuts a slit in the skin of your dog with its mouthpiece and sticks its proboscis into the wound. Then it sucks the blood of its victim and at the same time introduces an anaesthetic into the wound, so that the dog does not notice that he is being bitten. The secretion also acts as an anti-inflammatory agent which blocks the immune system of the host, thereby preventing the wound from closing and enabling the blood flow to continue.

During its meal, the tick excretes the undigested blood through its bowel into the wound of its host, which is what causes the previously mentioned transfer of pathogens.

Unfortunately, there are no vaccinations which work against some of these diseases, so you just need to prevent them as best you can, using the measures which are available to you.

One of the most proven remedies is the tick collar. The best-known of these include the Scalibor collar, which has the active ingredient Deltamethrin and the Preventic collar which contains Amitraz. Both collars are neurotoxic and work by continually emitting the active substance through the fat layer of the skin. It takes about a week to get the full benefit but it lasts for between four and six months.

The main advantage of these collars is that the toxic effect is released slowly into your dog and is therefore gentler on his body. If your dog is intolerant to the ingredients or the collar causes side effects, you can remove it immediately. You should also take off the collar when he goes swimming as the active substance can harm aquatic animals.

Spot-on substances, that you dab onto the neck of your dog, work much quicker. These also remain effective for up to four months. The disadvantage of these is that your dog is subject to the whole toxic effect of the preparation at once. If your dog proves to be intolerant towards it or if it causes side-effects, there is little you can do about it.

Both solutions involve using nerve agents so you must decide for yourself if you want to give your dog any of these toxins. In addition, when you stroke your dog, you will also come into contact with these toxins to a lesser extent. Therefore, you need to be careful with their use, particularly if a cat lives in the same house as your Labrador, because they can be very poisonous for your feline pet. Be sure to read the instructions on the packet carefully or speak to your vet about it before you use anything – something which I would advise every owner to do.

The very popular amber collar is harmless for both your dog and the ticks. It is not scientifically proven that they work.

Another popular household remedy is garlic, which is rubbed into the dog. This, as well as other remedies such as essential oils, lavender and lemons is also ineffective.

Bogacare seems to be a promising natural remedy, which can be used on a collar or as a spot-on compound. However, tests are still in the early stages here.

If your dog should get bitten by a tick, despite all your efforts, it is important to remove the tick immediately. It does not matter whether you use a tick tweezer, card or lasso or normal household tweezers. Use the tool with which you feel most comfortable as all of them work equally well.

I personally prefer the tick tweezers and I describe below how best to get rid of ticks with them.

- Firstly, make a space around the tick by pushing the fur around the area to the side.

- Place the tweezers (or whatever you are using) as close to the skin as possible and surround the tick.

- Pull the tick out quickly, but whatever you do, do not pull it out with a jerk. Ticks do not have a screw thread, so there is no need to twist it while pulling it out.

- The best result is when you are able to remove its biting apparatus intact. If not, there is no need to panic. Do not try to remove it another way as you could cause more harm than good. Leave it in, after a while it will fall out by itself.

- Destroy the tick by burning, squashing (I recommend doing that outside the house between tissues) or dissolving it in alcohol. You should never put it into your household rubbish alive or flush it down the toilet, as ticks are very hardy little insects.

- **No-Go:** Never use other aids, such as nail polish remover, alcohol, oil, fire or glue. If you pour and of those onto the tick, you will cause it unnecessary stress, which could cause it to vomit into the wound and release even more pathogens into your dog's blood stream. In addition, you could injure your dog, particularly if you use fire.

Finally, I want to emphasise that the best agent against sicknesses caused by tick bites is regular inspection of the fur. There are no preparations presently on the market that I could recommend, as all of them have side effects or they are not proven effective. The earlier you discover the tick, the less time it has to introduce pathogens into your dog's body. Not every tick bite causes sickness. Only 0.1 – 5% of ticks carry the ESME-Virus within them.

But what can you do if your dog gets sick? If your Labrador starts to show symptoms after a tick bite, such as fever, fatigue or vomiting, you should contact your vet immediately. These symptoms could appear up to three weeks after the bite as the incubation period can last that long. Only your vet can confirm whether or not it is a sickness which has come from a tick bite. In order to give your vet the most accurate information, make a note of when you noticed and removed the tick. I usually also take a photo of it, so that the vet can see which kind of tick it is and is able to exclude a few sicknesses from the outset.

You should also check for a few weeks after that if the bite has healed properly. In most cases, I can say that such a bite heals without problems or consequences. Make sure that you do not panic. Stay calm and be careful while removing the tick.

FLEAS

Fleas also belong to the insect family and are true survivors. Their natural habitat is meadows and bushes, but they like to live in homes too and can live there all year long. Just like ticks and mites, the fleas wait for hosts and then jump onto them as they pass by. Even though they are only 3 millimetres long, they can jump up to 1 metre away and reach a height of 25 centimetres — a great distance for such a small creature.

There are thousands of different types of fleas in the world, but the German pet dog is mostly only sought by one particular type: the cat flea, whose favourite hosts are dogs and cats. However, if either of those do not happen to be available, they are quite happy to attach themselves to humans.

Contrary to popular belief, flea infestation has nothing to do with bad hygiene. Most pet dogs become infected through contact with other dogs or wild animals, such as hedgehogs, and bring them home where they usually breed rapidly. A female flea usually starts to lay eggs directly after its first blood meal and can continue to lay up to 50 eggs per day. The eggs fall out of the dog's fur and lie on the grass, carpet or other household textiles until they hatch about a week later. The larvae crawl into small cracks and after about 10 days are ready to find themselves a new host. In that time, a single flea could have laid up to about 850 more eggs.

The most important thing about flea infestation is that you catch it early so that you do not have a real invasion of fleas in the house. But how do you recognise a flea infestation?

The first sign is of course when you see an increase in your dog scratching himself as the flea's saliva causes a strong itch. Some dogs start to bite themselves, which often causes injury. Not every dog scratches himself enough to be noticed. There may be very little itchiness if it is only a light infestation, but in the meantime, masses of eggs will be falling onto the carpet, the sofa, your cushions and many other places in your home.

I have taken to checking for fleas during my daily fur examination. In addition to normal brushing, I always have a flea comb ready which has very fine, close teeth, with which I comb against the direction of growth. Then I shake the comb onto a piece of moist kitchen roll and take a good look at what is there. If I see small black-brown spots, I squeeze them carefully. If they turn rust brown to red, then it is likely to be flea excrement (digested blood). If the spots do not turn reddish, it is probably just normal dirt.

I do this test on a few different places and that way I can get a good picture of whether or not my dogs have fleas.

If this test indicates that your dog has an infestation, you need to act quickly as it can be said that only 5% of the fleas are actually on your dog. The other 95% are to be found as fleas, larvae or eggs in the surrounding area. For this reason, it is essential that the whole region around your dog be treated. Larvae can live for up to 6 months, without nourishment, in a crease in the sofa and are only waiting to find another host to jump onto.

Because only a fraction of the infestation is found on your dog, it is important not to rely solely on flea collars or spot-on preparations. They will only serve to ensure that the fleas want to escape from your dog and find a safer place to wait until the coast is clear. In the worst case, they could decide to choose you as a substitute host.

I do not need to tell you that this is not a good situation. But how can you challenge flea infestation successfully? I suggest following these three steps:

1. **Kill the fleas on your Labrador**

    Contact your vet immediately and ask him which agent is best to fight the infestation. On the one hand you need an insecticide (mostly in the form of a shampoo, spray or powder), which kills the fleas. As this agent alone will not kill all the fleas, you also need an inhibitor to prevent their development. To ensure that both compounds work at optimum levels you will need to repeat the process at specific intervals. You should discuss exactly what dosage and at what intervals with your vet as these preparations are poisonous. If necessary, you should also treat other animals who live in the household with you. Be aware that tick preparations and some flea preparations can be fatal to cats. Your vet will know exactly what is needed and will give you the right advice.

2. **Eliminate the flea brood in the area**

   Once you have treated the fleas on your dog, you should start attacking the fleas, eggs and larvae in the area which your dog frequents.

   Wash all floors daily (including the corners) with a wet mop and vacuum all carpets, upholstery and other furniture. Get rid of the dust bag immediately. You can smother it with anti-flea powder if you wish.

   Wash all dog blankets, throws, cushions and covers at least at 60°C. You could use a chemical cleaner in addition to that (for example on sofa covers or carpets). Remember to clean your dog's stuffed animals too.

   Wash all textiles at a minimum of 60°C.

   Treat all surfaces where your dog lies and spray his blankets etc. with a special anti-flea powder or an environmental spray. Please take the advice of your vet about which to use and find out about the use of a so-called fogger which is a room spray which can kill fleas, eggs and larvae.

Remember to clean garages, cupboards, cars thoroughly and any other places where your dog may have recently been.

Even though it may seem difficult, if not impossible, you will need to keep this up for at least three months so that you can be sure you have caught all the eggs and larvae. If not, you have pre-programmed the next flea infestation.

3. Take preventive action

In addition to dealing with the fleas I would also recommend using a special anti-parasitic formula to ensure that all the extra work and costs in fighting the fleas is worth it. Ask your vet which remedy is most suitable for your dog. I personally prefer repelling anti-parasitic agents which prevent the flea from biting in the first place. However, as this is a poisonous pesticide, you should check with your vet that it will work quickly but gently on your Labrador.

In all the years I have been living together with dogs I have never had a flea infestation and I am very grateful for that. However, I know from those who have been through it how exhausting it can be for both humans and animals. Everyone I have spoken to who has suffered from a recurrence of the infestation, said that they did not adhere 100% to the recommended measures. I can only advise: If you happen to get fleas into the house, grit your teeth and hold out for the full three months, otherwise you will end up having the same problem again within a very short time.

GASTRO-INTESTINAL DISORDERS

Just like we humans, your dog can suffer from gastro-intestinal disorders. In this chapter I will describe the four most common gastro-intestinal problems which can be found in pet dogs.

Some owners are not always aware that they put their dogs into a danger which is quite avoidable, and I would like to change that. Sometimes it is the small things which you can do which can ensure that your Labrador is able to live a healthier life.

I will explain exactly what those things are on the following pages.

GASTRIC DILATATION VOLVULUS

Twisted stomach is one of the most-feared sicknesses which dogs can suffer from. If untreated (in this case that means unoperated), it can lead very quickly to the death of your dog.

Most dog owners have heard of it, but few know what causes it, how to recognise it and what to do about it.

It is mostly large breeds who suffer from twisted stomach, to which group the Labrador belongs. However, smaller breeds can also be affected. Apart from that, older dogs and in particular male dogs, are most prone to getting it.

As the name suggests, gastric torsion occurs when the stomach makes a complete turn inside the body, completely closing up the bowel entrance, oesophagus and blood vessels. If this occurs, there are no first aid methods which you can use to help your dog. The only thing which will help him is to get hold of a vet, or even better, an animal clinic, as quickly as possible so that he can have an operation to resolve it. The sooner the better.

If you see the following symptoms in your Labrador, you should act immediately.

- Your dog has a bloated stomach. In later stages it can even look like a drum.

- Your dog is very agitated.

- He refuses his food.

- His saliva production increases.

- He tries to vomit but without success.

Luckily there are a few ways to prevent twisted stomach. Here are a few examples:

- Divide his daily ration into several smaller portions rather than giving it all to him at once.

- Avoid allowing him to play and frolic directly after he has eaten. Your dog should remain quiet for at least 30 minutes after his meal.

If you stick to these two tips, there is little probability that your Labrador will ever suffer from a twisted stomach.

DIARRHOEA

Diarrhoea in dogs, much as in humans, is when there is an increased frequency of bowel movement where the consistency is mostly soft to runny.

It is a very unspecific symptom of any illness as it often happens with a variation of conditions, ranging from harmless to serious. In most cases, however, it is more harmless and disappears within a few days.

The reasons for this could be simply that your dog ate too fast or too much, so that his stomach could not tolerate it, or if he has a sensitive nature, he may have reacted sensitively towards stress, excitement or some changes in living conditions.

The biggest danger with diarrhoea is dehydration, so you should ensure that his water bowl is always filled.

As a second step, I suggest that you make him fast for a day (at least 24 hours), really giving him nothing to eat, not even a treat! This will give your dog time for his intestines to recover. On the following day, start by giving him a small portion of light food. A good example of this could be boiled rice with cooked chicken (important: without bones!) and cottage cheese. Most dogs love it, but if your dog is not so keen, you could add some vegetables or broth to the rice for some taste, but not so much broth as it could be too spicy for him.

You can increase the portions on the following days and when his condition has improved, you can go back to his normal food, step by step by reducing the amount of light food and increasing the amount of his normal food.

If the diarrhoea has not improved after two days, or is mixed with blood, you should contact your vet, particularly if he is showing other symptoms, such as vomiting and fever. Puppies are in increased danger, because dehydration could easily turn into a life-threatening condition. Keep a strict eye on your puppy and be prepared to contact your vet even earlier if he looks lethargic. If he is behaving within normal boundaries, eating normally and wants to play, there should be no reason to worry.

Avoid giving him medicines which are meant for humans at all costs. Many of them have strong side-effects or could even be fatal. If you really want to give your dog something, ask your chemist for a probiotic or electrolytes which are suitable for dogs. Again, do not give him anything which you have bought for your own use.

WORMS

Every dog which is kept properly and is allowed to play and sniff around, who is taken for walks and is allowed to run on fields and grassy patches will get worms sooner or later – that is unavoidable.

With all these activities, your dog will come into contact with the excrement of other dogs and animals. They ingest the worm eggs through the nose or the mouth. Stroking your dog, or allowing him to lick your hand could also pass the eggs onto you and infect you too.

You will not notice that your Labrador is suffering from worms until quite late. He will show symptoms of diarrhoea, loss of appetite and itching of the anus. You will probably notice it when your dog "sledges" along the ground, meaning he slides along the ground in the sitting position.

If your dog becomes infested by worms, you will need to make a worm cure immediately. This is a chemical treatment that you can only get from your vet as it is only available on prescription. The amount of repetitions you need to give depends on the compound, the severity of the infestation and the weight of your dog. For this reason, you should follow exactly the directions of your vet.

Today's worm cures are luckily a lot less strenuous than they were a few years ago. Most dogs are almost free of recognisable side-effects. However, your dog will certainly suffer from some changes to his bowel flora through the strong medicine.

Unfortunately, there is no prophylaxis or vaccine against worm infestation at present. This means that a dog can have another bout of worms as soon as 24 hours after finishing the worm treatment.

For this reason, many vets suggest using de-worming treatments regularly – every three to four months – so that the parasites have no chance of survival, even if there are no apparent symptoms.

However, this recommendation is not without its critics as the pharmaceutical companies have not yet carried out any long-term studies about the regular use of their treatments. It is not yet clear how the continual use of their compounds will affect your dog.

If you want to avoid giving your dog worm tablets his whole life, but at the same time be sure that he has not become affected, there is one other effective alternative: A faeces analysis.

For this you should collect stool samples on three consecutive days. A single sample would probably not be enough as you cannot see the worm eggs in every stool. Send the samples to a veterinary medicine laboratory or to your vet and have them analysed for parasites. If the results are positive there is no alternative but to administer another dose of the cure. If the results are negative, you can rest assured and if you wish you can repeat the analysis every three to four months.

This involves a significant amount of effort on the part of the dog owner, but the method is much less strenuous for your dog. An analysis costs between 15 and 30 Euros and has the advantage that your dog does not need to undergo unnecessary medical treatment.

Decide for yourself which method you prefer. You can either treat your dog when he tests positive for the infestation or you give him regular prophylactic treatments, or as a third alternative you can have his stools regularly examined for parasites.

POISONOUS SUBSTANCES AND OTHER PROBLEMATIC THINGS

Did you know that there are many foodstuffs which we humans can eat without problems but which are dangerous, if not fatal for your Labrador?

You should never feed your dog any of the following foodstuffs, as they could be life-threatening for him:

- **Avocado**: Dogs could choke if they swallow the stone. There are heated discussions about the effects of the fruit, although there is no scientific proof of the exact dangers.

- **Onions**: The sulphur contained in onions can destroy the red corpuscles in your dog's blood, so never give him your food leftovers. It does not matter if they are raw, cooked or dried.

- **Chocolate & Cocoa**: Cocoa (including chocolate) contains theobromine, which is poisonous for dogs. The darker the chocolate, the greater the proportion of cocoa and therefore the more poisonous the chocolate becomes.

- **Stone fruit**: There is also danger here regarding the stone in the fruit which can cause choking. Most stones are also sharp-edged and can cause injury to the oesophagus, stomach and intestinal mucosa. In some cases, it may even cause intestinal blockage. If your dog bites into the stone, it can release the hydrogen cyanide contained within it, which is also fatal for humans.

- **Grapes and Raisins**: Grapes and raisins contain oxalic acid which can lead to a fatal kidney failure.

- **Raw pork**: The Aujeszky's Disease virus, which can be found in raw pork, is incurable for dogs and is always fatal.

- **Alcohol**: Self-evidently, alcohol can lead to your dog suffering from liver and kidney failure.

- **Caffeine**: Caffeine contains Methyl-xanthines which can be fatal to the nervous system of your dog. Coffee and tea are therefore taboo.

The following foodstuffs are not usually fatal but are poisonous for your four-legged friend and could lead to serious problems:

- **Bacon**: Particularly fatty foods, such as bacon or poultry skin cause metabolic disorders which can cause problems with the kidneys or pancreas.

- **Poultry bones**: Dogs should never be given poultry bones, no matter whether cooked or raw. The thin bones split quickly and can get stuck in their throats.

- **Raw beans**: The toxin Phasin inhibits protein synthesis and can cause the red corpuscles to stick together. If you are going to feed your dog beans, ensure that you cook them first.

- **Raw solanaceous plants**: Raw potatoes, tomatoes and aubergines should never be given to your dog. They can cause diarrhoea, vomiting and brain disorders. The most dangerous part of the plant is the skin. However, these vegetables are no longer a problem once they are cooked.

- **Milk**: As many dogs are have a lactose intolerance, you should not give them any milk which contains lactose.

- **Salt**: Giving salt to your dog can cause them to develop kidney problems.

This was a summary of the main and most dangerous substances for your dog. If you notice that your Labrador is not able to cope with other foods, you should stop feeding it to him.

CANCERS

Current studies show that one in every four dogs suffers from a tumour at some time in his life. Every second dog over 10 years of age dies of cancer. This makes cancer undisputedly the most common cause of death in dogs.

It is not exactly clear what causes this, whether it be the consequences of living with humans, increased life expectancy, over-breeding or simply the improved and more intensive veterinary medicine available. What we do know is that some breeds suffer more often with cancer than others. Experts call this a genetic predisposition. Luckily, your Labrador is not one of these breeds but also here, cancers are not improbable.

Happily, there are also many therapies which can significantly extend the life expectancy of such dogs. Tumours can be surgically removed and their growth can be inhibited by radiation or chemo therapies. Radio and immune therapies are also among today's remedies which may enable an increase in the life expectancy of your Labrador or even cure him.

Dog owners should always weigh the benefits of increasing the length of their dog's life against the quality of his life. Extending his life through surgery or medicines, even if the quality of his life is badly impaired, may help the owner but does not always help his pet. Even if it is difficult, an owner has to be able to make the right choice for his animal.

The best care is better than any therapy, but there are varying opinions about what that should look like. Vets have not been able to establish a link between castration and a reduction in cancer. Castrated animals become just as ill as their "intact" cousins. The only link that vets have been able to establish is that older dogs are more prone to cancer than young ones.

Correct nutrition has also been linked to cancer care. However, this has not been scientifically proven. For this reason, I cannot offer you any recommendations on the best care for your dog in this respect.

That said, I can give you a few tips as to how you can recognise a cancer early. Early detection is very important as tumours spread quickly in dogs and therefore every minute counts in improving the chances of curing him.

Below you will find the most common signs that your Labrador could have a tumour:

- **Lumps on or under the skin:** When stroking your dog, be aware of any hardening, lumps or bumps on or under the skin of your Labrador. These can be found anywhere on the body.

- **Loss of appetite and unusual loss of weight:** Loss of appetite does not necessarily mean that there is a tumour. However, if it continues over a period of time, you need to have your dog examined. If your dog suddenly loses weight without changing his eating habits, there is definitely a reason to become concerned, as a malignant tumour would change the metabolism of your Labrador.

- **Frequent diarrhoea, blood in the vomit or blood in the diarrhoea:** If you see any of these symptoms you should contact your vet. The same applies if your Labrador has trouble urinating or defecating.

- **Lethargy or noticeable loss of stamina:** Many owners believe that these symptoms are part of growing old. This is also true, but if the symptoms come suddenly and strongly, you should take notice.

- **Changes in behaviour:** If your Labrador suddenly becomes withdrawn or is suddenly particularly clingy, this can also be a symptom.

All these symptoms could be, but are not necessarily, hints that your Labrador has cancer. It would not do any harm to have them checked anyway by your vet. Do not panic as these symptoms can also apply to much less serious disorders.

FEVER

The borderline to a fever is not as exact as with us humans. A healthy Labrador can have an optimum temperature of between 37.5°C and 39°C.

I would suggest taking your dog's temperature several times while he is healthy, so that you can tell if he is becoming sick. Make sure that he is lying quietly as stress or physical exertion can raise the temperature for a short time.

We speak generally of a "light fever" if the temperature is between 39°C and 40°C, but here there is no need to worry. As I mentioned previously, this could be due to stress or physical exertion.

If his temperature rises above 40°C, you can usually feel the heat coming off your dog. He could start to show outward signs of becoming unwell, such as loss of appetite or general lethargy.

You should contact your vet if his temperature exceeds 41°C. It could be dangerous for your Labrador to have a fever for too long.

If his temperature exceeds 42°C this could be very dangerous as the body's own proteins start to clump together – a process which cannot be reversed. At the latest, you should now be contacting your vet or even a pet clinic.

Having a fever does not have to be a bad thing. It is the way that your body destroys pathogens. In addition, it shows that your dog's immune system is working. Fever reduction medicines should not be used unless the fever becomes very high or remains for a long time. Again, never use medicines which are meant for humans, they can be fatal for animals.

How do you measure the temperature on your dog?

The simplest way is with a normal thermometer. I bought one especially for my dogs so that we humans do not have to use the same one. I use a disposable cover to reduce the amount of cleaning necessary afterwards. The best kind of thermometer to buy is one with a flexible tip, they are more comfortable for your dog and at the same you can reduce the danger of injury.

Dampen the thermometer slightly before use and ensure that it is not too cold. Hold your dog's tail firmly and lift it slightly. Insert the thermometer and wait for the signal before you remove it and check the temperature.

It is best to practise this procedure from puppy age onwards and praise him for standing still. Follow the procedures which you use for other health screening examinations.

If you do not have a thermometer handy, you can recognise a fever by observing the following symptoms:

- Your dog is panting a lot, even though it is not hot.

- The insides of your dog's ears feel warmer than usual, even hot.

- You notice that your dog is drinking much more than usual even though it is not very hot, or he stops drinking altogether.

- When stroking him, he feels warmer than usual, particularly around the nose.

- Your dog generally looks exhausted without having had much physical exertion.

If you see any of the above symptoms, you can assume that your Labrador has a fever. Watch him carefully. If you have the feeling that it is getting worse or that it remains for too long a time, you should contact your vet.

VACCINATIONS

The subject of vaccinations is as much of a subject of intense discussion and disagreement as it is with humans. However, in contrast to humans, there is no general compulsory vaccination programme, so it is up to each owner to decide whether to have his dog vaccinated or not.

Of course, every owner wants the best for his dog, but there is a great divide in opinions as to how this can be achieved. A vaccination, depending on the active ingredient, can have a good to very good protection against bacteria as well as viral diseases. However, they do not only protect them from catching them but can also even help to eradicate or at least to repress them. If a pathogen cannot find a host over an extended period of time, the population of this pathogen reduces.

For example, in Germany rabies has been eradicated since 2008. That means that you do not have to have your Labrador vaccinated against rabies. However, if you want to travel out of the country with him, you may find it necessary for him to be vaccinated. It is important that you can provide a valid rabies vaccination certificate if your Labrador has bitten another animal or even a human. If not, you may find that he has to be euthanised.

The Standing Committee of Veterinary Medicine's Immunisation Committee (known in Germany as the StIKoVet) regularly issues recommendations regarding vaccinations in two forms: Core and non-core vaccinations. Core vaccinations are (according to the StIKoVet) essential vaccinations which are important because a disease has become prevalent for which there are few or no treatments.

Core vaccinations include:
- Rabies
- Distemper
- Infectious Canine Hepatitis
- Parvoviruses
- Leptospirosis

The following vaccinations are less essential and are considered to be non-core:
- Parainfluenza (kennel cough)
- Lyme Borreliosis
- Babesiosis
- Leishmaniasis

- Bordetella bronchiseptica

The non-core vaccinations are also normally only for serious pathogens. However, these disorders often occur regionally and the vaccinations are often not effective for long.

If you decide to have your dog vaccinated, it is important that he gets the primary as well as the subsequent booster injections. The primary vaccination will build up immunity to particular pathogens in your dog's body. The booster injections will ensure continuing protection.

Only healthy dogs should be immunised. Dogs which are sick should not be immunised due to their weakened immune systems. It is also necessary for your dog always to have a thorough examination and a blood test before immunisation.

You should ensure that your puppy receives his primary vaccinations at between 8 and 15 months. The procedure and costs can be determined in consultation with your vet. You should also discuss the appointments for his booster injections early and perhaps arrange for your vet to send you a reminder.

CASTRATION

Many owners expect castration to be a panacea against all kinds of behavioural difficulties, particularly with male dogs. With female dogs, castration is considered more for hygiene reasons, mainly to avoid the inconvenience of her being on heat. In reality, there is a boom in castrations in Germany at the present time and many vets consider it to be a routine intervention, which can be advantageous for many reasons. They give the impression that you are doing a "good thing" for your dog by allowing a castration.

Of course, it is up to you whether you want your dog to be castrated. However, it is important that you think carefully about the subject, considering the pros and cons and what actually happens during castration. You need to have all the information before you can make a decision in the best interests of your dog.

When we speak of castration, we are talking about a veterinary intervention which removes the gonads of your dog. In male dogs it is their testicles and by females the ovaries, fallopian tube, the womb and the cervix are all removed. Castration is a permanent intervention which cannot be reversed. It is carried out under full anaesthetic, which can always carry some risk and there could also be some side effects.

Both the ovaries and testicles produce hormones which are absolutely necessary for the physical and psychological development of your dog, so should never be carried out before puberty. In addition, sexual hormones have a significant influence on the bone structure so castrating an animal too early often leads to joint problems and hip displacement.

The puberty of a Labrador usually begins at 7 months (often earlier with female dogs) and can last up to the end of the second or even third year. Contrary to common belief, it does not end when a dog is fully grown. It lasts much longer than that. How long depends not only on the breed but also from environmental factors and it is difficult to generalise. Large dogs, to which the Labrador belongs, usually need more time than smaller breeds. Female dogs should never be castrated before they have had their first heat, otherwise they tend to show immature behaviour all their lives.

Many owners believe falsely that they can resolve behavioural problems or prevent cancers with a castration. I can assure you that castration does not resolve behavioural issues. Neither does it help reduce behavioural difficulties on the lead. Nor does it reduce dominance or aggressiveness issues (unless both are due solely to the dog's sex drive). A castration also has no influence at all on territorial protective behaviour.

What many owners do not know is that the sexual behaviour of your dog is already anchored in his brain and cannot be rectified by a castration. A dog which often rubs himself on cushions or on other dogs would continue to do so after a castration. In this case, as with other problematic behaviour, only intensive behavioural training can help.

Many owners also do not know that there are also many unwanted side effects which a castration can cause

- **Obesity**: About 50% of all castrated dogs are obese, which can cause problems such as joint or heart disorders.
- **Personality Change**: The missing hormones can significantly change the personality of your dog, for example he may become lethargic or show general disinterest.

- **Increased ferocity**: Female dogs in particular tend to show increased aggressiveness towards each other.
- **Immature behaviour**: When a dog has been castrated too early, he may never grow up properly and shows immature behaviour all his life.
- **Fur changes:** Almost 30% of female dogs show a dullness in their fur.
- **Incontinence:** About 50% of all female dogs suffer from incontinence when they have been castrated.
- **Ear Infections:** About 30% of all castrated dogs show an increase in ear infections compared to their non-castrated fellows.
- **Bullying**: Other dogs which have not been castrated, and in particular males, will bully a castrated dog.

However, there are also positive effects which can be achieved through a castration. There is, for example, a reliable protection against pregnancies and reproduction generally. Female dogs no longer have their heat which is popular with many owners for hygiene reasons and there will also be no more phantom pregnancies with all their related issues. Male dogs which are castrated no longer have to deal with hormone-induced stress.

There is no scientific proof that the risk of cancers is reduced through castration. Even the feared mammary cancers in female dogs can only be reduced if a dog is castrated before its first heat. Even then, the risk of an uncastrated dog contracting mammary cancer is only 2%.

If you do decide on a castration, I recommend that you shop around as the prices at various vets can vary greatly. For males, the costs can vary between 150 and 250 euros. As the intervention is more extensive, the costs are higher for females and you can pay as much as 450 euros.

More importantly, you should ensure that your dog is thoroughly examined before the castration, because only healthy animals should undergo such an operation. This includes an examination for parasites.

Shortly before the operation you must ensure that your dog does not eat anything for at least 12 hours.

You should not feed your dog even on the evening before the procedure (if it is more than 12 hours before the operation). On the day of the operation, he should not drink anything either.

I have described two methods of castration below, so that you have an idea what happens during the procedure:

- For a male dog, the pubic area is shaved, disinfected and sterilised, ready for castration. The vet pulls the testicles forwards and opens them with a scalpel. He pulls out the testicles together with the spermatic cord and ties them up. Now he separates the testicles from the spermatic cord and removes them. Lastly, he unbinds the spermatic cord and sews up the wound.
- With a female dog the belly is shaved, disinfected and sterilised. The scalpel cut starts just under the belly button and along the lower abdomen. In most cases, the vet removes the ovaries, fallopian tubes, the womb and the cervix. The inner wound is

sewn up using absorbable sutures and the outer wound is closed with non-absorbable sutures.

After about 10 days, you will have to return to the vet to have the outer sutures removed. The inner sutures will dissolve by themselves.

Directly after the operation, your dog will sleep for another hour or two. When he wakes up, he will be very groggy and will be in a lot of pain. Therefore, it is important that you give him all the painkillers which your vet has prescribed. Dogs are unable to tell us when they are in pain. They are quiet and do not move much; very few of them whine or squeak.

It is up to you whether you want your dog to go through this. I hope to have given you some information in this chapter which can help you with your decision.

DISEASES TYPICAL FOR YOUR BREED

Unfortunately, due to their intensive breeding, Labradors suffer from certain conditions specific to their breed. It is advisable that you speak about those concerns with the breeder and find out how previous litters have been affected with them.

The most common of those conditions are as follows:

- **Hip Displacement**: Unfortunately, deformities of the hip have been all too prominent in the German Shepherd and it is now also being diagnosed more often with the Labrador. The propensity to suffer from hip displacement is mostly genetic, but can also be made worse through false feeding. Young dogs should not start too early with climbing stairs, walking on slippery floors or being encouraged to jump around too much.

- **Eye Diseases**: The cataract is a hereditary disease which is often found in Golden Retrievers, the consequences of which can lead to blindness. Treatment of this should be discussed in each case individually. Also, this breed can suffer from progressive retinal atrophy, which is untreatable.

- **Labrador Myopathy:** Dogs who suffer from this hereditary disease become tired very quickly during exercise. They start to stagger and can even collapse. This disease is not treatable and it is important to give your dog enough quiet time, during which he can normally recuperate fully.

CHECKLIST: FOR A HEALTHY DOG LIFE

- ☐ Am I feeding my Labrador appropriately?
- ☐ Is his weight normal?
- ☐ Does my dog always have access to fresh and clean water?
- ☐ Is my Labrador living in a clean environment? (bowls, sleeping place, toys etc.)
- ☐ Is he getting his regular examinations and do I know his normal temperature? Do I attend his appointments conscientiously? (e.g. vaccinations)
- ☐ Am I taking care of my Labrador's fur regularly and checking him for ticks?
- ☐ Is my Labrador getting enough exercise? Is he being physically challenged? Is he able to frolic, run and play? Am I offering him enough variety on his walks?
- ☐ Am I challenging this clever animal enough intellectually? Does he enjoy working and want more?

- [ ] Can I, in all honesty, say that my Labrador is happy with me or would he be better off somewhere else?

CHECKLIST: DOG FIRST AID KIT

- ☐ Medium to combat/heal wound infection (I recommend iodine ointment or Bepanthen – call the vet if in doubt)
- ☐ Dressing material suitable for dogs
- ☐ Paw shoes
- ☐ Waterproof plaster
- ☐ Compresses and bandages
- ☐ Thermometer (with disposable covers)
- ☐ Tick tweezers (or similar tool for removing ticks)
- ☐ Torch
- ☐ Optional blood clotting pen
- ☐ Soft muzzle
- ☐ Disposable gloves
- ☐ Tweezers

- Chapter 5 -

SPECIAL CHAPTER: MAKING YOUR OWN DOG FOOD

I personally take great pleasure in treating my dogs to a homemade snack or meal.

On the following pages I will introduce you to my 10 most favourite recipes so that you can really spoil your four-legged friend, knowing that he is going to enjoy them. In addition to being tasty, they include everything your Labrador needs to maintain his health.

Have fun following the recipes!

RECIPE 1: APPLE AND CARROT CRACKERS

Ingredients:
- 1 jar of baby carrot puree (approx. 125g)
- 2 jars of baby apple puree (approx. 125g)
- 200g wholemeal fruit muesli (without sugar, raisins or currents)
- 75g wholemeal flour
- 25g wheat bran
- 50g linseed whole grain
- 2 tbsp. brewer's yeast
- 2 tbsp. organic honey

Preparation:

1. Boil the linseed briefly in a little water until it makes a sticky mass.

2. Mix all the ingredients into the mass, one by one. It may be simpler to blend the muesli into the puree before adding to the linseed mass.

3. Put the mixture into baking moulds. I like to put mine into dog bone-shaped moulds. As an alternative, you could make small balls and lay them onto the baking paper.

4. Bake the crackers at 120°C for about 35-45 minutes.

5. Allow them to cool before you give them to your dog.

With this recipe you are giving your Labrador a real vitamin boost. It is also a reasonable snack at only 300 kcal per 100g.

RECIPE 2: WILD POTATO COOKIES

Ingredients:
- 200g potato flour
- 100g minced game (as an alternative you can use beef or chicken hearts)
- 2 eggs
- 2 tbsp rapeseed oil
- Approx. 50ml water

Preparation:
1. Mix all ingredients together.
2. Roll the mixture to about a finger-width in height and cut out the cookies in any shape you wish.
3. Lay the cookies onto baking paper on a baking tray.
4. Bake at 160°C for approx. 25 minutes.
5. Allow to cool after baking, then they are ready to serve.

RECIPE 3: LUNG WITH RICE

Ingredients:
- 250g beef lung (preferably fresh from the butcher)
- 125g round grain rice
- 1 carrot
- 1 banana
- 1 cored apple
- 1 tbsp olive oil

Preparation:
1. Cut the beef lung into small pieces and boil it together with the rice for about 20 minutes in 250ml water.
2. Cut the carrot, banana and apple into small pieces and place in a mixer. Mix together with the olive oil.
3. Add to the rice and lung.
4. Serve when cool.

RECIPE 4: CHICKEN WITH MILLET AND EGG

Ingredients:
- 200g chicken or turkey breast
- 1 boiled egg
- 150g millet
- 1-5 lettuce leaves
- A little olive oil
- 1 tsp fresh parsley

Preparation:
1. Cook the chicken breast thoroughly in a saucepan of water.
2. In the meantime, brown the millet in a pan with the olive oil. Then add a little water and boil it up.
3. Turn the heat onto the lowest setting and allow the millet to simmer for about 12 minutes. Remove and drain.
4. Chop the egg, parsley and lettuce leaves into a bowl and add them to the drained millet.
5. Cut the cooked and cooled meat into bite-sized pieces and mix together with the millet and other ingredients.
6. Allow to cool before serving.

RECIPE 5: RICE MEATBALLS

Ingredients:
- 150g minced beef
- 1 egg
- 40g carrot
- 40g courgette
- 50g rice
- 1 slice wholemeal bread
- 1 slice toast bread

Preparation:
1. Soak the toast bread in water
2. Shred the carrot and courgette
3. Cut the wholemeal bread into small squares
4. Press the surplus water out of the soaked toast bread
5. Mix all ingredients together into a homogenous mass.
6. Place the mass into a cake tin.
7. Bake at 200°C for 30 minutes.
8. Allow the cake to cook before serving.

RECIPE 6: BEEF MIX

Ingredients:
- 100g beef gullet
- 40g beef spleen
- 40g green beef rumen
- 60g buckwheat
- 1 carrot
- 1/2 cored apple
- 1 tbsp rapeseed oil

Preparation:
1. Cut the gullet into bite-sized pieces and steam at a low temperature.
2. Cut the spleen and rumen into bite-sized pieces but do not steam them.
3. Boil the buckwheat according to the instructions on the packet.
4. Steam the carrot in a bath of water and then puree it.
5. Grate the apple.
6. Mix all the ingredients together with the oil and the healthy beef mix is ready to serve.

RECIPE 7: WILD TURKEY (BARF)

Ingredients:
- 2 turkey necks (preferably fresh from the butcher)
- 40g turkey liver
- 100g turkey goulash
- 40g broccoli
- 1 carrot
- 1 tbsp dried sage
- 1 tbsp rapeseed oil

Preparation:
1. Cut the meat into portions and mix together.
2. Steam the broccoli lightly (raw broccoli can cause flatulence) and cut into small pieces.
3. Grate the carrot
4. Mix the carrot and broccoli and puree them.
5. Fold the sage and oil into the mass.
6. Mix everything together with the meat.

RECIPE 8: ITALIAN TURKEY

Ingredients:
- 300g turkey
- 60g buckwheat noodles
- 1 carrot
- 1 jar of grated beetroot
- 1 tbsp linseed meal
- 1 tbsp rapeseed oil

Preparation:
1. Chop the turkey into rough pieces and steam it gently until cooked.
2. Boil the noodles until soft.
3. Shred the carrot.
4. Mix all ingredients together and allow to cool before serving.

RECIPE 9: DOG ICE-CREAM WITH BANANA AND APPLE

Ingredients:
- 1 banana
- 1 apple
- 1 pack of cottage cheese
- 1 tbsp lactose-free yoghurt

Preparation:
1. Puree the banana and apple (after coring it – you do not need to peel it).
2. Mix the puree with the cottage cheese and yoghurt.
3. Fill small containers with the mass and put them in the freezer.

You can give your dog a real treat in warm weather with this recipe. I chose these two fruits because my dogs love them the most but you can choose any fruits you wish. The ice-cream is meant only to be a treat and should not replace a meal. I always give this to my dogs outside to avoid the mess.

RECIPE 10: DOG ICE-CREAM WITH LIVER SAUSAGE AND OAT FLAKES

Ingredients:
- 1 piece of liver sausage
- 20g oat flakes
- 1 pack cottage cheese
- 1 tbsp lactose-free yoghurt

Preparation:
1. Mix all the ingredients together.
2. Fill small containers with the mass and put them in the freezer.

- Chapter 6 -

CONCLUSION

You've done it! By reading the previous chapters, you have learned a lot about the nutrition and care of your Labrador.

This knowledge should not only help you to give your Labrador the correct nutrition but will ensure that you keep a cool head should your dog get sick. In addition, you have learned how to take care of your Labrador and know that occasional fur brushing is not enough. You know how to examine your dog's eyes and ears, his mouth and paws, his fur and his skin.

You know what you need to watch out for in order to recognise a parasite infestation in good time. In addition, you have learned to understand what is normal for your dog and what you need to have checked by the vet. You have obtained a well-stocked range of care products and a first-aid kit which is suitable for your dog.

You have learned a lot about his nutrition and know what to watch out for when buying pre-prepared foods. You know the advantages and disadvantages of alternative feeding, such as home-cooked foods as well as BARF, vegetarian or vegan foods. You know how much water your dog needs and have learned some simple tricks to motivate him to drink. The recipes you have learned will allow you to treat your dog and make him very happy. My best tip is to give him the ice-cream on very hot days – your Labrador will be unbelievably thankful to you!

You both have my sincerest good wishes and I hope that my tips about sicknesses never have to be used! But if so, I am sure that you will now recognise them early enough.

All the best,

Claudia

BOOK RECOMMENDATION FOR YOU

Get the first volume now and find out how to train your Labrador puppy.

Labrador Training – Dog Training for your Labrador puppy

The training of dogs is often...
- »... confused with classical dog training drills.
- »... only considered necessary for demanding dogs.
- »... mocked by other dog owners.
- »... replaced by anti-authoritarian methods.
- »... considered too difficult to achieve without experience.

What constitutes dog training and what is it good for? And how can you and your Labrador profit from it without having any experience?

The most important thing is to understand how a dog sees his world, what is "normal" for him and how you can use this to your advantage. In addition, the characteristics of each breed are significant when you get beyond the basic training phase. Your Labrador will show characterristics which are different to those of a Pug, for example, and this is predominantly what you need to consider during training.

Read about background information, read experience reports and obtain step-by-step instructions and secret tips which are tailor-made for your Labrador

Get the second volume now and find out how to train your grown-up Labrador!

Labrador Training Vol 2 – Dog Training for your grown-up Labrador

Dog training is often ...
»... confused with classic basic training of puppies
»... considered only suitable for particularly gifted dogs
»... considered too difficult to achieve without experience
»... replaced by anti-authoritarian methods.
»... considered too difficult to achieve without experience.

What constitutes dog training and what is it good for? And how can you and your Labrador profit from it without having any experience?

Do you sometimes have the feeling that your dog has too much energy and does not feel fully stimulated, no matter how often you walk with him? Then dog training is the right thing for you. The simple but very effective methods of physical and mental training that you will read about in this guide will help you to stimulate your Labrador, in an appropriate way for his species, while at the same time having fun.

Read about background information, read experience reports and obtain step-by-step instructions and secret tips which are tailor-made for your Labrador

DID YOU ENJOY MY BOOK?

Now you have read my book, you know how to care for your Labrador correctly and how to avoid or deal with possible ailments which may affect him. This is why I am asking you now for a small favour. Customer reviews are an important part of every product offered by Amazon. It is the first thing that customers look at and, more often than not, is the main reason whether or not they decide to buy the product. Considering the endless number of products available at Amazon, this factor is becoming increasingly important.

If you liked my book, I would be more than grateful if you could leave your review by Amazon. How do you do that? Just click on the "Write a customer review"-button (as shown below), which you find on the Amazon product page of my book or your orders site:

Review this product

Share your thoughts with other customers

> Write a customer review

Just write a short review as to whether you particularly liked my book or if there is something I can improve on. It will not take more than 2 minutes, honestly!

Be assured, I will read every review personally. It will help me a lot to improve my books and to tailor them to your wishes.

For this I say to you:

Thank you very much!

Yours
Claudia

SPACE FOR YOUR NOTES

REFERENCES

Winkler, Sabine: So lernt mein Hund: Der Schlüssel für die erfolgreiche Erziehung und Ausbildung. 3rd edition. Stuttgart: Kosmos Verlag

Möller, Anja; Braun, Astrid: Labrador Retriever: Auswahl, Haltung, Erziehung, Beschäftigung. 1st edition. Stuttgart: Kosmos Verlag 2016

Schlegel-Kofler, Katharina: Sportskanone mit Familiensinn. 4th edition. München: GRÄFE UND UNZER Verlag 2016

Rütter, Martin; Buisman, Andrea: Hundetraining mit Martin Rütter. 2nd edition. Stuttgart: Kosmos Verlag 2014

Fichtlmeier, Anton: Suchen und Apportieren: Denksport für Hunde. 1st edition. Stuttgart: Kosmos Verlag 2015

Schlegl-Kofler, Katharina: Apportieren: Das einzigartige Step-by-Step-Programm. 1st edition. München: Gräfe und Unzer Verlag 2018

Rütter, Martin; Buismann, Andrea: Hunde beschäftigen mit Martin Rütter: Spiele für jedes Mensch-Hund-Team. 1st edition. Stuttgart: Kosmos Verlag 2016

Theby, Viviane; Hares, Michaela: Das große Schnüffelbuch: Nasenspiele für Hunde (Das besondere Hundebuch). 2nd edition. Nerdlen/Daun: Kynos Verlag 2011

Schmidt-Röger, Heike: Das grosse Praxishandbuch. 6th edition. München: Gräfe und Unzer Verlag 2013

Laukner, Anna: Hunde pflegen: Einfach – richtig – schön. 1st edition. Stuttgart: Eugen Ulmer Verlag 2009

Kohtz-Walkemeyer, Marianne: BARF für Hunde: Den besten Freund gesund ernähren. 1st edition. München Gräfer und Unzer Verlag 2014

Dr. Hartmann, Michael: Patient Hund: Krankheiten vorbeugen, erkennen, behandeln. 1st edition. Reutlingen: Oertel & Spörer Verlag 2015

Dr. med. vet. Bucksch, Martin: Gesunde Ernährung für Hunde: Fertigfutter oder selbstgemacht – gesundes

Futter für jeden Hund. 1st edition. Stuttgart: Kosmos Verlag 2017

Zentek, Jürgen: Hunde richtig füttern. 3rd edition. Stuttgart: Eugen Ulmer Verlag 2012

DISCLAIMER

©2021, Claudia Kaiser

1st Edition

All rights reserved. Reprinting, of all or part of this book, is not permitted. No part of this book may be reproduced or copied in any form or by any means without written permission from the author or publisher. Publisher: GbR, Martin Seidel und Corinna Krupp, Bachstraße 37, 53498 Bad Breisig, Germany, email: info@expertengruppeverlag.de, Cover photo: www.depositphoto.com. The information provided within this book is for general information purposes only. It does not represent any recommendation or application of the methods mentioned within. The information in this book does not purport to imply or guarantee its completeness, accuracy, or topicality. This book in no way replaces the competent recommendations of, or care given by, a dog school. The author and publisher do not assume and hereby disclaims any liability for damages or disruption caused by the use of the information given herein.

Printed in Great Britain
by Amazon

A Real Mate

THE MOVING STORY
OF NGUYEN VAN TE
AND JIM ELLIS

Geoff Sims

an ABC BOOK

To all people who have lost hope

Published by ABC Enterprises for the
AUSTRALIAN BROADCASTING CORPORATION
20 Atchison Street (Box 8888) Crows Nest NSW 2065

Copyright © Geoff Sims 1991

First published 1991

All rights reserved. No part of this publication
may be reproduced, stored in a retrieval system or
transmitted in any form or by any means
electronic, mechanical, photocopying, recording or
otherwise, without the prior written permission of
The Australian Broadcasting Corporation

National Library of Australia
Cataloguing-in-Publication entry
Sims, Geoff, 1948–
  A real mate.

  ISBN 0 7333 0091 X.

  1. Nguyen Van Te. 2. Ellis, Jim, Major. 3. Vietnamese
  Conflict, 1961–1975 — Refugees — Biography. 4.
  Refugees — Vietnam — Biography. 5. Refugees — Australia
  — Biography. I. Title.

959.7043092

Designed by Kathleen Phelps
Set in 11/12 pt Chelmsford by Midland Typesetters, Maryborough, Victoria
Printed and bound in Australia by The Book Printer, Maryborough, Victoria
4-1695

Contents

	Acknowledgments	iv
	Map of Hong Kong	v
	Pronunciation Guide	vi
1	VBPs	1
2	Sunk	17
3	The Jolly Cop	36
4	Nouc Mam	56
5	Intelligence	68
6	The Cup	86
7	Chicken Wings	100
8	For Freedom	116
9	The Voyage	133
10	Home Again	150
11	Reunion	167
	Postscript	185

Acknowledgments

People named in this book for their help and humanity will expect no special acknowledgment. Nor will many others not named, and some not even mentioned. The outcome of this story is their thanks, but on behalf of Nguyen Van Te and his family, I thank them deeply anyway.

ABC Television News and Current Affairs and ABC Books deserve recognition for allowing me to persist with a story that has involved becoming part of it—not just reporting it.

I also thank the Office of Multicultural Affairs in Canberra for its support in writing this book, and Canon Australia for the use of the PC on which I wrote it.

To my good friends Te and Jim, your families and to my own family, I thank you all for your patience and encouragement.

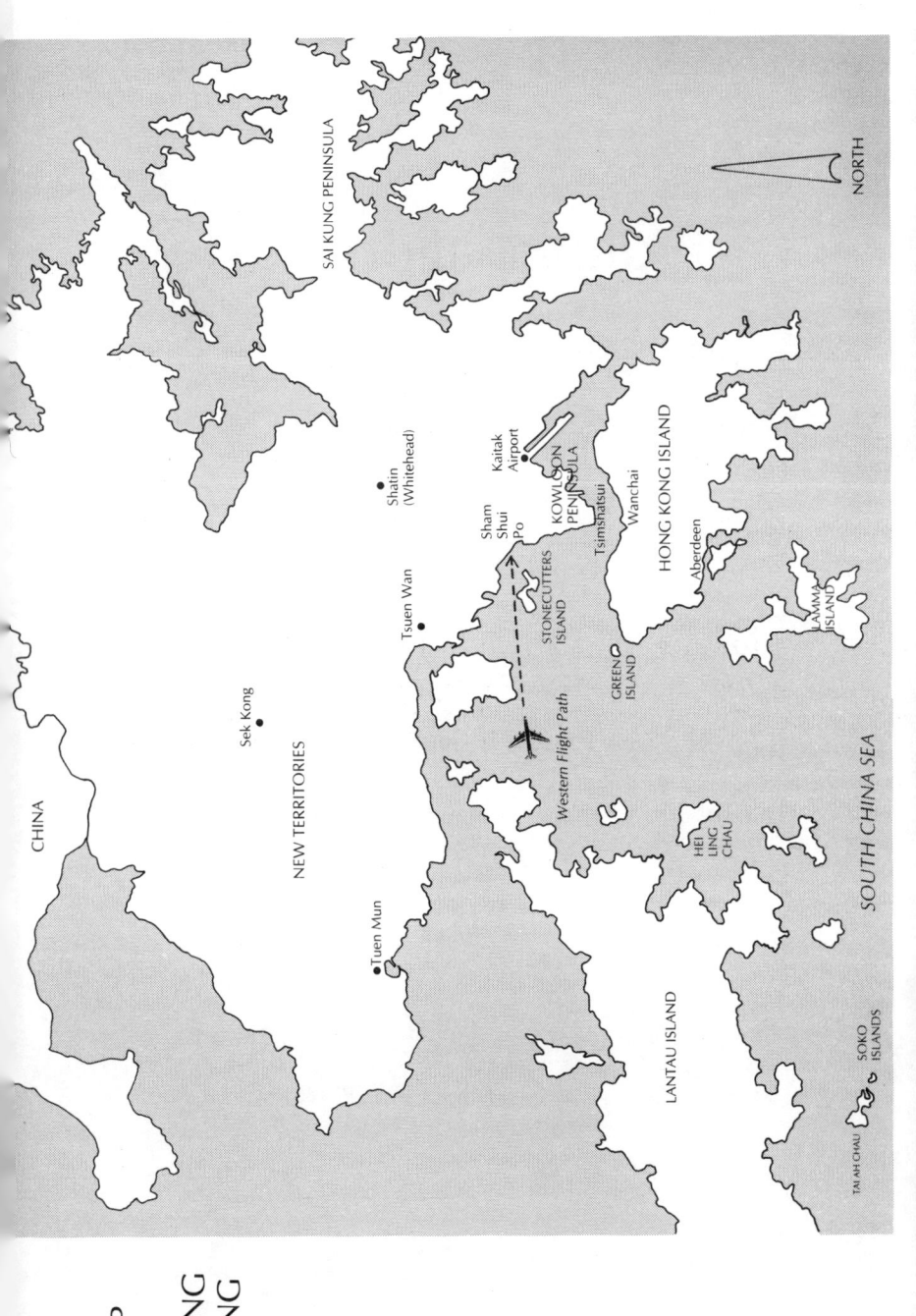

Pronunciation Guide

Nguyen Van Te　　　NGWIN VUN TAY ('ng' as in song)

His wife

Thi Tho　　　TEE TOH

Their children

Vuong　　　VWOONG

Thuy Vy　　　TWEE VEE

Thu Thao　　　TOOH TOW ('ow' as in 'now')

Duy Huy　　　DWEE HEE

Duy Khang　　　DWEE KAHNG

His wife's sister

Mai Phuong　　　MIGH FWOONG

1
VBPs

The tiny island was swarming with people. Six thousand of them, ant-like figures from this distance, had overrun it in only two days.

Tai Ah Chau was only a few hundred metres from end to end. Until now it had been populated by one elderly Cantonese couple who'd fled the teeming masses of Hong Kong proper to live out the remainder of their lives on their little island paradise.

The transformation from paradise to something approaching an oriental kingdom of hell had been rapid and dramatic. The crumbling two-storey brick house just back from the small dockside had given them a magnificent view of the beach and across the bay, across the pontoons supporting the nets for their fish farms. Now each pontoon was permanently guarded by a barking chow dog, pacing up and down, frustrated by its restricted movement, its isolation, and ready to drive off anyone set on a free fish dinner.

In their attempt at self-sufficiency, the old Cantonese couple had brought six dairy cows to the island and had allowed them to wander about, grazing in safety. There had been no need for fences. The cattle could never be far away.

Now there were only two cows left. The other four cows had been chased and cornered among rocks, then beaten and stabbed to death with sharpened sticks and knives lashed to boat poles.

After weeks at sea, many of these people were desperate. They had families to feed, and would do it which ever way they could.

We sped toward the beach on the inflatable boat. The ants on the sand, among the rocks and trees, became people—survivors, it seemed, washed ashore as if the rest of civilisation had perished.

Pieces of cloth, the rags they had worn or sheltered under from the blazing sun all those weeks at sea, were draped between branches, giving shade or drying after a saltwater bath.

Among the rocks there were small fires. People were cooking.

There was less swarming now. Most people sat in groups, lifeless. We were still too far off to see their expressions.

The young police inspector driving the inflatable eased back the throttle so he could guide the craft through ten or more wooden wrecks at anchor a couple of hundred metres off the beach. Each looked about to sink. None was painted. They were made of bare wood, bleached by the salt and the sun, broken and rotting, some with boards missing only a few centimetres above the water line, each one overcrowded with men, women and children and many with babies on their mothers' breasts.

The people squatted among makeshift awnings, bodies pressed shoulder to shoulder, staring at these strange white people with the television equipment.

One young woman was in the water, holding on to the anchor line. She may have been washing, cooling off or just trying to get some space. She watched without movement or expression as we passed, as if we were aliens, as well we might have been.

Beneath a flapping canopy on another boat a woman squatted with her head over a chipped enamel basin. Others around her paid no attention to her, nor she to them, and the passing white people may not have existed. She washed and combed the lather through her long black hair and the action seemed so incongruous. Here was vanity in the midst of abject hopelessness. Or was she simply attending to personal hygiene and self-respect?

Some children called out "Coca Cola" to us. A nose or two ran but the children appeared well enough, smiling and agile. One straddled a jib and called out "American!" It could have meant he thought we were American or that's where he believed he was headed.

Men perched on tillers, watching us go. One tended a smoking brazier. Another was making for the beach, swimming with one arm, holding a big plastic water bottle with the other.

The young English police inspector watched in silence.

"Why aren't these people ashore?" I asked him.

"Policy," he said. "We don't let them land unless their boats are actually sinking. There's enough of them on the island already. Too many, in fact, way too many."

"But all these boats look as if they *are* sinking," I said.

"No, these ones are okay. They're safe enough inshore. Look over there," he said, pointing toward the dockside near the old Cantonese couple's house. Wreck after wreck scarred the beach, some wooden, some steel, the hulks half-buried in the sand. "How those ones ever made it from Vietnam is beyond me."

A big steel barge was anchored off the beach, lifting wrecks out of the water with a crane and dropping them into its open hold, to be taken away and burnt.

We wove our way through the anchored boats toward the dock. There were probably 500 people watching us go, 500 wretched souls within a stone's throw of land and they were not allowed to set foot on it.

"They'll be processed eventually," said the police inspector. "Right now we've got our hands full on the island."

Even before we landed we could hear orders being shouted in Cantonese at people who didn't understand a word of it. The neatly pressed khaki uniforms of the Cantonese men and women of the Royal Hong Kong Police stood out among the rags that clad the boat people squatting on the landing. Some of the police waved batons as they shouted at two men here, two men there, to get them in line for their rations. Crates of canned pilchards were stacked on the landing. There were biscuits, too—even condensed milk occasionally. Wiry little Vietnamese men scurried to fetch them, urged on more by the wave of the batons than the incomprehensible orders, and then melted back into the vegetation that led to the beaches.

It was near midday and the heat and humidity were oppressive. This was the typhoon season when Hong Kong is best avoided. A young mother slumped against a wall, weak and exhausted, her baby falling off the breast.

A generator competed with the din of a million unseen insects, their cacophony rising and falling as the fierce sun beat down then disappeared for a moment behind a cloud.

Trying to make himself heard above all of this, a cheery Cantonese policeman tried to entertain the masses of boat people squatting as they waited for their rations. He would hold up his fingers and count them off in Cantonese, encouraging the people to mimic him. "Yut, yee, sam, sey," he would say for "one, two, three, four", then point to his eyes, his nose, his boots and say the Cantonese words for them. With a smile he would point at his belly and say, "ho sek fan", which meant "good food", and gesture the next to take his rations.

The island had no water supply. The Royal Navy was bringing in tanks and supplying them, but the water was limited and under constant guard.

Another white police inspector in his late twenties came over. "Patrick Hodson," he said. "Welcome to paradise."

The buzz of a high-powered outboard motor rose above the insects, the generator and the Cantonese lessons. Beyond the barge lifting wrecks into its hold, one of the police inflatables was heading off a heavily laden craft that had weighed anchor and was trying to make a run for the beach.

"You've got to have eyes in the back of your head," Inspector Hodson said. "The poor buggers are getting pretty desperate out there but they'll just have to wait. You can see for yourself what it's like here. The trouble is, day or night, nothing's safe. I won't even let my officers move anywhere on their own. It's just too bloody dangerous."

Another police craft had drawn alongside the wharf and about twenty boat people were climbing the broken steps to the landing.

"They've just been intercepted," said Hodson. "They're luckier than most. Their boat was sinking so they've been allowed to land."

Most appeared to be under 30 years old. There were a few children. All were ragged. Most had slivers of sticking plaster on their temples in the belief that it prevented or cured the headaches that accompanied seasickness.

"Do any of the boat people speak English?" I asked the inspector.

"Only one," he said. "They nearly all come from North Vietnam and they've never had any contact with English.

Hardly any of them speak Cantonese either. It's a real problem."

Inspector Hodson called over one of the Cantonese officers, a chubby chap with a scowl that he seemed to effect to give him some authority. "See if you can find the VBP who speaks English, will you?"

The officer scowled and repeated "English VBP" before waddling up the narrow path between two big boulders in the direction of the noise from the generator. There were several other police, men and women, coming and going along the path.

"VBP?" I asked.

"Vietnamese boat person. It's a bit of a mouthful but we can't call them refugees because they're illegal immigrants. This VBP, the one who speaks English, is a nice little bloke. Only been here a few days. Don't know what we'd do without him. His English is a bit rusty but not bad all the same. Says he used to be an interpreter for the Americans and Australians during the Vietnam war. Might be of interest to you."

Inspector Hodson's shirt was wet with sweat and his face glistened. I could feel the trickles of sweat down my own face and I felt clammy all over. The typhoon season was quite a change from the winter I had left behind in Sydney, but the British police officer seemed to be doing no better.

"A bit hotter than the old country?" I teased.

"Not really," he said.

"Sure. The typhoon season is hell in the Home Counties."

"The Home Counties are not home to me. I was born in Kenya and grew up there. Lived there longer than I did in the UK."

Touché.

The scowling officer was coming down the path with a small Vietnamese man, grimy but less ragged than most of the VBPs.

"Ah," said Inspector Hodson. "Mr Te, this gentleman is from the Australian Broadcasting Corporation. You know some Australians, don't you? Or at least you used to know some. Mr Sims has come to Tai Ah Chau to make a report for Australian television. Would you mind helping him?"

The little man stepped forward, limping on his right leg. His face broadened into a huge open smile and he put out his hand. "I am honoured to help Australian," he said as we shook hands. "I work as interpreter for Australian officers during war. Very good men. Please. My English not so good now. Long time not speak English. But happy to help Australian. Honoured to help Australian."

It was, of course, a huge bonus for an Australian reporter. Not only had I been presented with an English-speaking person, but the only one among the 6000 boat people on the island, and he actually had a connection with Australia. Or so he said. He was, in a selfish journalistic sense, a godsend. And in me he saw an unlikely angel of mercy.

Nguyen Van Te was on his way to freedom and neither of us knew it.

We followed the path that led past the tumbledown building the police were using as their island base. It was here that the generator was drumming away, the noise being carried across a little bay formed by two low, rocky headlands. The beach was strewn with wrecks and wreckage. A rusted steel hulk about 20 metres long was firmly embedded. Wooden craft, beached at high water, had sunk into the sand with successive tidefalls. The skeletal frames of some others lay exposed, like the ribs of stranded whales long decomposed.

People were still living on many of the craft. There was no other shelter. The British Army had supplied tents but these had not been erected. Canopies were stretched across any rigging that had survived. Washing lines stretched from stem to stern. A man was cooking something over a fire in an old can on the after deck of one boat.

A little further up the beach, just beyond the high water mark, wooden hulls had been turned over and propped up to provide shelter. Wasted people huddled underneath them in the shade. There was little movement.

Nguyen Van Te flapped along the sand beside me, his right foot at 45 degrees to his left, the legacy, I was later to find out, of a bout of polio. He was wearing drill shirt and trousers and a pair of scuffs, but a complete set of clothes nevertheless and they were a lot less ragged than most of the others had.

"That my boat there," he said with obvious pride, pointing to the shell of an open wooden boat at the far end of the beach. It was barely 6 metres long. The keel was well into the sand, the topsides of the planking only a few centimetres above the water line, and it was a reasonable guess that she'd taken water many times.

On this wreck Nguyen Van Te and fifteen others had left Vietnam near the China border on 14 April of this year, 1989, and had spent the next two months making their way along the coast of China until they were intercepted by police in Hong Kong waters.

Among those fifteen people were three of Te's five children—his son, Vuong, aged 16, and daughters, Thuy Vy, aged 13, and Thu Thao who'd celebrated her eighth birthday on board the boat four days before they arrived in Hong Kong. Te's sister-in-law, Mai Phuong, was also on board, deputising for her sister, Te's wife, who had stayed behind in Vietnam to look after the two younger boys, aged four and two. The younger one had polio and was too sick to travel.

Te and his boatload were picked up by the Hong Kong police at 4.30 p.m. on 15 June 1989. In one of many coincidences that punctuate this story, the timing of his arrival meant that his plight would gain attention during a broadcast the following week—Refugee Week.

Nguyen Van Te leaned against the side of the boat and the broad smile gave way to a worried frown. His voice dropped to a whisper, not that any other Vietnamese on Tai Ah Chau could understand English, even if any happened to be within earshot.

"Life very bad in Vietnam," he said. "I worry for the security for my family and myself. Maybe the government find out my circumstances during the war. Maybe they take me away."

"Away?" I asked.

"Re-education. Sometimes they take people away and the people never come back."

"When did you decide to escape?"

"30 April 1975—the day the communists took over Saigon. That day we try to get to American compound in Saigon to get helicopter lift to aircraft carrier leaving Saigon. Too many people."

"That was fourteen years ago. Why suddenly make a run for it now? They've left you alone all this time, haven't they?"

"Yes, but situation very bad now. People still disappear."

"But why decide to leave now with your wife and two young boys left behind?"

"Decision not just now. We try to escape from Vietnam many times. Sometimes my wife and me before we have children, many times since then. Never we succeed."

Still in a whisper, but now with that big smile replacing the frown, Te added, "When I find new life in freedom country, then my wife and two little ones come for family reunification."

There were no "ifs" about it. It was "when". There were more than 50,000 other VBPs ahead of him in Hong Kong. Many had been there for years. The chances of ever being "screened in" as a refugee were negligible. Te, his three children and his sister-in-law were among the last to arrive in Hong Kong and therefore the most likely to be forced to board an aircraft taking them back to Vietnam. This was what the Hong Kong government was threatening to do. "Forced repatriation" was to become the official policy.

And yet here was the diminutive Mr Nguyen Van Te convinced that he and his family were already on the way to a "freedom country".

"What do you hope to do?" I asked him. "Where do you want to go?"

"I think," he said, "the best, I want to go to Australia—refugee—because I know very well Australian and the Australian know well me. My document already in the Migration Department in Australia and also in the Australian Embassy in Hanoi."

"Do you think you qualify as a refugee?" I asked.

"Ah, yes," said Te confidently, then added, in case he'd sounded too cocky, "I don't know. That's as your delegation decides."

At the end of the interview he said, "I think we just here temporarily. I accept it temporarily, not for long time. It is very hard for us but I accept that. Not very long, I think, I and my family will be transferred to other place, and maybe the Australians will collect me as a refugee."

His face broadened into the most open, irresistible smile, and it was with that part of the interview and that smile I ended the report that was broadcast in Australia.

Before we left Nguyen Van Te on the beach at Tai Ah Chau he told me of an Australian army major he had allegedly worked for during the war. In the sand he wrote the name, "Maj. E.J. Ellis".

"My old boss," Te said. "Very good man. I not see him since sixteen years ago. Sometimes I got letters from him in Australia, but not since many years ago. I want contact him, but maybe he pass away already."

We were short of time and my cameraman, David Brill, and soundman, Chang Chun-yuen, had gone off through the wrecks to get more shots of the wretched boat people huddled under their upturned hulls.

I agonised over what this man that I had only just met had told me.

His writing the Australian officer's name in the sand had been very moving. It would also make compelling television—a castaway among the damned, appealing to one man from another country, another culture, a man he hadn't seen for sixteen years.

But was it just a ploy? If I were in this VBP's position I'd be prepared to try anything, to come up with the name of anybody from the past, any name that might lead to help. Surely it wouldn't be too difficult to name some foreign officer from all those years ago and make a convincing appeal.

Even if this Major Ellis existed, so what if his former interpreter was now stranded in Hong Kong? What could this Australian officer from a war not favourably remembered do to help? And what an enormous burden to place on the shoulders of a man I had never met. Any compassionate person might want to help, but what could he do except perhaps build up impossible expectations? There were 50,000 other VBPs ahead of Nguyen Van Te, and nobody jumps queues like that.

The sequence of Te's writing the name in the sand was never recorded. When the report was broadcast, the name of this Major E.J. Ellis, living or dead, was not mentioned. What I didn't know was that a glimpse of this Vietnamese man known as Te would not impose a burden on another man. It would lift one.

My hotel room faced west down Hong Kong harbour. The island of Tai Ah Chau was way out of view but I could see Green Island and Stonecutters Island where there were more boat people in detention, and I could see the old Star Ferries moored way down the western end of the harbour, midway between Hong Kong Island and the mainland.

The disused ferries, once used to carry passengers between Hong Kong Island and Tsimshatsui on the tip of the Kowloon peninsula, were home now to a couple of thousand boat people until more camps could be set up in the New Territories toward the China border. Boat people, months after setting out from Vietnam, were still afloat in heat and squalor, within sight of this bustling city and unable to set foot on land—even in a concentration camp.

I had not been sent to Hong Kong to cover the boat people. That had been my idea after I'd arrived. Various world powers and agencies were gathering in Geneva to discuss the plight of the Vietnamese boat people in Hong Kong and the colonial government's proposal for forcible repatriation.

I had been sent to Hong Kong to cover reaction to the upheavals in China and the crushing of the pro-democracy movement with the tanks in Tienanmen Square in Beijing.

My hotel room had become a kind of transit camp in itself. ABC correspondents and camera crews were passing through, picking up and dumping off gear as they came and went to Beijing, Shanghai, Guangzhou. Equipment was stacked down one wall, along the sofa and across the desk. Laundry bags lined another wall, waiting for their owners to collect them on the next shuttle.

I had inherited the room from John Mills, the ABC's Singapore correspondent, who'd stayed here on his way out of Beijing. I now passed it on to Max Uechtritz, taking some R and R in Hong Kong before heading back to Sydney from Beijing.

I packed the tapes we'd recorded on Tai Ah Chau and went down to the lobby with David Brill and Chang Chun-yuen. They had been a terrific crew. All three of us had met in Hong Kong for the first time. David, working freelance at the time, had turned up in Hong Kong "on spec" and was now staying on. Chun was part of one of the ABC's Singapore-based crews and he was going home, called up for a national service military exercise.

We said our goodbyes and I grabbed a taxi to Kaitak Airport, leaving the failed revolution in China and the marooned boat people in Hong Kong behind me.

It was only really in Sydney when I was going through the tapes that the magnitude of the problem of the boat people hit me, a delayed reaction that comes when you experience some great human tragedy which overwhelms you at the time but fails to make its full impact until you step outside the unreality of it all. You plug on, doing a job of work, neither unaware nor insensitive to the suffering of your fellow human beings but operating as if by remote control, trying to capture it as you see it and hear it and feel it before the moment is lost. You walk into people's lives and out again, entering and exiting the domain of the cursed, an intruder from the other side. You probably had a few beers and a laugh in your own world the previous night; you go, get the job done, and then conveniently step outside the wall of hopelessness that separates you from the damned, and you go back to a comfortable hotel to wash down the experience with a few beers and go to sleep in a fresh bed, wondering how you're going to pull the report together and wishing you'd done this and that, but scarcely dwelling on what those poor bastards are going through or what will happen to them.

The reaction comes later.

It had happened to me many times before, most vividly after the Ethiopian famine in 1984. People had died there, in front of the camera, young and old alike. Sad, dreamy big eyes, looking out of a child's face in a skull held limply to a body that was just a bag of bones, would half close, reopen, then close down forever, as if that last attempt to keep them open had sapped the final reserve of energy, and another life was gone in just the blink of an eyelid.

I watched the never-ending funeral processions there in Ethiopia, the bodies bundled in rag and borne aloft by those who were only a stumble from following them. In the south of the country I watched frail old herdspeople forgoing any food in order for the younger generations to survive this awful famine.

It was disturbing to witness these things, but the full impact was to follow. When the privileged intruder had vanished, stepping into and out of this world of death and dying, the effect was suddenly felt. The images, the moans and pathetic coughs in the silence, the filth in the barren sand and soil, the rats and insects that thrived, the stench, the overpowering combination of sight and sound and smell was numbing to experience and devastating to recall.

I remember taking one story back to the comfort and safety of London and simply breaking down in sobs as I viewed the tapes. Maybe it is that such large-scale human tragedy is incomprehensible without contrast. Transposed back into familiar and secure territory, surrounded by one's own happy and healthy children, the memory becomes more vivid than the experience.

Back in Sydney on 21 June 1989, the same thing was happening. The Vietnamese boat people had not died before the camera but the images of despair were haunting. There were the faces against the meshed windows, children behind barbed wire, the people nobody wanted or knew what to do with. Whatever the problems were in Vietnam, whatever the illusions under which its citizens were fleeing in hope to Hong Kong, the jailing of men, women and children was no solution.

Many more who were nobodies were incarcerated in Thailand, and VBPs were washing up in Malaysia, Indonesia, the Philippines, South Korea, Macau and Singapore. There were also the boat people from Cambodia, who'd survived the Indochinese war and the most awful postwar period, and those from Laos.

In June of 1989, according to the United Nations High Commissioner for Refugees, there were close on 200,000 Indochinese boat people held in countries that didn't want them. Among them was that little man with the deformed leg over on the Hong Kong island of Tai Ah Chau.

Nguyen Van Te had given me a letter addressed to a niece in Marrickville in Sydney and asked me to post it. I told my wife and children about him and said I would deliver the letter personally. I also told them I would see if the army had any record of a Major E.J. Ellis.

The report on the boat people on the island of Tai Ah Chau was broadcast throughout Australia on ABC TV's "7. 30 Report" on the night of Thursday, 22 June. The piece ran five minutes and 52 seconds. Mr Nguyen Van Te appeared for 23 seconds, and spoke for just 15 seconds at the end of the item.

The following morning I paced around the house, trying to unwind from a busy fortnight away from home. Those boat people were everywhere, those poor bloody wretches staring at me from behind the wire wherever I turned.

It had been just a fortnight away and I was taking a day off to pace around my suburban plot, comfortable and secure in a country in which I simply happened to be born. The boat people happened to have been born in another— and they weren't taking a day off. To them, one day was much the same as another, and they paced, if at all, with barbed wire separating them from the world, or on disused ferries going nowhere, on remote islands, or—if they were still on their boats—unable to do any pacing at all.

I would drive to Marrickville later in the day, I decided, and take the letter from the man on Tai Ah Chau to his niece.

The chill winter morning gave way to a warm day and I sat in the garden trying to read a newspaper. The children were at school and my wife was running her small kindergarten in the bedsit flat up the backyard when one of the "7.30 Report" producers rang.

"Mark here. That Vietnamese bloke in the piece last night, the bloke who reckoned he used to work for the Australian Army . . . "

"Yes?"

"You wouldn't have an address for him in Hong Kong where someone could write to him, I suppose? A letter would never find him, would it?"

"Who wants to write to him?"

"Some ex-army officer, a lieutenant-colonel, retired. He phoned last night after he saw the tail end of the piece. Left a message on the answer-phone saying he recognised his old interpreter. He asked for an address to write to— even suggested he would try to sponsor the Vietnamese bloke. Sounded very excited."

"What's his name?" I asked.

"Ah, it's here on the phone log somewhere . . . " he said, "hang on a minute."

If it was a minute or an hour I couldn't say. It seemed

to take forever—I could hear the paper rustling and the general hubbub of the office and I could hear my own heart beating.

"There was a number for him down at Bungendore, near Canberra . . . here it is. His name is Lieutenant-Colonel Jim Ellis."

I sprinted up the rough stone steps and burst into Jayne's kindergarten, shouting and blubbering. "Fantastic news!" I said. "The army officer that Vietnamese boat person told me about saw the piece on the box last night and recognised him. He phoned up and is even prepared to sponsor him!"

Jayne and the six kindergarten kids were preparing to cook some biscuits in the shape of piggies that they'd stamped out of pastry. Flour covered most of them, teacher included, from head to foot. I grabbed Jayne and hugged her and then held her at arm's length and we laughed at each other, both now covered in flour. Six little faces looked up at us, probably wondering what strange things grown-ups were.

"I must go down to the house and phone this old bloke," I said and bounded out of the kindergarten, down the stone steps three at a time.

I dialled the number at Bungendore and waited. And waited. There was no answer. There was no answer again when I phoned that night.

For the next ten days I phoned, every day and every night, and the calls remained unanswered.

The lieutenant-colonel, I began to fear, had got cold feet. Moved by the sight of some poor underling from a war fought and forgotten nearly a generation ago, the retired officer had then realised in the cold light of the following morning that sponsoring a migrant would carry a huge financial burden, but, moreover, a commitment he would rather not take into his retirement.

The Vietnamese interpreter had been a decent chap, but in the end he'd backed the wrong side and that was *his* problem.

Vietnamese faces showed up more and more commonly as I approached Marrickville, one of several Sydney suburbs that had absorbed the displaced Vietnamese.

The house on Livingstone Road where Te's niece supposedly lived showed no sign of life and the letter he'd given me in Hong Kong would have to remain undelivered. I banged on the door again and this time I could hear feet shuffling inside. A thin old Vietnamese woman opened the door and said something I couldn't understand.

"I have a letter," I said, "from a man called Mr Nguyen Van Te. He gave it to me in Hong Kong and asked me to post it to this address. It's for Miss Nguyen Thi Hu'ong."

It was obvious the old woman didn't understand a word of it, so I showed her the envelope. She held it up to the light, brought it toward her face then held it away, apparently unable to decipher the writing. She jabbered something at me with a mouthful of gold teeth and shuffled back inside.

I waited on the verandah until a young man came around the side of the house and I showed him the letter. He led me back down the driveway at the side of the house and into the kitchen where several people were preparing lunch. The young man called a woman over. She appeared to be about 30 years old and I guessed she'd spent nearly all of them in Vietnam because her English was nonexistent, but it appeared she was the niece. I explained to the young man how I'd met Te on Tai Ah Chau and he translated it, or at least spoke in Vietnamese to the one I presumed was the niece. Whether any of the original message survived the translation was doubtful, but I assured them Te was well and I was hoping we might be able to help him.

On the way back to the office I felt quite despondent. I wasn't even sure the woman who'd taken the letter was Te's niece, my colonel had vanished, and the high hopes of helping that little man in Hong Kong were leading nowhere.

On the evening of Monday, 3 July, I tried phoning Bungendore as I had done for the previous ten days and I waited for the answer that had never come.

The phone rang several times. The receiver was lifted and a voice said, "This is Jim Ellis."

"At last," I said, "I was beginning to think you didn't exist. Geoff Sims from the '7.30 Report'. You phoned the week before last."

"Yes," he said, "my old friend Te. I couldn't believe my eyes when I saw him. I thought he was dead. It's just wonderful to find out after all these years that he's alive."

Ellis paused and went on, "I'm sorry you haven't been able to get hold of me. We had to go to Queensland the day after we saw your program. We only got back last night."

There was no question of his having got cold feet. The sincerity in his voice was absolutely convincing.

"He's one of us," he said, "not just another boat person. I did two tours of duty in Vietnam and he worked with me both times. I couldn't have done without him. I've got to get him out."

"He mentioned you," I said. "He even wrote your name in the sand beside his boat. I didn't use it in the report because I didn't want to put this Major Ellis on the spot."

Ellis laughed for the first time. "It was a million-to-one chance that I saw him at all. His face appeared on the screen and was gone in a flash. Gosh, his eyes will be like saucers when he finds out. I've got to let him know I'll push as hard as I can to help him. Have you got an address for him?"

"He's on a remote island," I said. "There's nothing there, not even water, and certainly no postal service. But I made some pretty good contacts in Hong Kong and I reckon we can find him. Getting him out will be another matter. But let me come down and show you the whole report and we can talk about it."

"That would be great," he said.

"What puzzles me a little," I said, "is that he was just an interpreter, wasn't he?"

Ellis paused. "Te was more than an interpreter. I learnt Vietnamese in Australia and spoke it fluently before I went over there. Te was more like my right hand. We worked together, just the two of us. I was in Intelligence. I couldn't have done without him."

Ellis paused again before giving an Australian's absolute approval. "He's a real mate."

2
Sunk

Lake George stretched out to the right as an almost endless field. The fences ran down from the main road to cut the lake into paddocks when it was dry, as it was when we drove down to Bungendore. There was water way out there and the fences were eventually inundated, but for the most part the lake was lake in name only.

It was said that Lake George filled not when there had been heavy rains in the catchment but when the water drained away from another continent, and, conversely, when Lake George was dry it had emptied by some subterranean mystery into another part of the world. If the theory held true, today there may have been water aplenty in Ethiopia or Bangladesh.

We drove into and out of Bungendore in the blink of an eye, the little town on the New South Wales side of the border with the Australian Capital Territory. We crossed the stream that cuts off the road every time the word rain is mentioned, and drove up the escarpment that overlooks the lake. The wind was howling from the southwest and it was icy.

A line of mailboxes stood on posts along The Forest Road at the intersection. Four-gallon drums, boxes, some that looked like dog kennels, probably twenty in all, marked the turn-off. We turned to the right, then, a few hundred metres on, the white railing fence and the sign "Y-not" indicated the entrance to the home of Lieutenant-Colonel E.J. Ellis (rtd).

"I don't know what we're letting ourselves in for," I said to the camera crew. "He sounded absolutely straight on the phone, but he may be a crusty old bugger so we'd better be prepared to salute and stand to attention to do the interview, sir."

The house was flat on the ground and just back from the escarpment. The wind blew straight across at the house and there in the driveway was the figure of this old warrior. Lt-Col Jim Ellis was not the conventional retired army officer. He was dressed in bush boots, jeans and and old grey jumper with a floppy collar and no shape. He was there with hand outstretched and he welcomed us into the house and the warmth of the log fire.

Above the fireplace was a lacquer portrait by the Vietnamese artist Ngoc. On each side of the fireplace stood a big brass shell casing, both of them Soviet-made D74 Howitzers. The three items were brought back from Colonel Ellis's second tour in Vietnam. These were the only reminders of a military career that had spanned thirty years and had seen him serve in Malaya, Singapore, Borneo and Hong Kong, apart from Vietnam.

"I've put all that stuff away," he was to tell me later. "I'm not in the army any more. I'm doing now what I did before I was called up. I was a farrier then and I'm a farrier now. I've always loved being around horses and putting shoes on them is about all I want out of life now."

Jim Ellis was neither crusty nor even old. He'd retired from the army six years ago when he was 48. "I'd simply had enough," he explained. "I'd never been ambitious. I'd gone further than I ever really expected to go, and I didn't see much point in sitting in an office, pushing paper across a desk and waiting for another commission. The horses were calling me."

So Jim Ellis, Lt-Col (rtd), was 54: I was 41, a year older than Mr Nguyen Van Te. We were a very unlikely mix. One was a conscript who'd successfully continued a career in the army after his call-up period expired but then retired early; one was a conscript who'd managed to avoid conscription, and one was a civilian who'd been unfit for conscription because of his leg—yet had worked for a foreign power in the civil war in his own country and was now a non-person. The three of us had been drawn together by chance.

Ellis's wife, Glenda, made a pot of tea, clucking about the kitchen, only a little less excited than her husband. Ellis sat down to watch the replay of the report he'd all but missed and his eyes were alight.

There, in big close-up, was the face of Nguyen Van Te saying, " . . . the best, I want to go to Australia—refugee—because I know very well Australian and the Australian know well me . . . maybe the Australians will collect me as a refugee."

It was the first time Ellis had seen the full report. When Te's brief appeal finished with that big smile, Ellis said, "Gosh, that's exactly how he would say it. Poor old chap. That's wonderful. That's great. It means he's alive, and to be in Hong Kong is just tremendous because he's so close to the end of his journey. It's taken him fourteen years to get there."

"He's also in grave danger of being sent back to Vietnam," I said.

"That can't be allowed to happen. I really thought he was dead. No, that can't be allowed to happen."

Jim Ellis explained the odds against seeing the report.

"Most of the day I'm out fixing up horses' feet," he said, "and the only time people can get hold of a farrier is at night. So normally at night when the telephone rings it's for me and I answer, but on this occasion Glenda answered, and at that moment Te came on the screen. I was so excited that I screamed out and jumped up and down and called my wife off the telephone, telling her 'It's Te! It's Te!' She'd never met him of course but she knew Te through me and she came running in and I said, 'It's Te! It's Te!' and she said, 'Well what are you going to do about it?' I rang the ABC in Canberra straight away and they gave me the number at your office."

"How well did you know Te?" I asked.

"I knew him very, very well. We lived together every day of our lives. I speak Vietnamese so I was very involved with him on both my tours of Vietnam. The first time he worked for me in a one-to-one situation, and the second time he worked for me more or less voluntarily to assist me with the terms of technical equipment that I had difficulty with. I was working in Intelligence, and the knowledge that Te had helped me in that way alone would have placed him in great danger subsequently. He had served first of all the government of the Republic of Vietnam—that's the South—but not only that, a foreign government, and the recriminations against him would have been enormous.

"I don't think people in this country would understand, but there is no future in a country like Vietnam for someone with Te's background."

"You know it's virtually impossible for a boat person in Hong Kong to be recognised as a refugee? Most of them are fleeing economic hardship, not persecution, in Vietnam and that doesn't make them refugees. Do you reckon you can make out a special case for Te?"

"Te *is* special. He put himself in grave danger really by just serving the Australian government in Vietnam. If the Hanoi government had found out, they would have sent him off for 're-education', and his family would certainly have been split up. If this is what happened, somehow he must have got them together and managed to keep them together, to keep them alive through fourteen years, and then get them to Hong Kong. And there he is now, looking at the Union Jack all over the place—the flag that's part of the one he served when he served Australia. He would have a vision of freedom. It can't be denied to him."

Ellis showed me a photograph of himself as a major with Te, taken in Vung Tau in 1972. "That's him," he said, "grinning like a Cheshire cat. It's terrific to see he's still smiling after all he's been through, poor old chap."

It was not the first time Jim Ellis had referred to the man fourteen years his junior as that "poor old chap", nor would it be the last.

The young civilian interpreter, Nguyen Van Te, and Major Jim Ellis in Vung Tau soon after Jim began his first tour of duty in July 1970

"I have a few other bits and pieces somewhere but this was the only photo I could turn up for the moment. As I say, I put all that army life behind me. Most people around here don't even know I was in it. They just know me as Jim Ellis the farrier."

He put the photograph away, saying, "I really thought Te was dead. We exchanged letters for a time, but the last time I heard from him was in 1973 when I was back at Puckapunyal. Te wrote to me and enclosed a photo. I wrote back but never got another letter in return. I was sure they'd caught up with him and he'd been shot or had never survived re-education. And now, by a million-to-one chance, I see just a glimpse of him on television. The poor old chap isn't dead. He's a refugee now because he served Australia. He's got to be brought to Australia. He deserves that—he and his family."

We packed up the camera and lighting equipment and Jim Ellis sat there, eyes bright and still fixed on the place where he'd seen Te's face appear on the television monitor.

We sat down together to share a bowl of hot broth and Glenda said, "Jim ought to be in bed. He only got out of bed because he's so excited about seeing Te and because he wasn't going to let you down, but this bronchitis has knocked him for six. He'll probably collapse the moment you leave."

Jim, obviously a bit embarrassed at being publicly mothered, said, "It's all right. I'm okay. I'll have a rest a bit later."

"What are you prepared to do," I asked him, "to see that Te and his family have a chance of resettlement here?"

"Well, I'll have to approach the government, put it on an official footing, attempt to have him recognised as a refugee, and if I can't do that, have him sponsored as an immigrant. But now that I know he's alive I have to do everything I can."

"What chance would he have back in Vietnam if he were forcibly repatriated—which seems his most likely fate?"

"It's difficult to say but if the government in Vietnam were to realise that they'd missed him the first time round, they certainly wouldn't miss him the second time round."

"Would he adapt readily if he were to come to Australia?"

"He's very adaptable. I think the man's record stands for

itself. To have done what he's done shows independence and determination—which should ensure that when he and his family come to this country they wouldn't become a burden on society."

"He was helpful, charming, co-operative," I said, "in the brief period we spent with him, but you shared a war with him. What sort of a bloke is he?"

"He's a great mate," said the retired officer of his interpreter, "and I'm looking forward to the doors opening at the airport at Mascot and him stepping out of Customs and me singing out to him in Vietnamese, and I want to see the expression on his face when he arrives in this country. It'll be marvellous."

We left Jim Ellis standing in the doorway, waving us goodbye as the wind cut across the land and straight through any mortal creature in its path. The cold brought on another prolonged coughing spasm, and Glenda was now tugging at Jim's sleeve to get him inside.

Before we'd all stepped outside, Jim and I had discussed a multiple attack at finding Te through some people I'd met in Hong Kong. He would write letters and I would send them off with covering letters. I'd also make some calls to Hong Kong, and Jim and I would approach the Immigration Department in Canberra.

It was Wednesday, and all of this would have to wait until Friday because tomorrow I'd be tied up all day editing the piece we'd just recorded with Jim.

We drove off "Y-not" and on to The Forest Road, rearranging cartons of farm eggs Glenda had presented us with, and which now looked in danger of being crushed under camera boxes.

As we drove back down the escarpment, past Lake George, 300 kilometres to Sydney, one thing above all else that Jim Ellis had said kept going through my head: "Te is a religious man from a devout Catholic family and it's looking as if someone, somewhere, wants this all to happen."

The date was 5 July 1989.

The item went to air on the "7.30 Report" the following night, a simple story about the recognition of a wartime mate many years later. It was a follow-up story of hope. It moved people around the country to respond overwhelmingly in many positive ways. To the best of my knowledge, nobody ever disputed the genuineness of either party.

It was beginning to look like plain sailing for one VBP. He'd been remarkably lucky, not for the first time on this journey that had taken him fourteen years, but luck was not the only element in Te's favour. He had also been uncannily perceptive and able to turn things to his advantage.

Te should not have been on dry land at all the day I set foot on Tai Ah Chau. We should never have met.

When Nguyen Van Te and his boatload saw the big Hong Kong Marine Police boat, they took no evasive action, made no mad rush for land. This was not the end of their run for freedom, just another stage in its achievement, a moment of relief; not the end of their hopes but a time for renewing them.

Te's boat was with three others when the police spotted them. Te and his fellow travellers saw the tall buildings ahead of them, beyond the police boat, before they realised that they were in Hong Kong—not Macau as they'd expected. They were actually under the flight path into Kaitak Airport before the police picked them up. The little sailing boat, weighed down to the gunwales with sixteen people, their possessions and the seawater that kept coming in, had done its job. It had never been expected to take them around the world. Hong Kong had been its intended destination, and it had got them there all safe and sound.

Along the way they had seen the wreckage of many boats that had not lasted the distance. They had once come out of a cove and seen the bodies of two men and a woman floating face-down among pieces of a broken boat. The bodies could have been Chinese or Vietnamese but Te and his group were too scared to investigate. They got away as quickly as they could, sculling, paddling with their hands, in case the deaths and wreckage were the work of pirates waiting for another boatload of victims.

When Te and his people saw the Hong Kong police, they were only too happy to hand themselves over.

The big police launch circled them several times. An officer with a loudhailer called out in English and Cantonese, "Stop. Pull down your sails. Turn off the engines."

The four craft were taken in tow, and all but two of the Vietnamese were left on each boat. The police boat towed them southwest for more than two hours, away from the buildings they'd seen briefly on Hong Kong Island.

One of the Cantonese police officers handed out notices printed in Vietnamese, Cantonese and English. The boat people were advised that they would be detained in a camp for illegal immigrants where conditions would be lacking, that there was no future in stopping and that they should consider voluntarily pushing on—out of Hong Kong waters—or face the prospect of being put on a plane and sent back to Hanoi.

Like most of the other newly arrived Vietnamese, Te and his boatload thought this was largely bluff. Conditions couldn't be all that bad. Maybe a little patience would be required; eventually freedom would come.

At Tai Ah Chau the police boat stopped 100 metres or more from the beach. Here the police boat and the little wooden hulls were separated. Te's boat was lashed to another larger boat at anchor. It was not Vietnamese, but a Chinese junk that had been bought by another group of Vietnamese after their own boat had sunk along the Chinese coast. Te and the others were allowed to board the junk, but they were not allowed to land.

The junk was taking water more than Te's own boat and those on board knew it would sink if they didn't bail it out. When some of them started bailing, Te told them to stop—but he didn't tell them why. He had already worked out that seaworthy craft were not allowed to land, and that keeping the junk afloat meant keeping himself and his fellow travellers at anchor indefinitely.

"We must bail the water out," they told him.

"No," he said, "let the water rise. It will not sink."

Throughout the night, and the following day and night, the water kept rising. In the early hours of the next morning, when the water was almost over the sides, Te told the police, "This junk is sinking. We must go ashore."

The police said, "Okay. Use the oars. Go to the wharf and tie up there but don't leave the junk."

They slipped the ropes that attached the old junk to their own little boat and paddled toward the shore in the dark. As they did, they agreed in whispers to sink the junk at first light. By the time they'd tied up, the water level inside and outside was much the same.

As the sun began to appear over the sea, Te and the others slid into the water and worked their way around the broken wharf to the beach. The junk, now half submerged, was later lifted by crane into a barge and taken away to be destroyed.

Te's little boat, relieved of its load, had not taken too much water overnight, but was a danger to other craft in the bay. The police took it in tow and ran it up the sand.

Many other boat people were to ask Te, "How come you were allowed to go ashore so quickly when you could have kept the junk afloat by bailing out the water?"

"Ah," said Te, "The water was coming in much too quickly for us to bail it out. We could have drowned."

There were two main beaches on the island of Tai Ah Chau. The bigger one was where we'd first arrived, where the people on shore were living among the rocks and overhanging trees on which they draped their makeshift canopies, and where, 100 metres offshore, most of those who'd been refused permission to land were kept on their craft, tantalisingly in sight of land beyond their reach.

Most of the boat people here, like the great majority of Vietnamese making it to Hong Kong, were from what used to be North Vietnam, or from the ports of Da Nang and Hue in the northern part of what used to be South Vietnam. It was purely the logic of geography that sent them on the northern route to the outside world. By the same logic, those leaving the coast further south traditionally headed southwards, to Thailand, Malaysia or Indonesia.

In the years since the end of the war, the divisions between the two communities were as deep as ever. Partition of Vietnam in 1954 into the communist North and the capitalist South had been a national wound, opened up by civil war that followed, and unhealed by reunification. Now, all Vietnamese boat people—whatever their past loyalties and ideologies—shared a common dream of getting to the Western world, to the capitalist society one side had espoused and the other had despised. Yet the deep enmity between the southerners and the northerners remained.

Those from the south feared their countrymen from the north; they were afraid of persecution at home, and now it could be even worse in Hong Kong. The numbers were stacked against them, nine to one, or more.

But fear of the northerners was also felt by another group among the boat people—the ethnic Chinese from Vietnam. They had always been resented by the ethnic Vietnamese because the Chinese were the dominant traders and merchants, and were resented even more as fat cats and capitalist roaders by the communist rulers.

On the second, smaller beach on Tai Ah Chau, the southerners and the ethnic Chinese had grouped together for safety. It was this little beach which the police post overlooked, and the police were happy to see this self-segregation: they welcomed anything that prevented friction; the police had enough on their hands.

When Te's boat was towed ashore, the police were not on a sightseeing cruise. They chose the shortest distance possible. It just happened that the direct run took the little boat straight up the sand of the smaller beach, where Te's group would be accepted into a sympathetic community—under the watchful eye of the police.

"Incredible," said Jim, "absolutely amazing. The phone hasn't stopped since the moment the program ended. I've had calls from all sorts of people, some I haven't seen or thought of for twenty years, others I've never met or never heard of. They've all been supportive. I've had people from interstate who've called up just to wish me luck, strangers saying their faith in humankind has been restored. I've had people promising money if it'll help, someone who's offered Te a job when he gets here, somebody else who says Te and his family can stay in a house he's got down the coast somewhere, a barrister who's offering his services gratis, and some old duck who wants to marry both of us."

"Look what you've started," I said.

"No, *you* started it."

"No, I merely reported it."

"Well, somebody else seems to be directing it."

At the ABC the response from viewers had been much the same, all of them giving encouragement and support.

I'd expected a few calls from extremists, the rabid right-wingers never shy about calling broadcasting organisations and pouring out their racist hatred. The so-called "immigration debate" had been running and the xenophobia that lies very close to the surface of many an Anglo-Celtic Australian skin had begun to fester. It was time to stem the floodtide of Asians, many had been saying, and it was entirely predictable that some of the nutters would call up the "7.30 Report" condemning that "pinko army bloke" for trying to bring in another family of "gook slopeheads".

But in the great number of phone calls that were taken at the ABC at Gore Hill in Sydney the night of the broadcast and the following day, there was not one solitary call of opposition. Even the reliable and regular bigot callers must have realised the justification for helping this Vietnamese man and his family was simply unchallengeable.

In Canberra the high viewership of the "7.30 Report" would prove to be particularly valuable. It would mean the politicians and bureaucrats with whom we would deal would be familiar with the case and, we hoped, sympathetic when we approached them. It was time to act.

The top priority was to find Te. Before any proper application on his behalf could be made he would need to supply names and details of those of his immediate family with him. But in July of 1989 a letter addressed to Mr Nguyen Van Te, Vietnamese Boat Person, c/o Tai Ah Chau, Hong Kong, would have little chance of ever reaching the island.

We would try several other ways to make contact with him.

"First," I told Jim Ellis in one of many phone calls that would be made over a period of nine months, "I'll try to get hold of the cop in charge of Tai Ah Chau. I never met him but I spoke to him by phone a couple of times and he was helpful. He and the other cops laid on several craft for us on both trips to the island. One of them actually came from Tasmania—a Tasmanian cop in Hong Kong—so they were very cooperative. We had a beer with a few of them last time on board the command craft, *Police Launch Four*, a bloody great steel thing that was like a small warship. I'm sure this guy or one of the others there would pass on a letter to Te."

"Great," said Jim. "You've got his address?"

"Yes. His name is Chief Inspector Nick Angell. He doesn't sound too angelic—more like a Second World War sergeant-major. Address your letter to Te, care of him, send it to me and I'll post it off with a covering letter. I'll try to get hold of him by phone in the meantime."

"I'll get it off to you tomorrow."

"We should also try the Australian Consul-General in Hong Kong. His name is Geoff Bentley. I interviewed him about the flood of immigration applications they were getting in Hong Kong after the Beijing massacre. He was not at all a precious diplomat—very open and media aware. He said to call him at any time. I did when I went over to Taipei to do a piece on the Taiwanese gloating over the crackdown in China. I needed some contacts there and he was very helpful. I'm sure he will be again."

"Letter number two in the post."

"The bloke who took us over to Tai Ah Chau the second time is also worth a try. His name is Bill Wyllie, a very wealthy businessman from Perth who's into corporate rescue and that sort of stuff in Hong Kong. You know Hutchisons, one of the big companies there?"

"Yep. They got into big trouble a year or two ago, didn't they?"

"Wyllie came in and turned the company around."

"How does a wealthy businessman fit in with helping a Vietnamese boat person?" Jim asked. "Te's family business was pig farming. Does this bloke want some inside information on pork futures?"

"I don't think his interests are that diverse," I said. "But the other side to this tycoon is that he was a Salvation Army kid. His parents apparently farmed him off to the Salvos and he grew up with what he considers a great debt to charity. He's president or chairman of the Salvos in Hong Kong now, a very helpful bloke, generous and a great lateral thinker. When we were on the island we watched the police handing out cans of pilchards as rations to the boat people. Wyllie immediately picked up the fact that all of us missed— there were cans but no can openers. So what did he do? Got his secretary to send over a couple of cartons of them through the marine police. If he can help with Te, I'm sure he will."

"That's three letters. I'm getting writer's cramp already.

I don't know if my old farrier's hands can hold a pen straight."

"Then don't get your old farrier to write them. Do it yourself."

"Okay, boss, I'm writing."

"I'll let you know how I get on with the calls."

The letters penned by the old farrier's hands arrived in the next post. They were elegantly handwritten and thoughtfully composed.

The one he wrote to Te in our three-pronged attack was simple and very moving. To the great mate he hadn't seen for 16 years and had presumed dead, Jim Ellis wrote, on 8 July 1989:

Anh Te Than Men [Most esteemed brother Te],

Mr Geoffrey Sims of Australian Television has given me the good news that you are in Hong Kong.

My old friend, we must act quickly to have the Australian Government bring you to my country. But first must have some information.

Please carefully answer the questions I have listed below and send them to me:

1. The name of everyone in your family with you in Hong Kong.
2. Their sex and age.
3. Their relationship to you.
4. The names and adresses of any relatives you have in Australia.
5. What work you would like to do in Australia.

Anh Te Than Men, it is so long ago since I have seen you but I recognised you at once. I am old and gray. We have all been very busy trying to arrange for you to come to Australia. I hope we can rescue you soon.

Please give my respects to your family.

Your friend,

Anh Ly [Brother Ly, the transliteration of Ellis]

On Tai Ah Chau the boat people were processed cursorily. The number of people on each boat was what mattered, purely for purposes of allocating the food rations.

E. J. ELLIS.
"Y-Not", The Forest Road.
Bungendore, N.S.W. 2621
(P.O. Box 66, Bungendore, 2621)

7th July '89.

Anh Lê Thân Mên,

Mr Geoffry Sims of Australian Television has given me the good news that you are in Hong Kong. My old friend, we must act quickly to have the Australian Government bring you to my country. But first I must have some information.

Please carefully answer the questions I have listed below and send them to me:-

1. The name of everyone in your family with you in Hong Kong.

2. Their sex and age.

3. Their relationship to you.

4. The names and addresses of any relatives you have in Australia.

5. What work you would like to do in Australia.

Anh Lê Thân Mên, It is so long ago since I have seen you but I recognised you at once. I am old and gray. We have all been very busy trying to arrange for you to come to Australia. I hope we can rescue you soon. Please give my respects to your family,

your friend
Anh Ly

The letter Jim Ellis wrote on 7 July 1989, to the great mate he hadn't seen for 16 years and had presumed dead

SUNK

Nguyen Van Te hobbled up the small beach, weaving between the wrecks, watching the men return from the wharf landing, weighed down with bags and boxes of rations. He watched them disappear among the trees and rocks which they had made home. He left the rest of his family with the others from his boat and made his way to the police command post at the end of the beach.

"Excuse me," he said to one of the English inspectors. "My family have just arrived on Tai Ah Chau with me. We are hungry. Please can we have some rations?"

The inspector was stunned. "Where did you learn English?" he asked.

With a big grin, Te said, "I used to work for American and Australian forces in Vietnam War."

"God!" said the inspector. "You're the only one here who does speak it. Do you want a job?"

"Excuse me?"

"Would you be prepared to do a bit of interpreting?"

"Yes, of course," said Te. "I want to help my people, but I am concerned for the security of my family."

"So you should be. There are some pretty wild characters here. Keep your wits about you and you'll be okay. You're safe enough on the little beach. We'll keep an eye on you anyway."

Te was also concerned about shelter for his family. The boat was now useless to them. What was left of it lay half buried in the sand and couldn't even be upturned to make a lean-to the way others had done with theirs. Te, his children, sister-in-law and the eleven others from his boat slept on the beach under the stars for the first three nights until they were issued with a tent. They collected their rations of canned pilchards, biscuits and beans every two days, and the water brought by a naval ship. Once or twice they cooked some fish that someone had caught. That was the only fresh food they got. Te interpreted for the police and it helped relieve the boredom of life on this barren island. But it was no way to live.

After a week, Te complained to a young police inspector. "I cannot live like a mountain man," he said. "Please, why are we not transferred to a refugee camp?"

"You mean a detention centre," the inspector corrected him. "You're not a refugee yet. There's a big difference."

Others who'd arrived later than Te had already been transferred. Te suspected the delay was due solely to his usefulness to the police on Tai Ah Chau. He was right.

"What are we going to do for an interpreter if you leave us?" the police officer asked.

Te knew he was over a barrel. He hoped that cooperating with the police might be to his eventual advantage but he would never have any hope of being classifed as a refugee if he didn't get off the island and at least have his arrival officially noted.

On Monday, 3 July, just over a fortnight after reaching Hong Kong and being stuck on this little island, he made the police an offer. "Let my family go to a detention centre," he said, "and I will stay on Tai Ah Chau and help for maybe couple of months."

The police had been kind and sympathetic, but they could not be expected to deprive themselves of the one and only English-speaking Vietnamese.

At the Australian end things appeared to be humming along. I'd made contact with a public relations officer at the Immigration Department in Canberra who'd seen the program and was supportive of what we were trying to do. By coincidence she'd worked as a journalist in Hong Kong and we had several mutual acquaintances. By even greater coincidence she was married to an Australian army officer who'd worked under one Lt-Col Jim Ellis and confirmed Jim's bona fides.

I'd also phoned Geoff Bentley, the Consul-General in Hong Kong, and faxed him Jim's letter to Te. I had a VHS copy of the program made and I put it in the post to him. He was fascinated to hear of this chance recognition, and impressed by Jim's aim to get Te to Australia. He promised to do what he could, but cautioned against too much optimism. Since June of 1988 it had become almost impossible for a boat person to be "screened in", the term for being declared a refugee.

I'd also phoned Bill Wyllie, the Australian businessman in Hong Kong, who had just come from a lunch to promote trade between Hong Kong and Australia. The speaker at that lunch had sat next to Wyllie and they knew each other well. The speaker had been Geoff Bentley.

I faxed him a copy of Jim's letter to Te and put another VHS copy of the program in the mail. Wyllie was quite excited by it all. Without his kindness in taking us to Tai Ah Chau in his own luxury boat we'd never have come across Te, and Wyllie was obviously pleased to be involved.

"I know a couple of ladies through the Salvos who go in and out of these places for the boat people," he said. "I'll see if they go out to the Soko Islands to Tai Ah Chau. If they don't, they'll know some way of getting the letter to Te and finding out the details of those with him. I'll stay in touch with Geoff Bentley."

The attempts to get hold of Chief Inspector Nick Angell were less successful. Every time I'd called he'd been out of telephone contact or off duty, and the other police officers I'd met had been equally impossible to locate.

On 11 July I finally reached Angell by phone. "Be glad to help," he said by cellular phone from *PL4*, the big command boat. "Trouble is, don't know where your man is. Been transferred. Big group of 'em. Gone to Sek Kong, I think. Not sure. Left here four days ago."

Gone. Lost among 50,000 boat people. Te had got his wish to be transferred to a detention centre but in doing so he had inadvertently set back a rescue mission about which he knew nothing.

It was a huge disappointment. Inspector Angell said he'd try to find out where Te had gone but he wouldn't like to guarantee results. If Te had gone to Sek Kong, where a tent city was being built on the runway of an old airfield in the New Territories close to the border with China, there might be some hope of locating him. If Te had been sent elsewhere, it might prove much more difficult.

"I'm police," he said. "We run Tai Ah Chau. We run Sek Kong. CSD runs most of the others."

"CSD?"

"Correctional Services Department. Expect they've got Nguyens running out of their backsides. Common name. Maybe he'll turn up. Don't know. Expect they could do with an interpreter if he does. Bit thin on the ground, English-speaking VBPs. Send me the letter. Do what I can. No promises."

I tried phoning Jim to share the disappointment. He'd been off to the Immigration Department to start the wheels turning, to find out the best approach to having Te brought to Australia, either as a refugee or sponsored. There was no answer. As it happened, Jim was in a particularly buoyant mood and had just dropped a letter in the post to share news of an encouraging development the previous night. It was one that would have a significant influence on the course of events.

Jim had been called by the former President of the Returned Services League, Sir William Keys, an enlightened man whose commitment to improving multicultural affairs was unquestioned, and which placed him at odds with some of the League's present leadership. Sir William was a man of great influence. He lived in Queanbeyan near Canberra and was known to be well connected and well respected in the national capital.

The same day I learned we'd lost Te, Jim was writing to me:

Dear Geoffrey,

Another coincidence! I had a call from a girl I haven't seen in 20 yrs last night. She said she is a house guest of Sir William Keys and that Sir William gave her my number and would like to speak to me when she finished! Sir William asked me to give him full details (which I've done today) so that he can put the case for Te as he said, "at a very high level". I am becoming optimistic.

Regards, Jim. 11 Jul '89

E.J. ELLIS.
"Y-Not", The Forest Road.
Bungendore, N.S.W. 2621
(P.O. Box 66, Bungendore, 2621)

11th July, 1989.

Dear Sir William,

Thank you for your kind offer of support for my old friend Nguyễn Văn Tế. I have enclosed some writings which explain the background to his case. I do not have full details of his family group at this time but I am working on getting them.

Your assistance will be greatly appreciated — good luck and God bless you.

Yours faithfully,

Jim Ellis

Dear Geoffrey, Another 'coincidence'! I had a call from a girl I haven't seen in 20 yrs last night. She said she is a house guest of Sir William Keys and that Sir William gave her my number and would like to speak to me when she finished! Sir William asked me to give him full details (which I've done today) so that he can put the case for Tế as he said, "at a very high level." I am becoming optimistic.

Regards, Jim "Jul'89"

A copy of the letter Jim wrote to thank Sir William Keys, with a note to me scribbled at the bottom

3

The Jolly Cop

Three hundred people were crammed into a stone building about three times the size of an average home's living room in most Western countries. They slept four to a single bunk with a board for a mattress and the bunks were stacked four high. They not only slept on them, they spent the day sitting on them. The only other space was the gap between the rows of bunks. There was nowhere to wash. There was little light or ventilation. The heat and humidity were stifling.

The building was just one of several. For ten minutes each afternoon the people held in this and the other buildings were allowed out and into an exercise cage topped with barbed wire.

Green Island, just a stone's throw off the western tip of Hong Kong Island, was the official point of entry to the boat people, a "restricted area" inaccessible to the media. It was here that the rudimentary processing was done—a basic sausage-machine approach, one might say in Hong Kong's defence, by necessity. Hundreds more boat people were arriving in Hong Kong waters every day. People talked about the "record day" when 2000 made the run into Hong Kong territorial waters after grouping and sheltering from a typhoon along the China coast.

Among the 300 people in that stone building on 7 July 1989 were Te and his family, transferred after spending nineteen days on Tai Ah Chau. The police had respected his appeal and not before time; things were getting dramatically worse. Several women had been raped, fighting was common, stabbings were increasing, and in the absence of sanitary conditions cholera could break out at any time.

Te and the others from his boat arrived at about 3.00 p.m. They had travelled in the heat of the day, crammed among 500 people on one landing barge being moved hither and yon from Tai Ah Chau. It had been hot and airless in the barge and there had been no canopy to screen out the fierce sun. Still, anything would be better than spending another moment over there.

Te had believed the transfer to Green Island would signal an improvement on that lifestyle. It was hardly that.

On Tai Ah Chau he'd been forced to live, as he said, "like a mountain man". The transfer to Green Island, he later told me, "was like moving into a monkey house".

Led into one end of the crowded hut, little Thu Thao, the younger daughter, was stopped by a Vietnamese woman carrying out the work of the authorities. In one movement the woman, armed with a big pair of scissors, pulled the little girl's long black hair together and snipped it off at the neck then applied some thick, white, gooey substance on the scalp. It was presumed to be a treatment for head-lice but there was no evidence of lice and no explanation was given. It was simply standard procedure. Everyone had to accept it.

The whole family were still non-persons. Their names were of little relevance, merely part of a verification procedure to the authorities. People were given numbers by which they would be identified as Vietnamese boat persons, but not even the numbers were given out lightly.

"Name? Occupation? How did you get to Hong Kong?" an apparently disinterested Cantonese official asked each one in turn through an interpreter. "What village did you come from? Show it on this map." Then a map of a different scale was produced. "Show the village on this map," was the order. If the person failed to find it readily the official would pounce. "Show me! Show me!" he would demand, and then suddenly produce a Vietnamese bank note, folded over to reveal only a corner or perhaps the serial number. "How much money?" he would shout.

Even the children would have to answer accurately and quickly. Any hesitation and the whole group from a given boat would be removed, presumed to be not Vietnamese boat people but exiles from China posing as Vietnamese, and the policy for dealing with those who fled China had been long established: they were taken out to the border at Lowu and handed over to the authorities of the People's Republic.

Te had worked out the vetting process and the kinds of questions they would face. There was no reason for fear, but he rehearsed his group to make sure there were no slips or hesitation.

The day after they arrived on Green Island they passed the test and their presence in Hong Kong was officially recorded, three weeks after they first entered the territory. The boat number was registered as 411/16. It was the 411th Vietnamese boat to be registered by the Corrective Services Department in 1989 and there were sixteen people on board. Te was recorded as number 12 on the boat and his own personal number was thus 411/12/89. The rest of the family were numbered consecutively.

At least they now existed.

Inside the stone building that night, somehow disregarding the 300 others and their din, Te and his family were able to celebrate with what seemed to them a banquet. Gone was the steady diet of canned pilchards, biscuits and beans. On Green Island they were served a meal they had dreamed of for many weeks.

It was little more than rice but it was like manna.

"Can't find him, I'm afraid," said Geoff Bentley, the Consul-General. "They've moved thousands of them all over the place because of the typhoon and because the numbers keep growing. We'll find him but at the moment he could be anywhere."

There was little comfort in that—or in part of the contents of a letter I received from Bill Wyllie, the businessman. It was written the day Te was transferred to Green Island.

"I expect you have been following events up here and will be aware that boat people are continuing to flood into Hong Kong. The latest estimates by government are that they now expect the total number to balloon to approximately 75,000 by the end of the year and the temporary base which we saw in the Sokos [where we met Te among 6000 on Tai Ah Chau] has been suggested as being capable of taking at least another 30,000!"

In Canberra Jim Ellis learnt that a "case officer" in the Immigration Department had been assigned to deal with

Te's intended application. It sounded as if the department was taking the matter seriously.

Jim had also written to the Australian Ambassador to Hanoi to see if there was any record of the application Te told me he'd made there. If nothing more, it might provide all the names and details of the family members with him in Hong Kong and we could get things moving even before Te turned up in one detention centre or another—if he ever did.

It was now nearing the end of July. Weeks had passed and we'd heard nothing. The threat of enforced repatriation was looming. Three hundred boat people, persuaded that there was no hope of resettlement anywhere, had boarded an international carrier at Kaitak Airport and were on their way back to Hanoi. It was said they'd gone back voluntarily in spite of the fear of persecution on return to the country they'd turned their backs on.

Their voluntary return was taken by some as a convenient way of softening the blow of enforced repatriations that would have to come.

From Green Island the people from boat 411/16 had been sent once more by landing craft, once more packed in like the canned pilchards they hoped they would never see again, with 500 other numbered people. They crossed the harbour under the western flight approach to Kaitak Airport and were herded off in the New Territories. Then followed a journey by truck to Sek Kong, the old airfield that had undergone a sudden personality change.

The perimeter fence had been replaced with chain-link mesh three or four metres high, topped with coiled barbed wire. Doubled security gates had been installed. So had high security lights. Tents—hundreds and hundreds of them—had been put up along the entire length of the runway.

When Te and the others, all of them identified by their newly acquired numbers, were delivered at Sek Kong the number system suddenly didn't apply. All the new arrivals were grouped here and there according to their family name, with no reference to the boat on which they'd arrived in Hong Kong.

A REAL MATE

In the confusion, Te's sister-in-law, Mai Phuong, whose surname is Tran, was separated from Te and his children. The officials weren't interested in hearing stories. Protests would have to wait. Mai Phuong was led away with another group with whom she'd had no association at all.

Te and his children were told to wait with some other new arrivals where they stood. An interpreter, half Vietnamese, half Cantonese, said in Vietnamese, "Anyone speak English or Cantonese?"

About half a dozen stepped forward. Te joined them.

The interpreter said, "English or Cantonese?"

All but Te said, "Cantonese," and were taken aside to give their details.

In Vietnamese, the interepreter said to Te, "What about you?

"I speak some English," Te said.

The interpreter called over a Chinese police inspector.

"Good afternoon," he said in English to Te. "How's your English?"

Te didn't want to sound too confident. "I speak a little bit," he said.

The Chinese police inspector then called over an English inspector, the administrative officer of the camp. Inspector Peter Wheaton was a ruddy faced, jovial man, the sort of " 'ullo, 'ullo, 'ullo, what's this then?" English bobby. He was pleasant and gentle, yet wielded considerable power. He was a compassionate copper, as long as he wasn't crossed.

Inspector Wheaton looked at the much smaller man standing before him. "Speak English, do you? What's your name?—and don't give me your number."

Te said softly, "My name is Nguyen Van Te. I used to work as interpreter during the Vietnam war."

Wheaton said, "Well, would you please do it again? You'll get paid and you'll get more food."

Te said, "I don't worry about that. I just want to help my people. Already in Hong Kong I interpret for police on Tai Ah Chau."

"Very good," said Inspector Wheaton. "We could do with your help here. All the people in the camp are restricted to certain areas. We can't have them going anywhere they choose or there'd be even more chaos. But I'll give you a card that'll allow you to go wherever you like in the camp."

THE JOLLY COP

The jolly cop, Hong Kong Police Inspector Peter Wheaton, and interpreter/postman Nguyen Van Te at Sek Kong, New Territories, Hong Kong, July 1989

"I'll be happy to help," said Te, "but first I have a proposition."

The ruddy faced police inspector said, "Oh yes? Pay, more food, open access to the whole camp, plus police protection—not enough? You drive a hard bargain."

Te gave him that winning smile. "I already tell you I am happy to help," he said, "but my sister-in-law, my wife's sister, came with me to look after the children, particularly my little daughter. Now we have been separated. She goes to single women's quarters. I would like us to reunite."

"No, I'm sorry," the police inspector replied firmly. "She's your sister-in-law, not part of your immediate family. I'm not allowed to let you all live together in the one tent. Rules are rules, simple as that." He paused. The stern expression relaxed and the jovial one replaced it. "I'll just have to turn a blind eye, I suppose."

The old airfield was divided into four sections. Sections one and two were already full to capacity, section three was filling rapidly and section four was being hastily prepared. Within two weeks the airfield would have 7500 people living within the perimeter fencing. They would be transferred here from Tai Ah Chau and the old Star Ferries as new arrivals took their places.

There were two types of military tents—or huts, as they were known—that had been supplied by the British army. The bigger variety held 52 people, the smaller one held 30. The policy was to group families in the smaller huts wherever possible.

Day and night it was hot on the flat land surrounded by the steep and rugged hills of the New Territories. The humidity hung between the peaks, trapping the heat that rose from the airfield. The huts were like saunas. The privacy they afforded was not worth the cost. Almost without exception their occupants rolled up the sides in the hope of catching any breath of air. Sek Kong was awash with canopies rather than tents.

For bedding, each two people were allocated one sheet of plywood between them to place on a base of sandbags. They shared one army blanket but most chose to sleep on the bare bedboard. There was no need of warmth at night and the blankets were more useful tied to the tops of the tent poles to make a ceiling that helped keep the heat out by day.

Here, at least, was space. Confinement to an overcrowded building on Green Island for even a couple of days was overpowering. At Sek Kong people could move about within their own designated areas, they weren't stacked on bunks four high, and Te's own privileged position gave him even greater freedom.

The food had also taken a turn for the better. Hot meals were prepared en masse outside the camp and brought in for distribution. There were meals of rice with meat, fish and fresh vegetables. Nobody was known to complain of being overfed, but the food was edible, varied enough and adequate for most. A week's rations also included one orange, a can of condensed milk and some biscuits. People were not getting sick here in such numbers as they were on Tai Ah Chau.

For clothing, the boat people were on their own. Along the way to Hong Kong many had discarded their clothes, believing the Hong Kong government would supply them with new and fancy clothing if they arrived in threads. Where the rumour originated is unknown but those in threads stayed in threads.

The morning after Te and his family arrived at Sek Kong they awoke and stepped out from under the canopy that was officially called "B/49". A messenger told Te he was required to report to Inspector Wheaton and the deputy commandant of the camp, Chief Inspector David Mackersy, at the command post.

"Get your pay and food," they told him. "Collect your things and we'll move you to one of the big huts we've reserved for the interpreters. It's better for security reasons."

To their disbelief, Te declined the offer. He told them, "I don't feel threatened. There are five strong, younger men from my boat around me in our hut. I feel safe enough. Maybe later, if security becomes terrible, I would like transfer."

"Suit yourself," Inspector Wheaton said, "but we've kept all the other interpreters together so far. There's group A and group B. You will be head of group B."

If they suspected Te's motives for keeping a bit of distance between himself and the other interpreters they didn't let on. But if trouble did break out—as was almost inevitable—Te wouldn't want to be identified with a group supplying the police with information about troublemakers. Co-operation was one thing, collaboration another.

In one of his first assignments, Te organised a clinic and first-aid parade for one big group. It would turn out to his great advantage, helping him into another job much later.

Long before it did, and less than a fortnight after Te's arrival at Sek Kong, the typhoon signals were hoisted over Hong Kong. The numbers indicated the strength and direction from which the typhoon was approaching across the South China Sea. It showed no sign of veering away from Hong Kong. Ships prepared to leave port and ride the typhoon out at sea. Small craft, the junks and sampans, the Westerners' gin palaces and speedboats, all headed into the typhoon shelters. Shopkeepers got out the boards to seal up their windows. On the hillsides across the territory, squatters weighted down their wood and corrugated iron hovels with rocks and pieces of steel.

It happened several times every typhoon season and everybody went through the same ritual preparation, knowing that the big winds usually turned away at the last moment and petered out or did their damage somewhere else. But every now and then there was a big one, a mean one, single-minded in its determination to flatten as much of Hong Kong as it could, to sink as many ships as possible, destroy buildings, knock over the trees, send the squatters and their huts into a tangle of mud and grief with massive hillslides. And if the typhoon didn't succeed on its run across the territory the first time, it would make another determined onslaught as the huge spiralling wind came back the other way. The tent-city detention centre of Sek Kong would have no defence against a semi-serious storm, let alone a typhoon.

It was near the end of July as the typhoon bore in toward Hong Kong, and the decision was made to move the 7500 people now occupying the Sek Kong airfield to greater safety.

In one day this vast number of people was moved in a never-ending convoy of army trucks and small buses the 40 kilometres along often narrow and winding roads from Sek Kong to Shatin detention centre further to the east.

As a logistical exercise it was a great success, but it was no help in our attempts to locate the disappearing Mr Nguyen Van Te.

"Thought we had him," said Geoff Bentley by phone from Hong Kong. "Thought he must have ended up at Sek Kong, but they've all been moved again because of another typhoon and we can't find anyone with any record of his name—or his number, if he's got one."

Once more the Consul-General assured me Te would turn up sooner or later and all obstacles would be overcome. He'd now seen the copies of the programs I'd sent him. "Many cases we get are difficult because of this or that, something's just not right, the details are patently untrue or there's something fishy. Just once in a while you get a case like this which is simple and straightforward and so convincingly right and good that you know it'll work out just because it should."

I phoned Chief Inspector Nick Angell again and again. He'd received the letters from Jim and me and had sent them to the police at Sek Kong, though he reminded me about the typhoon and said he'd heard nothing about Te's whereabouts.

I phoned Bill Wyllie's office and spoke to Mrs Lynn D'Souza, his personal assistant who'd been willingly recruited to the cause of finding Te. She'd also heard that Sek Kong was the most likely place he'd ended up and she was making her own enquiries.

August now rolled around. Jim received a letter dated the first of the month from the Australian Embassy in Hanoi. It was from the First Secretary (Immigration). Jim read me the letter over the phone:

Dear Lieutenant-Colonel Ellis,

The Ambassador has asked me to reply to your letter of 7 July 1989, concerning your former employee Nguyen Van Te.

 I have had no immediate success in finding any record of Mr Te's application. As the operations of the Vietnam/Australia Migration Program are based in the Australian Embassy in Bangkok, an immigration application lodged by him could have been forwarded to Bangkok. To assist my (and Bangkok's) search, could you please let me know
—Mr Te's date of birth
—When he lodged his application at the Embassy in Hanoi
—The date he left Vietnam/arrived in Hong Kong.

Jim's frustration was beginning to tell. "I can tell them the answer to the first question; he was born on 20 January

Lieutenant-Colonel E.J. Ellis
P.O. Box 66
BUGENDORE, N.S.W. 2621

AUSTRALIAN EMBASSY
HANOI
01 Aug 1989

Dear Lieutenant-Colonel Ellis,

      The Ambassador has asked me to reply to your letter of 7 July 1989, concerning your former employee Nguyen Van Te.

      I have had no immediate success in finding any record of Mr. Te's application. As the operations of the Vietnam/Australia Migration Program are based in the Australian Embassy in Bangkok, an immigration application lodged by him could have been forwarded to Bangkok. To assist my (and Bangkok's) search, could you please let me know

- Mr. Te's date of birth
- When he lodged his application at the Embassy in Hanoi
- The date he left Vietnam/arrived in Hong Kong.

Yours sincerely,

Eleanor Higgs
First Secretary
(Immigration)

A letter to Jim from the Australian Embassy in Hanoi, saying that they had no record of Te's immigration application

From: Lieutenant-Colonel E.J. Ellis.

"Y-Not", The Forest Road,
Bungendore, N.S.W. 2621
(P.O. Box 66, Bungendore, 2621)

10th August, 1989.

Dear Ms Higgs,
Thank you for your letter in regard to my friend Nguyễn-Văn-Tê. I have enclosed a copy of the application Tê claims to have forwarded to the Embassy in Hà Nội on 27th July, 1988. I have notated details of a fifth child on the copy giving details of the relevant record entry references on the child's birth certificate issued by officials of Đồng Nai Province.

I hope this will be of some help in finding the original application.

yours faithfully,
Jim Ellis

Jim's reply, in which he enclosed the little information he had about Te

1949. I can tell the answer to the last question because he told you in Hong Kong; he left Vietnam on 14 April 1989 and arrived in Hong Kong on 15 June. I can't answer the second question because he didn't tell you the date he lodged his application in Hanoi.

"Really, what do they expect? I've seen a glimpse of him on television six weeks ago and we haven't been able to find him since.

"I think I'll just call the Governor of Hong Kong and tell him, 'Put Nguyen Van Te on the line, old chap. You're holding him somewhere there, I believe, at Her Majesty's pleasure, God bless the dear old girl, of course, and since you're her representative there, just send a bearer with a cleft stick and a cellular telephone.' "

Shatin detention centre, officially known as Whitehead, was hopelessly incapable of coping with the huge influx. It sprawled over part of the Sai Kung peninsula, a purpose-built concentration camp by another name, divided into sections for different categories of the same group of people nobody wanted.

Even by the normal methods of stacking bunks and doubling up sleepers to four to a single bed, there were twice as many people as Whitehead could provide for. The permanent huts were bulging to meet the numbers suddenly imposed on them.

When the rain came, pushed ahead of the typhoon, it came in torrents. Thousands of people were forced to squat, day or night. There was no room for them to lie down. If they were lucky they might have a sheet of newspaper on which to squat, but a sheet of newspaper is a negligible barrier against the filth in which they squatted.

At Whitehead Te accepted without hesitation the offer of accommodation for himself and his family in the interpreters' hut, guarded by police. He was concerned that some might see him as a collaborator because of his close relations with the police, but better to have their protection than to be defenceless.

Te reasoned that the interpreters more likely to be seen as collaborators were the ones who spoke Cantonese, because it was the Chinese police, not the whites, who were regarded as brutal and therefore hated by the majority of the internees. If the Cantonese police were despised, it was probably a reflection of mutual Asian prejudices: in Vietnam the minority ethnic Chinese were resented by the majority Vietnamese; in Hong Kong, particularly in the areas around the detention centres, the local Cantonese were staging mass protests calling for the boat people to be sent packing.

In any case Te was more concerned that he or his family could become victims of the attacks on people known to come from the old South Vietnam, or that they might simply get caught up in violence spreading uncontrolled throughout the place. Fights were breaking out, brought on as much by the pressure of the living conditions as by any identifiable disputes. Encroaching on someone's confined space could leave either party slashed savagely with a knife or maimed with a meat cleaver or beaten senseless with a folding chair.

Armed theft went unchecked; failure to comply with a demand to hand over your clothes could leave you not just naked but run through with a knife or sharpened stick. Gangs formed and fought each other like small armies.

People were being murdered. Others suffered terrible wounds.

Te and his family endured Whitehead for an interminable week until the typhoon passed. He joked that the place was so-named because that's what you could be left with—if you survived.

The 7500 boat people from Sek Kong were packed up and moved out of Whitehead back to the old airfield. There was less urgency than on the outward journey to beat the typhoon, and the operation this time took two days.

When Te and his family arrived back at Sek Kong on the second day they found the huts, or tents, had been re-erected by the army, but many of the sheets of plywood that served as beds had already been grabbed. Some of the first to arrive back in the camp had helped themselves to the luxury of one whole sheet of plywood where previously they'd had to share. It meant many were left with the bare sandbags to sleep on.

Te resumed his interpreting duties and life began to settle down a little after a few days. Te went to Inspector Wheaton and said, "I think maybe I try to contact the Australian Consulate."

"Why?" the inspector asked.

"I worked for the Australian Army in Vietnam and I would like to contact the Consulate. Maybe they would give me a chance."

On 8 August Te attended a Mass given every Wednesday by a Canadian priest called Father Robert. As the Mass was just beginning, the two Police Inspectors, Wheaton and Mackersy, appeared and signalled Te over.

"Quick!" Inspector Wheaton said, his ruddy face alive with optimism. "You have a phone call!"

The three of them rushed to the command post and Te picked up the phone, a facility beyond the reach of normal detainees.

"My name is Lynn D'Souza. I work for Mr Bill Wyllie, who took Mr Geoffrey Sims and an Australian television team to Tai Ah Chau where they met you in June. There are people trying to help you. Your old boss, Lieutenant-Colonel Ellis, saw you on the television program and he's trying to arrange for you to go to Australia. We must get the details of members of the family with you."

By Te's account, it would be hard to say who among the three of them in that police command post—the two jailers and the inmate—was most excited. Te gave Lynn D'Souza the information, thanked her and handed the phone back to one of the policemen. The two big English police officers and one little Vietnamese nobody, two of them able to come and go as they pleased, one of them just a number in a cage, whooped in delight as if they'd all been set free.

How Lynn D'Souza had tracked Te down remains a mystery. "I just asked a few questions here and there," she told me later. "It wasn't very difficult." In truth she had used her initiative and her connections and she'd been persistent, the qualities, as any corporate head will agree, that set a top personal assistant apart from the rest.

After she'd spoken to Te she wasted no time, and a couple of hours later Inspector Wheaton took another call for Te and put him on the line.

It was the Australian Consul-General. "Are you Te?" he asked.

"Yes, I am Nguyen Van Te."

"Did you work for the Australian Army?"
"Yes."
"Did you know a Captain Ellis?"
"No, he was Major Ellis. I know he was a major. He was my own boss."
"Good," said the Consul, "we may be able to help you."

At Bungendore, Jim hung his hammers and files and cutters on the wall of the shed, took a last look at the fading embers in the brazier, stretched an aching back and said to himself, "That'll do it for the day."

It was already dark, and the chill of the wind over the escarpment brought the effective temperature below freezing. He picked out a split log from the wheelbarrow outside the front door of his house and stepped inside as the phone rang. "It'll be Mrs Whatsername from over the hill," he said to himself. "Her daughter's pony has thrown a shoe and the whole world has fallen apart . . . "

"Colonel Ellis," said the female voice at the other end, "you don't know me but I have news about your friend Te. My name is Lynn D'Souza and I work for Mr Wyllie. I've found Te. He's in a camp at Sek Kong and he and his family are well—or as well as can be expected. I've spoken to the Consul-General and he's on to it. I'm sure you must be very happy."

It was, of course, an understatement.

By the time Jim called me to pass on the news, his excitement was barely contained. "Found him at last!" he said. "Te's at Sek Kong. He's been from Tai Ah Chau to Green Island to Sek Kong to Shatin and back again. And you know who found him? Bill Wyllie's personal assistant. You can see why he employs her."

The following day Geoff Bentley called me to let me know that he'd spoken to Te and the processing could begin with the details of Te's family members with him.

At almost precisely the time he was calling, Te was taking delivery of an opened letter, delivered to him by a representative of the Hong Kong office of the United Nations High Commissioner for Refugees. Inside the envelope were two letters, the one from Jim and the covering letter I had sent a month earlier via Chief Inspector Nick Angell who ran

SHEK-KONG. 10th August 1989.
FROM NGUYEN-VAN.TE
HUT: B39 FAM.1949.
SHEK KONG CAMP
.DETENTION CENTRE

TO: MR G.R BENTLEY
CONSUL. GENERAL
AUSTRALIAN CONSULATE GENERAL.
HONG-KONG.

Dear sir.

It was a great honor and gracefull for me to had a telephone conversation with you on the afternoon of 10th August. Now I have very pleased in enclosing the family particular for which you asked.

Now in here HK there are five members in my family consist of myself, my son, my two daughters and my un-married sister in law. These details are on the attached sheet of paper. There is also a picture of my family.

Please try to understand my mistake English. Because of it was so long time I haven't had the occasion to use english.

Many thanks for your help and look forward to meeting you and express my appreciation personally.

your sincerely
Nguyen-van Te

Te's letter to the Australian Consul-General in Hong Kong, August 1989

Tai Ah Chau. The two letters had been chasing Te from one location to another.

For any detained boat person, getting a letter at all was always a big event. It might be good news, a hint of help from a relative living abroad, it might be money from home, or simply some distraction from the routine of being locked up.

Te folded back the opened lid of the envelope carefully and removed the contents. He saw the ABC letterhead first and then he saw on the attached letter the handwriting of his old boss, his old mate.

"The first time I saw Jim Ellis's letter," he later told me, "I was so surprised. I was so happy, I grabbed the letter, ran to the command post and showed it to Inspectors Wheaton and Mackersy. 'Would you believe it!' I said. They said, 'Oh you've got a very good chance now. Do what they want as soon as possible.' "

Te didn't do much interpreting that day. He painstakingly wrote some letters. The first one thanked Mrs D'Souza for her kind efforts. The second one he wrote was to the Consul-General.

> Dear Sir,
>
> It was a great honor and gracefull for me to had a telephone conversation with you. Now I have very please in enclosing the family particular for which you asked.
>
> Now in here HK there are five members in my family consist of myself, my son, my two daughters and my unmarried sister in law. These details are on the attached sheet of paper. There is also a picture of my family.
>
> Please try to understand my mistake English. Because of it was so long time I haven't had the occasion to use English.
>
> Many thanks for your help and look forward to meeting you and express my appreciation personally.

The third letter was the most joyous to write, but the shortest because all of the things that had to be said could be said briefly without any chance of misunderstanding. It was also the only one he wrote in Vietnamese.

Esteemed Brother Ly,

Right now I am here (Hong Kong). It is like being incarcerated but I have you helping me. I am now confident that for me and my family everything will be fine.

The day we meet one another again is then not so far away, is it?

We are all well.

I hope you and your family are healthy and happy.

Faithfully, Te.

It marked the first exchange of communication in sixteen years.

Lynn D'Souza's discovery of Te, seven long weeks after he first appeared on the "7.30 Report" and Jim Ellis caught that glimpse of him, gave rise to great optimism, but in reality all that had happened was that Te had been found. Te was still just another VBP—number 411/12/89—just another illegal immigrant, and about number 50,000 back in the queue.

"I thought now I would definitely be resettled in Australia," Te told me later. "But we knew nothing about screening."

Screening was the process of evaluating a VBP's claim to being a refugee. It was the aim of all boat people to be screened *in*, meaning to achieve the status of refugee, but since a stiffening of policy by the Hong Kong government on 18 June 1988 it was next to impossible.

Screening *out* was almost automatic. It meant confirming the status of illegal immigrant and with it permanent incarceration. Repatriation, enforced or voluntary, was the only other likely consequence of being screened out.

The two European police officers gave Te some firm advice. "Don't let anyone know about the interest in your case. Don't even tell any other police officers. Don't even tell your family."

Their concern was easy to understand. If word got out, someone was bound to suspect that Te was being rewarded for spying on his own countrymen. With a knife between his ribs Te would have a great deal of trouble convincing an attacker that his old boss was behind any special treatment. And now was not the time to reveal his past anyway.

"I was dying to share the news with my family," he later told me. After nearly two months in one camp after another they would be as ready for a hopeful sign as he had been, but he could not expose any of them to the risk of inadvertently letting a word slip. It was in their own interests to be kept in the dark.

Day after day Te kept his secret to himself. He went about his interpreting duties and he was given the important and trusted position of handling mail, incoming and outgoing. To many of the detainees communication was everything. Any suspicion that the messenger was interfering with mail could prove fatal.

A week after sending off his family particulars to the Australian Consul-General, Te could no longer keep his silence. He decided he could not endanger his children by telling them. Mai Phuong, his sister-in-law, was the only adult. She would have to share his burden.

"I have a secret," he told her in a whisper as they walked a discreet distance away from the hut and tried to look casual about it. "If you promise to keep the secret I will tell it to you. If you do tell we may be killed."

Mai Phuong agreed and he told her what had happened. He told her about his old boss and that the Australians he had known in Vietnam were good people. Australia must be a good country. They were very lucky.

Te told Inspector Wheaton that he had been unable to keep the secret any longer but Mai Phuong would not tell anyone. The police inspector was not concerned about her trustworthiness but the risk of one misplaced word. "Better move you all to the interpreters' hut," he said.

"No, thank you," said Te, declining the offer for the second time, "that might make people more suspicious."

4

Nouc Mam

Major Ernest James Ellis was in love with Vietnam long before he was sent there in July of 1970. He knew well in advance that he was going and he knew why. It wasn't a mission simply to fight a war in someone else's backyard. His would be a job not of battle but of persuasion. Jim Ellis was bound for Vung Tau, way down south and well away from the fighting, to become commander of the local detachment of the Civil Affairs Unit of the Australian army. The job was to build bridges to the local community, to win hearts and minds.

The sound of the language appealed to him. Tonal, nasal and staccato, it was beyond the capability, application or even interest of most foreign soldiers. In any case, they'd only be there for a limited period, then out again. They could learn a bit of bar talk and bargaining technique. They could learn enough to get about, get a beer, get laid and get home again—hopefully. For anything more demanding they could rely on the army's interpreters.

Major Ellis learnt Vietnamese at the Royal Australian Air Force School of Languages at Point Cook on the outskirts of Melbourne, and was fluent before he arrived in Vung Tau.

Vietnam was even more beautiful than the country he'd fallen in love with from books and pictures and film. In Vung Tau the streets were wide and tree-lined, there was the scent of frangipanni in the air, there were hibiscus and other colorful flowers, and palms and flowering trees and fruits of the tropics everywhere. There were beaches and hills and enough of the flavour of colonial French architecture to spice the oriental, and a gracefulness about the place and the people that belied the state of war.

When Major Ellis arrived in Vung Tau he could speak

their language, but for the first few days he refrained from advertising the fact. In Australia he could learn a foreign language, but reach merely a superficial understanding of the culture to which the language belonged. That could be achieved only with exposure to the culture and with some expert guidance. Where the other foreign soldiers needed interpreters because they could not speak the language, Major Ellis wanted an expert interpreter because he could. If his mission of winning hearts and minds was to have any hope of succeeding, he would need to know and respect local ways, and not be just another ignorant foreigner. It would be a difficult enough task as it was.

Major Jim Ellis was 35. When he took over the Civil Affairs Unit in Vung Tau in 1970, Nguyen Van Te was already on the payroll. Te was 21, a civilian on contract to a United States company called Pacific Architects and Engineers, and seconded to the Australian army the year before Jim arrived. He was paid about the same rate as an enlisted corporal.

Te's background made him ideal for the job. He came from a strong Catholic, and therefore anti-communist, family that had fled the North after the country was partitioned. They were among 5000 people—half their entire village of Tra Co in Quang Ninh province—who followed the local priest to the North Vietnamese port of Haiphong and boarded an American aircraft carrier, part of a United Nations effort, to take them south.

They left Tra Co behind forever, the family village on the southern bank of the river border with China. They left behind a border which could be crossed on foot at low tide, and which, after the Vietnam war had ended, would see the Vietnamese and Chinese armies facing each other for much of the time from the late 1970s until it was reopened in 1988.

Te and his family became refugees in their own country. They had fled the communist North because of the fear of religious persecution. Thirty-three years later, Te would leave the country altogether, this time fearing political persecution.

Te's parents had run a pig-farming business in the north. Now they re-established it in the south, near Bien Hoa. Te was schooled nearby and helped them run the family business. After he finished school he studied English at college. He was exempted from military service in South Vietnam because of his polio disability and was engaged by the United States contractors, P.A. and E.

Major Jim Ellis and the officer he was replacing, Major Geoff Lofthouse, were already in the Civil Affairs Unit office when Te reported for duty about 8.00 a.m. on Jim's first day in the job. The two officers had a handover period of one week and Major Ellis was keen to use it to the full; in seven days he'd be on his own and there'd be no point in wishing he'd sorted out this or that before his predecessor had left. Te's presence was barely acknowledged, but clear in his recollection.

"Jim wore his black beret at an odd angle. He was a thin man. Major Lofthouse was plump. It was interesting to see them together. Major Ellis looked straight ahead into the distance, seeing nothing, listening all the time.

"I thought, my body is not much good, my polio leg is bad, I am a small man, but one thing I have is a good pair of eyes. I can tell a lot about a person's character by appearance, and they say thin people are difficult. This will be interesting."

During the week-long handover, Te made himself scarce. The two officers were trying to sort things out and the interpreter was not needed. There would be time later for Te to come to terms with this thin and potentially difficult new boss. It would come soon enough and it may not be easy.

Paranoia prevailed at the time. The South Vietnamese were terrified at the possible outcome of the war. There were agents and double agents and double-double agents and opportunists. Te was sure he was trusted by the outgoing officer but he suspected the replacement would take a bit of convincing.

As soon as Major Lofthouse had gone, Te found there was cause for concern. Major Ellis completely rearranged the office. Saying little, and still looking off into the distance, Jim threw out everything. He cleaned off shelves, filing cabinets, emptied out the desk. Everything was taken off the top of the desk except two pens, two pieces of paper, no more.

Jim then spoke to Te. "You'd better introduce me to some people," he said in English. "I can't get on with the aid projects until I know who we're dealing with. You're the interpreter, let's get cracking."

Major Ellis and Nguyen Van Te got into the Jeep and headed into town. Jim was driving and didn't say a word until they met the local priest. Te introduced them in English. Jim spoke to the priest in Vietnamese.

"I was very surprised," Te recalled. "He spoke it well. Accent very good."

About a week went by before Jim looked straight at Te, directly into his eyes and not into the distance. "I think it's about time you showed me where we can get a decent cup of coffee around here. Come on, mate, let's go."

The interpreter beamed. "I knew we would get on well after that. He called me 'mate'."

The aid projects were riddled with corruption. The Civil Affairs Unit was involved in schemes to build four extra classrooms and a library at Vung Tau High School, accommodation for Vietnamese veterans and widows, an orphanage, clinics, water installations and other practical self-help projects reminiscent of Graham Greene's "Ugly American". In most of them there was something bent going on.

On the outskirts of Vung Tau, the unit levelled a sand-dune and divided the hectare they'd created into twenty smaller blocks for families of Vietnamese veterans and widows. The unit provided the basic building materials—cement, steel reinforcing rods, mesh, timber and galvanised iron—and put the work out to contractors. The materials, in a country at war, were like gold. It was a fact of life that the contractors routinely overestimated their requirements and kept whatever they could get away with. There was a flourishing black market, for example, in "rebar", as the steel reinforcing rods were known. It was the only way most builders could get it.

Jim Ellis could speak the language but Te became his eyes and his ears. If the contractors weren't watched, they would pour the concrete walls and floors without putting in the rebar. In the finished building it would be impossible to tell—until a wall fell down.

"Don't let the bastards get away with anything," Jim told Te.

"Not so easy," Te explained. "If we don't give them a

bit extra, they will take it out of the building. Better to let them get away with a little bit than let the buildings collapse. We can't watch them all the time."

Te took Jim all over Vung Tau. Virtually daily they would bump along in the Jeep, doing the rounds of the aid projects and their contacts, ending with coffee and somewhere along the line having another cultural lesson that Jim would put to use in his second tour, if not his first.

Te from the start was eager to show his country and his culture to this new officer, the thin man who already spoke his language. Like most Vietnamese Te was fiercely proud of his culture, his heritage, and it was an opportunity and a privilege to share it with an unusually interested and informed foreigner.

The more Te exposed the culture to him, the more Jim soaked it up. He learnt and practised the circuitous ways in which things were achieved. Where in a Western society requests were made directly, here the protocols were different. It might take time to get what you wanted, but play by the foreigner's rules and you got nowhere. It might be frustrating. Too bad. Treat it as a game. Learn the Asian way, the Vietnamese way. It was a challenge and it was enjoyable because mutual respect would develop. It also worked.

One of the best lessons was about give-and-take, about compromise, and it would have its application much later. Over one of their earliest cups of coffee, Te told the story to Jim. It was about a host and his honoured guest at a dinner party . . .

Between the two men was a plate on which a whole steamed fish had been served. It smelt delicious, the flavour of the moist flesh enhanced by garlic, ginger and lemon grass. Some people preferred the tail, some the thick meat behind the gills. In Vietnamese custom, the flesh under the fish's eye was considered the greatest delicacy.

The host offered this morsel to his honoured guest. "No, thank you," said the guest, "you have provided this marvellous meal, so you deserve the most favoured portion."

"Not at all," said the host. "It is an honour to have you to dinner. We cannot have you as our guest and not let you have the delicacy."

The two men continued to defer to each other. "No,

you must have it," said one. "No, you," said the other.

Each knew how the matter would eventually be resolved, as it could have been at the start, but neither was anxious to bring the conclusion forward. It was simply the way things were done.

Backwards and forwards the two men insisted politely until the honoured guest said, "My good friend, you must have the flesh under the eye there. I insist. I will not be offended. There will be no conflict. You see," he said, turning the fish over, "there are two eyes. There is one for each of us."

Jim and Te laughed a lot. The thin man had proved himself to be not too difficult after all. He had made his polaroid camera available to Te to do a bit of moonlighting and Te would take pictures of anybody willing to pay. There might be a war on, but there is something that's magnetic about photographic portraits in many Asian countries, and a war in Vietnam wasn't going to stop a desire that's more like a compulsion.

People posed for Te against flowerbeds, against fountains, outside churches, at the beach. They were always similar poses. There was a steady stream of clients, fascinated by the speed of the polaroid process that reproduced an image on the spot. They could not resist it.

Jim laughed at the posing and was never sure who posed more—Te or his photographic subjects.

Jim didn't laugh so much when Te drove the Jeep. "He was a terrible driver in his youth," Jim told me. "I used to call him Terrible Te whenever he got behind the wheel. He saw himself as a film star and seemed to believe he was indestructible. He scared the hell out of me."

Jim got his revenge for Te's driving more often than he would have liked, and usually at sunset when they were making a run back into Vung Tau from the countryside. Snipers and ambushes were commonplace. Someone would fire in total safety from one or two hundred metres back from the road at passing vehicles, knowing that no-one in his right mind would stop and give chase with the light fading.

The routine was a simple and standard procedure used in many wars and revolutions in many countries: drive like hell at dusk, put your foot down and go. If you're going to provide them with a shooting gallery, give the buggers the fastest moving target you can manage. With Te beside him, Jim would do just that, and Te would find out what stunt driving was really like.

There was another occasion that Jim found particularly rewarding.

The usual chaotic traffic outside Vung Tau on the road to Baria was barely moving, held up by an American refrigerated truck. The road was narrow and the oncoming traffic prevented Jim from overtaking the truck. Between the Jeep and the truck was a small motorbike, one of the step-through models that buzz in and out of traffic in many Asian cities, causing countless accidents.

Jim and Te watched in astonishment as the motorbike drew alongside the refrigerated truck and the pillion passenger took hold and pulled himself aboard. In broad daylight he swung the lever on the back door open, climbed inside the refrigerator and started throwing out foodstuffs to the rider still on the bike. What the rider couldn't stuff into a bag across his shoulder, he let fall; they would turn back for it later. Hams, steaks, cartons of frozen hamburgers and other booty hit the road. The driver of the truck was oblivious.

"We can't let them get away with that!" said Jim, drawing his revolver and firing in the air.

The man who'd boarded the truck leapt off, ran across a field and into scrub. The rider swerved off the road and tried to follow.

So did Jim. "Bastards!" he yelled. "Hang on, Te!"

Te was not only hanging on. He had slid off the seat and compressed himself into a ball on the floor of the Jeep. He was terrified.

Te was in for a bruising ride.

The motorcyclist, weaving and wobbling his little bike, the tiny engine buzzing like a swarm of bees, tried to thread his way in and out of any obstacles that might impede the chase, but Jim was just getting into the swing of it. With his right foot flat to the floor and his left hand on the steering wheel, Jim drew his revolver and fired again over the bonnet of the Jeep. This time he aimed closer, as he said, "to scare the tripe out of the thieving little bugger". It did more than that.

Te's muffled yell came up from the floor. "Stop! Stop! These are not ordinary thieves. These guys are gangsters. They'll find me and get me!"

Jim fired once more, missing the bike by a fraction, then slowed and turned back for the main road. Only after the vehicle was back on the surfaced road did Te uncoil himself and get up from the floor.

Jim later recalled it as a moment of sweet revenge. "When Terrible Te eventually stuck his head up, you should have seen his face," he laughed. "It was the only time I ever saw Te frightened."

In years to come Te would find out what real fear was like.

The first time I met Jim Ellis in his house surprisingly devoid of military memorabilia, he had produced a photograph of himself and Te taken nineteen years earlier in Vung Tau. In the weeks that went by, he found some other photographic records from his Vietnam tours. Among them were reminders of himself, Te—and the high-flying pig.

Over coffee one evening Jim had told Te that he was keen to help in projects that were simpler, less formal and more direct than the building works that the Civil Affairs Unit (CAU) was involved in. He wanted to offer support at a lower level, to help small communities become more self-sufficient. It would not to be at the expense of the existing projects, but in addition to them. Jim wanted Te to keep his eyes and ears open for any such likely project. Through the close Catholic community it came readily.

A priest was planning to move his parishioners south to escape the fighting, and was setting up a temporary village in swampland on the Vung Tau peninsula. Like Te's family, these villagers had also fled once from the North, near Hanoi, ending up not far from the Australian Army base at Nui Dat. In all, about 200 people would be uprooted and moved to this godforsaken swamp which offered purgatory as a respite from the war. But the priest was determined that his people would make it home. They were villagers who could not be absorbed into a bigger community. They had no choice. It was this or nothing.

In July of 1970, soon after he took over the Civil Affairs

Unit, Jim, his deputy Lieutenant Greg Brown, and Te found the priest already at work with an advance group of the villagers, draining the swamp and preparing the ground for planting vegetables.

In just six months, with the unofficial help of the CAU and strongly supported by Father Jim Boberg of the Australian Logistics Support Group, the village was running. The simple economic base was the production of vegetables, livestock and fishing. There were chickens and pigs, and if there was one thing that was dear to Te's heart it was pigs.

He and Jim and Lieutenant Brown went out to the swamp to meet the priest and see how things were progressing. They saw displaced people at work in a no-man's-land and there was already a sense of community in the chaos. The priest was proud that the villagers were doing it for themselves. It would all come together. God willing.

The Australians and their nominal interpreter paced around the swamp village with the priest, watching men and women bent double in the mud and slime, digging trenches, scooping with their bare hands, cutting and lashing bamboo poles together for a dozen different reasons and making a track four kilometres long through the swamp to the road between Vung Tau and Baria. The basic village houses, of course, were taking shape around a place of worship.

Chickens, ducks and geese squawked in and out of the villagers' feet. The birds were owned by individual families.

The pigs were different. They were held as communal property, a traditional though slightly contradictory concept in a group fleeing communism. In a makeshift sty were six pigs. Te leaned on a railing and studied them while the priest impressed upon the two Australian army officers the conviction that this village would be self-sufficient.

When the priest excused himself and went off to talk to one of his parishioners, Jim said to Te, "You couldn't help yourself, could you? You and pigs—it's like a bee around a honey-pot!" He laughed and slapped Te on the shoulder. "Get your eyes off them, Anh Te. This is not a shopping trip. We're here to help."

Te laughed, then frowned, then beamed again. "But we *can* help, Anh Ly. There are six pigs, okay? When six pigs get eaten, how many will there be?"

"What are you getting at?"

"Look at the pigs. What do you see?"

"I see pigs," said Jim. "When I see pigs I see pigs. I see muddy, hairy things that smell. That's what I see. Pigs."

"What do you see about these pigs?" asked Te seriously.

"Pigs. Muddy, hairy things and they smell. Anh Te, I know you can take a while to come to the point, but I also know that when pigs are involved, you have stars in your eyes. You might see bacon and pickled pork and crackling and trotters. All I see is pigs. And the smell is not getting any better while we stand here talking about them."

"When six pigs are no more," said Te, "when the village people have eaten them, there will be no market or shop where they can buy more. Look at the pigs," he said once more to Jim. "They are all sows."

Then came the idea of airlifting a boar.

Back in Vung Tau, Jim and Lieutenant Brown contacted USAID officials and by a combination of begging and buying, a big and impressive boar was procured. In a crate slung under an Australian Army Iroquois helicopter, the boar was dropped into the village, squealing and snorting and showering pig poop before the crate hit the ground.

Jim, Greg Brown, Te and Father Boberg were there to make the official handover to the village through the priest. All the villagers turned out for the ceremony. There were endless speeches of gratitude and there were celebrations. There was also recognition of a simple and singularly appropriate example of "aid". It didn't change the course of the war but that was never the mission. The exercise was to win hearts and minds.

The swamp village flourished. When Jim Ellis left Vietnam at the end of his first tour in January 1971, the village had grown to more than 1300 adults and 300 children.

There may still be some survivors of that village who remember the thin Australian soldier who spoke Vietnamese and the interpreter who wasn't needed but knew that in war, in peace, and in animal husbandry, it takes two to tango.

There may also be some survivors of the airlifted "aid boar", a muddy, hairy, smelly beast that didn't like to waste time. Within six months of his arrival, the six sows had produced 24 offspring.

A few days before Te's 22nd birthday, Anh Ly said goodbye to Anh Te. Jim was returning to Australia to go to staff college. He didn't know whether he'd ever be returning to Vietnam, or if the two would ever meet again.

There was the customary farewell party and if there's one thing Te loves, apart from pigs, it's parties. Te has seen more farewell parties than most. He also learnt, the hard way, to avoid the excesses common to Australian farewells—at home or abroad.

Once was enough. It was a memorable hangover, thanks to those Australian soldiers with powerful thirsts and empty legs. Te tried to keep up with them, drinking beer with his Australian companions to be polite, and cognac which was a hangover of another sort from the French past. The combination was devastating, but unlike most others who went on to repeat the self-destruction time and time again, Te was permanently reminded of the experience. Unlike others whose memories of headaches and upset stomachs tend to blur in the repetitition of the assault, Te would heed the lesson. "Never again," he said. "Three days later my knees were still sore."

Jim drove himself to the airport at Vung Tau for the short flight to Saigon and the long flight home. Te sat beside him, sad to be farewelling his good friend, but looking forward to driving back to base like a movie star and getting one of his friends to take a polaroid picture of himself at the wheel.

"Remember the *nouc mam?*" Jim asked him when they reached the airport. Te noticed that Jim was beginning to look into the distance again, as he had done for the first week or so after his arrival in Vietnam.

"Yes," Te said, laughing. "It was the only time you ever got angry with me."

Here at Vung Tau airport they had waited for a light aircraft to take Jim to Saigon, as they were doing now. Jim had acquired an old-time quart bottle of *nouc mam*, a sauce flavoured strongly with garlic and chilli and considered a necessary complement to fish dishes. It was to be presented to the Nha family, his instructors in the Vietnamese language at Point Cook and now back in Saigon. Te and Jim had sat on a bench, the precious bottle on the concrete between them as they reminisced and laughed about the things they'd done. The little Air America four-seater arrived and Jim stood. Te followed, but in his enthusiasm to wish Jim a good trip, he'd forgotten the bottle of *nouc mam* and kicked it over. It smashed on the concrete and Jim was left to go to Saigon to visit friends empty-handed, which, as Te had taught him, was culturally inept in Vietnam.

"Clumsy bugger!" said Jim. "Look what you've done. You've left me with nothing to take to my old professor. Do you know what I went through to get that bloody stuff?"

Te's jabbered but sincere apologies fell on deaf ears. Jim turned and boarded the small aircraft. It was the only time there was ever any ill-feeling between them.

But that was months ago. Now they were at Vung Tau airport again and this time it was goodbye. Jim had met Te's family and had been welcomed into it. He was leaving a loyal and trusted friend, a man with whom he could also share a laugh.

"No more coffees by the front beach, Anh Ly," Te said.

"No more bloody pigs," said Jim.

"No more shooting at gangsters," said Te.

"And no more bloody *nouc mam!*"

Te laughed, still a bit embarrassed about the incident. "Do you forgive me now?"

Jim held the smaller man by the shoulders and looked him sternly in the face. "I suppose I'd better," he said and they both laughed and hugged without inhibition. "Look after yourself and your family, Anh Te."

"You too, Anh Ly. Give my regards to your wife. Please write if you have time."

And Jim was gone.

5
Intelligence

The so-called Vietnamisation of the war was well underway. The foreign forces were handing over to the South Vietnamese regulars, moving to a support role, then being withdrawn. The anti-war movement in the West was already signalling the end of foreign involvement and the subsequent collapse of the South. Nguyen Van Te continued to work for Jim Ellis's replacement at the Vung Tau detachment of the Australian Civil Affairs Unit until October 1971. He then returned to the American contractors, P.A. and E., and through them was assigned to another interpreting job for the United States forces.

Jim went through the Army's Staff College at Point Lonsdale, Queenscliffe, in Victoria and was posted to the military establishment at Puckapunyal. He and Te continued to exchange letters frequently.

In July of 1972, at the height of the disillusionment with the war, Major Jim Ellis was posted back to Vietnam, this time as an intelligence officer. Once more it was not a combat role, though he would see a great deal of action and be decorated for his efforts. His mission was to gather information about enemy equipment, and to gather the equipment itself.

Supposedly identical arms of Soviet design were being made in various countries, including China, but the standards were as varied as the places of manufacture. Captured equipment could produce intelligence immediately, and lead to more by a process of deduction. Standards of production could be worked out, but so could far more detail. It was relatively simple to establish precisely which factory in which country had produced a piece of equipment, but also which month it was produced, and, if a big enough sample were available, the rate of production.

The Chinese-made arms and equipment of Soviet design were of great interest. China was making everything from small arms to tanks, anti-aircraft guns and armoured personnel carriers. What the Chinese supplied to the Vietnamese communists could be very telling. It could reflect the state of relations between the two countries, Chinese philosophy about the war, and the capability of its own defence.

The Vietnamese communists were supplied with arms from many Eastern bloc countries. The heavy equipment they were given was generally taken to be obsolescent; the tanks and artillery shipped to North Vietnam were rarely the latest models. But the discovery of a change in models or suppliers could be important intelligence. It was a way of assessing China's production capability and its own military strength. An increase in the numbers of Chinese-made equipment could mean China supported a more determined thrust against the South. More important, it could mean the Chinese were fully armed with equipment about which the West knew little or nothing.

It was the period of China's opening up, soon after Richard Nixon's first visit, and nobody could anticipate where it would lead. It was vital to understand China's relations with Vietnam. It was also crucial to evaluate China's military might.

There was another reason for wanting to get hold of captured equipment. Australia was keen to replace the French missile system known as ENTAC and was on the verge of buying the American "Red Eye". But the surface-to-air system that was showing most concern around the world was the SA-7, a shoulder-controlled weapon of Soviet design. It was successfully accounting for more United States helicopters in Vietnam than the Americans cared to admit. Getting hold of an SA-7 could lead to reverse engineering and possibly copying the weapon in Australia.

Jim Ellis's task was "to find and obtain foreign weapons technology". He was assigned to the Captured Materiel Exploitation Centre (CMEC) at Tan Son Nhut airbase at Saigon. It was a multinational organisation, and the United States, of course, was keenly interested in this intelligence.

From the Defence Department's Joint Intelligence Office (JIO) in Canberra, Major Ellis was given a shopping list as if he were going into a supermarket rather than a war zone. The stuff was there, wasn't it? He could just go and help himself, pass it through the check-out counter and whistle for a taxi to take it home. They'd give it for free anyway. After all we were helping them in their bloody war, weren't we? We could find out what the commie buggers were up to and reverse-engineer it; work out the specifications, the quality of the forging of the metals, and turn out replicas at the Weapons Research Establishment at Salisbury in South Australia or the branch at Tottenham in Victoria.

"They didn't want much," Jim told me later. "Genuine working models, unmarked by war or hail damage, all packed in grease and shipped off home in a bloody great floating shopping-trolley."

Jim knew Te's help could be considerable. The cultural lessons on the last tour had been important in the hearts and minds exercise, and they'd be important again this time. Here was a country at war, riddled with corruption and run by warlords, the regional commanders, the generals. You wouldn't get anywhere walking up to them and saying, "Hey, man, gimme a tank". The Americans couldn't do it with a fistful of dollars, and Jim was empty-handed.

Jim needed Te to make sense of the technical details that related to weapons and equipment. Such captured data would be almost as revealing as the equipment itself, but by the time it had gone through several translations it could get very confusing. For example, the details of a Chinese copy of a Soviet-designed tank would eventually emerge in a version of Vietnamese in the handbooks supplied to Hanoi. One need only think of the operating instructions that are translated into English and accompany many domestic appliances made in Asia to imagine the scale of the problem.

Jim wrote to Te to let him know he was coming back and that he would like to see him. The letter was never received. When Jim got back to South Vietnam, however, he tracked Te down through P.A. and E. Te was stunned to hear from his old mate, and every bit as excited. They met at a coffee shop in Saigon and chattered on, filling in the gaps, then went to dinner. Te's family were at Bien Hoa.

"Anh Te," Jim said, "I am back here to gather information

about the things the communists are using against the South. Some of the information will be very technical and I may have trouble understanding the terms. I know you are working again for P.A. and E. but I need someone I can trust and I know I can trust my brother Te. Will you help me?"

Te smiled. "Of course I will help you. Did you think I would not help you?"

"No," said Jim, "but the war is at a critical stage. The future may not be easy."

"The present also is not easy," said Te, "but we are like brothers. Of course I will help you."

The thin Australian major was the odd man out at the Captured Materiel Exploitation Centre at Tan Son Nhut airbase. It was run by the South Vietnamese but the United States was heavily involved. It was South Vietnam's war, the Americans were the big backers, and Australia was on the brink of "bringing the boys back home". One lone Australian officer was in no position to help himself to captured equipment or to make any demands.

What the Americans failed to get by request, they would try to buy, often with huge amounts of dollars, and in a war there is no better lubricant than hard currency. Major Jim Ellis's slush fund could run to a bottle of *nouc mam* or occasionally a case of beer. He traded favours for a slouch hat on several occasions. Australian camouflage raincoats were also a form of currency. "The South Vietnamese and the Americans loved them," he said, "even though the bloody things didn't keep the rain out."

His preferred method was cultural persuasion.

Alone among the South Vietnamese and Americans at the CMEC in Saigon, the Australian intelligence officer seemed to have everything against him—a huge shopping-list and an empty wallet. Balanced against these disadvantages, there were benefits from operating on his own. He could be absorbed among the Americans and call on many of their facilities. He could also move about independently, exploiting his familiarity with the culture.

When it came to meeting the requirements of his shopping list, Jim was well placed. At the Captured Materiel Exploitation Centre he would get copies of reports on every tactical action in the war. He would know who was involved, the strength of the adversaries, the progress of actions, and be able to assess whether battles—imminent or already underway—might involve some of the heavy stuff he was looking for.

In one of those quirks of war, the lone Australian was actually more potent than the South Vietnamese with whom he was working. In a diary entry dated 3 August 1972 on the Perfume River in Military Region One, Major Ellis wrote, "I discovered the reason the ARVN [Army of the Republic of Vietnam] members of CMEC refuse to go to these areas. They receive no allowances and apparently cannot afford to find their own accommodation and meals."

"They never left Tan Son Nhut," he told me later. "If one of the divisions involved in the battle didn't bring the stuff back, it simply stayed on the battlefield until it was stolen, vandalised or destroyed. The South Vietnamese in the field were making a fortune selling the stuff as trophies to the GIs."

Jim set up agents in the capital and in all major regions. He received independent reports and he traded with the American Central Intelligence Agency. "It was a bit like swapping stamps," he said. "You can't trade if you don't have anything to trade. I had to gather my own intelligence in order to trade a bit of theirs—and the place was swarming with CIA."

A lot of technical information came into Jim's hands—specifications, operating instructions, even battle plans. This is where Te came in. "I had to know exactly what they meant," Jim said. "If I'd simply handed over the documents to the South Vietnamese or the Americans, asking them, 'Is this interesting?', they'd have said, 'No', and kept it to themselves, whatever it was. Te was vital."

Jim covered every part of South Vietnam. "I made at least 100 trips," he said. "When I got on to something, I couldn't wait. I would go over to the aviation company and head off up-country, usually with some of the American 'advisers', sometimes on my own, and usually when a battle was underway. If I'd hung about in Saigon waiting for the end, the local South Vietnamese commander in the battle would have got hold of the equipment and it would have become much more difficult to prize it out of him. Or the stuff would be nicked or vandalised and become useless to us."

It's on the shopping list but how do I send it home? Major Ellis examines a captured Soviet-made tank.

Tagging along with the Americans had its minor comforts. "If the shit hit the fan I'd get into their bunker," Jim told me. But it wasn't always available.

Major Ellis was deafened in one ear while witnessing battles from which he would procure captured equipment. The officer he had replaced in Vietnam moved to the Army's Inspectorate of Establishments in Canberra and later wrote to the Department of Repatriation and Compensation to support Jim's claim. "Major Ellis's duties were extremely dangerous ones requiring his presence during every major battle fought by the South Vietnamese Army in the period. He was subjected to artillery, mortar and rocket bombardment on many occasions."

Major Ellis was decorated three times by the Government of the United States and five times by the South Vietnamese government.

Major Ellis mockingly warns a British major who's also got his eye on the Chinese-made armoured personnel carrier. Perfume River, 1972

On 12 November 1972, his vehicle was involved in a grenade attack in the northern province of Thua Thien. Another vehicle, a little Renault taxi, was struck in the same attack and set on fire. Major Ellis pulled the unconscious driver out of the burning wreck and was decorated with the South Vietnamese Military Life Saving Medal. "It was the only award that meant anything," he said. "They handed out decorations all the time just for length of service, for doing the job. On this occasion I managed to save some poor bugger's life."

The election of the Whitlam government on 2 December 1972 marked the end of Australian involvement in the war, but not immediately. The boys would be coming home early in the new year, but not Major Jim Ellis. His intelligence mission would continue, although with the withdrawal of Australian troops he could not, in theory, remain.

When the boys came home, one platoon stayed on to guard the Australian Embassy in Saigon. Major Ellis stayed on, too, designated as Assistant Military Attache (Technical). It was an artificial position. He was theoretically attached to the Embassy but was never accredited. He reported to the head of the Joint Intelligence Office in Canberra.

Nguyen Van Te had stopped working for the American contractors late in 1972 and returned to the family home and piggery in Bien Hoa. His wife was pregnant with their first child. Jim called on the family or met Te in Saigon every week or so and Te continued to translate documents for him.

Many of them came from equipment Jim obtained after a huge battle in Military Region One, headquartered in the ancient capital, Hue. Jim put his success at acquiring the equipment down to Te's cultural lesson about the host, the guest and the fish.

It was a massive battle. The cream of the South Vietnamese troops—ARVN, the Army of the Republic of Vietnam—had three divisions of 12,000 men each, 36,000 of their best, stacked against 50–60,000 North Vietnamese regulars. Between them was the Tok Han River. Each side had heavy artillery backing, and the South Vietnamese also had air support. They were to slug it out for several days.

In one 30-hour pounding by heavy artillery, with each side hurling huge shells and missiles at the other, the losses were enormous. One entire ARVN battalion lost every tank and armoured personnel carrier, but it was the way that the North Vietnamese destroyed them that was of greatest interest to Major Ellis.

What Jim had his eyes on were the Type-59 Tanks on the North Vietnamese side of the Tok Han River. They were the Chinese version of the T-54 tanks that the Soviet Union had been producing since 1949. T-54s were quite common, but the Type-59 was in great demand. Close analysis of a Type-59 could reveal a lot about China's production capability . . . if only Jim could get his hands on one.

The losses on both sides were devastating. North and South both claimed victory but there was no winner in this battle. The fields on both sides of the river were strewn with the wreckage of so much heavy engineering—the tanks and APCs, the wheels, steels tracks, armour plating, gun barrels. The landscape had been transformed into a moonscape with craters left by the huge artillery charges.

The communist forces picked up their dead and wounded and slipped sideways into Cambodia, and the South Vietnamese army was left there, stunned and depleted. Every hill, taken and retaken as the battle had proceeded, was left adorned with flags proclaiming the victory neither side had won.

When the protagonists had gone, there was a rush for the mechanical pickings that were the spoils of war. Several Chinese-made Type-59 Tanks had survived the battle, immobilised but intact. By Jim's assessment, only one was a "goer".

The South Vietnamese commander of Military Region One, General Truong, would claim the equipment as his own—not the army's, not South Vietnam's. "Even if you could get President Thieu on the phone," said Jim, "and have him order the general to hand over the equipment, the general would stall forever. He knew the Americans wanted the stuff and had a bag of gold to pay for it. The USA paid $US100,000 for the loan of a Type-59 Tank for twelve months!"

Jim was determined he would get a Type-59 Tank but he knew it was pointless asking for one. He would be seen as just another crass foreigner loaded with money. He would have to be different. He would adapt Te's lesson about the fish.

Jim went over the battlefield and checked out what he could, then approached the general and said in Vietnamese, "Congratulations on your victory. It was very decisive. You have sent the communists retreating in shame across the Cambodian border."

"Thank you," said the general, who'd already met Jim and knew he was shopping. "You speak the language well. What is your interest in the battle?"

"My country is keen to examine some of the equipment the communists have left behind."

"So is everybody else," said the general.

"I am particularly interested in the tanks," said Jim, "the Type-59s the Chinese are making."

"So is everybody else. The Americans are willing to pay big money for them."

"I come from Australia, as you know. I have no money to pay for them."

"In any case," said the general, "I couldn't let you have a Type-59. There are too few and they are too precious. The best I could let you have is a T-54, you know, the Russian-made tank."

"I know them," said Jim. "I would be grateful for one if you would let me choose one."

"Yes, which one on the battlefield do you want?"

"That one over there," said Jim pointing at a tank he'd checked out earlier, "that T-54 over there."

"Oh, *that* T-54," said the general. "Yes, my Australian friend, you may have that old tank."

The smiles they exchanged were mere twinkles in the eye. Each knew it was not a Soviet T-54 at all, but a Chinese Type-59, and each knew that the other knew. Jim had put into practice the cultural lesson Te had given him and been rewarded for it.

The tank was even presented with a plaque attached to it. The inscription read something like, "This captured T-54 tank of Soviet manufacture is presented to the Australian Army by the Army of the Republic of South Vietnam", but the poignancy was lost on the curators of the Armoured Corps Museum in Melbourne where the tank ended up, and still lies today.

Many years later Jim heard that the inscribed plaque had been chiselled off the tank "because the South Vietnamese had obviously misinterpreted the captured tank and its country of origin". An official letter to Major Ellis said, "We had little trouble identifying the tank as a Type-59".

The Type-59 was only part of the pickings. Jim had also acquired an APC, an armoured personnel carrier, and sent off "a signal" letting the Joint Intelligence Office in Canberra know.

"Terrific news," came the reply. "Send it home!"

"What do they expect?" Jim wondered. "Shall I just pop it in the post?"

Here was Major Jim Ellis, on his own in a war zone and in possession of two very large and heavy objects. They were not even near a port. While Jim was arranging—in return for a case of beer here, a slouch hat there, a camouflage raincoat somewhere else—to get the two items brought to the port of Da Nang on a flat-top barge, JIO in Canberra was sending another signal saying a cargo ship was being despatched forthwith.

When the ship *John Monash* eventually arrived at Da Nang from Singapore, there was no crane to lift the tank or the APC aboard, and the ship had sailed without chains or shackles with which to secure them. If they moved about in the hold, as they would have done if not tied down, the *John Monash* would almost certainly have rolled, taking itself, the tank, the APC and all aboard to the bottom of the South China Sea. The ship had already had one brush with a typhoon on the way into port.

Jim persuaded a South Korean firm to use its 60 tonne floating crane to get the heavy items aboard the *John Monash*, and out of his own pocket bought chains and shackles.

By this time another signal had arrived from JIO in Canberra, informing Major E.J. Ellis that the captured military equipment had to be "in quarantine condition for entry to Australia".

"That topped everything," said Jim. "I'd got the bloody things, got them to Da Nang, got them aboard the ship and even got them tied down. And now I had to make sure they didn't have a speck of dirt or feathers on them and hadn't run through any Vietnamese chook poop on their way into battle."

When the ship eventually left with the APC and the tank aboard, Jim made his way back to Saigon, then visited Te and his family at Bien Hoa. It was a country at war but here among friends there was a sense of sanity.

Te pointed proudly at a new lot of piglets. For some reason Jim was reminded of his mission. The captured equipment—in or out of quarantine condition—would help establish that the Chinese were not as advanced as the West had suspected. They were, in fact, about thirty years behind in their technology. "Anh Te," said Jim, "you've got to laugh."

Major Jim Ellis later got hold of an SA-7, a Soviet-made, heat-seeking surface-to-air missile. It was procured with no claim to cultural niceties. He didn't even get it from a battlefield.

"I pinched it from the Americans," he told me. "It was in a store at Tan Son Nhut. I was running out of time to get one any other way, so I thought, okay, if I get caught I'll be kicked out but it's a risk I have to take."

He packed it in a box, and, knowing it would be searched on the way out of the airport, draped an Australian flag over it. At the boom gate at the airport perimeter fence, Jim told the South Vietnamese security guard, "This is the body of an Australian soldier killed up-country. I have to take the body to the Australian Embassy, then bring it back out here to send to Australia."

The security guard lifted the flag to see the box underneath. He put his hand on the lid then drew it away. Jim drove the missile to the Australian Embassy, prepared the shipping documents declaring the weapon was safe for transportation and drove back to Tan Son Nhut, with the Australian flag once more draped across the box.

The sentry at the boom gate blew his whistle and called out a guard of honour. The South Vietnamese soldiers stood in line and saluted a box bound for Melbourne. They were unaware they were saluting a stolen surface-to-air missile, and they should have been a little suspicious. The last of the Australian soldiers had been withdrawn from Vietnam two months earlier.

In April of 1973 it was all over. The so-called Assistant Military Attache (Technical) was being withdrawn three months early at his own request because his wife, Glenda, was sick.

As it was, the timing was none too soon. An official letter said later, "It was necessary to issue an order restricting Major Ellis's participation in further military actions just prior to his return to Australia. This was done because his situation was becoming too hazardous and the political consequences of him becoming a casualty at that time were too great."

Jim drove up to Bien Hoa to say goodbye to Te, his wife who was still pregnant with their first child, and his parents. Te and Jim met outside the cathedral and went on to the house attached to the piggery. Life was reasonably comfortable with the income from the piggery and a small plantation. To the family Jim presented a refrigerator he'd acquired, and penicillin that was surplus to Embassy needs. It was like gold to a Vietnamese pig-farmer.

Jim ate with the family in a mood of sadness he was unable to change. "Te wanted to know what would happen to him," said Jim. "I told him it was inevitable that the communists would take over but he would be okay. I had no way of guaranteeing it, of course. I thought maybe the communists would hang a few generals but the likes of Te would be too small-fry to worry about. It was much later that I became concerned. Helping the foreign forces could have landed Te in some real trouble if they'd found out."

They met again in Saigon just before Jim's departure. Symbolically their last meeting was on Freedom Street, and Major Jim Ellis was heading back to what Te described as a freedom country. It seemed an odd description at the time to Jim. He'd asked in February to be allowed to go home once he'd acquired the SA-7 and then held the fort, as it were, during the United States withdrawal. Permission was granted, but because of some diplomatic pique and apparent resentment at Jim's unaccredited attachment, Australian Embassy officials had refused to authorise an air ticket for him, and Major Ellis, the intelligence officer who'd stuck his neck out for his country, been shelled and half-deafened for his troubles, and been decorated by two other countries, was forced to leave a personal cheque as security against his ticket home from the war.

"Goodbye, old friend, my brother Te," said Jim.

"Goodbye, Anh Ly," said Te.

They hugged and Jim walked away, out of Vietnam, out of this crazy war and back to the country where returning veterans had been spat on only a few months earlier. If any of it was to make sense, now was not the time.

Te's first child was born six weeks after Jim left. Overjoyed that his first-born was a son, Te wrote to Jim to share the news. The family enterprise ticked over and, with the war with two more years still to run, Te put his association with the United States and Australian forces behind him and absorbed himself in the family and its business. He was a civilian, a disabled pig-farmer, useless to either side in a war.

A month after Jim Ellis returned to Australia, he received a letter from the Australian Embassy in Saigon.

Dear Jim,

Attached is your cheque for $US697 which you lodged with the Embassy prior to your departure on 7 April 1973.

As it turned out there was a cable dated 4 April which allocated the funds and approved the travel. This cable was kept in the Military Section.

Sorry for the inconvenience this has caused.

Hope you are enjoying being home.

Regards,

R.L. Cox, Attache (Property).

Jim turned the letter over, then read it again. He had been designated Assistant Military Attache, and it was the Military Section of the Embassy that had withheld the approval for his ticket home. As if by poetic justice, Jim later became the head of the Army's technical intelligence section in the Joint Intelligence Office which had sent him off to Vietnam with that impossible shopping list.

Te and Jim exchanged letters for three months. On 25 August 1973 Te wrote to Jim at Puckapunyal enclosing photographs of that beaming smile and saying, "I hope you will become ambassador and come back to Vietnam".

Biên Hoà ngày 25-08-1973

Anh Ly thân mến.

Có lẽ Tế phải viết bằng tiếng Anh, nhưng lâu quá thông dụng nên gặp khó khăn.

Tế luôn luôn mong Anh Ly và gia-đình gặp nhiều may mắn và khỏe mạnh. Bây giờ ở đây (VN) trời đang mưa mùa, mưa nhiều lắm, suốt ngày suốt đêm, mưa làm Tế nhớ anh Ly nhiều lắm, làm sao Tế quên được tách café thật nóng tại Kaki, Cười. Trong lúc Anh Ly tại VN đã dạy cho Tế nhiều bài học về đời sống rất quí-giá.

Bây giờ anh Ly đang làm gì? và ở đâu. Anh Ly có nhớ đến Tế bao giờ không?

Sau khi Anh Ly về úc có nhiều bạn gái của Tế muốn gặp anh Ly để nói

On 25 August 1973, Te wrote a letter to Jim at Puckapunyal, saying that he hoped Jim would return to Vietnam. In it he enclosed a photo of his beloved truck.

chuyến và đi Vũng Tàu tắm biển.

Anh Ly ơi: Có bao giờ trở lại VN nữa không? Tế mong rằng: trong tương lai, Anh Ly sẽ là Đại sứ Úc Tại Nam Việt Nam (The Saigon) có lẽ lúc ấy tế sẽ sung sướng lắm vì gặp lại Anh Ly. Nhưng bây giờ chỉ là một giấc mơ!

Tế dừng lại đây nhé chúc Anh Ly và gia đình mạnh khỏe may mắn giàu mạnh.

Thân mến
Tố.

AUSTRALIAN EMBASSY
SAIGON

In reply quote No. 3/IP

26 April 1973

Dear Jim,

    Attached is your cheque for $US697 which you lodged with the Embassy prior to your departure on 7 April 1973.

    As it turned out there was a cable dated 4 April which allocated the funds and approved the travel. This cable was kept in the Military Section.

    Sorry for the inconvenience this has caused.

    Hope you are enjoying being home.

Regards

(H.E. Cox)
Attaché (Property)

An apologetic letter from the Australian Embassy in Saigon, which arrived a month after Jim got back from the war in 1973

It was the last Jim would hear of his old mate for the next sixteen years. Jim Ellis was promoted to lieutenant-colonel, but at the age of 48 left the army behind for good. Into the civilian lifestyle, resumed after a career of thirty years that began with conscription, Jim would carry an enormous burden of guilt. He became convinced that Te had died or been killed, or, at the very least, been taken away and forgotten in the purges that were called "re-education". Whichever fate had befallen Te, Jim Ellis blamed himself.

6

The Cup

"Get your things together," said Inspector Wheaton. "You're on your way to Hei Ling Chau to be screened, and I'll bet you," he added with a smile on his ruddy face, "you'll be screened in."

It was 29 August 1989, three weeks after Vietnamese boat person number 411/12/89, had been located at Sek Kong in the New Territories of Hong Kong. No-one but his sister-in-law, Mai Phuong, knew about the interest shown in his case by the Australian Consulate-General. Te simply carried on his job as interpreter and postman for the police who ran the camp and had taken a shine to him. He picked up his pay at the rate of $HK125 a month ($A22), and, as always, avoided trouble.

"I'm doing my best for you," Inspector Wheaton told him. "I've asked the police in the camp at Hei Ling Chau to look after you." Such a request was virtually an order.

Te and his family had another of their many tearful farewells. Jailer and inmate celebrated another step on the way to Te's freedom, unaware there were many steps—and many stumbles—still to come.

They were also parting company with the other eleven people with whom they'd shared the little boat all the way from Vietnam. Some of them carried the few belongings of Te and his family up to the wire fence and watched as the gates parted and were closed again. Through the wire they had one last contact. Mai Phuong and Thuy Vy cried. Te cried too.

From the big camp that only recently was an airfield they were taken by police bus to a pier near Sham Shui Po, once more underneath the flight path to Kaitak Airport. "One day, maybe soon," Te told his children, "we will up there, too, on our way to Australia, the freedom country.

THE CUP

Soon, I am confident, we will be screened in."

They boarded the police launch and then wove out through the junks and sampans, the big lighters and barges loading and unloading the ships of many flags at anchor in Hong Kong harbour. Past Stonecutters Island they went, past the old Star Ferries that were now prison hulks, moored in the lee of the island with thousands of Vietnamese kept on board. Past more old ferries tied up at the western end of the harbour they went, and past Green Island where they were first intercepted, where they'd seen the highrise buildings of Hong Kong Island and mistaken it for Macau.

The police launch disgorged them at Hei Ling Chau, a tiny island previously known for only one thing. On its steep rocky top were several imposing stone buildings, the place of banishment or reform for some of the colony's many drug addicts, the ones who'd chased too many dragons on the narcotics of the poppy.

Hei Ling Chau now housed a second breed of the unwanted, equally unwelcome in any other part of the colony and preferably disposable. If either group had to be tolerated at all, few Hong Kong residents could think of a better location for them than this remote island, inaccessible and silent.

The two were segregated; the drug addicts here, the boat people there. High wire fences impeded any unlikely fraternising. Hei Ling Chau was run by the Correctional Services Department (CSD) in a no-nonsense way. There was precious little to laugh about. The process here was screening. Get 'em in, get 'em done, get 'em out again. Next!

Te was brought before the CSD's chief officer, a Chinese man whose stony expression fitted the environment. When he spoke, his face softened. In English, he said to Te, "We are authorised to help you. We know the reason you've been transferred to this place and I know you used to work for the Australian Army. At the longest, you will be here two weeks. If you have any worries, tell me. Don't let anyone know your background. Don't let anyone know that people are trying to help you. Don't even tell your children— especially don't tell your children."

Te and his family were shown into a concrete building twenty metres long and ten metres wide. The bunks were stacked three high, with three people to each bunk. There were 200 people in this one block.

The closeness of the Vietnamese family unit without doubt saved many people from succumbing to the awfulness of their environment—from simply going mad. Family members comforted, consoled and counselled each other. They kept themselves together, concentrating on each other's welfare, though each was just a disposable number in a big leaderless flock. There was violence, sometimes serious and widespread, but it seemed to me that it was not an indictment, rather a vindication of the patience of these people—because there was so little, not so much, in conditions that were sub-human.

The extended Vietnamese family, a feature of Asian cultures, is more like an ever-extending family. People are recognised as blood relatives long after the common blood has thinned out or been contaminated by generations of other generations. Relatives of friends have almost the same claim to recognition, and unrelated people from the same village are regarded almost as members of the family, even though the village might have a population of 10,000 people.

Yet among 50,000 boat people in Hong Kong at the time, most of whom came from north Vietnam, Te frequently came across people he knew or was related to. In the hut in which he now found himself on Hei Ling Chau, he recognised ten people from his village who'd been in Hong Kong for well over a year and had still not been granted their first screening interview. He also found a female cousin, or rather she found him.

By the time Te and his family had been brought into the concrete hut it was too late for the evening meal. He was also told by the hut leader that all bunks had been taken, and hut leaders were quite feudal—as the regional warlords had been during the Vietnam war; Te and his family would have to sleep on the floor. Too bad. Last in, first learn your place.

A woman in her forties was on the top bunk nearby. She heard the voices and stared down to recognise one of the speakers. "Young cousin Te!" she shouted and called to another man, another cousin; the fathers of all three of them were brothers.

The ever-extending family syndrome proved to be a big

help. Suddenly a meal was produced, and space was found on the bunks. Te and his son Vuong could share the narrow strip of plywood with the male cousin, and another piece of ply was found for Mai Phuong, Thuy Vy and Thu Thao to share.

It wasn't luxury but it was a step up from the bleak prospect of going to sleep on an empty stomach on the floor.

If variety eases the boredom of incarceration, if change can be a relief from despair, Te and his family were better off than most. They had not been restricted to the same four walls. Hei Ling Chau was now the fifth detention centre they had seen from the inside in two-and-a-half months.

Their hut was another mass of bodies and sweat and smells and noise. There was wailing and there were groans, fighting and rape. Gangs backing the hut leaders fought gangs wanting to topple them. Other gangs fought each other, for distraction or for sport. People hid any gold and valuables wherever they could. The Correctional Services Department had given up trying to maintain order at night. At 9.00 p.m. the officers locked the doors on the 200 people in each concrete hut and left them to sort themselves out until 7.00 a.m. the following day. Then they would allow the boat people into a fenced exercise yard. If there was any blood to clean up, the VBPs could do it themselves.

In Te's case, a senior CSD officer, sometimes Chinese, sometimes British, checked every couple of days and warned him to be very careful. "If the gangsters fight," he would be told, "let them. If they want your clothes, give them. Don't argue. Clothes can be replaced. Your life can't. You won't be here much longer."

Te was given a new number to remember. His boat number was 411/89. Now he was given a personal number by the CSD. For the moment the man known as Nguyen Van Te should forget his name and remember his new number, 13541. He liked his name better, but he was quick to see that he had been given "a very interesting number".

Everybody else, as far as he could tell, had been given a number higher than 30,000. Each morning the CSD staff would display the numbers of those to be interviewed for screening, and there was never a number as low as the one given to Te.

His cousins also noticed. "How come your number is so low?" they asked him.

"I don't know," he replied.

On the fifth night Te thought his number, so to speak, was up.

Lying on the plywood bunk with Vuong and the male cousin, Te half dozed. In this warehouse of bodies, sleep was impossible. He felt the bunks move slightly as someone climbed up. He felt a hand on his leg, and before he could move or cry out he felt something very sharp pressed into his back. It was a warning and to challenge it might cost him his life. Te felt a hand slide up his legs, around his waist, up and across his chest then down his back. He felt the sharpened object pressed slightly harder into his back then suddenly withdrawn as the man jumped down and ran off on cat's feet into the mass of bunks and bodies. Te saw the man and the cloth tied round his face. He knew he would never recognise him, and he knew it was better that he couldn't. Whatever the man was after, he didn't get. And Te was alive to face the next challenge.

Each day the personal numbers of the people to undergo their screening interviews that day would be posted on a wall. No names were listed, only numbers. The first interview was usually very cursory. The numbered person would be required to give his or her name and the number of people in the group to a low-ranking CSD officer, then be ordered: "Return to your bunk". Even so, the VBPs would prepare their stories and rehearse them to make sure there was no conflict among the group members' versions.

When Te saw his number, 13541, posted on the wall on the morning of his seventh day at Hei Ling Chau, he shuffled the few pieces of paper that might be relevant: his identity card from Vietnam and the letters Jim and I had written.

The children were not required at this stage, only Te and Mai Phuong. Each faced not a low-ranking officer but an inspector, a male for Te and a female inspector for Mai Phuong, both of them Chinese. Te made the running.

"Good morning, sir." he said. "How are you today?"

"Same as usual," said the inspector, looking up briefly from Te's file before him on the desk.

Attached to the back of the file Te could see a letter

from his policeman friend at Sek Kong, Inspector Wheaton. As near as he can recall, it read:

> Mr Nguyen Van Te worked as interpreter/translator for the Australian Army and for the United States contractor, P.A. and E., during the Vietnam War. Here at Sek Kong he has worked for us an interpreter and postal officer. His behaviour has been excellent. On behalf of the Command Board I would recommend he be screened in. The Australian Consulate-General has already been in contact with us and is concerned for him.

Te thought, no wonder Inspector Wheaton had wanted to place a bet that I would be screened in!

"Do you have any other papers?" asked the CSD inspector.

"Certainly, sir," said Te. He looked at another Chinese man, who was apparently an interpreter, standing beside the inspector's desk. To Te the event resembled a court case. The interviewing officer was the judge, the interpreter was a lawyer for the prosecution, and Te was the accused.

"I have an idea, sir," said Te to the inspector.

"What's that?"

"We do the interview in English. We are both speaking English now. I'm sorry I don't speak Cantonese."

"Never mind that," said the inspector, looking first at the little man before him and then to the interpreter. The inspector said something to him in Cantonese. Te waited, smiling. The interpreter abruptly stood up, shook Te by the hand and walked out of the room.

First victory to me, Te thought. I've just succeeded in having the prosecutor dismissed. Now it's just me and the judge.

"Have you any letters?" said the inspector, knowing full well that Te did.

"Yes," said Te proudly, "I have letters from my old boss, Major Ellis, and from an Australian television reporter."

"May I make copies?"

"Certainly, sir."

"Did you know it would be very difficult to be screened in in Hong Kong?"

"I knew it would not be easy."

"Tell me the main reason you left Vietnam."

"As you know, sir, I used to work for Australia and America. Since communists took over the South I live in fear."

"What do you think will happen to you if you are repatriated to Vietnam?"

"Ah," said Te, "I definitely think that on humanitarian grounds I will not be sent back. I would be given terrible time by the communist government."

The CSD inspector wanted to know Te's history from the first move south with the Catholic villagers following Dien Bien Phu, and what happened to Te after he ceased to work for the foreigners.

"Did you go to re-education camp?" asked the inspector.

"No," said Te, and added, beaming, "I hide my background."

"How?"

"Nearly three years before the North took over the South I stopped working for Australians and Americans. I went back to my village 100 kilometres from Vung Tau and work on my parents' pig farm and small plantation. Good Catholic community. Bad communications. My secret safe there."

"Then why did you live in fear?"

"One very close friend worked as interpreter for American company called Phoenix. It was CIA agency. When war ended in 1975 he reported his background to the communist authorities. That same day he disappeared. No further word since. For fourteen years I worry. Same could happen to me."

The CSD inspector read the letters and one from the Consul-General in Te's file. "I don't promise anything," he said, "but I'll do my best for you. You have very strong support."

Instead of the cursory question and answer session that usually constituted the preliminary interview, Te's had lasted nearly half a day.

"Would you now help your sister-in-law?"

"Yes, of course," said Te.

He went into the other room where the female CSD inspector sat opposite Mai Phuong. Te put his hand on his sister-in-law's shoulder and said in English, not for her but for the inspector, "Good people are helping us."

Suddenly the interviewing officer snapped, "Why did she leave?"

THE CUP

Mai Phuong sat silent. Te said, "May I answer for her?" The woman relaxed. "Yes, please," she said.

Te explained how Mai Phuong had come along as proxy mother while her sister waited in Vietnam with the younger boy suffering polio, and his brother. Te added, "Her father was an officer in the South Vietnamese police. After the North took over the South he was put in a re-education camp for three years. He fell sick and nearly died. The communists released him, expecting him to die within a week, but God didn't do what the communists wanted. He's still alive today.

"The whole family suffered. Mai Phuong was forced to work in the fields without pay while her father was in re-education. The communists called the workers in the fields 'happy volunteers'.

"Even at school she was punished because her father had been a policeman in South Vietnam, but she had no part in the war. She was only 11 years old when it ended.

"My wife says Mai Phuong became isolated from her own age group and wanted to escape as much as we did. When my wife knew I was leaving with the three older children she said to Mai Phuong 'I have a way for you to leave Vietnam. The youngest boy is too sick to travel. I will stay with him and keep the next youngest for company for him. Will you go with Te and look after the three older children for me?' Mai Phuong was already very close to the children. We one big family, so she agreed."

The inspector asked Mai Phuong, "Is this true?"

"Yes," said Mai Phuong. It was all she said or was required to say.

"We must stop now and continue tomorrow," said the inspector. "I have twenty others to interview."

When Te and his family left the interview room, somebody waiting in the queue said, "How come you spent so long in there?" Another demanded, "How come you got to see an inspector?"

They turned to each other in the queue, all of them from North Vietnam, and started saying, "He must be a spy. He must have a Yankee skeleton hidden in the cupboard."

Te stopped. "It doesn't work here even if you were a Yankee spy. They say a CIA spy named Tinh was here before you people arrived. He spent eighteen years in jail in Hanoi after he was caught by the North. He finally escaped to Hong Kong but Immigration Department here interviewed him seven times and still didn't believe him."

The door to the room where the interviews with males were conducted opened and the CSD inspector walked out briskly through the queue. He stopped in front of Te and shook him by the hand. "Goodbye. Good luck. I must leave now."

Te was as stunned as the others. The officials never shook hands with the boat people.

"What's so special about you?" demanded one of the VBPs.

"Nothing special," said Te. "I'm same like you."

"How come they didn't interview your children then?" shouted another. "They always ask kids over five years old, just to check out the story and ask, 'Did your father tell you last night to say that?'"

'I don't know," said Te. "Maybe they too busy. Maybe they ask tomorrow."

That night Te slept little. He lay on the plywood waiting for the sound of any approach, for any movement of the bunk, for the feel of the sharpened object in his back or at his throat. He felt Vuong beside him and he listened to his son's breathing. He raised his head slowly but often to check that Mai Phuong, Thuy Vy and Thu Thao were safe. He heard the muffled footsteps of the gangsters on the prowl, he heard moans and wondered if they'd claimed another victim for the sake of a gold ring or revenge.

When 7.00 a.m. finally came round and the doors were opened, his heart was still pounding. It had been an exhausting night doing nothing except staying alert—and praying.

Their numbers were posted again that morning. Mai Phuong was called in to see the same CSD officer she'd seen the day before. Te was left outside to face the taunts again in the queue outside the interview rooms.

"Yankee skeleton! Yankee skeleton!" the North Vietnamese chanted.

Te decided that to ignore the taunts would be to plead guilty. He stopped and replied, quietly but firmly, "If I had a Yankee skeleton I could write to Vietnamese people already in United States and then US will come and let my whole family into United States easily."

"How did you learn English?" one demanded.

"I am a teacher of languages." Te had deliberately spoken with a northern accent which he'd learned from his parents.

"Where did you teach?"

"Before reunification I taught in Haiphong. Afterwards I move to Ho Chi Minh City."

Before the people in the queue could grill him any further, the CSD officer appeared and called Te away. "We need you to help us interview your sister-in-law."

They spent the whole morning completing forms, filling out particulars, explaining and justifying Mai Phuong's presence in place of her sister, Te's wife. "We are Asian people, like you," Te told the interviewing officer. "We have very strong family ties. I know you understand."

At midday the interviewing officer shook their hands again and wished them luck. The results could be expected in about fourteen days.

Te considered asking the CSD chief to isolate the family from those who had taunted him, but decided against it. The accusers would conclude that isolation was an admission of guilt. It would be better to take his chances in the hut.

The night passed slowly once more, locked in with the 200 others at 9.00 p.m. and left to their mercy. Te may have disarmed them with his performance, his two cousins may have had some influence because they'd been there longer, but after that night it would not matter.

The following morning Hei Ling Chau underwent another transformation. The drug addicts remained undisturbed, but every Vietnamese boat person, all 3000 of them, were moved off the island and split up once more at Whitehead, the sprawling, purpose-built detention centre at Shatin.

Cholera had broken out on Tai Ah Chau, the island where Te spent his first period of incarceration in Hong Kong three months earlier. It had only been a matter of time before the disease spread across the tiny island, through the VBPs living, as Te had said, like mountain men.

Te and his family were off to Shatin again, and the people from Tai Ah Chau were being moved on to Hei Ling Chau in the hope of containing the disease.

"We've lost him again," said the Consul-General. "First it was typhoons, now it's cholera. All I can tell you is that we're on to it. I've had dinner with the UNHCR chief and he assures me he's doing what he can. I've also spoken to Geoff Barnes, the Government Secretary who's like the minister in charge of the boat people, and he understands our concern.

"Whatever happens, Te will have to go through the screening process. They all have to. The problem is the numbers. The government can't keep up. There are many Vietnamese who arrived around the time screening was introduced 15 months ago and they still haven't been interviewed. Hopefully your man won't have to wait that long. But there are no guarantees.

"Incidentally Barnes says the boat people are coming in at such a rate that they need a new camp every four days."

I phoned Jim Ellis at Bungendore to pass on the news, frustrating as it was. "Geoff Bentley really seems to be pushing," I said.

"Someone's pushing this end, too," said Jim.

"That would make a change. They haven't told us anything we didn't already know, so far."

"They might have a bit more incentive now. Remember Sir William Keys said he would take it up 'at a very high level'? Well you know who he meant?"

"Some senior public servant, I suppose."

"Bugger the public service," said Jim. "He's got the Prime Minister on to it. Good old Bill. He's got Bob Hawke to back it, and apparently Hawkey's insisted the Minister keep him fully informed."

"That's terrific as far as the processes here are concerned. But Te hasn't even been screened yet and Geoff Bentley can't guarantee that the Hong Kong government will bring the case forward."

"You can bet he's let them know the Prime Minister of Australia wants this man out, and I think they'll play ball. The Brits could say 'Screw you, he can take his turn' but I doubt it. I think they'll give him some priority."

Te and his family were taken with the 3000 others from Hei Ling Chau by open barge to Shatin, a shuttle service that took days to complete. They were moved into the newly completed Stage 3 section of Whitehead. Big huts made of galvanised sheeting were divided in two, 174 people in each end, with one huge spotlight that burnt all day and all night in the centre of the hut. The people might have been battery chickens.

By day the steel huts were like ovens, windowless and with little ventilation. By night, under the spotlight, they didn't cool down either. The risk of fire was enormous. Many of the boat people had tapped into the electricity supply and were creating short circuits with pens and fencing wire to boil water. Wires carrying 240 volts trailed everywhere, over the bunks and the people in them, across the floor.

The frames of the bunks had been installed before the arrivals from Hei Ling Chau but in the haste to get the people off the island and replace them with those from Tai Ah Chau the bunks had not been completed. There were stacks of plywood that would form the bases of the bunk beds but a gang immediately claimed the ply as its own. One of the leaders stood triumphantly on a stack. Vuong tried to take a sheet. Several of the gangsters pounced on him, a lone, vulnerable teenager. They threw him to the floor and kicked him.

Vuong wanted to stand up for himself but his father pulled him away. "Don't fight, Vuong," Te told him, "we don't need to sleep on bunks. We can sleep on blankets outside the hut. It will be cooler anyway. Some of these people are criminals. They were stealing and killing in Vietnam. Let them have the plywood. If you fight they will kill you."

The day after Te and his family arrived at Whitehead, Te wrote to Inspector Wheaton, the police officer who had befriended him at Sek Kong.

> Activities are so confustion and it's so dangerous to my family. Sir, so that I do not like to send you the signal SOS I and my family do not feel any safety and peaceful. I would like to move to somewhere better safe. I hope you and your family are well.
>
> Kind regards,
>
> Nguyen Van Te

He gave the letter to a lawyer working for the UNHCR and asked him to post it.

Te took his family outside the hut and slept on the blankets they'd managed to get. Three times the hands came at night, feeling his body, searching, running over each of his fingers for any rings, pressing any lumps in his clothing for gold that had been hidden. He saw the gangsters, two or three at a time, masked and armed with sharpened steel or with heavy bars. "Roll over," they would bark, "lie there, don't shout, don't move!"

The voices would carry through the night air but no-one but the foolish dared challenge them. No help would come anyway.

One night a woman called out, "Robbers!" as her husband lay on his bunk with a gangster holding a sharpened object against the man's back, demanding gold. "We all woke up," Te told me later. "Everybody banged on their beds. We shouted. The gangster shoved the steel into the man's back. There was blood everywhere. The robber ran off. The CSD officers came but he was never caught."

There was more fighting every day. Conditions were appalling. The toilets had not been completed before the latest influx, and the portable ones were totally inadequate, overflowing, unreachable through the filth that surrounded them.

Te could find no CSD officer who spoke English. There was no talk of screening any more. It was as if everybody here had been discarded without hope. Here he was no special case, just another body, another number in a huge game the authorities were losing. The quality of life was so miserable Te and his family could not eat. It was their lowest ebb.

It was several days before Inspector Wheaton received Te's letter. He read it with alarm, knowing Te had declined favoured treatment at Sek Kong and therefore things at Whitehead must be pretty bad. He sent it back to the chief CSD officer at Whitehead with a note on the back of the envelope:

> Personal friend, interpreter and postmaster. Please look after him and especially his children—let them know at the request of Peter Wheaton. Please assist as much as possible/as soon as possible. Many thanks.

THE CUP

Te and his family endured Whitehead for ten days before word went round that a list of people screened in would soon emerge. For the first time there was a sense of hope. For the first time in ten days, a sense of irony appeared. The escape from Vietnam into the unknown had been a huge gamble, and many Vietnamese love nothing better. Win or lose, the results were about to be posted. "The Cup! The Cup!" people chanted. "Who will win the Cup?"

On 21 September 1989 the CSD sent a Cantonese/Vietnamese interpreter into Te's compound. He told the husbands or fathers in each family group to come forward as 'principals'. They were made to wait together in front of some bunks. An official casually thumbed a sheet of paper. Te could see numbers on it, and guessed they were the personal numbers given by the CSD on Hei Ling Chau.

The official spoke to the interpreter, who then turned to the group of principals and called several numbers but asked for no acknowledgment from the people represented by the numbers. Sometimes the people shouted out anyway. Others kept the news to themselves.

"Number 13541," the interpreter called, then went on to the next one. Only Te and his male cousin, sitting on the top bunk, knew the number was Te's. The cousin gently kicked Te in the back but said nothing. Nor did Te. His heart pounded and it was all he could do to stop his face opening into that huge smile.

When the CSD officer and interpreter had left, Te walked nonchalantly outside the hut. After a suitable time had passed he found his male cousin and said, "Would you come for a walk with me?"

They walked slowly, side by side, not saying a word. When nobody else was around, the cousin said, hiding his excitement and his envy, "I bet there is good news for you." There was not much else to say.

Te left it for an hour before he went up to the CSD office. "My number is 13541," he said, "I heard you want to see me."

A CSD officer replied in English, "Yes, come in. I have to tell you to bring your things up here tomorrow morning. You will be moved to another camp at Tuen Mun. You and your sister-in-law have been screened in."

They had won the Cup.

7

Chicken Wings

The odds against being screened in were overwhelming. Getting through on the first interview was nearly unheard of. Rejection of the claim for refugee status was almost automatic. It was usually only on appeal, if at all, that a person would be screened in.

"Winning the Cup" on the strength of the first interview was the ultimate dividend. Passing the post on appeal left you on a winner, but the going was impossibly slow.

The Hong Kong government's threat to repatriate all Vietnamese screened out was being repeated almost daily, and it meant a flight back to Hanoi was on the cards for most. It would be a journey against their protests, and almost certainly the first flight of their lives.

In the vivid jargon of the camps, it was argued that the screening process forcibly prepared these flightless creatures to leave the ground. When a boat person's attempt to be screened in failed, the others would say, "You've been given your first chicken wing." When the appeal also failed, they would chorus, "That's your second chicken wing. Prepare for take-off."

There were no chicken wings for Te.

On the night of 21 September 1989, Te slept with his secret. He told no-one, not even Mai Phuong nor his male cousin that tomorrow they would be leaving. It was just another night at this place of horror, just one more night to survive. Tomorrow they would move to a place where they would be elevated to the status of refugee. In this netherworld it was like being crowned emperor.

Te was up before 7.00 a.m. and trying to behave as if it were a normal day. At 7.30 he woke the others. "Come on," he said quietly, "Pack up everything you have. Do it quickly."

Mai Phuong said sleepily, "Why?"

"No arguments," said Te. "Come quickly."

To his male cousin he said, "Please, will you and some of the others you know come with us to the truck there? We are being moved in about ten minutes. You guessed it. We've been screened in. Don't tell anyone. I will come back and visit you."

The truck alone was enough to start a buzz around the camp. When Te and his family moved toward it, their few possessions in their hands, and surrounded by the cousin and his friends, a crowd formed quickly. "You won the Cup!" somebody shouted.

Recalling the moment, Te beamed as he said, "I don't know how to describe my happy!"

CSD officials arrived for Te's protection. They put the few bags in the back of the truck. They helped the family aboard and two of the CSD staff got in with them. Te waved to his cousins and friends as the truck moved away to another section to pick up some other Cup winners.

Te was amused to hear some left behind saying, "You know how he got screened in? He's half Chinese."

Te shouted to his cousin, "Good luck to you! I'm now entering freedom. I'll never be in jail again!"

The military truck rattled out of Whitehead, through Shatin and on to the coastal expressway that leads westwards through the factories and residential blocks, the great ugly masses of concrete forever springing up to keep pace with a population constantly exploding. Through Tsuen Wan, a city in itself, the truck bumped along, belching out diesel fumes into an atmosphere already barely fit for breathing, past the high smoke stacks of the world's biggest desalination plant at Lok-On-Pai.

The air pollution didn't bother Te. "I could feel the air of freedom in my lungs," he said.

At Tuen Mun, an urban mass described as one of the new towns in the far west of the New Territories, the truck turned into Hing Ping Street, flanked by street stalls at the corner of the main road. The narrow street wound up a slight hill, through tropical green vegetation, papaws growing on the roadside.

The truck slowed past a police post on the left, and then stopped at some high double gates. Te and his family saw, to their disbelief, the sign saying "Tuen Mun Closed Centre" and the high fences topped with barbed wire, rusting and patched up where they had obviously been breached many times over.

Te gasped as the gates swung open and the truck passed through. "Hold on," he said to himself, "we're going back into jail!"

The gates clanged shut behind the truck, and Te and his family were inside a cage once more. The high expectations were shattered. They were refugees now, weren't they? Refugees were a cut above the masses of illegal immigrants. They had fled religious or political persecution or the fear it, and their status had been acknowledged. So why the fences and gates and barbed wire and police?

Te, Mai Phuong and the three children climbed off the truck and stared about them, as if shell-shocked. The place was overrun with people and sadly lacking in facilities. It was no better than the others. Out the front, just behind the wire and in the open air, was a line of taps. People washed themselves and their clothes in the cold water on the concrete slab. The accommodation blocks were huts of bricks and iron and had been around since the Second World War.

An officer ushered them into the office of the head of the camp. "Be careful," he told them. "You may be in danger. We have all sorts in here. Some of them arrived before the screening process began. Anybody who arrived before June 1988 was automatically a refugee. There are many bad people, gangsters and drug pushers. They seem all right to begin with. They offer you a cigarette today, and tomorrow they give you one that's been drugged. Pretty soon you're hooked, and that means you're theirs. You need the drug and you'll do anything in order to get it. They can make you a gangster in no time. I've seen good, ordinary people become addicted, and soon they're robbers and gangsters like the others, just to meet their addiction."

It was not the introduction Te had expected to his new status as refugee.

"Don't be too alarmed," the head man told him, "just careful. Things are looking good for you. I'd hate to see you blow it."

"Why so many people here?" Te asked.

"Remember," he was told, "refugees are still illegal immigrants. They're not free Hong Kong citizens. They're just refugees waiting for some third country to accept them, and there are thousands in the queue. Those who arrived before the cut-off date were declared refugees but nobody wants them, and they may be in for a long wait yet before somebody takes them. Some have been in Hong Kong for years.

"I hear your chances are better than that. The first thing is to get you your Alien Registration Card. It means everything. You'll be able to come and go as you like, as long as you're back inside before the curfew at 10 o'clock each night. I don't know how long you'll be here but things could be worse. You won't be here forever."

Jim the farrier took another wheelbarrow load of split firewood from the stack that doubled as a windbreak on the southwestern corner of his plot. The garden had started to come to life with the signs of spring but it was still very cold at night and much too early to brave a night without the fire.

He placed a couple of logs on the embers and sat back, stiff from wrestling horses in the wind. It always upset them. Their predators could take advantage of the wind and catch them unawares, and though they may be a bit short on predators at Bungendore, the instinctive worry still prevailed. They were always nervous in the wind, and a jumpy horse on the end of a hoof makes a farrier very vulnerable when he's holding that hoof between his own legs.

"A horse's leg is solid muscle," he'd told me, "so strong and fast you'd never follow a kick with your eye. If I've got the hoof wedged between my knees, banging in nails or filing it and I feel the horse pull the leg back, I go with it. If the horse does decide to kick, there's no distance between the foot and me. Try to go against it when the horse pulls back, and the hoof will hit you at a million miles an hour.

"You usually learn the hard way, but one lesson is enough. So when I'm working on a horse's foot and the leg tenses and moves, I'm riding every movement, sitting on a piston.

It means I'm less likely to get a kick in the arse, but at the end of a day working in the wind with nervous horses I'm the one who's fit for the knacker's yard."

He picked up a copy of a country newspaper and turned to the section advertising clearing sales, a feature of bush life and more like a social event. People would travel considerable distances to see and be seen at the auction of property belonging to some deceased estate, or to some other landowner who'd gone broke.

"Here's an anvil and some other bits and pieces I wouldn't mind taking a look at," he muttered to himself when the phone rang.

"Hullo, this is Jim Ellis," he said.

He could hear the noise of the long-distance line, and then a voice said, "Will you accept a collect call from a Mr Nguyen Van Te?"

Jim was stunned. "Yes, yes, of course I will."

"Go ahead, please," said the operator. There was silence.

"Go ahead, please," she repeated.

Then a voice said quietly, "Anh Ly. Te speaking!"

There is simply no way of gauging the excitement they both felt. A year after he made the call, Te remembered it vividly. "It was the first time in sixteen years that I had heard his voice. It had not changed much at all. I was so happy I could hardly speak."

The moment they had stopped speaking, Jim phoned me. His excitement undoubtedly matched Te's. "I've just had a phone call from Hong Kong!" he said. "It was Te! He's been screened in, he's got his refugee ticket and he sounds terrific. We both had trouble speaking."

"How on earth did he phone you?"

"My number was on the letter you sent him, and as soon as he'd got his refugee ID card he walked down to a supermarket somewhere near the camp and placed a reverse-charge call—he's no bloody fool. There we were, first time we'd spoken to each other since 1973."

"What did you tell him?"

"I told him he was a television star. He liked that. I also told him the Prime Minister of Australia had had a hand in helping him. He couldn't believe it. He said, 'How about that!' I told him 'Geoffrey Sims and I are coming to see you in Hong Kong and see if we can speed things up a bit. You're on your way to Australia,' and he said, 'I always know I can rely on my old boss. He's my mate.' "

The hut Te and his family shared with 200 other people was dilapidated and even more dangerous than the previous ones, not simply because of the gangsters. There were electric wires everywhere. "Everybody was stealing electricity," he recalled. "Very dangerous. One hut burnt down the previous year." Each time the CSD officials came around the people would hide their appliances, then bring them out when the coast was clear.

There was, however, one great luxury. Te and his family were allocated four separate bunks. Actual mattresses. Not plywood sheets. Not blankets on sandbags. Not cardboard. The two girls would share, but for the first time since they left Vietnam in April, Te, Mai Phuong and Vuong would each have a proper bed.

Te climbed on to the top bunk that first night after phoning his old Aussie mate and settled into his first peaceful sleep on his own in more than five months.

Just after midnight he found he was no longer alone. Another body was crouched over him and the hands were feeling everywhere.

"Who is it?" he yelled in fright before he thought of the knives and sharpened steel he had felt pressed into his back on other occasions. This time he was lucky. There was no weapon. The man jumped down and disappeared in the human warehouse. He had taken nothing.

"Don't yell out next time," others told him in the morning. "Stay cool. They're usually armed."

Te was not to let it get him down. It was only a matter of time now. He could already see the vastness of Australia in his mind's eye. He had a cultural background of Confucian patience and Catholic faith. Always look on the bright side. There is light at the end of the tunnel. Now we have separate bunks. Now we can come and go as we like. We can taste freedom. We are only in jail overnight.

Within days, Mai Phuong discovered another relative was also at Tuen Mun and was using her freedom to make some money. She had got a job on an assembly line in a watch factory at the Wai Hing industrial area. Through her, Mai

Phuong also found work at the watch factory. It got her out of the camp all day and she could help supplement the food they were given. She could also help lift her spirits and those of the children by shedding some of the tired old rags and replacing them with new clothes. It was an indulgence guaranteed to restore a bit of the dignity lost in the dehumanising conditions in which they'd been living.

Te also indulged himself a little and threw caution to the wind at the same time. He bought two bed lamps and connected them to the spaghetti of illegal wiring. It was dangerous and Te had to hide the lamps whenever CSD officials came around, but a lamp on his own individual bed! It was almost like home.

Te also wanted to indulge his sense of freedom. He wanted to stretch his wings, his own wings, not chicken wings. He left the children in the care of another relative he'd discovered in the camp and strode out through the gates to the little supermarket with the telephone and dialled Inspector Wheaton at Sek Kong.

"Good morning, sir. Te speaking. I'm not VBP any more. I got the refugee status. You win your bet. I would like to come and visit you at Sek Kong. You can meet a free man."

Armed with cakes, Te made his way alone from Tuen Mun to Sek Kong by minibus, the first time he had travelled independently in months. He savoured the privilege, the freedom to move about without restriction.

Everywhere he looked there was activity, the industry of daily life in Hong Kong. The traffic, as always, was impossible, clogged with many varieties of passenger transport, industrial vans and trucks, the vehicles carrying steel and concrete and timber and bamboo scaffolding for more and more construction jobs, and all the produce trucks bringing in live pigs and chickens and fish and vegetables from the New Territories and from China.

The small bus almost disappeared in Yuen Long, another formless mini-city of concrete blocks from a giant's playpen, then passed through some of the smaller traditional villages with their temples and fish farms and cherry trees. Te soaked up the sights of the Hakka women with their wide-brimmed hats, the hawkers, the men and women carrying great loads suspended from each end of bamboo poles across their shoulders. They moved with a rhythm as the poles flexed under the load, making the bearers spring along rather than walk.

At Sek Kong, Te was now on the outside looking in. At the main gate, the police enthusiastically greeted the interpreter/postman who had got lucky. Te showed off his new refugee card. One of the police ran off to find Inspector Wheaton.

The other interpreters he'd left behind, those who spoke Cantonese, crowded around him. "What's it like on the outside?" they all wanted to know. "Can you go out?" one asked incredulously.

"Of course," said Te, "Look at me. I have gone out of Tuen Mun and I am here now. I can leave the centre any time I like except during the overnight curfew."

The other interpreters parted for the arrival of the imposing, ruddy-faced figure of Peter Wheaton, beaming down on the man who was not much more than half his size. He picked Te up by the shoulders and held him at arm's length as if he were weightless. "Great news!" he said. "I wish I'd had a few dollars on the bet. I had a feeling you'd breeze through the screening."

The big inspector put Te down and they shook hands vigorously, no longer the jailer and the inmate but two free men.

"Come over to the office," the policeman said. "This calls for a cup of tea."

Te was enjoying his new status immensely. He wanted to see his friends and relatives, not to gloat but to share his trip to freedom and to give them hope.

"I know this will come as a disappointment to you, Te," said the inspector, "but I must warn you not to go into the camp. Keep to the offices and the main gate. Visit whoever you like here but not in the camp proper. It's not like it was. You got out just in time. Four days after you left Sek Kong, the place blew up."

It had started over a disputed result and a one-point victory in a volleyball game. The two teams had been drawn from boat people from the northern Vietnamese port of Haiphong and from Quang Ninh, further north. The disputed result opened up provincial rivalries and in no time had turned into an open battle that spread through the airfield camp.

Tent pegs made of angle iron had been flattened and sharpened and turned into formidable swords. Other weapons, produced over the months the camp had existed and secreted here and there, sometimes buried, were brought out. Several people were chopped or clubbed to death. There were many terrible wounds as the battle spread beyond the two groups of volleyball supporters and thousands became involved.

The police were powerless to stop it. For two days they allowed no food into the camp and hoped that hunger would bring the bloodbath to an end but the chopping and stabbing and beating continued without let-up.

"After two days," Inspector Wheaton told Te, "we had to cut the fences to allow the women and children out. You don't know how lucky you were to leave when you did."

"It's about time we went to Hong Kong," I said to Jim. "I've got the okay. The head of the department has given his approval, so we'd better go and see if you've got the right Mr Nguyen. It could turn into a comedy if you haven't."

"It's him all right. I recognised his black hair and he recognised mine because it used to be. Are you going to tell him we're coming?"

"I think we'll give him a bit of a surprise. I want to see his reaction when he lays his eyes on you. The viewers might enjoy it, too."

"When do we go?"

"I thought we might meet the Prime Minister first. He's big on multicultural affairs at the moment and he's had more than a passing interest in this story. It was he who gave the hurry-up. I'm sure Bill Keys can arrange a meeting. I'll give him a call."

On 5 October 1989, several days later, we were standing in a room adjoining the office of the Prime Minister of Australia. Sir William Keys was present. I had driven down to Canberra with cameraman Geoff Clegg and soundman Steve Barnes and picked up Jim at Bungendore on the way. In strode Bob Hawke saying "G'day Bill! G'day Geoff! G'day Jim! Well what a remarkable set of circumstances. Tremendous isn't it!"

"And your intervention," said Sir William, "speeded things up."

"Just absolutely thrilled to be able to help to accelerate things."

"Te phoned me the other night," said Jim, "and I told him 'you have the Prime Minister to thank', and he couldn't understand how an ordinary person like me could get to the Prime Minister."

"Tell him you know an influential go-between," Bob Hawke laughed. "Bill wrote to me, and if he says something's worth looking at, I know it is, because over all the years I've known him he's never abused the relationship, and so I saw it and thought immediately 'this ought to be fixed'. So what I then did was let Senator Ray [at that time the Minister for Immigration] know that this ought to be looked at within the normal rules and it was something we were able to expedite. It just is a great human story."

There may have been a vote or two in it for him, but the ethnic vote was Labor's already and Hawke's credentials in the area of multiculturalism were sound. He didn't seek publicity over his intervention in Te's case; it was I who set up his meeting with Jim Ellis. If Hawke gained, so be it. The Opposition had itself raised the so-called 'immigration debate' and had managed in the doing to come dangerously close to vilifying every Asian in or out of Australia. The more the coalition tried to explain its position, the more it offended Asian Australians, other minority groups, enlightened whites and Australia's neighbours.

Te's case clearly deserved to go ahead without complication or delay. The only concern Jim and I had about giving any politician credit—and we discussed it at length—was that political intervention should have been required at all.

The more Hong Kong threatened forcible repatriation, the more Hanoi protested that the proposal was a violation of human rights. It was barefaced hypocrisy, coming from a government which continued to act repressively against its opponents fourteen years after the war had ended. Respect for human rights in Vietnam did not exist, nor did Hanoi concern itself with the welfare of its citizens who'd fled.

The communists were presiding over a nation in collapse. Reunification had been achieved but had brought no prosperity. The boat people continued to flee, abandoning their own country to its poverty and creating a huge burden on the countries or territories where they landed. It was obvious that the solution did not lie in jailing them, sending them back, or even in expecting other countries to take them in by the thousand, but in removing the reasons for the departures, by making Vietnam a country its people would not want to leave.

There was a strong argument that the United States had a lot to answer for. It had supported the corrupt capitalist governments, propped them up, waged war against the North, raped, bombed and poisoned the countryside, then retreated in failure, leaving the dead, maimed and bereaved of both sides, and a nation in ruin. We'd had a hand in that, too. The great Western allies had gone in like cowboys on another movie set that had strange, Asian extras who were irrelevant in their own civil war. And now the United States refused to accept the overwhelming moral responsibility for helping rebuild the country. It had backed the losers, and would not hear of lending a hand to those who'd won a country with no economy and no future.

Washington and Hanoi continued their mutual hatred, each aware that the only way Vietnam could get on its feet was with the help of the world's richest nation.

For Hanoi, the loss of some of its citizens was unpreventable. They would find ways of leaving. You could re-educate them, jail them, persecute them, hassle them, you could round them up and bring them back before they got too far, but some would always get away, and a sizeable number of officials would get rich on the bribes they accepted to let it happen. Once they'd got as far as Hong Kong or Thailand or Malaysia or the Philippines or Indonesia, forget 'em. Forget the fact that among them, among the gangsters and criminals, the opportunists and layabouts, were some fine brains the country could ill-afford to lose.

Hanoi didn't want its people back again. They were somebody else's problem now, some other country's responsibility to house and feed and look after. There were fewer mouths to feed in Vietnam.

The only way the communist government would

countenance accepting them back was if there was a bounty attached to each one of them—a price on the heads of its own people. The British rulers of Hong Kong would have to pay a bounty for Vietnam to receive Vietnamese citizens. The money would be considered "aid" for the redevelopment of the economy and the provision of facilities in the localities to which boat people were returned. When Hong Kong got round to sending back fifty-one boat people by force at the end of the year, provoking a huge international outcry, the British government paid the Vietnamese government $826 a head. It is doubtful that any of the $42,126 ended up in Haiphong where the majority of the people came from and returned to.

Vietnam was an ongoing mess, screwed by one imperialist force after another and now screwing itself in independence.

A Vietnamese song of unity called "Mother of Vietnam" that was around just before the war ended has these lines:

> One thousand years occupied by China,
> One hundred years by France,
> Twenty years of civil war
> All Vietnam, get rid of the foreign forces
> and stop the civil war.

The foreign occupation and war had ended. There was triumph in that, but unity had brought none of the other promises of independent nationhood. It was, and remains, a sad and disillusioning outcome for a people whose love of their country is matched by few others.

The influence that foreign intervention had on creating Vietnam's tragedy was overpowering. It reinforced the division of a nation and prolonged a war in which foreigners should have had no part.

And here I was, accidentally caught up in an event brought about by a war in which I declined to participate. Here I was, reminded of the range of medical conditions I contrived in order to have myself declared unfit for military service so I could avoid going to that senseless bloody war.

It had happened more than half my lifetime ago. That painful skiing accident when I'd gone arse over breakfast at

Kosciusko the winter before the medical; chipped ankle bones, God, I could hardly walk (when I thought about it). That rash, psoriasis for sure; you could imagine how it would play up in the tropics, doctor, just look at it now (now that I've spent the night scratching my bum raw). And blind, talk about blind! Watch me stuff up that eye chart (I've been practising which letters to confuse for weeks).

Armed with a certificate from a sympathetic local doctor I stumbled and limped into the medical examination rooms in Kent Street, as I recall, in Sydney, and peered over the top of the bulletproof lenses I'd borrowed. What a motley lot. They looked as if they'd just come back from a war!

These unappealing examples of mindless youth were in varying stages of undress, having undergone a cursory count of toes and testicles. They would be ordered to cough while the medico seemed to weigh the scrotum resting on the palm of his hand. What did that tell? I wondered. Would he reveal to you the grand mass of your testicles so you could go into battle knowing precisely how much lighter you'd be when you had your balls shot off? Not for me. I didn't want statistical testicles. I wanted them right where they were, 20 years old, freshly matured and active. I wanted to hang on to them. I was puny, but I was having fun. Bugger the war.

These other battered wrecks of youth were already on their way. You could tell that. What exposed skin that wasn't boil-ridden was scarred or tattoed. There were probably twenty of us in that room and the other nineteen wouldn't have had a complete set of teeth between them.

Over the tops of these armoured lenses, even through them, what I saw compounded a philosophical objection to conscription and the war. I didn't want politicians telling me some Asian people unknown to me were my enemy. Why were they enemy? These ragged youths here were equally alien to me. You can try to talk *them* into going along with the domino theory and forward defence. Just leave me out of it.

By the time my turn came, I'd completely gone into character. I limped and grimaced and groaned when the large, gruff man in the dustcoat pressed and prodded my ankle. I'd been to the loo and given my bum a top-up of scratching and it was a most impressive pair of blotched

CHICKEN WINGS

```
                    COMMONWEALTH OF AUSTRALIA
             DEPARTMENT OF LABOUR AND NATIONAL SERVICE

   Mr. Geoffrey R. Sims,
   33 Consett Street,
   CONCORD WEST.  N.S.W.  2138
                                                    - 6 NOV 1968


   Registration No. 11229993


   Dear Sir,
              I am writing to tell you that you do not meet the standards of fitness required of
   persons called upon to render service under the National Service Act.

              You should preserve this letter carefully in case it should be necessary to
   produce it at any time as evidence that you are not required for service.

                              Yours faithfully,


                                  RASmee

                              Registrar
```

The official letter from the Department of Labour and National Service, telling me I wasn't fit to go to war, November 1968

cheeks that I presented. As for the eye chart, I could barely find it, and when I did I strained and squinted and then got all the O's and C's and Q's expertly mixed up and all the N's, M's and Z's arse-about-face.

What a thespian performance, I thought, although the doctor's credentials probably needed a more thorough checking than my ailments. The Department of Labour and National Service should have sought a second opinion on both of us. The doctor filled out the answers in a questionnaire without referring to me, except once when he looked out through pouchy eyes and read the question, "Have you ever volunteered for military service?" Even then he gave me no time to respond. "Like any other half-bright young man," he said, "the answer, obviously, is no. Good, that does that."

When he'd finished and was shuffling the papers, I dared to ask, "Can you give me a clue? It could be life or death, you know."

"I'm not at liberty to give out that information," he said gruffly. "It's confidential."

"Just a hint?"

"I'm not allowed to, I told you," he said. "You'll be notified in due course."

That's it, I thought, and turned to walk out the door. I'm in. Conscientious objection's the next step. They'll have to drag me away.

The gruff voice behind me had lost its edge when the doctor said to my back, "You're in the clear, son. If I were you I'd go out and get pissed tonight."

I suspect he took his own advice that night. I suspect he did most nights.

The official letter arrived from the Department of Labour and National Service some weeks later. I still have it. My registration number was 11229993. The form letter reads:

Dear Sir,

I am writing to tell you that you do not meet the standards of fitness required of persons called upon to render service under the National Service Act.

You should preserve this letter carefully in case it should be necessary to produce it at any time as evidence that you are not required for service.

Yours faithfully,

Registrar

It was signed in what looked to me then and looks to me today the writing of about a nine-year-old child, "R.A.Smee".

The letter was dated 6 November 1968. I was 20.

Twenty-one years later, here was the draft-dodger caught up with the retired lieutenant-colonel and his attempt to bring to Australia a person who'd backed the wrong side in a war in which we did not belong.

How to rationalise it? Well, Australia *was* involved, whether I opposed it or not; Australia had a responsibility to look after a bloke who'd helped Australia's commitment. The question of whether or not we should absorb those fleeing poverty alone did not arise, but we did have an obligation to help someone fearing persecution because of what he did serving Australia.

No problem.

On Friday, 6 October 1989, the domestic airline service was almost non-existent because of the strike, then subsequent resignation, of most of the pilots in Australia. Jim Ellis, Lt-Col (Rtd), arrived in Sydney from Canberra on a RAAF flight. "I thought we must be going to Vietnam again," he said. "It's nice there this time of the year.

"I can just see Te now. His face will light up and he'll probably knock me flat when he sees me. I wonder what he's been up to all these years, how he survived the transition, and how he got out of Vietnam. I really thought he was dead, poor old chap."

8

For Freedom

Everyone knew the end was near. Win or lose, it was just about over. The South was in disarray, fallen apart, with the escape routes diminishing by the minute. The North had seen the foreigners driven off, the southern capitalist-roaders pocketing the silver from the national table and fleeing with it.

In Saigon all eyes were either looking north for the communists' approach, or to the United States Embassy compound where passage through the gates held the promise of evacuation to the world's mightiest country, the one that had stuffed up this one.

It was 25 April 1975, Anzac Day, and Te had read the signs better than most. For two years he'd hardly mentioned his association with the Australian or United States forces and become once more a villager and second-generation pig farmer. It was a Catholic village after all, and the communists couldn't get much out of such a tight-knit community. The villagers had closed ranks and Te was just villager Te, whether or not they knew he'd worked for the foreigners.

Te left his wife, Thi To, with their son, Vuong, who was not yet two years old, and Te's parents at the family piggery in Bien Hoa and set off for Saigon on the little step-through motorbike. He had his connections with the United States forces, though by now it was doubtful that they would be any use to him. The formality of showing passes to get through the compound gates had gone by the board. Anyone who squeezed through stood a good chance of a helicopter ride to a US ship offshore. He'd heard it was pandemonium at the US compound but he'd see for himself before trying to get there with Thi To and Vuong.

The traffic into Saigon proved impossible and impassable,

even to a step-through bike. There was a solid mass of people and vehicles as far as his eye could see, and Te knew that he'd left his run too late. The United States Embassy compound was not the escape route for him, his wife and their young son. But he would not give up. For the next fourteen years he would try time and time again to escape.

The day after Te turned back from the congested road to Saigon, one of his uncles offered to help get them aboard a merchant ship on which he was a crewman. They declined the offer in fear of seasickness. Boat person Te was really a reluctant sailor, but news that the communist forces were knocking on Saigon's door soon left him with the realisation that the only way out was by sea.

It was too late to take up his uncle's offer. The merchant ship had already left. At Vung Tau, Te, Thi To, Vuong and Te's parents boarded a small fishing boat with other friends— forty-two people in all on a boat 12 metres long—and headed out to sea. They were 20 kilometres out of sight of land when they heard on shortwave radio that the Americans were pulling out their nationals and many others. It merely confirmed what they could see and hear. The sky was alive with helicopters running an airborne shuttle service between the United States Embassy compound and an aircraft carrier.

The sea, too, was buzzing with activity. Many fishing boats were doing the same as the one on which Te and his family were crammed. They were following the helicopters toward the carrier in the hope that they'd be able to scramble aboard.

With little warning, the forty-two people on the fishing boat suddenly became forty-three. Both mother and child were doing fine, but the escape plan, proceeding so well, was thrown into reverse. In Vietnamese culture, a birth on any voyage is a bad omen, a signal to turn back, and the skipper did exactly that.

On their way toward land, against the tide of fishing boats heading out to sea, someone on board another boat shouted, "Why have you turned back? It's too late—the communists have overrun Vung Tau!"

The skipper of Te's boat wrestled with the superstition, then turned the boat around. After several days they were caught by a big wave that broke across the little craft, nearly capsizing it. Te's group, skipper and all, panicked. They should have heeded the sign of the baby's birth and gone back to land, communists or not. On this they had to agree.

Once more the skipper turned the boat about. When they came in sight of land and the water shallowed they dropped anchor so that they could agree on a plan of action before they reached Vung Tau. A few hundred metres off, they could see a bigger boat, maybe 20 metres long, also lying at anchor. Never mind Vung Tau, they decided. This bigger boat might still allow them to escape to sea and reach the American aircraft carrier.

As they approached the bigger boat, the presence of only two people on board, as far as they could tell, stirred the superstitions again. Why were all other boats loaded to the gunwales and making their way as quickly as possible to the carrier when this boat seemed to have only a man of about 40 and presumably a son about 10 years old on board, and be lying at anchor, going nowhere?

The explanation was also unsettling. "The owner gave me the boat," the man on board said. "When we got to the American aircraft carrier, he jumped aboard and said, 'You can keep my boat.' "

"Why didn't you go with him?" someone asked.

"My wife and kids are still at home," he said.

"Why didn't you take them with you?" someone else asked, and then another asked, "Why are you anchored here then, when you could be fetching the rest of your family?"

Whatever the answers were, Te didn't hear. His eyes were on a pistol the man had in his belt. "He's South Vietnamese police," said Te to a friend beside him. "Who cares what he's up to? Let's fox him. We'll jump aboard and force him to take us to the carrier."

Te's friend jumped aboard as the two boats bobbed about and spoke briefly to the man. He thought better about using force with a man packing a pistol, and jumped back. As he did, the man started the engine, the son pulled up the anchor and away they went. Where they were going was impossible to tell, but it was down the coast, not out to sea.

Te's skipper once more dropped anchor and the passengers spent the night wondering what fate awaited them when they landed at a place that had been home to them but was now in the hands of the enemy.

The following day they made their way slowly back to Vung Tau, the place where Australians and Americans had been abundant only a few years earlier. On the fishing pier, Te saw his first North Vietnamese soldier, machine gun in his hands, just waiting for them.

Will he kill us? Te wondered. Will he just mow us down in the boat and let it sink with all of us aboard? Or will he let us land first, then shoot us and watch us topple backwards into the water?

No, he won't shoot us, thought Te. The communists have just had a big victory. They've won the war. We are no threat to him. If there are to be killings, they'll start with the generals, not the villagers. I hope.

Te let his parents do the talking. They had come from North Vietnam and would speak with the same accent as the soldier from the north.

The soldier spoke gently, softly. He asked them where their village was and why they had left. The answer that they had been afraid made him speak even more gently. "You have no reason to be afraid," he reassured them.

Te wondered, how on earth did gentle people like this one beat the South Vietnamese forces? Then he noticed the soldier had his eye on Te's watch. It was one that had been bought in Hong Kong as a gift for Te in 1971 by an Australian soldier, Bob Dowling, the driver for Jim Ellis's replacement in the Civil Affairs Unit.

"Would you sell your watch to me, your brother?" he asked Te.

"The watch is not very good," Te lied. It was a self-winding Seiko clockwork watch that would become obsolete within a few years with the advent of the quartz movement, but which was still valuable in 1975. "In any case it is the only one in the whole family. I would not like to lose it."

The soldier merely smiled and looked away.

One by one they climbed on to the pier and went their separate ways. The North Vietnamese soldier ignored them.

Te and his family went to a village nearby, to the home of another relative with whom Te had left his small truck. It was still there. So were the relatives, and as they entered the home, the village seemed unaffected by the takeover.

The family ate their first proper meal in five days.

When the meal was finished, Te went upstairs to a balcony that overlooked the village. It was here that fear really set in, where the gentleness of the voice and manner of that soldier on the pier was shattered. From what he saw before him, Te knew that if his past were uncovered, it could be the end for him.

The village was now festooned with liberation flags. The victorious communists were more and more apparent. Some of them walked about with loudhailers. The message was the same, and was repeated over and over.

"Any people here who worked for the Thieu regime and the foreign forces must report to the new government of Vietnam. If they don't, they will face the consequences. Come out now. Do not try to hide your past. It will do you no good."

Te went out, but not to surrender himself to the new government. Instead he went to the home of the friend who had worked in Vung Tau for a Central Intelligence Agency front called Phoenix. They watched as people reported by the thousand. There were former South Vietnamese soldiers, police officers and public servants, defeated and forlorn. Te and the friend went outside the house and sat on the grass where no-one could hear them.

"Some people around here know we worked for the foreign powers," said the friend. "They could betray us. It might be better to give ourselves up."

"If I do," said Te, "I won't do it here. I want to go back to my own village at Bien Hoa and then consider my position."

The two separated. Te gathered his family together and set off for Bien Hoa. The truck became useless to them only a few kilometres down the road. The road bridge linking the island of Vung Tau to Baria and Saigon had been sabotaged by the South Vietnamese in a vain attempt to stop the communists. Te and the family crossed the river by small passenger ferry, then transferred to a public bus to take them home.

There were many control points along the way. The driver would have to stop, a communist soldier would board the bus and study the faces of the passengers. If the soldiers were looking for anyone in particular they didn't say. If they were trying to show who was boss, they succeeded.

The family home had remained intact, the pigs had been fed by a cousin, and village life proceeded in spite of the din of the loudspeakers mounted on three-wheeled motor scooters. "We have beaten the strongest and richest enemy in the world," the message came, loud, distorted and crackling above the noise of the engines. "Now we will rebuild our country better—ten times better—than even Ho Chi Minh wanted." The messages always quoted Uncle Ho: "Nothing is more valuable than freedom and independence."

Te told his wife, "I have made the decision that I won't report to the new authorities."

"That has to be your decision," Thi To replied. "I will support you in your decision, whatever it is, though I can't decide for you. But it is a good village, a good Catholic village, and not many know you worked for the Australians and Americans. In any case you stopped working for them in 1972, three years ago. We must pray."

Every day the official reports said many more of the traitors and collaborators had been taken away for re-education. It took different forms. Ordinary citizens had to go one or two days a week for usually two or three months to a place near the village where the words of Ho Chin Minh and the other slogans blasted out over loudspeakers. The more serious offenders were taken away, sometimes never to return.

The new authorities wanted to break up big communities, to create "new economic zones" away from any established areas, sometimes 100 kilometres or so deep in the forests. It was part of the grand plan for reconstructing the country. It never led to the genocide practised by Pol Pot in neighbouring Cambodia, but the new rulers tried to force people to leave the cities, the towns and villages. They called for volunteers and then nominated people when too few came forward voluntarily.

Te was volunteered five times to work for a week at a time building huts out of small trees in a "new economic zone". He had not come under suspicion; he was simply volunteered, and he went, rather than risk investigation of his past. His wife told the authorities, "The family cannot run its business for the good of the country with my husband gone. We have only one and a half labourers—myself and my husband who is disabled from polio." Eventually they were exempted.

The new rulers tried all sorts of threats to get people to cooperate in the development of the new economic zones. They stood over families or whole villages and said, "You must go or face the consequences." Sometimes the intimidation was enough. Sometimes the officials would demand money for the good of the great proletarian cause in return for exemptions. If a relative, say a high-ranking former army or police officer, were in a re-education camp, they would promise the family he would be released if they moved to a new economic zone. They would cut off power supplies to a village that refused to cooperate. They tried this with Te's village, knowing it was dependent on power for crushing the root vegetable manioc, or cassava, but the villagers refused to go.

In that first year of Hanoi's rule, Te tried several times to escape but was thwarted each time.

In 1978 another opportunity presented itself. By now Te and Thi To had had their first daughter. Thuy Vy was two years old, and this time Te and his family would all get a free ride on an escape mission with eleven of Saigon's relatively wealthy Chinese community. All Te had to do was organise it.

The Chinese involved traded with Te's family and trusted them. They each gave Te one ounce of gold as their share in the costs of arranging and preparing a boat for a journey that would take them south, the standard escape route. Te had heard of a boat supplier at Phan Ri, about 170 kilometres along the coast to the north of Vung Tau. Te's wife hid the Chinese gold in loaves of bread, and off they set on the little step-through motorbike, taking the prized local bread with them.

The boatman they met behaved oddly from the start. He told them it was too risky to deal direct with them, and insisted on using a go-between. Then he agreed, without introducing any third person, to take the boat down to Vung Tau. Now we're getting somewhere, Te thought, the man is merely frightened and with good cause. The boatman had been recommended, Te reminded himself, and so he gave over the five ounces of gold demanded as a deposit.

Te and Thi To returned to Saigon to let the Chinese group

know what had happened. Fine, the leader said, we'll go ahead. Te and Thi To went into a famous Catholic church in the Saigon suburb of Binh Trieu. "Dear God," Te prayed, "please help me. I don't want to end up in jail. I might die in jail. In three days the boat will be at Vung Tau. Please make everything work out successfully."

The following day they went down to Vung Tau on the little bike. "This place has many happy memories for both of us," said Thi To. "Let us enjoy ourselves while we can." They spent the days lazing at the Front Beach, enjoying each other's company in perfect weather. When the boat arrived they would send for the rest of the family and be gone before the authorities could become suspicious.

Then a woman with big news of the boat found them. "The boat has gone," she said. "The owner took another group, not your Chinese friends, about 20 kilometres off Phan Ri, then found they had little fuel. He turned back and when they landed told them they must separate until it was safe to try again. He had their gold and he has your deposit. He has sold the boat twice, and now he has disappeared with the proceeds."

Te knew that he had to confront the Chinese and explain how their five ounces of gold had gone for good. He hid the remaining six ounces of gold in the chassis of the motorbike to take back with him to Saigon to face the music. What will they do to me? he worried. Will they believe me? Am I to die at the hands of the Triads?

Once more seated at the big round table with the Chinese men, Te explained how they'd all been cheated. Without expression, eleven pairs of eyes held him. Will I ever get out of here alive? he wondered. I could just disappear and no-one would ever know what they did with me. "Here are the remaining six ounces of gold," said Te, pushing the rings and other bits into the middle of the table. "I am sorry the other five ounces are gone forever. All I can say is, I did my best."

The oldest among them leant forward slowly and retrieved the pieces of gold. "Six ounces," he said. "We gave you eleven, and now you give us only six back." He shook his head and divided the gold into one ounce lots. He left four in front of himself and pushed two across the table to Te. "Take it," he said, "for your troubles and for petrol. Thank you for trying."

Te tried again in 1979. He and Vuong would try to leave with another group by boat from central south Vietnam, again heading south. Thi To left young Thuy Vy with Te's parents and accompanied them to the coastal village to say goodbye. She wished them well. "We will all be together again soon," she said.

It would be sooner than she thought.

Te and Vuong found some of the villagers with whom they'd be travelling. Te and Vuong, who was now six, were hidden with another woman passenger in the back room of a house where they were to remain until nightfall. There was little they could do but listen for the approach of the authorities, tipped off that something was going on. Te heard no footsteps, but the others in the main part of the house were whispering, then arguing, and the conversation was easy to hear through the wall.

"The boat is not theirs," Te whispered to Vuong. "They've stolen it!"

In a village such as this, everyone would know who owned every boat, and if a boat went missing, word would soon travel. Te thought, we're cooped up like chickens, ready for slaughter. He had already paid an ounce of gold as deposit and knew there was no hope of getting a refund.

Holding Vuong's hand, Te emerged from the back room and before the astonished villagers could tell him to get back into hiding he said, "I don't feel I can continue. I have already paid my deposit, but I cannot go on." This is no time for discussion, he thought, and kept on walking slowly through the house.

"We cannot let you go," said one of the villagers as he passed by. "If somebody sees you and realises you are not from around here, our plan may be discovered."

Te and Vuong kept on walking. "No," he said, "if something goes wrong with your plan it is better for all of us if I am away from here."

Out through the door they went, not looking back but expecting any moment to be grabbed from behind. They were out in the open now and still on their own. They crossed the main road and walked 5 kilometres before they managed to get a ride in a passing truck. The woman passenger in the cabin of the truck said to Te, "I know you don't come from around here. What have you been up to?"

"Just visiting relatives," said Te.

"Nonsense," said the woman. "You're trying to escape!" then laughed out loud.

Te and Vuong climbed into the back of the truck and proceeded another 15 kilometres to a town where Thi To was awaiting word that they had successfuly left.Vietnam.

It was nearly sunset when they arrived.

Te helped Vuong to the roadside, then offered to pay the woman and her husband for the ride. "Put it away," she said. "Good luck to you if you do get away," and waved as her husband drove off.

Te found his wife the next day and told her the story as they walked around an open market, buying cakes. They would be inconspicuous; the town was big enough and far enough away from where the boat was to have departed. As they walked about the square, disappointed that another escape attempt had ended in failure, they chose to concentrate on the positive aspect that they were together again, sooner than Thi To had predicted.

A big group of people surrounding a smaller bunch appeared, becoming more noisy as they approached. Children were yelling, "Escaping! Escaping! They stole a boat and they've been caught escaping!" In the middle of the group, Te recognised the villagers from the house in which he'd hidden. In making their escape, they'd tried to steal some fuel from a fishing boat that doubled as a coastal patrol boat. A savage fight had followed and one man had been killed.

Te had one overpowering thought: let's get out of here!

Te leaned over the concrete wall of the sty and looked with pride at the big fat sow and the six piglets all buttoned on to her teats. They were a symbol of prosperity, and nationalising all enterprises had done nothing to change that. In any case, nationalisation had been a clumsy and impossible undertaking. Pig farmers by and large remained pig farmers. Even the new rulers realised experience and expertise counted for a lot.

There was also the small family plantation down the road. It may have been nationalised, but the system was so bent that private cash sales were commonplace. There were ways and means of defeating the checks and counts and stocktakes and yield expectations. Everyone was into it. Cheating was a national pastime and now more refined than ever under a socialist state.

Te and his family lived reasonably well. Their accommodation next to the piggery was adequate, even by Western standards. They ate well, thanks largely to the self-sufficiency that rewarded their efforts with the piggery and the plantation, and what produce they were able to sell or trade. The family lived together, worked together and cared for each other.

They lived adequately, even prosperously, compared to many. Where the overwhelming majority of boat people were deemed to be merely "economic" refugees, people fleeing poverty and squalor, Te and his family had reasonable comfort. They loved the village and the people in it. They were, after all, family, or damn near it.

What they felt their lives lacked was not material. I have asked Te many times why they left, when so much of him still wants to be there, still *is* there, and will remain there regardless of whether he makes a fortune in Australia. The answer is always the same. It may have become automatic. Some may say it is the response a person in his position would feel he ought to give. But the conviction is difficult to question. Each time he is asked, he answers, firmly and without hesitation: "For freedom!"

It is a reminder of a concept which, at the end of the twentieth century, is rare, fragile, and one we take for granted.

Te and Thi To continued to enlarge their family. Vuong was now eight, Thuy Vy five, and they now had two other children—a daughter, Thu Thao, aged three, and a new baby son, Duy Huy. The year was 1984. It was time to try once more to reach a "freedom country".

Te and a friend hatched a plan to have a new boat built in Vung Tau; to hell with this business of leaving from a strange village in a strange part of the country. The boat would be 11 metres long and would take its registration number from another smaller boat the friend owned and would scuttle. It was easier and less suspicious than applying for a new registration number. Te paid five ounces of gold to take his whole family, and another two-tenths of an ounce to become a registered fisherman so he could try to learn a few of the ropes.

Not long after the boat was finished, two of its other backers died. It was tragic for their families, and a bad omen for the others. The plan was therefore doomed, as was Te's first attempt during which the woman had given birth.

Te and his friend persisted but before they could get everything together, the oil pump failed and the engine exploded. "I know about engines," Te later explained. "The oil pump is like the heart of the engine. When the heart stops, everything stops."

The friend was determined. "We'll repair it," he said, "but it will cost money. There will be only two seats for you now—yourself and your son. We will have to sell the others to pay for the repairs. You will also have to supply a good compass, binoculars and some naval maps."

Te agreed reluctantly but was equally determined, after so many failures, to see it through. After all, the partner was a friend and they were on home territory. When he produced the required navigational aids, his friend told him, "Don't go far. We will leave within a week."

"I'm ready to go now," said Te. "Put me in the forward hold, put the deckboards on and nail me in! I've had enough delays."

"No, that's too risky. Stay somewhere locally. I'll get word to you when I have the others ready to go."

Several days later, Te learnt the friend had left without him. With Te's ounce of gold, the binoculars, compass and maps, the friend had fled, taking some of his brothers and sisters with him.

A month later, Te received a letter of apology from the dubious friend who'd now reached Malaysia. "I was very angry," said Te, "very disappointed that he lied and cheated. But he's still my friend. Now he lives in Canada."

Something seemed to be saying, go north. Maybe I'm a slow learner, Te told himself, but going south just doesn't work out. It's cost me a fortune and always ended in failure. Even if we'd ever got underway, we'd have faced at least five days against the elements in the South China Sea; we'd face typhoons and pirates, we'd have to take large quantities of food to last the distance, and who knows where we'd end up? The solution is obvious: we'll go north, stay close to the coast of China, and head for Hong Kong.

Te made five exploratory trips to the north. His connections were good. His parents were from the border region, he'd been born there, his entire village had its roots there. He could speak with a northern accent, and there were many friends and relatives with whom he could stay. Until recently there were travel restrictions, but these had now been eased so that Vietnamese citizens had the luxury of being able to move about within their own country for up to thirty days. The border, however, remained a restricted area.

The husband of a cousin, himself an experienced skipper, arranged the trip. A small boat would be found. When everything was ready, he would send a coded telegram to Te at Bien Hoa. It would say, "Please send workers to the fields".

"I cannot go with you," said Thi To. "I must stay here to look after the little ones. Duy Khang is so sick. He could not travel with this polio. Duy Huy will stay to keep him company. You must take Vuong with you. In two years he will be drafted and probably sent off to fight in Cambodia if you don't. Mai Phuong will come with you and look after the girls."

"This time," said Te, "I am feeling confident."

"What about this 'screening' they talk about in Hong Kong?"

"Don't worry about that, my darling. You know I worked for Australia and the United States. If we can get to Hong Kong I think we'll have a chance of being resettled, and the family can be reunited."

The telegram arrived. The workers were required in the fields. It meant the boat would leave in one week. For the first time, Thi To, a pillar of support to Te, started crying uncontrollably. It was infectious. Soon everybody was crying, parents, grandparents and children. Three generations were about to be split up, perhaps never to see each other again.

The children did not want to go. Thuy Vy was most upset, sobbing and wailing, knowing that she had no choice: if her parents said do it, she would have to do it; defiance of a child's parents was almost unheard of in Vietnamese culture.

Even Te started crying.

"Stop it!" he said. "Everybody please stop crying! We can't get our future off to a good start with so many tears. Please listen to me. This is very important. We must look to the future. We have tried many times before, but this time I believe we'll be successful. Things have never looked so good before. We must be optimistic. It is our custom.

"Even if we get caught, the worst we can expect is jail. Very few people caught escaping are executed.

"We will hug the coast. If the going gets rough, we will stop in wherever we can. We will not have to face the open sea.

"The opportunity is in our hands to find a better future, a life of freedom. You three children must come because it improves the chances of the rest of the family being allowed to be resettled with us. Now look on the bright side, for heaven's sake. Everybody cheer up. Everybody pray that soon we may have a new life."

Train travel in Vietnam was as corrupt as everything else. If you wanted to buy advance tickets you would usually have to buy them on the black market, or stand in line for three days. Te had learnt this on his exploratory trips to the north to arrange the boat. He now had four sleeping berth tickets from Saigon (as everybody still called Ho Chi Minh City) to Hanoi and Haiphong. The others travelling with them came from the same village and had made similar arrangements.

The family hugged and sobbed and said goodbye in their home. Thi To and Te's parents would not come to the station for fear of raising any suspicions. Thi To took Thu Thao, the younger daughter, into the kitchen and whispered a secret message for her to have hope and courage.

One by one, Vuong, Thuy Vy, Thu Thao and Mai Phuong

were ferried to the bus station by Te and a friend using their little little motorbikes. There was no turning and waving. It was simply one last goodbye inside the door, then off.

"It was the toughest time of my life," Te later recalled, "very hard—far harder than anything on the trip or in the camps in Hong Kong."

The other travellers from the village had arrived at the train station in Ho Chi Minh City before Te and his family, each carrying one small overnight bag with a couple of changes of clothing, walked on to the platform. They were at different ends of the station. Deliberately, they had chosen different carriages in which to travel.

The old diesel-engined train was filthy, inside and out, but at least it went. Slowly it headed north, sometimes along the coast beside the sandy beaches that looked idyllic. The line crossed many rivers that still showed the scars of war; the wreckage of many bridges blown up by one side or the other, bomb craters now forming great mud puddles.

Not far north of Bien Hoa, Te recognised the vestiges of jungle that held one of his favourite childhood memories. Elephants were still common here in the 1950s. They flourished in the thick vegetation and wallowed in the rivers. In 1957, Te recalled, some of the American so-called advisers hunted here. If they couldn't bag a Viet Cong guerilla, they might bring down a jumbo and take home its tusks as trophies. On one occasion, with the help of Vietnamese spotters and beaters, a big bull elephant was killed here and all the villagers feasted on the meat. The elephant had been doing no harm, and its death probably jeopardised the survival of the entire herd, but bravado was big in the 1950s, and the mindless slaughter of a bull elephant in the jungle was the stuff of boyhood dreams in East and West alike.

Vuong had come alive on the train, running from the engine through to the last carriage, playing games with imaginary people and creatures. The trauma of leaving home had abated. This was an adventure.

Te sat on the three-tiered bunks with the girls as the train pulled into another small village station. There was no catering on board the train. Each time it stopped, local village people hawking hot food, fruit and drinks would swarm aboard, then often not leap off until the old diesel engine had picked up quite a bit of speed on the way out of the station. Te loved the process. He treated the family to local delicacies, and sold mangoes bought in the south for a considerable profit in the north where they were not available.

In central North Vietnam the train went through many tunnels. The evidence of the war was clear passing in and out of them. Scrap metal was piled up, recognisable pieces of tanks and other tracked vehicles, trucks and shells.

Without warning, a rock was lobbed through the window and hurt someone in a group on the next row of bunks. It happened often, Te was told. Groups of kids with nothing better to do waited beside the line and threw things at passing trains, as idle kids do in most countries. Here, though, it was more serious. Whole volleys of rocks could be expected to rain down through the open windows, so regularly that it was now customary to travel at night with metal shutters across all windows, no matter how hot it was. It took three days to get to Hanoi, a distance of about 1700 kilometres. There they changed to another train to take them down to the port of Haiphong and were met by a cousin. They stayed in his house for two days. The eleven others who'd come up from Bien Hoa to join them on the boat waited in the safety of the Catholic church. They then split up and stayed in hiding in earthen huts at Van Ninh in Quang Ninh province to await the boat.

Three mysterious northerners had been foisted on them, supposedly guides to get them from the village, through the fields and down to the beach to rendezvous with the boat that would take them away at night.

Te thought of all the other attempts and tried to put them out of his mind. Be optimistic. This would be the successful one. Just look at the deal he had got on the price of their passage. It was normally one ounce per head, plus another one-tenth of an ounce per family. Te had agreed to this, on condition that Thu Thao travelled free because she was so small, and that the family surcharge was waived. He'd paid 1.2 ounces in advance, keeping the remaining 2.8 ounces until he saw the boat. The gold, and their remaining stash, was secreted inside belts, the hems of the girls' dresses, the cuffs of trousers. Everything was in order. They were just waiting for the signal.

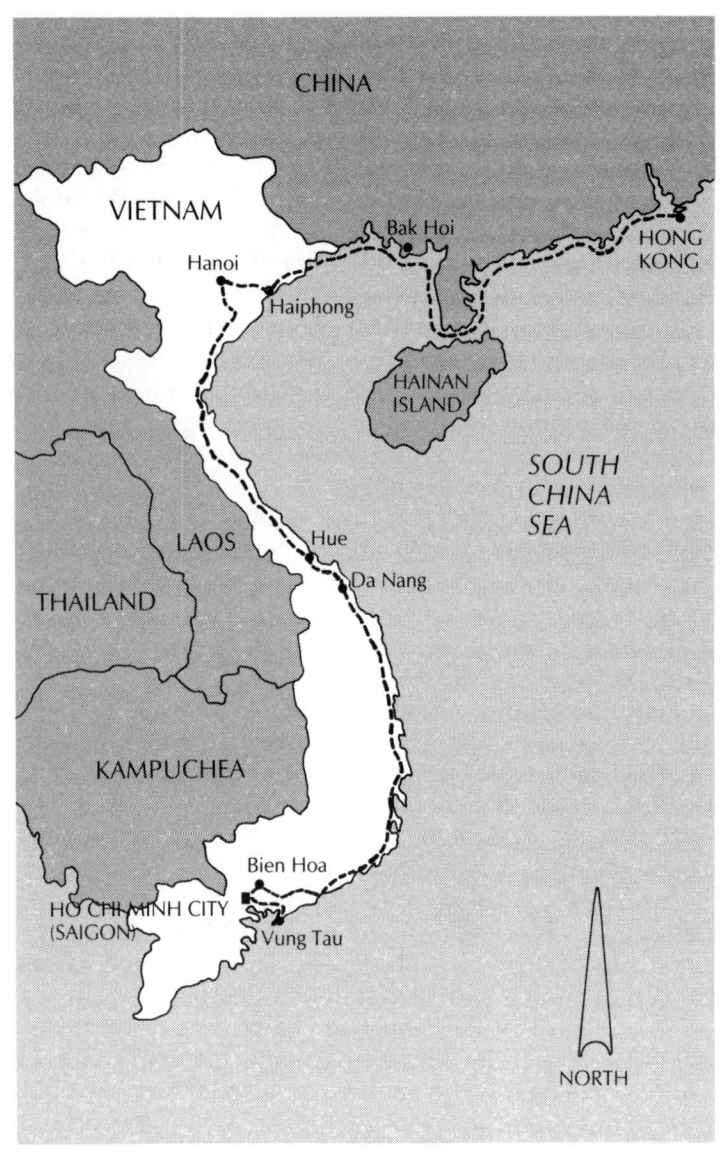

---- Te's route to freedom

9

The Voyage

Te and Mai Phuong dressed themselves and the three children as the field labourers and fishermen and their families would dress in Quang Ninh province. Closer examination would show that even though Te had worked in the piggery and on the small plantation, and even though Mai Phuong had been forced to work in the fields in the new economic zones, their hands were not the rough and calloused hands of the local labourers and fishermen. They hoped it wouldn't come to that. If it did, Te could do the talking. He could speak with the local accent and explain that his size and his disabled leg restricted the amount of heavy work he could do—not that he wanted to draw too much attention to his limp; it made him too noticeable, too easily identified.

Te couldn't help noticing the contrast. One of the guides, a strong and wiry youth about 18 years old, long-haired, with eyes more like a Japanese, had huge, rough hands. They looked as if his pastime was punching holes through reinforced concrete.

It was late in the afternoon of 13 April 1989 when the guides appeared at the two earthen huts. "Time to go," one of them said. "We must leave now. Long walk. Some now, some in fading light, some in darkness." He spoke with a northern accent but strongly flavoured with Chinese. It must be common, Te reassured himself, so close to the border.

A big bamboo fence surrounded the village. The two groups, each led by a guide, walked behind the fence and into the rice fields. Nobody spoke. Nobody wanted to attract any attention. They were just workers going home at the end of the day.

The rice fields, flat for irrigation and controlled drainage, stretched for several kilometres. Where the adjacent land began to rise and was not terraced to create more fields, the vegetation remained thick and green.

After two hours the sun dropped quickly behind a small hill. The lights of another village could be seen away to the left. Everyone was tired and thirsty. In the half-light, Te scooped up water from a stream. As he drank from his cupped hands, the guide took hold of his arm and said, "Hurry. Remember this. We are at a very dangerous point. We must press on so we can meet the other group at an agreed spot near the boat."

Little Thu Thao was near collapse. Vuong lifted her on to his back and they set off again, Te limping at the rear of the line.

The light had gone completely now. In the darkness they crossed a little stream. There was no bridge and they had to walk through knee-deep water. Carrying his shoes, Te felt the cold water and the slime and stones under his feet. It sent a shiver up his back. There was no moon. "It was very creepy," he recalled.

"Stop!" they heard the guide say. "I think we're being followed." The guide carried a big knife commonly used in the fields for slashing, and Te thought, I bet he knows how to use it.

They melted back off the track into the vegetation and listened. Te could hear nothing but the cacophony of frogs and insects in the field, and he could smell the strong muddy odour. It reminded him of the smells of the countryside during his childhood in the north. He and his young friends often played in the fields, and when the big frogs came out in the wet season they would catch them and sell them as food. It was always a great adventure for boys, and quite profitable. Crouched at the side of the track, Te thought of many of his old playmates that he knew had been killed in the war.

"Come on," said the guide. "I think it is safe."

In single file they trudged along in the darkness, Thu Thao clinging to her big brother's back. Te limped along at the tail-end, thinking: if I am grabbed from behind, the rest of the group will never know.

"Stop!" the guide said again. "Get off the path, lie down in the scrub and listen!"

Te could feel the inside of a communist jail, and thought of the perversity of the regime's propaganda. They say there are no jails, he thought, only re-education centres to help people become good citizens, but many people have lost their lives becoming good citizens and if we are discovered we could be next.

He felt the guide's big rough hand in the darkness. "Look over there," the guide said, pointing into the gloom. Te struggled to follow the direction in which the claw was pointing, and saw the faint beam of a torch about 400 metres away. "We must move back another 100 metres off the track, and no noise."

When they had settled deeper in the scrub, the guide lit a cigarette, one locally made and very pungent. "How can you light that thing when we're supposed to be making ourselves disappear?" Te asked. "People on the other side of the fields would see you light up, and even if they didn't, they'd sure smell that awful tobacco. Stop it, please. You are putting us all in danger."

"I need a smoke," the young guide replied and took a deep draw on the foul cigarette, but relented and stubbed it out.

Te could hear Vuong's breathing, accelerated from having to carry his little sister. We are both extremes here, Te thought, I am the oldest and Thu Thao is the youngest; we must not give up.

"If there is no sign of being followed after fifteen minutes," said the guide, "we will press on."

In the darkness, even though they had had time to adapt to it, they could barely make out each other's shapes. Te pulled Thu Thao against him and tried to reassure her. Mai Phuong cuddled Thuy Vy. They were all tired and frightened.

"Maybe it was a fisherman carrying a torch," said the guide after several minutes. "Maybe it was not security. Let's move on."

It was now 8.30 p.m. They had been walking for four hours in fear and silence, and half of it in darkness. They rounded another small hill and the guide stopped them. As he shone his torch on his watch, they could hear the sounds of waves and feel a very slight sea breeze. "We are approaching the place where we will meet the other group. Maybe one hour more. We have made up a little of the time we lost when we waited beside the track. We'll stop for five minutes."

Thu Thao's head began to roll back. Te grabbed her and gave her a water bottle. "Drink only a little bit," he told her.

Soon they were on their way again, stumbling in the darkness. Now they could hear the wash of the sea, then it disappeared as the track wound in from the coast. In much less than an hour the guide said, "This is it. Sit, keep quiet. Don't move. I'll find the other group."

It was so dark that all they could see was the tall grass in front of their faces. The guide picked up a clod of earth, threw it into the black night and was gone.

Their hearts were thumping. Everyone was afraid he'd abandoned them. He's got his cut already, thought Te; even though I only paid a deposit, the others paid the full amount and he's already taken his commission. Abandoned in the darkness and the long grass, they could be anywhere. Even in daylight they would have no hope of finding their way out.

A loud whistle came from some way off, and then the flash of a torch. Some of Te's group were on their knees praying. We've been discovered, they thought; it's all over.

They waited for another whistle, another torch flash, but none came. They heard movement through the long grass, and thought: how can we defend ourselves when we can't even see our attackers? In his strange accent, the guide said, "I have some information about the other group. They are safe. They will join us soon."

Presently they heard footsteps through the grass. The other group arrived, each relieved to see the other, and they were led, all together at last, down to the beach. "The tide is rising," said the guide. "The boat will come in half an hour."

The group of sixteen from Te's village sat on the sand and looked out beyond the sound of the lapping waves. Nobody spoke but they shared the same fears and relief on the brink of their illegal departure from their motherland.

Somebody coughed, then another. "Silence!" ordered the guide, but the coughs caught on. Several more started to cough. "Quiet! Stop your damned noise!"

"Shut up, yourself!" (cough) "How do you expect us to stop coughing?"

THE VOYAGE

Soon they were arguing more noisily than the coughs.

"Everybody stop arguing, please!" said Te. "You are making more and more noise. If you have to cough, cover your mouth and do it as quietly as possible, but there's no point in everybody arguing about it."

"Look!" said one of the guides and everyone strained to see what he had seen. Vuong said he could vaguely make out a mast without a sail. The guide flashed his torch across the water in its direction and someone out there returned the signal.

The guide breathed a pungent cigarette over Te and demanded, "Quick! You promised to pay us the rest of the gold when you saw the boat. There it is. Pay up your 2.8 ounces. Don't try to trick us."

Te and Mai Phuong had pressed the gold into some sticky rice cakes before they left. They had lost so much on previous attempts, they weren't going to lose this. If necessary they would eat the rice cakes, rings and all, and recover the gold when it passed through them.

"We are honest people," Te told the guide. "There is nothing wrong with our gold. You can test it with a flame right now."

One of the guides produced a cigarette lighter and held the flame against the sides of the rings he was holding between his fingers. Any normal fingers would be scorched, Te thought, but not these calloused claws. The rings showed no discoloration under the heat; they were genuine. The guide put them in his pocket.

The boat had now bottomed in the shallow water and people were climbing aboard, one by one. Each person carried a little bag with two changes of clothes, some rice cakes, sweets and a bottle of water. As Te clambered in, the last one to board, he thought: this boat will either take us to a freedom country—or be a coffin for all of us.

By feel, and occasionally by torchlight, they found their way into a half-cabin and perched like chickens roosting inside. They could see little but it was obvious the boat was only about 6 metres long and two in the beam, a tiny craft for sixteen passengers and the three guides. Whoever had brought the boat into the beach had now disappeared.

They could see the silhouette of someone poling the boat away from the beach and they could feel the sway of the boat each time he pushed down hard on the long oar he was using as a pole. The two young male guides were both swearing about the absence of wind. They poled for about an hour, obviously keeping close inshore, until a slight breeze came up. Some of the men helped the guides, or crew as they had now become, to raise a sail from the single mast. Immediately the boat picked up speed.

All the passengers were ordered to stay inside the tiny half-cabin, only a couple of metres square. Two of the stronger men were told to squat near the mast in case their help was needed. The shapes of other small boats could be made out on the water, and occasionally one showed a light. One of the crew started singing the way local fishermen sang.

They appeared to be making reasonable progress for about two hours and then the wind dropped. "Bloody hell!"—or about as close as the Vietnamese curse comes—said one of the crew. "Pull down the sail! We'll have to row the bloody thing!"

The crewman with the big hands put an oar over the stern and used the twisting motion of sculling to propel the boat very slowly through the water. Several of the group from Te's Catholic village fell into silent prayers for the wind to come up again.

"Bloody hell, I'm hungry!" said the male guide with the girl companion. He'd now assumed the role of captain.

"You're hungry!" said one of the villagers. "We're all hungry. None of us has had any dinner and we've walked for five hours. Don't you start complaining."

"Everyone please keep quiet," said Te. "Arguing will do no good. We can live without food tomorrow. It is known that a man can live for seven days and a woman for nine days without food, only water. None of us is about to starve. Just keep praying for some wind."

In sullen, bored, cramped silence the group roosted in the half-cabin while the crew took turns sculling and cursing at the same time. It was midnight and the younger ones, exhausted by the long walk, had long ago slumped against the nearest body. Some of the adults dozed. A woman tried to fan herself but gave up in the restricted space. Inside the half-cabin the air was still and close. When the breeze came up, they smelt it before they could feel it.

"Hoist the sail!" cried the captain, seized by the opportunity for some drama. "Move! Move! Let's not waste it!"

The sail filled and the little boat responded quickly. "If this wind keeps up," said Te, "what time will we leave Vietnamese territorial waters?"

"About sunrise—another six hours away. Now cook me some food!" he said, turning to the girl who, Te learned later, was the man's fiancée. "I'm starving. Cook something for me."

One of the group took pity on the girl and passed the man a rice cake. He swallowed it greedily and said, "Good cake. Give me more!" He was given two more by the group, and after he'd eaten them, turned to his fiancée and demanded once more, "Food! Cook me some rice!" Obediently she produced a small brazier and cooked for him on the stern of the boat.

Soon after the captain had had his meal, the wind changed direction and he tacked frequently to maintain the correct direction. In doing so, they found themselves among a group of fishing boats. "Everybody stay inside," said the captain. He turned to a passing fishing boat and yelled, "No wind when you want it, too much when you get it, and no bloody fish! Have you seen any escaping fishing boats? Many have been lost this month."

"Don't worry about them," a voice yelled back, "the more that go, the better. It leaves more fish for us."

After several hours of tacking, the wind dropped. It was now daylight and there was no sign of land. They still had not entered Chinese waters. "We are near the border," said the captain. "Patrols are likely. We might have to go back, hide somewhere and continue tonight."

"No, let's keep going," said Te. "I'm sure it's more dangerous to go back." The others agreed. They would not remain becalmed forever.

A stronger wind came up eventually, the sail was hoisted once more and the little boat, as far as they could tell, was heading in the right direction but bouncing quite violently. Several of the adults, including reluctant boat-person Te, were seasick. Confinement in the small cabin helped bring it on, and some were unable to reach the side in time.

They had no bearings, but China could not be far off. The wind eased—but now they were quickly swallowed up in dense fog.

I hope we haven't strayed into a shipping lane, Te thought.

Thunk, thunk, thunk. They could hear the diesel engine somewhere out there in the fog. Thunk, thunk, thunk. The noise could be coming from almost anywhere. The fog deceived the sense of direction. At least it was clear the noise was coming from no supertanker.

"It's a Chinese fishing boat," said the captain. "That's good news! The coast will be over to the left; the fishing boat means the open sea. I have fished around here many times. I don't need a compass. The fog doesn't bother me. As long as I can hear the Chinese fishing boats I can work out where we are. We'll land on a Chinese beach this afternoon. I can tell you we are safe now."

Safe, thought Te, when we're lost in fog? If ever I go back to Saigon to visit, I'll go by air!

The boat was awash and people were constantly bailing. The planks had opened up and some of the caulking had fallen out. In the strong wind, the boat had taken water over the sides, too. Everyone was wet, but hopes had risen with the captain's confidence that a landing in China was imminent.

When the fog lifted, they saw a beach in the distance. Te and the others from his village had the same thought: this is the first time I have ever been outside my own country. They had successfully left at last.

There were boats of many designs that Te had never seen before. Apart from the junks and sampans there were barges and lighters and fishing boats with fat bellies and square sterns, big motorised rafts of bamboo that carried enormous weights and seemed impossible to steer.

On the beach, bent figures were raking thousands of fish to dry on concrete slabs. Big, rubbery jellyfish had been piled, also to dry, in holes in the sand. The stench coming from the land did little to help recovery from seasickness.

A little way along was a village. Before they could land, an old Chinese man brought his sailing boat alongside and ran it into the sand. The wind had come up and the skipper

THE VOYAGE

of Te's boat was having trouble getting to the beach. The man said in Vietnamese, "If you have any Vietnamese currency, I can change it for you. I go to Vietnam often to buy fish and I can pay for it in local currency. If you don't change your money here, nobody further along the coast will want it. It will be worthless."

The old Chinese man helped them beach the boat. "You can leave the boat here for a short while," he said, "but a strong wind is coming up and you'll be safer anchoring on the other side of the harbour. The authorities here won't stop you going into the village if you want to buy some things, but please don't steal anything."

It was wonderful to be on dry land. Everyone was wobbly, uncertain on sea legs, but relieved in the knowledge that they had finally set foot on a foreign shore. They changed some money at a rate they found mutually agreeable. The old man said, "Maybe you would like to buy an engine for your boat. The wind is good but it is unreliable."

"Wind!" said the captain. "I've had enough of wind. Yes, let's get an engine. But first let's get some food. I'm starving."

The boat people wobbled off into the village. The locals paid them little attention. Most spoke Vietnamese as well as their Chinese dialect, and the boat people were able to buy sugar cane, some fresh vegetables, cake and rice. On the way back to the boat they picked up some dried fish left on a slab of concrete.

The wind was strengthening, as the old man had predicted. The boat people and their three guides or crew climbed aboard and poled their way out of the shallows and over to the safer anchorage. When they started to cook on the little brazier, they were beckoned by some Chinese men on another boat at anchor. "Come and join us," the men shouted. "Come and share some rice and tea with us."

It was a much bigger boat and comfortably accommodated everyone. The two Chinese men listened to the story of the escape and the problems of relying on the wind. They advised the Vietnamese escapees, as the old man had done, to have a small diesel engine fitted. The Chinese engines were cheap, simple, reliable and need not be used if the wind were favourable.

"Bloody hell!" said the captain of Te's boat. "You all must

buy an engine and more food tomorrow before we go any further."

"No," said Te, "that's not the deal. We've already paid once and you were to supply food and buy an engine out of what we've already paid. Now we discover you had only 10 kilograms of rice on board when you were supposed to have 200. We've paid once and we're not paying again. You must pay."

"If you don't buy an engine and more food, I'll sail the boat back to Vietnam!"

Te said, "You don't own the boat. We all do. We bought it. You now work for us, don't you agree?"

"Okay, you own the bloody boat but you can't sail it. I'll ask you to buy an engine and more food. Will you do it?"

"No," said the diminutive Nguyen Van Te, "and we terminate your services."

The two young men and the fiancée of one of them took their belongings and left.

Good riddance, thought Te and all the others from his village. Now what do we do for a skipper?

"It will cost," said the man on the bigger boat, "but we've done it many times before. We have many satisfied customers." He handed Te a book full of Vietnamese names. "We towed all of them up to Bak Hoi harbour. This boat is strong. We can tow yours, too. In Bak Hoi you can have an engine fitted cheaper than here. It's a bigger harbour—more boats, more boatyards. Half an ounce of gold is all we charge to tow you there."

Te read through the book he'd been handed. He recognised the names of people from his own district. He also read a letter from a Vietnamese person in Hong Kong thanking the man for his help in getting there. He put the letter aside and looked at the food in front of the man. "You live better in China than people do in Vietnam," said Te, half absent-mindedly.

"Maybe," said the man, "but there are too many men in China. It is very difficult to find a woman suitable for marriage. Even if I could find a good woman, I couldn't afford to marry her."

Te felt sorry for the man. If he is so honest, Te decided, he must be trustworthy. The man had also shared a very good meal with strangers, and it could not have been purely to drum up business. "Okay," said Te, "for half an ounce of gold you will take us to this place, Bak Hoi. First we must get some more fish and rice."

Cramped as they were on the small boat, the people from Bien Hoa slept well with full stomachs and without the cursing captain and his crew. It was peaceful without them. In Bak Hoi they would have an engine fitted to the little boat and try to find someone to act as skipper on the long journey to Hong Kong.

They left, under tow, about 8.00 p.m., having stocked up on food and water in the village. A few kilometres out of the harbour, the bigger boat stopped and dropped anchor. There were three people on board, plus Te and Thu Thao. "Now you must pay us the half ounce in gold," said the man with whom they'd been dealing.

Te gave a gold ring that weighed one-twentieth of an ounce, and made up the difference with the watch he'd declined to sell to the North Vietnamese soldier on the pier at Vung Tau. Te had treasured the watch for eight years. He thought of the Australian soldier, Bob Dowling, who'd given it to him. Sorry, Bob, he thought, I'm sure you would understand. I only have my wedding ring left, and that will have to go soon, too.

The three Chinese men examined the ring and the watch, heating the gold with a cigarette lighter to see if it were genuine, and set off up the coast. It would take one day and one night to reach Bak Hoi, travelling non-stop, they told Te, if all went well. Te and little Thu Thao stayed on the bigger boat. It was slightly more stable and they could do with the break. On board the smaller boat, Vuong, Thuy Vy and Mai Phuong took their turns bailing out. It had to be done continuously.

It was some time after midnight when the wind built up and the boat ran into heavy rain. Te looked on as the man in charge shone the torch on his newly acquired watch. It hurt to be reminded that he had lost it forever and he felt as if he had betrayed a friend, but the storm struck so violently there was little time to feel guilty. The big boat strained under the load of the smaller craft and had to ease back for fear of pulling it under a big wave. On both boats, everyone feared they would capsize.

The man in charge knew the coast well and found a small, sheltered fishing harbour and dropped anchor. Te and Thu Thao stayed on board. One of the crew threw off the line to the smaller boat and told them to drop anchor 100 metres away, in case the boat dragged its anchor in the wind and heavy sea. Even in the protection of the harbour, the storm was like a small typhoon. The temperature had dropped markedly and everyone on both boats was wet through.

For two days they waited for the weather to improve. It was a particularly depressing period for Te and his family, the only time he seriously questioned what he had undertaken. "I couldn't sleep," he recalled. "Always I worried about my family still in Vietnam. It was like a different world away. I thought, we may all lose our lives, and it is my responsibility. Maybe I made a crazy decision to take the children from their mother and the motherland. We were making a reasonable living, and if the government discovered my background, maybe I'd get a few years in a re-education centre but I'd probably survive—others have.

"Why did I take on this dangerous trip when I could not know or plan anything? Now I can't go back. I always thought it would only take a few days before we reached a freedom land, but here we are, still in a communist country, and my wife doesn't know if I'm alive or dead.

"I remembered saying goodbye to my parents, my wife and the two little boys. So many tears. Everybody cried. Everybody has a country and a home. Now I have left behind my country, my home, my wife and two kids, my mother and father, and I'm sitting here, wet and cold and responsible for the safety of my oldest son, my two daughters and my sister-in-law."

Thu Thao sat beside him, leaning on him, looking sad as she had done most of the time since they left their village, and saying nothing.

Te recalled, "I kept thinking our lives were on a movie screen, and when the film ends, we will all pass away."

He was still thinking of movies, as he had done for many years, but the scenes in which he used to imagine himself as a movie star driving Major Jim Ellis's Jeep in

Vung Tau had always had happy endings.

One of the other two men on the bigger boat brought him back to reality. "The weather is improving. We'll start off again tonight."

"Why not today?" asked Te.

"The police might give us some trouble. It's safer to go at night."

"Let's get going as soon as we can," said Te. "I'm sure we are all depressed waiting here day after day."

When the sun went down, the sea lit up as all the fishing boats headed out for the first time in days. Hundreds of boats, maybe thousands, had set out from ports and anchorages where they'd waited out the storm. As Te remembers it, "It was like a city on the sea."

The towing boat motored over to the little Vietnamese one and secured a line. They set off about 9.00 p.m., in weather that had improved so radically that the water was flat and dead calm, throwing up the lights of this floating city.

About 3.00 a.m. the owner told Te, "Maybe we can reach Bak Hoi before sunrise." They moved along the coast, leaving the fishing boats going further out to sea.

After two hours, there was another mass of lights on the water. The travellers could make out the shapes of big ocean-going ships, going nowhere, and then the silhouettes of the heavy anchor chains and lines attached to mooring buoys. For navigation lights, one of the crew tied battery-powered torches to each side of the towing boat. Nobody seemed to bother with the internationally recognised colours of red for port and green for starboard. The towing boat slowed, and the owner said to Te, "Better you and your little girl get back on board your own boat now. Put the anchor down. At sunrise, do whatever you can manage with the sail or the oar to move inside the harbour. This is Bak Hoi."

Whatever we can manage! Te thought. To the best of my knowledge, not one of us has ever been to sea before, most of us have never been on a boat before—I know I haven't, and I seem to have taken over the leadership of this expedition!

They dropped the anchor and waited, not quite knowing what they were waiting for. Was it the daylight? Was someone likely to come and help—a harbour patrol boat, perhaps? Or were they to wait until some sea-going vessel failed to see this little, bobbing boat, or possibly see it but be unable to manoeuvre around it and go straight over it?

At daybreak, these sixteen frightened and helpless foreigners watched as boat after boat, ship after ship, came out of the harbour mouth and headed along the coast or out to sea. They waited and waited. There couldn't be so many boats in the whole world as were still coming out of Bak Hoi harbour. We must try to go against the tide of boats and get inside the harbour, Te thought.

What followed is probably still the talk of that Chinese port. Those who saw the little Vietnamese boat trying to enter the harbour would most likely throw back their heads in laughter every time they remembered it. Even Te is able to see the humour in it now. He wasn't at the time. He was terrified, like the others on board.

They tried with an oar over the stern, but sculling is a practised technique. Twisting and kicking back the tip of the oar to propel the boat forward but stop it corkscrewing is not something you acquire in one emergency lesson. It is true that old women on board sampans in many Asian ports do it with ease, but it is equally true they did not learn at their first attempt entering a busy harbour.

The boat zig-zagged across the harbour mouth, missing and being missed by the steady stream of much bigger vessels coming out. Te tried his hand at sculling, he and others tried paddling the boat, they put up the sail and worried for a moment that they would not stop until they were washed up in the Philippines. People on passing boats gaped and cursed. Others gathered on the harbour wall to witness the impromptu aquatic circus.

Te, a man not inclined to swear, thought: I know what that skipper who has now gone back to Vietnam would say. Bloody hell!

When they finally found themselves and their boat inside the harbour walls it was difficult to apportion any credit. To Te, it merely consolidated his Catholicism. He had witnessed a miracle.

When he looked around him, he wasn't so sure.

One end of the harbour was packed with other Vietnamese boats and boat people. It couldn't possibly be a good sign. Were they all being assembled here so that the People's Republic could take action against them collectively? Had the three men who'd towed them here and suddenly left them been doing the work of the Chinese police?

As Te's mind raced, two Chinese police officers appeared on the harbour wall and climbed on to the boat. It was then that Te remembered he was wearing a Chinese People's Liberation Army shirt that one of the men on the towing boat had given him.

"Any drugs or weapons?" one of the police officers demanded in Vietnamese. Te's heart sank. Dear God, he thought, now we're drug runners or criminals. Maybe they'll also think I've murdered a soldier and stolen the shirt off his back.

"Everybody keep still," the Chinese policeman ordered. He and his colleague searched the small boat from stem to stern, emptying all bags, lifting loose deckboards, feeling behind the frames and reaching into the bilge.

"How did you get here?" asked the police officer. "Did any Chinese fishing boats tow you? They shouldn't, you know. It's against the law." Without waiting for answers, as if he had asked the questions simply because he was required to do so, he went on, "You really ought to get yourselves an engine. If you have any gold, I can put you on to someone who'll do it well and charge you a reasonable price. Otherwise you'd better leave your boat here and see if you can get a ride on a bigger one."

"We have only one-tenth of an ounce of gold left," said Te, "and we need it to buy food."

"Then you'd better see if you can get a ride with someone else."

Easier said than done, thought Te. There is seldom any room on any boat leaving Vietnam. They are usually dangerously overloaded to minimise the costs. Sixteen people would not easily fit aboard another boat, even if they could afford the going rate of two-tenths of an ounce per person from there to Hong Kong.

On one of the many other boats in Bak Hoi harbour, Mai Phuong found an old friend who was kind enough to give her another one-tenth of an ounce of gold. With it they bought 100 kilograms of rice and picked up some dried fish left on the drying slabs on the foreshore.

For two days they waited in the harbour for something to happen. They knew they could not sail the boat on their own, nor could they afford an engine, and that left them with the choice of trying to find another boat willing to take them, or finding another skipper. Neither seemed likely.

Te noticed some people working on the engine of a boat about twice the size as his. "I've worked on diesel engines on my small plantation," he told them. "Maybe I can help you." In return for getting the engine going again, Te asked the group to take them to Hong Kong.

"Only you and your family," said the leader of the group, but Te had now assumed responsibility for the eleven others on his boat and decided he could not abandon them.

On the second day they found two experienced sailing families who had been forced to sell their boat to buy food. There were nine people in all. Te and his group agreed to take them—twenty-six people on a boat 6 metres long. They set off immediately, paddling out of the harbour in the still air. The temperature was about 40° Celsius.

By sunset they had travelled only about 20 kilometres. They dropped anchor and those who could swim—Te, Vuong, and two others—swam ashore to beg some food and fresh water from the Chinese villagers.

After three days they were still no more than 50 kilometres from Bak Hoi. At a small village, the captain gave up. "We'll never reach Hong Kong without an engine," he said. "You're on your own." With that, the two additional families picked up their luggage and left.

Te and several of his own villagers also went ashore. Penniless and without an engine or a skipper, they were stuck in a foreign country that didn't want them. They could go neither forward nor back, and they could not stay here either. Te had even traded his wedding ring for food. But it was here that Te's group had one of the greatest strokes of luck on their remarkable journey. In the village they met the kind, local police officer, a young country cop who had lived in Vietnam for some years and spoke the language. Te explained their predicament, not knowing what kind of reaction he would get.

"No money, no captain, little food," repeated the young Chinese policeman. "You are about a quarter of the way to Hong Kong. You can give up, go back and face the consequences. Or you can go back, scrounge some more gold and sneak out again overland. If you want to try this course, I will help you."

There was really no choice at all.

10

Home Again

"You cannot all stay on the boat," said the country cop. "It is not good for the children. I live with my parents near the village. The women and girls can stay with us. You need not be afraid. This is not Thailand."

There was, of course, an element of risk, but Mai Phuong would be with Thuy Vy and Thu Thao, and Te knew she would look after them as if they were her own.

Running a shuttle service on his little motorbike, the policeman transported the women and girls to his house about 4 kilometres from where the boat lay at anchor. The men and boys slept on the boat.

In the morning, the shuttle service was repeated in reverse. The women and girls had had a night of comparative luxury. "They gave us food—even a mosquito net," said Mai Phuong.

"Bring your boat along the beach closer to the house if you can," the policeman said. "It will be more convenient for everybody."

Te took control. "Put up the sail," said the reluctant sailor who had now become the interim skipper, and the boat, caught by a gust, sped off the wrong way. "We'll tack," he said, enjoying the use of these new nautical terms, and the sail flapped and spun around as the boat continued the wrong way. After several attempts they brought the boat on course and managed to tack along the beach to a spot near the policeman's house. "That day," said Te, "I became a sailor."

The policeman said to Te, "I will take you back to near the border by bus. You alone will go from this boat, but you will travel with a Vietnamese woman from another boat and two boys whose father has gone ahead to try to get some money. I will meet you again after two weeks. The women and children from your boat can stay with me and my parents. The men can sleep on the boat, but we will look after them."

The policeman said Te could pay him two-tenths of an ounce of gold on his return. Te calculated it was a generous offer. It would barely cover the man's costs—possibly even leave him out of pocket.

The policeman paid for the bus fares for himself, Te and the others travelling back to Vietnam. They changed buses three times, then stopped about 20 kilometres from the border at a village. The policeman bought them all a big meal at a restaurant, gave them their onward bus tickets and handed each of them a packet of cigarettes, including Te, who doesn't normally smoke. "If you get nervous," he said, "smoke them. Or use them to buy favours."

He showed them a hotel in the village and said, "I will meet you here two weeks from today. Knock at room number 138. If you get back here within two weeks a friend of mine will receive you. He does not speak Vietnamese but he understands it and he knows what's going on. Wait here until I return."

The policeman gave each of them 10 Chinese yuan—the equivalent of a few dollars—and waited with them until the bus arrived. "He got on board the bus and offered the driver a cigarette," Te recalled. "I think he also gave the driver some money."

There were three checkpoints before the border. A Chinese official would board the bus, point at individuals and call them off the bus. There would be body searches and the luggage would be examined.

"What have you been doing in our country?" one official asked.

"Visiting relatives for Ancestors' Day in March," Te lied.

At the border, another official said, "You entered our country without permission. Where are your papers?"

"We lost them, sir," Te said, tempted to light up a cigarette to counter his nerves.

"Make sure you don't lose them next time. Off you go."

Te was now allowed to enter the Trading Zone on the Chinese side of the border. He walked straight through with the Vietnamese woman that the Chinese policeman had helped. With many other Vietnamese returning from a shopping spree in the Zone, they crossed the river by ferry back into their own country. His fellow travellers were armed with electric fans, clocks, rice cookers, radios, vacuum flasks, bicycles, cloth and medicine. Te was empty-handed.

At the Vietnamese Customs checkpoint, an official refused to let Te and the woman in. "Where's your return ticket, the one you were issued in Vietnam?" he demanded. "Prove to me that you didn't leave Vietnam illegally."

"The Chinese police took everything," Te lied. "They took our tickets and our Vietnamese ID and wouldn't give them back. Please have a cigarette. Take the whole packet."

The official did just that, and with an inclination of his head directed Te and the woman through. Te was back in his motherland—but at the wrong end of it and without the money to get down to Bien Hoa where he hoped he'd be able to scratch up some more gold. In the border area, he remembered, there was a woman who was a friend of his parents, and was now widowed. Her husband had been down to Bien Hoa to visit Te's parents soon after reunification, when those from the north were allowed to visit the south, but not the other way around.

The widow, eager to hear news from her friends in the south, welcomed Te and his travelling companion into her home. She fed them well and they began to relax, talking about old times. There was a little noise from one of the other rooms in the house. It was her daughter, the widow explained. She had some friends over.

Speaking softly, Te told the widow he had to get to his village then back into China quickly because his children were waiting for him. She listened attentively to his description of his escape and the series of events that had gone wrong. He was her friends' son and of course she would help. Of course she would lend him the money to get a train ticket.

About 9.00 p.m. it was all arranged. He would leave for Hanoi, the first stage in the journey, in the morning. The widow poured another cup of gunpowder tea. Somebody started hammering on the door of the house.

"This is the police!" a voice shouted. "Don't move. The house is surrounded. If you try to escape we will shoot."

Te was not about to move. He was frozen where he sat. As the police burst through the door, his one thought was: If they arrest me, what will happen to the children in China?

The police rushed past Te and the widow and into the room in which the widow's daughter was entertaining "some friends". As the police marched the friends out, Te counted them. There were forty. The daughter, an apparently ideologically motivated student, had been running a service from the privacy and comfort of her own home, arranging escapes from Vietnam.

The police seized the identity documents of everybody in the house, took names and details, then gave the obligatory lecture. "Do not try to leave your motherland. As Ho Chi Minh said, 'Nothing is more valuable than freedom and independence.' "

At the local police station the following day, the widow was fined 120,000 piastres (about A$40) for having strangers in the house without reporting their presence. Whether she was aware of what her daughter was doing or not—or even if she herself were involved—was apparently not an issue. Each person had to pay 7500 piastres (A$1.50) for the return of his or her ID.

In all honesty, Te was able to tell the police, "I am not trying to escape. I am on my way south after visiting the north." Even more truthfully he was able to say, "I can't wait to get home."

Te said goodbye to the widow and the woman with whom he'd left China and got the first bus to Hanoi. At the railway station, the ticket seller told him he couldn't catch a train for three days. "I'll pay to get one sooner," Te said, slipping another 5000 piastre note (A$1) inside the wad of 60,000 piastres (A$12), and the ticket was his.

Three uncomfortable days and nights later he was setting foot in his own Bien Hoa province. The station was about 5 kilometres from his village but he dared not approach it until he had heard if it was safe to do so. He waited in another village a kilometre from his own and asked a friend to fetch his wife.

It was the first word Thi To had had in the weeks since saying goodbye to her husband, her children and her sister. Here he was back in Bien Hoa, and the others—her flesh and blood—were off in China somewhere with a policeman they'd never met before. She was distraught. "Thi To was more upset than when we left Vietnam," Te recalled. "She cried and cried and cried."

"What are you going to do?" Thi To asked him. "So many people know you escaped. I know it is a good village, but you are taking a big risk by coming back."

"We must get more gold to buy an engine," Te said. "Each person on the boat has given me a note asking their parents and relatives to give two-tenths of an ounce of gold. I also need to find a new skipper for the boat. I can't do all the running around and yet not be seen. Come. We must be brave. We are going back to our village—and no hiding."

Te borrowed the friend's step-through motorbike and buzzed back into his village with Thi To riding pillion.

"Many people watched us ride in," he recalled. "Someone shouted, 'Look! Te has come back again!' but nobody told the authorities. It is a village of friends."

Te swept up the two younger boys he'd left behind with his wife. He hugged them and hugged his parents who'd begun to assume the worst. It was a great relief to know he, Mai Phuong and the three children were well, even if the trip had had many disappointments.

Te was home, but he was just passing through. He could not risk arousing too many suspicions and he could not leave the others in China a moment longer than necessary. In two days and nights he was able to present the notes from the others on the boat and gather the gold he calculated they would need to make it to Hong Kong. More than that, Te found a skipper in his own village—a man of 60 who had migrated south with Te's parents after partition, was an experienced seaman, and knew the border area well.

Te said goodbye to his wife, sons and parents once more, feeling, in a sense, mission accomplished—or at least this part of it. "This time I must succeed," Te told Thi To. "We will meet again in a freedom country. We both must believe. We both must pray."

With folded bank notes in the lining of cigarette packets, gold rings and flattened plate hidden in belt seams, trouser cuffs and pressed into a tin of balm, Te and the skipper made the long journey north to the border. They bribed officials to let them leave Vietnam and enter the China Trading Zone, a walled area, and they watched a Chinese trader the skipper had known for many years slide some money into the back pocket of another official to let them enter China proper.

That left them only about 200 kilometres from Te's children, but still with all those road checkpoints between them. To travel by road to the hotel where they would meet the Chinese policeman would be tempting fate too much. They would try to get around the sensitive area near the border by sea. The Chinese trader would arrange it—for half an ounce of gold.

Dressing Te and the skipper as fishermen, down to the carrybags the local fishermen used, he led them on a four-hour walk down a river to pick up a little boat that was waiting for them. It was one of three rowing boats travelling down that section of the river in the early hours of the morning, supposedly on their way to pick up the larger fishing boats near the coast. There was safety in numbers, Te thought, until the light of a checkpoint appeared around a bend in the river and then another torch indicated that all three boats should stop.

There was no hope of making a run for it. Any suggestion of failing to cooperate would most likely bring a volley of bullets. Te hoped a bit of fast talking and possibly another bribe would be the better bet, but as the first two boats pulled in to the checkpoint, the official waved Te's boat on. Te and the skipper were only too happy to oblige.

When they got to the coast it was still dark. They left the little Chinese boat and walked along the beach toward the village as the sun was coming up. Te could see the boat which had pulled his boat to Bak Hoi, now lying at anchor. There was no sign of life aboard it. Te and the skipper waited, hoping to catch a ride on one of the many Vietnamese boats bound to come along.

It was then that the police arrested them.

"You boat people?" asked the police officer.

"Yes."

"Then where's your boat? If you're Vietnamese boat people, you can keep on going toward Hong Kong. If you don't have a boat, we'll send you back to Vietnam."

"The boat is coming along behind us," said Te in a speech he had rehearsed over and over in his mind. "It was very cramped. We got off to walk along the beach for a while so we could stretch our legs."

"You sure?"

"Sure. Why?"

"Some Vietnamese have killed two Chinese fishermen and stolen the engine out of their boat. How do we know it wasn't you?"

"If we had killed anybody and stolen an engine," said Te, "would we be strolling along the beach? Wouldn't we be going as fast as possible away from here?"

"Okay," said the police officer, "but give me your ID just in case. If your boat doesn't arrive by tonight you can sleep outside the house at the control point."

It was Te who did all the talking. The skipper was fully occupied controlling the panic he felt. He was older and more inclined to worry, and, thought Te, more likely to land them in trouble simply by looking guilty at every opportunity.

"Go and find a Vietnamese boat," said Te when the police officer was out of earshot. "Any one will do, as long as the people on board are prepared to say we've been travelling all along with them. It's the only way the police officer will give our IDs back."

The skipper shuffled off down the beach toward Vietnam, looking as if he were about to confess to murdering the two Chinese fishermen. Te followed. They had little trouble persuading those on a passing Vietnamese boat to say they had been passengers since they left their own country. The police officer returned the IDs and Te and the skipper set off with the Vietnamese boatload.

They went no more than 200 metres to where the other boat lay at anchor, the one that had towed them to Bak Hoi. The owners had returned, and agreed, for four-tenths of an ounce, to take Te and the skipper toward Bak Hoi. They would be towing no other boat this time, and they could set off as soon as the tide lifted her off the sand.

It would be too much to expect plain sailing. One hundred kilometres or so along the way, the boat took a buffeting from strong winds and the price was loaded by another tenth of an ounce, but at last it was possible to put Te and the skipper out south of the harbour where they could meet up with the village cop at the hotel.

They made it back to his house by bus—by several buses—and there they found that the rest of Te's family and the others from the boat had succumbed to nothing more serious than boredom. They had been well fed and cared for by the family of a man they barely knew, an officer of the law in a country they had entered illegally.

Through contacts of the Vietnamese-speaking policeman, they bought a single-cylinder diesel engine and had it fitted to their little leaky boat for the journey to Hong Kong, still more than 700 kilometres away. With the luxury of an engine and now their third skipper—a man who was competent, if a little inclined to worry—they set off yet again for that British territory.

When they left, the police officer who had helped them took the trouble to travel all the way to Bien Hoa to let Te's wife know of their safe departure. He still communicates regularly with Te but the man is unable to write in the Roman alphabet, so although he can speak Vietnamese, he can't write it. He writes in Chinese, and a Chinese friend Te has made in Canberra translates the calligraphy into English, then reverses the process when Te replies.

The skipper's inclination to worry about the dangers of escaping was not unwarranted. Since 1985 he had been like this: he had lost much of his will to live and had come to expect the worst at every turn.

A big wooden boat had left Vung Tau in that year with fifty-two people on board. The boat was about 12 metres long and 4 metres in the beam, a sailing boat with a diesel engine. It had as reasonable a chance as most did heading for Indonesia or Malaysia.

Te was supposed to have been on board that trip and to have taken Vuong along with him. He would have been the only English-speaker, and his role would have been to communicate with foreign vessels in the busy international waterways. The money had all been paid and all intending travellers were awaiting word of the date on which a bribed official would let the boat leave. When word came, it happened to be the lunar new year, a time when gambling is almost mandatory, when the coming year is best welcomed by a manifestation of luck. If you are lucky then, it is said the luck will carry you through the year.

The night the boat left, Te played cards at a friend's place.

A REAL MATE

The game went on and on and luck seemed to be playing into Te's hands. It got later and later. Te could not let his wife know where he was; there were no telephones. In the morning he trudged home, having won and lost most of his winnings, but still in front. Thi To was furious.

"While you were out wasting your time playing cards," she told him, "you missed the boat. The people came to tell you it was time to board. They had to leave last night, and you were nowhere to be found."

Te tried to laugh it off. "Maybe it was not supposed to be my turn to leave," he said. "Maybe a fortune teller would say, 'next time is the right time.' "

Thi To was unimpressed. Te remained "in bad odour" for some time.

The weeks went by, then months. There was no word from the boat or its fifty-two passengers. If they had got to Indonesia or Malaysia, some message would eventually have found its way back to the relatives, but no message ever came. The boat and all on board had been seen leaving Vung Tau on the night of the lunar new year and they disappeared without trace.

The skipper now with Te in China in 1989 and given to nerves at any sign of danger, had lost three sons on that boat in 1985.

Beyond the southern coastline that they continued to hug, China was a country in turmoil. The death of Hu Yaobang, the former General Secretary of the Chinese Communist Party, the day after Te had set foot in China in April, had prompted the ill-fated pro-democracy movement. It wasn't too noticeable on the coast, but in the big cities the call for reform was being taken into the streets.

On Sunday, 4 June 1989 the tanks rolled across Tienanmen Square in Beijing. Students, holding out for weeks in the hope that their protest would eventually win out, were crushed. The People's Army had acted violently against the people.

On Monday, television audiences around the world were stunned by the brutality of the action brought by satellite into their living rooms. To look into the mysterious Middle Kingdom in crisis was spellbinding. World media organisations were already in force in Beijing and now sent reinforcements to Hong Kong.

On Tuesday, Ian Macintosh, the head of ABC Television News, said to me, "How quickly can you get to the airport?" He didn't require an answer. Ian had been ABC bureau chief in London when I was posted there in mid-1984 and when I went off to cover the uprising against apartheid in South Africa, the Ethiopian famine and one or two other events.

I arrived that night at Kaitak Airport along with many other correspondents and camera crews. The mission initially was to cover reaction in Hong Kong and Taiwan to the unfolding developments in China.

Hong Kong was in an advanced state of the jitters. With only eight years to go before the British territory was to be handed back to China, Beijing's guarantees on Hong Kong's future as a capitalist port and trading centre now appeared dubious at best. If Deng Xiaoping could send in the tanks against students in the capital of China, why would Hong Kong be safe?

In Taiwan, the Nationalist Chinese were already gloating over the repression on the mainland where they'd governed until the communists threw them out in 1949. Never trust a communist, they were saying to whoever would listen. We told you not to woo Beijing. We told you not to abandon Taipei.

On Wednesday I used a freelance local cameraman and Chang Chun-yuen, a Singapore-based ABC sound recordist and videotape editor, now in Hong Kong after a turbulent time in Beijing. We shot and satellited a news report that included a commemoration service at the Hong Kong stock exchange to honour the dead in Tienanmen Square, a big protest rally, and some rioting that broke out in an area called Mongkok, where opportunists used the tension as an excuse to loot shops and throw petrol bombs at police.

On Thursday I made contact with David Brill, a seasoned ABC cameraman now working freelance, and attracted to Hong Kong by the action in China. For the next fortnight the three of us—David, Chun and I—would work together. We organised visas for Taiwan and for China, should we need them, then shot, edited and satellited another news piece on evacuations by Qantas from Beijing and Shanghai.

A REAL MATE

At Kaitak I met the Australian Consul-General, Geoff Bentley, and arranged to see him at his office the following day.

On Friday we shot and satellited another news piece, this time on the flood of applications by people from Hong Kong and the Portuguese territory, Macau, wanting to migrate to Australia. Long before the doors to the Australian Consulate-General opened, high above the harbour at Wanchai, there was a huge crush of people waiting to get into the lifts; when the doors opened, there was no turning back.

The Consul-General was open and helpful, "media-friendly", and although he said, "Call me any time if I can do anything", I'm sure neither of us thought we would ever have any further contact.

On Saturday and Sunday we turned from the events in China and their effects on Hong Kong, and started concentrating on the other issue, the Vietnamese boat people. An international conference was about to get underway in Geneva and the British had already made clear their proposal to start sending the boat people back to Vietnam by force. I would do a background piece showing the stark reality of the conditions in which the boat people lived in Hong Kong, the flood of new arrivals, and the attitude of Hong Kong people to what they saw as an invasion. My colleague in London, David Ransom, would go to Geneva to cover the conference.

We shot pictures of the so-called detention centres and the faces and the fingers at the wire. At Sham Shui Po, not far back from the tourist hotel and shopping area of Tsim Sha Tsui and directly under the flight path into Kaitak Airport, thousands of people were squashed into the hot metal huts surrounded by fences topped with barbed wire. If the term "concentration camp" is too strong, too emotive, as some would say, I am unable to find a more suitable one. A dictionary definition of a concentration camp as a place where non-combatants or political prisoners are interned is wholly accurate. Adolf Hitler and the Nazis have no claim to exclusivity over the term.

We drove around the New Territories and found that the old airfield at Sek Kong was being converted into another camp. The wire fences were going up, the tents were being brought in and erected. In the towns and villages we found the slogans and the signs of protest against the Vietnamese influx. On the harbour we found the protest convoys of small freighters and barges, junks and sampans noisily and colourfully showing their opposition to the other boat people, the ones from Vietnam.

In the evening I made contact with the Hong Kong Government Information Services and arranged to be taken on a big police boat to witness the interception of some of the Vietnamese boats arriving in Hong Kong waters the following day. Everyone knew they were coming. A rumour had spread that if boat people arrived in Hong Kong before the Geneva conference got underway, they would be screened in as refugees under an amnesty. It was untrue, but it didn't stop the frantic run into Hong Kong waters, made all the more desperate by Typhoon Dot, which had delayed many boats from Vietnam, forcing them to seek shelter along the China coast.

On Monday, 12 June, we arrived at the Marine Police base at Aberdeen near the famous floating restaurants of Hong Kong, and were told we would be taken to the Soko Islands which bordered China's territorial waters. We were to share the police launch with teams from the BBC and ITN and several newspapers.

Through the entrance of the Marine Police base was a doorway leading to a vast shed, like an aircraft hangar, that opened on to the police wharf. Presumably it was used normally for storing launches and other craft and equipment. At this time it housed well over a thousand Vietnamese people. They were squatting shoulder to shoulder, the knees of one pressed into the back of the one in front. Some had the luxury of a piece of cardboard or a sheet of paper on the hard floor. There were people of all ages, brought here by police boat from the island group we were about to visit. They had spent the entire weekend squatting in their own filth, waiting for Typhoon Dot to pass.

Before our police launch arrived they were marshalled out into the open on the pier to await barges to take them back out to the desolate island, Tai Ah Chau. The Cantonese police officers, men and women, barked orders incomprehensible to the Vietnamese and waved their long truncheons to indicate they should stand up, sit down, squash up here, move in there.

A REAL MATE

All the police wore surgical masks, as if they were dealing with diseased animals or sub-humans, and, I thought, it was unnecessarily insulting. If the masks were intended to filter any offensive smell, then everyone in Hong Kong should wear one constantly. If they were intended as a prophylactic, what were they to prevent? The people had been kept here because of a typhoon, not because of an outbreak of disease. There was, as yet, no sign of cholera.

Among the faces, forlorn and sapped of life, was the incongruous mask of a painted lady, a former Saigon bar girl now in her thirties. She had no possessions at all, no bag, no change of clothing—nothing, except a make-up kit. She squatted on the pier with all the rest of them, but was the only one with any make-up—it was heavy about the eyes and her lips were bright red. "I want to go to America now!" she said defiantly in English as the camera swung on to her. In my report I apparently upset one or two feminists by referring to her as a destitute prostitute, but no apologies are due. That's what she was, and she propositioned several men in my presence.

After several hours at sea, patrolling the territorial border between Hong Kong and China and keeping in radio contact with the Marine Police command boat, we had witnessed the interception of only one Vietnamese boat. It was a rusting old river barge that should never have survived the war, much less a passage of 1000 kilometres or so to Hong Kong, overcrowded with more than 200 people above and below deck.

All the other boats expected to arrive to beat the rumoured amnesty had not materialised. They must be still coming, having ducked for cover from the typhoon.

The embarrassment of the police and Government Information Services (GIS) people on board was obvious. They offered to land us at the island of Tai Ah Chau, to show us where the people in the shed back at the Marine Police base at Aberdeen had arrived a few days earlier, and where all new arrivals would first go. The BBC and ITN correspondents angrily refused the offer. They had come to witness mass interceptions and nothing less would do.

I accepted the offer; it seemed pointless to demand interceptions if there were no boats to intercept. It seemed equally obvious to me that shots of the barren island would tie in pertinently with the hangar full of wretched people at Aberdeen.

We went ashore by one of the police inflatables—just us, some newspaper journalists and, as I recall, a couple making an amateur production for a Scandinavian charity. We wove our way through the wrecks of many Vietnamese boats. The island was deserted, except for the old Chinese couple who lived there, a few police and about ten boat people from the one boat intercepted earlier in the day. They huddled in an old concrete hut that had probably been there since World War Two.

When we returned to the big police patrol boat, some of the correspondents were still complaining that they had been cheated, their day wasted. In the wheelhouse of the boat, I quietly suggested a "face-saving" solution to the senior police officer and the GIS official—and saving face is the art of Oriental compromise. The solution, I suggested, lay in offering to take us all to see the old Star Ferries now used as floating detention centres in Hong Kong harbour. They would have to get approval, the officials said, and they started making calls by radio and cellular telephone. In the end the peace proposal was approved and accepted, and David, Chun and I were able to get another powerful sequence which we would otherwise have been denied.

The item was satellited to Sydney on Tuesday, 13 June, and broadcast on the "7.30 Report" the same night. As it went to air, Mr Nguyen Van Te and his boatload were unknowingly entering Hong Kong waters. The sister piece from Geneva was broadcast the following day—the day on which Te and the others were intercepted and taken to Tai Ah Chau.

As the unknown Mr Nguyen Van Te was being picked up by the Hong Kong police, we were heading in the other direction to Taipei to shoot a news piece on the Taiwanese response to the clampdown in Beijing. We returned the same day, edited the following day, and went on to shoot a longer "7.30 Report" piece on the future of Hong Kong in view of the uncertainty in China.

An old friend in Hong Kong suggested that a successful Perth businessman who'd been in Hong Kong for many years might be worth approaching for an opinion. The businessman was involved in investments and corporate rescue and had kept his confidence in Hong Kong during the Cultural Revolution and other periods of upheaval. The man was Bill Wyllie and he agreed to do an interview after the Queen's Birthday long weekend.

In the meantime I decided that before we returned to Sydney we should do another piece on the Vietnamese boat people, a follow-up on the deserted island we had visited. The people who had been moved into the Aberdeen Marine Police shed because of the typhoon had now been dumped back on the island. Their numbers had been swollen by the mass of new arrivals who had taken shelter along the China coast—the people the marine police had taken us out, without success, to intercept.

The contrast between the island in its deserted state and now swarming with 6000 people would make a strong item. It was Sunday, 18 June, and if some other justification were needed for a second piece on the boat people, it was the first day of Refugee Week.

The idea was straightforward enough. Its execution was not.

The Queen's birthday, in the dying days of this last colonial outpost, worked heavily against us. The civil servants had gone off for the day, no doubt to raise a glass of pink gin loyally to Her Majesty, and, to keep up tradition, a few more to themselves. Officially the place just closed down.

The Government Information Services were under instructions to show the world the strain under which Hong Kong coped with the huge numbers of boat people, but not this weekend, thanks; come back next week, world, the boat people will still be here, and maybe we can offer a "press facility" such as a ride on a police launch to Tai Ah Chau. I tried the Royal Air Force; twenty years earlier I had lived in Hong Kong and the RAF occasionally made helicopters available. Not now, sorry; Queen's birthday.

I was reminded of a line that was popular among the sub-colony of "China Watchers" in Hong Kong in the 'sixties. "China will never bother to invade Hong Kong to take it over," they would say. "It will take just one phone call." Sitting here, in this colony seized by royal paralysis, I thought: you could frustrate the hell out of Deng Xiaoping by inviting him to make that call on a Queen's birthday weekend; there'd be no-one in Hong Kong to threaten—or even answer the telephone. Oh, how the little tyrant would lose face.

I phoned Chief Inspector Nick Angell on *Police Launch 4*, the command vessel in the Soko Island group. "Can't help you," he said. "Nothing due over from Aberdeen for a couple of days. Nothing to stop you coming under your own steam, though, if you can find a way of getting here. Tai Ah Chau is public property—not restricted, yet. Can't stop you landing here—if you can get here."

On a summer long weekend in Hong Kong, finding a suitable boat that's not already booked up is not easy. Chang Chun-yuen and I walked along the waterfront from Sheung Wan to the Star Ferry terminal. The best piece of advice we could get was to go back toward the Macau Ferry terminal and try the operators of some of the wallah-wallahs, the bobbing launches best known for transporting overnight workers, revellers and drunks from one side of the harbour to the other after the Star Ferry stops running around midnight.

Through the multilingual skills of Chun, we struck a deal with the old couple on the only wallah-wallah we could find that was not in use. In Cantonese, Chun explained where we wanted to go and that the skipper would have to wait and bring us back. Chun went through it several times until we were all clear about what it involved.

We went back to the hotel to pick up David and all the camera gear and walked back down the waterfront to the wallah-wallah. It was like a cork in the big harbour swell, bouncing and rolling as we tried to hold it against the stone wall and load the gear. Once on board we had to wedge some of the equipment and hold the rest to prevent damage—and we were only a few metres out.

The old skipper and his wife, both grinning gold teeth at us, turned away from the harbour wall and headed out, straight across to Kowloon. We should have been going to the left, to the west and out of the harbour. Something had got confused in the negotiations. We never worked out what; Chun's Cantonese is excellent and we had even shown the old couple a map of where we wanted them to take us. But only now did they seem to realise it meant leaving the harbour, and their boat, they insisted, was not suitable. We were inclined to agree. Back to the harbour wall we went, money refunded, sorry, sorry, make mistake.

"Shall we give up?" we all seemed to say at once.

"Maybe we'll have to leave it till after the long weekend," said David.

"We can't," I said. "We won't have time. We still have to finish shooting the piece on Hong Kong's future, and we leave on Tuesday evening. It has to be today or tomorrow or not at all."

We trudged back to the hotel with the gear. "One last card," I said to David and Chun, "is Bill Wyllie. He offered to take us out on his boat if we had time before we left. The trouble is, he said he was going away for the long weeekend."

I phoned the Wyllie residence at Shek-O without much hope. Bill, in fact, had not gone away. "Sure," he said when I explained our frustrations, "love to take you. We were going to take the boat out tomorrow anyway. I'll send the car for you at nine in the morning."

The car was a Rolls Royce, gleaming blue and straight from the showroom floor. The chauffeur picked us up and delivered us to the residence at Shek-O where the boat, matching the Rolls in luxury but decidedly more space-age in design, was waiting.

It was thus that we were finally transported, with the Moet et Chandon chilling, to Tai Ah Chau. I had set out to do a story of contrasts on the island of boat people. The greatest contrast was in the style of our arrival.

I offer this diarised table of events merely as another illustration of the work of the hand of fate in the life of Mr Nguyen Van Te—the chances against our meeting, and the brief television appearance that led to his freedom.

11
Reunion

Jim Ellis's eyes were as bright as the lights of Hong Kong below us. Somewhere down there in all that glitter and noise and confusion, out of place in a British colony which, itself, was out of place and out of time, was his old mate.

The big aircraft came in by the western approach path, over Sham Shui Po "detention centre", skimming some of the most densely populated blocks in the world, dropping into Kaitak Airport without so much as a rooftop washline or television antenna caught in the undercarriage. The wheels hit the runway with enough of it still stretched out in front of us, so that with full reverse thrust and heavy braking, there was no need to dip the nose in the harbour where the runway ran out.

It was a perfectly normal landing at Kaitak. There are only degrees of excitement in arriving in Hong Kong; it is never dull.

Waiting for us were the crew from the ABC's Singapore office, Chang Chun-yuen, who had worked with me on the previous trip, and the cameraman, Sebastian Phua, who had been in Beijing at the time. Chun, having been involved in the other reports on the boat people—and having heard and recorded Te's appeal—was immediately caught up in the story of two great mates. He had also briefed Sebastian.

The following morning we set out to find Te. It was Sunday, 8 October. He had no idea we were in Hong Kong and I wasn't about to spoil the reunion by giving him any warning. Nor would I "go through the proper channels" and let the authorities know, in case someone told him. If we were going to bring Nguyen Van Te and Lt-Col Jim Ellis together after sixteen years, we were going to do it as a surprise.

We took the MTR (Mass Transit Railway) to Tsuen Wan, the end of the line and not even halfway to Tuen Mun.

We transferred to a New Territories taxi (green as opposed to the red ones on Hong Kong island and the Kowloon peninsula). Chun explained in Cantonese where we wanted to go, to the place in Tuen Mun where those Vietnamese boat people were kept. The driver knew it well, he said; everybody knew where the Vietnamese were kept. Roughly 20 kilometres later we had wound our way around the coastline to Tuen Mun—and kept on going.

"Wasn't that Tuen Mun?" Chun asked the driver.

"Oh that?" the driver replied. "I think so."

It took several runs at Tuen Mun, complicated by divided roads and roadworks, many stops and endless conversations with local people who had no idea where the boat people place was but couldn't bring themselves to admit it.

Finally we turned from the main road into Hing Ping Street, more by a process of elimination than good direction, and drove slowly between the barrows and bicycles and people shuffling, shuffling, shuffling. Among the oriental faces, mostly Cantonese of course, and a few Hakkas, there were now the distinct features of many Vietnamese. We could not be far from the place where Te, at last report, was being kept.

The taxi drove in past the police post where no-one took the slightest notice of us, and almost up to the sign that read, somewhat puzzlingly to us, "Tuen Mun Closed Centre". Vietnamese faces were on both sides of the high, rusting wire. There were double, prison-style gates in front of us, and, further up the hill, another set of gates.

What Te was doing in a "closed centre" now that he was a refugee was beyond us. It was much later that I was given an explanation, which I present as a tribute to the logic of the bureaucratic mind. The closed camp at Tuen Mun, you see, was really an open centre for people who'd been screened in, so that once they'd been screened in, they could go in and out of the open centre, but if they went out (those who'd been screened in), they had to be back in again by 10.00 p.m. when the open centre was closed until 7.00 a.m., at which time the closed centre would be reopened, and those who'd been kept in could go out again. I'm assured by Valerie O of the Government Information Services that in June of 1990 the name was changed to the Tuen Mun Refugee Centre. Officially it became, at last, an open camp, but only for six months before it was closed again, this time permanently.

Such enlightenment had not reached Tuen Mun when we arrived in search of Mr Nguyen Van Te.

Nobody paid us any attention until Sebastian and Chun got out of the taxi with their camera gear. Two Cantonese policemen were immediately on to us, and—even more intimidating—a diminutive policewoman. "What are you doing? Who authorised this? Back behind the police post with the camera!" she barked, or rather squeaked, with menace. She may have been half our size but she didn't invite challenge.

I asked the crew to move back while Jim and I tried to explain why two "kweilos" or foreign devils and a camera crew would want to be trespassing on her little domain. We told it straight: Jim was a former officer in the Australian Army in Vietnam and was helping one of the VBPs who'd been screened in. We believed the man was in this camp.

The policewoman appeared neither to comprehend nor be interested. "Could you please try to find out if he is here," we begged. We wrote his full name and his alien number on a piece of paper and gave it to her. She looked us in the eyes contemptuously, said, "I try. Stay here," and walked up the hill to the top gate.

There we waited, with high expectations and a great deal of anxiety. We might have the wrong camp. Te had been moved about so many times that he could have been shunted off somewhere else since his last letter—maybe several times. Or maybe he was here, but the policewoman would not bother to find out, and we could be standing here all day, two silly kweilos being shown who's boss.

As the minutes went by, the bigger worry was whether Te had survived. There was violence everywhere he'd been sent and it was increasing. Resentments, jealousies, sometimes the result of rumours or half-truths, had led to many savage attacks on people. What if his background had become known among the North Vietnamese majority? Or if his rapid screening had upset just one of the many thousands ahead of him in the queue?

What if, after his amazing escape, the two months between Vietnam and Hong Kong, and the three months since his old wartime officer had caught a glimpse of him on television,

Te had perished behind those awful fences, with freedom almost within grasp?

Jim Ellis was unconsciously rocking backwards and forwards on the balls of his feet, excited, apprehensive, looking from one set of gates to the other and then to his watch. "Poor old chap," he muttered about the man who was fourteen years his junior.

We heard the announcement over the centre's public address system. We heard the sharp voice of the tiny Cantonese policewoman reading out his alien number and mispronouncing his name, and we knew she was as uncertain as we were that this was the right camp. If there was a register of names of the people kept here at Tuen Mun, nobody seemed able to find it. In any case, the surname Nguyen would have taken up most of it.

"Poor old chap," said Jim, looking once more from one gate to another and then to his watch.

Small groups of Vietnamese people were coming and going in Hing Ping Street, giving us curious looks and continuing on their way.

Without warning there was a huge bang, then another and a rat-a-tat-tat like machine-gun fire. We all jumped. The bangs came from the downhill side of the camp. There were more bursts and puffs of smoke, not in the camp itself but in the village just below. We could see banners in Chinese and I suddenly realised we were witnessing no gun battle but the fireworks to celebrate the "Double Ten", the tenth day of the tenth month, the day on which the Chinese Nationalists each year try to ignore the fact that the communists chased them off the mainland to Taiwan in 1949. The celebrations were starting two days early because of the weekend, and Chinese people seldom need an excuse to bring out the fireworks. The Nationalists in particular need little encouragement to abbreviate the celebrations of their arch rivals, the Communists, whose national day is 1 October and whose celebrations continue up to the eve of the Nationalists' day.

Jim looked to the top gate, down to the bottom gate and then at his watch and the waiting was all over.

Te appeared at the top gate, a comical little figure in an oversize khaki shirt, but we heard him before we saw him. His yell must have woken the entire camp from its

REUNION

Reunion! Two great mates from the Vietnam war are reunited after 16 years. Hing Ping Street, Tuen Mun, Hong Kong, October 1989

torpor and probably half of Tuen Mun as well. At a hundred metres or so, his face was an enormous smile. We could see him straighten up on his good leg, as if it gave him some improved ability to accept what his eyes were telling him.

Te's hands, clasping the letters Jim and I had written to him, went up to his head and I can still hear the yell, so trembling, so penetrating, so loud and genuine that it froze us where we stood, and he kept yelling all the way down the hill. Without inhibition or embarrassment he ran, his bad leg flapping like a bird's broken wing and all out of coordination, at this strange white man that none of the boat people had ever seen before.

A REAL MATE

Jim was tugging at his hair, yelling back, his face like a child's, bright with excitement, as Te flung himself, full-speed, at him. The force would have knocked most mortals to the ground.

Te's arms were locked around Jim's neck, his legs wrapped around Jim's waist, and they laughed and yelled at each other in Vietnamese, probably neither of them understanding a word of what they were saying or hearing.

Still spinning around, Jim slapped this little wrap-around figure on the back, then held him at arm's length and said in English, "Ah, let's look at you!" and they beamed at each other like father and son.

Sixteen years had gone by, a reunion of two great mates, but more than that. It was one human being presenting to another the precious gift of freedom. It was an astonishing event to witness, and a privilege to be able to share it with others through the medium of television.

They sat down on a brick retaining wall outside the camp, now jabbering with so much to say, now silent because words seemed so hopelessly inadequate. Te's oldest son, Vuong, looked on, awkward in his adolescence and somewhat puzzled at this strange white man his father had so often spoken about, who was now speaking their language.

It was some minutes before Jim became aware of Vuong's presence. Eyes bright with some secret reserve of excitement, Jim exclaimed in Vietnamese, "Vuong! You must be Vuong!"

Vuong muttered an embarrassed, "Yes," as Jim jumped up from the retaining wall and held him and looked at him.

"Look at the size of you!" said Jim. "The last time I saw your mum and dad must have been a month or so before you were born, and look at you now!"

"He bigger than me already," said Te proudly. "You like to meet my daughters and my sister-in-law?"

"Of course. Where are they?"

"You wait here. I bring them."

Te was gone for much longer than we expected, and when he returned we could see why. The two girls and their aunt emerged from a hut shared with a couple of

REUNION

Another few steps toward freedom. Jim leads Te, Thu Thao, Vuong and Thuy Vy away from Tuen Mun. Te's sister-in-law, Mai Phuong, was working the day of the reunion.

hundred others behind the wire, yet managed to look as if they were off to a ball. Te himself had found a freshly pressed shirt, but the real contrast was the sight of these immaculate girls against the chain-link mesh and barbed wire. It was obvious Te wanted them to look their best to meet his great friend, and he succeeded.

Jim was animated as he spoke to each one in turn in Vietnamese, a man delighting in the discovery of his grandchildren.

"Where can we all go and get some morning tea?" Jim asked Te.

"This way," said Te. "We walk."

Jim takes his old friend under his wing outside Tuen Mun detention centre, October 1989

Jim and his extended family. Only moments after meeting Te's children, Jim cracks a joke in Vietnamese.

The two men walked in front down Hing Ping Street, holding hands, as is quite normal and acceptable in many cultures. They chatted mostly about Te's wife, Thi To, and how much Te wanted to have the whole family together again. Vuong, the girls and their aunt walked behind until we got to the level crossing at the New Territories tramline when they all held hands and crossed as one.

Over tea and cakes, an otherwise happy event, Vuong's sadness became apparent. He could understand his father's euphoria, but Vuong's heart was elsewhere.

"He missing his mother very much," said Te. "They very close. He worry all the time his mother never leave Vietnam."

"She will," said Jim emphatically. To Vuong, he said in Vietnamese, "Your mother will join us in Australia. Maybe this year, maybe next year, we don't know exactly when, but she *will* come to Australia—your mother and your little brothers."

"First we have to get you to Australia," I said to Te. "We can't do much today because it's Sunday, but tomorrow we'll try to get things moving. I'll get on to the Australian Consulate-General first thing in the morning. Have you been interviewed by them yet or been given any forms to fill out?"

"Not yet. They say I must see the United Nations High Commissioner for Refugees for registration first."

"I thought you were already classified as a refugee."

"By Hong Kong government. Now I must register with UNHCR."

"I would've thought that would be automatic. You mean you're a refugee as far as Hong Kong is concerned, but Australia can't start processing your application until the UNHCR agrees with Hong Kong's assessment of you? When might that happen?"

"I must go to UNHCR at Yaumatei on Tuesday morning. A minibus is taking us."

"We'd better meet you there and see if we can speed things up a little."

Back up Hing Ping Street, before we parted, Jim Ellis swept his arms around the family in a collective embrace, the way a mother hen shields her brood. "These are our people," he said. "We're going to get them to our country."

They stood in the middle of the road waving as we drove

off in a green taxi, back down this nondescript little street, the name of which has probably never appeared in print before. There was nothing remarkable about it at all, except for the camp that existed at its top end. By the time we turned into the main street, Te and his family would be be-hind the wire once more, but at least with some renewed hope.

To the Cantonese people in the bustle at the intersection, it was just another day. They shuffled this way and that, they clanked along on their heavyweight bicycles, carried big loads on bamboo poles, they bought and they sold. The taxi slowed to go through this mass of people. A man pushing a barrow with a huge block of ice on it crossed in front of the taxi and was soon swallowed up in the crowd.

Jim lurched forward in the back of the taxi. His eyes brimming, he gasped, "Oh my god!"

Delayed reaction, I thought. The retired lieutenant-colonel, the tough old soldier, was overcome by the emotion of this reunion and all that had led up to it. I knew him well enough by now to know he had never wavered in his commitment to help his old mate. He could simply bottle his feelings no longer.

"That bloody block of ice!" he said, choking on his own voice. "Where would you ever see a block of ice like that in Australia these days? I haven't seen one like that since Vietnam. I'm sorry. I'll be okay in a moment."

The significance of the block of ice escaped me. It was common in marketplaces all over Asia to see the stuff delivered, spiked and split expertly into cubes and chunks and chips and then packed around fish and other foodstuffs. The blocks were over a metre long, half a metre high and a quarter of a metre thick, delivered on trucks and then moved on barrows.

"Ever seen an Iroquois helicopter?" Jim asked, pulling himself together. "They're big ones, used all the time in Vietnam when the war was on. They'd come and go, great waves of the things with open sides, disgorging and picking up people and all sorts of loads.

"We were upcountry one day, moving six big blocks of ice just like the one on that barrow. We had them stacked sideways across the floor of the helicopter in a pyramid formation—three on the bottom, two in the middle, and another one on top.

"We had a full load, but some South Vietnamese soldier wanted a ride so we said, 'Climb in if you can find room to sit'. He scrambled into the chopper and perched on the top block of ice. It was the only bit of space left.

"We lifted straight up off the ground, and maybe a thousand feet up banked steeply to get our direction. As we did, the top block of ice, with the Vietnamese bloke still on it, went sliding out the door. It happened too quickly for any of us to grab him.

"We watched the poor bugger ride the thing all the way to the ground. What a thing to be reminded of today, of all days."

A multi-storey car park seemed an odd location for the Hong Kong offices of the United Nations High Commissioner for Refugees—unless a second wave of Vietnamese boat people was expected to arrive in amphibious landing barges. The Yaumatei car park in Shanghai Street, Kowloon, was a scruffy run-down building in a part of Hong Kong that showed no knowledge of the existence of mops and paintbrushes. The adjacent area, Mong Kok, was better known for its rate of grime and crime, but it was a close-run thing.

All sorts of international agencies were housed in this building or had set up temporarily to deal with the boat people screened in or those who had arrived in Hong Kong before screening began. Hundreds of boat people were being processed daily in barely controlled confusion. Interviews here, medical checks over there, go down there for registration, fill out your forms in the next room, one urine sample in this beaker, please, down the road at this address for your TB check.

Australian immigration staff, poached from the consulate in Kuala Lumpur, had set up desks and files in corridors. Australia alone was preparing to take a batch of between 1300 and 1600 boat people, many of whom had been waiting for years.

"My immigration officer, Graham Hainey, will be there," the Consul-General had told me. "I'll let him know that he may have an extra for a medical."

Nguyen Van Te and his family group arrived by minibus,

as arranged. Te clutched a bag of documents, new and old. Some had survived since his days with P.A. and E., letters of reference, birth certificates, marriage certificate, driver's licence, identity document, and more recently acquired, his alien registration card and the letters from Jim and myself.

Jim and Te met almost as if it were the reunion again. A whole day had passed while we shot other material in Hong Kong and made contact with the consulate, the UNHCR and others.

Jim showed Te and his family into the lift and up to where we'd established previously that the first interview would take place. It was not easy. With all the governments, agencies and departments involved, the language problems and sheer weight of numbers, it struck me that applications could easily end up in the wrong tray or pigeonhole. It was not difficult to imagine the wrong Nguyen being sent to this country, the wrong Tran being sent there. For all we could tell, as people were directed from one door to another, told to wait here, hand this in somewhere else, thousands of boat people may have been lost in this very building for years.

It is beyond doubt that the presence of a television camera, some diplomatic influence and the word that a Prime Minister was particularly interested in this case helped achieve in one day a complete process that would normally have taken weeks or even months.

First the registration with the UNHCR meant an interview and forms to fill out, then a meeting with the immigration officer of the Australian Consulate-General, Graham Hainey, and his consul, Andrew Metcalfe; some meetings with senior UNHCR officials; then a medical check done through another agency, the Intergovernmental Committee for Migration. The medical officer, Dr Chris Reynolds, by coincidence an Australian, agreed to do a mock medical for the camera. "We'll have to book him in for a proper one, but not for a few weeks, the way things are looking," he said, checking ears, nose and throat, then said, "Well, he's here now—we might as well do it for real, urine sample and all."

At lunch, Jim sat with Te in a small park on Nathan Road and filled out the applications for migration to Australia, then went back to the car park for Te's official interview with the Australian migration officer.

There was one more thing to do that day—Te had to be X-rayed for TB, but as we all could see, it was little more than a formality.

We loaded Thu Thao, Thuy Vy, Vuong and Mai Phuong aboard the minibus to take them back to the camp they would have to endure only a little longer. As he climbed into the bus, Te waved and said, "Thank you, thank you. See you soon. See you very soon in Australia."

"And I'll be there waiting for you," said Jim. Ignoring the perils of Hong Kong traffic, he stood in the middle of the road and waved until the bus was out of sight.

Chief Inspector Nicholas Francis Angell was exactly as he sounded, and as accurately as he had described himself. "Big and bald, can't miss me. See you at the Mariners' Club. Probably be in the bar, having a snort, mm? Need one. Look forward to meeting this Lieutenant-Colonel Ellis."

His neck was the size of a rugby forward's thigh, shoulders as broad as a full front row, a shining pate sticking out of a very large T-shirt. The voice was that of a drill sergeant-major and his laugh went 'Waw waw'!

"Worked 72 hours straight," he said when we met him at the bar having a snort. "Snowed under, mm? Bogged down. Boat people. More boat people than we now what to do with, mm? Lucky chap, this friend or yours. Bloody lucky!"

It was the last part of the round of meeting people and thanking them for their help. We had met and thanked Lynn D'Souza, Bill Wyllie's assistant, and had lunch with the Consul-General. "Should be out in a matter of weeks at the most," Geoff Bentley told us confidently.

Now we were going to unwind with a drink with the police inspector who had sent on our first letters to Te when he was moved from Tai Ah Chau to Sek Kong.

"Not many blighters as lucky as yours, mm? Odd, this."

"What's odd?" Jim asked.

"Drinking with a journalist," said the police inspector. "Have a motto, mm? Never trust a journalist!"

"Wise," I said. "He might tell the truth."

"Let's eat. Got to eat. Starving! Put the menu away. Know it backwards, mm! Steak; excellent. Snails; must have the snails. Waiter! Snails all round!"

His wife arrived about the same time as the snails.

"Light of my life!" he said, introducing her. "Light of my life, mm! Must have a drop of red with snails. Not *with* snails, I should say, *in* snails!" And so he sloshed a quarter of a bottle of claret into his snails and exhorted us both to join him. We declined.

"Must come back to the flat and have a snort," he said after the meal. "No question about it. Could do with a drink. Got the taste now. Waw waw!"

Jim and I looked at each other. What the heck, we were going home tomorrow, and it was obvious this guy wasn't going to take no for an answer.

Chief Inspector Angell commanded his ageing Mercedes as if it were a Roman chariot. It sped up Piper's Hill in Kowloon, the old engine working hard as the charioteer went up and down through the gears and yelled curses at other motorists. The light of his life seemed unimpressed.

Inside the flat we were led on to a veranda. Jim was assigned to an old lounge chair, I was installed on a wicker one that had a cushion stuffed down a hole worn in the centre of its base, and there we were pinned without hope of departure until the very large policeman wearied in the early hours of the morning. He was as liberal with his wine as he was insistent at our staying, and the light of his life went out, to bed.

"Just another one. Bulgarian. Bit fruity. Full-bodied. Like me. Waw waw!"

A fat gecko on the ceiling laughed back at him.

"You've got to watch those fellas," said Jim. "We used them a lot in Vietnam. Intelligence gathering."

"Geckos?" said the big policeman. "Intelligence gathering?"

"We had them specially trained," said Jim. "We used to let them go in the rooms of anyone we suspected might be worth listening to."

"Don't get it," said the inspector, "Aussie sense of humour, mm? What good's a gecko in intelligence gathering, mm?"

"They looked like ordinary geckos," said Jim, "but we used to equip them with tiny radio transmitters."

"Pulling my leg?"

"No," said Jim, "we used to stick the transmitters up their arses."

Before we weaved off into the early morning in search of a taxi, Chief Inspector Nicholas Francis Angell said to Jim, "Thing is, still don't understand. You're a lieutenant-colonel. The Vietnamese you recognised on telly is a civilian interpreter, mm? What's so special about this guy?"

"Don't you see it?" said Jim. "Haven't you worked it out yet? He's the one who shot the president!"

When Te walked back into the camp, aglow from seeing Jim again, there was good news for him. He'd been offered a job.

Ten days earlier a social worker in the camp at Tuen Mun, a Chinese woman working for a group called Community and Family Services International, had asked him to apply for a job as interpreter/translator. The position would carry some counselling responsibilities for which she thought Te would be well suited.

While we were helping Te and his family with their processing, the group had sent a message to the camp telling Te he had got the job. He would mediate in family disputes and interpret for Vietnamese refugees brought before the Hong Kong courts to answer charges of stealing and other offences. It was an interesting job and he took it happily, but it won't be for long, he thought; soon I'll be in Australia.

It was 13 October 1989 the day Jim and I arrived back in Australia—Friday the 13th as it happened—always a good day for air travel. There were seats aplenty on the flight.

"Don't walk under any black cats today," I said to Jim as we parted at Sydney.

"Don't let any ladders cross your path," he called and headed off for his flight to Canberra.

A few days later I phoned Jim to let him know how the editing was going. He could hardly speak at first, then opened up.

"It's brought a lot back," he said hoarsely. "I took over from a brilliant guy on the second tour in Vietnam—in fact I had to go up and bring him back so he could be pushed sideways in a non-job. His one flaw was that he loved to get himself in the papers when we were supposed to be doing a quiet job.

"He took enormous risks in Vietnam—we both did—and he never got over being pulled out and, in effect, demoted. A few years after I came home, I had lunch with him. His name was Clarke, Major Rex Clarke. We discussed how we both thought we'd been manipulated by the head of the Joint Intelligence Office in Canberra who would take the glory while we risked our necks.

"It really hurt Rex. It had hurt him for years. We had lunch on the Friday, and on the Sunday he phoned the police in Canberra, gave his address and said, 'There's been a shooting accident.' As the police walked up his driveway, he put a revolver in his mouth and blew the top of his head off.

"It was such a terrible waste. The man was brilliant.

"To make matters worse, there was no military funeral, not even uniforms at his funeral. We had to go in mufti.

"Rex was another casualty of the war, and it's all come back to me.

"At least we know Te's all right. For years after we lost contact I assumed the worst—that he'd been killed, and I held myself responsible because of some of the tricky things I got him to do. It's been a huge relief to find he's okay. That's the up side. Remembering poor old Rex is the down side."

The program on the reunion of Jim and Te went to air on 23 October 1989. The response, as far as I have been able to judge, was singularly approving. Many people seemed to take encouragement and inspiration from a simple story of human relationships. Te and his family would be in Australia, I confidently predicted, "this month or next month".

Two days after the broadcast, Jenny Hoskin phoned from the press office of the Immigration Department. "Lovely story," she said. "That reunion had everybody I know in tears. The problem is, he can't come—not just yet anyway. The results of Te's medical have come back. He's absolutely riddled with TB."

I phoned Te at once at the number at his new job.

"No," he said, "I don't have TB. I *did* have it last year in Vietnam, but I was treated and cured. Maybe old scars showed up, but I don't have TB."

It was a fortnight before Te was given the follow-up X-ray, and the big group of Vietnamese refugees Australia had accepted left Hong Kong without him and his family, who had to wait with him.

It took until 11 December 1989—ironically the day before Hong Kong forcibly repatriated its first batch of boat people—before the authorities accepted the results of their own X-rays.

Christmas came and went. I received a very touching card from Te's wife, Thi To, thanking me for helping her husband, children and her sister, but they were all still in Hong Kong and I was powerless. Thanks for what? I thought.

Then the month of January 1990 also slipped by without result. All we could establish through any of our contacts was that "some of the documentation seems to have been mislaid". Precisely what the documentation was, or which of the many agencies now involved in the case had mislaid it, remains a mystery.

On 5 February 1990, Geoff Bentley phoned me with a simple message: "He's cleared."

Still another month went by before the arrangements were finalised. On 1 March Te was given a big send-off at the Tuen Mun office of Community and Family Services International. His police friends from Sek Kong joined in. One of Te's colleagues, a Filipina of Chinese extraction, played the guitar and sang. Te requested "Love Is Blue" because it was popular in Vung Tau all those years ago and reminded him of Jim Ellis.

The next day Te and his family were moved into the Transit Centre at Kaitak Airport for three more nights before they boarded their flight to Sydney.

"How come you win the Cup?" another refugee asked him. "Nobody ever wins so quickly."

"Just lucky," said Te.

"No. I know you. You were on television. Australian program shown here in Hong Kong. Hey, you're *lucky.*"

Te, Vuong, Thuy Vy, Thu Thao and Mai Phuong boarded Qantas flight 28 on the night of 6 March 1990. It was the first time any of them had been on board an aircraft, except

Te, whose only experience of air travel was on a military Caribou and a helicopter with Jim.

Mai Phuong and the two girls sat together. Vuong sat on one side of his father. Te was seated next to a middle-aged woman who was a seasoned traveller. He introduced himself, saying, "We are refugees, going to make a new home in Australia. This is our first time on a passenger plane. It is very strange. Please help me—tell me what to do."

"How exciting!" she said. "Now don't do anything at all, dear. Just make sure your seat belts are on, and relax. There's nothing to be afraid of. I'll hold your hand till the plane takes off. How wonderful!"

Postscript

Jim Ellis was at Sydney Airport to meet Te, Vuong, Thuy Vy, Thu Thao and Mai Phuong when they arrived on 8 March 1990. I was also there with a "7.30 Report" crew.

Together we flew to Canberra where they were welcomed by an Immigration Department official and representatives of the Catholic welfare service.

We drove the family to their new home, a house they would rent from the government, in a typical Australian suburban community sprinkled with refugees from various countries. The house had been fully furnished by Jim and the church.

The day after Te arrived, he was offered and accepted a temporary position in the Department of Health and Community Services, where he worked for several months until he took up a permanent position with Australia Post.

The children attended special English classes and settled into schooling. Mai Phuong did a course in English and continued in her role as proxy mother to her sister's children.

On 11 May 1991, Jim went to Canberra and helped Te lodge the applications for his wife and two younger boys to join him under the Family Reunification Scheme. I was able to meet them at the Immigration Department; by another coincidence, I was in Canberra that day attending the national Thorn-EMI Television Awards, at which the programs involving Te and Jim were highly commended.

Many months went by, many calls were made, many letters written, and much waiting done. The family adapted quickly to life in Australia, but it was only part of a family.

At 10.00 p.m. on Saturday 2 March 1991, Karen Stanley of the Australian Embassy in Bangkok, which handles Vietnamese immigration applications on behalf of the embassy in Hanoi, phoned me at home in Sydney. She, too, had been caught up in the story. "I have great news," she said. "Te's wife, Thi To, is finally on the Vietnamese government's exit permit list. It means we can now officially gain access to her. There will be health checks and other formalities and it may take a few months, and of course Te will have to pay their fares, but I have no reason to believe there will be any problem with her and the two little boys."

I phoned Te immediately.

"I am so excited," he said.

I left a message at Jim's house telling him the news. When he called back, he said simply, "It's been worth it, hasn't it!"